Y0-CRG-332

The Collected Works of Gerard Manley Hopkins
Volume II

CORRESPONDENCE

Gerard Manley Hopkins, April 1888.

Gerard Manley Hopkins

CORRESPONDENCE

Volume II

1882–1889

Letters on the Death of Gerard Manley Hopkins

Edited by

R. K. R. THORNTON

and

CATHERINE PHILLIPS

OXFORD
UNIVERSITY PRESS

Great Clarendon Street, Oxford OX2 6DP,
United Kingdom

Oxford University Press is a department of the University of Oxford.
It furthers the University's objective of excellence in research, scholarship,
and education by publishing worldwide. Oxford is a registered trade mark of
Oxford University Press in the UK and in certain other countries.

First published in 2013

Impression: 2

British Library Cataloguing in Publication Data
Data available

ISBN 978–0–19–953399–2

Printed in Great Britain by
CPI Group (UK) Ltd, Croydon, CR0 4YY

CONTENTS

Volume II

LIST OF LETTERS

The listing is chronological and includes letters both from and to GMH; those written to him and the correspondence of friends and family after his death are here differentiated by italic. Conjectural dates are in square brackets.

1883

1887

1889

Letters on the Death of GMH, 1889–1890

LIST OF ILLUSTRATIONS

1882

I January [1882] to his Mother

FL, no. XCIII, p. 162 Bodleian, MS Eng. lett. e. 41, fos. 79d–e^v

Manresa House, Roehampton, S.W. New Year's Day.

My dearest mother, — I wish you all a very happy new year. But I am distressed and disturbed to hear of this sickness of yours, though Lionel says you were somewhat better yesterday. I am the more troubled because I am hourly expecting ~~my r~~ ^orders^ to return to Liverpool. One of our Fathers, who was for the best part of two years my yokemate on that laborious mission, ~~has~~ died ^there^ yesterday ^~~th~~^night after a short sickness, in harness and in his prime.[1] I am saddened by this death, for he was particularly good to me; he used to come up to me and say "Gerard, you are a good soul" and ~~said~~ that I was a comfort to him in his troubles. His place must now be supplied and it must be by one of two, both in this house; I feel little doubt it will be by me and that this is probably the last night I shall spend at Roehampton.

I do not know whether you got the January number of the ~~m~~Month, but if you did I am sorry to say that you must put no trust in the music headed "original". The Thirteenth Century composer if he saw it wd. scarcely know it and would not acknowledge it for his own. What a thing it is that even in publishing ~~a~~ an antiquity, a piece of music every note interesting and precious from its ~~age~~ date, people must change, adulterate, and modernise! If the editor of the Month were a musician he would have been aware of this and would not have allowed it, at all events without warning the reader. The effect of the original is totally lost by the change for instance

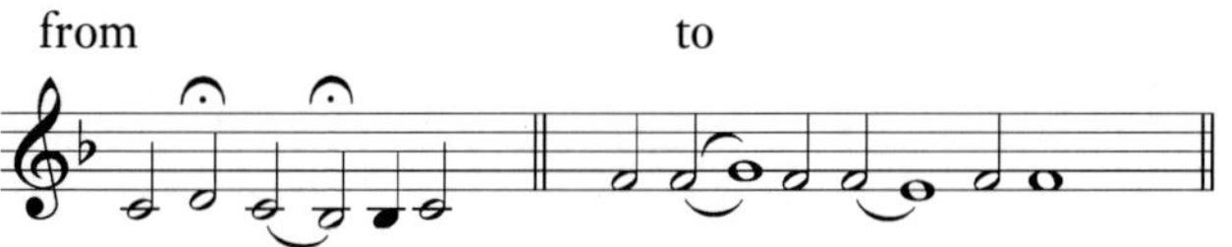

The first is characteristic, fresh, and quaint; the second a platitude. The true original is in the 7th Mode, the Young Men's Mode or Angelic Mode, the natural scale of G,[2] and I had wanted Grace to see the effect. But now it is all a mess.

Aunt Kate[3] tells me she has lost £400.
Believe me your loving son Gerard.

[1] William Hilton was educated at the English College at Lisbon, ordained *c.*1860. After four or five years working at St Chad's, Birmingham, he was given charge of the mission at Nuneaton until 1877, when he entered the Society of Jesus. He studied theology at St Beuno's and was then appointed to Liverpool in Aug. 1880. He died on 31 Dec. 1882 of typhoid caught from attending parishioners.
[2] The Mixolydian mode, said by some medieval theorists to be appropriate to adolescents because of its high range and leaps.
[3] The widow of the Revd Thomas Marsland Hopkins. See Biographical Register.

28 January 1882 from Richard Watson Dixon to GMH

CRWD, no. XXII A, p. 100 Campion Hall, D 28/1/82
Addressed to 'The Rev[d]. | Gerard Hopkins S.J. | Manresa House, | Roehampton, | S.W. London'. PM CARLISLE JA 28 82, LONDON JA 30 82.

Hayton Vicarage, Carlisle | 28 Jan. 1882
My dear Friend,

This is intended not to be an answer to your last immensely valuable Letter: but an acknowledgment of the Song which I have received from your Sister: & also is written because I feel as if it were long since I wrote to you. The Song[1] seems to me singularly beautiful & proper to the words: which words are too much honoured in being wedded to such music. I have the air running in my head. My daughters have been trying it many times over, & are charmed with it. I am making a copy of it for one of them who is away since it came.

I cannot help, since I began this, taking up your last long letter to read again. As to the first part of it, in which you speak of your poetry, and its relation to your profession, I cannot but take courage to hope that the day will come, when so health-breathing and purely powerful a faculty as you have been gifted with may find its proper issue in the world. Bridges struck the truth long ago when he said to me that your poems more carried him out of himself than those of any one. I have again and again felt the same: & am certain that as a means of serving, I will not say your cause, but religion, you cannot have a more powerful instrument than your own verses. They have, of course with all possible differences of originality on both sides, the quality which Taine has marked in Milton: & which is more to be noted in his minor pieces than the great ones, of admiration — I forget Taine's expression, but it means admiration (or in you other emotions also) which reaches its fulness & completeness in giving the exact aspect of the thing it takes: so that a peculiar contentation is felt.[2]

To take another point in your letter, I have seen Cobbett's Reformation,[3] indeed read a good deal of it. A great deal of it is true: the general view that the Reformation was not an admirable thing is true: but the reasons for which Cobbett thinks so are not very high: he thinks that the expediency of the Ref^n was inexpedient: was a mistake in calculation: or rather that no account was taken of public expediency in the haste of private expediency. He is an indignant utilitarian: nothing more: & his indignation has no other expression than sheer abuse, which is wearisome in a while, unskilful & disgusting. What he says about pauperism is true enough.

Following y^r. criticism (and also Bridges, who said much the same when he read it) I have much altered the beginning of Septimius & Alcander, and also cut away much of that grind of a description of Rome. But the most important thing I have done at it is to add six verses to the end, to deepen the moral; at the suggestion of something that you said. You may remember that it ended with Love handing back Alcander to Reason, so that he knew Septimius & Hypatia kneeling by him dying. I add[4]

> They reasoned too: as on his death they gazed,
> One hideous (common / mutual) thought their bosoms raised,
> Which out of being smote the only good
> That he had gained in all — their gratitude.
> "So is it best for us," Septimius said:
> Hypatia looked, and nodded o'er the dead.

I s^d. like to have y^r. opinion on this.

Your classification of the modern poet schools seems to me to hold: & especially I like what you say of Wordsworth. But I must now stop.

Ever your affectionate Friend
R W Dixon

[1] 'Sky that rollest ever'. See letter of 1–16 Dec. 1881.

[2] Although Taine's *History of English Literature*, translated in 1871 by H. van Laun, has a sizeable chapter on Milton in its first volume, and phrases and sentences from it could be applied to GMH, nothing exactly matches what RWD remembers.

[3] This responds to a question in his letter to RWD of 1–16 Dec. 1881; see n. 14.

[4] The end suggested here is substantially that of the printed version, though the second line above was altered to: Love sent one thought that both their bosoms raised.

1–3 February 1882 to Robert Bridges

LRB, no. LXXX, p. 140 Bodleian, Dep. Bridges, vol. 91, fos. 188–189v

Manresa House, Roehampton, S.W. Feb. 1 1882.

Dearest Bridges, — I was of course delighted to get your letter and think you must now surely soon be going to be quite strong and well.

I have no time for more than ~~a~~ business-like letter writing. At the beginning of Lent I am to take duty at Preston[1] (St. Ignatius's will do for the address) and from ~~a~~ the Fourth Sunday in Lent (March 19) to Palm Sunday (April 2) I am to help in mission-services to be given at Maryport[2] on the coast of Cumberland (not so far from Carlisle). I am ^now^ therefore closely employed preparing discourses and instructions. After that I ought to return here, but it may easily happen that some need fixes me elsewhere. I am, as you must remember, ~~as~~ like a novice, have been to town only to see the dentist, and could not hope to visit you. You might come and see me and the place is worth seeing, but it could be very seldom. In no case ~~would~~ does my probation last beyond August.

The winter has been very mild. Our primroses have been more than a fortnight in bloom ^and laurels are beginning to flower^. It is unnatural and I want to see it colder.

I find the life trying — weakening, I mean. But the calm of mind is delightful: I am afraid I shall leave it behind.

I should hardly wish you to send me your poem here.[3] Either send it to me at Preston or keep it awhile. I am sorry to put off the pleasure, but the time does not suit. I may add that the right to secrecy in ~~lett~~ correspondence which, as you know, we Jesuits surrender . . . the sentence would be tedious to finish: what I mean is that the right to ~~have~~ read our letters claimed by the Society of its subjects but mostly not exercised is here a ~~gr~~ realised fact; so consult your own taste about what you will say and leave unsaid.

I shall never rest till you change the ^third^ line in the sonnet "In all things beautiful": it weakens and disfigures an otherwise perfect work. Can you not say something like:

As but to watch her folds fall how they do,
And all { her ways are / that comes is } past expectancy — ?[4]

And I hold to the metrical ~~er~~ objections I made to some lines in the poem about ~~Ris~~^Fly^ing Flames.[5]

I believe I told you that you must be mistaken about the stanza-nature of terza rima being quite unknown to English poets. Shelley certainly has one or more pieces in that measure printed in stanzas and as a boy I published in Once a Week a piece called Winter with the Gulf Stream[6] (it was such another winter as this) in ~~that~~ the same (but in eights) and so printed. I borrowed also the contrivance of ending with a couplet, which has the convenience of ravelling up the rhymes. Treated in this stanza form the terza rima is one of the simplest of measures as it is one of the most beautiful: at each stanza's end you can either rest or go on with equally charming effect. Indeed I think I must try it again.

Yesterday Feb. 2 it froze. We had a holiday and I took two Frenchmen[7] to the ^South^ Kensington museums. The frost fog ~~mix~~ red with smoke made it so dark that we cd. scarcely be said to see. Amidst the bewildering wealth of beautiful things my attention was fixed by the casts from Michael Angelo, the David, two figures of slaves for Julius II's tomb, a Madonna, and others. I thought of the advantage, for which nothing can completely make up, ^you have^ of seeing these things on the spot. In the arts of painting and sculpture I am, even when most I admire, always convinced of a great shortcoming: nothing has been done yet at all equal to what one can easily conceive being done. For instance for ~~a~~ work to be perfect there ought to be the sense of beauty in the highest degree both in the ~~individual~~ ^artist^ and in the age, the ^style and^ keepings of which the artist employs. Now the keepings of the age in which for instance Raphael and Angelo lived were rich, but unsatisfactory in the extreme. And they were both far from having a pure sense of beauty. Besides which they have several other great shortcomings. But in poetry and perhaps in music unbetterable works have been produced. No room to go on nor time either. But talking of perfection, could you not get rid of Test in "Thou didst delight"? Look here: rhyme on first and durst and you will get something very good. I dare not tell you my ~~own~~ thought, for it wd. be to defeat my own purpose, but do it yourself, simple, suitable, and sweet.[8] Write about things in Italy. Your ever affectionate friend Gerard M. Hopkins S.J.

[1] Established by the Anglo-Saxons on the shores of the River Ribble, Preston was an important 17th-c. port and later centre of textile manufacture in the 19th c. Charles Dickens's Coketown (*Hard Times*) was based on it.

[2] Maryport. See letter below to RB of 3–4 Apr. 1882, n. 2.

[3] *Prometheus the Firegiver.*

[4] In their final form (*P.W.*, i, *G of L*, 31) these lines are:

'Tis joy to watch the folds fall as they do,
And all that comes is past expectancy.

[5] The lyric 'O my vague desires' (*P.W.*, ii, bk. iii. 1). RB also used it towards the end of his *Prometheus*.

[6] In the issue of 14 Feb. 1863, p. 210. His poem is in the traditional *terza rima* stanza—three lines with the middle line rhyming with the first and last lines of the succeeding stanza—but with eight-syllable lines. See *CW* viii. RWD's *Mano* is in *terza rima*, but not set out in stanzas.

[7] MS 'Frenchman'.

[8] The first reading was (*Poems*, 1880):

Thou didst delight my eyes:
Yet who am I ? nor best
Nor first nor last to test
Thy charm, thy bloom to prize; . . .

The final form (*P.W.*, vol. ii, book iii. 12) is:

Thou didst delight my eyes:
Yet who am I ? nor first
Nor last nor best, that durst
Once dream of thee for prize; . . .

1–3 February 1882 to Richard Watson Dixon

CRWD, no. XXIII, p. 101 Bodleian, Dep. Bridges, vol. 93, fos. 95–97v
Addressed to 'The Rev. | Canon Dixon | Hayton Vicarage | Carlisle'. PM PUTNEY S.W. FE 3 82. Written on one small folded sheet.

Manresa House, Roehampton, S.W. Feb. 1 1882.

My dear Friend, — I was almost writing to you when your letter came. I am now very busy; for after taking some duty at Preston (St. Ignatius's) from the First Sunday in Lent, I am to go to Maryport in Cumberland to help in ~~a~~ mission-services to be carried on there for the fortnight before Palm Sunday: I am therefore at work preparing instructions and other discourses. I should return here after that unless countermanded.

I ^do^ certainly think that the added lines to Too Much Friendship throw ~~back~~ ^a vein^ of much deeper pathos and interest back through the whole story. I should like however the 4th of them to end with "— gratitude", omitting "their", as more crisp and pointed — something like

"That all that grief had earned him — gratitude."

I think also that Septimius should speak either more reservedly, without us, as: ~~"It was~~

> " 'It was the best to ~~m~~^b^e' Septimius said" —

or else more cynically, something like:

> " 'He rests — and we may rest' Septimius said".[1]

I ~~sh~~^w^ould remark that you have made Septimius of beautiful character and worthy of being Alcander's friend early in the story, but from the moment when he 'refused the bat and ~~I~~ chose the dove', which though it was not selfish was far from being unselfish (if I may speak so illogically), he may be supposed to have declined and Hypatia to have ~~corrup~~ corrupted him. About her there is no difficulty and the situation itself puts her in a more odious light.

My mind is much employed at present on the subject of Sacrifice, about which I am getting together some materials, ~~poss~~ with a view possibly to write about it some day: I do not know of course but I fancy it may be the case that nothing at all exhaustive or satisfactory has been written on it either ~~treated~~ speculatively or historically. Something my brother, who is a Chinese scholar, furnished me the other day reminded me of ^two^ lines in an early poem of yours. A certain pious and devoted prince of early times called T'ang offered himself as a propitiatory sacrifice in a great drought for the sake of his people. He went ~~to the place~~ of "in a plain carriage, drawn by white horses, clad in rushes, in the ~~guil~~ guise of a sacrificial victim, . . . to a forest of mulberry trees, and there prayed".[2] Now was it a fancy or was it fo~~unded~~^llowing^ ~~on~~ some tradition that made you say:

> I took weak waterweeds to fold
> About my sacrificial dress —?[3]

and if the latter what?

Bridges has been writing to me from Florence about your poem of "Mano"~~.~~ and says that "it is a marvellous work, full of the richest things, and quite unlike anything else", but that he has not room to describe it, with more, all of which makes me of course eager to see it; but that cannot be yet.

I should not have thought that Cobbett was mer~~l~~ely a utilitarian. His seemingly heartfelt remarks about love of country for instance (^I mean^ patriotism) and its dependence on beauty of buildings and historic monuments ~~seem~~ ^are^ those of a man who ha~~d~~^s^ other ideals than ~~that of~~ utility.

I am very glad indeed you are so well pleased with the music. I shall hope to send you one[4] or two more of your pieces some day. My sister tells me she has had from you a very flattering letter.

The winter has been so mild with us that primroses have been in bloom in our shrubberies for three weeks or so.

Believe me your affectionate friend Gerard Hopkins S.J.
Feb. 3 1882.

[1] These suggestions were not adopted in the version printed.

[2] GMH is quoting from James Legge's *The Religions of China* (London, 1880), 54–5, where it describes 'an incident in the life of T'ang, which, though not in the Shu, has been handed down by the historian Sze-ma Ch'ien and others. For seven years after his accession (B.C. 1766–1760), there was a great drought and famine. It was suggested at last by some one that a human victim should be offered in sacrifice to Heaven, and prayer made for rain. T'ang said, "If a man must be the victim, I will be he." He fasted, cut off his hair and nails, and in a plain carriage, drawn by white horses, clad in rushes, in the guise of a sacrificial victim, he proceeded to a forest of mulberry trees, and there prayed, asking to what error or crime of his life the calamity was owing. He had not done speaking when a copious rain fell.'

[3] 'Dream', *C.C.*, 58, ll. 9–10.

[4] 'or' written in error for 'one'.

22 February 1882 from John Henry Newman to GMH

FL, no. C23, p. 411 Campion Hall and MS copy in Birmingham Oratory, N 22/2/82

Written on a card with a coloured picture of laburnum. Addressed to 'The Revd F^{r} Hopkins SJ | St Wilfrid's Catholic Church | Preston'. PM BIRMINGHAM FE 22 82, PRESTON FE 23 82.

Thank you sincerely for the kindness of your remembrance, and for the kindness of your letter.

J H Card. Newman
Feb 22 | 1882.

26 March 1882 to Richard Watson Dixon

CRWD, no. XXIV, p. 103 Bodleian, Dep. Bridges, vol. 93, fos. 98–9
Written on one small page with printed heading.

Our Lady and St. Patrick's, | Maryport. [*printed heading*]

March 26 1882.
My dear Friend, — I mean to be at Carlisle ^tomorrow^ by the train which reaches there at 12.25 # and to leave it for Preston at about 4: could I hope to meet you? If not I can employ myself at the Cathedral and otherwise of course. The chance may never occur again. Believe me yours affectionately Gerard Hopkins S.J.

If you missed me at the station you might find me at the Cathedral perhaps.

Palm Sunday [2 April] 1882 to Richard Watson Dixon

CRWD, no. XXV, p. 104 Bodleian, Dep. Bridges, vol. 93, fos. 100–2
Addressed to 'The Rev. Canon Dixon | Hayton Vicarage | Carlisle'. PM PRESTON AP 2 82. Written on one small folded sheet.

St. Wilfrid's, Preston. Palm Sunday 1882.

My dear Friend, — I am still lingering at Preston, expecting to go south tomorrow or next day. I was detained here and closely employed, or I shd. have dropped you a line before to thank you, which I never did, for your kind entertainment at Carlisle.

I wish our meeting cd. have been longer for several reasons, but to name one, I fancied you were shy and that time would have been needed for this to wear off. I think that for myself I have very little shyness left in me, but I cannot communicate my own feeling to another.

I have nothing more to say now, but when I see anything settled you shall hear. In the meantime as long as I am at Roehampton, at least in the character of a novice, I do not ask to see Mano or anything important of yours — which nevertheless, in MS or print, I do of course earnestly hope to see. Believe me your affectionate friend Gerard M. Hopkins S.J.

3–4 April 1882 to Robert Bridges

LRB, no. LXXXI, p. 143 Bodleian, Dep. Bridges, vol. 91, fos. 190–191v

St. Wilfrid's, Preston. April 3 1882.

I hope, my dear heart, you are now really better; not better, well; strong, vigorous, lusty, beefish, as apt to pull an oar[1] as to turn ~~y~~ a sonnet with the best in either kind. And we may now shortly hope to meet. For I suppose I shall be at Roehampton tomorrow. The address is Manresa (not Manresca) House — it is called after the place where St. Ignatius lived for a year doing penance in a cave —, Roehampton, S.W.

At the beginning of Lent I came from Roehampton here to stop a gap and do some parish work; I then went to Maryport on the coast of Cumberland, to take part in a Mission, which is something like a Revival without the hysteria and the heresy, and it had the effect of bringing me out and making me speak very plainly and strongly (I enjoyed that, for I dearly like calling a spade a spade): it was the first thing of the sort I had been employed in;[2] but no~~w~~ more of this now. On my way back I was detained here to hear confessions again.

I came by Carlisle and made an appointment with Canon Dixon, so that we spent some hours together, and he gave me dinner and shewed me the Cathedral. Partly through this sightseeing and more through shyness on his part (not on mine) we did not get much intimate or even interesting talk. I was amused when his hat twice blew off in English Street to watch his behaviour. I wish I could have been with him longer.

I have been reading Purcell's Life in the Great Musicians series:[3] you should.

I forget if I told you that Grace set ~~so~~ music to "Sometimes when my Lady".[4] It is characteristic, with an old fashioned and suitable flavour about it.

Believe me your loving friend Gerard.

If the best comes to the best you are already home and free to see me, but do not come this week of course. Let me have a line first.

April 4 — I forgot to tell you that Canon Dixon was married ~~las~~ in February.[5]

It is a pity you did not write to me while I was here. I must go back tomorrow.

[1] RB had been stroke in the Corpus eight at Oxford (i.e. the oarsman who sits nearest the stern and sets the timing for the other rowers in the eight-man crew).

[2] GMH was at Maryport 12–26 Mar. He said mass on 12 Mar. and gave sermons on 19 and 26 Mar. The *Tablet* recorded that the mission had been very well attended with more than 900 Easter Communions, forty or fifty aspirants consecrated Children of Mary, and Confirmation administered by the Bishop to 200 persons. The *Maryport Advertiser and Weekly News* (24 Mar. 1882) reported of the inauguration of the Children of Mary: 'the candidates wearing white veils, occupied seats in the lady chapel. The Rev. Father Hopkins preached an appropriate and eloquent sermon. The choir having been strengthened by some professional singers, the Benediction service was exceedingly well sung, . . . upwards of 750 persons were present at the service.' (Thomas, 200.)

[3] By William Hayman Cummings, one of the original committee of the Purcell Society, founded 21 Feb. 1876 (London, 1881).

[4] 'Sometimes when my lady sits by me', a poem by RB.

[5] On 9 Feb. 1882 RWD married Matilda Routledge, the eldest daughter of the publisher.

13 April 1882 from Richard Watson Dixon to GMH

CRWD, no. XXV A, p. 104 Campion Hall, D 13/4/82
Addressed to 'The Rev. | G. Hopkins S.J. | Manresa House, | Roehampton, | London'. PM CARLISLE AP 14 81, LONDON AP 15 81.

Hayton, Carlisle | 13 Ap. 1882

My dear Friend,

I ought to have written before: but things have been in the way: to say how very glad I am to have seen you & to have a full knowledge what you are like. So far as I can remember, you are very like the boy of Highgate. I dare say I seemed "shy": I have an unfortunate manner: & am constantly told that I am too quiet: I have often tried to overcome it: but the effort is always apparent to those with whom I am, & never succeeds. You must therefore forgive it: it is not from want of feeling or affection.

I feel the death of Rossetti most acutely.[1] I have known him for twenty years: he was one of my dearest friends, though I only saw much of him at one period, & that not a long one. It leaves an awful blank.

I am now called out, so good bye: wishing you every possible happiness, & among others that you may soon be at liberty to write, & may write poems.

I am My dear Friend
Ever your affec^{te}
R. W. Dixon

[1] He died 10 Apr. 1882.

6 May 1882 to Alexander William Mowbray Baillie

FL, no. CXXXVIII, p. 248 UCD L 47
One folded sheet and one half sheet.

Manresa House, Roehampton, S.W. May 6 1882.

Dearest Baillie, — We parted in Bond Street, when a schoolfellow who had not met you since school days came up and discovered himself and introduced his wife (you must always have been a favourite). After that I returned to Liverpool, but was shortly ordered to Glasgow, where I was for two months. Though Glasgow is repulsive to live in yet there are alleviations: the streets and buildings are fine and the people lively. The poor Irish, among whom my duties lay, are mostly from the North of Ireland, scarcely distinguishable in tongue from the Scotch and at Glasgow ~~greatly~~ ^still further^ Scoticised. They are found by all who have to deal with them very attractive; for, though always very drunken and at present very Fenian,[1] they are warm-hearted and give a far heartier welcome than those of Liverpool. I found myself very much at home with them. It is also pleasant to hear Scotch spoken, though indeed it is the accent only and not the dialect that now one hears, excepting a few idioms and words. From Glasgow I came here to make what we call the tertianship or third year of noviceship, before taking the last vows. It began ~~with~~ in October and will end on Aug. 15. In Lent we went out to preach 'missions' and retreats: my business lay on the coast of Cumberland and on my return I found your letter, to which I shall now reply.

You see that we are not far and perhaps you might see your way to a visit; for I could not go to London without business now, being like a novice again. The grounds look well and would have looked better if the late terrible gale had not felled our trees and blasted our foliage — a thing I never saw before: they say the complaint is widespread. If you can, let me have a card beforehand, but one day is pretty much as another: Sundays ~~is per~~ and Wednesdays are commonly the freest and the afternoon better than the morning, the earlier ^in it^ the better.

I always liked and admired poor Green.[2] He seemed to me upright in mind and life. I wish I had made more of the opportunities I had of seeing him in my 10 months at Oxford, for he lived close by. His fortune fell first on Knox and then on Hegel and he was ~~bor~~ meant for better things. Probably if he had lived longer he would have written something that wd. have done the same.

What you ~~say~~ ^write^ about the wide knowledge of antiquity in the last century is true, I am sure. I do not know what to say except that they cared less for minute scholarship. But in the century before that ^too^ what a knowledge educated men had! for instance of mythology. However there must have been textbooks now superseded. Did you ever know any one, any young man at all events, read Lipsius de Magnitudine Romana[3] (is it not called? You see I do not even know the title)? ^Such books as^ this would have ~~been~~ served the purpose of modern classical dictionaries. But this is not all: Addis (by the by, he is now fellow or professor of the new Irish ~~Uni~~ University)[4] used to ask what philosophy good or bad — what system — did we ever learn at Oxford?

About Egyptian — but I think we must talk the rest.

I heard from Garrett[5] not so long since. He is going or gone to Tasmania on business for six months. Hobart, Tasmania is, as theological theses say, his 'necessary and sufficient' address. In India 'Calcutta' or Bengal would find him. Strange that what wd. miss at Putney should hit in the whole of Bengal. (However the right Indian Address is Bengal Club, Calcutta.)

Poor Forster![6] I suppose everyone respects him, but I believe his retirement is a way out of difficulties. However I see no papers now.

Believe me your affectionate friend Gerard M. Hopkins S.J.

Ah! you will have heard the Nibelungs' Ring.[7] You must tell me your impressions.

[1] i.e. Irish nationalists prepared to support violent action; so called from the society formed by John O'Mahony in 1868, which took its name from the Fianna, a 2nd- and 3rd-c. band of warriors.

[2] Thomas Hill Green (1836–82; *ODNB*), former tutor of GMH, fellow of Balliol, and White's Professor of Moral Philosophy from 1878, who died on 26 Mar. 1882. He was a man of character and influence, and is perhaps best known for his criticism of Hume's philosophy and the posthumous *Prolegomena to Ethics*. See *CW* iv. 51–3.

[3] *De Militia Romana* (1595).

[4] Addis was elected Fellow in Mental and Moral Philosophy of the Royal University of Ireland in Apr. 1882, but resigned in Oct. of the same year. Although the Catholic University of Ireland was founded in 1854 with John Henry Newman as its first rector, it declined after he left in 1857, but was re-formed in 1880 with the establishment of the Royal University of Ireland, of which University College Dublin, at which GMH was shortly to teach, was a constituent college.

[5] See letter to Garrett of 22 Mar. 1872 and Biographical Register.

[6] The strongly moral and usually moderate William Edward Forster (1818–86; *ODNB*), whose 1870 bill had established the system of national education in England, had been appointed by Gladstone chief secretary for Ireland in 1880, at one of the most difficult times in Ireland's history. In 1880 he failed to carry the Compensation for Disturbance Bill, which was designed to compensate tenants who had been evicted (it

went through the Commons but was thrown out by the House of Lords) and he also failed to recognize the importance of Parnell. In Oct. 1881, Charles Stewart Parnell, President of the Land League, which had been formed to give Irish farmers the right to own the land they worked on, gave warnings of violence in response to the inadequacies of the 1881 Second Land Bill. Parnell was imprisoned in Kilmainham gaol (Dublin) under emergency measures 'on reasonable suspicion' of encouraging violence. By Apr. 1882 Gladstone wanted him out of gaol to calm popular protest, and negotiated the 'Kilmainham treaty', which agreed that in exchange for his release and a government promise to help with tenants' arrears of rent, Parnell would denounce violence and appeal for law and order. Forster resigned in protest on 2 May 1882. His replacement, Lord Frederick Charles Cavendish, was murdered in Phoenix Park on 6 May 1882.

[7] In May 1882, the impresario Alfred Schulz-Curtius presented Angelo Neumann's touring company in a performance of the cycle of four operas, *Der Ring des Nibelungen*, by Richard Wagner (1813–83) at Her Majesty's Theatre. It was the first complete performance in England and was conducted by Anton Seidel. During Act III of *Die Walküre* the bass singer of the part of Wotan, Emil Scaria, broke down and lost his memory, though he later recovered.

15 May 1882 to Robert Bridges

LRB, no. LXXXII, p. 144 Bodleian, Dep. Bridges, vol. 91, fos. 192–3

Manresa House, Roehampton, S.W. May 15 1882.

Dearest Bridges, — ~~w~~Will Thursday, which is Ascension Day, do? Come in the afternoon, the earlier the better. But if it rains I should say put it off.

The weather is most bleak and I should like you to see our grounds to advantage, which on a day like this can never be; but besides, the great gale of the 30th felled three of our trees and blighted the foliage in a way I never saw before.[1] The lime tops are almost bare: the young leaves being withered have been falling in the East winds of late and on the ground look like ~~dry~~ tealeaves after boiling dried.

But we have a remarkable show of buttercups. I suppose you would not see the like in Italy.

We have also three remarkable pictures of great size by a lady, a sort of "new departure".[2]

Perhaps what I took for Manresca was Manrexa, but that is wrong too: x and s are not the same in Spanish, though x and j are.

I would say Wednesday, our usual weekly holiday, but this week I do not feel quite sure about it.

I suppose Mrs. Molesworth did not ~~fol~~ forward my last letter. On second thoughts I suppose she did. Anyhow you got it.

Strictly, any day would do. But I am chary of my time for study, which now thickens as the time thins.

Believe me yours Gerard M Hopkins S.J.

By the by, your note is dated the 12th: it bears today's postmark.

[1] The gale affected the South coast and home counties (i.e. those nearest London: Middlesex, Surrey, Kent, and Essex, and possibly Hertfordshire and Sussex). It was strongest between 4.00 and 8.00 p.m in London, whipping the raised level of the Thames into substantial waves, felling trees and chimneys. Though it caused only two deaths in the capital, there were a number of casualties along the south coast, where trees fell onto buildings, boats were capsized, and people drowned (*The Times*, 1 May 1882, 6 f.).

[2] Probably by Madam Courtauld-Arendrup (1846–1934; *ODNB*), whose visits are recorded in the porter's journals. Edith Courtauld lost her mother in a horrific riding accident when she was 9. When a young woman she was given a studio by her father in a field opposite their home and with some assistance and much experimentation and determination, she became an artist. She was for a brief time part of the St John's Wood art circle and lived in a rented house and studio at 35 Grove End Road. In Egypt with her father in 1872 in order to see Eastern scenery for her paintings, she met S. Adolph Arendrup, a Lieutenant-Colonel in the Egyptian army. They were married in Paris and settled in Cairo. Arendrup was killed in 1875 and, after the birth of their son, Axel, Edith returned to Britain. She exhibited large paintings at the Royal Academy and the Dudley Gallery and became a generous and important patron of the Catholic Church in London, among other things establishing a church and religious house at Wimbledon. She also worked among the poor in Dublin. Her one picture preserved in illustration, a milking scene in Madeira, shows her style as realist and competent. The titles and whereabouts of the paintings which she gave to Roehampton on 29 Oct. 1881 are now unknown but among her religious paintings are ones with titles such as *The First Palm Sunday* (National Gallery, Victoria, Australia), *Earth hath lost her King* (RA 1874), *Peter went out and wept bitterly*, *Daybreak on Mount Calvary* (both RA 1872), and a life-size painting of St Ignatius that was hung in the chapel and then the stairwell at Manresa House.

5 June 1882 to Robert Bridges

LRB, no. LXXXIII, p. 145 Bodleian, Dep. Bridges, vol. 91, fos. 194–5

Manresa House, Roehampton, S.W. June 5 '82.

Dearest Bridges, — My heart warmed towards that little Bertie Molesworth[1] (I do not mean by this that he is so very small), so that if you were to bring him again I shd. be glad to see him. (But I am afraid he felt dull. He is shy I dare say.) However I expect he is no longer with you. It cannot be denied nevertheless that the presence of a third person is a restraint upon confidential talk.

Davis the gardener was discontented that I would not let you buy his peaches: he wd. have let you have them on reasonable terms, he said.[2]

I have been studying the cuckoo's song.[3] I find it to ~~be~~ v~~e~~ary much. In the first place cuckoos do not always sing (or the same cuckoo does not always sing) at the same pitch or in the same key: there are, so to say, alto cuckoos and tenor cuckoos. In particular they sing lower in flying and the interval is then also least, it being an effort to them to strike the higher note, which is therefore more variable than the other. When they perch they sing wrong at first, I mean they correct their first try, raising the upper note. The interval varies as much as from less than a minor third to nearly as much as a common fourth and this last is the ~~inter? s~~ tune when the bird is in loud and good song.

About the book I will not write.[4]

Your affectionate friend Gerard M. Hopkins S.J.

[1] Son of RB's eldest sister Maria. The porter's journal shows that RB visited on 18 May.

[2] RB vividly remembered the incident, including his explanation in *The Testament of Beauty*, Book IV, *Ethick*, ll. 406–58 (1928). As a Tertian GMH was forbidden to eat between meals. When he acquiesced to RB's insistence, it was so as not to offend against charity (J. F. Cotter, *Hopkins Annual* 1993, p. 107).

[3] See GMH's poetic fragment 'Repeat that, repeat'.

[4] The MS of *Prometheus the Firegiver.*

7 June 1882 to Robert Bridges

LRB, no. LXXXIV, p. 146 Bodleian, Dep. Bridges, vol. 91, fos. 196–197[v]

Manresa House, Roehampton, S.W. June 7 1882.

Dearest Bridges, — You might surely have guessed that I had some reason for my silence. It was not want of admiration.

(1) I hope Mrs. Molesworth will not long be laid up. But if she were to be so she would not wish to keep you every afternoon at home. (2) Your niece can do the very thing she has come to do when you give her the opportunity by your absence. (3) There are houses at Roehampton, Barnes, Richmond, Twickenham, Ham, Petersham, Kew, Isleworth, Mortlake, Wimbledon, all near us. (5) Canon Dixon: you have answered this admirably. (6) Your brother: and this. (7) The club: "this is past and present"; then not future, such as the rest of this week or next.

I have revised ~~tw~~ nearly twice through. The worst is that one seasons over a thing and one's first verjuice flattens into ~~flattery~~ ^slobber^ and sweet sylla~~bu~~ bub. Or one ripens; yet there is something in "the first sprightly runnings".[1]

Your affectionate friend Gerard M. Hopkins S.J.

Tomorrow, Corpus Christi,[2] you must not come: I shd. be engaged.

I see I have ~~left~~ overlooked 4. the Turkish baths. ~~I do not kno~~ Instead of answering — but by the by too many Turkish baths are not good. An old gentleman (commercial) that I gave a retreat to here nearly died in one.

You were asking me about my own writing. You perhaps forget my mentioning my beginning an ode in honour of Fr. Edmund Campion's martyrdom.[3] Little is done, but I hope to be able to go on with it and that it will not be inferior to the two other odes. It is dithyrambic or what they used to call Pindaric (which as we have Pindar now is unPindaric),[4] I mean in ^variable^ stanzas and not ~~st~~ antistrophic; ~~It has~~ like Alexander's Feast or Lycidas. It has ^some^ new rhythmical effects.

But if I must write about Prometheus, then I will shortly ^say^, what it seems scarcely necessary to say, how beautiful and masterly it is, what a sense of style, unknown in our age, in the phrasing and the verse, how vigorous the thought, and how Greek, whether you wished it or not, the choruses, and yet so fresh.

[1] Dryden, *Aureng-Zebe*, IV. i. 42.

[2] The feast of 'the body of Christ', 8 June, was especially important to GMH (see also notes in *CW* v and vii). See letters to RB of 10–11 and 16 June 1882.

[3] See letter to RB of 16–17 Sept. 1881.

[4] Pindar (532–443 BC), a much admired Greek lyric poet, whose diction is exceptionally bold and vigorous and whose forms complex; for some years he was also much misunderstood under the influence of Abraham Cowley (1618–67; *ODNB*), who wrote *Pindarique Odes* (1656), based on a superficial reading of the originals. Although Pindar's ode was as different from Cowley's, said Edmund Gosse, 'as a crystal from a jelly-fish' (*Life of William Congreve* (London, 1888), 159), Cowley's version, an abrupt, irregular, amorphous, and exalted ode, was much imitated, until Congreve pointed out the error in his *A Pindaric Ode to the Queen with a Discourse on the Pindaric Ode* (1706). 'Pindaric' for a time became synonymous with rhapsodic irregularity, rather like the dithyrambic, with its wild, vehement, and boisterous nature. Dryden's 'Alexander's Feast' (1697) was influenced by Cowley but Milton's 'Lycidas' (1637) has a careful development nearer to the genuine Pindaric structure of strophe, antistrophe, and epode.

10–11 June 1882 to Robert Bridges

LRB, no. LXXXV, p. 147 Bodleian, Dep. Bridges, vol. 91, fos. 198–199v

Manresa House, Roehampton, S.W. June 10 1882.

Dearest Bridges, — It was a needless and tedious frenzy (no, the phrase is not like Flatman's "serene and rapturous joys" to which poor Purcell had to drudge the music):[1] another train came ~~a~~ up on that train's tail, and indeed it was a dull duncery that overhung us both not to see that its being Ascot day ensured countless more trains and not fewer. There was a lovely and passionate scene (for about the space of the last trump) between me and a tallish gentleman (I daresay he was a cardsharper) in ~~the~~ ^your^ carriage who was by way of being you; I smiled, I murmured with my lips at him, I waved farewells, but he would not give in, till with burning shame (though the whole thing was, ~~I~~ as I say, like the duels of archangels)[2] I saw suddenly what I was doing.

I wish our procession ~~had been~~, since you were to see it, had been better: I find it is agreed it was heavy and dead. Now a Corpus Christi procession shd. be stately indeed, but it shd. be brisk and joyous. But I grieve more, I am vexed, that you had not a book to follow the words sung~~:~~. the office is by St. Thomas[3] and contains all his hymns, I think. These hymns, though they have the imperfect rhetoric and weakness in idiom of all medieval Latin verse (except, say, the Dies Irae: I do not mean weakness in ~~Cicer~~ classical idiom — that does not matter — but want of feeling for or command of any idiom), are nevertheless remarkable works of genius and would have given meaning to the whole, even to the music, much more to the rite.

It is long since such things had any significance for you. But what is strange and unpleasant is that you sometimes speak ~~of~~ as if they had in reality none for me and you were only waiting with a certain disgust till I ^too^ should be disgusted ^with myself^ enough to throw off the mask. You said something of the sort walking on the Cowley Road when we were last at Oxford together — in '79 it must have been. Yet I can hardly think you do not think I am in earnest. And let me say, to take no higher ground, that without earnestness there is nothing sound or beautiful in character and that a cynical vein much indulged ~~?~~ coarsens everything in us. Not that you do ~~in~~ overindulge this vein in other matters: why then does it bulk out in that diseased and varicose way in this?[4]

Believe me your affectionate friend Gerard Hopkins S.J.

June 11 — Since writing the above I have luckily come across the enclosed, which contains some of the hymns.

Remember me very kindly to Mrs. Molesworth, who is, I hope, better. Also to Mr. Woolrych. Must meet him next time I am at — but I shall never be there by the by now.

I am just starting for Brentford.

[1] Purcell set to music Thomas Flatman's ode, 'On the King's return to White-hall after his Summer's Progress', in 1684. The poem opens: 'From these serene and rapturous joys | A country life alone can give, | Exempt from tumult and from noise, | Where Kings forget the trouble of their reigns, | And are almost as happy as their humble swains, | By feeling that they live:' (*Caroline Poets*, ed. G. Saintsbury, 3 vols. (1905–21), iii. 277–8).

[2] i.e. performed quietly. See Jude: 9: 'When Michael the archangel disputing with the devil, contending about the body of Moses, he durst not bring against him the judgement of railing speech, but said, The Lord command thee.'

[3] In 1264 Pope Urban IV commissioned Thomas Aquinas to compose an office for the Feast of Corpus Christi.

[4] The comment seems to have hit its mark. See letter of 26–7 Nov. 1882.

16 June 1882 to Robert Bridges

LRB, no. LXXXVI, p. 149 Bodleian, Dep. Bridges, vol. 91, fos. 200–201v

Manresa House, Roehampton, S.W. June 16 1882.

Dearest Bridges, — But at any rate do not come on Sunday —, for I shall be away taking duty at Westminster.

Put S.W. after Roehampton: your last note had five postmarks, one of them very sinister, as if there had been some struggling or straying.

Corpus Xti[1] differs from all other feasts in this, that its reason and occasion is ~~a~~ present. The first Christmas Day, the first Palm Sunday, Holy Thursday 'in Caena Domini', Easter^,^ ~~Sun Day~~ Whitsunday, and so on were ~~festivities~~ to those who took part in them festivities de praesenti {*of the immediate moment*}, but now, to us, they are anniversaries and commemorations only. But Corpus Christi is the feast of the Real Presence:; ~~and~~ therefore ^it is^ the most purely joyous of solemnities. Naturally the Blessed Sacrament is carried in procession ^at it^, as you saw. But the procession has more meaning and mystery than this: it represents the process of the Incarnation and the world's redemption. As Christ went forth from the bosom of the Father as the ~~Lanb~~ Lamb of God and eucharistic victim to die upon the altar of the cross for the world's ransom; then rising returned leading the procession of the flock redeemed / so in this ceremony his body in statu victimali {*in the role of victim*} is carried to the ~~a~~Altar of Repose as it is called and back to the tabernacle at the high altar, which will represent the bosom of the godhead. The procession out may represent the cooperation of the angels, ^or of the^ patriarchs~~,~~ and prophets, the return the Church Catholic from Christ's death to the end of time. If these things are mismanaged, as they mostly are, it is not for want of significance in the ceremony.

Prometheus has been twice revised~~,~~. ~~w~~Whether I shall want to keep it longer I cannot say yet. We want alas! a touch of his trade this bitter June. This morning not only the air is most nipping; the very look is of a winter frostfog. ~~My~~

My best love to Canon Dixon, whom I hope soon to see.
Your affectionate friend Gerard Hopkins S.J.

[1] GMH distinguishes the Catholic festivals here. At Corpus Christi {*the body of Christ*}, a feast established in 1264, the participants celebrate that at the Eucharist the body and blood of Christ are present in the sacraments—the Real Presence. The other feasts merely commemorate the anniversaries: Christmas, now usually celebrated on 25 Dec., celebrates the birth of Christ; Palm Sunday, the last Sunday in Lent and the beginning of Holy Week, remembers his entry into Jerusalem; Holy Thursday (or Maundy Thursday) recalls the Last Supper ('Caena Domini' meaning 'the Lord's supper') at which the ceremony of the Eucharist was initiated; Easter remembers the crucifixion and resurrection of Christ; Whitsunday commemorates the descent of the Holy Ghost on the Apostles. *The Catholic Encyclopedia* (<www.newadvent.org/cathen/>) has thorough and scholarly information on each.

17 August 1882 to Fathers William Shapter, SJ, Charles De Lapasture, SJ, Francis Goldie, SJ[1]

'Four Newfound Letters: An Annotated Edition, with a Fragment of Another Letter', ed. Joseph J. Feeney, SJ, *HQ* 33/1–2 (1996), 3–17 Gonzaga 1:1
(discovered by Bischoff in Beaumont College Archives, 1949)
Addressed to 'The Rev. [*bracketed*] William Shapter | Charles de Lapasture | Francis Goldie [*bracket closed*] S.J. | St. Wilfrid's | Preston.' PM PUTNEY S.W. AU17 82 and PRESTON AU18 82. Envelope has the name of Gabriel Billot in ink in a hand not GMH's on the front and Elizth Hothersall and Thos Bolton in pencil on the reverse in another hand. One folded sheet and one half sheet, six sides.

Manresa House, Roehampton, S.W. Aug. 17 1882.
Pax Christi.

My hearties,[2] — I am going to answer "the three of yez" under one trouble — no, no, not trouble, not trouble: pleasure is the word — under one pleasure. This pleasure ~~must~~ shall be brief, because, ~~the~~ according to the one of yez, I am to call to yez on my way to Glasgow ~~to~~ so very shortly.[3] ~~This~~ However this is to know more than the Provincial knows, who told me the day before yesterday that he wd. in a day or two let me hear where he should have decided to put me.[4]

The ceremony of the vows took place at St. Joseph's, by the chicane of Fr. Minister[5] the quasi-parochus, who thinks all is grist that comes to his mill. It was thought striking and edifying by those who witnessed it, but I was one of the performers. For myself my feelings were mixed. Sometimes I thought last vows were an eventus nullus {*a non-event*} and made no difference. Then too I remembered that once I had hoped to be professed and that is always a ^sad^ heartache to me.[6] Then again and finally I thought the other thing was better, because our Lord says: Nonne qui recumbit? Ego autem ~~sum~~ in medio vestrum ^sum^ sicut qui ministrat {*The one at table, surely? Yet here I am among you as one who serves!*}.[7] Now this is in confidence to the three of yez.

Charles Gordon[8] flew back to his post by the earliest conveyances yesterday: his heart was never here. Mine is: at least I shall never be so happy, I am afraid, again as I have been under "Viewy Bob"[9] (it is solemnly true that he was so called among the clergy before he came to us). (Bar of course occasional rapture of a visit ~~to~~ ^under^ roof of present company.) De Würtzburg[10] is, I believe, going back today. Wm. Kenny[11] is to be sub-min. at Beaumont. George his brother[12] and Fr. Anderdon[13] are to go to the Holy Name. Fr. Chandlery[14] is to be praef. stud. at Glasgow, but is lingering here in the doctor's hands. Gavin[15] everybody but the Provincial says is going to Mount Street. The two Frenchmen Pères Plantier[16] and Gavoty[17] went away yesterday almost blubbering, good souls — let us say almost founding in tears.[18]

After our vows we got agate[19] among the novices, charming boys they are. One of them[20] is 68 years of age. There was an entertainment in the evening, in the society's wellknown style of gingerbread jokes and a rococo gilding of piety and tears and fond farewells, but still the general effect very nice. Alas, my style wants unction; that is what it is.

Now the difficulty is to get down simply and stately too from the plural onto the singular, for I have something to say which concerns only the one third or, so to say, East Riding[21] of you. Let me distinguish cum communi {*within the group*} the Poet, the Ascetic, and the Antiquary.[22] And for fear of mistakes I shall say that the Antiquary, to whom I want to speak, is also associated with Bilious Bouts. More ~~clar~~ ^clear^ly to individualise him let Observation with Extensive View Survey Mankind[23] from Caledonia stern and wild to the soft skies and slobbering sunshine of Italy. If now I throw in a perspective of the fine arts, of Harrogate, of Oxford old and new, of St. Frideswide, of Blessed John this and Venerable Robert that, I believe the saddle will be found with the girths taut on the right horse. Good. Then I have to say that poor Henry Bellamy[24] has suddenly lost his father by an accident and is very anxious to get prayers for him. He died a Protestant; still prayers may do much, all that is necessary in fact: in these cases I always pray backwards, if you understand, and God allows discount. It is really a great light. You ask him to have granted the grace and the difference of tense is only to you.[25] This message and these remarks do after all then concern all of you.

I should have told you that Gavin is going to Ripon to take duty for three weeks;[26] so much is settled.

Best love to Fr. Dykes,[27] Fr. Little,[28] and who is it is supplying? No matter: remember me to him and dilute the cordiality to the degree of our acquaintance; for it is preposterous to maintain with Rodriguez[29] on Particular Friendship and Affection to Parents that . . . you see my drift.

To conclude then, for I am tedious, very many thanks to you all for yr. kind~~ness~~ wishes and all, and most to the one that did it handsomest: that is only fair, is it? and breaks no bones. By the tenour of this I gather I must be in good spirits—a thing never to be granted if I can help it, it saps sympathy and importance. Believe me yours jointly and affectionately in Christ Gerard M. Hopkins S.J.

P.S. Whichever of you gets this first — at any rate push it about between the three of you like the three Graiae did their ~~own~~ ^one^ eye.[30] See Greek mythology.

Or like Hunt the Slipper.[31]

[1] William Shapter (1847–1928), Charles de Lapasture (1839–1923), Francis Goldie (1836–1912), former fellows of GMH at various Jesuit institutions, had sent their good wishes when he pronounced his Final Vows as a Jesuit on 15 Aug. Our thanks to Joseph J. Feeney, SJ, who edited the *HQ* publication, for untangling the complexities of this allusive letter. Most of these notes closely follow his, and those seeking further detail can consult his extensive bibliography.

[2] The phrase 'my hearties' (and perhaps 'the three of yez') may be a private joke on their contemporary, Henry Schomberg Kerr, SJ (1838–95), who was a Navy Commander before becoming a Jesuit and never lost his naval ways. His obituary says: 'It was considered that the discipline which he had first to obey and afterwards to direct in the navy would give him great facility in the control of the scholars [at Beaumont College], as it had previously rendered him a most effective organizer of public works in the noviceship. Perhaps the same hand was felt to be a little too firm in enforcing discipline at Beaumont.' GMH, Shapter, de Lapasture, and Goldie had all been in the same community with Kerr, and GMH and Goldie had experienced Kerr (a second-year novice) as 'organizer of public works in the noviceship'.

[3] GMH never got to Glasgow; leaving Roehampton on 22 Aug., he spent a week at Worcester (where he enjoyed an art exhibition), and on 31 Aug. arrived at Stonyhurst College.

[4] GMH was to teach the Classics to a university level, preparing some thirty-five students, called the 'Secular', 'Lay, or Gentlemen Philosophers' (as distinct from the Jesuit philosophers), for the External BA of the University of London.

[5] Frederick C. Hopkins, SJ (1844–1923). No relation though he shared the surname; contemporary, and often classmate of GMH. At Roehampton he was 'minister' (vice-rector) of the Jesuits and 'quasi-parochus' (acting pastor) of the parish. In 1887 he sailed to British Honduras as a missionary, and in 1899 became its bishop.

[6] This statement solves a long-standing riddle for GMH scholars: was GMH disappointed by not being professed? See James F. Cotter and Joseph J. Feeney, SJ, 'Forum', in *HQ* 11 (1984–5), 45–7.

[7] Luke 22: 27. When Jesus was asked at the Last Supper who is greater, the one sitting down to eat or the one serving, he answered, as GMH quotes from the Vulgate and we translate from the *Jerusalem Bible*.

[8] Charles Gordon, SJ (1831–1911). A Scots gentleman-farmer, Gordon became a Papal Zouave (a unit formed in 1861 of young, unmarried, Roman Catholic men, who volunteered to assist Pope Pius IX in his struggle against the Italian Risorgimento), entered the Jesuits at 38, was administrator in South Africa and Glasgow, and as bishop (1889) worked in Jamaica aiding poor farmers and advising the government on education. He began tertianship with GMH but left early, on 19 Dec., when sent as minister to Glasgow, where he later founded St Aloysius College.

[9] Robert Whitty, SJ (1817–95), GMH's Tertian Instructor. Irish-born, he was a diocesan priest in England and from 1850 Vicar-General of the Westminster diocese under Cardinal Wiseman. He became a Jesuit in 1857, and was professor of Canon Law at St Beuno's, superior of Jesuits in Scotland, assistant to the English Provincial, subsecretary in Rome, English Provincial, Instructor of Tertians (1881–6), and English Assistant to the Jesuit General. He was cheerful, sympathetic, 'quiet and amiable'; 'his views were singularly open' and his advice prized. As for 'Viewy Bob': 'his thoughts beguiled him into many views and theories, and his very fertility in suggesting different and sometimes conflicting plans and methods, without determining any particular one to be adopted, caused a certain amount of confusion and delay in his administration of the affairs of the diocese, as also during after life, in his rule of the Province' (*LLNN* 23 (1895–6), 345–57).

[10] Edmund de Würtzburg, SJ (1840–1906). Born in Athens of noble Bavarian lineage and cousin to the Duke of Norfolk, de (or von) Würtzburg was 'a robust and active missionary priest' who, despite weak heart and eyes, was a military chaplain in South Africa and worked in Yorkshire for thirty years, mainly among the poor of Chesterfield (1879–1901 and 1903–6).

[11] William Kenny, SJ (1844–1915). Canadian by birth, he entered the English Province and was an assistant administrator (including 'subminister' or assistant

vice-rector) at Beaumont, Mount St Mary's, Liverpool, and Roehampton. A holy and cheerful man though 'quick-tempered at times', he had a 'most charming personality' and 'great sympathy for others'.

[12] George Kenny, SJ (1840–1912). A Canadian and brother of William, he was a barrister in Halifax before entering the Society in Canada. After two years at Holy Name Parish, Manchester, he returned to North America as professor and rector in Canada and the United States. A distinguished preacher, he was 'bright, cheery, and brimful of charity'.

[13] William H. Anderdon, SJ (1816–90). A holy and devoted Anglican vicar, he became a Catholic in 1850, a diocesan priest in 1853, served as secretary to his uncle, Cardinal (then Archbishop) Manning, and became a Jesuit in 1872. A noted preacher, retreat-giver, and writer.

[14] Peter Chandlery, SJ (1846–1925). He was headmaster (praef. stud.) at Liverpool and Glasgow, professor of theology at St Beuno's, secretary (in Italy) to the Jesuit General's English Assistant, editor of *LLNN*, writer, and retreat-giver. He enjoyed sketching, loved Italy, and had a 'deep piety' and 'habitual good humour'.

[15] Michael Gavin, SJ (1843–1919). Irish by birth, he was ordained with GMH, taught theology at St Beuno's, and in 1882 went to Mount Street (London) to serve at the Farm Street Church for thirty-six years as preacher, lecturer, writer, and director of the Men's Sodality (a spiritual association). A painstaking worker, he had a 'delightful old-world courtesy' (*LLNN*).

[16] Emile Plantier, SJ (1846–1924). A member of the Lyons Province, he was headmaster or chaplain of schools in Marseilles and Lyons, directed groups interested in social problems, served in several parishes, and in 1920–2 worked with Action Populaire near Paris.

[17] Ernest Gavoty, SJ (1847–1929). From the Lyons Province, he taught or did minor administration at schools in Lyons, Cairo (Egypt), and Avignon, then was minister or curate at Jesuit houses and parishes in central and southern France.

[18] They were returning to a France whose government attacked or expelled the Jesuits in 1764, 1828, 1843, 1880 (two years before this letter), and 1901; Jesuits were seen variously as successful schoolmasters, and/or as influential, controversial, and politically dangerous priests.

[19] The Lancashire term to 'get agate' meaning to 'get going' would be appropriate to his Preston audience.

[20] James Cuddon (1816–96). Actually 66 years old, Cuddon was a successful barrister who after his wife's death in 1881 entered the Jesuits on 16 Mar. 1882, but because of ill health left the order on 24 Oct. 1882.

[21] Yorkshire was divided into three parts ('thridings'), the East, the West, and the North Riding.

[22] 'The Poet' was probably Shapter and 'the Ascetic' de Lapasture; 'the Antiquary' was certainly Goldie, who had studied philosophy at Ushaw College (near Durham, perhaps close enough to Scotland to be 'Caledonia'), did theology in Italy, served in Harrogate for seven years as a diocesan priest, worked as a Jesuit in the parish at Oxford (where he succeeded GMH), and by 1882 had already published *The Life of Blessed John Berchmans* and booklets on 'The Story of St. Frideswide, Virgin and Patroness of Oxford' and 'A Bygone Oxford'.

[23] A parody of the opening couplet of Samuel Johnson's 'The Vanity of Human Wishes'; GMH quotes the same couplet in the letter to RB of 26–28 Oct. 1880.

[24] Henry Ernest Bellamy (1861–1932) was a convert who had been a member of the Oxford Catholic Club and known GMH (1879–80) and Goldie (1879–80) at St Aloysius Church. GMH, as the Club's spiritual director, took part in its meetings from Dec. 1878 to Oct. 1879. Bellamy's niece, Ethel F. Bellamy (letter in Bischoff

Collection, Gonzaga) wrote that he went to be trained as a Roman Catholic priest, gave that up and went to America, where he was a professor of music, returned to England and joined the D'Oyly Carte Opera Company. He sang small baritone roles in Gilbert and Sullivan operas in 1888–94 and in 1896–7 and served as business manager for several D'Oyly Carte companies before retiring as the company's sole Business Manager in 1920. He and GMH appear in a group photograph of 1879, and see the letter to him of 21 Jan. 1889.

[25] GMH's argument is philosophically careful: God, as spirit, is not limited by matter nor (therefore) by time; a human can thus pray for something now, have the prayer heard by a timeless God, and 'answered' even in what seems (to the human) the past. GMH makes a similar point in his sonnet 'Henry Purcell'.

[26] For temporary pastoral work (or 'supply'); there was no Jesuit house there.

[27] Thomas Dykes, SJ (1820–88). An Anglican priest whose wife died soon after marriage, he became a Catholic in 1851 and almost immediately a Jesuit; as professor, curate, rector, and builder, he was 'active, cheerful, genial', highly logical, and 'an universal favourite by his kindness, his genial manner, and excellent preaching'. Highly successful at Mount St Mary's, he was GMH's rector there (1877–8) and at the time of the letter, rector at Preston. GMH called him 'a good friend of mine and very hospitable' in the letter to RWD of 24 Sept. 1881.

[28] Thomas Little, SJ (1835–85). After Stonyhurst and the Jamaica and Guyana missions, he worked in Preston from 1880 until his death. He had been GMH's subminister at Stonyhurst (1870–2).

[29] Alphonsus Rodriguez (1526–1616), Jesuit priest and ascetical writer, not to be confused with the laybrother of the same name (*c.*1533–1617) honoured in GMH's sonnet. In his three-volume *Practice of Perfection and Christian Virtues*, read in the past by Jesuit novices, Rodriguez cautions against 'particular friendships' with fellow religious and 'inordinate affection for kindred', writing, e.g., that 'a good religious . . . must try to avoid as far as he can all manner of intercourse with his kinsmen' and not be corrupted by their 'useless conversation' (i. 257; ii. 427, 436). Like GMH, many Jesuits find Rodriguez's asceticism monastic, excessive, and inhuman.

[30] The Graiae (or Graeae)—'the old women'—were sisters of the Gorgons and grey-haired from birth; among them, they had only one tooth and one eye, which they shared.

[31] A Victorian parlour game in which players sit in a circle pretending to mend shoes; when an outsider brings a slipper to be 'mended', the others secretly pass the slipper around until someone is caught holding it.

26–7 September 1882 to Robert Bridges

LRB, no. LXXXVII, p. 150 Bodleian, Dep. Bridges, vol. 91, fos. 202–5

Stonyhurst College, Blackburn. Sept. 26 1882.

My dearest Bridges, — I must break this mournful silence. I began a letter yesterday, but am not pleased with it and now shall be brief.

I have been here[1] since this month came in. My appointment is to teach our "philosophers" (like ~~i~~undergraduate students) Latin, Greek, and perhaps hereafter English (when I know more about it) for the London B.A. degree. My pupils will be here with the next month. The Provincial[2] further added that what time was left over I might employ in writing one or other of the books I had named to him. But very little time will be left over and I cd. never make time. Indeed now, with nothing to do but prepare, I cannot get forward with my ode. But one must hope against hope.

I did in my last week at Roehampton write 16 ~~rough~~ pages of a rough draft of a commentary on ~~the~~ St. Ignatius' Spiritual Exercises. This ^work^ would interest none but a Jesuit, but to me it is interesting enough and, as you see, it is very professional.[3]

I shall try and read the Greek tragic poets, but it is sad how slow I am. I am now in the Agamemnon and Supplices (Aeschylus's, I mean). How noble is the style! I have made some emendations which seem to be great improvements. But what I pay most attention to is the art of the choric parts, for this was one of the subjects on which I had proposed to write, the art of the Greek lyric poets, including of course the lyric parts of dramatic poets. I have not time at present to tell you what the leading idea or my leading discovery is. In part of course my work here may serve me for the books I should like to write.[4]

The Provincial gave me leave to go to any one of our houses I liked till my term began. I did go for a week to Worcester, where there was, by the by, a very well worth seeing exhibition, but then I thought it better to come here at once. He said moreover that if I wanted to go elsewhere I was to apply to him. He would no doubt readily have given me leave to visit you and, had there been the possibility of saying mass, I might therefore have seen Yattenden. But it was not to be.

I wish I could show you this place. It is upon my word worth seeing. The new college, though~~,~~ there is no real beauty in the design, is nevertheless imposing and the furniture and fittings are a joy to see. There is always a stirring scene, contractors, builders, masons, bricklayers, carpenters, stonecutters and carvers, all on the spot; a traction engine twice a day fetches stone from a quarry on the fells; engines of all sorts send ~~out~~ their gross and foulsmelling smoke all over us; cranes keep swinging; and so on. There are acres of flat roof ~~from~~ which, when the air is not thick, as unhappily it mostly is, ~~one sees~~ ^com^mands a noble view of this Lancashire landscape, Pendle Hill, Ribblesdale, the fells, and all round, bleakish but solemn and beautiful. There is a garden # with a bowling green, walled in by massive yew hedges, a bowered yew-walk, two real Queen Ann summerhouses, observatories under government,[5] orchards, ~~graperies~~ vineries; greenhouses, workshops, a plungebath, fivescourts,[6] a mill, a farm, a fine cricketfield besides a huge playground; then the old ~~mas~~ mansion, ponds, towers, quadrangles, fine cielings, chapels, a church, a fine library, museums, MSS illuminated and otherwise, coins, works of art; then two other dependent establishment[s], one a furlong, the other 3/4 a mile off; the river Hodder with lovely fairyland views, especially at the bathingplace, the Ribble too, the Calder, Whalley with an abbey, Clitheroe with a castle, Ribchester with a strange old chapel and Roman remains; schoolboys and animation, philosophers and foppery (not to be taken too seriously) a jackdaw, ^a^ rookery, goldfish, a Clough with waterfalls, fishing, grouse, an anemometer,[7] a sunshine guage, a sundial, an icosihedron, statuary, magneti~~sm~~c instruments, a laboratory, gymnasium, ambulacrum, studio, fine engravings, Arundel chromos, Lancashire talked with naïveté on the premises (~~W~~ Hoo said this and hoo did that[8]) — and, what caps all, if I were shewing it you, as I hope to do (I have to shew it ^too^ often: it takes from an hour and a half to three hours: I do it with more pride than pleasure) you could not make me wretched now by either stealing or buying fruit.

I want to hear about Yattenden (or Yattendon?).[9] And when will Prometheus be out?

I should be sorry to think you did nothing down there but literary work: could you not be a magistrate? This would be honourable and valuable public duty~~?~~. Consider it.

I am your affectionate friend Gerard M. Hopkins S.J.
Sept. 27 1882.

[1] He remained on the staff there till Feb. 1884. He taught Greek and Latin to candidates for the external Intermediate and Degree examinations of the University of London.

[2] Father Edward Ignatius Purbrick (1830–1914). He was born in Birmingham and educated at King Edward VI's Grammar school and Christ Church, Oxford. He converted to Catholicism in 1850 and entered the Jesuit novitiate in 1851, and was ordained priest in 1864. He became Rector of Stonyhurst in 1869, Visitor to the Canadian mission 1879, and Provincial of the English Province 1880–8; Instructor of Tertians 1888–9; 1895–7, Superior of the new college at Wimbledon; 1897, Provincial of New York and Maryland Province. He returned to England in 1903 in failing health. He then became Spiritual Father at Clongowes and Liverpool in 1904; Instructor of Tertians in New York in 1906 and finally, from 1907 to 1914, Spiritual Father at Manchester (Thomas, 90).

[3] Devlin commented on these notes that while they are too incomplete to constitute a commentary, their 'main interest is in their personal reliving of the Christian and Catholic revelation in the light of the Exercises', especially 'the great sacrifice' (*S*, 107). See *CW* v.

[4] This is the first mention of his long-term projects on Greek lyric, choruses, the Pindaric, and the Dorian measure, which emerged from his discussion with Fr Purbrick. Further moments in the long and, as it turned out, never-finished progress of these projects can be found in letters of 18–19 Oct. 1882 to RB, 14 Jan. 1883 to AMWB, 2–4 Oct. 1886 to RB, 21–2 Oct. 1886 to RB, 28 Oct. 1886 to RB, 7 Nov. 1886 to Patmore, 11 Dec. 1886 to RB, 23 Dec. 1886 to AMWB, 20 Jan. 1887 to Patmore, 1 May 1887 to RB, 30 July 1887 to RB.

[5] Serious astronomical observations were made at Stonyhurst; some of the Jesuits took part in international astronomical expeditions, and the school was one of the first in the country to teach science subjects.

[6] There are still fives courts at Stonyhurst, as at several public schools. Fives is an esoteric game, rather like squash, with gloved hands for rackets.

[7] Of this list of facilities, the anemometer is the wind gauge; the icosahedron (misspelt by GMH) is a twenty-sided solid contained by twenty equilateral triangles; the ambulacrum was (at Stonyhurst) the covered playground used in wet weather; and the Arundel chromos (most of them still there) are a collection of chromolithographic prints by the Arundel Society, which was founded in 1848 (it ceased in 1897) to 'promote the knowledge of art by copying and publishing important works of ancient masters'.

[8] The feminine third person pronoun 'hoo' derives directly from the Old English 'heo' and survived in Lancashire well into the 20th c.

[9] Mrs Bridges wrote to Abbott: 'My father, Alfred Waterhouse the architect, bought Yattendon estate in 1876. He built himself a house on the hill above the village, and there we went to live in April 1881. The eighteenth-century Manor House was then to let—and this was just when RB was looking about for a country house to settle in with his mother. One thing that made him think it would suit her was its close proximity to the church. They settled there in 1882, about September. I don't know how to fix the exact date, but I know RB was living there by 29 October 1882, when my brother, Paul Waterhouse, came of age. RB later became a member of the local (Bradfield) Board of Guardians.'

[Early October 1882] to Robert Bridges

LRB, no. LXXXVIII, p. 152 Bodleian, Dep. Bridges, vol. 91, fos. 207–208^{v}

[Stonyhurst College, Blackburn.]

Dearest Bridges, — You are in the infinite leisure of Yattenden and you do not write.[1]

I send with this the air to <u>I have loved flowers that fade</u>.[2] A young Mr. Fitzpatrick is going to put me an accompaniment to it, but in the meantime I want you to see the tune. Playing it is of little use, unless it were on the violin; the snapping of a piano cannot give the extreme smoothness I mean: it must be sung. If you do not like it I think it must be a misunderstanding, for properly rendered I believe it could not fail to please you.

I want to go # ^on^ with the study of harmony, but now my # scholastic work is ~~beg~~ beginning and at first at all events I fear I shall ~~have~~ ^not^ have time even for necessities, let alone luxuries or rather bywork.

I have finished the Leaden and Golden Echoes (meant for a maidens' song in St. Winefred) and am pleased with it: I shall send it you when I have put the last touches; it would be rash to send it today.

I want to see Prometheus out and when published for people here to see it. Remember me very kindly to Mrs. Molesworth and believe me your affectionate friend Gerard M. Hopkins S.J.

Better let me have it soon back, and then if you like it you cd. afterwards have an accompanied copy.

[1] RB was particularly busy at this time, 'settling in' at Yattendon.

[2] Not known to be extant; but see *CW* vi for GMH's music.

16 October 1882 to Robert Bridges

LRB, no. LXXXIX, p. 153 Bodleian, Dep. Bridges, vol. 91, fos. 206^{r-v}, 209

Look at this: Saturday Review Oct. 14 1882~~,~~: The Sorrows of Prince Bismarck:[1] "On some luckless day the bookseller sends out his catalogue, with such items as 'Love Lies Bleeding. By G. Hopkins. Pages unopened <this is wrong: it should be uncut>.[2] Autograph poem and inscription by the author. Published at Five Shillings. Fourpence.' Then these catalogues fall into the hands of Hopkins and his friends, and there is wailing and shrieking on Parnassus". It seems to be meant for me. Andrew Lang[3] perhaps~~,~~ ^or^ somebody who knows of me through you ~~rather than~~. It shews by the by what a shocking bad name mine would be to publish under. For in itself Love Lies Bleeding is a good title, for instance for a Shaksperian comedy. Be careful not to betray me to suspects and dangerous people.

"G. Hopkins." Oct. 16 1882.

[4]I suppose then you are more confirmed at Yattendon than before and so I am more likely to see you there.

Were there two sheets in your letter or three? For the last begins with a small letter~~; though ^it is true^ the first ends with a blank and the sense goes right on~~ as though it were a continuation, though nothing is wanting to the sense, it is true, and the first sheet ends with a stop and a blank after it.

[1] An unsigned would-be-witty article. The three sorrows are: the infliction on him by authors of presentation copies (and herein comes the extract made by GMH); the printing of books in 'unpatriotic legible Roman characters'; and attempts at phonetic spelling.

[2] 'Unopened' is right.

[3] Andrew Lang (1844–1912: *ODNB*) was a prolific author, editor, translator, and reviewer, and friend of RB—it was his review of RB which prompted renewed contact between GMH and RB. His earliest volume was *Ballads and Lyrics of Old France* (1872) and in 1881 he published the voguish *XXXII Ballades of Blue China*. RB showed him some of GMH's poems, but GMH dreaded the publicity. See letters to RB of 21 Oct. 1882, 26–7 Nov. 1882, and 18–19 Aug. 1888.

[4] This separate leaf was misplaced by RB and thought by Abbott to belong here or hereabouts. But there is most of a page remaining blank after 'Oct. 16 1882' and the papers are of slightly different sizes; so it is probably not a continuation of the letter above. It is perhaps a note included with the MS of 'The Leaden Echo'. RB placed the letter we date 16 Oct. 1882 before the letter we assign to early Oct. 1882 and this separate leaf afterwards.

18–19 October 1882 to Robert Bridges

LRB, no. XC, p. 154 Bodleian, Dep. Bridges, vol. 91, fos. 210–214[v]

Stonyhurst College, Blackburn. [*embossed heading*]
Oct. 18 1882.

Dearest Bridges, — I have read of Whitman's (1) "Pete"[1] in the library at Bedford Square (and perhaps something else; if so I forget), which you pointed out; (2) two pieces in the Athenaeum ^or Academy^, one on the Man-of-War Bird, the other beginning "Spirit that formed this scene";[2] (3) short extracts in a review by Saintsbury in the Academy:[3] this is all I remember. I cannot have read ~~six pieces~~ more than half a dozen pieces at most.

This, though very little, is quite enough to give a strong impression of his marked and original manner and way s of thought and ^in particular^ of his rhythm. It might be even enough, I ~~wi~~^sha^ll not deny, to originate or, ~~m~~^much more^, influence another's style: they say the French trace their whole modern school of landscape to a single piece of Constable's exhibited at the Salon early this century.[4]

The question then is ^only^ about the fact. But first I may as well say what I should not otherwise have said, that I always knew in my heart ~~that~~ Walt Whitman's mind ~~was~~ ^to be^ more like my own than any other man's living. As he is a very great scoundrel this is not a pleasant confession. And this also makes me the more ~~cur~~^desir^ous to read him and the more determined tha~~n~~t I will not.

Nevertheless I believe that you are quite mistaken about this piece~~,~~ and that on second thoughts you will find the fancied ~~imitation~~ ^resemblance^ diminish and the imitation disappear.[5]

And first of the rhythm. Of course I saw that there was to the eye something in my long lines like his, that the one would remind people of the other. And both are in irregular rhythms. There the likeness ends. ~~So far~~ The pieces of his I read were mostly in an irregular ~~pr~~ rhythmic prose: that is what they are thought to be meant for and what they seemed to me to be. Here is a fragment of a line I remember: "or a handkerchief designedly dropped".[6] This is in a dactylic rhythm — or let us say anapaestic; for it is a great convenience in English to assume that the stress is always ~~on~~ ^at^ the end of the foot; the consequence of which assumption is that in ordinary verse there are only two English feet possible, the iamb and the anapaest, and even in my regular sprung rhythm only one additional, the fourth paeon:[7] for convenience' sake assuming this, then the above fragment is anapaestic — "ór å hánd | kerchief . . . | . desígn | edly drópped" — and there is a break down, a designed break of rhythm, after "handkerchief", done no doubt that the line may not become downright verse, as it would be if he had said "or a handkerchief purposely dropped". Now you can of course say that he meant ^pure^ verse and that the foot is a paeon — "ór å hánd | kerchief desígn | edly drópped"; ^or^ that he means, without fuss, what I should achieve by looping the syllable de and calling ~~it~~ ^that foot^ an outriding foot — for the result might be attained either way. Here then I must make the answer which will apply here and to all like cases and to the ~~resemblances~~ ^examples^ which may be found up and down the poets of the use of sprung rhythm — if they could have done it they would~~;~~: sprung rhythm ~~is so~~, once you hear it, is so eminently natural ^a thing^ and so effective ^a thing^ that if they had known of it they would have used it. Many people, as ~~they~~ ^we^ say, have been "burning", but they all missed it; they took it up and mislaid it again. So far as I know — I am enquiring and presently I shall be able to speak more decidedly — it existed in full force in Anglo saxon verse and in great beauty; in a degraded and doggrel shape in Piers Ploughman[8] (I am reading that famous poem and am coming to the conclusion that it is not worth reading); Greene[9] was the last who employed it at all consciously and he never continuously; then it disappeared — for one cadence in it ^here and there^ is ~~nothing~~ not sprung rhythm and one swallow does not make a spring.[10] (I put aside Milton's case, for it is altogether singular.)

In a matter like this ~~to do~~ a thing does not exist, ~~unless it consci~~ is not done unless it is wittingly and willingly done; to recognise the form you are employing and to mean it is everything. To apply this: there is (I suppose, but you will know) no sign that Whitman means to use paeons ~~ou~~ or outriding feet where these breaks in rhythm occur; it seems to me a mere extravagance to think he means people to understand ^of themselves^ what ~~even when pointed out~~ they are slow to understand even when marked or pointed out. If he does not mean it then he does not do it; or in short what he means to write ^—^ and writes — is rhythmic prose and that only. And after all, you probably grant this.

Good. Now ^prose^ rhythm~~ic~~ ~~prose~~ i~~s~~n English is always one of two things (allowing my convention about scanning upwards or from slack to stress and not from stress to slack) — either iambic or anapaestic. You may make a third measure (let us call it) by intermixing them. One of these three simple ~~rhythms~~ ^measures^ then, all iambic or all anapaestic or mingled iambic and anapaestic, is what he in every case means to write. He dreams of no other~~. In fact the piece "Spirit that formed this scene" was to the best of my recollection real verse and~~ and he means a rugged or, as he calls it in that very piece~~,~~ "Spirit that formed this scene" (which is very instructive and should be ~~seen~~ ^read^ on this ^very^ subject), a "savage" art and rhythm.

Extremes meet, and (I must for truth's sake say what sounds pride) ~~his~~ ^this^ savage~~ or~~ ^ry^ ~~or~~ ^of his^ art, ^this rhythm^ in its last ruggedness and decomposition into common prose, comes near the last elaboration of mine. For that piece of mine is ~~most~~ ^very^ highly wrought. The ^long^ lines are not ^rhythm^ run to seed: everything is weighed and timed in them. Wait till they have taken hold of your ear and you will find it so. No, but what it is like is ~~G~~ ^the rhythm of^ Greek tragic chor~~al~~^uses^~~ rhythm ~~or of Pindar~~ic rhythm~~: ~~that~~ ^which^ is pure sprung rhythm. And that has the same changes of cadence from point to point as this piece. If you want to try it, read one~~, mark the stresse~~ till you have settled the true places of the stress, mark these, then read it aloud, and you will see. Without this these choruses are prose bewitched; with it they are sprung rhythm like that piece of mine.

Besides, why did you not say ~~b~~Binsey Poplars was like Whitman? The present piece is in the same kind and vein, but developed, an advance. The lines and the stanzas (of which there are two in each poem and having much the same relation to one another) are both longer, but the two pieces are greatly alike: just look. If so how is this a being untrue to myself? I am sure it is no such thing.

The above remarks are not meant to run down Whitman. His ~~rugged~~ ^"savage"^ style has advantages, and he has chosen it; he says so. But you cannot eat your cake and keep it: he eats his offhand, I keep ~~it~~ mine ~~long~~. It makes a very great difference. Neither do I deny all resemblance. In particular I noticed in "Spirit that formed this scene" a preference for the alexandrine. I have the same preference: I came to ~~de~~ it by degrees, I did not take it from him.

About diction the matter does not allow me so clearly to point out my independence as about rhythm. I cannot think that the present piece owes anything to him. I hope not, here especially, for it is not even ^spoken^ in my own person but in that of St. Winefred's maidens. It ought to sound like the thoughts of a good but lively girl and not at all like — not at all like Walt Whitman. But perhaps your mind may have changed by this.

I wish I had not spent so much time in defending the piece.

Believe me your affectionate friend Gerard.

Oct. 19 1882. I am not sure I shall not ask C. D. to let me see at least one packet of Mano. He should, every one should now, use one of these reproductive processes: it is next to printing and at least it secures one against irretrievable loss by the post. All our masters here use the gelatine process[11] for flying sheets etc.

1 For Whitman see letter to Bridges of 29–30 Jan. 1879, n. 3. 'Pete' is 'Come up From the Fields Father' (*Leaves of Grass, Drum-Taps*). RB lived at 52 Bedford Square while he was practising medicine in London. He had a copy of the first edition of *Leaves of Grass*.

2 'To the Man-of-War-Bird' and 'Spirit that form'd this Scene' were also from *Leaves of Grass*. The latter was printed in *The Academy* of 24 Sept. 1881 from the *New York Critic* of 10 Sept. 1881 and headed 'Original Verse'.

3 A review of *Leaves of Grass* in the revised edition of 10 Oct. 1874, pp. 398–400. (On 24 June 1876 there is, in the same paper, a less important review of *Two Rivulets* by Edmund W. Gosse.)

4 Three pictures by John Constable (1776–1837; *ODNB*) were exhibited at the Paris Salon of 1824—*The Hay Wain*, *A View near London (Hampstead Heath)*, and *The Lock on the Stour*. They were not sent by the artist, but by a French speculator who had bought them at the Royal Academy.

5 'The Leaden Echo and the Golden Echo', dated: Stonyhurst, Oct. 1882.

6 Saintsbury had quoted Whitman's description of the grass:

> It is the handkerchief of the Lord;
> A scented gift and remembrance designedly dropt,
> Bearing the owner's name someway in the corners, that we
> May see and remark, and say Whose?

[7] The paeon is a metrical foot of four syllables, one of which is long and the rest short; according to where the long syllable occurs, it is named first, second, third, or fourth paeon.

[8] *Piers Plowman*, a late 14th-c. English narrative poem in unrhymed alliterative verse by William Langland (*c.*1325–*c.*1390; *ODNB*) of which different versions were published by Walter Skeat in 1867, 1869, and 1873.

[9] Robert Greene (?1560–92). A writer of pamphlets, romances (including *Pandosto*), and five plays, among them *The Honorable Historie of Friar Bacon and Friar Bungay*. His plays and poems had been edited by Alexander Dyce in 1831 and an edition of the complete works was currently being prepared by Alexander B. Grosart (1881–6).

[10] Quoting from Aristotle's *Nicomachean Ethics*, on which GMH had made extensive notes in his undergraduate days (Campion Hall MS G1; see *CW* vi).

[11] An early copying method in which an original, written or drawn in aniline ink on paper, is transferred to a cake of gelatin softened with glycerin, and impressions are taken from this onto ordinary paper.

21 October 1882 to Robert Bridges

LRB, no. XCI, p. 158 Bodleian, Dep. Bridges, vol. 91, fos. 215–16

Stonyhurst College, Blackburn. [*embossed heading*]
Oct. 21 1882.

My dearest Bridges, — All you say shall be attended to, but in some of your criticisms you are, I think, not quite at the vein or in the "humour" of the piece. The question of what they call run-on lines and the rhymes or other final words ~~concluding them~~ ^belonging^ is difficult. I find it a hardship to alter "~~soarin~~ ^sighs^ soaring, soaring sighs":[1] I quite believed it to be a hit; like "mobled queen" good.[2]

Spite — no, bless me, I never said spite. A sally I should call that; though if the G. was intentional no doubt he ~~oug~~ ^was^ wrong and ought not to have done it.[3]

My de-Whitmaniser crossed you on the road.[4] I believe it was stern and a bit of a mouther.

If I should ever be mentioned between you, propitiate Lang, set me right with him; not in the literary way but personally; make him understand that those snags that are in my style are not in my heart and temper.

"Nay, what we lighthanded" etc[5] means "Nay more: the seed that we so carelessly and freely flung into the dull furrow, and then forgot it, will have come to ear meantime" etc. No more at present. Yours affectionate friend Gerard M. Hopkins S.J.

[1] This line from the 'Golden Echo' was not altered:

And with sighs soaring, soaring sighs deliver
Them, . . .

[2] *Hamlet*, II. ii. 522.
[3] See letter to RB of 16 Oct. 1882.
[4] See previous letter to RB, 18–19 Oct. 1882.
[5] From the 'Golden Echo':

Nay, what we had lighthanded left in surly the mere mould
Will have waked and have waxed and have walked with the wind what while we slept, . . .

4 November 1882 to Robert Bridges

LRB, no. XCII, p. 159 Bodleian, Dep. Bridges, vol. 91, fos. 217–218v

Stonyhurst College, Blackburn. Nov. 4 1881.

Dearest Bridges, — I return *Π.Π.*,[1] for ~~I sh~~ my mind is dull and museless and I shd. do no good by keeping it longer and delaying you.

The opening is now richer than before.[2] But the four first lines ~~aplease me as little as~~ seem to me perhaps the worst in the play, whereas the frontispiece, Pindar says, *χρὴ θέμεν τηλαυγές* {*should set a far-shining front*}.[3] The second line I except: it is Miltonic and fine.

The piece about Greek art does not much please me. It strikes me as ~~wha~~ written in what I call ~~P~~Castalian or Parnassian, that is the language of poetry draping prose thought, ~~I objecte~~ ^a fine rhetoric,^ such as there is a good deal of in Wordsworth's blank verse~~.~~ (against his principles, by the by). I objected in the same way to the account of Rome in C.D.'s <u>Too much Friendship</u>[4] and he called it "that <u>grind</u>" and struck it out.

The blotching of the copy ~~I fin~~ with countless corrections is a heavy toll on its charm in reading. I want to see i~~n~~t in plain print.

Although on the one hand the action is so good and its unity so well kept and on the other hand the style so beautiful I have doubts about ~~its~~ ^the play's^ acting.[5] Experience only can decide; but I do not think it has in a high degree a nameless quality which is of the first importance both in oratory and drama: I sometimes call it <u>bidding</u>. I mean the art or virtue of saying everything right <u>to</u> ^or <u>at</u>^ the hearer, interesting him, holding him in the attitude of correspondent or addressed ^or at least concerned^, making it everywhere an act of intercourse~~.~~ — and of discarding everything that does not bid, does not tell. I think one may gain much of this by practice. I do not know if I make myself plain. It is most difficult to combine this bidding, such a fugitive thing, with a monumental style. Your style is monumental. But it can be done: witness Greek plays — and Shakspere's, but those are more monumental and less in bidding, his more bidding and less monumental. I fancy the French drama eminently succeeds in this ~~way~~ ^combination^, but the success is not what we should be content with, the rank of the result not being very high. This will be of more importance in your ~~n~~Nero.

The "O my vague desires" is a unique and wonderful creation, which would never, I sh~~d~~ould think, be forgotten.[6]

Believe me your affectionate friend Gerard M. Hopkins S.J.

P.S. In printing I hope you are not going to give in to that piece of German unlogic of writing "red white and blue", "fish flesh fowl or good red herring" without stops. The German printers are the worst masters ~~and~~ in punctuation that you could take. They ditch their sentences with commas where they ~~cannot be~~ break the sense's neck and they leave them out where it is wailing for them. It is worse than writing Virgil Vergil.

[1] The Greek initials of RB's *Prometheus the Firegiver* (1883), *Προμηθεύς Πυρφόρος*.

[2] Abbott and Mrs Bridges could find no MS of *Prometheus the Firegiver.* The opening lines in the first edition of 1883 are:

> From high Olympus and the domeless courts,
> Where mighty Zeus our angry king confirms
> The Fates' decrees and bends the will of the gods,
> I come: and on the earth step with glad foot.

In the final form (*P.W.*, i) 'etherial' takes the place of 'domeless'.

[3] Pindar, *Olympians*, vi. 3–4. The opening is (in the translation by the Revd Francis David Morice in *Olympian and Pythian Odes of Pindar*, 1876), 'As who would frame some gorgeous hall, | Uprears its porch with shapely wall | On golden pillars hung: | Our song's proud front must glitter from afar.'

[4] Canon Dixon's *Too Much Friendship, The Story of Septimius and Alcander* (*The Last Poems of Richard Watson Dixon, D.D.*, . . . 1905).

[5] *Prometheus the Firegiver* was a masque rather than a play. It was acted, probably for the only time, at a boys' grammar school near Newbury, a performance that RB saw.

[6] Mentioned here because part of the *Prometheus.*

16 November 1882 to *Nature*

CRWD, p. 161
Letter published in *Nature*, 27 (16 Nov. 1882), 53

"A Curious Halo"

The phenomenon described by M. Dechevrens[1] as often witnessed in China, I have several times seen in this country, namely, beams or spokes in the eastern sky about sunset, springing from a point due opposite to the sun. The appearance is not very strongly marked, and I used to think I must have been mistaken, till I came to see the true explanation, which was the same as that furnished by your correspondent.

There seems no reason why the phenomenon should not be common, and perhaps if looked out for it would be found to be. But who looks east at sunset? Something in the same way everybody has seen the rainbow; but the solar halo, which is really commoner, few people, not readers of scientific works, have ever seen at all. The appearance in question is due to cloud-shadows in an unusual perspective and in a clear sky; now shadow may not only be seen carried by misty, mealy, dusty, or smoky air near the ground, but even on almost every bright day, by seemingly clear air high overhead. Therefore, if this sunset phenomenon is much commoner in China, there must one would think, be some other reason for it than that the sky of England is not heavily charged enough with vapour to carry shadow. Rather it is too much charged, and the edge of the shadow becomes lost with distance and with the thickening of the air towards the horizon before the convergence of the beams eastwards is marked enough to catch the eye.

I may remark that things common at home have sometimes first been remarked abroad. The stars in snow were first observed in the polar regions; it was thought that they only arose there, but now everyone sees them with the naked eye on his coatsleeve.

GERARD HOPKINS.
Stonyhurst College

[1] The letter is a comment on a letter from Fr Marc Dechevrens in the issue of 9 Nov. 1882, pp. 30–1, which itself continues a correspondence from 20 and 27 July. It is one of a series of four letters to *Nature*: 16 Nov. 1882, 15[12] Nov. 1883, 3 Jan. 1884 [21 Dec. 1883], and 30[19] Oct. 1884.

26–7 November 1882 to Robert Bridges

LRB, no. XCIII, p. 161 Bodleian, Dep. Bridges, vol. 91, fos. 219–22

Stonyhurst College, Blackburn.

Nov. 26 1882. And "in spite of the boasted civilisation of this so-called nineteenth century" this letter cannot even start from here for more than 24 hours[1] nor reach you before Tuesday morning; nor could it indeed if you lived at ~~bre~~Blackburn.

Dearest Bridges, — This is to be a mere jottery. And first if you like to send Prometheus I will ^review and^ reply as fast as I can.

I wrote to Lang and he is going presently to write to me on the subject of Dragons. I ~~en~~ return his letter to you. We are on terms of mother's milk.

Yes, I do wish I could have seen Yattendon.

I have written to Canon Dixon. I hardly dare to undertake anything about Mano, because I have somewhat rashly promised to revise for style's sake a historical work by one of ours, which cannot but take a great deal of time, I am afraid.

Of course I do and must pay attention to ~~wha~~ your criticisms on the Echos~~. The~~ and everything else. I ~~was~~ ^am^ however somewhat dismayed about that piece and have laid it aside for a while. I cannot satisfy myself about the first line.[2] You must know that words like charm and enchantment will not do: the thought is of ~~a physical hindra~~ beauty as of something that can be physically kept and lost and by physical things only, like keys; then the things must come from the mundus muliebris {*world of women*}; and thirdly they must not be markedly oldfashioned. You will see that this limits the choice of words very much indeed. However I shall make some changes. Back[3] is not pretty, but it gives that feeling of physical constraint ~~tha~~ which I want. More of this perhaps hereafter.

I never saw Hall Caine's sonnet book. I saw some ~~rew~~ review of it. He has written a memoir of Rossetti.[4]

I always said Gosse was a good fellow and I am glad you speak of him so. I should like to meet him. So I should a little Marzials.[5] Did you tell me or is it my fancy that Marzials looks like a Jew?

Can you really mean that Π.Π. is to appear this month ? — and not this year? There are now only four more days of the month. If you mean that, revision must be done by return — no, by calculation ~~of~~ on my fingers the thing is chronologically impossible.

Talking of chronologically impossible and long words ~~Mr~~. ^the Rev.^ Wm. Barnes, good soul, of Dorset-dialect poems (in which there is more true poetry than in Burns; I do not say of course vigour or passion or humour or a lot of things, but the soul of poetry, which I believe few Scotchmen ~~a~~ have got) has published a "Speech~~lore~~ craft of English Speech"[6] = ~~G~~ English Grammar, written in an unknown tongue, a sort of modern Anglosaxon, beyond all that Furnival[7] in his wildest Forewords ever dreamed. He does not ~~say~~ ^see^ the utter hopelessness of the thing. It makes one weep to think what English might have been; for in spite of all that Shakspere and Milton have done with the compound I cannot doubt that no beauty in a language ~~is~~ can make up for want of purity. In fact I am learning Anglosaxon and it is a vastly superior thing to what we have now. But the madness of ~~tryin~~ an almost unknown man trying to do what the three estates of the realm ~~cou~~together could never accomplish! He calls degrees of comparison pitches of suchness: we <u>ought</u> to call them so, but alas!

My sisters met Wooldridge[8] at dinner at Hampstead.

I daresay you made a capital speech. Everyone shd. at least be able to speak on an occasion.

When I reproached you for treating me as if I were not in earnest I meant, and I mean now, to open up no further question; it was only of the injustice to myself I was thinking then. But "pain" is not the word: it was a mild rebuke to you for being so unreasonable towards me. However ~~when~~ a man ^who^ is deeply in earnest ~~he does~~ ^is^ not very eager to assert his earnest ~~les~~ ness, as they say when a man is really certain he no longer disputes ~~and~~ ^but^ is indifferent. And that is all I say now, that to think a man in my position is not in earnest is unreasonable and is to make difficulties. But if you have made them and can solve them, by a solution which must be wrong, no matter.

The sonnet you ask about is the ~~faultie~~ greatest offender in its way that you could have found. It was written in my Welsh days, in my salad days, when I was fascinated with <u>cynghanedd</u> or consonant-chime, and, ~~like~~ ^as in^ Welsh <u>englyns</u>, ~~the~~ "the sense", as one of themselves said, "gets the worst of it"; ^in this case^ it exists but is far from glaring. To answer in detail:[9]

The word is <u>more</u> and is a midline rhyme to <u>score</u>, as in the next line <u>round</u> is meant in some way to rhyme to <u>down</u>. "Rash-fresh more" (it is dreadful to explain these things in cold blood) ^means^ a headlong and exciting new snatch of singing, resumption ~~of~~ ^by^ the lark~~'s~~ ^of his^ song, which by turns ~~it intermits~~ ^he^ gives over and takes up again all day long, and this goes on, the sonnet says, through all time, ~~with its~~

~~never~~ ^without ever^ losing its first ~~fresh old~~ freshness, being a thing both new and old. Repair means the same thing, renewal, resumption. The skein and coil are the lark's song, which from his height gives the impression (not to me only) of something falling to the earth and not vertically quite but tricklingly or wavingly, something as a skein of silk ribbed by ~~bein~~ having been tightly wound on a narrow card or a notched holder or ^as^ fishing[2]tackle or twi[1]ne ~~unwound~~ unwinding from a reel or winch:* [*GMH footnote:* * or ^as^ pearls strung on a horsehair.] the laps or folds are the notes or short measures and bars of them. The same is called a score in the musical sense of score and this score is "writ Upon a liquid sky Trembling to welcome it", only not horizontally. The ~~bird~~ ^lark^ in wild glee races the reel round, paying ~~out~~ or dealing out and down the turns of the skein or coil right to the earth floor, the ground, where it lies in a heap, as it were, or rather is ^all^ ~~r~~wound off on ^to^ another winch, reel, ~~or~~ bobbin, or spool in Fancy's eye by the moment the bird touches earth and so is ready for a fresh unwinding at the next flight. There is, you see, plenty meant; but the saying of it smells, I fear, of the lamp, of salad oil, and, what is nastier, in one line somewhat of Robert Browning. I felt ~~that in the labour of~~ even at the time that in the endless labour of recasting those lines I had lost the freshness I wanted and which indeed the subject demands. "As a dare-gale skylark" is better in that respect. The peerage would be well earned. — Crisp means almost crisped, namely with notes.

Believe me your affectionate friend Gerard Hopkins S.J.
Nov. 27 1882.

[1] 26 Nov. was a Sunday, so there was no postal collection until Monday.

[2] The first line, in MS 'A', is:

> How to kẽep—O is there any any, is there nowhere knõwn any any brooch or clasp, catch, kẽy to keep
> Back . . .

[3] *The Leaden Echo*:

> . . . or key to keep
> Back beauty, keep it, beauty, beauty, beauty, . . . from vanishing away?

In *The Golden Echo* this theme is answered:

> . . . beauty-in-the-ghost, deliver it, early now, long before death
> Give beauty back, beauty, beauty, beauty, back to God, beauty's self and beauty's giver.

[4] *Recollections of Dante Gabriel Rossetti* (1882).

[5] Theo Marzials (1850–1920) was the son of the pastor of the French Protestant church in London. He was a poet and musician. From 1870 to 1882 he worked in the British Museum, where he was friendly with Coventry Patmore and Edmund

Gosse. He wrote music to work by Christina Rossetti and Swinburne (the latter's 'Ask nothing more of me, Sweet' became a popular ballad of the 1880s).

[6] *An Outline of English Speech-craft*, 1878. Barnes was always a student and lover of robust words. In 1854 he published a philological grammar, 'grounded upon English, and formed from a comparison of more than sixty languages. Being an introduction to the science of grammar and a help to grammars of all languages, especially English, Latin, and Greek'. His *Grammar and Glossary of the Dorset Dialect*, with 'the history, outspreading, and bearings of South-western English', was published by the Philological Society in 1863.

[7] See letter to his mother of 24 Dec. 1881, n. 6. In pursuit of primary texts to help with the construction of the *Oxford English Dictionary*, Furnivall founded several literary societies, including the Early English Text Society, of whose 250 volumes he edited a substantial number with vigour if not scholarly care. His sometimes contentious energy did not make him a careful editor but his editions and influence made careful editors of many others.

[8] Harry Ellis Wooldridge (1845–1917; *ODNB*), friend of RB. See Biographical Register.

[9] The sonnet is 'The Sea and the Skylark' (Rhyl, May 1877). The original version, in 'A', ll. 3–8, ran as follows:

By flood, by fall, low-lull-off or all roar
Frequenting there while moon shall wear and wend;

Left hand, off land, I hear the lark ascend
With rash-fresh more, repair of skein and score,
Race wild reel round, crisp coil deal down to floor,
And spill music till there's none left to spend.

These lines were much altered.

28 November 1882 to Richard Watson Dixon

Bodleian. In the Bridges collection of letters to Dixon, Dep. Bridges, vol. 91, fo. 103^{r-v} an envelope exists with no dated postmark, but the annotation in pencil 'Nov 28 82' and an accompanying note in pencil saying 'This letter omitted'.

1 December 1882 to Robert Bridges

LRB, no. XCIV, p. 165 Bodleian, Dep. Bridges, vol. 91, fos. 223–4

Stonyhurst, Blackburn. Dec. 1 S̶ 1882.

Dearest Bridges, — You shall have Π.Π. back soon. I do not feel as if I could make any criticism of value, my mind not being fresh.

I still do not like domeless.[1] It is not archaeologically right, though I believe the so-called Tomb or Treasury of Atreus[2] has a rude dome;

neither does it convey much image to my mind. And I cannot see but the fourth line is poor and halting. It must be meant to express by its rhythm the act of alighting[2] briskly,[1] but most readers will miss this and will only find it halt, as I do even with that in view.

I agree with you that English compounds do not ~~sp~~ seem real single words or properly unified till by some change in form ^or^ spelling or slur in pronun~~t~~^c^iation the~~y~~^ir^ construction is disguised. This seems in English a point ~~in~~ craved for and insisted on, that words shall be single ^and specific^ marks for things, whether self-significant or not; and it is noticeable how unmeaning our topographical names are or soon become, while those in Celtic languages are so transparent~~.~~ — not that their unmeaningness is any virtue, rather a vice; still it shews the tendency. But your instances are not fair: if icebergs had been common in British seas a name would have been found for them either not compounded or at[3] or if compound as good as iceberg is or better and certainly a great deal better than icelump, which is caricature. Thimble is singler than thumbstall (I do not believe it comes from ~~it~~ ^that^ but from thumb-le), but it is a meaner word. The absurdity of 'finger ha~~a~~^u^t' is not in its being a compound but in ~~the~~ ^its^ impropriety, in the particular trope employed. Fingerhood or indeed fingerstall seem to me to be well enough. Potato is certainly one of the ~~most~~ ugliest and most laughable words in the language and cannot ^well^ be used in verse, ^whereas^ earthapple is stately: ~~it~~ ^potato^ has one virtue only, the being specific.

If one is to bandy plays upon names Burns might mean ~~s~~^S^calds and Barnes ~~of~~ ~~g~~^G^ranaries of Plenty. I have a cousin by the by called Barne or Barnes.[4]

The very worst compound ever I heard in English was Tyndal's word clangtint = klangfarbe in German = timbre in French for the quality of musical instruments.[5]

Your affectionate friend Gerard M. Hopkins S.J.

[1] See letter of 4 Nov. 1882.

[2] The treasury of Atreus or tomb of Agamemnon dates from *c.*1550 BC. At 13.5 metres high and 14.5 metres wide inside, it was the one of the largest domes in the ancient world.

[3] 'at all'?

[4] See letter to his mother of 29 July 1865.

[5] The word was proposed to translate Helmholz's 'Klangfarbe' by John Tyndall (1820–93; *ODNB*) in a series of lectures collected in *Sound* (1867), 118. GMH had met Tyndall, an avid mountaineer, while visiting Switzerland in 1868. See letter to his mother of 20–21 Sept. 1874 and *CW* iii.

7 December 1882 to Robert Bridges

LRB, no. XCV, p. 166 Bodleian, Dep. Bridges, vol. 91, fos. 225–6

Stonyhurst, Blackburn. Dec. 7 1882.

Dearest Bridges, — Briefly: your letter is dated the ~~5~~4th, it has two Newbury postmarks of the 5th, a Blackburn one of the 6th, and I got it this morning. I posted Π.Π. and a letter on the 4th and you, I hope, got them on the 5th: let me know that the book is not lost. It is absurd that a letter posted at latest on Tuesday shd. not reach me till Thursday and . . but not to pursue my thought, let me, if you have not already done so, hear that all is right.

Did you see the transit yesterday?[1] With a smoked glass you could, if it was fine: he~~ar~~^re^ it snowed all day.

Do I understand you to say that since you have been at Yattendon some one you know has drowned himself?

Yours G. M. H.

It wd. be strange if τέχνη {*art*} and τύχη {*chance*}[2] together did not bring some fine results out of any ^lot of^ caleidoscopic elements; still to me a pure language seems a finer thing than a mixed one — till the mixture becomes imperceptible.

[1] A transit of Venus across the face of the sun visible from the UK. Such transits occur rarely but in pairs; in 1761 and 1769, in 1874 and 1882, and in 2004 and 2012.

[2] Continuing the discussion of compounds. *Passim* in Aristotle and Plato: 'art (or science)' and 'chance (or luck)'.

15 December 1882 from Richard Watson Dixon to GMH

CRWD, no. XXV B, p. 105 Campion Hall, D 15/12/82

Addressed to 'The Rev^{d}. | Gerard Hopkins S.J. | Stonyhurst College, | Blackburn'. PM CARLISLE DE 16 81, PRESTON DE 16 82, WHALLEY DE 17 82.

Hayton Vicarage Carlisle | 15 Dec. 1882

My dear Friend,[1]

I have been longer in answering you than I intended from the gladness that it was to me to see your handwriting again. I am very glad to hear that you are employed in some teaching & literary work, even though it may not be exactly of the kind that I at least should be able by acquirements to be able to judge of. My own experience is that any teaching, any literary work is good for the mind: provided that it be literary, by which I include philosophy & exclude mathematics. I hear from Bridges that you have sent him a "very fine" poem:[2] wh. is excellent news. You speak of Mano.[3] I am revising him from Bridges's suggestions: & find it rather a toil: I only give off days to it. I have not quite reached the end of Book 1. Bridges likes it, & has taken vast pains about it. Nearly everything he says is right. I am also going on with my Church History: & am in the middle of the year 1551.

Rossetti's death is a very sad thing indeed. Hall Caine's book[4] contains a short contribution from me, at his request, to say what ~~his~~ ^R.'s^ share in the Oxford & Cambridge Magazine was, & gives one or two other recollections. I agree with much of what you say of Rossetti. He was a man of extraordinary gifts: who rose at once, very early, to a great development, & then stood still, through some lack. He has however made a mark.

I have heard a good deal from Bridges lately: mostly concerning Mano. His Prometheus seems to me a very good poem: particularly the choruses: extremely Greek in feeling. The difficulty seems to me the impossible state of things, without fire, what the story supposes.

As to Tennyson's Promise of May:[5] I should suppose that it failed from want of interest, though I speak only on hearsay. It seems to have had no plot: or only a slight single plot, & a wretched lot of characters: & to have been written in prose. How Tennyson could waste his time in writing a thing of that sort is a greater wonder than that it should fail. The only thing he could do for the ~~stage~~ ^drama^ wd. be to try to reform it; but that wd. not be by writing in prose the adventure of the cold blooded sort of being that might have figured in one of the Nineteenth Century Magazine's "Symposiums". At present the sooner the lingering falsity is got rid of that the acted drama is in any way an exhibition of noble passion, or a vehicle of wit, fancy, imagination, or good writing, the better. Let it be frankly acknowledged to be what it is, without the slightest pretence to be anything else: viz. a paradise of baseness & folly, merely jolly & idiotic: but of art an extinct kind: having less to do with poetry than waxworks have.

Tennyson's Queen Mary[6] (the best I suppose of his "dramatic works") shewed very little ability of any sort. There was no dramatic knowledge: but that was not to be expected: but there was no dramatic <u>tone</u>: no go, no vigour. The speeches were all about five lines long, & hooked on to one another in the way of direct reply mostly: & these unsatisfactory morsels were interspersed with monstrous sermons, three pages long! And the incidents that were <u>related</u> (not acted) instead of being brought in with force, or at least conversationally, were brought in in the way of "making a statement". I send you a Photograph, asking for one in return.[7] Ever your affecte friend

R W Dixon

[1] Presumably an answer to the letter of 28 Nov. 1882.
[2] Perhaps 'The Leaden Echo and the Golden Echo'.
[3] Published in 1883 by the firm of George Routledge, his new father-in-law.
[4] *Recollections of Dante Gabriel Rossetti*, by T. Hall Caine (London, 1882). RWD's contribution is on pp. 36–40.
[5] 'The Promise of May' was included in the volume *Locksley Hall Sixty Years After* (1886).
[6] *Queen Mary* (published 1875, produced 1876) was, like his other historical plays of the late period, a generally acknowledged failure.
[7] Not with the letter, and we cannot know precisely which photographs were exchanged.

20 December 1882 to Robert Bridges

LRB, no. XCVI, p. 166 Bodleian, Dep. Bridges, vol. 91, fos. 227–9

Stonyhurst, Blackburn. Dec. 20 1882.

Dearest Bridges, — You misunderstand about those four opening lines: I did not want them replaced by others but ^only^ in some places reworded. I have told you of my objection to domeless. If there were some reason for it why do you not tell me? A court I suppose to be any large ~~ar piece~~ room or space of a building upon the ground floor and imperfectly closed. About the being on the ground floor I do not feel quite sure, about the being imperfectly ^closed^ — above or around — I do. Courts can seldom be domed in any case, so that it is needless to tell us that those on Olympus are domeless. No: better to say the kamptuliconless[1] — courts or Minton's-encaustic-tile-less courts or vulcanisèd-india-rubberless ^courts^. This would strike a keynote at once and bespeak attention. And if the critics said those things did not belong to the period you would have (as you have now with domeless) the overwhelming answer, that you never said they did but the contrary, and that Prometheus, who was at once a prophet and as a mechanician more than equal to Edison[2] and the Jablochkoff candle and the Moc-main Patent Lever Truss with self-adjusting ^duplex^ gear and attachments, meant to say that emphatically they had not got those improvements on Olympus and he did not ~~mean~~ ^intend^ that they should. But if you cannot see your way to this "frank" treatment and are inclined to think that fault might be found with domeless, then remember that that fault is found in your first line.

I seem to be in a griggish[3] mood; it must be because holidays have begun. Your last letter was depressed, but I do not want you to be depressed but to bring out ^your^ beautiful work as soon as possible. However to return to those four first lines. I wanted no account of the journey through the air, but that, since the fourth line was meant to be descriptive and to suit the ~~acti~~ word to the action, ~~th~~ it should suit the word to the action better — the action of alighting ~~to~~ on earth. That was all. For as things now are it is to me like ~~an arm~~ ^a man^ dragging a lame leg after him. Could it not end somehow with a double ending like "gladly alighting". I have a line in St. Winefred on a like occasion (this is a six-footer of course) "Shall fling their crutches from them, on heels of air departing".[4]

I am at present in a state of weakness, I do not well know why. Believe me your affectionate friend Gerard Hopkins S.J.

[1] Kamptulicon was a floor-covering invented in 1843 and generally available by 1855 in which India rubber and ground cork are pressed together. A variety of additional substances such as gutta-percha, sawdust, resins, and asphalt have been used in its manufacture. Herbert Minton's firm made the most famous of the encaustic floor tiles available from *c.*1860, using medieval techniques of inlaying different colours in a background tile. Vulcanized India rubber was developed in the middle of the 19th c. and was a treatment of rubber by sulphur, accelerators, and antidegradant products to form a flexible, heat-resistant, and durable material of numerous uses in machinery, waterproof clothes, medical tubes and masks, and ultimately car tyres.

[2] Thomas Edison (1847–1931), the inventor and developer of numerous products including the vacuum-sealed light bulb, the phonograph, and rudimentary films. An aggressive advocate of DC (direct electrical current) power distribution, in Jan. 1882 he opened the first steam-generated power station at Holborn Viaduct in London. The Jablochkoff candle, invented in 1870 by Paul Jablochkoff, was one of the first electric lamps. White's Moc-main patent lever truss was for sufferers of hernia.

[3] A 'grig' is an extravagantly lively person, full of frolic and jest.

[4] The printed line is: 'Their crutches shall cast from them, | on heels of air departing' (l. 23 of fragment C of 'St. Winefred's Well').

1883

4–5 January 1883 to Robert Bridges

LRB, no. XCVII, p. 168 Bodleian, Dep. Bridges, vol. 92, fos. 1–4ᵛ

Stonyhurst College, Blackburn. Jan. 4 188~~2~~^3^.

Dearest Bridges, — Since our holidays began I have been in a wretched state of weakness and weariness, I can't tell why, always drowzy and incapable of reading or thinking to any effect. And this must be why I was, before that, able to do so little on your Prometheus.

I think the sonnet a fine work,[1] but should like the phrasing to be more exquisite in lines 2, 4, and perhaps elsewhere. Still it has to me an unspontaneous artificial air. I cannot consider the goblet and "golden foil" a success. It is out of keeping with sons of toil ^and the unadornment of their brides^. It is obscure too: it means, I suppose, that the goblet is of gold and that this gold sets off and is set off by the colour of the wine. This much resemblance there is, that as the goblet draws or ^~~or~~ swallows up and^ sort-of-drinks the liquid ~~the~~ and the liquid at the same time swallows up and sort-of-drinks the material of the goblet so the body ~~swallows sleep a~~ absorbs sleep and sleep the body. But the images of gold and crimson are out of keeping: brilliancy is ^only^ in the way. You were, you say, driven to it: I protest, and with indignation, at your saying I was driven to the same image. With more truth might it be said that ~~the i~~ ^my^ sonnet might have been written expressly for the ~~s~~ image's sake.[2] But the image is not the same ^as yours^ and I do not mean by foil set-off at all; I mean foil in its ~~literal~~ sense of leaf or tinsel, and no other word whatever will give the effect I want. Shaken goldfoil gives ~~up~~ ^off^ broad glares like sheet lightning and also, and this is true of nothing else, owing to its zigzag dints and creasings and network of small many cornered facets, a sort of fork lightning too. Moreover as it is the first rhyme, presumably it ~~required~~ ^engendered^ the others and not they it. This reminds me that I hold you to be wrong about 'vulgar', that is obvious or necessary, rhymes. It follows from your principle that if a word # has only ^one^ rhyme in the language it cannot be used in selfrespecting poetry at all. The truth seems to me that a problem is set to all, how to use that ^same^ pair (or ~~th~~ triplet or any set) of rhymes, which are invariable, to the finest and most natural effect. It is nothing that the reader can say / He had to say it, there was no other rhyme: you answer / Shew me what better I could have said if there had been a million. Hereby, I may tell you, hangs a very profound question treated by Duns Scotus, who shews that freedom is compatible with necessity. And besides, common sense tells you that though if you ~~you~~ say A_1 you cannot help saying A_2 yet you ~~need not say~~ ^can help saying^ A_1+A_2 at all; you could have said B_1+B_2 or C_1+C_2 etc. And is not music a sort of rhyming on seven rhymes and does that make it vulgar? The variety is more, but the principle the same. Come, you are as much cast in this matter as Lawes was ^in the Belt case^ — though I am grievously afraid there was a miscarriage of justice in that ~~case~~ ^trial^; not that I like to side against a judge's sentence.[3]

Jan. 5 — Hall Caine's ~~lectur~~ "Disquisition" on Rossetti's picture of Dante's Dream bought by the city of Liverpool reached me this morning, I suppose from the author.[4] Noel Paton[5] is quoted as saying, with ^goodnatured^ gush, that it may be ranked with the Madonna di San Sisto. Now, you know, it may not, and I am considering whether I shall tell Hall Caine so.

To return to your sonnet, could you not find another rhyme? the~~a~~re is spoil, despoil, turmoil, not to speak of coil, boil, parboil, and ~~Hol~~ Hoyle on whist — the very sight of which dreary jugglery brings on yawns with me.

You speak of writing the sonnet in prose first. I read the other day that Virgil wrote the Aeneid in prose. Do you often do so? Is it a good plan? If it is I will try it; it may help on my flagging and almost spent powers. Years ago ~~a~~ one of ours, a pupil of mine, was to write some ^English^ verses for me, to be recited: he had a real vein. He ~~ha~~ said he had no thoughts, but that if I would furnish ~~them~~ ^some^ he would versify them. I did so and the effect was very surprising to me to find my own thoughts, with no variation to speak of, expressed in good verses quite unlike mine.

The sonnet on Purcell means this: 1–4. I hope~~d~~ Purcell is not damned for being a Protestant, because I love his genius. 5–8. And that not so much for gifts he shares, even though it shd. be in higher measure, with other musicians as for ~~in~~ his own individuality. 9–14. So that while he is aiming only at impressing me his hearer with the meaning in hand I am looking out ~~for~~ meanwhile for his specific, his individual markings and mottlings, "the sakes of him". It is as when a bird think~~s~~^ing^ only of soaring spreads its wings: ~~but~~ a beholder may happen then to have his attention drawn ^by the act^ to the plumage displayed. — In particular, the first lines mean: May ~~he~~ ^Purcell^, O may he have died a good death and that ~~spirit~~ soul which I love so much and which breathes ~~so~~ or stirs so unmistakeably in his works have ~~passed away and~~ parted from the body and passed away, centuries since though I ~~me~~ frame the wish, in peace with God! so that the ^heavy^ condemnation under which he outwardly or nominally lay for being out of the true Church may in consequence of his good intentions have been reversed. "Low lays him" is merely "lays him low", that is / strikes him heavily, weighs upon him. (I daresay this will strike you as more professional than you had anticipated.) It is somewhat dismaying to find I am so unintelligible ^though^, especially in one of my very best pieces. "Listed", by the by, is "enlisted". "Sakes" is hazardous: about that point I was more bent on saying my say than on being understood in it. The "moonmarks" belong to the image only of course, not to the application; I mean not detailedly: I was thinking of a bird's quill feathers. One thing disquiets me: I meant "fair fall" to mean fair (fortune be)fall;[6] it has since struck me that perhaps ~~it can only fair~~ "fair" is an adjective proper and in the predicate and can only be used in cases like "fair fall the day", that is, may the day fall, turn out, fair. My line will yield a sense that way indeed, but I never meant it so. Do you know any passage decisive on this?

Would that I had Purcell's music here.

Did you see Vernon Lee's paper in the December Contemp.?[7] I don't like it. She professes herself a disciple of a Mr. Edmund Gurney, who by way of reaction against the gush of programmes ("sturdy old tone-poet" — "~~imita~~ inimitable drollery of the semi demiquavers in the dominant minor" and so on) says that we enjoy music because our apish ancestors serenaded their Juliet-apes of the period in rudimentary recitatives and our emotions are ~~a~~ ^the^ survival — that sexual business will ^in short^ be found by roking[8] the pot. This is to ~~react~~ ^swing^ from pap to poison. Would that I had my materials ready to talk sense. Yours affectionately Gerard Hopkins S.J.

Jan. 5 1883

Is it not too much for two lines running to have the rhythm reversed in the 4th foot? as your 13 and 14. Perhaps not. Twelfth night.[9]

[1] RB substantially rewrote the sonnet, leaving out the foil and the goblet. The octave in the 1889 edition of *The Growth of Love*, with the diagonal slashes used in that edition to punctuate, ran:

Sweet sleep/ dear unadornéd bride of toil/
Whom in the dusk of night mens bodies low
Lie to receive/ and thy loved coming know/
Closing the cloudy gate on days turmoil:
Thou through the lost ways enterest to despoil
The ready spirit and on worn flesh bestow
Such comfort as through trembling souls will flow
When Gods Welldone doth all their sins assoil.

[2] 'God's Grandeur':

The world is charged with the grandeur of God.
It will flame out, like shining from shook foil;
It gathers to a greatness, like the ooze of oil
Crushed.

[3] The libel case of *Belt* v. *Lawes* ended on 27 Dec. 1882 in a verdict for the plaintiff, with £5,000 damages. The libel complained of stated that certain busts and pieces of sculpture attributed to Mr Belt, and claimed by him, were executed by other persons in his employ. The application for a new trial was refused (though Lord Chief Justice Coleridge, besides considering the damages excessive, thought there had been a gross miscarriage of justice) but the damages were reduced to £500. In Mar. 1884, however, the Court of Appeal confirmed the verdict of the jury, and restored the original damages. For an interesting account of this case see chapter 3 of Sir Charles Oman's *Things I Have Seen* (London, 1933).

[4] Hall Caine, according to his *Recollections of Dante Gabriel Rossetti* (1882), was largely responsible for the sale of this picture to Liverpool, and quotes Sir Noel Paton: 'I was so dumbfounded by the beauty of that great picture of Rossetti's, called "Dante's Dream", that I was unable to give any expression to the emotions it excited—emotions such as I do not think any other picture, except the "Madonna di San Sisto" at Dresden, ever stirred within me'.

[5] Joseph Noel Paton (1821–1901; *ODNB*), a popular Scottish artist, who frequently chose subjects from fairy tales or history. He exhibited a number of pictures at the Royal Academy. At this time he was engaged in painting religious subjects.

[6] The sonnet opens:

Have fair fallen, O fair, fair have fallen, so dear
To me, so arch-especial a spirit as heaves in Henry Purcell,

[7] 'Vernon Lee', pseudonym of Violet Paget (1856–1935; *ODNB*), art historian and woman of letters; 'Impersonality and Evolution in Music', *Contemporary Review* (Dec. 1882), 840–58. GMH's account is very different from those conclusions of Gurney's that Lee praises and even further from her position. Lee praises Gurney for suggesting in his *Power of Sound* (1880) that music is 'the most formal and ideal of all arts, unique in the fact that the form it creates resembles and signifies nothing beyond itself' (p. 846). She suggests that the argument should be taken further, that, as the Russian Formalists were to argue for literary forms, musical form evolves; 'art is affected by civilization; it absorbs from it and is constrained by it; but it has physico-mental necessities of its own, which determine what it may absorb and by what it may be constrained' (p. 858). See letter to RB of 22 June 1879 for Edmund Gurney.

[8] See *EDD*, 'rauk', to stir, poke about, search.

[9] GMH notes that the day is Twelfth Night, marking the coming of Epiphany and an end to the Twelve Days of Christmas, traditionally a period of reversals and misrule, when RB's reversed rhythms would be appropriate.

14 January 1883 to Alexander William Mowbray Baillie

FL, no. CXXXIX, p. 250 UCD L 48
Two folded sheets and a half sheet of paper watermarked 'A Pirie & Sons'; 10 sides.

Stonyhurst College, Blackburn. Jan. 14 1883.

Dearest Baillie, — I believe I am writing chiefly to withdraw something ~~I~~I said at our last meeting, though if there had been nothing to withdraw still I ought to write; but blackguardry stamps my whole behaviour to you from first to last.

Strong words are seldom much good and the more of heat the less of reason. The strong word I repent of using was that if ever there was a humbug it was Swedenborg. What I might reasonably have said (and what I really meant) was that Swedenborgianism (what a word!) is humbug. But I ought not to have seemed to imply that Swedenborg[1] himself was an impostor or anything of the nature of Cagliostro,[2] for so far as I know there is no ~~reason~~ ^ground^ for saying this. He had some very str#ange experiences: how he came by them no matter, but he may have related them faithfully. It is however a great folly of his followers to build on them. His first dealing w#ith the other world took place at an eating-house in London, where after a very heavy dinner (so he is quoted as saying in his journal) he saw the cieling (or the floor) covered with hideous reptiles. Then he was aware of a light in a corner of the room and of a luminous figure which sternly said to him "Do not eat so much". After that he began to receive communications. The circumstances suggest delirium tremens, as everyone must feel. Whatever the explanation, no sensible man would feel happy in a religion which began to be revealed in that way.

I am here to coach classics for the London University Intermediate (say Moderations) and B.A. (say Greats) examinations. I like my pupils and do not wholly dislike the work, but I fall into or continue in a heavy weary state of body and mind in which my go is gone (the elegance of that phrase! ~~a~~ as Thackeray says, it makes one think what vast sums must have been spent on my education!), ~~and~~ I make no way with what I read, and seem but half a man. It is a sad thing to say. I try, and am even meant to try, in my spare time (and ~~one whose~~ ^if^ I were fresher or if it were anyone but my self there would be a good deal of spare time taking short and long together) to write some books; but I find myself so tired or so harassed I ~~make no~~ fear they will never be written. The one that would interest you most is ~~one~~ on the Greek Lyric Art or on, more narrowly, the art of the choric and lyric parts of the Gk. plays.[3] I want it to be in two parts, one the metre, the other the style. It is, I am afraid, too ambitious of me, so little of a scholar as I am; only I think what I should say would th^r^ow a new light and that if I did not perhaps no one else would. But it is a laborious business and why shd. I undertake it? There are, I believe, learned books lately written in Germany on the choric metres and music, which if I could see and read them would either serve me or quench me; but on the other head I do not anticipate being anticipated — so to say. My thought is that ~~besi~~ in ~~the~~ ^any^ lyric passage of the tragic poets (perhaps not so much in Euripides as the others) there are — usually; I will not say always, it is not likely — two strains of thought running together and like counterpointed; the over-thought that which everybody, editors, see (when one does see any-thing — which in the great corruption of the text and original obscurity of the diction is not everywhere) and which might for instance be abridged or paraphrased in square marginal blocks as in some books carefully ~~edi~~ written; the other, the underthought, ~~suggested~~ ^con-veyed^ chiefly in the choice of metaphors etc used and often only half realised by the poet himself, ~~and~~ not necessarily having any connection with the subject in hand but usually having a connection and suggested by some circumstance of the scene or of the story. I cannot prove that this is ~~a reality~~ ^really so^ except by a large induction of examples and perhaps not irrefragably even then nor without examples can I even make my meaning plain. I will give only one, the chorus with which Aeschylus' ~~Supplices~~ Suppliants begins. The underthought which plays through this is that the Danaids[4] flying from their cousins are like their own ancestress Io teazed by the gadfly and caressed by Zeus and the rest of that foolery. E.g *δίαν δὲ λιποῦσαι | χθόνα σύγχορτον Συρίᾳ φεύγομεν* {*the land divine whose pastures march with Syria, we have quitted in exile*}:[5] the suggestion is of a herd of cows feeding next a herd of bulls. Shortly follows a mention of Io and her story. Then comes *δέξαισθ' ἱκέτην | τὸν θηλυγενῆ στόλον αἰδοίῳ | πνεύματι χώρας* {*receive as suppliants this company of womankind with the reverent spirit of the land*};[6] this alludes to the *ἐπίπνοια* {*engendering breath*}[7] by which Epaphus was conceived — *ἀρσενοπληθῆ δ' | ἑσμὸν ὑβριστὴν Αἰγυπτογενῆ* etc {*but the thronging swarm of wanton men born of Aegyptus . . .* }:[8] this suggests the gadfly. Perhaps what I ought to say is that the underthought is commonly an echo or shadow of the over-thought, something like canons and repetitions in music, treated in a

~~some~~ different manner, but that sometimes it may be independent of it. I find this same principle of composition in St. James' and St. Peter's and St. Jude's Epistles,[9] an undercurrent ^of thought^ governing the choice of images used. Perhaps I spoke of this to you before.

I could write more, but have written enough now. Tell me about the Rossetti exhibition; but you need not enlarge on Dante's Dream or on Mr. Rae's pictures,[10] for these I have seen. In an old letter of yours, many years ~~ago~~ ^old^ (I have been reading them again), you speak of Pindar, taking exception to some things and giving examples. I do not on the whole agree with your objections and should defend the ~~inele~~ *examples. [*GMH footnote*:* It turns on their explanation. If the explanation suits them it defends them.] This sort of thing I should explain ~~if~~ in that book ^if it^ were written. I shd. also give some fancy music to some choruses and odes, plainchant, not an attempted reproduction of Gk. music but as a means of bringing out the rhythm.

Be very interesting and entertaining: what else could a letter of yours be? Meanwhile and ever after believe me your affectionate ~~friend~~ ^and^ grateful friend Gerard #Hopkins S.J.

[1] Emanuel Swedenborg (1688–1772) trained as a scientist and tried to find a scientific explanation of the universe. In middle age he began working on mystical subjects. GMH objected to his appointing himself interpreter of Scripture, which he did after a series of visions. The first of these GMH describes, omitting in his account that the reptiles or worms were considered by Swedenborg to be a purging of his overeating.

[2] The ninth edition of the *Encyclopaedia Britannica* (1876) describes Count Alessandro di Cagliostro (1743–95), as 'the arch-impostor of modern times'. It was said to be the alias of Giuseppe Balsamo, an Italian traveller, impostor, forger, charlatan, mason, and the subject of operas and books, including an essay by Thomas Carlyle collected in his *Miscellaneous Essays* from *Fraser's Magazine* of 1833 (July and Aug.).

[3] This is his long-term project on Greek lyric, choruses, and the Dorian measure, which emerged from his discussion with Fr Purbrick. See letters of 26–7 Sept. and 18–19 Oct. 1882, and 2–4 , 21–2 and 28 Oct. 1886 to RB, 7 Nov. 1886 to Patmore, 11 Dec. 1886 to RB, 23 Dec. 1886 to Baillie, 20 Jan. 1887 to Patmore, and 1 May 1887 and 30 July 1887 to RB.

[4] Hera, in jealousy at Zeus's infidelity with Io, changed her into a heifer and set a gadfly to chase her all over the world. Epaphus (whose name is said by Liddell and Scott to derive from the word meaning 'to handle') was the son of Io and Zeus, who had, as Robert Graves has it, '*touched* her to some purpose' (*The Greek Myths* (London, 1992), section 56). The Danaids, descendents of Io, were the fifty daughters of Danaus, twin brother of Aegyptus, who had fifty sons. Aegyptus proposed to marry his sons to their cousins to solve a dispute, but Danaus rightly suspected a plot, and the Danaids fled, pursued by the sons of Aegyptus, all but one of whom were killed by their prospective Danaid brides.

5 Aeschylus, *Suppl.* 4 f.
6 Ibid. 27 ff. [in v. 27 Heath's conjecture δέξασθ' is generally accepted].
7 Ibid. 17.
8 Ibid. 29 f.
9 i.e the books of the New Testament.
10 See letter of 14–15 May 1881.

28–9 January 1883 to Robert Bridges

LRB, no. XCVIII, p. 172 Bodleian, Dep. Bridges, vol. 92, fos. 5–7

Stonyhurst College, Blackburn. Jan. 28 1883.

Dearest Bridges, — Lang may have spoken in print about vulgar rhymes, but I ~~understood you~~ referred to something you said by word of mouth, as I understood you, ^to the same effect^ at Roehampton when we were talking over ~~some~~ ^a^ chorus of Π.Π. and I had wanted you to avail yourself of some rhyme like measure and pleasure. But it is no matter now.

It turned out not to be Hall Caine himself # who sent me the pamphlet. I mildly remonstrated ^with him^ against ~~the~~ Noel Paton's matching Dante's Dream with the Sistine Madonna. However in his answer Hall Caine said he agreed with me. He lives in London now. There is a great deal of nonsense ^about that set^, often it sickens one~~,~~ (though Rossetti himself I think had little of it); but still I disapprove of damfooling people. I think it is wrong, narrows the mind, and like a 'parvifying glass' makes us see things smaller than the nat~~ura~~ural size. And I do not like your calling Matthew Arnold Mr. Kidglove Cocksure. I have more reason # than you for disagreeing with him[1] and thinking him very wrong, but nevertheless I am sure he is a rare genius and a great critic.

You do not seem quite to have understood my question about Fair fall, but whether you understood it or not at any rate you have answered it and set me at rest. The quotation from L.L.L. is decisive.[2] "Fair befall your ~~face"~~ mask" must have the same construction as "Fair fall the face beneath it". Now "~~F~~fair befall" certainly means 'Fair fortune, ~~what is fair~~ all that is fair, nothing but what is fair / befall' and "fair" is there a substantive and governs the verb. So therefore it is and does in "Fair fall", which is what I wanted. (Fair is of course a substantive in My fair and Shakespeare says "And every fair from fair sometimes declines".)[3] This being so I am unwilling to alter that line, for if it ~~can~~ ^will^ only stand, and it will, ~~as I hoped,~~ it pleases me much.

You should have been more explicit about the origin of music.

I try to get a bit of strumming every day now. Somebody left with me a volume of Bach's Fugues and, though it is like beginning at the end, as an exercise in dead reading I think it is very good for me and perhaps some day I shall find ~~myself~~ that I can read music pretty easily. If you like to be so good as to send me what you offer, some pieces of Purcell, it will be, as the Irish say when they beg, "the biggest charty you ever did in your life". I will send them ^back^ and even soon, if you wish.

Believe me your affectionate friend Gerard Hopkins S.J.
Jan. 29.

[1] Perhaps a reference to GMH's misconception that Arnold had been the eminent critic who had criticized his poems to Hall Caine. See Letter to RB of 27 Apr. 1881.

[2] 'Now fair befall your mask!—fair fall the face it covers!' (*Love's Labour's Lost*, II. i. 124).

[3] Sonnet 18, l. 7.

9 February 1883 [fragment] to Richard Watson Dixon

CRWD, no. XXVI, p. 107 Bodleian, Dep. Bridges, vol. 93, fo. 105$^{r\text{–}v}$
One small sheet. No salutation or address since the first part is missing.

This private printing of Prometheus[1] may turn out unfortunate. I have myself no taste for what is called dainty in the get-up of books and am altogether wanting in the spirit of a ~~biblio~~ bookhunter. 10s. seems like what is called a prohibitive price. I could not recommend our library to get ~~the~~ ^such a^ book and till the second edition I shall not see the poem in print.

I do not so strongly feel the objection about the fireless state supposed. Some of the people of New Guinea were lately for some time, a generation perhaps, without fire: they were very wretched and a disease of the gums spread among them, still they lived. Perhaps you mean that the poem makes the fire not only wanting in fact but even unprocurable from nature. But it is agreed that it is very hard to raise it and one may make, ~~some~~ ^in^ favour of the myth, some allowance for a malignant providence which always ~~with~~ easily baffled men's efforts, in that direction.

Is it not an objection or do you avail yourself of the fact, that Mano means Hand? Perhaps I might shortly, say at Easter, if it were convenient to you, see at least some portion of it. Believe me your affectionate friend Gerard Hopkins S.J.

Feb. 9 1883.

[1] Privately printed by H. Daniel in 1883, in an edition of 100 copies. (Charles) Henry Olive Daniel (1836–1919; *ODNB*), fellow and later provost of Worcester College, Oxford, had begun printing books as a boy and at Oxford began fine printing in 1874, well before Morris's Kelmscott Press, though it did not rival the latter in design and innovation. He printed a number of RB's works. See *CPRB*, 107, for a quotation from RB's commonplace book explaining the financial benefits of Daniel's printing.

3–10 February 1883 to Robert Bridges

LRB, no. XCIX, p. 173 Bodleian, Dep. Bridges, vol. 92, fos. 8–12[v]

Stonyhurst College, Blackburn. ✠ Feb. 3 1883.

Dearest Bridges, — I cd. not venture to ask that our library should subscribe ~~for~~ half a sovereign for an édition de luxe of a new book by an almost unknown author; still less could I expect, nor shd. I like, you to present me, that is our library, with a copy.[1] Here then is ^ a ^downright^ deadlock and there is nothing for it but for me to wait for the second edition and then, like Brewer[2] in the Mutual Friend, "see how things look".

Many thanks for the anthems. I remember now that I heard the first at Magdalen.[3] Did you remark that the first 9 notes of the Hallelujah are, with a slight ~~ex~~ change, the beginning of Cease ~~of~~ your funning?[4]

This is a terrible business about my sonnet "Have fair fallen", for I find that I still 'make myself misunderstood'. Have is not a plural at all, far from it. It is ~~an~~ ^the singular^ imperative (or optative if you like) of the past, a thing possible and actual both in logic and grammar, but naturally ^a^ rare ^one^. As in the second person we say "Have done" or in making appointments "Have had your dinner beforehand", so one can say in the third person not only "Fair fall" of what is present or future but also "Have fair fallen" of what is past. The same thought (which ~~is~~ plays a great part in my ^own^ mind and action) is more clearly expressed in the last stanza but one of the Eurydice, where you remarked it.

I quite understand what you ~~say~~ ^mean^ about gentlem~~a~~^e^n and "damfools"; it is a very striking thing and I could say much on the subject. I shall not say ^that^ much, but I ~~will~~ say this: if a gentleman feels that to be what we call a gentleman is a thing essentially higher than without being a gentleman to be ever so great an artist or ~~philosopher~~ ^~~th~~ thinker^ or if, to put it another way, an artist or thinker feels that were he to become in those ways ever so great he wd. still essentially be lower than a gentleman that was no artist and no thinker~~,~~ — and yet to be a gentleman is but on the brim of morals and rather ^a thing^ of manners than of morals properly~~,~~ — then how much more must art and philosophy and manners and breeding and everything else in the world be below the least degree of true virtue. This is that chastity of mind which seems to ~~be the~~ lie at the very heart and be the parent of all other good, the see^ing^ at once what is best, ~~and~~ ^the^ ~~to~~ hold^ing^ to that, and the not allowing anything else whatever to be even heard pleading to the contrary. Christ's life and character are such as appeal to all the world's admiration, but there is one insight St. Paul gives ^~~into~~^ ~~it that~~ ^us^ of it which is very secret and seems to ~~be~~ ^me^ more touching and constraining than everything else is:[5] This mind he says, was in Christ Jesus — he means as man: being in the form of God — that is, finding ^~~himself~~^, as in the first instant of his incarnation he did, his human nature informed by the godhead — he thought it nevertheless no snatching-matter ^for him^ to be equal with God, but annihilated himself; taking the form of servant; ~~he could~~ that is, he could not but see what he was, God, but he would ~~be~~ ^see^ it as if he did not see it~~,~~ and be it as if he were not and instead of snatching at once at what ~~was~~ all the time was his, ~~and~~ ^or^ was himself, he emptied or exhausted himself ~~of,~~ so far as that was possible, of godhead and behaved ^only^ as ~~a creature, servant~~ ^God's^ slave, as ~~a~~ ^his^ creature, as man, which also he was, and ^then^ being in the guise of man humbled himself to death, the death of the cross. It is this holding of himself back, and not snatching at the ^truest and^ highest good, the good that was his right, nay his possession from a past eternity in his other nature, his own being and self, which seems to me the root of all his holiness and the imitation of this the root of all moral good in other men. I agree then, and vehemently, ~~with you~~ that a gentleman, if there is such a thing on earth, is in the position to despise the poet, were he Dante or Shakspere, and the painter, were he Angelo or Apelles,[6] for anything in him that shewed him not to be a gentleman. He is in the position to do it, I say, but if he is a gentleman perhaps this is what he will not do. Which leads me to another remark.

The quality of a gentleman ~~seems to me~~ ^is^ so very fine a thing that it seems to me one should not be at all hasty in concluding that one possesses it. People assume that they have it, take it quite for granted, and ~~rea~~ claim the acknowledgment from others: now I should say that this also is 'no snatching-matter'. And the more a man ~~realizes~~ ^feels^ what it means and is — and ^to feel^ this is certainly some part of it — the more backward he will be to think he can have realised in himself anything so perfect. It is true, there is nothing like the truth and "the good that does itself not know scarce is";[7] so the perfect gentleman will know that he is the perfect gentleman. But few can be in the position to know this and, being imperfect gentleman, it will perhaps be a point of their gentlemanliness, for a gentleman is modest, to feel that they are not perfect gentlemen.

By the by if the English race had done nothing else, yet if they left the world the notion of a gentleman, they would have done a great service to mankind.

As a fact poets and men of art are, I am sorry to say, by no means necessarily or commonly gentlemen. For gentlemen do not pander to lust ~~n~~or other basenesses nor, as you say, give themselves airs and affectations nor do other things to be found in ~~their~~ ^modern^ works. And this adds a charm to everything Canon Dixon writes, that you feel he is a gentleman and thinks like one. But now I have prosed my prose and long enough. Believe me your affectionate friend Gerard M. Hopkins S.J.

Feb. 10 1883.

I am rueful and remorseful about P. F.[8] But what else could come of handmade Dutch paper? I regret that Daniel[9] made his offer. And I hope the 2nd edition will be this one's Jacob.[10]

[1] *Prometheus the Firegiver* | Printed at the Private Press of | H. Daniel | Fellow of Worcester College | Oxford | 1883. 100 copies were printed.

[2] Brewer, with Boots, is part of the sycophantic group surrounding the Veneerings in Dickens's *Our Mutual Friend* (1864–5). See bk. 2, ch. 3.

[3] Magdalen College, Oxford, founded 1458, and with a still-active chapel and choir.

[4] There are numerous 'Hallelujah' anthems. 'Cease your funning' is an old English air, incorporated in Gay's *Beggars' Opera* (1728).

[5] Philippians 2: 5–11.

[6] The greatest poets, and the greatest artists: Dante Alighieri (*c.*1265–1321), William Shakespeare (1564–1616; *ODNB*), Michelangelo Buonarroti (1475–1564),

and Apelles of Kos, who worked in the 4th c. BC and was considered by Pliny the Elder to be the greatest of painters.

[7] Patmore, *Victories of Love* (1863), 'The Wedding Sermon', ll. 1–2.

[8] i.e. *Prometheus the Firegiver*.

[9] For Daniel, see letter to RWD of 9 Feb. 1883.

[10] Jacob is a type of the eternally blessed. Although a second son, he was materially far more successful than his twin brother Esau, who was born first to Rebecca and Isaac (see Genesis 25 ff.).

27 February 1883 from John Henry Newman to GMH

FL, no. C24, p. 412 Campion Hall, N 27/2/83 and MS copy in Birmingham Oratory

Addressed to 'The Rev. F[r] Hopkins SJ | Stonyhurst College | Blackburn'. PM BIRMINGHAM FE 27 83, BLACKBURN FE 28 83, WHALLEY FE 28 83.

Febr. 27. 1883

Dear F[r] Hopkins

Thank you very much for your remembrance of my birthday, and also for the complimentary proposal you make in behalf of my Grammar of Assent.[1]

But I cannot accept it, because I do not feel the need of it, and I could not, as a matter of conscience, allow you to undertake a work which I could not but consider at once onerous and unnecessary. ~~It~~ ^The book^ has succeeded in twelve years far more than I expected. It has reached five full editions. It is being translated in India into some of the native tongues — broken into portions and commented on.[2] It is frequently referred to in periodical home publications — only last Saturday week with considerable praise in the Spectator[3] — Of course those who read only so much of it as they can reach while cutting open the leaves, will make great mistakes about it, as D[r] Stanley has[4] — but, if it is worth anything, it will survive paper cutters, and if it is worthless, a comment, however brilliant, will not do more than gain for it a short galvanic life, which has no charms for me. Therefore, sensible as I am of your kindness, I will not accept it

Remember me warmly to my friends at Stonyhurst, and believe me,
Very truly yours
John H Card. Newman

[1] First published in 1870. GMH's letter to Newman is not extant, but see Newman to GMH, 26 Apr. 1883.

[2] By Simeon Wilberforce O'Neill, who went as a missionary to India and was granted permission to bring out a version of the last chapter of Newman's *Grammar of Assent* with comments on passages which 'require explanation to natives of this

country'. See his letter of thanks to Newman from Lahore of 15 Aug. 1882 (*LDJHN*, xxx. 123).

[3] In a review of Mivart's *Nature and Thought* in the *Spectator*, 17 Feb. 1883, p. 238.

[4] In 'Religious Movements of the Nineteenth Century', *Edinburgh Review* (Apr. 1881), 314. Arthur Stanley (1815–81; *ODNB*), Dean of Westminster, had first heard Newman preach while he was an undergraduate at Oxford in the 1830s.

Easter Monday [26 March]–27 March 1883 to Robert Bridges

LRB, no. C, p. 176 Bodleian, Dep. Bridges, vol. 92, fos. 13–14v

St. Wilfrid's, Preston (home tomorrow). Easter Monday [26 March] 1883.

Dearest Bridges, — To remove fatal false impressions your last (from Pangbourn) should have been answered at once, but that could not well be. It was too bad of you to think I was writing to tell you you were no gentleman; that you should be saying, like Mrs. Malaprop, whom I saw amusingly played lately, "Me, that~~,~~ means me, ~~sir~~ ^Captain Absolute^".[1] It is true, remarks of universal application must ~~also~~ apply even to present company and one ~~ma~~ ^cannot^ well help remembering that ^they do^; I cannot say "all must die" and politely except my hearers and myself; but beyond this I did not aim at you. No, if I had wanted a conspicuous instance of a ~~bad~~ blackguard I should have ~~giv~~^tak^en myself, ~~(but and told~~ ^as I was going to do and to tell^ a good story too thereanent, but refrained because I thought it might look as if I wanted to draw a faint protest from you and because humility is such a very sensitive thing the least touch smutches it and well meant attempts to keep it from jolting, like the ~~a~~Ark when the cattle shook it, do more harm than good;[2] but all the same I shd. have been sadly sincere and sadly truthful.

Further the only reason why I struck out say to write mean was because say came just before that.

And indeed how many many times must you have misunderstood me not in my sonnets only but in moral, social, personal matters! It must be so, I see now. But it would embitter life if we knew of the misunderstandings put upon us; it would mine at least.

About the artist and the gentleman I have said my say.

The interpretation of St. Paul Phil. ii 5 sqq. was, as it stands, my own.[3] At least I thought so, but I see that ^some^ modern Catholic commentators, as Beelen (who published a N.T. grammar) and ~~S~~Bp. MacEvilly, give it or nearly so.[4] Older commentators led mainly by St. Austin take ~~ἁρπαγην or~~ ἁρπαγμον ~~(whichever it is)~~ and rapinam for robbery, that is / Christ being God thought it no ~~robbery~~ sin to be what he was and yet humbled himself etc; but this requires a strong adversative particle in the Greek, wh. there is not. I got the sense of ἁρπαγ~~ην~~^μον^ {*snatching matter*} from Jowett or some modern critic: it in reality adds force to St. Austin's interpretation, which otherwise I was following. St. John Chrysostom[5] seems to have come ~~very~~ ^still^ near^er^ the sense I gave.

Human nature in me seems to[6]
feel [?a certain malignant] joy
that
tell

I have had a late very pleasant letter from him. He says you are not altogether recovered; that one night you seemed quite ill, though recovered next morning. Still if I were you I shd. not dwell on it.

The weather in these parts continues winterly, atrociously so.

I have completed one sonnet,[7] since I came north one — and three triolets, which have been published, but they have the taint of jest and ~~would~~ ^dare^ not meet your eye.[8] The sonnet is a companion to "I remember a house" (in which write "build this ~~house~~ ^world^ of Wales" for "make"): perhaps I may enclose it. I am always jaded, I cannot tell why, and my vein ~~can~~ shews no ~~se~~ signs of ever flowing again.

Believe me your affectionate friend Gerard M. Hopkins S.J. March 27.

[1] Both are characters in Richard Brinsley Sheridan's *The Rivals* (1775).

[2] 2 Samuel 6: 6: 'And when they came to Nachom's threshingfloor, Uzzah put forth his hand to the ark of God and took hold of it; for the oxen shook it. 7. And the anger of the Lord was kindled against Uzzah; and God smote him there for his error, and there he died by the ark of God' (*AV*; *Douay* says 'the oxen kicked and made it lean aside').

[3] See letter of 3–10 Feb. 1883, where he translates the Greek as 'snatching-matter'. Other versions that have been suggested include 'robbery', 'possession', and 'something to be ostentatiously displayed'.

[4] Jan Theodore Beelen (1807–84) published *Grammatica graecitatis Novi Testamentis* (1857) as well as a *Commentarius in epistolam S. Pauli ad Philippenses* (2nd edn. 1852) and a translation of the New Testament (3 vols., 1859–69). John MacEvilly (1816–1902: *ODNB*), archbishop of Tuam, Ireland, wrote *An Exposition of the Epistles of St. Paul,* in which he agreed with Beelen's view of the passage in question: Christ 'did not with eager tenacity retain the external form and equality with God the Father, which he possessed; but, by taking on himself human nature and the appearance of man, veiled his Divine glory and Majesty; thus humbling himself, which is a powerful motive for humiliation on our part. The Greek word "for robbery", ἁρπαγμον, favours this interpretation' (6th edn., 1898, ii. 12).

[5] Homily 6 on Philippians by St John Chrysostom (*c*.347–407), archbishop of Constantinople, called 'golden-mouthed' (*Χρυσόστομος*) for his eloquence.

[6] Of four lines beginning this side of the leaf, the first is left, with two words of the second, and the rest has been scratched out with a knife, no doubt by RB. The passage must have been about RWD.

[7] 'Ribblesdale' ('Stonyhurst, 1881'). Companion to 'In the Valley of the Elwy'.

[8] *λέγεταί τι καινόν* {*Is there any news today?*}, 'Cockle's Antibilious pills', and 'The Child is Father to the Man' (Wordsworth), published in *The Stonyhurst Magazine*, 1/9 (Mar. 1883), 162, signed with the pseudonym BRAN. See letter to RB of 24 Oct. 1883 and *CW* viii.

19 April 1883 to Robert Bridges

LRB, no. CI, 178 Bodleian, Dep. Bridges, vol. 92, fos. 15–16

Stonyhurst, April 19 1883. I am writing with a glass tube pen ~~and~~ homemade and homebrewed ink.

Dearest Bridges, — I wish you would write; it makes me disconsolate punctually every morning to get no letter.

I want to know if you know any one who knows music, counterpoint, thoroughly, or, what comes to the same thing, if you know Stainer[1] thoroughly, enough to ask him a favour. For I shall shortly have finished an exercise in the second species[2] in two parts on "Pray, Goody, please to moderate",[3] pretty elaborate, and I want to know on authority if it is correct and if not where.[4] It has taken much time and I shall never write anything so long again by way of exercise. It is rather, not very, pretty.

I shall of course be glad to see Nero. Is there then to be a Second Part?[5] You forgot that I had read the triolet in MS. It is witty in the lent[6] century but one sense of that word. I do not see that the anagrams in it are of any importance.

No more now. Your affectionate friend Gerard M. Hopkins S.J.

[1] Sir John Stainer (1840–1901; *ODNB*). Despite losing the sight in one eye as a child, he was a prolific composer, writer of books on music theory and history, and an organist. As a youth, his beautiful voice won him a place as a chorister at St Paul's; he spent two years under the guidance of Sir Frederick Gore Ouseley as organist at St Michael's, Tenbury, and then went up to Oxford, where he became organist at Magdalen College in 1860, and of the University in 1861. He was one of a group of artists and musicians with whom Bridges was friendly while he was a medical student in London. GMH obtained Stainer's *Theory of Harmony* (1871). In 1889 Stainer succeeded Sir Frederick Gore Ouseley as Professor of Music at Oxford.

[2] i.e. two notes in one voice against one in the other. This is the way Johann Joseph Fux taught counterpoint (based on the practice of Palestrina) in his *Gradus ad Parnassum* of 1725.

[3] See letter to RB of 8 Apr. 1879 n. 9 on 'Pray, Goody'.
[4] See letter of 29 May 1883.
[5] *Nero* was published in 1884: the second part in 1894.
[6] MS 'lent'= last?

26 April 1883 from John Henry Newman to GMH

FL, no. C25, p. 412 — Campion Hall, N 26/4/83 and MS copy in Birmingham Oratory

Addressed to 'The Rev. | Fr Hopkins S.J. | Stonyhurst College | Blackburn'. PM BROMSGROVE AP 26 83, CARNFORTH 27 AP 83, BLACKBURN AP 27 83.

Rednall | April 26/83

Dear Fr Hopkins

In spite of your kind denial,[1] I still do & must think that a comment is a compliment, and to say that a comment may be appended to my small book because one may be made ^on^ Aristotle ought to make me blush ^purple^! As to India, I suppose all ^English^ books, even Goody Two Shoes,[2] are so unlike its literary atmosphere, that a comment is but one aspect of translation

I must still say that you paid me a very kind compliment. You seem to think compliments must be insincere: is it so?

Most truly yours
John H Card. Newman

[1] See Newman's letter of 27 Feb. 1883 for his earlier response to GMH's proposal.
[2] *The History of Little Goody Two Shoes*, a well-known children's tale of virtue rewarded, was published anonymously in 1765. Goldsmith, Giles Jones, and its publisher John Newbery have been proposed as author. Marcus Clarke's pantomime *Goody Two Shoes* was produced at the Theatre Royal Melbourne in 1870.

11 May 1883 to Robert Bridges

LRB, no. CII, p. 179 — Bodleian, Dep. Bridges, vol. 92, fos. 17–18v

Stonyhurst College, | Blackburn. [*embossed heading*]
May 11 1883.

Dearest Bridges, — Here then is this blessed thing, which has cost more trouble than it is worth.[1] Try it yourself. Sometimes when I play it at my own pace and with my own expression I think it very good in parts and at other times and when somebody else plays it it seems to me a meaningless maundering and a wandering in a wilderness.

I think from what you say it had better not go to Stainer, though as he was my contemporary and I knew him by sight I feel drawn to him.

We hang up polyglot poems in honour of the Blessed Virgin this month. I am on one in English in three-foot couplets.[2] I do not suppose I shall ~~either~~ find it either convenient or desirable to send you a copy. ~~Unl~~ It is partly a compromise ~~b~~with popular taste, and it is too true that the highest subjects are not those on which it is easy to reach ^one's^ highest.

The cold half kills me.

Your affectionate friend Gerard Hopkins S.J.

Though the favour will be, directly speaking, to you I shall be very grateful to your friend.[3] U^W^hat I want is that he should mark any mistakes he may find and make any remarks he may think proper, on the margin or elsewhere. Whitsunday. I have sealed it up, but you may put onto it that the bass sounds better an octave lower or doubled.

Your letter has come, on which I have to remark —

Some of my rhymes I regret, but they are past ~~chan~~ changing, grubs in amber: there are only a few of these;

Others are unassailable;

Some others again there are which malignity may munch at but the Muses love. To this class belongs what you quote. You will grant that there are things in verse which may be read right or wrong, which depend for their effect upon pronunciation. For instance here if I had rhymed drew her to to her I should have meant it to be read tó her and not to hér, though in itself the latter is just as possible. You will also grant that in drew her, rightly read, the h is evanescent. Good. Now then endured may be read with little or with well marked circumflex — endũred something like en-dew-ered. And[4]

[1] The exercise in counterpoint, 'Pray Goody'.

[2] 'The Blessed Virgin compared to the Air we Breathe'. 'Stonyhurst, May '83.' He did send RB a copy; see letters to RWD of 25–9 June 1883 and to RB of 24–5 Oct. 1883.

[3] RB cut out the name of this friend whenever it subsequently occurred. It seems to have had about seven letters; GMH's reference later to the *Athenaeum* (1–2 Apr. 1885) suggests that perhaps it was Walter Parratt, whom RB knew and to whom he contemplated sending in 1897 verse by Henry Newbolt for music. Parratt (1841–1924; *ODNB*) was an organist and composer, fellow of Magdalen College, Oxford and private organist to Queen Victoria and then the King's Master of Music. He was a professor at the Royal College of Music, very influential in the training of organists throughout Britain and a composer of church music.

[4] Most unfortunately the rest of this postscript is missing. GMH and RB were obviously discussing the rhymes in stanza 14 of 'The Wreck of the Deutschland'. In his notes on 'Rhymes' in the first edition, pp. 109–10, Bridges says that 'when he indulges in freaks, his childishness is incredible', and adds, probably referring to the above exchange, that GMH 'did not escape full criticism, and ample ridicule, for such things in his lifetime', going on to quote from the above letter.

18 May 1883 to Robert Bridges

LRB, no. CIII, p. 180 Bodleian, Dep. Bridges, vol. 92, fos. 19–20

Stonyhurst College, | Blackburn. [*embossed heading*]
May 18 1883.
(fine day, with a solar halo; holiday; our boys to have a match)

Dearest Bridges, — Fine bass! I should think so. But did you never hear Pray Goody before? I am glad I have introduced it to you. (I think it far better to take fine things like that to practise on than the maundering exercises in books.) And it is but one ~~ou~~ ^out^ of a host of such masculine and (what some one called) earnest melodies, little known here and abroad I suppose totally unknown. It is simple truth that no German since Mozart has been capable of anything of the sort. The Germans are great and I believe unsu~~pr~~-passable in expressing mood and feeling, but for the bone, frame, and charpente {*frame (work)*} of music they cannot come up to this kind of thing.

On the contrary anything that Simcox[1] says is important. But for rhymes like those search the scriptures, thumb the poets, and you will find they readily allow monosyllables and dissyllables like higher and fire to rhyme.* [*GMH footnote*: *You will say a monosyllable cannot rhyme to a monosyllable and a disyllable both at once, in the same stanza, that is. But if it can ever, then one of the two is accommodated to the other; and if one can be so can two or if one to one then one to two. Do you see the reasoning?[2]] It is true it is not very consistent of me to appeal to them when I profess to follow a more excellent way;[3] still when I am told so and so is indefensible I must shew that it is defensible. Authority justifies it and the pronunciation can be so adjusted as to satisfy the ear. What is serious, you seem to think I took the objection overseriously. And now I think I am going out by woods and waters alone. ~~Yours~~ Yours Gerard.

[1] George Augustus Simcox (1841–1905) had been at Corpus 1858–62, took a 1st in Greats, and became a fellow of Queen's College, lecturer, and librarian. His best-known work is a *History of Latin Literature from Ennius to Boethius* (2 vols., 1883), but he also wrote a *Prometheus Unbound, a Tragedy* (1867), various shorter poems and romances, and edited classical texts with his younger brother. GMH told his mother that 'besides being amiable [he] is the most eccentric and witty man I ever met' (20 Oct. 1869). He also reviewed books for *The Academy*.

[2] This footnote is written in pale blue pencil.

[3] GMH is quoting from 1 Corinthians 12: 31.

29 May 1883 to Robert Bridges

LRB, no. CIV, p. 181 Bodleian, Dep. Bridges, vol. 92, fos. 21–22[v]

Stonyhurst College, | Blackburn. [*embossed heading*]
May 29 1883.

Dearest Bridges, — I am very grateful and greatly indebted to your friend — .[1] His judgment and notes are also reassuring, for the composition is in fact ~~the~~ ^my^ second exercise and no more, ~~un~~ in the species my first (~~I~~'tis true I took trouble over it) and the objections he makes are to things Dr. Bridge's[2] book had ~~not~~ warned me against either not properly or not at all. Here indeed is a difficulty: I do not know if there are or where I can find examples (and the examples of the great masters are the soul of education) of existing counterpoint~~,~~ — if such ^a^ thing~~s~~ ~~do~~ ^does^ exist — ; not short exercises in books (and of these I have only seen Dr. B's). Thus ?Mr. — [3] speaks of "figures repeated two or three times": now~~,~~ I, bless us all, put these in for beauties, ~~as als~~ especially in a passage he marks as monotonous (and so it is if I ought to have kept changing). Clearly they are against the spirit of the kind of composition; though according to that of others, as fugue. How ^then^ am I to advance without models? Somewhere ~~they~~ ^models^ must be. And if he could tell me where, I should be glad. I hesitate ~~ab~~ over your offer to get him to write: it might entangle him in more than he meant and he will be in this busy world busy. Of course I should like it in itself.

I took to counterpoint not for itself but as the solid foundation of harmony. But I soon began to suspect it was only an invention of theorists and ~~a~~ ^a would-be or^ fancy-music, for what is written in it? Not even the preludes to Bach's fugues. There are two-part preludes which seem as if they ought to be in the second or third species[4] and are not, the rules are in smithereens: then WHAT IS in true counterpoint?

I meant to be as conservative as Mr. — [3] could be and my accidentals I always intended not to be chromatic but fragments of related keys, I did not always know what.

I have exhibited a poem,[5] which I hope to send you when I can copy it, but it is longish for copying. Yours Gerard.

[1] Name deleted by RB. See note 3 to 11 May 1883.

[2] Either *Counterpoint* (1877) or *Double Counterpoint and Canon* (1877) by John Frederick Bridge.

[3] Name deleted by RB.

[4] i.e. four notes against one, and syncopation.

[5] 'The Blessed Virgin Compared to the Air We Breathe'. See letters to RWD of 25–9 June 1883 and to RB of 24–5 Oct. 1883.

9–10 June 1883 to Grace Hopkins

Renascence, 31 (1979), 196–7 HRHRC, Container 1.5

Stonyhurst, June 9 1883.

My dearest Grace, — I feel though at a distance some of the force of this dreadful blow by which once more death shows its power ^suddenly^ to darken ^our^ hopes and disenchant us.[1] But the firmest and most fruitful ^ground of^ comfort is to look on everything that has happened, your meeting with Henry Weber, your engagement, the ~~time~~ ^months^ that ha~~p~~ve since past, and his death, as things providential, always meant (more than permitted) ^by God^ to be and their times and circumstances appointed. On your part there is, I presume, nothing that you regret to have said or done (setting aside mere trifles) and, though I do not know, yet I should judge that to him his love for you and betrothal had been a steadying and purifying thing rather than other wise. If so, then for your spell of brightness and happiness, great while it lasted, to end for him in death and for you~~r~~ in a deep disappointment marks it as a sorrow more especially of God's sending and of which he undertakes to be the comforter. For consider this: say all had gone well, he had recovered and thriven, and you had married and lived a long happy prosperous life together and reared your children, would not this be of God's giving and would you not have returned him and been bound to return him thanks for the blessings bestowed? It was a thing quite possible, you were hoping for and looking forward to it. Now, poor child, this is for ever gone and without a warning at one blow swept away: is it not plain that God our Lord knows what he does and in striking so hard pities your poor heart and means for you something far better, the brighter that seeming future was the better this real one? But you are not to think, my dear, that you are somehow to be made happy some day for being unhappy this: there is no sense in that. What God means is that you shall greatly gain if you will be humble and patient. And patience means that grief shall not make you exacting or selfish or in good time unfit you for ordinary duty. It has this effect on some people; it makes mere wrecks of them. It is not said to them Blessed are the mourn,[2] for they shall be comforted.

I shall say mass for Henry Weber's repose tomorrow and another day: I hope it may avail him and if so, whatever you may think, he will be grateful to his betrothed's brother for it.

To your letter~~, with which I~~ ^(I liked it all and^ agreed with it) I do not answer now and I have not written this without tears. Good-bye, dearest child, and believe me your loving brother Gerard.

I will shortly write to my mother. I am well. I have to preach at Preston tomorrow week.[3]

June 10 — I said mass for Henry Weber this morning and during the mass I felt ~~ther~~ ^strong^ly those motions from God (as I believe them to be) which I have often before now received ~~a~~touching the condition of the departed, by which was signified that it was well with him. I have also warnings sometimes of an approaching death: I had such a one lately, but it was slight and I paid little attention to it.

[1] See letter to RB of 5–6 Aug. 1883, which explains the situation.

[2] Hopkins probably mis-writes rather than misquotes 'Blessed are they that mourn' from Matthew 5: 5.

[3] The documents mentioned here, Grace's letter, the letter to his mother, and his sermon, have not survived.

28 June 1883 (fragment) to Robert Bridges

LRB, no. CV, p. 182 Bodleian, Dep. Bridges, vol. 92, fo. 23

Stonyhurst. June 28 1883.

Dearest Bridges, — I send Purcell herewith and my thanks and regret for having kept the piece so long. It shd. have gone yesterday, I swear it should, but as I was just going to pack it I was despatched to take a party of people over the college, which lasted till post time was past. Before . . . [1]

[1] A fragment: the bottom of the leaf is torn off.

25–9 June 1883 to Richard Watson Dixon

CRWD, no. XXVII, p. 107 Bodleian, Dep. Bridges, vol. 93, fos. 106–109[v]
Addressed to 'The Rev. Canon Dixon | Hayton Vicarage | Carlisle'. No readable PM. One folded sheet.

Stonyhurst, Blackburn. June 25 1883.

My dear Friend, — I am ashamed to think how long I have let you go unanswered: it was bitter winter weather, I remember you said, when you wrote; but the winter was very late this year. It came March 20.

I have little to say. I enclose one sonnet,[1] meant as a companion to one beginning "I remember a house",[2] which perhaps you have. You will see that the first words begin a lyric of yours — or perhaps those are "Earth, <u>sad</u> Earth".[3] During May I was asked to write something in honour of the Blessed Virgin, it being the custom to hang up ~~o~~ verse-compositions "in the tongues" (which sometimes are far fetched, for people gravitate to us from odd quarters): I did a piece[4] in the same metre as "Blue in the mists all day",[5] but I have not leisure to copy it.

Both your new poem and Bridges' linger.[6]

We have duly got your History, but till holiday time I shall not look at it. Reading history is very laborious to me: I can only digest ~~and~~ ^or^ remember a little at a time.

My time, as I have said before this, is not so closely employed but that someone else in my place might not do a good deal, but I cannot, and I see no grounded prospect of my ever doing much not only in poetry but in anything at all. At times I do feel this sadly and bitterly, but it is God's will and though no change that I can foresee will happen yet perhaps some may that I do not foresee. — I fumble a little at music, at counterpoint, ^of^ which in course of time I shall come to know something; for this, like every other study, after some drudgery yields up its secrets, which seem inpenetrable at first. If I could get to accompany my own airs I should, so to say, enter into a new kingdom at once, for I have plenty of ~~airs~~ tunes ready.

Your health is, I hope, good, for when you wrote you were suffering greatly from the cold. We have had drought in Lancashire, a rare thing: now the fine weather is broken up and there is much rain.

In the sonnet enclosed "louchèd" is a coinage of mine and is to mean much the same as slouched, slouching. And I mean "throng" for an adjective as we use it here in Lancashire.

This is but a scrub of a letter, but I could not make it longer or better now. Believe me your affectionate friend Gerard M. Hopkins S.J.

June 28 1883.

June 29 — I mislaid this under books yesterday and it was not posted — I suppose that I might light upon this, as I have this very minute — Athenaeum for June 9 "Literary Gossip[7] . . . Canon Dixon's new poem, entitled 'Mano: a Poetical History', is ~~b~~ written in terza rima, the measure being treated more upon structural principles than it has generally been in English. The time is the close of the tenth century, when there was a general expectation of the end of the world. The hero is a Norman knight, a precursor of the Normans who conquered Italy and S~~e~~^i^cily in the next century, and the scenes are laid partly in Normandy, partly in Italy. The famous Gerbert, who became Pope and was a reputed magician, is among the characters."

[1] 'Ribblesdale'. See *CW* viii.

Ribblesdale

"Vanitati enim creatura subjecta est, non volens sed propter eum qui subjecit eam in spe" cum praecc. et sqq. Rom. viii 20. {*'For the creature was made subject to vanity, not willingly, but by reason of him who hath subjected the same in hope' along with what precedes and follows Romans 8: 20.*}

Earth, sweet Earth, sweet landscape with leavès throng
And louchèd low grass, heaven that dost appeal
To, with no tongue to plead, no heart to feel,
That canst but only be, but dost that long.
Thou canst but be, but that thou well dost; strong
Thy plea with him who dealt, nay does now deal
Thy lovely dale down ~~d~~ thus and thus lets reel
Thy river and o'er gives all to rack or wrong.
But what is ~~Nature's~~ ^Earth's^ eye, tongue, or heart else, where
Else, but in dear and doggèd man?—Ah, the heir,
To his own self-bent so bound, so tied to his turn,
To thriftless reave both ~~this~~ ^our^ rich round world bare
And none reck of world after—this bids wear
Earth brows of such care, care and dear concern.
Stonyhurst 1883

[2] 'In the Valley of the Elwy'.

[3] The lyric 'Mercy' from *H.O.* (*S.P.*, 59), begins:

> Earth, sad earth, thou roamest
> Through the day and night.

[4] 'The Blessed Virgin compared to the Air we Breathe'.
[5] 'Nature and Man', *Lyrical Poems* (*S.P.*, 116–20).
[6] RWD's *Mano* and RB's *Prometheus the Firegiver* are both long, though GMH probably intended the kinder meaning.
[7] What GMH gives is the whole note.

26 July 1883 to Robert Bridges

LRB, no. CVI, p. 183 Bodleian, Dep. Bridges, vol. 92, fos. 24–5

Stonyhurst, Blackburn. July 26 1883.

Dearest Bridges, — What I enclose is I dare say quite too[1]
long; if so ~~le~~
wise unsuita[ble]
be suppressed,
reads to me
like a family
is what Mrs [?Waterhouse]
wanted; rath[er]
one. Perhaps
er than once
might pass.
I made the
it some time
mon was put
I was forced
matter needing
on and not
ly. If Mrs W[aterhouse]

[*next page, where beginnings of lines are missing*]

to try.
ne and gone.
had meant
ou [?]; I wanted
e-books,
e strictness.

[*missing line*]

Our year begins with ~~at~~ autumn and the appointments for this college will be made public on the 1st of next month. It seems likely that I shall be removed; where I have no notion. But I have long been Fortune's football and am blowing up the bladder of resolution big and buxom for another kick of her foot. I shall be sorry to leave Stonyhurst; but go or stay, there is no likelihood of my ever doing anything to last. And I do not know how it is, I have no disease, but I am always tired, always jaded, though work is not heavy, and the impulse to do anything fails me or has in it no continuance.

Weather has been very wet and cold and has made me ill a little.

Believe me your affectionate friend Gerard.

[1] From here onwards almost half the first leaf of this letter was cut off by RB, leaving the beginnings of lines on the first side and the ends of lines on the second; the blanks, therefore, are unavoidable. The lines on the first side are of about three or four words, and on the second side, where the writing is in a different direction, about five to seven words. The matter of the letter can, however, to some degree be recovered. Mrs Waterhouse was compiling a *Book of Prayers* (finished in 1884), and it was suggested that GMH should contribute. This he did: but the Prayer he sent (evidently with some diffidence) was held to be out of keeping with the undoctrinal tone of the rest of the book, and was not included. RB pasted it into MS A, and indexed it as 'a prayer written for protestants'. It is printed in *CW* v. For further remarks by GMH on the subject, see letter to RB of 24–5 Oct. 1883.

5–6 August 1883 to Robert Bridges

LRB, no. CVII, p. 183 Bodleian, Dep. Bridges, vol. 92, fos. 26–28v

Stonyhurst, Blackburn.
Aug. 5 1883.

Dearest Bridges, — Though you are long and deeply in my debt, yet having things to tell you I write again.

The holidays are come and from the ~~climax~~ ^height^ of buzz and bustle we have been suddenly steeped in the dankness of ditchwater. I have leave of absence and on Thursday probably am going to Hampstead and presently to Holland for a few days with my people: ~~and~~ to explain how this comes about I must go back.

You may have met my cousin Magdalen. She lived with her widowed mother Mrs. Marsland Hopkins and her elder sister and brother at

Oxford in Holywell Street. There she became engaged to Archibald Commeline then an undergraduate of Magdalen~~.~~. I used to meet him there, but remember him indistinctly: he is a great friend of Sir Gore Ouseley's.[1] She was married to him on the 7th of last June from my father's house. Of course my sisters were to be among the bridesmaids, but Grace was not so and this was the reason.

When my people were abroad last year they met at Montreux on (I think) the Lake of Geneva a young man Henry Weber son to a doctor at Sensburg in East Prussia. He was attracted by Grace's playing and, the weather keeping them in, was constantly at her piano: when they parted, though they had known each other for less than a fortnight, they were both deeply in love. ~~His~~ In spite of his frail health, his uncertain prospects, and the obvious reasons against such a match my father and mother could not refuse to let it be an engagement. After some illusory rallies, just when Grace and he had persuaded themselves that he was to recover and all would be well, suddenly at the last, he died. The news reached Grace on the very eve of Magdalen's wedding. It was an overwhelming blow. Magdalen wished the wedding to be put off, but that was neither possible nor desirable; ~~only~~ but a gloom was cast over the day and Grace kept her room. She then set her heart on seeing her lover's grave. An escort was found for her as far as Berlin and at the station nearest Sensburg Mrs. Weber met her. Now she is with them and they treat her like one of themselves. Mrs. Weber wd. seem by all accounts to be a very sweet person. I have had a letter from Grace from Sensburg. My father and mother are going to fetch her home and that is how I am to go to Holland. As at present arranged I am to go to Hampstead on Thursday.

The first of this month was our Speechday or 'Great Academy' to which guests come. Among them was Coventry Patmore: he came two days before and stayed till the day after and the Rector put him into my hands, so that I saw a good deal of him.[2] But as ~~he knows or~~ your friend —[3] knows him well I suppose I need not describe him, and moreover you affect an absence of interest in him. ~~I~~ On my mentioning you ~~y~~ he expressed at once his admiration of your poetry but knew it only from revie[ws] and had tried without suc[ce]ss to get it from his booksell[er] or publisher and I could not properly direct him about it. I wish you would let me know in what form it now is obtainable: the titles I mean, for I have had the books but they are not here, I think. I told him of Prometheus: ~~I suppose~~ will there be any spare copies buyable? I took him all my MS of Dixon, of whom he had never heard, and made an enthusiastic convert of him. Before bringing out ~~this~~ this autumn the

~~last~~ next edition of his own poems, which, he says, is likely to be the last in his lifetime, he is going to send them to me for suggestions: I do not know but it was bragging to mention this; however now there it is, all blubbering in wet ink. ~~I~~

I suppose it will be more than a fortn[ig]ht before I am at Stonyhurst again. My appointment is ~~ne~~ renewed.

Believe me your affectionate friend Gerard Hopkins S.J. Aug. 6 1883.
Tell me about Mr. —[4]

[1] See Biographical Register.

[2] GMH's sketch of Patmore, dated 'Aug. 1 1883', is reproduced in *LPM*, 355. See also *CW* vi.

[3] Name cut out by RB, which has also caused the other deletions on the verso of the page, which it is however possible to conjecture. Edmund Gosse? 'Gosse named Coventry Patmore . . . as one of the three most formative friendships of these early years' (Anne Thwaite, *Edmund Gosse: A Literary Landscape 1849–1928* (London, 1984), 227). Gosse, Patmore, and Bridges were all members of the Savile Club. Gosse was also very friendly with the Waterhouses, RB's neighbours and landlords, shortly to become his in-laws.

[4] Name cut out by RB, but see letter of 11 May 1883, n. 3.

10 August 1883 to Robert Bridges

LRB, no. CVIII, p. 185 Bodleian, Dep. Bridges, vol. 92, fo. 29

The Holy Name, Oxford Road, Manchester. Aug. 10 1883.

Dearest Bridges, — I cannot be at Hampstead on Monday the 13th now nor till Wednesday or Thursday. A sudden need brought me here and keeps me. I am sorry you tore up that letter: why not have let me have the pennyworth?[1] Patmore lives at Hastings: I shd. think that address enough but shall come to hear more. Yours Gerard Hopkins.

[1] The cost of the penny postage.

12 August 1883 from Richard Watson Dixon to GMH

CRWD, no. XXVII A, p. 110 Campion Hall, D 12/8/83
Addressed to 'The Rev^{d}. | Gerard Hopkins, S.J. | Stonyhurst, | Blackburn'. PM CARLISLE AU 13 83, PRESTON AU 13 83, BLACKBURN AU 14 83, WHALLEY AU 14 83.

Hayton Vicarage, | Carlisle. 12 Aug 1883

My dear Friend,

I have left your last kind & interesting letter too long unanswered: & now I am not, I feel, in spirits to answer it: but I have a little time on hand, & you have been, & are, much in my thoughts: therefore I write, but having little to say.

I like the Sonnet on Earth the Creature,[1] which you sent, very much, as I do all your work: it has the rareness, the sweetness that is in all: & could have been written by none other. Of the other poem which you mention, on Our Lady, it is probably the same that Bridges has mentioned to me, saying that it is "admirable", "Our Lady compared to the Air we breathe".

Thank you very much for copying that notice of my poem from the Athenæum. The book is out, & I hope to send you a copy in a day or two. I want your judgment of it.

Bridges' poem came to me two days ago. It reads splendidly, especially the choruses: & (what is I sd. think extremely difficult) the verse for verse dialogue. He has managed the plot also excellently. By the way, what do you understand by "unity of action"? The phrase is used by Hall Caine in a good article on Shakespeare in the Contemporary[2] in a way that I do not understand of it. I forget his exact words, something like the end being harmonious with the inception. I thought it meant having a single plot. Greek dramas have a single plot.

I have been reading over some of poor Rossetti's work. There is something very grieving in most of it. I thought, though it must seem presumptuous, that many of the sonnets might have been improved.

I wish the present run, or rather rush, upon the Sonnet were over. It is a bore to see the inevitable "regular structure" week after week in all the "cultured" organs, the fifth verse for ever virtuously turning the others, as it were, inside out. But I must not reopen the subject with you, to bore you.

Do you happen to know Rowe's Lucan?[3] It seems to me the finest version made in that age: the versification far better than Dryden, & more of a direct advance from him than Pope, which was rather another kind (I think) than an advance on Dryden.

Thank you for procuring my Church History: I hope if you read it, that there may be nothing to offend you. I trust not. I am going on with it, & am in the year 1551,[4] a dreadful time.

With all good wishes and affectionate regards, I am ever your affectionate Friend R. W. Dixon

[1] i.e. 'Ribblesdale'.

[2] For June 1883 (pp. 883–900), *Two Aspects of Shakespeare's Art*.

[3] Nicholas Rowe (1674–1718), whose translation of Lucan's *Pharsalia* was first published in 1718 [1719].

[4] In 1551 England was under a regency council, and the reign of Edward VI (1547–53) was marked by riot, rebellion, political infighting, reformation of the church under the fervently Protestant king, and anxieties over the fate of the crown.

12 August 1883 to Richard Watson Dixon

CRWD, no. XXVIII, p. 111 Bodleian, Dep. Bridges, vol. 93, fos. 110–113v
Addressed to 'The Rev. Canon Dixon | St. Mary's Vicarage | Hayton Vicarage | Carlisle'. PM MANCHESTER AU 13 83. One folded sheet.

The Holy Name, Oxford Rd., Manchester. Aug. 12 1883.

My dear friend, — I am here filling a gap and take the opportunity of letting you know that two days before our 'Great Academies', that is the speechday with which our Stonyhurst scholastic year ends, Coventry Patmore came to visit us and stayed three or four days. The Rector gave me charge of him and I saw a good deal of him and had a good deal of talk. He knew and expressed great admiration of Bridges' Muse upon the strength of extracts in reviews only, ^not^ having till that time ~~not~~ been able to get the poems from his bookseller; but of you he ~~n~~^k^new nothing, not even your name. I brought him all I had of yours in MS and he read it all. He told me he was very slow in taking in a new poet, even the meaning, much more the effect and spirit; he said ~~after a first reading~~ "~~One~~ ^I^ feels oneself in presence of a new mind, a new spirit, but beyond that at a first reading I am not yet accustomed to the strange atmosphere". This he said after a little reading of the MS. Then he became much taken up with Love's Consolation and that made the most impression. He was in fact completely won by it and pointed out passages with the insight of ~~one ^a man^ who~~ the predestined reader. In the end he told me when I next wrote to you to express to you 'the immense pleasure the reading of your poems had given him'; he was amazed and sorry he had never known anything of them before. I furnished him with titles and publisher and told him to expect Mano's coming out. He would have ^it^ that Morris must have borrowed from you, but I told him I thought that it was a ^case of^ parallel growth. His conversation was of course full of interest. He is fastidious and searching in his criticism. Of his friend Aubrey de Vere[1] he said, assenting to a remark of mine, "He has all the gifts that make a poet excepting only that last degree of individuality which is the most essential of all". Of Browning, whom he can no longer bring himself to read, he said ~~the~~ something the same but severer. I suppose I am more tolerant or more inclined to admire than he is, but in listening to him I had that malignant satisfaction which lies in h~~av~~^ear^ing one's worst surmises confirmed — the joy Mrs. Candour's audience must have felt when she discussed M~~iss~~^rs^. Vermilion and Miss Evergreen.[2]

I expect on Thursday to go to my father's at Hampstead and in a week's time to Holland for a week. I suppose I shall be back at Stonyhurst by the beginning of next month. I am reappointed for the ensuing year, I am happy to say.

Believe me your affectionate friend Gerard Hopkins S.J.

I shall see Bridges at Hampstead, I expect.

By the by Patmore has a very great admiration for Dorset Barnes.

[1] Aubrey de Vere (1814–1902), poet and critic. See *ODNB*. He had been converted to Catholicism in 1851 and was Professor of English Literature in the Catholic University, Dublin. In 1864 he had urged Coventry Patmore, who needed a change of scene, to go on holiday with him to Rome.

[2] Sheridan, *The School for Scandal* (1777), II. ii. It should be 'Miss Vermillion' and 'Mrs. Evergreen'.

12 August 1883 to Coventry Patmore

FL, no. CLXIII, p. 295 — Durham University Library, Abbott MS 181
Single folded sheet watermarked A PIRIE & SONS

The Holy Name, Oxford Road, Manchester. Aug. 12 1883.

My dear Mr Patmore, — I expect to go to town on Thursday and not to be back at Stonyhurst till about the beginning of next month: I tell you this for fear your books should have ~~come~~ ^gone^ or should hereafter go to Stonyhurst without acknowledgment. I have written to

Canon Dixon and to Bridges. Bridges would send you his pamphlets (that is his poems exclusive of the sonnets, I think, and Prometheus) if he knew your address. I am going to ~~send~~ ^address^ this to Hastings; I should think that would do.

Believe me yours sincerely Gerard M. Hopkins S.J. [*The salutation was blotted so GMH wrote it out again.*]

[13 August 1883] from Richard Watson Dixon to GMH

CRWD, p. v. Stonyhurst College Library. Pasted into a copy of Dixon's *Mano* (1883).

Hayton, Carlisle

Your letter crossed one that I sent to Stonyhurst.
Many thanks for your delightful letter.
In extreme haste,

Ever yours
R W Dixon

14 August 1883 from Coventry Patmore to GMH

Campion Hall, P 14/8/83
Envelope only, addressed to 'Rev[d] Gerard Hopkins, S.J. | Stonyhurst College, | Blackburn'. Re-addressed to 'Church of the Holy Name | Oxford Road | Manchester'. PM HASTINGS AU 14 83, PRESTON AU 14 83, BLACKBURN AU 14 83, WHALLEY AU 15 83, MANCHESTER AU 16 83, and franked with 1d postage due stamp.

15–16 Aug. 1883 to Richard Watson Dixon

CRWD, no. XXIX, p. 112 Bodleian, Dep. Bridges, vol. 93, fos. 113–117[v]
Addressed to 'The Rev. R. W. Dixon | St. Mary's Vicarage | Hayton | Carlisle'. PM MANCHESTER AU 16 83. Two folded sheets.

The Holy Name, Oxford Road, Manchester. Aug. 15 1883.

My dear friend, — Your letter was brought me from Stonyhurst by hand yesterday and your book[1] came by parcel post today: for both I heartily thank you. I have nearly finished the first Book, but at a first reading it would be too soon to ~~say~~ speak. The style is more consistently archaic than I had expected: this style easily lends itself to pathetic effects but not so easily to powerful ones. A pageant of beauties passes before my mind ~~a~~as I read, but, much as Mr. Patmore ~~read~~ ^said^, I need time ~~to~~ and rereading ~~for them~~ to take the effect fairly in. So I will wait a while before writing further.

By 'unity of action'[2] I understand (but I am not advised of ~~that~~ ^the^ subject) not simplicity of plot (in the ordinary sense of simple, that is ~~the having little or no complexity~~ the opposite of complex~~,~~^)^ ~~but only in the sense of unity~~ but connectedness of plot. There is unity of action, as I understand, if the plot turns on one event, incident, or, to speak more technically, motive and all its ~~terms and~~ parts and details bear on that and are relevant to ~~it~~ ^that^: if they are irrelevant or disconnected or involve by-issues then the unity of action is impaired. So I have been accustomed to understand the phrase. The plot in some Greek plays is simple, slight, in the extreme~~,~~: the Agamemnon for instance ~~has~~ ^is^ what we should call rather a scene than a plot, a scene leading ^up^ to and then leading off from one incident, the hero's murder; but the unity of action is also extreme, for almost every word said and thing done leads up to, turns on, influences, or is influenced by this. But in this play there is ~~the~~ also the 'unity of place' and, by a conventional abridgment, the semblance of 'unity of time'. Where, as in the ~~Ion of~~ Eumenides, these ^two^ unities are not observed the plot becomes more complicated. The plot, quite in our modern sense ^of plot^, is well enough marked in the Oedipus King though the unities of time and place are there observed. In general I take it that other things being alike unity of action is higher the more complex the plot; it is the more difficult to effect and therefore the more valuable ~~than~~ when effected. We judge so of everything. In practice something must be sacrificed, and on what shall be sacrificed temperaments differ and discover their differences. The incidents for instance of Goethe's Faust are fascinating, but the unity of action, the~~ir~~ bearing ^of all these^ on one common lesson the play is to teach or effect it is to produce, is not telling at first ^sight^ and is perhaps — I ~~do not~~ have no opinion — really defective. The Gk. ~~plays~~ ^dramas^ are on the other hand well concentrated, but the play of incident and character is often slight: one does not quote from them either stage-effects or types of character. But my thoughts are unverified and undigested.

A friend recommended me if I met with them to read L. Stevenson's stories, the New Arabian Nights[3] and others since. I read a story by him in Longman's, I think, and a paper by him on Romance.[4] His doctrine, if I apprehend him, is something ~~this~~ like this. The essence of Romance is incident and that only, the type of pure Romance the Arabian Nights: those stories have no moral, no character-drawing, they turn ~~on~~ altogether on interesting ~~in~~ incident. The incidents must of[5] course have a connection, but it need be nothing more than that they happen to the same person, are aggravations and so on. As history consists essentially of events likely or unlikely, consequences of causes chronicled before or what may be called chance, just retributions or nothing of the sort, so Romance, which is fictitious history, consists of event, of incident. His own stories are written on this principle: they are very good and he has # all the gifts a writer of fiction should have, including those ^he holds^ unessential, as characterisation, and at first you notice no more than an ordinary well told story, but on looking back in the light of this doctrine you see that the persons illustrate the incident or strain of incidents, the plot, the story, not the story and incidents the persons. There was a tale ~~in~~ ^of his^ called the Treasure of Fourvières[6] or something like that; it is the ~~tale~~ ^story^ of an old treasure found, lost, and found again. The finding of the treasure acts of course ~~upon~~ and rather for the worse ^upon^ the finder, a retired French doctor, and his wife; the loss cures them; you wait to see the effect of the refinding: but not at all, the story abruptly ends — because its hero was, so to say, this triplet of incidents. His own remarks on the strength and weakness of the Waverleys are excellent. But I have been giving my own version of the doctrine (which is, I think, clearly true) rather ~~than what I remem~~ ^than his^ for I do not remember well enough what he says.

Now I think Shakspere's drama is more in this sense romantic than the Greek and that if the unity of action is not so marked (as it is not) the interest of romance, arising from a well calculated strain of incidents, is greater. You remember the scene or episode of the little Indian boy in the Midsummer Night: it is, I think, an allegory, to which, in writing once on the play, I believed I had found the clue, but whether I was right or wrong the meaning must have in any case been, and Shakspere must have known it wd. be, dark or invisible to most beholders or readers; yet he let it stand, just, as I suppose, because it is interesting as an incident in the story, not that it throws any light on the main plot or helps the unity of action, but rather, at all events~~,~~ superficially, hinders it. I could write much more but must stop. I am shortly starting for London, where my address is Oak Hill, Hampstead, N.W. I am going to let Mr. Patmore know Mano is out: I heard from him this morning. Believe me gratefully and affectionately your friend Gerard Hopkins S.J.

Aug. 16.

[1] *Mano.*

[2] The 'Three unities' were developed into a somewhat prescriptive system, by 16th-c. Italian critics and 17th-c. French classical dramatists, from suggestions in Aristotle's *Poetics*. Aristotle indeed requires a 'unity of action', whereby the action of a tragedy should be complete, whole, and contain only things relevant to its one central issue; but a 'unity of time' (confining the action to twenty-four hours) is merely mentioned by Aristotle and 'unity of place' (keeping to one scene only) not at all. Many of the Greek plays which Aristotle knew, and many English dramas, do not slavishly observe the unities.

[3] Robert Louis Stevenson. Published in 1882 (reviewed in the *Athenaeum* of 12 Aug.).

[4] 'A Gossip on Romance', *Longman's Magazine*, Nov. 1882, pp. 69–79. Reprinted in *Memories and Portraits* (1887).

[5] MS 'have'.

[6] 'The Treasure of Franchard', *Longman's Magazine*, Apr. and May, 1883. Reprinted in *The Merry Men* (1887).

16 August 1883 to Coventry Patmore

FL, no. CLXIV, p. 295 Durham University Library, Abbott MS 182
Single folded sheet.

The Holy Name, Oxford Road, Manchester. Aug. 16 1883.

My dear Mr. Patmore, — Your letter[1] crossed mine and reached me from Stonyhurst this morning. I am just starting for London, where, if any necessity should arise, my address for a week will be Oak Hill, Hampstead, N.W. I write now to tell you that yesterday I received Mano: a Poetical History: of the Time of the Close of the Tenth Century: Concerning the Adventures of a Norman Knight: which fell part in Normandy part in Italy: in Four Books: by Richard Watson Dixon (Routledge 1883). It is in terza rima: an address to the Reader in the same measure draws attention to the measure itself, which has been written so that each triplet shall be, as it should be, a sort of stanza, with a rest — this being Dante's, "the master"'s, law in composition. In R. W. D. this is due to Bridges (to whom by initials the book is dedicated): he got the author to rewrite it, so as to bring that out and his suggestions were, so the Canon told me, invaluable and almost always right. The style is more archaic than I approve; I look on archaism as a blight; but it is a better one than Swinburne's or Morris's, mastered, made his own, and in fact a style and not a trick like writing in italics or long s's ("Confider (ij) O my foul" as I have seen in a Puseyite spiritual book: one does and must and at bottom is meant by the people who do this to, mentally ^~~to~~^ hear, and then translitterate, Confider idge O my fowl). Of course I have not read it all, but can say that if you get it you will not repent.

Prometheus the Firegiver[2] also, on Dutch handmade etc, published by subscription 10s. 6d., ~~at~~ ^from^ Mr. Daniel of Worcester College's private press, awaits me at my father's house and, as I have read and weighed and given counsel on that, I can say that to me it appears a work of standard and classical beauty, rather to be named with Comus and Samson Agonistes than with other attempts in the same line. I do not know how soon a Christian edition is to come out.

Thanking you for your kind letter ^and for your prized books^ I remain yours very sincerely Gerard M. Hopkins S.J.

Canon Dixon has a hateful and incurable fancy for rhyming Lord to awed, here to idea etc and, what takes away all excuse, he nevertheless uses the ordinary licence of rhyming s's proper or sharp to s's flat or z's, th proper to th = dh and so on.

[1] This letter is missing, but see envelope for 14 Aug. 1883.

[2] See letter to RB of 3–10 Feb. 1883.

19 August 1883 from Coventry Patmore to GMH

FL, no. CLXIV A, p. 296 Campion Hall, P 19/8/83

Addressed to 'Rev[d] Gerard M. Hopkins, S.J. | Oak Hill, | Hampstead, | London'. PM HASTINGS AU 19 83.

Hastings. Aug. 19, 1883.

My dear Sir,

Many thanks for your letter & its information about the poems. I shall send for "Mano", and shall be delighted to receive Bridges verses. The above address is sufficient. I quite agree with you about the archaism wh. so many of our best living poets affect; and also, in the main, about rhymes. Such as Lord with awed are absolutely unpardonable. What you say of "Prometheus the Fire-Giver" makes me very curious to see it. Perhaps when you have done with it you will kindly let me have the loan of it for a day or two.

If you could come & spend a night here, I need not say that I should have the greatest pleasure in seeing you again.

Yours very truly
C. Patmore

22 August 1883 to Coventry Patmore

FL, no. CLXV, p. 297 Durham University Library, Abbott MS 183
Single folded sheet watermarked H K MAYOR | SUPERFINE

OAK HILL, | HAMPSTEAD, N.W. [*embossed address*]
Aug. 22 1883.

My dear Mr. Patmore, — I send you Prometheus. When you have quite done with it send it to me at Stonyhurst. On a fresh reading I feel I have in no way overpraised it and I believe your judgment will agree with mine. Read particularly the passage about the ~~rooks~~ ^rooks^ and herons,[1] Prometheus' speech "Thou sayst I am mad",[2] his history of fire,[3] Argeia's remonstrance about Salmoneus and the lightning,[4] the Agonistes-like chorus "O miserable man",[5] the fire-scene,[6] the last chorus ^with^ "O my vague desires" — but I am like the Guide to North Wales: "on the extreme right the visitor will not fail to observe" etc.

About rhymes — to imperfect rhymes my objection is my own and personal only; to what are called cockney rhymes with suppressed r's I object cum communi criticorum {*with the general body of critics*}, though they have Keats's (in this matter) slight and boyish authority; but what I am clear about is that it is altogether in~~defensi~~^excusa^ble ~~is~~ to combine the two sorts, the defence of ~~one of which is~~ ^either being^ the over^throw^ of the other.

Bridges has been here. He has done another tragedy (Roman)[7] and is at work on a third (medieval).[8] His pamphlet-~~b~~poems will reach you, but not the Growth of Love sonnets, which I believe he delays reissuing till the set shall be complete. But at present you will have a surfeit of my friends.

I should greatly enjoy availing myself of your kindly offered hospitality, but cannot do so now: I must from Holland make haste back to my duties. Believe me yours very sincerely

Gerard M. Hopkins S.J.

[1] ll. 152–9.
[2] ll. 436–504.
[3] ll. 569–607.
[4] ll. 918–39.
[5] ll. 1171–1232.
[6] ll. 1257 sqq.
[7] The First Part of *Nero*.
[8] *Palicio*, 'A Romantic Drama in Five Acts in the Elizabethan manner'.

24 August 1883 from Richard Watson Dixon to GMH

CRWD, no. XXIX A, p. 115 Campion Hall, D 24/8/83
Addressed to 'The Rev. | Gerard Hopkins S.J. | Oak Hill, | Hampstead , | N.W. London'. PM CARLISLE AU 24 83, LONDON AU 25 83.

Hayton Vicarage, Carlisle. | 24 Aug. 1883.

My dear Friend,

I write a line in haste to thank you for your immensely interesting Letter. Your remarks on Unity of action are, I think, the truth: i.e. that so far from that being the same thing as singleness of plot, it may be ~~highest~~ most perfect in a plot complicated with incidents, or a mixture of two or three plots or stories: as in, e.g. the Merchant of Venice, where you have the story of the Merchant & Jew, that of the Caskets, & that (a very slight one) of Lorenzo & Jessica. But still, as a fact, the Greek plays, out of wh. the Unity was evolved as a law of the drama, have only one plot or story. I conclude that Shakespeare held that unity might be preserved — essential unity — while complications & mixture of plots might be admitted, & as you say, increase the value of the unity, ultimately preserved, by the difficulty added, ^and even by the apparent breach of unity.^

I have nothing to write but this acknowledgement: and therewith to thank you very warmly for interesting Mr. Patmore in my poems. He sends me a message through you in your last letter. Please thank him, whenever you write. I read part of the Angel in the House very long ago, & remember being pleased especially with a description of a "stony-built sky". I am not sure of the exactness of my memory of the phrase: but it was a very forcibly life-like one.[1]

I hope you may enjoy your trip to Holland: a land that I have desired with desire to see.

Ever your affectionate friend
R. W. Dixon.

[1] His memory is faulty; there is no such phrase in the poem. Perhaps he is thinking of 'His faith's a rock-built citadel' in Book II, Canto vi, 'The Love Letter'.

11 September 1883 to Robert Bridges

LRB, no. CIX, p. 186 Bodleian, Dep. Bridges, vol. 92, fo. 30^{r-v}
Postcard addressed to 'Robert Bridges Esq. | Yattendon | Newbury | Berks'. PM Oxford SP 11 83 603 and CHIEVELEY SP 12 83

St. Giles's, Oxford. Sept. 11 1883.

It is a dreadful disappointment, but it was to be. The train at Reading did certainly seem earlier than there was any need, but I got into it without suspicion: I was whirled past Pangbourn, and by the time you were there, if you went, was almost at Oxford. The worst of it is I do not even see how another opportunity is ever to occur. G. M. H. To Stonyhurst tomorrow.

14 September 1883 from Coventry Patmore to GMH[1]

FL, no. CLXV A, p. 298

Hastings. Sept. 14. 1883.

My dear Sir,

I return 'Prometheus' with many thanks. I have read it twice, and in part thrice, with increasing admiration of its pure style, high finish, and many other fine qualities. Many poems, with inferior claims, have become English classics.

I have written for 'Mano', but have not yet got it.

Yours very truly
Coventry Patmore.

[1] This letter is not with the others to Patmore in Campion Hall and is evidently the letter which Bridges had begged to be allowed to keep, referred to at the end of GMH's letter of 23 Sept. 1883. See also a letter of 7 May 1884 to RB from Patmore, printed in Champneys, ii. 247.

14 September 1883 to Coventry Patmore

FL, no. CLXVI, p. 298 Durham University Library, Abbott MS 184
Single folded sheet watermarked H K MAYOR | SUPERFINE.

~~OAK HILL, | HAMPSTEAD, N.W.~~ [*embossed address*]
Stonyhurst, Blackburn, Sept. 14 1883.

My dear Mr. Patmore, — I returned the night before last and next morning opened the parcel from Bell's containing your handsome volumes[1] (to praise now the picture for the frame) and thank you for them on the College's account and my own. And since then I have read a great part of the Angel in the House. Much of it I remember without reading ~~and~~ (I do not say word for word) and of the rest there is little I do not at least remember to have read; though I believe I never read it but once.

And now I feel that the task I have undertaken is a dangerous and an over-honourable one and perhaps it was presumptuous to accept it: now however I must go through with it and even quickly. It will be best for me therefore to send you anything that shall strike me at, say, a volume's end and not to wait till I have read the whole. It emboldens me somewhat to find that you have forestalled some of the suggestions that I shd. have made: there was for instance something I did not quite like in the garden scene with the Wiltshire Butterflies[2] (that incident indeed is now left in a certain irrelevance, but it is better so) which has disappeared and you have softened the first over severity of "That's Lais",[3] against which I cd. have quoted the artless beauty of what the Newcastle lass in Merry may the Keel Row says of her lover's dancing and the dimple in his chin.

As my business is now to find faults, not beauties, and as if I wanted to feature out my admiration I shd. have to adduce ^the^ volumes themselves, I want it to be taken as said.

Canon Dixon ~~con~~ wishes me to thank you for your kind words.

Alexander Wood has sent me a pamphlet of his in Italian on the University question.[4]

Since my time is short the remarks I make will be briefly jotted. You will excuse this: otherwise ~~as my time is occupied~~ ^I foresee^ they wd. not get done at all.

Believe me yours very sincerely Gerard Hopkins S.J.

[1] *Poems*, 4 vols. (1879), the copies still at Stonyhurst, to which GMH was to spend much time meticulously suggesting amendments and improvements.

[2] See Book I, Canto iv, 'The Morning Call', 2 (1906, p. 27). The passage, in 1863, ran:

Across the Hall
She took me; and we laugh'd and talk'd
About the Flower-show and the Ball.
Their pinks had won a spade for prize;
But this was gallantly withdrawn
For 'Jones on Wiltshire Butterflies'!

[3] Book II, Canto ii, Preludes, III. The version of 1879 is the same as that of 1863 (1906, p. 88). 'Merry May the Keel Row' is infrequently used as the title of 'Weel May the Keel Row', the Tyneside song which praises in simple terms the 'bonny' keelman.

[4] For Alexander Wood (1845–1912), second son of Capt. John Denniston Wood, RN, of Largo, Fifeshire, see the article by Fr J. H. Crehan, 'More Light on Gerard Hopkins', *The Month* (Oct. 1953), 205–14. Of this pamphlet in Italian, he says: 'The pamphlet . . . was clearly directed towards the formation of an enlightened opinion among Roman ecclesiastics upon the question of Catholic attendance at Oxford.' It was thus directed against the views of Manning. Alexander Wood of the Somersetshire Archaeological Society is credited with the translation from Italian of books on *The Pope and Italy* (1882) and *The Vatican and the Quirinal* (1882).

18 September 1883 from Coventry Patmore to GMH

FL, no. CLXVI A, p. 300 Campion Hall, P 18/9/83
Addressed to 'Rev[d] Gerard Hopkins, S.J. | Stonyhurst College, | Blackburn'.
PM HASTINGS SP 18 83, BLACKBURN SP 19 83, WHALLEY SP 19 83.

Hastings. Sept. 18. 1883.

My dear Sir,

I thank you for your kind letter of the 14th, which I ought to have acknowledged sooner, but just at this time of the year I get poisoned by the perfume of a huge magnolia which covers the house, and a bad sick headache must be my excuse to you.

I expect that, as you go through the poems, you will find that I have removed many of the things you objected to. Since the earlier editions the whole work has been revised by me with extreme care and every verbal fault that I could see amended. But your quick sense and new eye will find many defects wh. escaped me, and, as far as the time allows, — for I expect to begin printing very shortly — I shall make full use of your suggestions.

Yours ever truly
C. Patmore.
Rev[d]. Gerard Hopkins, S.J.

23 September 1883 to Coventry Patmore

FL, no. CLXVII, p. 300 Durham University Library, Abbott MS 185
Two large folded sheets and one half sheet watermarked Caxton EMPIRE QUALITY or a figure of Britannia, five leaves, written only on the rectos.

Stonyhurst College, Blackburn. Sept. 23 1883.

My dear Mr. Patmore, — Time presses on us both and I send, ~~as~~ hurriedly put together, my remarks on the Angel in the House. In making them first I blush at my own boldness; next I know that they may be mistaken and that your judgment on the matter is better than mine, and even where you may be ready to agree with me, still some flaws are flies in amber, ~~and are~~ embedded in excellence~~,~~ which must perish in removing them.

I have one serious fault to find and on that I lay so much stress that I could even wish you were put to some inconvenience and delay rather than that the poem should go down to posterity with it. I shall speak of it last or put it off, so that you may consider and, if necess~~ity~~ary, change ^in the meantime^ the trifling points which follow.

(1) The poem is without a title.[1] Neither in the headlines nor ^on a^ flyleaf ~~does~~ nor table of contents nor anywhere does "The Angel in the House" appear; only on the general titlepage in this shape, clearly a reference only: "Poems. By Coventry Patmore. Vol. II. Angel in the House" — without "the".

(2) Stops are omitted by the printer at the end of several stanzas. I have not marked them except at p. 122, last line, where I am not sure if anything is omitted or not.[2]

(3) It deserves consideration whether it is not more natural and unaffected to write walked and talked than walk'd and talk'd (and though ~~than tho'~~ ^and^ through than tho' and thro'), keeping the accent for the older form walkèd and talkèd when you use it. It seems ~~more~~ reasonable that the ~~rule~~ exception should be marked, not the rule, and now a days the contraction is the rule, the full form the exception.[3]

(4) P. 3 "And he's too sage to kick or rear" is infra dignitatem {*undignified*}. I know that this '~~Induction~~ ^Prologue^' must be pitched homelier than the poem proper, as the pieces of plays introduced by Shakspere into plays are and so forth, but there is a mean: this seems to me below it and to become jocular. Perhaps a change of construction and removing "and he's" might get rid of ~~what~~ the fault I find.[4]

(5) P. 28 “Or the fool’s not worth a groan”: the same objection. It reads to me like a poor joke.[5]

(6) P. 44 “Each other helps her and is glad”: there is a clumsiness and what they call a ‘false relation’ in music, arising from “each other”. Could it not be “The others help her and are glad” or something like that?[6]

(7) P. 51 no. 1 — You will not alter it, I know, but I protest nevertheless against the exaggeration and sophistry of this piece. The ~~arg~~ form of argument is that favourite one with rhetoricians, to compare the best of A with not the best of B and then conclude that A is better than B. The stanza at foot of p. 52 contains the refutation of that at top of p. 53; for if woman by her own way reaches truth as well ^as —^ and you suggest better than — man, then, by parity, man ~~by~~ ^in^ his own way loves as deeply as — and by suggestion deeper than — wo~~m~~-man. I have no room ~~for~~ to say all.[7]

(8) P. 56 “Discuss’d” ~~is~~ ^seems to me^ prosaic. The language ^of the line^ has an exact propriety, I know, but that is not enough: propriety of ~~la~~ diction is the special excellence and attainment of rhetoric; poetry must have, down to its least separable part, an individualising touch — and so the rest of the quatrain has. But my judgment on the matter ~~only~~ ~~s~~ which “the very looking straight at mars” allows me to lay no stress on it.[8]

(9) P. 54 (out of order) “lost or won”: is it not better “won or lost”?[9]

(10) P. 67 no. 3 The breaking of the sense across the metre is excessive. It is like ~~a~~ choking. Some of it was suitable, I am aware, but not so much as to destroy music. Perhaps one instance less would make it right.[10]

(11) P. 73 I find “Heaven and Earth” very obscure and a little sour.

Here and elsewhere you use the word “mode”, which is to my ear frigid[11] (e.g. p. 147 first line).

(12) P. 84 “As old processions” etc. The image has no great felicity, it seems to me, and has a conventional ring. You will see without my ~~f~~ needing to explain further.[12]

(13) P. 98 “Link catching link”: only goods trains do this, passenger trains are locked rigidly.[13]

(14) P. 117 “Sin” “men”. This rhyme is neither correct ~~nor~~ in itself nor covered by convention.[14]

(15) P. 135 The image of the harp is obscure. ~~Some~~ There are in fact breath instruments and the harp is not one of them. What goes before is obscure too and the reader, at the crisis, baffled by the unintelligible.[15]

(16) The Prologue: rose is rhymed on twice: did you mean this?[16]

(17) P. 154 Why must the bird be he when she is meant?[17]

(18) P. 167 “Is Felix there” shd. be (in your text) in inverted commas, shd. it not?[18]

(19) P. 173 “Raised in the dance” obscure. Mists are raised: is that meant?[19]

(20) P. 176 “Pure”. The construction, at a close, is unsatisfactory: shd. it not be “And pure” and the line modified accordingly?[20]

(21) P. 183 ~~“Than~~ third line “Than” shd. be “That”, should it not?[21]

(22) P. 216 The fourth line halts much.[22]

(23) P. 225 “that they’ve been there” seems to me slovenly.[23]

(24) P. 226 “Disappointment” it seems to me shd. be recast. The more it is considered the more the thought appears a fallacy, nothing. Of course the man sought in one at a time: if so there is no antithesis. I suppose he ought to have sought there longer, deeper: then that ought to have been said. Neither can it be assumed that ~~it~~ ^he^ was necessarily to be rewarded in the first woman sought.[24]

(25) ~~“Her~~ P. 230 “Her virtue all virtue so endears” is only endurable by slurring “all”; but that wants emphasis. Would not “Her virtue virtue” do?[25]

(26) P. 234 “Vague”: would not “dark” be more respectful?[26]

(27) Next page — the last line is unmusical.[27]

(28) P. 241 The ~~sun~~ moon is eclipsed by shadow, the sun cannot be.[28]

(29) “I stopp’d once” needlessly halting, it seems to me.[29]

(30) ^Ibidem^ Sir John’s Old Hall. No point that I see in the image: it ought if possible to be something having a bearing on the sight that followed.[30]

(31) P. 252 “too long regarded”: the sense hovers between dazzling ^of the eyesight^ and something mental, and you seem afraid to fix your thought.[31]

(32) P. 215 (out of order) No point in “Scotland”: it shd. be something homelike and familiar against ~~som~~ what is outlandish and the word shd. ~~begin with~~ alliterate with something near it, most naturally with “Cathay”.[32]

I reserve my most serious difficulty for want of time and so catch this post. Believe me, with misgivings for the overfreedom of what I have written, yours very sincerely Gerard Hopkins S.J.

Bridges was much gratified by what you wrote and begs to keep the letter.[33]

[1] It is given one in 1885. Patmore has gone methodically through the letter, marking any criticism he has acted upon with the word ‘Done’ in pencil, and putting a cross on those he does not accept. ‘Done’ is written through GMH’s points 2, 4, 5, 6, 8, 9, 18, 21, 23, 25, 26, 28, 29 and crosses through the rest.

[2] To this line a semicolon is added in 1885.

[3] No alteration.

[4] Book I, 'The Prologue, I' . In 1885 'prance' is substituted for 'kick': but 'kick' is restored in the edition of 1894, p. 3.

[5] Book I, Canto ii, 'Mary and Mildred', 4:

We who are married, let us own
A bachelor's chief thought in life
Is, or the fool's not worth a groan,
To win a woman for his wife.
I kept the custom. I confess
I never went to Ball, or Fête,
Or Show, but in pursuit express
Of my predestinated mate[.]

In 1885 (and 1906, p. 17) the first four lines are omitted, and the section begins with a rehandling of l. 5:

I laugh'd and sigh'd: for I confess . . .

[6] Book I, Canto iv, 'The Morning Call', Preludes, II. The passage ran:

Boon Nature to the woman bows;
She walks in all its glory clad,
And, chief herself of earthly shows,
Each other helps her, and is glad[.]

In 1885 (and 1906, p. 26) this was strengthened:

Boon Nature to the woman bows;
She walks in earth's whole glory clad,
And, chiefest far herself of shows,
All others help her, and are glad[.]

[7] Book I, Canto v, 'The Violets', Preludes, I. Unchanged in 1885 (1906, pp. 30–1).

[8] Book I, Canto v, 'The Violets'. In 1885 (1906, p. 33) 'Discuss'd by gossips at their tea', became 'The guess of gossips at their tea'.

[9] Book I, Canto v, 'The Violets', Preludes, II. In 1885 (1906, p. 31) 'Love, lost or won, is countless gain', becomes 'Love, won or lost, is countless gain'.

[10] Book I, Canto vi, 'The Dean', 3. No change in 1885 (1906, p. 39).

[11] Book I, Canto vii, 'Ætna and the Moon', Preludes, II. Unaltered in 1885 (1906, p. 42) save for omission of a comma.

[12] Book I, Canto viii, 'Sarum Plain', I. Unaltered in 1885 (1906, p. 48), save for change in position of a comma.

[13] Book I, Canto ix, 'Sahara', 3. Unchanged in 1885 (1906, p. 55).

[14] Book I, Canto xi, 'The Dance', Preludes, II. No alteration in 1885 (1906, p. 66).

[15] Book I, Canto xii, 'The Abdication', 4. No alteration in 1885 (1906, p. 75).

[16] Book II, The Prologue, ll. 10 and 12, ll. 46 and 48. Unchanged in 1885 (1906, pp. 77–8).

[17] Book II, Canto ii, 'The Course of True Love', Preludes, I. The maiden is compared to the bird of the first eight lines, and the bird is referred to as 'he'. Unchanged in 1885 (1906, p. 85).

[18] Book II, Canto ii, 'The Course of True Love', 7. Inverted commas added in 1885 (1906, p. 92).

[19] Book II, Canto iii, 'The County Ball', 2. Unchanged in 1885 (1906, p. 95).

[20] Book II, Canto iii, 'The County Ball', 4. Unaltered in 1885 (1906, p. 97).

[21] Book II, Canto iv, 'Love in Idleness', 4. The misprint is corrected in 1885 (1906, p. 101).

[22] Book II, Canto viii, 'The Koh-i-noor', Preludes, I. The line in question, 'Myst'ries that light would more perplex', remains unaltered in 1885 (1906, p. 119).

[23] Book II, Canto ix, 'The Friends', Preludes, II.

> And go and brag that they've been there,
> becomes in 1885 (1906, p. 125)
> And go and brag they have been there.

[24] Book II, Canto ix, 'The Friends', Preludes, III. Unaltered in 1885; in 1906 (p. 125) 'What only can be found in one' has become 'What can be found in only one'.

[25] Book II, Canto ix, 'The Friends', 4. In 1885 (1906, p. 127) GMH's suggestion is adopted.

[26] Book II, Canto x, 'The Epitaph', Preludes, III.

> 'In heaven none marry.' Grant the most
> Which may by this vague word be meant,

'Dark' is substituted for 'vague' in 1885 (1906, p.130).

[27] Ibid. The line is: 'Where Now and Then are no more twain!' Unaltered in 1885 (1906, p. 130).

[28] There are eclipses of the sun. Book II, Canto xi, 'The Wedding', Preludes, I.

> And think, the sun of such delight
> From thine own shadow takes eclipse.

In 1885 (1906, p. 133) 'darkness' is substituted for 'shadow'.

[29] Book II, Canto xi, 'The Wedding', 3.

> I remember well
> I stopp'd once, with her Mother, there.

In 1885 (1906, p. 137), 'stopp'd' becomes 'stay'd'.

[30] Ibid., 'The Wedding', 4. Unaltered in 1885 (1906, p. 137).

[31] Book II, Canto xii, 'Husband and Wife', Preludes, II. In 1885 (1906, p. 139), unchanged.

[32] Book II, Canto viii, 'The Koh-i-noor', Preludes, I. Unaltered in 1885 (1906, p. 119).

[33] That is, the letter of 14 Sept. 1883 above.

24 September 1883 to Coventry Patmore

FL, no. CLXVIII, p. 306 Durham University Library, Abbott MS 186
Two and a half small folded sheets with embossed address and watermark H K MAYOR | SUPERFINE, ten sides.

~~OAK HILL, | HAMPSTEAD, N.W.~~ [*embossed address*]
Stonyhurst. Sept. 24 1883

My dear Mr. Patmore, — I have found since writing yesterday that the line "Her virtue all virtue so endears" may with forethought be so read as to run smoothly, even with a stress on "all". I think however that how to do this will not strike everybody and that the line will ^mostly^ be a stumbling-block in reading aloud.[1]

There is also some metrical objection to "Disappointment". The cadences "found in ~~one~~ ^none^", "found in one" strike one as identities, not rhymes: the~~re~~y are really rhymes, but there is a 'false relation' suggested. This correction would be easy.[2]

Also I am dissatisfied with ~~th~~ "Beauty" p. 159 sq.[3] The text and principle stated is noble and deeply true, the development seems to me a decline and a surrender. It comes to this: beautiful evil is found, but it is nature's monstrosity. Then is qui supplet locum idiotae {*he who occupies the place of the unlearned*},[4] the worldling, Philistine (or whatever he is to be called) answers: and all I have to add is that the monstrosity is very common, and so we are agreed. ^And^ so it wd. come to the same thing to say Beauty deludes or ~~Good disguises~~ ^# Ugliness does^. This was not to be granted. It is certain that in nature outward beauty is the proof of inward beauty, ~~in~~ outward good of inward good. ~~Beauty~~ ^Fineness^, proportion, of feature comes from a moulding force which succeeds in asserting itself over the resistance of cumbersome or ~~con~~^re^straining matter; the bloom of health comes from the ~~vitali~~ abundance of life, the great vitality within. The moulding force, the life, is the form in the philosophic sense, and in man this is the soul. But because its available activity is limited the matter it has to struggle with may be too much for it and the wax is either too cold and doughy (so to speak) and will not take ^or^ ~~is~~ ^is^ too hot and boil~~s~~^ing^ ~~and ^may^~~ blots~~s~~ out the stamp ~~upon~~ ^of^ the seal — I speak under an old but a very apposite image not easily improved. This explains why "ugly good" is found. But why do we find beautiful evil? Not by any freak of nature, nature is incapable of producing beautiful evil. The explanation is to be sought outside nature; it is old, simple, and the undeniable fact. It comes from wicked will, ^freedom of choice,^ abusing the beauty, the good of its nature. 'Thou wert' the Scripture says and ~~commenta~~ ^great^ writers apply it to the Devil 'the seal of resemblance'.[5] The instance is palmary and shews how far evil can be beautiful or beauty evil and what the phenomenon means~~,~~ when it occurs. — This at least is how the subject strikes me and I find it more interesting and pathetic so; it may be however that you think no otherwise, only that I have missed the turn of your thought.

Whether you agree with me or not about ~~all~~ the above points they are ^all^ trifles and altered or let stand little affect the poem. The following is the ~~point~~ matter ~~of~~ where I have to make a serious objection.

P. 202 "Women should be vain",[6] p. 217 "The Koh-i-noor" no. 1,[7] p. 251 "Because, although in act and word, . . . ~~all~~ unattain'd desert"[8] —

In the midst of a poem ~~on~~ undertaken under a kind of inspiration from God & to express what, being most excellent, most precious, most central and important and even obvious in human life, nevertheless no one has ever yet, unless passingly thought of expressing you introduce a vice, the germ of ~~a~~ widespread evils, and make the highest relish of pure love come from the base "smell of mortality". Everyone has some one fault he is tender to and vice he tolerates. We do this ourselves, but when another does it towards another vice not our own favourite (of tolerance, I do not say of commission) we are disgusted. The Saturday Review contrasting the Catholic and Protestant ideal of a schoolday came out with the frank truth, that it looked on chastity as a feminine virtue (= lewdness a masculine one: it was not quite so raw as I put it, but this was the meaning). Mommsen[9] a brilliant historian I find thinks great nations should break treaties. Dr. Ward[10] (in his younger days) said candour was anything but a saintly virtue (perhaps he did not but is misquoted: let it at least serve as an illustration). Then violence is admired and, above all, insolence and pride. But it is our baseness to admire anything evil. It seems to me we shd. in everything ~~be~~ side with virtue, even if we do not feel its charm, because good is good.

In particular how can anyone admire or (except in charity, as the greatest of sins, but in judgment and approval) tolerate vanity in women? Is it not the beginning of their saddest and most characteristic fall? What but vanity makes them first publish, then prostitute their charms? In Leonardo's ^famous picture^ "Modesty and Vanity"[11] is it not almost taken for granted that the one figure is that of a virgin, the other that of a courtezan? If modesty in women means two things at once, purity and humility, must not the pair of opposites be no great ~~a~~way apart, vanity from impurity? Who can think of the Blessed Virgin and of vanity? Then in one's experience, in my own, it seems to me that nothing in good women is more beautiful than ^just^ the absence of vanity and an earnestness of look and character which is better than beauty. It touches me (if I may give such an instance — I cannot easily give others) in my own sisters that when ~~she~~ ^they^ ~~sends ^lets^~~ let me see ~~her ^musical^~~ ^their^ compositions ~~which I with a brother's biased judgment~~ in music or painting, which I, with a brother's biassed judgment but still sincerely, admire, they seem to be altogether without vanity — yet they might be with reason vainer of these than of their looks, and towards a brother not be ashamed to shew it (and I towards them can hardly conceal mine): they are glad when I admire nevertheless. It is the same in literature as in life: the vain women in Shakspere are the impure minded too, like Beatrice (I do not know that I may not call her a hideous character); those whose chastity one could have trusted, like Desdemona, are free from vanity too.

It is a lover who speaks in the "Koh-i-noor", but that proves very little. He happens to be a good one, ~~but take a bad one~~ and therefore tolerates nothing worse than carelessness, talkativeness, and vanity;[12] but take a bad one: he will want the smell of mortality stronger. What does the ~~lover of his neighbour's wife love in~~ adulterer ~~do but~~ love in his neighbour's wife but her obligingness in committing adultery? Tennyson makes Guenevere say "The low sun makes the colour":[13] it is a happy touch and the whole passage is instructive. Those also who write of moral monsters born without a fault and ~~But th~~ "Let other~~s~~ bards of angels sing <in the House or elsewhere> Bright suns without a spot; But thou art no such perfect thing: Rejoice that thou art not",[14] these people never saw and had lost the idea of holiness~~,~~ and are no authority.

You will say that everything else, her own words and what others say of her, shew that in Honoria there was in reality no vanity and that your ~~words~~ lines are not be ~~so~~ taken in such grim earnest. But the truth seems to me to be that in writing you were really in two inconsistent moods, a lower and a higher, and that the record of both is in your pages.

Naturally a lurking error appears in more places than one and a false principle gives rise to false consequences. An ideal becomes an idol and false worship sets in. So I call it at p. 251, where it is said that a wife calls her husband lord by courtesy, meaning, as I understand, only by courtesy and "not with her least consent of will" to his being so.[15] But he is her lord. If it is courtesy only and no consent then a wife's lowliness is hypocrisy and Christian marriage a comedy, a piece of pretence. How much more truly and touchingly did you make Mrs. Graham speak! But if she was right then the contrary is wrong. Perhaps I misunderstand the passage: I hope I do, but then I hope you will prevent other people misunderstanding it. And now pernicious doctrines and practice are abroad and the other day the papers said a wretched being refused in church to say the words "and obey": if it had been a Catholic wedding and I the priest I would have let the sacrilege go no further.

~~The passage~~ Honoria's letter in the "Love-letters" pp. 202, 203 by itself would be well enough, it contains its own correction ("I hope in jest"), though the incident always struck me as very trivial ~~though~~ ^if also^ very natural, and I on no account want to lose the lovely turn "But I was very dull, dear friend" and what follows;[16] but the other two convey, it seems to me, though in small quantities, a poison. And they may be quoted in support of evil and do mischief commended by the lustre of your name (I hope it will be illustrious then) years after you are dead.

If I have written strongly I am sure it is in a zeal for the poem. Believe me yours very sincerely Gerard Manley Hopkins S.J.

[1] See previous letter, n. 25.

[2] See previous letter, n. 24.

[3] Book II, Canto ii, 'The Course of True Love', Preludes, II. Unaltered in 1885 (1906, p. 88).

[4] GMH is quoting from the Vulgate: 1 Corinthians 14: 16.

[5] GMH is quoting from the Douay–Reims version of Ezekiel 28: 12.

[6] Book II, Canto vi, 'The Love-Letters', 3. Unaltered in 1885 (1906, p. 112).

[7] Book II, Canto viii, 'The Koh-i-noor', I (p. 217 should be p. 219). Unaltered in 1885 (1906, p. 121).

[8] Book II, Canto xii, 'Husband and Wife', Preludes, I. Unaltered in 1885 (1906, pp. 138–9).

[9] Christian Matthias Theodore Mommsen (1817–1903), whose *History of Rome* (7 vols., 1860) was on Oxford reading lists in the 1860s. See *CW* iv. 85.

[10] William George Ward (1812–82). See *CW* iv.14–15.

[11] Then in the Sciarra Palace. Antoine Claude Pasquin Valery, *Literary and Artistic Travels in Italy* (Paris, 1839), 565.

[12] The lines are:

'Her virtues please my virtuous mood,
'But what at all times I admire
'Is, not that she is wise and good,
'But just the thing which I desire.
'With versatility to sing
'The theme of love to any strain,
'If oft'nest she is anything,
'Be it careless, talkative, and vain.'

[13] 'Lancelot and Elaine', l. 134.

[14] Wordsworth, 'To—' (written at Rydal Mount, 1824, on Mrs Wordsworth), the first stanza.

[15] See p. 307, n. 3. The lines are:

Because, although in act and word
As lowly as a wife can be,
Her manners, when they call me lord,
Remind me 'tis by courtesy;
Not with her least consent of will,
Which would my proud affection hurt,
But by the noble style that still
Imputes an unattain'd desert.

[16] See n. 6 above.

24 September 1883 from Coventry Patmore to GMH

FL, no. CLXVIII A, p. 311 Campion Hall, P 24/9/83
Addressed to 'Rev. Gerard Hopkins, S.J. | Stonyhurst College, | Blackburn'. PM HASTINGS SP 25 83, BLACKBURN SP 26 83, WHALLEY SP 26 83.

Hastings. Sept. 24 1883.

My dear Sir,

I am exceedingly grateful to you for the trouble you are taking in sending me such carefully considered notes and suggestions, with nearly all of wh. I agree and ^nearly all of wh. I^ shall endeavour to adopt. I did not mean "vanity" however in the sense in which you read it. I meant Honoria's pleasure in her lover's delight in her beauty — a sense in which some great Doctor or Saint — I think St. Augustine — says that there was a little vanity in the Blessed Virgin. ^("Sweet to myself that am so sweet to thee)^[1] I confess that this kind of vanity seems to me to be the very ^daintiest^ beatitude and last beauty of the soul. I think the context of the passage you complain of indicates that Honoria is only "careless, talkative, and vain" in a sort of pure inebriation and abandonment of soul towards one person. This sort of vanity consists with and even implies humility. St. Theresa I think says that it requires more humility for the soul ~~for the~~ to discern and rejoice in its own beauty as a Goddess in the wisdom of God, than to call itself a miserable sinner. You will find a further apology for vanity in "De Natura Deorum" p. 179.[2] But, notwithstanding all this, it is a serious fault if the passage in question leaves such an impression as it does on your mind, and as I know it has left on the minds of some other readers. If I can I will set it right, but, at this distance of time from the composition of the poem it is very dangerous to make more than verbal alterations. I cannot recover the mood in wh. I wrote, and were I to remodel a passage, however short, I fear the alteration would look like a patch of a different colour. This may probably be my excuse for not ~~adopting~~ ^acting on^ one ~~of~~ or two of your strictures, though I think them quite right.

Believe me
yours very sincerely
Coventry Patmore

[1] *The Unknown Eros*, vii, 'The Azalea', last line. Any reference in Augustine on the vanity of the BVM has not been found. Individual Greek Fathers (Origen, St Basil the Great, St John Chrysostom, St Cyril of Alexandria) taught that Mary suffered from venial personal faults: such as ambition and vanity, doubt about the message of the Angel, lack of faith under the cross, etc. (Origen for example, in his Homily on Luke 17: 6–7, suggests that Mary was not holy from the beginning and had vanity within

her), but the more modern Catholic view agrees with GMH in seeing her without stain. Patmore may be thinking of the Magnificat (Luke 1: 46–55) and particularly the phrase 'all generations shall call me blessed', though GMH is by no means unusual in thinking Patmore's perspective rather odd.

[2] *The Unknown Eros*, Book II, xiii.

28–9 September 1883 to Coventry Patmore

FL, no. CLXIX, p. 312 Durham University Library, Abbott MS 187
One folded sheet watermarked A PIRIE & SONS and a small half sheet; six sides.

Stonyhurst. Sept. 28 '83.

My dear Mr. Patmore, — I was relieved by your kind letter of this morning, for indeed I began to fear I had, as people say, "done it this time". For you might not have taken my remarks, I am afraid intemperately expressed, in so gentle a spirit.

I did of course know that Honoria was to be vain towards her lover only and that her vanity would not exactly be the vice so called; I followed something of the subtlety; still I thought you had given incidentally some countenance to the vice. (I shd. say that I had seen something of the same sort before — that Barry Cornwall spoke of a fallen woman ^as^ having in her fall lost "vanity, gentleness", and something else; making it a grace of some sort, a virtue.)[1] But I must have read your lines in too gross a mood. You agree however that there is a likelihood of others falling into the same misunderstanding and we ought not to fire a forest (or the furze upon a common) in lighting a pastille.

It has also occurred to me that the piece beginning now "Where she succeeds" p. 51[2] formerly began

> I know not how to her it seems
> Or how to a perfect-judging eye,
> But as my loving thought esteems
> Man misdeserves his sweet ally.

You must have had some reason for striking this out, but at least it had this effect: it gave what followed a dramatic propriety and made it the expression of mood, a lover's mood, and not of the whole experience of life and a final and impersonal judgment. This seems to me to make all the difference and would, so far as I am concerned, remove the objection I feel against it.

I think I know very well what you mean when you speak of the danger and difficulty of making more than verbal alterations in works composed long ago and of a bygone mood not being to be recovered. For a time we keep the connection with our past feelings open; they recede, but still we have an insight into them; then something comes between and a long while after looking back, like the tail of train going round a sharp curve, you see your own self quite from outside. And even verbal alterations will be hazardous, for the ^stress of^ mood which dictated and justified the word or image has passed away.

I shall be more careful about making metrical objections. I used to object to things which satisfied Bridges and ^we^ came to the conclusion that ~~one's~~ our own pronunciation, by which everyone instinctively judges, might be at the bottom of the matter.

I do not know ~~now~~ ^either^ whether I was right about "discussed";[3] for now I do feel a certain relation between that word and "delicately hid" in the line before~~,~~: on these mutual bearings of words in a passage ~~the~~ the beauty of diction depends: and if so it ~~is~~ has no more ^only^ a rhetorical but also a poetical felicity.

Sept. 29 — I shall ~~now~~ very soon be in the thick of my work; I hope however to send my remarks on the Victories, ~~which will, I think, be few, soo~~ shortly: there will not, I think, be many to make.[4]

The British Association were here from Southport yesterday and the day before.[5]

Believe me yours very sincerely Gerard Hopkins S.J.

P.S. Of course "The Comparison" of which I have spoken above is full of insight; but if it is not fair, then all the insight in the world does not make up for the want of judgment and of truth. If this unfairness could be thrown on the lover, then the insight would be in place. Ruskin, it seems to me, has the insight of a dozen critics, but intemperance and wrongness undoes all ~~the~~ ^his^ good again.

How was it that Felix, after all his resolutions in "Love in Idleness", never went into Parliament?[6] (or does he?)—I suppose Honoria did not care for it, but for his fame as a poet.

[1] Barry Cornwall (pseudonym of Bryan Waller Procter, 1787–1874). In 'Within and Without: A London Lyric', he writes of a harlot dying on the streets (*Dramatic Scenes: with Other Poems*, 1857):

> She who is slain in the winter weather,
> Ah! she once had a village fame;
> Listened to love on the moonlit heather;
> Had gentleness, vanity, maiden shame[.]

[2] Book I, the beginning of Canto v, 'The Violets', Preludes, I, The Comparison.

[3] See letter of 23 Sept. 1883, n. 8.

[4] 'The Victories of Love' was the last section of what came to be known as *The Angel in the House*, published on its own in 1862, and as part of the whole poem in 1863. GMH's suggestions for corrections are in the next letter.

[5] The British Association for the Advancement of Science had held their meeting this year in Southport.

[6] The resolutions made in 'Love in Idleness' seem irresolutely followed even there.

7 October 1883 to Coventry Patmore

FL, no. CLXX, p. 314 Durham University Library, Abbott MS 188
One large folded sheet and a small half sheet, the small sheet watermarked A PIRIE; five sides.

Stonyhurst, Blackburn. Oct. 7 1883.

My dear Mr. Patmore, — You will have expected me to have written again before this; I wish I could have; but my work has begun and my brother is staying at the Green for a week and I am obliged to give him my afternoons. I now send, if not too late to be of use, my remarks on the Victories of Love.

(1) The titles to the letters are not consistently given.[1] It is "From Jane to her Mother": why not then "From Frederick to his Mother" and so throughout?

(2) P. 23 "Lowering" — shd. it not be "louring"? The two words are often confused, though different in spelling, sound, and meaning. Do you not mean the word we use of clouds, weather? It is, I suppose, much the same as "glouring", that is ~~flo~~ frowning.[2]

(3) P. 35 sq.[3] (on this and other passages where I make objections on the score of obscurity I have consulted my brother, and by this means cleared up some but confirmed myself on the others) — I understand the image of the lake to ~~mean~~ ^be^ this: men sometimes marry for beauty, but being married become deadened ^to^, lose their eye for, that and care only to satisfy their bodily cravings as they could do, beauty or no beauty: so a thirsty traveller is cheered by the sight of a lovely lake far off, ~~and~~ but coming to it cares for nothing but to quench his thirst at it. The context seems to require this sense, but I cannot see how it comes from the words. I suppose "a lovely lake far off" to mean a lake which far off is lovely. In what sense does it not fill the eye? Because far off it ~~is~~ looks small or because on coming near it looks less beautiful or what? And why "the exulting

eye”? Does it mean exulting in its beauty till the ^man^ comes near and then thinks ~~over~~ ^only^ of his thirst or exulting ~~in the prospect of drink~~ when he reaches it on attaining his desire? Is “inappreciably” used by a strain of language for <u>unappreciatively</u> or does it mean that he sips only an inappreciable little drop? And why ~~being~~ ^however^ thirsty is he disappointed with a whole lake and why being thirsty does he only sip? Then it is possible of course but very hard / to imagine ~~that~~ how a man could with the lips, that is / falling forward on hands and knees, drink from “the deep” of a lake, which can only be deep ~~at a sheer~~ where the bank is sheer. I must surely have missed the clew to the meaning, for all this is ~~so~~ far from the great felicity your figures have. I suppose I have, but then I think others will mostly miss it too.

(4) Below: “Whate’er her faults” etc means, I suppose, Honoria is one of those ~~by means of whom the last degree~~ ^who having received the highest degree of^ culture or civilisation (“the world’s last polish”) carry ~~it~~ ^that culture^ one degree higher ^still^ (“a novel grace”) and oblige all who aim at culture to follow them, so that they are ~~the civ~~ civilisation’s benefactors (“owes”). But it has a false suggestion of being a confusion for “Who to the world’s last polish owe”.[4]

(~~1~~5) P. 45. “^He^ suckles, with the hissing fly,~~”~~—The spider”: there shd. be no commas: you mean that God makes the fly the spider’s food, its suckl~~ing~~e or thing to suck; but they led me into thinking you meant / suckles, feeds, at once spider and fly, beast of prey and quarry.[5]

(6) P. 69 “who wed through love” must mean through a disappointment in love. But the words so naturally mean / out of love, that is / from loving the woman they wed and from no other motive~~,~~ (the very contrary of the fact here), that the ambiguity is grievous.[6]

(7) “With wickedness of lawful things” must mean, I suppose, “by pursuing lawful ~~pleasu~~ indulgences as fiercely as if they ^were^ some wickedness which got a zest from being forbidden”. It ~~seems~~ seems to me a harsh and disquieting expression; ~~the induct~~ perhaps I miss the meaning.[7]

(8) P. 106 “Men’s creeds” etc: the epigram seems to require “faiths” or “faith”. The line “If logic” etc has something forced and poor. In the passage alluded to it is ~~leav~~ Pharisees’ leaven, not ^the^ Devil’s.[8]

(9) P. 109 “intermediate” seems prosaic.[9]

(10) P. 116 “Our rustic grace” etc: surely that is a gross and graceless grace.[10]

(11) P. 159 “How strong” etc means, I suppose, how overwhelmingly true appears all that people say in her praise (and in general about her)! The transition to what follows is harsh and obscure.[11]

(12) P. 174 "The sort of Wife": the doctrine may be true, but the expression of it is hard. The Old Testament gives us great pictures of holy wifehood and through it ran the ancestry of Christ. But further Christ's words appear to apply to the future: they are always quoted so for the rest of the text. Cases ~~might~~ ^may^ occur, and divines treat them, of a ~~be~~ man or woman being bound to leave a bad wife or husband who is a grievous occasion of sin.[12]

(13) P. 199 "As one who fondly" etc: is the traveller sailing to or from port? The meaning and image differ greatly accordingly.[13]

(14) P. 229 "Every ambition" etc: this doctrine on a very dark matter may be as sound as the expression of it is certainly witty; but I could wish these four lines were left out. The thought is indicated clearly enough by what goes before and the epigram, undeniable in terms, which clinches it seems to me to lend itself more to abuse than use.[14]

(15) PP. 233~~,234~~ sqq.[15] The image ~~of the comets~~ I suppose to be a contrast between the long elliptic orbits of comets, with the sun almost at one end, and the short ones, practically circles, of the planets, with the sun at the centre. It might be clearer. But what follows is obscure in the extreme. I understand it to be this: married souls and virgin~~s~~ ^ones^ fall into ~~the~~ like (not opposite) errors if they # seek for their satisfaction first and foremost, the married in the marriagebed, virgins in ^the^ gratitude of those they benefit. Then the image of the shadows contains or suggests an infelicity. The only shadows of which what you say is true are our own: the shadows of birds, clouds etc do not infallibly escape or pursue us. But "~~the~~ shadows of the heavens" naturally means shadows of clouds or indeed images, not *shade* at all, of heavenly things. ^It is true it is a heavenly body, the sun, that makes us cast shadows.^

(16) P. 236 "Whereby the complex heavens" etc: if I understand this at all it seems to me a thought condensed beyond what literature will bear. I suppose it to mean: all the hierarchies of ^the^ angels do freely the things they must do, as stars play freely in necessary orbits.[16]

(17) P. 237 "Exuberent": why not "exuberant"?[17]

(18) Same page, higher "Nay more": perhaps the odd rhythm is of preference: otherwise it is very easy to shift "leave" into the next line.[18]

(19) Ib. "Take, in love's innocent gladness, part": it seems to me there should be no commas.[19]

(20) P. 244 "Caught, but a laurel or a stream": I suppose an allusion to Daphne and some other myth; but allusion is pushed to extremes here.[20]

There is such a world of wisdom and wit in this Wedding Sermon that I wish it to be as perfect and as lucid as it can be.

Believe me, in haste, very sincerely yours Gerard Hopkins S.J.

[1] No alteration made. As in the letter of the 23 Sept., Patmore has gone methodically through the letter, marking 'Done' in pencil any criticism he has acted upon, and putting a line across those he does not accept. 'Done' is written through Hopkins's points 2, 5, 15, 17, 18 and crosses through most of the rest.

[2] 'Victories of Love', iv (1906, p. 158). The verse became: 'For the black gun-deck's louring roof'.

[3] Ibid. vi (1906, p. 164): unchanged.

[4] Ibid.: unchanged.

> Whate'er her faults, she's one of those
> To whom the world's last polish owes
> A novel grace, which all who aspire
> To courtliest custom must acquire.

[5] Ibid. viii (1906, p. 168): the commas are omitted.

[6] Ibid. xi (1906, pp. 179–80): unchanged, save that a comma disappears after 'love'.

> Wed not one woman, oh, my Child,
> Because another has not smiled!
> * * * * *
> Ah, desperate folly! Yet, we know,
> Who wed through love wed mostly so.

[7] Ibid. xi (1906, p. 180): unchanged.

[8] Ibid. xvi (1906, p. 197): unchanged.

> 'Men's creeds should not their hopes condemn.
> 'Who wait for heaven to come to them
> 'Are little like to go to heaven,
> 'If logic's not the devil's leaven!'

[9] Ibid. xvii (1906, p. 198): unchanged.

> The clouds, the intermediate blue[.]

[10] Ibid. xviii (1906, p. 201): unchanged.

[11] Ibid., Book II, v (1906, p. 220): 'strong' becomes 'strange':

> How strange appear the words of all!
> The looks of those that live appal.

[12] Ibid., Book II, vii (1906, p. 227): unchanged.

> The sort of Wife the Law could make
> Might well be 'hated' for Love's sake,
> And left, like money, land or house;
> For out of Christ is no true spouse.

[13] Ibid., Book II, xi (1906, p. 238):

> For nothing of my state I know,
> But that t'ward heaven I seem to go,
> As one who fondly landward hies
> Along a deck that faster flies.

'Seaward' is substituted for 'faster'.

[14] Ibid., Book II, 'The Wedding Sermon', 2 (1906, p. 252, where the following lines are omitted between ll. 32 and 33):

Every ambition bears a curse,
And none, if height metes error, worse
Than his who sets his hope on more
Godliness than God made him for.

[15] Ibid., Book II, 'The Wedding Sermon', 5 (1906, p. 255): unchanged.

[16] Ibid., Book II, 'The Wedding Sermon', 6 (1906, p. 256): unchanged,

Whereby the complex heavens rejoice
In fruits of uncommanded choice.

[17] Ibid. This change is made.

[18] Ibid.

Nay, more, she bids him leave, for his spouse,
Even his heavenly Father's awe,

becomes (1906, p. 256)

Nay, more, she bids him, for his spouse,
Leave even his heavenly Father's awe[.]

[19] Ibid.: the commas disappear.

[20] Ibid., Book II, 'The Wedding Sermon', 8 (1906, p. 260): unchanged.

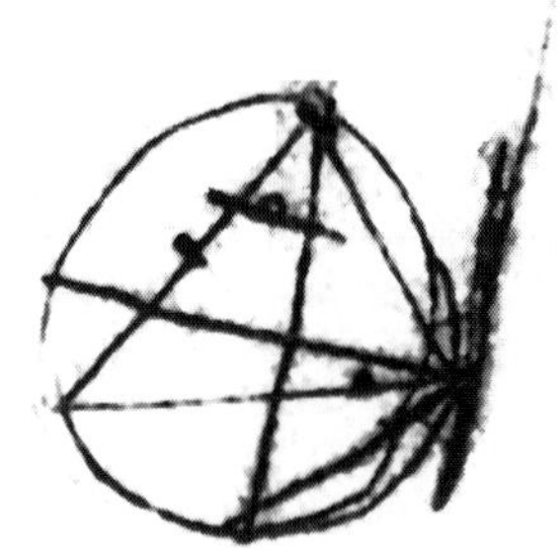

10 October 1883 from Coventry Patmore to GMH

FL, no. CLXX A, p. 319 Campion Hall, P 10/10/83
Addressed to 'Rev. Gerard Hopkins, S.J. | Stonyhurst College, | Blackburn'. PM HASTINGS OC 10 83, BLACKBURN OC 11 83, WHALLEY OC 11 83. Drawing on envelope of a circle with triangles within it, as if for geometry.

Hastings. Oct. 10. 1883

My dear Sir,

Thank you for your new batch of suggestions, which I see, at a glance, are very important. As it is now too late for the Autumn season my new edition will not be issued until the Spring, so that I shall not be printing for at least two months yet. I find it better not to take off the edge of the work of correction by familiarizing myself too much with your suggestions until I come to ^the^ actual labour; therefore I abstain from writing about individual points. The best way of recognising the consequence of your advice will be to act upon it as far as I may.

I am reading "Mano", but with some disappointment. It is full of vigour and manly and even great style; but I think that a reader, alert, as I am, to watch for indications of the inner motive of the poem, ought to be enabled to discover it more clearly than I am as yet able to do.

Yours ever truly
C. Patmore

11–14 October 1883 to Richard Watson Dixon

CRWD, no. XXX, p. 116 Bodleian, Dep. Bridges, vol. 93, fos. 119–120v
Addressed to 'The Rev. Canon Dixon | St. Mary's Vicarage | Hayton | Carlisle'. No readable PM. One folded sheet.

Stonyhurst, Blackburn. Oct. 11 1883.

My dear Friend, — This is not a proper letter but a line or so to say more shall be presently forthcoming with remarks on Mano. I took the book abroad with me, read it once cursorily, then began a more careful study, but this I interrupted on my return, for there was something pressing in the way of poetical criticism I had promised to do,[1] and in the meantime I lent it to one of my pupils, who has it now.

On the second reading the great beauty of the verse came out. I also found the archaism of the diction did not stand in the way of powerful effects, but allowed of vigorous and homely language, as in the line about the pull at the Roman rope.[2] Of imagery the beauties were countless. (What I am saying now is a mere gabble.) The story is tragic in the extreme. My present puzzle is that I cannot find the clew to it. Mano seems ~~my~~ ^some^ sort of type of man; an Adam, betrayed by a^n^ ~~woman~~ ^Eve^. Gerbert seems something of a serpent. I never cd. get out of my head that he was the "valley-wight":[3] if there is nothing in this you may be sure others will think so nevertheless. I could not interpret the dream of the rabbits, lovely as it is.[4] I cannot be reconciled to Mano's killing Joanna:[5] I do not see that he could be justified, terrible as the occasion was. Nor can I understand his falling away on the journey to Italy.[6] Pathos and strokes of the human heart abound throughout; the scene where Mano visits Blanche and her husband disguised comes back to me as particularly lovely in this respect;[7] but I will write no more remarks of my own till I get the book back. I shall now tell you what Mr. Patmore says.

Mano, he writes, "is full of vigour and manly and even great style; but I think that a reader, alert, as I am, to watch for indications of the inner motive of the poem, ought to be ~~able~~ enabled to discover it more clearly than I am as yet able to do". This seems to be my own difficulty. But more hereafter.

There has been and will be no time for my reading your history.

Believe me your affectionate friend Gerard Hopkins S.J.
Oct. 14 1883

I have again missed the post.

[1] His detailed criticism of *The Angel in the House*.

[2] Book I, canto XV, ll 40–2:

> The same that spread the Roman name and scope
> Furthest abroad, was he at first who dared
> The boldest pull against the Roman rope.

[3] The 'valley-wight' occurs in cantos X and XI of Book I.

[4] The dream of the rabbits is in Book IV, canto II.

[5] The climax and end of the story.

[6] Book II, canto V.

[7] Book IV, canto III.

24–5 October 1883 to Robert Bridges

LRB, no. CX, p. 186 Bodleian, Dep. Bridges, vol. 92, fos. 31–36v

Stonyhurst, Blackburn. Oct. 24 1883.

Dearest Bridges, — Thank you first for very kindly copying out the poem on the Blessed Virgin[1] and then for your letter.

You always do misunderstand me on matters like that prayer for Mrs. Waterhouse. I was not thinking of you and her, not, I mean, as using ~~those~~ ^the^ prayers in that book or of your opinions as mirrored in them, but of the buyers of the book and the public it was meant for; which public I suppose you and Mrs. W. to know the mind and need of better than I do and therefore to be right in admitting one thing and excluding another: now ~~for~~ ^in^ that public I regret, and surely I may, that it ~~now~~ can no longer be trusted to bear, to stomach, the clear expression of or the ~~th~~taking for granted even very elementary Christ~~e~~^ian^ doctrines. I did not realise this well enough, did not realise that distinct Christianity ~~wd~~ damages the sale and so the usefulness of a well meant book; but now that I do what ought I to be but sorry?[2]

But by the way you say something I want to remark on: "Even such a doctrine as the Incarnation may be believed by people like yourself", as a mystery, till it is formulated, but as soon as it is it seems dragged down to the world of pros and cons, and *as its mystery goes*, so does its hold on their minds". Italics the present writer's. You do not mean by mystery what a Catholic does. You mean an interesting uncertainty: ~~with~~ ^the^ ^un^certainty ceasing ~~ceases also~~ interest ~~also~~ ceases also. This happens in some things; to you in religion. But a Catholic by mystery means an incomprehensible certainty: without certainty, without formulation there is no interest (of ^course a doc^trine is valuable for other things than its interest, its interestingness, but I am speaking now of that); the clearer the formulation the greater the interest. At bottom the source of interest is the same in both cases, in your mind and in ours; it is the unknown, the reserve of truth beyond what the mind reaches ~~which it~~ ^and^ still feels to be behind. But the interest a Catholic feels is, if I may say so, of a far finer kind than yours. Yours turns out to be a curiosity only; curiosity satisfied, the trick found out (to be a little profane), the answer heard, it vanishes at once. But you know there are some ^solutions to^, say, chess problems~~,~~ ~~some~~ ^so^ beautifully ingenious, some resolutions of suspensions so lovely in music that even the feeling of interest is keenest when they are known and over, and ~~survives~~ for some time survives the discovery. How must it then be when the very answer is the most ~~pointed~~ ^tantalizing^ statement of the problem and the truth you are to rest in the most pointed putting of the difficulty! For if ~~explanations and figure metaphors are wanted~~ the Trinity, as ~~Freder~~ Francis Newman[3] somewhere says, is to be explained by grammar and by tropes, why then he could furnish explanations for himself; but then where wd. be the mystery? the true mystery, the incomprehensible one. At that pass one ~~could po~~ should point blank believe or disbelieve: he disbelieved; his brother, at the same pass, believed. There are three persons, each God and each the same, the one, the only God: to some people this is a "dogma", a word they almost chew, that is an equation in theology, the dull algebra of Schoolmen; to others it is news of their ~~three~~ dearest ^friend or^ friends, leaving them all their lives ~~in a~~ balance~~e~~^ing^ whether ~~to say~~ they have three heavenly friends or one — not that they have any doubt on the subject, but that their knowledge leaves their minds swinging; poised, but on the quiver. And this might be the ecstasy of interest, one ~~coul~~ would think. So too of the Incarnation, a mystery less incomprehensible, it is true: to you it comes to: Christ is in some sense God, in some sense he is not God — and your interest is in the uncertainty; to the Catholic it is: Christ is in every sense God and in every sense man, and the interest is in the locked and inseparable combination, or rather it is in the person in whom the combination has its place. Therefore we speak of the events of Christ's life as the mystery of the Nativity, the mystery of the ~~c~~Crucifixion and so on of a host; the mystery being always the same, that the child in the manger is God, the culprit on the gallows God, and so on. Otherwise birth and ~~crucifixion~~ ^death^ are not mysteries, nor is it any great mystery that a just man should ~~die~~ ^be crucified^, but that God should fascinates — with the interest of awe, of pity, of shame, of every harrowing feeling. But I have said enough.

Oct. 25 — Austin Dobson's triolet I knew well by quotation: I dare say it is the best the Rondeliers have done. The stupid fellow, to change it! Makes me think the worse of him. But yours may be carried, I think, a step farther: the fine subtlety of "Said my ear to my eye" is not broad enough for a skit.[4] I should put it into his own mouth and entitle it[5]

On t
from
the

Con-fo
I'll tak
Rose a
Confoun
Stop

Se[?] you
Confoun
I'll take
This origin
is full of
of condem
The 'heav
"violets"

[*A section here completely cut out*]

The expectations I raised in Mr. Patmore about Mano were my own~~: I had~~ and got from you: I had not then seen it. ~~Ia~~ ^A^fterwards however, when I had, I wrote to him that if he got it he wd. not be disappointed; whereas he is. I have not got it by me now and will not at present say more of it than this, that crowded as it is with beauties of the noblest sort, the deepest pathos and tragedy, besides a few touches of humour, ~~noble~~ finely conceived character, interest, romance, landscape, imagery, and unflagging music, still I am much of Mr. Patmore's mind: it ~~is or~~ either has not or else I have hitherto missed finding a leading thought to thread the beauties on — or almost worse, that I see ^one^ but it breaks and is unsatisfactory, namely that Mano is a kind of Adam and falls and also a kind of ~~s~~Second Adam and is crucified. I will write more hereafter.

I had not meant Mr. Patmore to know I wrote poetry, but since it has come naturally and unavoidably about there is no more to be said and you may therefore send me your book and I will point it and make a few corrections. You were right to leave out the marks: they were not consistent for one thing and are always offensive. ~~Stll~~ Still there must be some. Either I must invent a notation applied throughout as in music or else I must only mark where the reader is likely to mistake, and for the present this is what I shall do.

I have a great ~~m~~ deal more I could say, but must conclude. I am your affectionate friend Gerard Hopkins S.J.

I may presently but will not just yet avail myself of your kind offer of the loose Purcells.[6]

I have yet heard nothing particular about Grace.[7] She will settle ^down^ and be happy: she is too simple-minded and too sweetnatured to let herself be soured or enfeebled by a grief. She may even come to care for someone else, though no doubt she does not believe she ever could.

[1] 'The Blessed Virgin compared to the Air we Breathe'. See letter of 7 Mar. 1884. GMH had lost his copy of the poem. RB made a transcription from MS 'A' and sent this. GMH began to copy it into MS B but did not have time to complete it before moving to Dublin. In the move, he mislaid RB's transcription and sent the album to Coventry Patmore. Discouragingly, it was this poem, of which only one-third had been copied, that Patmore singled out for praise.

[2] In 1886 Mrs Waterhouse sent GMH a copy of the book. See the accompanying letter of 10 May 1886.

[3] Francis William Newman (1805–97; *ODNB*), younger brother of the cardinal. Like his brother he thought deeply about his religious convictions, but resigned his fellowship at Balliol in 1830 on finding that he could not give the assent to Anglican doctrine required of Oxford dons. He later became Professor of Latin at University College, London, 1846–63.

[4] Unknown, but obviously some form of skit on Dobson. Henry Austin Dobson changed his triolet to its present version:

I intended an Ode
  And it turned to a Sonnet,
It began *à la mode*,
I intended an Ode;

But Rose crossed the road
   In her latest new bonnet;
   I intended an Ode;
And it turned to a Sonnet.

'Urceus Exit', *Collected Poems* (London, 1913), 324 is the fifth of a group of triolets under the title 'Rose-Leaves', and in one version, which only appeared in *Proverbs in Porcelain* (1877), referred to its own form, so that lines 2 and 8 read 'And it turned into Triolets', and line 6 read 'With a bunch of fresh violets'. RB and GMH seem to be objecting to the eye-rhyme. Dobson's title refers to Horace's *Ars Poetica*, ll. 21–2: 'amphora coepit | institui; currente rota cur urceus exit?' {*it started out as a wine jar; as the wheel turns round why does a pot emerge?*}.

[5] Only a third of the next leaf remains, and one side has on it only the beginnings of a title and the lines of a triolet. The cut was evidently made intentionally by RB.

[6] i.e. unbound sheet music of pieces by Henry Purcell.

[7] See letter to RB of 5–6 Aug. 1883 and to Grace of 9–10 June 1883.

25–9 October 1883 to Coventry Patmore

FL, no. CLXXI, p. 319 Durham University Library, Abbott MS 189
Two large folded sheets, six sides written on.

Stonyhurst, Blackburn. Oct. 25 1883.

My dear Mr. Patmore, — I now make some remarks on the Amelia volume, which is a hotchpotch volume of new and old.

L'Allegro — The passage about Golden-Tongue is ~~sower~~ sour and to my taste flavours the whole too much, so that allegrezza {*liveliness*}is not quite the spirit or "instress" the poem conveys to me.[1]

P. 101 "And truth is dying because joy is dead": no doubt you mean what you say, but a plain man will be driven to believe it is a slip for "joy is dying because truth is dead". I do not ~~think~~ ^feel sure^ I take your meaning. I suppose it must be that joy holds the great secret, is an insight into the deepest truth, which being lost plainer and easier truths will follow.[2]

P. 102 "And judging . . School-Divines" — I can make nothing of this, but if before sending ~~this~~ ^my letter^ off I shd. find someone who can explain it I will let you know.[3]

~~The~~ Tamerton Church Tower is an unequal work. It is like Love's Labour Lost and Shakespere's earlier plays in this, that the dramatic power and grasp of "motive"* [*GMH footnote*: * I mean motif, leading thought, central idea.] is all there and mastered; but the execution ^is^ still to seek. Not all the execution, for the landscape ^or scenery^, which is the most part of the poem, is brilliant and perfect, but the songs. They seem to me forced and cold. The difficulty was one I have noticed before, to bring a lyric into a lyric, as a play into a play: one must subdue the ~~back~~ground or heighten the 'charge' or do something to difference the two; but I think it must be granted the difficulty has ^not^ been met nearly so well as by Tennyson in the Miller's Daughter. The ingenuity of the passage about Cupid's bow and the letters spelling "Kiss" is extreme, but extreme ingenuity and turns of pure fancy in art are in great danger of frigidity.[4] However, dramatically this is all right: the two characters might amuse themselves so; the main matter is ^made^ good, but the anise and cummin not. I have the modern taste about small waists too: they are odious to me. — I have made these remarks, but the poem will not now bear alteration.

The Yewberry — P. 144 "Joy then suffered":[5] I understand the paradox, but in many readings it never struck me till today; I had slipped over it as ~~y~~ if you had written "felt" or "enjoyed". And in general ^in^ this and all the early poems the acuteness of the intelligence is in excess of the instress or feeling and gives them a certain cold glitter.

I cannot make out whether Laura was Herbert's wife or ~~not~~ only betrothed. The story is much more tragic if his wife. Surely ~~this~~ ^it^ shd. be indicated which.

So too the reticence of the River is extreme. There are hints that the disappointed lover drowned himself, but I cannot feel sure of it. ~~But~~ ^Still^ I do not say that this ^mystery^ may not add ^more^ interest and greater awe; only for myself I shd. like to know.

The rainbow-~~test~~ standard in the first stanza is not decisive. On hilly ground a rainbow may stand wholly within a few acres. Perhaps a slight change of wording might turn what is unsatisfactory as a measurement into what ~~wd~~ what cd. be impressive as a picture.[6]

In the Girl of All Periods "skipping the wicked pages" may be from life but is unpleasant.[7] This piece seems to me not quite successful metrically either, though it is sparkling: it seems ~~it~~ ^the line^ ought to begin with the stress in the first foot — like: "Leave their nature, dress and talk like men", as in Tennyson's Vision of Sin; or else that mixed with the other. I do not undertake to recommend any change; but ~~it~~ ^the piece^ reads to me something like the rhyming passages in the Midsummer Night. And as there are only four light endings ~~of~~ out of thirty-eight it looks as if there ought to be none at all.

The Dream very whimsically ends without a rhyme, as if it were a fragment.[8] I do not know that the effect is bad neither do I feel that it is good. The last sentence is obscure; ~~I supp~~ I suppose it to mean: "Here (in the Paradise or dreamworld where she was) there is blushing for the ~~coldnes~~ coldness of lovers on earth and for the shameful spectacle of" etc.[9]

The Scorched Fly — on the sin of presumption.[10] ~~It~~ Penitents often ~~mention~~ accuse themselves of sinning with the hope to be forgiven; they seem to mention this as an aggravating circumstance, but divines ~~take~~ ^here^ notice that, taken as it stands, it rather shd. be called an extenuating ~~circumstance~~ one. And certainly if despair is a very aggravating circumstance ~~hope shd.~~ of sin hope shd. be an extenuation ~~of it~~. ~~And~~ ^Again,^ in the nature of things, mortal sin is an act of excommunication, a breaking off of relations, of charity or mutual regard between God and the sinner: now though this ~~is~~ excommunication is involved in every mortal sin it makes a difference, a vast ~~one~~ ^difference^, whether the sinner chooses it ~~or is~~ in itself or as bound up with something else, ~~does~~ ^decrees^ it formally or ^only^ by a necess~~ity~~ary implication, whether he wishes gold or pleasure and regrets that he can only get it by theft or fornication and still more regretfully and against his will ~~ex~~ consents to break off intercourse with God in getting it — whether he acts thus or, to take the opposite case of diabolical malice, means to excommunicate God and chooses theft or fornication as a ~~pro~~ way of doing it. The affectus {*disposition*} of disloyalty is the worst feature of an act of disobedience; the affectus, though ineffectual and inconsistent, of loyalty is the greatest mitigation of one. Now, as far as words go, this last is the state of mind of one who sins in hope of forgiveness: he wants to have ~~a ^his^ forbidden good and wants~~ an object forbidden and ~~would~~ if possible not to break off relations with God in consequence; if that cannot be and God forbids under pain of excommunication, yet he hopes that the excommunication may not last long.

However it is likely that those who accuse themselves of sinning in hope mean that they sinned in presumption; ~~as goo~~ mocking God, as good as telling him they know best what ~~is~~ matters and what does not matter and making themselves and not him, ^by^ a hideous perversion, the standard and fountain of morality. This was the sin of Adam and Eve, who, both in different ways, eat of the “Test-tree”, the Tree of the Knowledge of Good and Evil, the Tree-to-decide~~-what -is~~-right-and-wrong-by, if I may so interpret; Eve taking it as a challenge on God’s part which it was the most subtle and refined morality ^in her^ to ~~le~~ accept by an act of outward disobedience; Adam, not deceived about that but still deluded # into thinking God would admire his generosity in sinning out of charity to his wife.

It is of presumption then, not hope, ^that^ I interpret this poem, but the objection I have to make is ~~that~~, not that you say hope, for there is true and false hope, but that you use the very words which most excuse the sin and make the hope ~~well~~ ^seem^ true hope and wellfounded — "Sorrow for sin God's judgment stays".~~: for~~ ^Surely^ that is the truth and the only mistake is the man's taking for granted he will be sorry; which seems rather foolish than malignant. Could not this be better put? The poem being on so vital a point of morality should have nothing misleading in it.

Eros — ^In^ the third quatrain the rhythm very immature, especially "faith truly plight". Also "Touched by the zephyr" seems poor.[11]

The Sign of the Prophet Jonas — I withdraw my objection that the meaning might ~~m~~^d^isedify: perhaps the time is come when it needs to be spoken. But I ~~think~~ still think the poem sour and also so continuously ~~severe~~ obscure that it will be a stumblingblock to most readers; I need not point out particular difficulties or obscurities.[12]

The Kiss — Though this is a little gem of execution and will be a favourite, yet there is something about it that offends me. It is unreasonable, but I cannot help having a wish that Victor and Amanda might both once be well whipped.[13]

Semele — Does he say this to her or she to him, Jove, as it were, to Semele or Semele to Jove? The parable seems to require the first, the poem itself the second.[14]

In the Essay[15] I wd. recommend that marginal headings or something equivalent shd. be added: it greatly helps the reader in a matter so naturally difficult and dry. I will write further on this.

I have consulted two clearheaded men about the passage p. 102[16] — They could not clear it, but in talking to one of them I came to the conclusion it must mean this: and criticising complete strangers by those ^mild^ ~~prin~~principles ("lines"), unenforced by any sanction and ^so^ of counsel, not of precept, ~~which~~ that the ruthful ^tender-hearted^ spirit which is the essence of equity has long since ^prompted^ the theologians to lay down. But what and where are those principles?

Meanwhile another doubt has arisen — Amelia: "I touch the notes which music cannot reach".[17] One of my counsellors thought the notes were ~~the~~ ^a^ kiss upon Amelia's cheek; the other a flush of colour called out there by love in parting — according to the common analogy of colour and sound. In either case "touch the notes" I take to be the same as ~~sound~~ 'make them ~~sing~~ sound', as by touching keys or strings.

Believe me very sincerely yours Gerard Hopkins S.J.
Oct. 29 1883.

[1] Unaltered (1906, p. 370).
[2] 'L'Allegro' (1906, p. 369); unchanged.
[3] Ibid. (1906, p. 369). See below and next letter.
[4] Unaltered (1906, p. 373, no. 4).
[5] Unaltered (1906, p. 391): 'P. 144' should be 'P. 145'.
[6] Unaltered (1906, p. 396).
[7] 'The Girl of All Periods, An Idyll'. The poem is unchanged (1906, pp. 442–3). The lines particularly in question are:

> 'Yes, she had read the "Legend of the Ages",
> 'And George Sand too, skipping the wicked pages.'

[8] It is a fragment excised from an early version of 'The Victories of Love'.
[9] Unaltered (1906, p. 428).
[10] Omitted later, therefore given here:

> Who sins in hope; who, sinning, says,
> 'Sorrow for sin God's judgment stays!'
> Against God's Spirit he lies; quite stops
> Mercy with insult; dares, and drops,
> Like a scorch'd fly, that spins in vain
> Upon the axis of its pain,
> Then takes its doom, to limp and crawl,
> Blind and forgot, from fall to fall.

[11] Unaltered (1906, p. 429).
[12] This poem reappears later (with the first ten lines omitted) as *The Open Secret* (1906, 432–4).
[13] Unaltered (1906, pp. 435–6).
[14] Unaltered (1906, p. 438). See next letter.
[15] *Prefatory Study on English Metrical Law.*
[16] See above and n. 3.
[17] Unaltered (1906, p. 363).

31 October 1883 from Coventry Patmore to GMH

FL, no. CLXXI A, p. 324 Campion Hall, P 31/10/83
Addressed to 'Reverend Gerard Hopkins, S.J. | Stonyhurst College, | Blackburn'. PM HASTINGS OC 31 83, BLACKBURN NO 1 83, WHALLEY NO 1 83. Small drawing of box on envelope.

Hastings. Oct. 31. 1883.
My dear Sir,

Your careful and subtle fault-finding is the greatest praise my poetry has ever received. It makes me almost inclined to begin to sing again, after I thought I had given over.

I agree with all or very nearly all your objections. "Tamerton Church Tower" and "The Sign of the Prophet Jonah" are incorrigible. I should be sorry to condemn the first to total extinction, <u>but</u> "Jonah" must go — not on account of its extreme obscurity, but on account of its hopelessly ~~false~~ ^unpleasant^ <u>tone</u>, and also because I fear it is scarcely obscure enough. I have long, also, felt the objection you make to the "Scorch'd Fly", but I retained it in — or rather restored it to — my later editions because I thought it a good piece of execution. It shall go, however.

It is certainly "Jove" who speaks to "Semele". What you say about "The Kiss" is quite just, but there is no help for it, except extinction, wh. I think would be too severe a sentence. Your interpretation of the four lines in "L'Allegro" is what I meant. They are nearly verbatim from Hooker's Ecclesiastical Polity.[1] The "unsanction'd lines" or principles I understand to be those intuitions of orthodox humanity wh. always seem to go hand-in-hand with orthodox theology. — the female side of orthodoxy. "Gaude Maria Virgo, cunctas hæreses sola interemisti in universo mundo {*Rejoice O Virgin Mary, you who alone have struck a mortal blow against all the heresies throughout the world*}."[2] On all or nearly all the other queries or objections I shall try to act, so need not write about them, unless again to thank you for your great kindness.

I should like much to talk over "Mano" with you. My failure to see in it all that I was led to expect is very likely my own fault. It is full of very weighty merits and must not be lightly criticised.

Yours very truly
Coventry Patmore
Revd Gerard Hopkins, S.J.

[1] Patmore's lines are:

And judging outer strangers by
Those gentle and unsanction'd lines
To which remorse of equity
Of old hath moved the School divines.

His source is Hooker's 'Of the Laws of Ecclesiastical Polity', Book V, section 60 (*Works of Mr Richard Hooker* (London, 1821), ii.107): 'remorse of equity hath moved divers of the school-divines in these considerations, ingeniously to grant, that God, all merciful to such as are not in themselves able to desire baptism, imputeth the secret desire that others have in their behalf, and accepteth the same as theirs, rather than casteth away their souls for that which no man is able to help'.

[2] The Book of Hours (and the Breviary) records the 'Hours of the Virgin', with this as the Antiphon (a liturgical chant) to the Psalm 'Cantate Domino' in the third Nocturn of the Office of the Blessed Virgin Mary. See <medievalist.net/hourstxt/bvm1matd.htm>.

7–10 November 1883 to Coventry Patmore

FL, no. CLXXII, p. 325 Durham University Library, Abbott MS 190
Two large sheets folded and a half sheet; written on nine sides.

Stonyhurst. Nov. ~~6~~7 1883.

My dear Mr. Patmore, — It would be a calamity in literature if Tamerton Church Tower were suppressed and a consummation devoutly to be wished against, [1] but being to find fault I found the songs faulty, though I knew they could not now be altered. It is an early piece and so immature, but so is Love's Labour's Lost and others of Shakspere's ~~early~~ plays, which are faulty though they teem with genius and could never be spared. It is recognised by sound critics that poets ~~mature~~ ^ripen^ and that faults of youth and immaturity can be found in ~~their~~ works ^which are^ even master pieces in other ways. I say the same, in proportion, of the Kiss ^excepting that the objection I made there was ~~not~~ made on another ground^. We must also acknowledge that if we criticise in the rigour of justice no human work except short pieces of music and small examples in the arts of design could stand.

I now make some remarks on the Study on English Metrical Law. There are some things in this essay I do not find myself altogether in agreement with, but on these I do not touch; I only point out what seem to be overstatements or understatements and so forth upon the ground ~~taken~~ there taken.

P. 20 "With us, the places . . . coincide",[2] p. 22 "Let me now ask", with all that follows[3] — The treatment of English spoken accent here is unsatisfactory: you nowhere say what it is. Now if, as you say, the learned are pretty well agreed what the ^old^ Greek accent was, which no living ear ever heard, we must surely be able to know and say with certainty what the English is, which we cannot even dispute about without exhibiting as fast as we open our mouths. If some books say it is long quantity, that is so grossly stupid as to need no refutation; it is
◡́ — ◡́ — ◡́ —
enough to quote # words — "thorough paced blackguard, agonising
◡́ — ◡́ – – ◡́ — ◡́ – – ◡́ — ◡́ – –
headache, messengers, cattle market, illustrating, Billingsgate, Liverpool" and so on. But I do not remember ^ever^ hearing any sensible man say that. It is plain and, ~~is~~ so far as I know, ~~if~~ ^it is^ commonly agreed that it is stress. The Greek accent was a tonic accent, was tone, pitch of note: it may have included a stress, but essentially it was pitch. In like manner the English accent is emphatic accent, is stress: it commonly includes

clear pitch, but essentially it is stress. Pitch totally disappears in whispering, but our accent is perfectly given when we whisper. But perhaps one ought further to explain what stress is. Stress appears so elementary an idea as does not need and scarcely allows of definition; still this may be said of it, that it is the making a thing more, or making it markedly, what it already is; it is the bringing out its nature. Accordingly stress on a syllable (which is English accent proper) is the making much of that syllable, more than of others; stress on a word or sentence (which is emphasis) is the making much of that word or sentence, more than of others. Commonly and naturally what we emphasise we say louder, and the accented syllables, words, and so on are in fact what we catch first and lose last in a dist~~inc~~^an^t speaker; but this is not essential. Also what we emphasise we say clearer, more distinctly, and in fact to this is due the slurring in English of unaccented syllables; which is a beauty of the language, ~~and~~ ^so that^ only misguided people say Dev-il, six-pence distinctly; still even this is not essential. The accented syllable then is the one of which the nature is well brought out, whatever may become of the others. When the others are as well brought out then, but this is seldom, happens that which you so acutely point out, that the mind, as ~~in~~ it does to the tick tock of a clock, supplies ~~a~~ for a ~~certain spell~~ while that difference which has ceased to be marked ~~really~~ outwardly. And this is clearly seen in ~~music~~ ^singing^; for, however smoothly and equally the notes are sung, if the accent of the syllable does not fall on the accent, primary or secondary, of the bar — though in fact neither the note nor the syllable sung to it ~~is~~ ^were^ any louder than the rest — the effect is intolerable; if for instance instead of

we made it

I put aside of course ~~revers~~ syncopations and other calculated effects, as in all art.

It only remains to say that the stress~~es~~, the ictus, of our verse is founded on and in the beginning the very same as the stress which is our accent. In fact in smooth and simple and especially in strongly marked lyric measures, as, say, Poe's Raven, one may read on a long while together without a single discrepancy. And when ~~they~~ ^discrepancies^ do arise they begin so ~~imperceptibly~~ ^naturally^ that people may well not notice them: as suppose a man said in prose "A~~n~~ ~~interested gentleman~~ ^penniless adventurer^ is ~~never~~ ^often^ in ~~a~~ ~~difficulty~~ ^extremities^" — this can be seen to run into alternate strong and weak beats, say iambs or trochees, according to where you begin scanning; and perhaps people wd. not notice that every other strong beat, ~~at~~ every fourth syllable, that is, is really scarcely marked at all, ~~but~~ ^so^ inevitably does the mind supply it. This indeed falls into double-iambic or double-trochaic feet, or in music ^bars of^ four time, in which the first accent is stronger than the second, but from the same kind of sentences ~~less regularly~~ may also arise the blank stresses, as I am accustomed to call them, of the ten-syllable ^line^ and other lines; for in fact in Milton few lines have ~~ten really~~ ^five^ real stresses, one or two being blank, though in idea there are always five. — However you hold that the ten-syllable line ~~is~~ has three bars, I remember; but you will agree with what I have been saying.

I have written a great deal on this head, but all comes to this, that you ought ~~to~~, in my opinion, to say once clearly what English accent is and not, after quoting different views, leave the truth unexpressed as if there could be or in fact were any doubt about the matter.

(By the by, though I have done it above and it is a momentary convenience, it is a radically bad principle to call English feet iambs and trochees. In music it is still worse; it is a complete overturning of the meaning of words. A Greek would say that the ~~full~~ bar I have given of "Full fathom five" contained a spondee followed by a syncopated trochee—in Greek notation | –́ – | ⌞́ ∪ |—or was a syncopated fourth epitrite — | –́ – ⌞́ ∪ | whereas ^modern^ musical writers would, I suppose, ~~call~~ say it contained two trochees. Names ought to be invented for rhythmic feet. In modern verse much ~~confusion~~ ^harm^ does not arise from this ^confusion^ — though what you are saying at pp. 66 and 79 would not have needed so much explanation but for ~~this confusion~~ ^it^ —, but music is just the very place where the difference of ~~the~~ time-feet and rhythm-feet recognised in Greek poetry is still in force ~~force~~ and where therefore the established meaning of words ought rigidly to be kept to.)

P. 22, the paragraph on tonic accent — The best thing I have read on Greek accent is an essay by the late American Professor Hadley (in his collected Essays).[4] It seems to me that, looking at such facts as you here cite, we shall be justified in saying the acute tonic accent was the best marked pitch ~~of~~ in ~~the~~ ^each^ word; which pitch was commonly a rise (say of a fifth, ~~the~~ ^to the dominant^ — the most natural interval) from the keynote or readingnote; but sometimes a fall of, say, a fourth, to the same dominant, ~~below~~ I mean of course the octave of the other, below. In like manner the grave accent, which Hadley reasonably says means not a lower note, that is, one lower than the keynote or readingnote, but ^only^ one not so high as the acute above it, will commonly be a rise of, say, a ^major^ third, to the mediant, but sometimes a fall of, say, a minor third, to the submediant. ~~A~~ ^The^ circumflex is no doubt a sort of turn or shake, two notes to a syllable instead of one or a rise and fall instead of a rise only. It is to be remarked that men seem to have found it hard to reach the simple notion of a note. In the passage you quote at p. 15 Cicero says[5] there are only three sounds ^in music^, the turn, the rise, and the fall — for so I interpret him; and it is believed that our present musical notation arose from a complicated system of accents, rising, falling, and so on (~~A~~ a great variety of marks, now unnecessary, may be seen in books on the history of plain chant, e.g. Helmore's Primer in Novello's Music Primer series);[6] as though men first were struck by the change or passage of sound and later ^seized^ the points of departure and arrival. It is true this does not agree with what I have said above about the grave accent, but modern ~~writers~~ ^critics^, as Roby and Munro,[7] strongly suspect Cicero, Quintilian, and the Latin writers of bungling on the subject and misapplying Greek theory to Latin, and if it is true (but I have not verified it) what a friend told me of Lucretius, that he says distant objects do not appear smaller but only less distinct,[8] I could believe anything of a Roman writer.

As then the English accent is stress and yet we can make the stress on the ~~acce~~ unaccented syllables of an emphatic word more marked than on the accented of an unemphatic one, the general or rhetorical emphasis overriding the ~~syllabic~~ particular and syllabic, so in Greek no doubt it was possible for the accent to be ordinarily a ~~rising~~ ^high^ tone and yet for the lowest note of one word to be higher than the highest of another or even for the note usually raised on occasion to be lowered as markedly, the ~~rhe~~ general and rhetorical intonation here too ~~over~~ controlling and modifying the syllabic and particular. ~~And~~ More shortly, emphasis does not destroy our accent of stress nor need intonation have destroyed their accent of tone, and I should have liked something of the sort to be expressed here.

P. 30 "In song, we have gradually" etc[9] — Here I would say "Art advised of that?" for so far as I know it is not the fact. Grétry should not be trusted about the short compass of old songs, for French popular music is remarkable, it is said, for just this monotony and short compass, while ~~Engli~~ British is not. The Welsh air of the Camp, better known as "Of a noble race was Shenkin",[10] to my mind the most majestic pure melody that was ever ~~writt~~ composed, is of ~~extreme~~ ^great^ range, from G above the treble down to B ~~on the ledger line space~~ below the ledger line.[11] "And how should I your truelove know?" has one note less (as I used to know it). Maggie Lauder a fine air has the same, twelve notes. "Full fathom five" has the same; and twelve notes, that is an octave and the dominant above ~~it~~, is so natural a range that many airs must have it. Other things being alike, the greater the range the greater the room for fine effects. The rise or fall of an octave is a most vigorous effect and it is inconvenient not to be able to ~~do~~ ^set^ this on, say, any but the keynote. The Welsh air I have quoted, besides several splendid octave ~~effects~~ ^falls^, rises its whole range ^at once^ in one ~~bound~~ ^place^ and ten notes in another. You may of course have had real cases in your mind, but it is possible you were thinking of very low or very high notes in airs not of ~~quite~~ ^great^ range but set low or high for display's sake. For my part I am rather struck with the tameness of modern songs. It is true I seldom hear them.

P. 52 I should like you to reconsider the matter of alliteration in vowels. To my ear no alliteration is more marked or more beautiful, and I used to take it for granted as an obvious fact that every initial vowel lettered to every other before ever I knew that anything of the sort was practised in Anglo Saxon verse. I cannot agree that this alliteration is destroyed by using the same vowel. No doubt the effect is more beautiful, more artistic, with a change of vowels; still with the same one it is heard. How this alliteration arises is, I know, very hard to say, but to my ear there is no doubt about the fact.

But about Pope's line "And apt alliteration's artful aid" (if that is the line in full) there is more to be said.[12] Pope was the great master of metre of his day, as we know, but (like Tennyson in our day, who on his own ground is so strong but has made a sad mess of his classical experiments) he was nothing ultra crepidam {*out of his proper sphere*}[13] and here he seems to have gone ultra crepidam. He meant the line as a sample of the effect of alliteration, but in doing so he made two blunders. For first no doubt he thought, because every word began with a, therefore ~~at~~ every word began with the same ~~sound~~ ^vowel^. But in fact there are four initial vowels or three at the least in that line. The a in apt is the common English short a. The a in artful is the English broad a, a very different thing. The ai in aid is called long a in English, but is really one of the continental es, and is still more different. Then the initials of and and alliteration, if you bring them distinctly out, are the same as that of apt no doubt, but slurred, as we commonly pronounce them, they are ~~stil~~ another vowel still. And secondly if the vowel was really the same throughout then it was not the better but rather the worse for that. Still it seems to me that the line does alliterate and that Pope's ear heard that, though his reason was astray on the subject.

P. 56 "This metre[14] . . outlived the Anglo-Saxon language several centuries" — You know the attack made of ~~the~~ late on the name Anglo-Saxon. I think and I see that others think it is pedantic, but it seems to me that if ever an objection could be made to the use of the term "Anglo-Saxon language" without reserve or explanation it might be in this sentence. For "several centuries" cannot mean less than three; which would carry us back from Piers Ploughman to the Conquest. Now anyone can see by glancing at a few lines that the language of England before and after the Conquest for some time differed ~~only imp~~ ^only by^ almost imperceptible differences.

P. 63 note on Welsh verse — I shd. like to lay what I know of the facts shortly before ^you^, but will do it, if I can, in another letter.

P. 79 "Six real anapaests counting 'wrastling' as one"[15] — You must mean that "wrestling" is of three syllables and ^the last^ two of these enter into one of the anapaests, not that it is an anapaest as it stands: of itself it is rather a dactyl.

I forgot to say that in L'Allegro p. 101[16] the line "Between such friends as thou and I" is strange and, I rather think, indefensible grammar. You must mean are to be understood, but can it be understood when there is no verb in the other limb of the parallel? The odd use of I after prepositions in Shakspere is a colloquialism I should think inadmissible in such verse as this.

I will not write of Mano yet awhile.

Believe me, dear Mr. Patmore, yours very sincerely Gerard M. Hopkins S.J.

I will try and let you have my remarks on the Eros volume soon, if it is not too late. This being your ~~matu~~ ripest work I feel more distrust of my judgment upon it.

Nov. 10 1883.

Perhaps you do not know that the Latin writers exchanged and misapplied the Greek words arsis and thesis. ~~Thesis~~ Arsis is properly the rise of the foot in dancing or of the conductor's arm in beating time, thesis the fall of the same. Arsis therefore is the light part of the foot,

I call it the "slack"; thesis is the heavy or strong, the stress. For this reason some writers now refuse to say arsis and thesis and use ictus only. It is clear the Latin writers thought of arsis as effort, thesis as the fall to rest after effort.

[1] GMH is adapting the line from Hamlet's 'To be or not to be' soliloquy; *Hamlet* III. i .63–4: 'a consummation | Devoutly to be wish'd'.

[2] 'With us [the English], the places of the *metrical* accent or "ictus"—of the accent in the sense of change of tone, and of long quantity, coincide . . . '.

[3] 'Let me now ask, what do we mean by "accent", as the word is commonly used in speaking of its function in English verse? . . . Now, it seems to me that the only tenable view of that accent upon which it is allowed, with more or less distinctness, by all, that English metre depends, in contradistinction to the syllabic metre of the ancients, is the view which attributes to it the function of marking, *by whatever means*, certain isochronous intervals . . . . '.

[4] *Essays Philological and Critical, Selected from the Papers of James Hadley, LL.D.*, 1873. V. 'On Ancient Greek Rhythm and Metre' (1864). VI. 'On the Nature and Theory of the Greek Accent' (1869).

[5] Patmore's essay quotes a variant of Cicero's comment in his *Orator* (57–8): 'Mira est enim quaedam natura vocis cuius quidem e tribus omnino sonis, inflexo, acuto, gravi, tanta sit et tam suavis varietas perfecta in cantibus: est autem in dicendo etiam quidem cantus obscurior', which H. M. Hubbell in the Loeb edition of 1971 renders: 'For the voice possesses a marvelous quality, so that from merely three registers, high, low and intermediate, it produces such a rich variety of song. There is, moreover, even in speech, a sort of singing.'

[6] Thomas Helmore (1811–90), *Primer of Plainsong* (1877). Four other *Novello's Music Primers*, edited by Dr Stainer, were reviewed in the *Musical Times* of 1 Nov. 1877, p. 536. They were *The Art of Pianoforte Playing* by Ernest Pauer, *The Organ* by John Stainer, *The Rudiments of Music* by W. H. Cummings, and *The Elements of the Beautiful in Music* by Ernest Pauer.

[7] Henry John Roby (1830–1915), best remembered for his Latin grammar (1871–4), and Hugh Andrews Johnstone Munro (1819–85), most noted for his edition of Lucretius (1860, revised 1864). See *ODNB*.

[8] *De Rerum Natura*, v. 564 sqq., and possibly in part also v. 579–81.

[9] 'In song, we have gradually fallen into the adoption of an extent of scale, and a diversity of time, which is simply *nonsensical*; for such variations of tone and time correspond to no depths or transitions of feeling of which the human breast is cognisant. The *permanent* popular instinct, which is ever the best test of truth in art, recognises the falsehood of these extremes.' He then quotes Grétry [i.e. André Ernest Modeste Grétry (1741–1813)], on French popular music, in support.

[10] GMH refers to four songs here. 'Of a noble race was Shenkin' comes originally from D'Urfey's stage comedy *The Richmond Heiress* (1693), music for which was written by Purcell and John Eccles. It later appeared in John Gay's *The Beggar's Opera* and was also included in Edward Jones's collection of Welsh airs under the name 'The Camp' in 1794. 'And how should I your truelove know?' is a setting of Ophelia's song from *Hamlet*, Act IV. 'Maggie Lauder' is a traditional Scottish song, attributed to Francis Sempill. 'Full fathom five' is another setting of a Shakespeare song, this one from *The Tempest*, I. ii. 397–405.

[11] GMH seems interested in this span of a 17th. See letter to CP of 6–7 Dec. 1883, n. 6.

[12] Churchill, *The Prophecy of Famine* (1763), ll. 85–86:

> Who often, but without success, have pray'd
> For apt Alliteration's artful aid[.]

[13] The Greek artist Apelles is reported by Pliny (in *Natural History*, XXXV, ch. 10) to have said to a shoemaker who, having successfully corrected the drawing of a sandal, dared to criticize the drawing of a leg, 'ne supra crepidam iudicaret', which gave rise to the Latin tag 'ne sutor supra crepidam' {*let not the cobbler go above the sole*}, or in other words, stick to your last.

[14] That of accentual alliteration.

[15] In a discussion of four lines from Phaer's *Virgil.*

[16] This line is unaltered (1906, p. 368).

11 November 1883 from Coventry Patmore to GMH

FL, no. CLXXII A, p. 333 — Campion Hall, P 11/11/83

Hastings. Nov. 11. 1883.

My dear Sir,

I shall give your remarks on the metrical Essay my best consideration together with the rules of the "New Prosody", which Mr Bridges has promised to explain to me, before I reprint that Essay, which I propose to do, not in the next edn. of my Poems, but in a subsequent vol. consisting of three or four critical Essays wh. I wrote many years ago in the Edinburgh and other reviews;[1] meantime I will only say that much of the substance of your very valuable notes will come in rather as a development than as a correction of the ideas which I have endeavoured — with too much brevity perhaps — to express.

I did not intend to limit song to an octave, but to the natural compass of the human voice, male and female, wh. I suppose is about two octaves.

I must try to teach my ear to adopt your view of alliterative vowels. I do not see the way to it at present.

I fear I cannot alter the line in "L'Allegro", as it forms part of a strain of the very best music I ever wrote, and I never dare touch such passages so long after I have written them. If the grammar has hitherto been bad, please henceforth to consider it good.

> "As Poets of grammar, Lovers are
> The fountains of morality"![2]

May I trespass still further on your kindness by asking you to glance over the inclosed verses of my son,[3] who died lately, aged 22. They seem to me to be of really extraordinary promise and some of them to contain a good deal more than promise. But I must not trust myself in such a case. Do you think them good enough to publish, or shall I follow my present impression that it will be better to print only a few copies for his & my friends?

Yours very truly
Coventry Patmore
Rev. Gerard Hopkins.

[1] This volume was not published.
[2] *The Angel in the House*, Book I, Canto xi, Preludes, ii (1906, p. 65).
[3] For photograph and further detail about Henry Patmore (1860–24 Feb. 1883), see Champneys, i, chap. xxi.

14 November 1883 to Coventry Patmore

FL, no. CLXXIII, p. 335 Durham University Library, Abbott MS 191
Single folded sheet watermarked A PIRIE & SONS. Written on three sides.

Stonyhurst. Nov. 14 1883.

My dear Mr. Patmore, — I beg to acknowledge with thanks the receipt of the MS of your son's poetry. I will read and return it you as soon as I can. I hope also to send some remarks on the Unknown Eros: what I was going to add on the Study can wait. My time is besides short.

As for vowel alliteration, it is clearly not for you to accommodate your ear to mine. Besides if you do not agree with me now, it is likely there is some fundamental difference and we do not hear alike.

~~In~~ ^About^ that new prosody according to which I think English ~~po~~ verse might be written and by which Bridges has written parts of Prometheus, as well as some earlier poems, the most beautiful, I think, "Snow in London", I do not know that Bridges shares all my views; he would, I think, treat it as less strict than I should say it ought to be and has been freer in putting strong syllables in weak places and weak in strong ~~sometimes~~ than always pleases my ear.[1] As I look at it, it is a simple thing and capable of being ~~written~~ drawn up in a few strict rules, stricter, not looser than the common prosody. But though the rules would be few and strict, the freedom of motion in the rhythm gained under them would, as I believe, be very great. The converse at all events you will agree to and would insist on, that where there is much freedom of motion the laws which limit it should be strict.

Believe me yours very sincerely Gerard M. Hopkins S.J.

[1] See the note on the new prosody prefaced to Bridges's *Poems*, 3rd series (1880).

15 [12] November 1883 to *Nature*

CRWD, p. 161
Letter contributed to *Nature*, vol. 29, published 15 November 1883, p. 55.[1]

Shadow-Beams in the East at Sunset

The phenomenon of beams of shadow meeting in the east at sunset, treated of in the pages of NATURE some months since (at which time you did me the honour of inserting a letter of mine), was beautifully witnessed here to-day and yesterday. Both days were unusually clear; there was, nevertheless, a 'body' in the air, without which the propagation of the beams could not take place. Yesterday the sky was striped with cirrus cloud like the swaths of a hayfield; only in the east there was a bay or reach of clear blue sky, and in this the shadowbeams appeared, slender, colourless, and radiating every way like a fan wide open. This lasted from 3.30 to about 4.30. To-day the sky was cloudless, except for a low bank in the west; in the east was a 'cast' of blue mist, from which sprang alternate broad bands of rose colour and blue, slightly fringed. I was not able to look for them till about 4.30, when the sun was down, and they soon faded. I have not before seen this appearance so far north, but on the south coast, where I first saw it, I think it might often be witnessed. It is merely an effect of perspective, but a strange and beautiful one.

Stonyhurst College, November 12 GERARD HOPKINS

[1] One of a series of four letters to *Nature*: 16 Nov. 1882, 15 [12] Nov. 1883, 3 Jan. 1884 [21 Dec. 1883], and 30 [19] Oct. 1884.

19 November 1883 from Richard Watson Dixon to GMH

CRWD, no. XXX A, p. 117 Campion Hall, D 19/11/83
Addressed to 'The Rev^{d}. | Gerard Hopkins S.J. | Stonyhurst, | Blackburn'. PM CARLISLE NO 20 83, PRESTON NO 20 83, WHALLEY NO 21 83.

Hayton Vicarage. Carlisle | 19 Nov. 1883

My dear Friend,

I have kept you so long without answer, that I feel it impossible not to write now, though for aught I have to say I might have written long since.

Your opinion of Mano is not so favourable as I wish: & I do not know how to meet your main objection: but so far as I can judge myself, there should be a central motive in faith (in its human aspect fidelity) struggling with fate or accident & misunderstanding. I fear that this is not made apparent enough, since both you & Mr. Patmore have felt the same lack of something. With regard to Mano's conduct in the last scene, your objection never occurred to me. Perhaps you are right.

To turn to something else. I have lately written an account of Ireland in the reign of Edward vi for the third volume of my Church History. Do you happen to have any records of your Society at Stonyhurst bearing on that period? There were some Missionaries there, who were spoken of by Archb. Browne of Dublin in a sermon in 1551 or 1552. And there was a blind bishop, often called "the blind Scot" in State Papers, whose name was Waucop, Lat. Venantius, who was provided to Armagh when Cromer died, about 1542.[1] He was a doctor of Paris, present at Trent, and a remarkable man. He had a good deal to do with your Society, & I think lived in it at Paris at one time. I believe he died in Ireland about 1551.

You may possibly have heard from Bridges that I am about to leave Hayton for Warkworth, in Northumberland: to which the Bishop of Carlisle has presented me. I suppose I shall be there before Christmas.[2]

Do not take any trouble about the records. There are the names of some early members of your Order, who were in Ireland at that time, in one of the histories that I have here. They seem Spanish or Italian names. If nothing particular is known, I could not add to what I have said. But the history of the Society altogether in these isles is very little known: & I hope, as I go on, to do some sort of justice to its heroic devotion, even if the cause be not wholly my own.

I see, on looking at your letter again, that your judgment is not fully settled on Mano. What you say in praise of it is very gratifying. Can you send me anything of your own? Bridges has spoken of some not long since done.

I am ever
Your affectionate Friend
R. W. Dixon

[1] On the death of George Cromer (d. 1543) the Pope appointed Robert Waucop to the See of Armagh while Henry VIII appointed George Dowdall (1487–1558). Waucop, who was indeed called Venantius, was a Scot and blind and a learned graduate of the Sorbonne, died in 1551 and seems to have been Prelate only in title, but he is credited with introducing the Jesuits to Ireland in 1541.

[2] RWD was inducted in Warkworth Church on 30 Nov. 1883.

23–5 November 1883 to Coventry Patmore

FL, no. CLXXIV, p. 335 Durham University Library, Abbott MS 192
One folded sheet and two half sheets watermarked A PIRIE & SONS, written on seven sides.

Stonyhurst. Nov. 23 1883.

My dear Mr. Patmore, — In your son Henry you have lost a mind not only of wonderful promise but even of wonderful achievement. In the poems you have kindly lent me there may indeed be found some few immaturities, many expressions the ~~eh~~ echos of yours and one or two perhaps of those of other poets, and the thought, both in its spontaneous play and also from the channel of reading and education it had of course run in, such as well to mark the writer ~~as~~ ^for^ his father's son; still the general effect of their perusal is astonishment at a mind so mature, so masculine, so fresh, and so fastidiously independent: "sed erat" as the Breviary says of St. Agnes "senectus mentis immense" {*but in her immense wisdom she was old*}.[1] It is no disparagement to see in this (what I have seen in a remarkable degree in a young child) the unnatural maturity of consumption and the clearsightedness of approaching death, forestalling by the refinement of the body what would otherwise have come with years.

What first strikes in the poems is the spontaneous thoughtfulness, the utter freedom from the poetical fashion and poetical cant of this age and all that wilderness of words which one is lost in in every copy of ~~mag~~ magazine verses one comes across. Your example was however here a natural safeguard. The love of paradox, carried even to perversity, is due ~~to~~ also to his birth or his breeding. The disdainful avoidance of ~~all~~ affectation and vulgar effect leads sometimes ~~even~~ to the ineffective, as in the last couplet of the ^lines^ "O for that afternoon": he wd. have come to feel this. To me the three most beautiful ^pieces^ seem to be the sunset-poem,[2] the lines on Flora's violin,[3] and the Prologue.[4]

But if the poems have ^a^ shortcoming beyond points of detail it would be in flow, in the poetical impetus, and also in richness of diction: they are strong where this age is weak — I mean Swinburn and the popular poets and, I may say, Tennyson himself —, in thought and insight, but they are weak where the age is strong. He might have strengthened in this respect with growth or have compensated for the want by weight and mastery of thought, but I have an impression that, had he lived, he wd. have laid his chief stress elsewhere than in poetry. Naturally, being who he was, to ~~come~~ ^write^ poetry came to him first; his mind had been cradled in it; and even the metres he employs are those he was familiar with in you. But it seems to me, though it may look strained, that nowhere in those poems is there such a stroke of genius as the title to the piece on sunset.[5] I shd. say he had, and would have found himself to have, a command of prose style by which he could have achieved more even than by ~~his~~ that of poetry. The finest prose style is, in English at least, rarer, I should say, than the finest poetical.

About publishing I do not know what to advise. The poems are not likely to have any wide success; they would be caviare to the general — even of such readers as if their bulk were greater would be taken hold of by them; for in such a matter bulk counts. On the other hand it is sad that ~~his~~ such a mind should not have its record and that those who would be drawn ~~in~~to communion with it should ~~not~~ lose the opportunity.

One thing I should like to say. If the poems are published I suppose a memoir or notice of some sort would be prefixed, such perhaps as appeared with the Sunset-piece in the Athenaeum[6] and elsewhere. It was there said, and you repeated the same thing in speaking to me, that your son had, though idle, easily carried off the first prizes and places among his schoolfellows, his fellow students. You seemed to say this in his praise, but it is not to his praise. It is a fault which now he must repent of, and he would not wish his mind honoured at the expense of his will. I cannot see why that circumstance need be mentioned* [*GMH footnote*: * unless indeed it were by way of apology or reparation.] and in naming the matter, if you will pardon me, I seem to be doing what is friendly to his memory. I said mass for him ~~the other~~ ^yesterday^ morning.

I will return the packet very shortly. Believe me, dear Mr. Patmore, yours very sincerely Gerard M. Hopkins S.J.

Nov. 25 1883.

[1] The feast of St Agnes, who suffered martyrdom at the age of 13, is celebrated on 21 Jan. The Breviary says: 'Infanta quidem computabitur in annis, sed erat senectus mentis immensa' {*Childhood is computed in years but in her immense wisdom she was old.*}

[2] 'Lament of one who could go out only in a bath-chair, the doctor recommending the morning; but once, being out on a January afternoon, he felt some sadness at tasting a pleasure which he had almost forgotten.'

[3] The poem beginning:

> Love feels the breath with joy again
> Of moments when to breathe was pain.

[4] 'Prologue to Poems Mostly Unwritten'.

[5] See n. 2 above.

[6] The issue of 10 Mar. 1883. The short memoir is: 'The papers announce the death of a very young man, who was justly admired among a small private circle for his unusual attainments, and who could not have failed to have obtained a far wider fame had he lived a few years longer. Henry Patmore, son of Mr. Coventry Patmore, was educated at the college of St. Cuthbert, Ushaw, and he carried off year by year all its highest honours, and this with so much ease that he had the reputation of being the first in idleness as well as in talent and learning. He had an extraordinary poetic faculty, but little or no ambition to be known. Only two or three very short pieces have reached the public eye.'

26 November 1883 from Coventry Patmore to GMH

FL, no. CLXXIV A, p. 338 Campion Hall, P 26/11/83
Addressed to 'Rev[d]. Gerard Hopkins | Stonyhurst College, | Blackburn'. PM HASTINGS NO 27 83, BLACKBURN NO 28 83, WHALLEY NO 28 83.

Hastings. Nov. 26. 1883.
My dear Sir,

I need not tell you how much delight your opinion of my sons poems gives me. It almost confirms me, too, in the intention I have been lately forming of incorporating these verses with the new edition of my own poems.[1] From what you say I gather that, in doing so, I should not be at all sacrificing ^to the impulse of natural affection^ the harmony and equality of the whole collection. I should much like, however, to have your opinion on this point.

When I spoke of his "idleness", I only meant in regard of his school studies. He gave time & labour enough to them to carry him through brilliantly, and his idleness was higher work. I never came across a mind of anything like such contemplative power. In confidential talk with me he used to say things that took my breath away. It was like talking with a Saint Theresa or Saint Katherine. I learned more from him than he did from me.[2]

Yours ever truly
Coventry Patmore.

[1] Ten of Henry's poems were printed in the revised edition (third collected edition) of his father's *Poetical Works*, published in 1887. His poems, however, had already, in 1884, been printed at Henry Daniel's press at Oxford, in an edition of 125 copies, with a Biographical Note by Gertrude Patmore, and a further Note by Coventry Patmore.
[2] See n. 1 of letter to CP, 6–7 Dec. 1883.

26 November 1883 from Coventry Patmore to GMH

FL, no. CLXXIV B, p. 339 Campion Hall, P 26/11/83b

Hastings. Nov. 26. [1883]
My dear Sir,

In my note of this morning I omitted to thank you, as I do now, for your kind consideration in offering mass for my son Henry.

In connection, also, with what you say about his prose writing, I should have remarked that you are quite right in your ~~impressions~~ ^inferences^ from the few lines at the head of the Sunset poem. When he was between 18 & 19 he wrote a Greek story[1] which is not like anything in recent writing except Landor — of whom he had never read a word: — cold and severe outside, but white-hot within.

He wrote, also, a criticism, in the "Spectator", on the translators of Horace,[2] which for weight & sobriety of style was wonderful, considering his age.

Yours ever truly
C. Patmore

[1] Gertrude Patmore, in her small memoir of Henry, says of this: 'his time was chiefly taken up with a Grecian love tale, delicate and beautiful in thought, and executed in a powerful and original style'. It was called 'Anthusa'.
[2] *Spectator*, 19 Feb. 1881. An anonymous review of *Horace's Odes, Englished and Imitated by Various Hands*. Selected and edited by Charles W. F. Cooper. In the *Spectator* for 24 Dec. 1881 was printed Henry Patmore's 'Aglaia', and in the issue of 12 Aug. 1882, his 'Flora'.

6–7 December 1883 to Coventry Patmore

FL, no. CLXXV, p. 339 Durham University Library, Abbott MS 193
One large folded sheet and a half sheet, six sides.

Stonyhurst, Blackburn. Dec. 6 1883

My dear Mr. Patmore, — I was much afraid after my last letter that the words about idleness would have given you ~~just~~ pain and by their coarseness justly displeased you: this does not seem to have been the case and they were written moreover, as I see, under a misconception.

The thought of your son's poems being bound up with yours had struck me already. I did not name ~~I~~ it, because I did not at all know that you would like it. One or two perhaps are unsuited for publication: the Dream at least, being a trifle and of a passing interest, I should think he would not have printed himself. It is, to be sure, quaint and quaintly told, but then the vein ought to be worked longer to make it worth much.

What you say of your talk with your son is almost the very words of St. Austin about his son Adeodatus, who died at much the same age, I think.[1]

I send some remarks on the First Part of the Unknown Eros.[2]

The Proem, 4th line:[3] ~~wh~~ would not Cai[a]phas' words be more forcible without inversion? Milton produces such splendid effects by the very words of the Scripture, as in "Dust shalt thou eat all the days of thy life".[4]

~~The~~ ^St.^ Valentine p. 15[5] — I do not understand how May should be feminine unless Earth is to be masculine, and that is against all usage and the nature of the case and even the context. May is indeed a female name in English, but that is little difficulty. It looks to me like an oversight. I had to struggle with Bridges over something of the sort.

Winter — The rhymes in this piece (I have not examined the others in the same way) are the most scattered, I should think, ~~had ever~~ that could anywhere be found in English. Most p. 20 is, to speak musically, a 17th, green p. 22 a 19th.[6] No bad effect is produced by this, but then ~~I think a few~~ an unrhymed line here and there would not be noticed and I cannot satisfy myself that any effect ^at all^ is produced, that is to say that one hears the rhyme at that distance at all; yet I dare say ~~it is~~ ^one does^ really and make no objection to the execution of ~~an~~ a kind of art of which you are the master; I only remark the facts. But about the last line I am in great doubt: if I were commenting on you as an ancient classic I should swear you meant what I am going to say, but as you can tell me if I am wrong I ~~have some doubt~~ ^hesitate^; for it is most true what Newman says, that we are never so sure of ~~what~~ ^a thing that^ allows of immediate verification. Do you not then mean this? —

Of ether, moved by ether only, or
By
somethíng
stíll
more
tranquíl — ?

Each word rhyming. And if so would it not be better to print it as above?[7] for I ~~ha~~ am sure three readers out of ~~five~~ ^four^ will miss it altogether. To me the effect is charming and yet I do not feel certain the effect is after all not mine.

Felicia — I do not understand the name. Is it a ~~woman's~~ ^proper^ name or the neuter plural of felix? If the latter I do not see the exact point.[8]

Tristitia — This poem will assuredly be prized, even in ~~this~~ ^such a^ volume; yet it troubles me, for it seems to ~~be~~ ^me^ perverse and founded on ~~wh~~ an unreality. For first, taking all quite in earnest, as we must, we know that the blessed cannot mar their bliss by any grief, so that no promise is needed. Then the case supposed seems to be what they call a 'Spanish Case', one that cannot arise. A heathen, one who lived in the twilight of natural reason only, may be sentenced, I understand well enough, to the twilight of a sort of natural felicity; but a Christian, having light must, if he sinned, have sinned against light. For it is an intolerable doctrine, though many writers and preachers and even Newman in his well known sermon about Demas have* [*GMH footnote:* * I hope he does not, he only seems ~~at~~ to; still that is the superficial impression left.] countenanced it, that a man may somehow sin mortally by no particular mortal sin.[9] There would be no peace, no reasonable trust and hope possible if this were so. You seem besides to have given the antidote to that thought in the passage in the Angel in the House "Him most, but her most sensibly" and the rest.[10] What "gracious-seeming sin"[11] of ~~lo~~ inordinate love towards a wife could a man commit that would not fall under one of the Commandments? In which case it would have some obvious turpitude. We have in fact the case and it is the most famous of all cases. Adam sinned by love of his wife, that is he sinned for, ~~as~~ or through love of his wife; but, formally speaking, the sin was ~~the~~ one of disobedience and its act eating the apple. To him no doubt it seemed gracious, chivalrous, as we should say, to share Eve's fate; he even thought God would look at it in this light; but to us, the circumstances considered, the act appears grievous, selfish, for it ruined a race for the sake of two, ungenerous — that is towards God, and even its seeming chivalry was all gone within a[n] hour, when he said 'The woman thou gavest me' and so on. We must take your poem then as the lovely expression of an overstrained mood and, what is so common, an insight coupled with an oversight. But could this any way be indicated, so as to warn the reader?

Ought not the Azalea and the next poem to be transposed? The reader passes ~~in~~ through the same fluctuations as the ~~speaker~~ writer or speaker, but ends in believing the heroine is dead: then it should come after Departure.[12]

1867 — "Their Jew": this is a hard saying, all politics apart.[13] Many people speak so, but I cannot see how they can be justified. For Jew must be a reproach either for religion or for race. It cannot be for religion here, for Disraeli[14] was not by religion a Jew: he had been baptized ~~a~~ young and had always professed Christianity. His Christianity was a shadowy thing, I know, but so is that of thousands. If he believed in anyone I suppose that was Christ and did not, as Jews do, 'look for another'. It must then be for race. But that is no reproach but a glory, for Christ was a Jew. You will I know say that this dilemma is as fallacious a[s] most dilemmas are and that Jew is a reproach because the Jews have corrupted their race and nature, ~~and~~ ^so^ that it is their vices and their free acts we stigmatise when we call cheating 'jewing' — and that you mean that Disraeli in 1871 overreached and jewed his constituents. But what you say is wider than that and will be so taken and therefore it will sound unjust and passionate, the more as time goes on. For other things happened after 1867 and it is a very common feeling, even among those who in his lifetime opposed or detracted from Lord Beaconsfield, that he, of all eminent statesmen, was truly devoted to and truly promoted the honour of England; that he, a Jew born, was above all things a British patriot. This is the meaning of the primrose worship~~.~~ that goes on.

I think there is a great discrepancy of feeling in this volume — from this piece for instance and the Merry Murder,[15] which amount to animosity, to the ~~deep~~ ^sweet^ inward pathos and ^tears of^ devotion ~~of~~ ^in^ Victory in Defeat.

P. 75. "Stopp'd to stretch his legs" seems used contrary to idiom. It is rather 'rest his legs' you mean: it is people cramped by long sitting who stretch their legs.[16]

P. 77 — I wonder who is that "better Bard". Is it one of the Prophets?[17]

The rest as soon as I can. Believe me, dear Mr. Patmore, yours very sincerely Gerard Hopkins S.J.

Dec. 7.

P.S. P. 87. "Listener's": why the apostrophe?[18]

[1] Adeodatus, Augustine's brilliant son, died at the age of 16 in 388. See *Confessions*, bk. 9, section VI. E. B. Pusey's translation (1838) of the relevant section says: 'We joined with us the boy Adeodatus, born after the flesh, of my sin. Excellently hadst

Thou made him. He was not quite fifteen, and in wit surpassed many grave and learned men. I confess unto Thee Thy gifts, O Lord my God, Creator of all, and abundantly able to reform our deformities: for I had no part in that boy, but the sin. For that we brought him up in Thy discipline, it was Thou, none else, had inspired us with it. I confess unto Thee Thy gifts. There is a book of ours entitled The Master; it is a dialogue between him and me. Thou knowest that all there ascribed to the person conversing with me were his ideas, in his sixteenth year. Much besides, and yet more admirable, I found in him. That talent struck awe into me.'

[2] In the section of this letter where GMH makes remarks on the poetry, Patmore has noted whether he has acted on the suggestion or not, marking 'Done' or 'O' against each point. The 'Done' marks are against the comments on the 'Proem' and 'Felicia'.

[3] Unaltered (1906, p. 269): 'Expedient 'twas for all that One should die'.

[4] *Paradise Lost*, IX.178: 'And dust shalt eat all the days of thy Life.' GMH quotes the *AV* version of Genesis 3: 14, which would have been the version Milton used.

[5] Unaltered (1906, p. 274).

[6] In the poem 'Winter' as it appeared in Patmore's *Poems* (London, 1909), 276–7, the word 'most' (l. 3) rhymes with 'crost' (l. 19) and is thus seventeen lines apart (counting both ends, as in music); 'green' (l. 34) is likewise nineteen lines away from its rhyme 'seen' (l. 16). That distance in both poetry and music, is outside the norm.

[7] Unaltered (1906, p. 277):

the sphere
Of ether, moved by ether only, or
By something still more tranquil.

Frederick Page pointed out to Abbott that Patmore's comment on these verses ('It satisfied my ear; so I left it as it is': see next letter) is curious, because he had in mind a sentence from J. J. Garth Wilkinson's *Life of Swedenborg*, 1847, in which Wilkinson alluding to Swedenborg's imperturbability writes: 'The ether can only be moved by the ether, or by something still more movingly tranquil.'

[8] 'Felicia' became 'Beata' (1906, p. 278).

[9] In his 'Hopkins and Newman: Two Disagreements', *Christianity and Literature*, 57/3 (Spring 2008), 401–18, Fredric W. Schlatter discusses this point and suggests the sermon is Newman's 'The Duty of Self-denial', a sermon delivered in 1830 and printed in various editions of *Parochial and Plain Sermons* between 1834 and 1869.

[10] *The Angel in the House*, Book I, Canto X, 'Going to Church', 4 (1906, p. 62): 'Him [God] loved I most, But her I loved most sensibly.'

[11] vi, 'Tristitia', unaltered (1906, p. 281):

If thou alone should'st win
God's perfect bliss,
And I, beguiled by gracious-seeming sin,
Say, loving too much thee,
Love's last goal miss, . . .

[12] Order unaltered.

[13] xiii, 1867. Unaltered (1906, p. 291):

In the year of the great crime,
When the false English Nobles and their Jew,
By God demented, slew
The Trust they stood twice pledged to keep from wrong, . . .

[14] Benjamin Disraeli, Earl of Beaconsfield (1804–81; *ODNB*), British prime minister in 1868 and 1874–80, of Jewish descent but baptized as an Anglican in

1817. Egotistic, elitist, and charismatic, he was only rivalled by Gladstone as the most fascinating politician of the 19th c. For GMH he was everything in a national leader and politician that Gladstone was not. See letters of 30 Sept. 1867 and 14 May 1881.

[15] This title became '1880–85' (1906, xvii, p. 299). The poem is much altered and shortened.

[16] Ibid. (1906, p. 300):

> Should take the man who stopp'd to stretch his legs

became

> Should take the laggard who would stretch his legs.

[17] This phrase disappeared. Patmore had applied a version of 'il miglior fabbro' {*the better craftsman*}, the description of Arnaut Daniel in Dante's *Purgatorio* (26. 117), to Dante himself. See next letter.

[18] The apostrophe disappears.

9 December 1883 from Coventry Patmore to GMH

FL, no. CLXXV A, p. 344 Campion Hall, P 9/12/83
Addressed to 'Rev^{d}. Gerard Hopkins, S.J. | Stonyhurst College, | Blackburn'. PM HASTINGS DE 10 83, BLACKBURN DE 11 83, WHALLEY DE 11 83.

Hastings. Dec. 9. 1883.

My dear Sir,

I agree with almost all your criticisms on the Unknown Eros, but I fear that some of the most important cannot be acted on simply because they are so important. I dont feel up to any thing much beyond merely verbal corrections. In my present state of poetical incapacity — which has lasted for two or three years, & may probably be permanent, I could only act on your very just objections by extinguishing the poems affected with the faults you point out, which I should be loth to do, though, of course, I would do so, if the balance of good seemed to require it. But I think "Tristitia" may pass as the ^harmless^ expression of a poetic mood. That the "Merry Murder" exceeds the bounds of poetry I felt at the time I wrote it. The political action and inaction of England — her ministers & her people — during the last twenty years or more fill me with an actual thirst for vengeance — such vengeance as I have felt towards myself in former times, when I have asked with ardour that I might not go unpunished. And the greater life of the nation has created a proportionate indignation in me, and I ^sometimes^ long for some hideous catastrophe — though I & mine should be involved in it — which should wake the country from its more hideous [*illegible deletion*] sleep. I cannot see that the feeling is uncharitable since it bears the test of being applied to myself in like conditions; but I see that the expression of the feeling is not for verse. It is not among the "thoughts that voluntary move harmonious numbers".[1]

I hate (in all charity) Lord Beaconsfield more, if possible, than I hate Gladstone, and ^"Jew" or^ <u>any</u> stone seemed good enough to throw at such a dog. He had a strong dramatic sense of what a statesman ought to be (wh. Gladstone has not) and therefore is more to be blamed for abandoning all principle as soon as it conflicted with his personal interest. Do you remember the <u>details</u> of the passage of his Reform Bill in 1867? How it began by being a real work of defence against the tide of revolution, and how it ended — rather than Mr. Disraeli should go out of office — in actually consummating the revolution wh. the Radicals were only dreaming of?

"Better Bard" means Dante, who saw that Charity was not for the damned, and rejoiced in adding ~~actively~~ to the icy tears of the wretch who begged for news of the world he had left.

I used the name "Felicia" because it is a name, and suggests itself as the female of Felix. "Felicitas" would not have done. I will try for a better name.[2]

I do not think that the rhymes in the form of the Ode can be too much scattered, but, to compensate for the scattering they should be so numerous as to be always felt; and I am aware that in some of the Odes this condition has not been sufficiently attended to.

I had no especial intention in the seemingly anomalous metrical conclusion of "Winter". It satisfied my ear; so I left it as it is.

I believe you are right about the relative order of the "Azalea" & "Departure". I will see to it.

Yours ever truly
C. Patmore.
Rev. Gerard Hopkins, S.J.

[1] Milton, *Paradise Lost*, Bk. III, ll. 37–8.
[2] He chose Beata instead.

3 January 1884 [21 December 1883] to *Nature*

CRWD, pp. 162–6
Letter contributed to *Nature*, vol. 29, 3 January 1884, pp. 222–3.[1]

The Remarkable Sunsets

The body of evidence now brought in from all parts of the world must, I think, by this time have convinced Mr. Piazzi Smyth that the late sunrises and sunsets do need some explanation, more particular than he was willing to give them. With your leave I should like to point out from my own observations and those of others that, 'given a clear sky' and the other conditions put by Mr. Smyth, the sunrises and sunsets of other days, however bright and beautiful, have *not* given any such effects as were witnessed, to take an instance, here on Sunday night, December 16th. I shall speak chiefly of the sunsets.[2]

(1.) *These sunsets differ from others, first in their time and their place or quarter.* Sunset proper is, I suppose, the few minutes between the first dipping and the last disappearance of the sun's disk below the true horizon; the pageant or phenomena we call sunset, however, includes a great deal that goes on before and after this. The remarkable and specific features of the late sunsets have not been before or at sunset proper; they have been after-glows, and have lasted long, very long, after. To take instances from your number of the 13th ult., Mr. F. A. R. Russell notices that on November 28th, the sun having set at 3.55, one after-glow lasted till 5.10, and was then succeeded by another 'reaching high above the horizon'. The day before he mentions the after-glow as lasting to 5.20. On the 29th a 'foreglow' is reported as seen in London from 5.30 to 7.30, that is more than two hours before sunrise, which was at 7.43. On December 1st, sunset being at 3.53, Mr. Russell observed an after-glow till 5.35; on December 4th the first dawn at 6.5, the sun rising at 7.50; the next day dawn at the same time, sunrise 7.51; that evening, sunset being at 3.50, he observed not a glow only but 'spokes of rays from the glowing bank' at 4.45, that is to say, sunbeams, visible in the shape of sunbeams, 55 minutes after sunset. Mr. Johnston-Lavis speaks of the after glow at Naples as *at a maximum* an hour after sunset. Here at Stonyhurst on December 16th, the sun having set at 3.49, the glow was observed till 5.50. Now winter dawns and after-glows do not last from an hour to two hours, and still less so day after day, as these have done. The recent sunrises and sunsets then differ from others in duration.

They differ also in the quarter of the heavens where they are seen. The after-glows are not low lingering slips of light skirting the horizon, but high up in the sky, sometimes in the zenith.

I have further remarked that the deepest of the after-glow is in the south, whereas the sun below the horizon, is then northing. I see that other observers take notice of the same.

(2) *They differ in their periodic action or behaviour.* The flushes of crimson and other colours after ordinary sunsets are irregular, not the same nor at the same time for two days together; for they depend upon the accidental shapes and sizes and densities of the cloud-banks or

vapour-banks the sun is entering or freeing himself from, which vary and can never be alike from day to day. But these glows or flushes are noticed to be periodic before sunrise and after sunset. Mr. Russell furnishes exact estimates of the intervals of time, which he finds to be the same day after day.

(3) *They differ in the nature of the glow, which is both intense and lustreless*, and that both in the sky and on the earth. The glow is intense, this is what strikes every one; it has prolonged the daylight, and optically changed the season; it bathes the whole sky, it is mistaken for the reflection of a great fire; at the sundown itself and southwards from that on December 4, I took a note of it as more like inflamed flesh than the lucid reds of ordinary sunsets. On the same evening the fields facing west glowed as if overlaid with yellow wax.

But it is also lustreless. A bright sunset lines the clouds so that their brims look like gold, brass, bronze, or steel. It fetches out those dazzling flecks and spangles which people call fish-scales. It gives to a mackerel or dappled cloudrack the appearance of quilted crimson silk, or a ploughed field glazed with crimson ice. These effects may have been seen in the late sunsets, but they are not the specific after-glow; that is, without gloss or lustre.

The two things together, that is intensity of light and want of lustre, give to objects on the earth the peculiar illumination which may be seen in studios and other well-like rooms, and which itself affects the practice of painters and may be seen in their works, notably Rembrandt's, disguising or feebly showing the outlines and distinctions of things, but fetching out white surfaces and coloured stuffs with a rich and inward and seemingly self-luminous glow.

(4) *They differ in the regularity of their colouring*. Four colours in particular have been noticeable in these after-glows, and in a fixed order of time and place — orange, lowest and nearest the sundown; above this, and broader, green; above this, broader still, a variable red, ending in being crimson; above this a faint lilac. The lilac disappears; the green deepens, spreads and encroaches on the orange; and the red deepens, spreads, and encroaches on the green, till at last one red, varying downwards from crimson to scarlet or orange fills the west and south. The four colours I have named are mentioned in Lieut. G. N. Bittleson's letter from Umballa:[3] 'The sun goes down as usual and it gets nearly dark, and then a bright red and yellow and green and purple blaze comes in the sky and makes it lighter again.' I suppose the yellow here spoken of to be an orange yellow, and the purple to be what I have above called lilac.

Ordinary sunsets have not this order; this, so to say, fixed and limited palette. The green in particular, is low down when it appears. There is often a trace of olive between the sundown and the higher blue sky, but it never develops, that I remember, into a fresh green.

(5) *They differ in the colours themselves, which are impure and not of the spectrum.* The first orange and the last crimson flush are perhaps pure, or nearly so, but the two most remarkable glows, the green and the red, are not. The green is between an apple-green or pea-green (which are pure greens) and an olive (which is tertiary colour): it is vivid and beautiful, but not pure. The red is very impure, and not evenly laid on. On the 4th it appeared brown, like a strong light behind tortoiseshell, or Derbyshire alabaster. It has been well compared to the colour of incandescent iron. Sometimes it appears like a mixture of chalk with sand and muddy earths. The pigments for it would be ochre and Indian red.

Now the yellows, oranges, crimsons, purples, and greens of bright sunsets are beautifully pure. Tertiary colours may of course also be found in certain cases and places.

(6) *They differ in the texture of the coloured surfaces*, which are neither distinct cloud of recognised make nor yet translucent mediums. Mr. Russell's observations should here be read. I have further noticed streamers, fine ribbing or mackerelling, and other more curious textures, the colour varying with the texture.

In ordinary sunsets the yellows and greens and the lower reds look like glass, or coloured liquids, as pure as the blue. Other colours, or these in other parts, are distinct flushes or illuminations of cloud or landscape.

I subjoin an account of the sunset of the 16th, which was here very remarkable, from my own observations and those of one of the observatory staff.

A bright glow had been round the sun all day and became more remarkable towards sunset. It then had a silvery or steely look, with soft radiating streamers and little colour; its shape was mainly elliptical, the slightly longer axis being vertical; the size about 20° from the sun each way. There was a pale gold colour, brightening and fading by turns for ten minutes as the sun went down. After the sunset the horizon was, by 4.10, lined a long way by a glowing tawny light, not very pure in colour and distinctly textured in hummocks, bodies like a shoal of dolphins, or in what are called gadroons, or as the Japanese conventionally represent waves. The glowing vapour above this was as yet colourless; then this took a beautiful olive or celadon green, not so vivid as the previous day's, and delicately fluted; the green belt was broader than the orange, and pressed down on and contracted it. Above the green in turn appeared a red glow, broader and burlier in make; it was softly brindled, and in the ribs or bars the colour was rosier, in the channels where the blue of the sky shone through it was a mallow colour. Above this was a vague lilac. The red was first noticed 45° above the horizon, and spokes or beams could be seen in it, compared by one beholder to a man's open hand. By 4.45 the red had driven out the green, and, fusing with the remains of the orange, reached the horizon. By that time the east, which had a rose tinge, became of a duller red, compared to sand; according to my observation, the ground of the sky in the east was green or else tawny, and the crimson only in the clouds. A great sheet of heavy dark cloud, with a reefed or puckered make, drew off the west in the course of the pageant: the edge of this and the smaller pellets of cloud that filed across the bright field of the sundown caught a livid green. At 5 the red in the west was fainter, at 5.20 it became notably rosier and livelier; but it was never of a pure rose. A faint dusky blush was left as late as 5.30, or later. While these changes were going on in the sky, the landscape of Ribblesdale glowed with a frowning brown.

The two following observations seem to have to do with the same phenomena and their causes. For some weeks past on fine bright days, when the sun has been behind a big cloud and has sent up (perspectively speaking) the dark crown or paling of beams of shadow in such cases commonly to be seen, I have remarked, upon the ground of the sky, sometimes an amber, sometimes a soft rose colour, instead of the usual darkening of the blue. Also on moonlight nights, and particularly on December 14, a sort of brown or muddy cast, never before witnessed, has been seen by more than one observer, in the sky.

GERARD HOPKINS.

Stonyhurst College, December 21, 1883

[1] One of a series of four letters to *Nature*: 16 Nov. 1882, 15 [12] Nov. 1883, 3 Jan. 1884 [21 Dec. 1883], and 30 [19] Oct. 1884.

[2] See letter to Bridges of 1 Jan. 1885. The present letter, contained in the issue of 3 Jan. 1884, is part of a considerable correspondence in *Nature* on 'The Remarkable Sunsets', and is prefixed by an editorial note on the evidence about them and their cause that was rapidly being collected. Krakatoa, a small volcanic island between Java and Sumatra, a crater partly submerged in the sea, erupted 26–8 Aug. 1883, blowing most of the island to pieces, and several new islets were formed from the debris. For some months afterwards there were very fine sunsets, caused by the reflection downwards of the sun's rays from the upper atmosphere after sunset, this upper air over most of the world being affected by volcanic dust.

Professor C. Piozzi Smyth, the Astronomer Royal for Scotland, published a letter on the same topic in *Nature*, vol. 29 13 Dec. 1883, pp. 149–50, in which he wrote in a somewhat self-satisfied tone that the sunsets are quite unexceptional and that their like could have been witnessed by anyone who, like him, had cared to look for them. F. A. R. Russell wrote a lengthy set of notes on pp. 150–2 of the same issue. The 'NOTES' on p. 157 of the issue of 13 Dec. 1883 say that 'our readers in all parts of the world will render a service if they will communicate any similar facts they may have observed, giving, as far as possible, accurate dates'. It was not at this stage absolutely certain that Krakatoa was the cause, but 'In an article in Saturday's *Times*, Mr. Norman Lockyer shows that the body of evidence already to hand connects them with the eruption of Krakatoa'.

[3] Lieutenant G. H. Bittleston's letter was in the issue of 13 Dec. 1883, p. 152.

1884

3 January 1884 to Coventry Patmore

FL, no. CLXXVI, p. 346 Durham University Library, Abbott MS 194
One folded sheet and two half sheets watermarked A PIRIE & SONS, eight sides.

Stonyhurst. Jan. 3 1884.

My dear Mr. Patmore, — I have to wish you a happy and a fruitful new year and to add my last comments, on the second Book of the Unknown Eros, for which I have kept you waiting too long (till perhaps they are too late), but my time at the end of the year has been quite broken.

P. 119. Why "Zion"? Elsewhere pp. 142–144 you have "Sion", which here would alliterate also.[1]

P. 122. "The clearness" etc[2] — I am told some commentators give an interpretation of the text meant much like yours here. To me it seems perverse and ~~to ^a^ nullifying~~ ^a^ bringing of the sign to nothing. So far as I understand, our Lord says that his second coming shall be sudden, surprising, and unforeseen, but when it comes utterly unmistakeable; in that differing from his first coming and all other tokens of himself. However you seem to distinguish the first bid~~ to the feast~~ding to the feast from an^other^, after bidding, both belonging to Christ's second coming, according, I suppose, to Apoc. xx 5. I daresay this ~~inter~~ treatment is as well justified as any and do not wish you to make any alteration, but have spoken because I had marked the passage for comment.

~~Pp. 161~~ Pp. 161, 162, and elsewhere — Thou and you are freely mixed.[3] This is commonly thought a great inelegance and irregularity and, I must own, it seems so to me. Sometimes no doubt there is a reason for it, a subtlety in the change of relations expressed; but the reason ought to be strong to outweigh the obvious slovenliness. It is a lamentable thing that the educated have lost the thou and thee. Here in Lancashire one constantly hears it; but, except in a few common words like dost, wilt and so on, they use the form of the third person with it, as Thou comes. They mix the singular and plural, I think, but that according as they pass from a more to a less familiar address. So I find ~~in~~ too in one of Hardy's novels (or more ~~irreg~~ irregularly still) and also I think in Shakspere. But in a literary style the effect is different and not so available.

P. 167 "Far less" — It seems it should rather be "far more". And why "his wings": surely "her wings" or "its".[4]

This poem and the two next are such a new thing ^and belong to such a new atmosphere^ that I feel it as dangerous to criticise them almost as the Canticles. What I feel least at my ease about is a certain jesting humour, which does not seem to me quite ~~th~~ to hit the mark in this profoundly delicate matter, as for instance at p. 178 "I love him, as none surely e'er could love" etc,[5] which is not far from profane, and p. 180 "Gods in the abstract", and especially the word "well".[6] The last passage at all events admits of some slight rewording. A single touch in such a matter may be "by much too much". I repeated to someone what I had read in the life of St. Theresa or Blessed Margaret Mary,[7] that the saint had been at one time believed possessed and was exorcised and drenched with holy water; our Lord comforted her, telling her that the exorcisms were not directed against him and could do her no harm, and that he liked holy water. This, for a great familiarity, is credible. But I heard my friend repeat it "that he rather liked" etc — which is shocking.

Of the enigmas "Lines parallel" at p. 182 I can make nothing.[8] However I daresay you do not mean me to~~o~~.

Lastly in the "Child's Purchase" you have a refrain "Ora pro me" {*pray for me*}. But I have noticed that the introduction of a foreign phrase or refrain — I would not say a single word — ^into poetry^ invariably has a frigid effect; I nowhere remember an exception. At first hearing it is, I know, taking — vulgarly taking, if I may say so; but it is illegitimate. It destroys the seriousness of the style and makes it maccaronic. If you should on consideration agree with this the correction is easily made, I should think.[9]

As to the political poems in the First Book, I am glad they are to stand, but I wish the reader could be made to understand what you tell me, that they are to be taken historically, as the utterance of your then mood, not every word of which you would now necessarily stand by or, if it were to be done over again, repeat. And in this light the note at p. 56 is the worst offence of all,[10] because it is final and editorial, and yet it expresses as much passion or more than the poem, by the very figure of speech; for literally speaking ~~no one can~~ ^it is not true to^ say that the ~~upper~~ middle and upper classes were disfranchised, it is only in practical result that this could be ~~true~~ ^the case^. (By the by the poem contains something like its own refutation. It says what is most insightedly true, that the Best were best by exercise of their ^high^ functions and, as you once wrote elsewhere, "by having borne ~~it w~~ it well in mind"~~,~~: then it would seem that the lowest would be raised by having high functions entrusted to them. However I do not want to controvert,~~)~~ especially as I scarcely dispute the facts.)

There was some sort of a competitive examination held, I see, the other day with a prize for the best arrangement of living English writers in prose and verse: the winning selection and several others were printed in the Spectator. I think the prizewinner put Browning at the head of his list. In most lists Tennyson, Ruskin, Newman, Matthew Arnold, and Browning got high places. I saw your name nowhere. Indeed I believe you were not in the running. And when I read Remembered Grace, The Child's Purchase, Legem Tuam Dilexi and others of this volume I sigh to think that it is all one almost to be too full of meaning and to have none and to see very ~~high~~ ^deep^ and not to see at all, for nothing so profound as these can be found in the poets of this age, scarcely of any; and yet they are but little ~~un~~known and when the papers ~~gift~~ ^give^ a list of the contemporary English poets your name does not appear. And so I used to feel of Duns Scotus[11] when I used to read him with delight: he saw too far, he knew too much; his subtlety overshot his interests; a kind of feud ~~arises~~ ^arose^ between genius and talent, and the ruck of talent in the Schools finding ~~themselves~~ ^itself^, as his age passed by, less and less able to understand him, voted that there was nothing important to understand and so ^first^ misquoted and then refuted him. But I must conclude. Believe me, dear Mr. Patmore, yours very sincerely Gerard Hopkins S.J.

[1] This change was made. Patmore again marks the letter with either an 'O' or the word 'Done'. He wrote 'Done' beside the suggestions for pp. 119, 161–2, 167, and on the 'jesting humour'.

[2] *The Unknown Eros*, Book II. iv, *The Standards*. Unaltered (1906, p. 319):

> But know,
> The clearness then so marvellously increas'd,
> The light'ning shining Westward from the East,
> Is the great promised sign
> Of His victorious and divine
> Approach, whose coming in the clouds shall be,
> As erst was His humility,
> A stumbling unto some, the first bid to the Feast.

GMH refers to Revelation 20: 5, which says: 'But the rest of the dead lived not, till the thousand years were finished. This is the first resurrection' (Douay–Reims version).

[3] Ibid., Book II, xii, *Eros and Psyche*. The difficulty is avoided by making Psyche use consistently the singular pronouns and Eros the plural.

[4] Ibid.

> 'Tis hard for fly, in such a honied flood,
> To use his eyes, far less his wings or feet

becomes (1906, p. 340: Psyche is speaking)

> 'Tis hard for fly, in such a honied flood,
> To use her eyes, far more her wings or feet.

[5] Ibid., Book II, xiii. 'De Natura Deorum'. The passage, which is unaltered (1906, p. 345), continues:

> 'Our People's pompous but good-natured Jove.
> *He* used to send me stately overture;
> But marriage-bonds, till now, I never could endure!'

[6] Ibid.

> Gods, in the abstract, are, no doubt, most wise;
> But, in the concrete, well, they're mysteries!

becomes (1906, p. 346)

> Gods, in the abstract, are, no doubt, most wise;
> But, in the concrete, Girl, they're mysteries!

[7] GMH will have been reading a *Life of the Blessed Margaret Mary* by George Tickell, SJ, published in 1869, which recounts on p. 236 how 'She was supposed to be possessed or obsessed by the devil. Some threw holy water upon her, and made the sign of the Cross, to drive away the evil spirit. "But He by Whom I felt myself possessed," she remarks, with simplicity, "far from fleeing away, drew me more powerfully to Himself, saying, I love holy water, and I have so great an affection for the Cross, that I cannot refrain from uniting My self closely with souls who bear it as I did, and for the love of Me."'

[8] Ibid. Unaltered (1906, p. 347):

> Lines parallel meet sooner than some think;
> The least part oft is greater than the whole[.]

[9] Ibid., Book II, xvii. Unchanged.

[10] Ibid., Book I, xiii, 1867. The note ran:

> In this year the middle and upper classes were disfranchised by the Tory Government.

This became later:

> In this year the middle and upper classes were disfranchised by Mr. Disraeli's Government, and the final destruction of the liberties of England by the Act of 1884 rendered inevitable.

[11] See the discussion in *CW* v of GMH's attitude towards and use of Scotus.

5 January 1884 from Coventry Patmore to GMH

FL, no. CLXXVI A, p. 350 Campion Hall, P 5/1/84
Addressed to 'Rev[d]. Gerard Hopkins, S.J. | Stonyhurst College, | Blackburn'. PM HASTINGS JA 6 84, BLACKBURN JA 7 84, WHALLEY 84.

Hastings. January 5. 1884
My dear Sir,

As usual I agree with most of your remarks, though I may not be able to act on all those with which I agree because they would involve an amount of revision which could only be executed in the presence of the feeling which is gone past. All that is written — as far as I recollect — concerning the second coming of Our Lord may be interpreted, as far as concerns this little world in ourselves, by His coming to ^each of^ us <u>in the flesh</u> — that altogether marvellous and convincing sign ^("sudden, surprising, unforeseen, unmistakeable")^[1] destroying His enemies in us, reigning and giving thousandfold life to those in us that were alive; and raising many that were dead, and dreamed not that they would ever be called upon to give Him glory. As far as regards the greater and outer world, would not the prophecy be fulfilled by some great, authoritative and ~~convincing~~ ^convincing^ teaching of the esoteric doctrine involved in the Blessed Sacrament and whispered all through the Breviary[2] and the services of the Church? This would at once divide the world into two camps — one (containing nearly all learned and respectable people) to whom it would be ruin and a rock of scandal, and who would denounce it as infamous and blasphemous, as the first coming was denounced; the other — most of them Gentiles and not of the visible Church — who would instantly recognize it as the <u>present</u> fulfilment of all their desires? It is said that the Second Coming is as the lightning that shineth from the East (the Spirit) to the West (the flesh); for where the <u>Body</u> is there shall the Eagles ("Christians", according to St. Austin) be gathered together.[3] Our Lord replied to St. Peter "What if I choose that he (St. John) tarry till I come"[4] — words which seem to me to indicate how we are to take the prophecy of the Second Advent.

All this, I say, of course, subject to correction; but the view wholly satisfies me, and seems to me to be the highest and most moving as well as the most intelligible interpretation.

The word "well", p. 180, shall go out. Playfulness is not necessarily irreverent. It may be the highest reverence. But that is a touch beyond playfulness, and verges on the ~~deeply~~ disgusting slang you quote: "He rather liked etc."

Lines 10–14, p. 182 are meant by the Pythoness in a final burst of fun, to puzzle Psyche, not you.

I dont think that "Ora pro me" can be translated. The Ode consists of a somewhat inconsequent sequence of exclamatory sentences, and the strong break, caused by the Latin, helps to hide this fact from the reader.

As to what you note of the paragraph in the "Spectator", I shall not consider myself "out of the running" so long as there are a dozen men in England to think or speak of the "Unknown Eros" as you do. I fancy I must have a cavern in my brain where the love of popularity ought to be — wh. I may say without fear of the retort of "sour grapes", inasmuch as the "Angel" obtained for me, at one time, a very sufficient taste of public applause.

Yours ever truly & gratefully
C. Patmore.

[1] GMH's words. See previous letter.

[2] In the Roman Catholic Church the Breviary is the book comprising the liturgical texts of the Divine Office.

[3] Matthew 24: 28: 'Wheresoever the body shall be, there shall the eagles also be gathered together' (Douay–Reims version).

[4] John 21: 22: 'If I will that he tarry till I come, what is that to thee? follow thou me' (AV).

21 January 1884 from Coventry Patmore to GMH

FL, no. CLXXVI B, p. 351 Campion Hall, P 21/1/84
Addressed to 'Reverend Gerard Hopkins, S.J. | Stonyhurst College, | Blackburn'. PM HASTINGS JA 21 84, BLACKBURN JA 22 84.

Hastings. January 21,[1] 1884
My dear Sir,

Mr Bridges and Mr Gosse have excited much desire in me to see some of your Poems in MS. I have felt somewhat shy of taking the liberty of asking you, but Mr Bridges encourages me to hope that you will not refuse my request.

Yours very truly
C. Patmore
Rev. Gerard Hopkins, S.J.

[1] The date is altered by writing 21 over 18.

20 February 1884 to John Henry Newman

FL, no. XXXV, p. 63 Birmingham Oratory
University College, | 85 and 86, Stephen's Green, | Dublin. [*printed heading*]
Feb. 20 1884.

Your Eminence and Dearest Father, Pax Christi — I wish you a very bright tomorrow and health and happiness and the abundance of God's grace for the ensuing year.

I am writing from where I never thought to be, in a University for Catholic Ireland begun under your leadership, which has since those days indeed long and unhappily languished, but for which we now with God's help hope a continuation or restoration of success. In the events which have brought me here I recognise the hand of providence, but nevertheless have felt and feel an unfitness which ~~made~~ ^led^ me at first ^to^ try to decline the offer made me and now does not yet allow my spirits to rise to the level of the position and its duties. But perhaps the things of most promise with God begin with weakness and fear.

These buildings since you knew them have fallen into a deep dilapidation. They were a sort of wreck or ruin when our Fathers some months since came in and the costly last century ornamentation of flutes and festoons and Muses on the walls ~~are~~ ^is still^ much in contrast with the dinginess and dismantlement all round. Only one thing looks bright, and that no longer belongs to the College, the little Church of your building, the Byzantine style of which reminds me of the Oratory and bears your impress clearly enough.

I should have said in the beginning that I am to convey from Fr. Delany[1] the best wishes of all the College together with my own.

I remain your Eminence's affectionate son in Christ Gerard M. Hopkins S.J.

[1] Fr William Delany (1835–1924; *ODNB*) became President of University College in Oct. 1883. See *WHALB*, pp. 357 ff. and letter to GMH's mother 26 Nov. 1884.

29 February 1884 from John Henry Newman to GMH

FL, no. C26, p. 413 Campion Hall, N 29/2/84 and MS copy in Birmingham Oratory
Addressed to 'The Rev F[r] Hopkins S.J. | 85, 86 Stephen's Green | Dublin'. PM BIRMINGHAM FE 29 84.

Febr 29. 1884
Dear F[r] Hopkins

Thank you for your remembering my birthday and for your kind thoughts upon it.

I hope you find at Dublin an opening for work such as you desire and which suits you. I am sorry you can speak of dilapidation,

Most truly yours
J. H. Card. Newman

6 March 1884 from Coventry Patmore to GMH

FL, no. CLXXVI C, p. 351 Campion Hall, P 6/3/84
Addressed to 'Rev. Gerard Hopkins, S.J. | University College, | 85 & 86 Stephens Green | Dublin'. PM HASTINGS MR 6 84. H&K PACKET MR 7 84.

Hastings. March 6. 1884
My dear M[r] Hopkins,

I have just received your MSS. It may be sometime before you hear from me about them, as I expect to find in them something quite new, and I am conscious of my extreme slowness in taking fully in what is new. I suppose it comes of my all along having followed a single line of my own, that I am really the worst off-hand critic of really new work that I know. But, as one of the Greek poets,[1] I believe, says, "Slow is the wrath of Gods, but in the end not weak," so my judgment, though hard to make up, may rank perhaps with the judgment of the best of the "gallery Gods" when it is made up; for it is founded on the severe and instinctive principles which I believe I owe mainly to my Father's having taught me from my early boyhood a contempt for what is meretricious and a love for all the best models within my reach.

Do you henceforward reside in Dublin, or are you only there to take up your Fellowship?

Yours ever truly
Coventry Patmore.

[1] Aeschylus, *Prometheus Bound*. Patmore uses this paraphrase of an Aeschylean theme three times in his *Courage in Politics and Other Essays 1885–1896* (1921).

7 March 1884 to Robert Bridges

LRB, no. CXI, p. 189 Bodleian, Dep. Bridges, vol. 92, fos. 37–38v

University College, 85 & 86, Stephens Green, Dublin. March 7 1884 [*Printed address with date added by hand*]

My dearest Bridges, — Remark the above address: it is a new departure or a new arrival and at all events a new abode. I dare say you know nothing of it, but the fact is that, though unworthy of and unfit for the post, I have been elected Fellow of the ^Royal^ University of ~~Iel~~ Ireland in the department of classics.[1] I have a salary of £400 a year, but when I first contemplated the six examinations I have yearly to conduct, five of them running, ~~I thought that Ste-~~ and to the Matriculation there came up last year 750 candidates, I thought that Stephen's Green (the biggest square in Europe) paved with gold would not pay for it. It is an honour and an opening and has many bright sides, but at present it has also some dark ones and this in particular that I am not at all strong, not strong enough for the requirements, and do not see at all how I am to be^come^ so. But to talk of weather or health and especially to complain of them is poor work.

The house ~~is~~ we are in, the College, is a sort of ruin and for purposes of study very nearly naked. And I have more money to buy books than room to put them in.

I have been warmly welcomed and most kindly treated. But ~~D?~~ Dublin itself is a ~~u~~joyless place and I think in my heart as smoky as London is: I had fancied it quite different.[2] The Phoenix Park[3] is fine, but inconveniently ~~f?~~ far off. There are a few fine buildings.

It is only a few days since I sent the MS book[4] to Mr. Patmore (and ~~I~~ in packing I mislaid, I hope not lost, your copy of the poem "Wild air, world-mothering air",[5] so that I had to send that unfinished): he acknowledged it this morning.

I enclose a poem of Tennyson's which you may not have seen.[6] It has something in it like your Spring Odes and also some expressions like my sonnet on Spring.

I shall also enclose, if I can find, two triolets I wrote for the Stonyhurst Magazine;[7] for the third was not good, and they spoilt what point it had by changing the title. These ~~too~~ ^two^ under correction I like, but have fears that you will suspend them from a hooked nose: if you do, still I should maintain they were as good as yours beginning "All women born".[8]

Believe me your affectionate friend Gerard Hopkins S.J.

There was an Irish row over my election.[9]

[1] In the 1850s Newman had suggested the establishing of a Catholic university in Ireland but, moving from Dublin, he withdrew from the scheme in 1858. Very little progress was made until 1879 when a charter was granted for a royal university. There were several different proposals each with its Irish advocates but in 1882 it was decided that the university should be composed of several colleges. The Jesuit University College, to which GMH was attached, was opened in 1883. Like the University of London, it was primarily an examining body, only teaching a small proportion of the students who sat its papers. Since he was a Jesuit priest, GMH's salary did not go to him but to the college.

[2] GMH seems to have been unaware that RB had in fact worked in Dublin in 1873 and RB seems never to have enlightened him.

[3] Phoenix Park, situated 3 km north-west of Dublin city centre, is Europe's largest enclosed urban park, covering nearly 1,800 acres. Originally a royal hunting preserve, it has a resident herd of fallow deer. It was opened to the people of Dublin in 1745 by Lord Chesterfield, and in 1830 as an additional attraction one of the oldest zoos in the world was established there.

[4] MS B. In 1883, RB, fearing that in MS A he possessed the only copy of some of GMH's best poems, began to transcribe them into a second album (MS B). GMH worked on it several times, amending poems and transcribing new ones into it. These copies provide the 'text' for most of GMH's mature poetry. For more details see *CW* viii.

[5] 'The Blessed Virgin compared to the Air we Breathe'. See letter of 24–5 Oct. 1883 to RB and n. 1 to it.

[6] A newspaper cutting of 'Early Spring' (*Tiresias and Other Poems*, 1885; *Works*, 1909, p. 573).

[7] See letter to RB of 26 Mar. 1883.

[8] First printed in *Poems*, 1873.

[9] Fr Reffé, who was Dean of Studies at Blackrock, another of the Royal University's colleges, had also been a candidate, but Fr Delany, President of University College, objected to a cross appointment. Delany was anxious to secure GMH not only because he was known to be a good classicist but also because the college needed money and would benefit from GMH's salary of £400. GMH was elected by a vote

of 21 to 3 but was resented by members of the other colleges, who considered that University College was gaining too many new posts. He was also disliked simply because he was English and a convert.

20 March 1884 from Coventry Patmore to GMH

FL, no. CLXXVI D, p. 352 Campion Hall, P 20/3/84

Addressed to 'Revd Gerard Hopkins, S.J. | Stonyhurst College, | Blackburn', readdressed to 'Ireland | University College | 86 Stephen's Green, Dublin'. PM WHALLEY [MR] 29 84, H&K PACKET MR 30 1884.[1]

Hastings. March 20. 1884

My dear Mr. Hopkins, — I have read your poems — most of them several times — and find my first impression confirmed with each reading. It seems to me that the thought and feeling of these poems, if expressed without any obscuring novelty of mode, are such as ^often^ to require the whole attention to apprehend and digest them; and are therefore of a kind to appeal only to the few. But to the already sufficiently arduous character of such poetry you seem to me to have added the difficulty of following several entirely novel and simultaneous experiments in versification and construction, together with an altogether unprecedented system of alliteration and compound words; — any one of which novelties would be startling and productive of distraction from the poetic matter to be expressed.

System and learned theory are manifest in all these experiments; but they seem to me to be too manifest. To me they often darken the thought and feeling which all ^arts and^ artifices of language should only illustrate; and I often find it as hard to follow you as I have found ^it to follow^ the darkest parts of Browning — who, however, has not an equal excuse of philosophic system. "Thoughts that voluntary move harmonious numbers" is, I suppose, the best definition of poetry that ever was spoken.[2] Whenever your thoughts forget your theories they do so move, and no one ^who knows what poetry is^ can mistake them for anything but poetry. "The Blessed Virgin compared to the Air we breathe" and a few other pieces are exquisite to my mind, but, in these, you have attained to move almost unconsciously in your self-imposed shackles, and consequently the ear follows you without much interruption from the surprise of such novelties; and I can conceive that, after awhile, they would become additional delights. But I do not think that I could ever become sufficiently accustomed to your favourite Poem, "The Wreck of the Deutschland" to reconcile me to its strangenesses.

I do not think that your musical signs ⌒ ~ ⌒ etc. help at all. I fancy I ^should^ always read the passages in which they occur as you intend them to be read, without any such aid; and people ^who^ would not do so would not be practically helped by the notation.

I do not see how I can say more without going into the matter at very great length indeed; and, after all, I might very likely be wrong, for I see that Bridges[3] goes along with you where I cannot, & ^where^ I do not believe that I ever could; and I deliberately recognise in the author of "Prometheus" a sounder and more delicate taste than my own. You remember I only claimed to be a God among the Gallery Gods — i.e. the common run of "Nineteenth Century", "Fortnightly" & such critics. I feel absolutely sure that you ~~will~~ would never conciliate them — but Bridges' appreciation is a fact that I cannot get over. I cannot understand his not seeing defects in your system wh. I seem to see so clearly; and when I do not understand a man's ignorance, I obey the Philosopher and think myself ignorant of his understanding.[4] So please do not rely upon impressions which I distrust ~~in~~ myself.

I should like to keep the MS. a little longer, and shall be very glad if you will allow me to copy two or three small pieces for my own use. But I will not do this unless you tell me I may.

Your's ever truly
C. Patmore.

I have been quite out of working health for two or three months past; so have not done much yet to the new ed[n] wh. I suppose will come out in the Autumn.

[1] The envelope is more distressed than the other envelopes from Patmore, but whether from GMH carrying it in a pocket, or its postal travels, or modern readers consulting it is hard to say.

[2] Quoting Milton, *Paradise Lost*, III. 37–8.

[3] See Champneys, ii. 246–7, for two letters from Patmore to RB which mention GMH and his poems. In the first (2 May 1884) Patmore wrote: 'I am very glad to find that my feeling about my son's verses is supported by your opinion, to which, as I told Mr. Hopkins, I attach so much weight that I hesitate to give so absolute a verdict of dissent from some of his (Hopkins's) poetic novelties as I otherwise should give. To me his poetry has the effect of veins of pure gold imbedded in masses of unpracticable quartz. He assures me that his "thoughts involuntary moved" in such numbers, and that he did not write them from preconceived theories. I cannot understand it. His genius is however unmistakable, and is lovely and unique in its effects whenever he approximates to the ordinary rules of composition.' Later (7 May 1884) he writes: 'I wish I had not had to tell Hopkins of my objections. But I had either to be silent or to say the truth; and silence would have implied more difference than I felt. I have seldom felt so much attracted towards any man as I have been towards him, and I shall be more sorry than I can say if my criticisms have hurt him.'

[4] At the beginning of chapter 12 of Samuel Taylor Coleridge's *Biographia Literaria* (1817) he writes: 'In the perusal of philosophical works, I have been greatly benefited by a resolve, which, in the antithetic form and with the allowed quaintness of an adage or maxim, I have been accustomed to word thus: "*until you understand a writer's ignorance, presume yourself ignorant of his understanding.*"'

25 March 1884 to Richard Watson Dixon

CRWD, no. XXXI, p. 119 Bodleian, Dep. Bridges, vol. 93, fos. 121–3
One folded sheet.

University College. 85 & 86, Stephen's Green. Dublin. March 25 1884 [*Printed address with date added by hand*]

My dear friend, — In writing last (and I hope you got that letter: it was addressed to Hayton and contained my ~~ma~~riper thoughts of Mano)[1] I forgot to reply to some things you had spoken of.

The two Jesuits in Ireland were Frs. ~~Br~~ Paschasius Brouet or Broet and Alphonsus Salmeron, both of St. Ignatius's first companions.[2] Their mission to Ireland is well known, but it wd. be interesting to hear of it from the Government side. About the Blind Scot I consulted Fr. Wm. Forbes-Leith.[3] He is a learned and indefatigable historian and antiquary and it wd. even be well for you on such points to ~~try him~~ apply to him, for on ~~m~~ that period and in the matter of Scotch Catholics in particular he has an unflagging interest and first hand knowledge. He went quite lately to Simancas to "research". He has written a history of the Scotch Guard at the French court, edited Turgot's Life of Queen Margaret of Scotland, and is now busy on the annals of the Scotch Jesuits.[3] He never lets a minute ~~escape po~~ ^go idle^ and after his teaching-work at once returns to his own studies. He is to be found at Stonyhurst. ~~But~~ He knew all about the Blind Scot, but what he told me, if he told me anything particular, I have forgotten. But if necessary you can write and hear from himself.

Believe me your affectionate friend Gerard M. Hopkins S.J.

[1] This letter is missing, though RWD received it; see next letter and letter of 14 Apr. 1884. RWD had left for Warkworth by Dec. 1883, but he may well have kept it separate from the other letters and with his copy of *Mano*.

[2] Alphonsus Salmeron (1515–85), a Jesuit biblical scholar whose chief writings are commentaries on the Scriptures, was, in 1541, sent by Paul III with Pascase Broët (1500–62) as joint apostolic nuncio to Ireland. They landed on 23 Feb. 1542, and thirty-four days later they set sail for Dieppe on the way to Paris.

[3] William Forbes-Leith published *Narratives of Scottish Catholics under Mary Stuart and James VI* (1885), *The Life of Saint Cuthbert* (1888), and *Pre-Reformation Scholars in the XVIth Century* (1915).

25 March 1884 to Robert Bridges

LRB, no. CXII, p. 191 Bodleian, Dep. Bridges, vol. 92, fo. 89

University College, 85 & 86, Stephens Green, Dublin. March 25 1884 [*Printed address with date added by hand*]

Dearest Bridges, — Kindly forward the enclosed,[1] for I fear that a former letter, addressed to Hayton, may have miscarried (which however were such perdition as nothing else could ~~match~~ match); kindly also be damned to you for not writing and believe me affectionately yours Gerard M. Hopkins.

[1] Evidently the above letter to RWD, whose Warkworth address he did not yet know.

5 April 1884 from Coventry Patmore to GMH

FL, no. CLXXVI E, p. 354 Campion Hall, P 5/4/84
Addressed to 'Rev. Gerard Hopkins, S.J. | University College | 85 & 86 Stephens Green, Dublin'. PM HASTINGS AP 7 84, H&K PACKET AP 8 1884.

Hastings. April 5. 1884

My dear M[r] Hopkins,

At the very time your letter[1] came, this afternoon, I was feeling very anxious as to how you might have received my last. My difficulty in getting at anything very new is, as I said before, greater than that of most persons; and sometimes that difficulty seems insuperable. It struck me, however, at once, on reading your poems, that the key to them might be supplied by your own reading of them; and I trust some day to have the benefit of that assistance. I do not, however, feel at all sure that, even with such aid, I shall be able to enter into your spirit. The partiality and limitation of my appreciation of art often surprises myself. I have the most acute delight in some of the best music, but it seems a mere accident. Most of Beethoven, for example, seems to me to be simply noise; but when I do understand him I understand him indeed. It was twenty years before I could learn to see anything in Wordsworth's sonnets to the River Duddon.

What you say concerning your modes of composition disposes, at once, of some of what I thought were sound critical objections against writing upon theory etc. but <u>how</u> such modes, or at least some of them, as for example your alliterations, come to be the spontaneous expression of ^your^ poetical feeling, I cannot understand, and I do not think I ever shall.

I have never met with the "Potato ~~Patch~~ Poet",[2] and I fear I have not enough in me of "the native earth and real potato" to like him if I did. I cant help being a little amused by your claiming for your style the extreme of popular character. But after all perhaps that is the secret of my being so insensible to its peculiar merits. I never could understand "the people" — indeed, I may say with Sir Thomas Browne, that the People is the only entity which I sincerely hate. If you succeed in pleasing them with your potato-style as much as you do me when you write in your Ambrosia-manner (as in "Wild Air etc.") you may claim an almost incomparable universality of influence.

You will, in a few days, receive my sons Poems, wh. Mr Henry Daniel has printed for me. I shall reprint some of the best in my new edn. But when that will come out I know not. My brain, for some time past, has felt like a "flowery potato", and the blossoms of it would ^not^ harmonize with those of my "early" style, which is too full of "Wild Air etc."

Your's ever truly
C. Patmore

Pray let me have one line some day to say that, however much you may despise me, you are not offended.

[*Under the flap of the envelope the postscript:*] I told Mr Daniel to send your copy of Henry's poems to Stonyhurst. I suppose you will have it forwarded to you in Dublin.[3]

1 This letter, probably of 4 Apr., is missing.

2 Frederick Page in *Notes and Queries*, 184/8 (1943), 224, quotes Professor E. C. Mossner's *The Forgotten Hume* to the effect that William Wilkie (1721–72) was 'so successful in the new cultivation of tubers as to earn the covetable sobriquet of "potato," being variously known as the "potato minister," "the potato poet," or just plain "Potato Wilkie."' Wilkie, author of the *Epigoniad*, a turgid epic which earned him the name of 'the Scottish Homer', and *Fables* (1768), was 'rough and unpolished' and a man of extravagant eccentricity. A less likely candidate is James Russell Lowell (1819–91) whose 'What Mr Robinson Thinks' has the lines 'He draws his furrer ez straight ez he can, | An' into nobody's tater-patch pokes'. GMH had said to RB in his letter of 1 Dec. 1882 that 'Potato is certainly one of the ~~most~~ ugliest and most laughable words in the language and cannot ^well^ be used in verse, ^whereas^ earthapple is stately: ~~it~~ ^potato^ has one virtue only, the being specific.'

3 The copy (number 56 of 125) which Patmore sent to GMH is in the Irish Jesuit Archives, item J11/23. Tucked inside the front cover is a card which reads: 'Hastings, Easter, 1884. | With COVENTRY PATMORE'S compliments'.

14 April 1884 from Richard Watson Dixon to GMH

CRWD, no. XXXI A, p. 120 Campion Hall, D 14/4/84
Addressed to 'The Rev[d]. | Gerard Hopkins S.J. | University College, | 85 & 86 Stephen's Green, | Dublin'. PM ACKLINGTON AP 15 84, WARKWORTH AP 15 84, H&K PACKET AP 16 84.

Warkworth Vicarage, | Northumberland. 1884. | April 14.
My dear Friend,

I have been long in answering your Letters: and yet I take the first opportunity. I cannot say how glad I am to have your full judgment on Mano. There must be some difficulty about the poem at first sight, which may account for the various opinions of those who have written of it. It is a relief to me that it gains on you: what you say of the diction and imagery is extremely satisfactory, and gave me great pleasure.

With regard to yourself, I congratulate you on your change of scene & work, & on the honours that your learning has won for you.[1] The prospect of reading for examining others would be a pleasant one to me: at least if it involved re-reading books that I once read with the other motive ^of being examined^: for nothing seems more to refurnish the mind than reading old books again: I have no pupils now, having been transferred to Warkworth: & I miss them. It is good to be compelled to read the great books.

Thank you very much for your reference to your Friend Mr. Forbes: & for the trouble you have had about my historical enquiry. I shall avail myself of his help, when I come to look over my new volume: which is growing to completion. The doings of the Reformation in Ireland were abominable. I am about to fill up a gap that I left open in my Irish part, by putting in Bale's adventures in Ossory.[2]

I now send you a pamphlet of poems[3] which I have [*illegible deletion*] ^printed^ at Oxford, at Mr. Daniel's press, where Bridges printed Prometheus. You do not like printing of this limited sort, I know: but apart from that, I shall be glad to know what you think. The London public have given up reading poetry. In fact this is not a literary age: & there seems to be a sort of feeling to retire on Oxford & strive to win the young. You have seen some of the pieces.

I think you must have some poems of your own that I have not seen, & should be very glad to see, if ~~You~~ ^you^ could let me conveniently. Bridges perhaps has some. I will ask him, when I write.

I have received this morning from Coventry Patmore a copy of his son's Poems, printed also by Daniel.[4] They seem truly exquisite. Probably you know them. I have to thank you for them really.

I feel that this is a poor answer to your long and kind letter: and I do feel all the force & value of your criticism, being especially pleased that you think Mano's chief quality "humanity", a new critical term, I think: & a most happy one. Of this I have told Bridges, who agrees. Also I am delighted that you like the "characterisation": above all Mano himself. Lang in the Saturday[5] said his outline was not clear.

I have been trying to spell out a few Canons of Poetry: feeling, as every one does, the want of some sort of basis for criticism ~~to have~~: something definite in principles, to prevent it from being all guess work. Coleridge, I believe, said this was wanted, years ago. What do you think of this, the first?

For the two highest kinds of poetry, dramatic & heroic, blank verse is the only proper vehicle. And, conversely, blank verse is degraded, when it is used for any other kind of poetry.

Corollary. Inferior kinds of poetry, narrative, pastoral, didactic, "idyllic", and others employ an improper vehicle when they are written in blank verse. Blank verse has been more freely applied to these inferior kinds ~~than ever before~~ in the present age than ever before. In proportion as the two highest kinds have been disused, their proper metrical form has been transferred to others.

I may as well go on —

2. For long poems, that are not of the highest kind, the couplet measure or some stanza are proper.

3. Long poems ought ~~only~~ ^to^ be written in one measure only. The practice of breaking long narrative poems with lyrics, brought in by Scott & Byron, & universally continued now, is the gravest innovation.[6]

I have some more in mind: but what do you think of these? May be they are nought: but here is another —

Poems in any stanza are of inferior form to poems in ^the^ continuous measure of blank or even couplet verse.

With all affectionate regards
I am, My dear Friend,
Yours always
R. W. Dixon.

[1] His appointment to the Chair of Greek in the Royal University, Dublin.

[2] John Bale (1495–1563) was an evangelical polemicist and historian, made Bishop of Ossory in southern Ireland in 1552. He was an uncompromising Protestant and his *The Vocacyon of Johan Bale* (1552) chronicles part of his turbulent life.

[3] *Odes and Eclogues* by Richard Watson Dixon, Printed at Oxford by Henry Daniel (1884). 100 copies. Price 5 shillings.

[4] *Poems by Henry John Patmore*, with a biographical note by Gertrude Patmore. Henry Daniel: Oxford, 1884. 125 copies. See letter to CP of 26 Nov. 1883, n. 1.

[5] Andrew Lang wrote (anonymously) in the *Saturday Review* of 8 Sept. 1883 a long review, which told the story of *Mano* and concluded judiciously that 'We have read Canon Dixon's poem, if not constantly with ease, yet often with pleasure, and always with sympathy and respect for work so well wrought and so original'.

[6] By the date of this letter, the long poem in a single form, such as Wordsworth's *The Prelude*, or Tennyson's *Idylls of the King*, might have seemed old-fashioned, and the general mood was influenced by ideas such as that of Edgar Allan Poe that poetry can only be lyric and intense and therefore cannot be long. The sequence of lyrics, or the long poem interrupted by lyric, such as Tennyson's *Maud*, John Clare's *Child Harold*, or Whitman's *Leaves of Grass*, paved the way for the collage of Eliot's *The Waste Land*, and the *Cantos* of Ezra Pound.

16–19 April 1884 to Robert Bridges

LRB, no. CXIII, p. 191 Bodleian, Dep. Bridges, vol. 92, fos. 40–1

Clongowes-Wood College, Naas. [*Embossed heading*]
April 16 (back at University College, Stephen's Green tomorrow)

Dearest Bridges, — There could be no difficulty about the corrections, ~~I w~~ I could deal with that well enough, but I cannot spare much time; therefore I should not undertake ~~much~~ detailed criticism. But send the plays, both or one, nevertheless.[1]

I wish, I wish I could get on with my play.[2] Perhaps seeing yours may encourage me.

Mr. Patmore did not on the whole like my poems, was unconverted to them. He expressed high admiration for some, naming the one "Wild air, world-mothering air",*[3] [*GMH note*: *of which unluckily I had copied only a third.] but of the rest it seems he could not make anything.

Canon Dixon sends me from Warkworth a little volume of Daniel's printing.[4] I like the get-up better than Prometheus. It seems there is even some advantage in publishing in this way; at least he says so, but it would be tedious to explain how, AND WHAT DOES ANYTHING AT ~~All~~ ALL MATTER?

I cannot however hope that you will publish the two other ~~tragedie~~ plays ~~at~~ this way: I do think you ought to come before the public in the usual manner. I want also to ~~say~~ ^see^ P. F. republished.

The East wind is worse than in England.

I am in a great weakness. I cannot spend more time writing now, but am your affectionate friend Gerard M. Hopkins S.J.

The Century is an interesting serial. There is ^in it^ a saddening account of a young American poet called Sidney Lanier,[5] who had

^good^ notions about poetical form, ~~th~~ scansion etc, and died young, in struggling circumstances. The samples of his own were something like E. A. Poe, something like Whitman, and shewed, I thought, some genius, but not of a high order; but there was little ~~to~~ to judge from. I remark that when American poets introduce native trees, flowers, birds etc into their verse the effect to us is of a "ciphering" note on an organ.[6]

Stephen's Green. April 19.

[1] *Nero* and *The Return of Ulysses*.

[2] 'St Winefred's Well'.

[3] 'The Blessed Virgin compared to the Air we Breathe'.

[4] *Odes and Eclogues* (1884).

[5] Sidney Lanier (1842–81) was born in Macon, Georgia. He fought in the Civil War, then he and his brother acted as pilots aboard English blockade runners. Caught, he was imprisoned in Maryland, where he contracted tuberculosis. After short spells as a teacher and church musician, he returned to Macon, married, trained, and practised as a lawyer. He travelled widely in the south and west in search of better health and, recovering an early love of music, tried to find work in an orchestra, eventually joining the newly formed Peabody Orchestra in Baltimore, Maryland. His final years were spent in teaching English at Johns Hopkins University, where he wrote various essays on literary and musical subjects, including his *Science of English Verse* (1880) on relations between music and prosody. From 1867 he wrote and published poetry; his best-known poems use logaoedic dactyls: 'The Revenge of Hamish' (1878), 'The Marshes of Glynn', and 'Sunrise'. His other works included modern-day versions of chivalric tales to appeal to boys (he had three sons): *Froissart* (1878), *King Arthur* (1880), the *Mabinogion* (1881), and *Bishop Percy's Reliques* (1882), and two travelogues. He succumbed to tuberculosis in 1881, at the age of 39. The *Century Magazine*, the successor of *Scribner's*, contained, in the number for Apr. 1884, Lanier's portrait as a frontispiece, and a sketch of Lanier by William Hayes Ward (*Sidney Lanier* by Edwin Mims, 1905).

[6] 'Sounding of a single note, without any key being pressed down; this is sometimes called howling, or humming'; *OED*.

30 April 1884 to Robert Bridges

LRB, no. CXIV, p. 192 Bodleian, Dep. Bridges, vol. 92, fos. 42–3

University College, 85 & 86, Stephens Green, Dublin. April 30 1884 [*Printed address with date added by hand*]

Dearest Bridges, — The secret out: I too am engaged[1] on examination papers and must therefore be very brief.

First I am not the least surprised, not that I suspected anything but that nothing about marriage surprises me ever.

Next I am glad: I say every one should marry, and do not see why you did not, years ago, except that[2]

Thirdly you were waiting for Miss Waterhouse[3] to turn up,* [*GMH footnote*:*indeed to be born] which having happened and being to complete your happiness I am very glad of it and feel sure she must be ~~ch~~ ^both^ good and charming. ~~And~~ ^For^ I have reasons not altogether a priori for judging she is both. Of course I wish you both great joy and am your (the both of yiz) affectionate friend Gerard M. Hopkins S.J.

I am, I believe, recovering from a deep fit of nervous ~~po~~ prostration (I suppose I ought to call it): I did not know but I was dying.

[1] This is written in a bold hand, occupying most of the page before it continues on the verso.

[2] No break here; GMH is simply tabulating the three items of his letter.

[3] Mary Monica Waterhouse (1863–1949) was the elder daughter of the architect Alfred Waterhouse. The family were Anglican but Mrs Waterhouse had been raised as a Quaker. She and her daughters ran classes and provided facilities for local people in the village of Yattendon. Monica was musical and an expert calligrapher, whose book *A New Handwriting for Teachers* (1899) was influential in the style taught in schools. The couple had three children: Elizabeth (1887), Margaret (1889), and Edward (1892).

5 July 1884 to his Father

Lance Sieveking, *The Eye of the Beholder* (London, 1957), 281–2 and *The Month*, NS 19/5 (May 1958), 265–6 HRHRC

July 5th, 1844[1] Castlebar,[2] County Mayo.

My dearest Father, — I write from this remote place to wish you many happy returns of Monday. I have got a circular ticket which will take me over great part of Ireland. To be at Castlebar was no ~~part~~ ^item^ of my plan, but fortune does and should play a great part in travel. (More by token I have written a paper on Statistics ^~~and~~^, from another point of view than yours, which perhaps might appear in the Atlantis, when the new Atlantis appears: the ~~first~~ ^old^ Atlantis was published when ~~N~~Cardinal Newman was Rector of the Catholic University and was brilliant, but did not last long.) I ~~meant to~~ left Dublin this morning meaning to go to Westport on the coast, but fell in with a clergyman~~,~~ who, finding me to be a friend of a friend of his invited me to stay with him, which I gladly did. In the house live 3 curates, he being the eldest of them. I am to go by private car to Letterfrack[3] tomorrow and my driver, if after looking into my purse he agrees to be so, is momently expected to the conference. At Letterfrack on the Atlantic some of our people are staying. When I am tired of them or they of me I go on through Connemara to ~~Galw~~ Furbogh or Ferbo in Galway Bay, where are others of ours, and thence to Killarney, where there are again others, and so by degrees home. Part of the difficulty of telling you what I am g^d^oing lies in the pen, which makes it a labour to write.

The weather is close and sultry. There was heavy rain last night but all dried up. Thunderclouds hang about. Great part of the population are very pleasantly shod in their bare heels and stockinged in their bare shins. How gladly would I go so! The struggle I keep up with shoemakers, murderers by inches, I may say ever embitters my life.

~~The~~ It being market day the streets were full of people, but hitherto I have heard no Irish talked. But every one in the country parts and most markedly the smallest children, if asked a question, answer it by repeating the words without Yes or No. "Were you at school on Friday?" — "I was, sir." "You would be afraid to go in where the bull is?" — "I would not, sir." The effect is very pretty and pointed.

John Collins and I are agreed over our drive, 36 Irish miles, which are, so far as I can reckon, about ~~5~~46 English, for 17s. and driver 7s. 6d. I do not know that it is dear, but I feel that it is ruinous in my impoverished condition.

With best love to all believe me your loving son Gerard Manley Hopkins. S.J.

If you have not bought argosy braces don't: they are very ingenious and if you spent your life in picking up horseshoes, as Sandford[4] did and as Merton would not, you would find them convenient, but you will never draw an easy breath ~~with them~~ ^from the day you put them on^. I shall get rid of my cuirass on the earliest opportunity.[5]

[1] GMH misdated this to the year of his birth.

[2] Castlebar was on the railway from Dublin. It is the county town of Mayo in north-west Ireland. Michael Davitt founded the Irish National Land League there in 1879.

[3] Letterfrack is a small coastal village in Connemara, the county south-west of Mayo. It was founded by Quakers in the middle of the 19th c. and later (in 1913) was to become the site of Marconi's transatlantic radio receiver station.

[4] Thomas Day's *The History of Sandford and Merton* (3 vols., 1783–9) features the virtuous farmer's son Harry Sandford and the spoilt rich boy Tommy Merton.

[5] Argosy braces were widely marketed; they were elastic with an elaborate system of pulleys aimed to give freedom of movement; the advertisement said that they were 'the only Brace with which it is impossible to pull a Button'.

9 July 1884 from Richard Watson Dixon to GMH

CRWD, no. XXXIB, p. 122 Campion Hall, D 9/7/84
Addressed to 'The Rev. | Gerard Hopkins S.J. | University College, | 85 & 86 Stephen's Green, | Dublin'; re-addressed to 'Furbough | Spiddle [Spiddal] | Co Galway'. PM ACKLINGTON JY 9 84, WARKWORTH JY 9 84, H&K PACKET JY 10 84, DUBLIN JY 11 84, GALWAY JY 12 84.

Warkworth Vic. | 9 July 1884

My dear Friend,

Do not think because I have been long in writing that I have neglected you in thought. I have been & am distressed by the news of your illness, or at least prostration of strength: & have had you almost constantly in my mind. I wish it lay in my power to do anything. Will you let me know how you are? I have not yet written to your Friends about the Irish Mission, tho I had a very kind reply to my first letter from Mr. Forbes. I have been pushing on to the end of my 3d. vol. & the reign of Edward VI, & have now got to the last few pages; after that I shall write to some of them, certainly to Mr. Forbes.

It is not unlikely that Bridges will come to pay me a visit soon, but he has not fixed the time yet. I wish you could see this place.

Do you know anything of an American poet named Street?[1] He seems good from extracts.

I am glad of your good opinion of Odes & Eclogues.[2]

Ever your affec^te^ Friend
R. W. Dixon

[1] Presumably Alfred Billings Street (1811–81), author of *The Burning of Schenectady, and Other Poems* (1842), *Frontenac, or the Atotarbo of the Iroquois, a Metrical Romance* (1849), and *Forest Pictures in the Adirondacks* (1865).

[2] The letter containing this opinion is missing.

18 July 1884 to Robert Bridges

LRB, no. CXV, p. 193 Bodleian, Dep. Bridges, vol. 92, fos. 44–45v

Furbough House, near Galway. July 18 1884.

Dearest Bridges, — I must let you have a line now, I see, and write more hereafter. I ought to have answered you before, but indeed I hardly thought you were in earnest in proposing I should be your best man, pleasant and honourable as the position would be. But to show no other reasons why not, at the time you name I should be ~~in~~ about beginning my examination work and it ~~it~~ would be altogether impossible for me to ~~away from~~ ^be out of^ Ireland. However you do not want for friends better fitted to do the work than I.

I am here on holiday. I have been through Connemara, the fine scenery of which is less known than it should be. Yesterday I went to see the cliffs of Moher[1] on the coast of Clare, which to describe would be long and difficult. In returning across the Bay ~~I was~~ ^we were^ in some considerable danger of ~~my life~~ ^our lives^. Furbough House stands amidst beautiful woods, ~~a Paradis~~ ^an^ Eden in a wilderness of rocks and treeless waste.[2] The whole neighbourhood is most singular.

The weakness I am suffering from~~,~~ — it is that only, nervous weakness (or perhaps I ought not to say nervous at all, for I am not in any ~~way~~ unusual way nervous in the ~~usual~~ ^common^ understanding of the word) — continues and I see no ~~hope~~ ground for thinking I can, for a long time to come,[3] get ~~a~~ notably better of it, but I may reasonably hope that this pleasant holiday may set me up a little for a while. Your enquiries are very kind: there is no reason to be disquieted about me, though weakness is a very painful trial in itself. If I could have regular hard exercise it would be better for me.

The reason of course why I like men to marry is that a single life is a difficult, not altogether a natural life; to make it easily manageable special provision~~s~~, such as we have, ~~are~~ ^is^ needed, and most people cannot have this.

I shall begin my annual eight days' retreat in a few days and then return to Dublin.

Coventry Patmore has kept your MS book[4] a long time, as though it were to give himself the opportunity ~~for~~ ^of^ repentance for not admiring all the poems, and indeed appears to look on~~,~~ his condition as one of guilt and near ^to^ reprobation — which is very odd of him. And

I believe it will be of no avail and that like Esau and Antiochus[5] he will not get the grace and is in a fair way to die in his sins.

I find that 2557 is divisible by nothing ~~but 3~~ till you reach 20, beyond which I have not tried: what then can the length of the stanza be? And what is the subject of the poem?[6]

Believe me your affectionate friend Gerard M. Hopkins S.J.

Write University College, Stephen's Green: the number is unnecessary.

[1] Cliffs of Moher, County Clare. Still one of the most popular of Irish tourist attractions, the cliffs rise to a maximum height of 214 metres from which there are spectacular views inland and across to the Aran Islands.

[2] Presumably a reference to the Burren, described by the commander of English forces in the 17th c. as 'a country where there is not water enough to drown a man, wood enough to hang one, nor earth enough to bury him'. *The Memoirs of Edmund Ludlow*, ed. C. H. Firth, 2 vols. (Oxford, 1894), i. 292.

[3] This comma had followed 'time'.

[4] The MS book of GMH's poems. See letter to RB of 7 Mar. 1884.

[5] Esau was the elder fraternal twin of Jacob and sold him his birthright. Jacob tricked him out of their dying father's blessing. Genesis 27: 5–40. For Antiochus, 'a wicked root', see Gen. 27: 34–5, 1 Macc. 2: 48, 63. The Douai Bible has a note calling Antiochus 'that man of sin'.

[6] A reference to *Eros and Psyche* (1884; rev. and enlarged, 1894).

26 July 1884 from Coventry Patmore to GMH

FL, no. CLXXVI F, p. 356 Campion Hall, P 26/7/84

Addressed to 'Rev. Gerard Hopkins, S.J. | University College, | 85 & 86 Stephens Green, | Dublin'. PM HASTINGS JY 26 84, H&K PACKET JY 28 1884.

Hastings. July 26. 1884

Dear Mr Hopkins,

I have just had the great pleasure of making the acquaintance of your friend, Bridges, with whom I have left your MS. volume, having delayed so long returning ^it^, through dread of accident by post.

Bridges seemed supremely happy in his successful prosecution of love and poetry. The rate at which he is getting through his thousands and thousands of highly finished verses is to me wonderful. I doubt, however, whether he will touch "the crowd, incapable of perfectness".[1] He spoke with the sincerest admiration and love of your poetry.

I happened to be present at the Government's first attempt to get up a civil war last Monday.[2] The "procession" was at the outside 15,000 persons, of whom not 500 were countrymen. The amount of lying done by the liberal newspapers of the next morning exceeded all that I can remember of newspapers in that way.

Your's ever truly
Coventry Patmore

I have not yet repeated my reading of "Mano", but I mean to do so, though I have little hope of being able to see in it all that some who are quite as good judges as I am seem to see in it.

[1] Patmore begins his piece on *Prometheus the Firegiver* in *The St James's Gazette* (9 Mar. 1885 and 31 Dec. 1885) with this phrase. The essay is reprinted in *Courage in Politics*.

[2] A 'Reform Demonstration' of 21 July. The procession marched from the Thames Embankment to Hyde Park, where at six platforms it was addressed by Liberal MPs and others. *The Times* (which was sympathetic) estimated the number of agricultural labourers at 6,000; two independent witnesses thought the total number of demonstrators was 26,000.

3 August 1884 to Robert Bridges

LRB, no. CXVI, p. 194 Bodleian, Dep. Bridges, vol. 92, fos. 46–7

University College, 85 & 86, Stephen's Green, Dublin. Aug. 3 1884
[*Printed address with date added by hand*]

Dearest Bridges, — I am extremely glad to hear from both of you that you and Mr. Patmore were so well pleased with one another.

You did not, I hope, let him hear my remark about the MS book.[1]

That book would be the greatest boon to me, if you are so good as to offer it — a godsend and might lead to ~~more~~ my doing more. And if you were to complete "Wild air",[2] that would be the comble.[3] The former copy you made of it I must have, but it got mislaid in moving to Ireland.

Did you see there was in the book a "curtal-sonnet"[4] you had not had?

I enclose something very beautiful and almost unique.[5] I am hoping myself to publish a new and critical edition of St. Patrick's 'Confession', a work worthy to rank (except for length) with St. Austin's Confessions and the Imitation and more like St. Paul'~~s~~ and the Catholic Epistles than anything else I know, unless perhaps St. Clement of Rome.[6]

I am the better and fresher for my holiday: I do not know how long this improvement will last but say with St. Patrick as enclosed "Salvation is the Lord's". Believe me your affectionate friend Gerard M. Hopkins S.J.

[1] See above, letters of 7 Mar. 1884 and 18 July 1884.

[2] 'The Blessed Virgin compared to the Air we Breathe'. See letters to RB of 24 Oct. 1883 and 7 Mar. 1884.

[3] A variant of 'cumble', meaning high point, culmination. See *OED* under 'cumble'.

[4] 'Peace', Oxford 1879.

[5] St Patrick's Hymn, or 'Breastplate'—'a corslet of faith for the protection of body and soul against devils and men and vices'. For Old Irish text and translation see *Thesaurus Palaeohibernicus*, ed. Whitley Stokes and John Strachan, 2 vols. (Cambridge, 1901–3), ii. 354–8.

[6] Pope Clement I (*fl.* latter part of 1st c.), of whom the only genuine piece of writing extant is his letter to the church at Corinth, one of the earliest Christian documents outside the New Testament.

18 August 1884 from Coventry Patmore to GMH

FL, no. CLXXVI G, p. 356 Campion Hall, P 18/8/84
Addressed to 'The Rev[d] Gerard Hopkins, S.J. | University College, | 85 & 86 Stephens Green, | Dublin'. PM HASTINGS AU 18 84, H&K PACKET AU 19 84.

Hastings August 18. 1884
My dear M[r] Hopkins,

I am very glad to hear that you like the little translation.[1]

I am much interested in Bridges both personally and as a Poet. As a Poet he surprises me by his power of pouring forth, almost without any pauses for correction, thousands of verses all bearing the appearance of high finish. His first draft of "Eros and Psyche" is more complete than I could have made ~~it~~ such a poem after years of correction. He rises to a certain altitude — not the very highest but still very high — and can remain there as long as he chooses and apparently without any fatigue. It seems that "Prometheus" was written with the same ease; and yet to my mind it is the most finished poem of the kind since "Samson Agonistes".

Personally I am attracted to him, as I am to all really poetic minds, by — may I call it so? — a sort of sanctity of intellect, a power of perceiving an immense range of things rightly and of believing his perceptions, [*illegible deletion of 3 or 4 words*] because they are perceptions. A Poet, ^though^ without faith, still seems to me like the cartoon (defective, indeed, even as a cartoon) of a holy picture; and I confess that I feel much more at home with such a man than I do with many a very orthodox and exemplary member of the "visible" Church, who believes all and perceives nothing.

Pray let me have the music to the "Swan" when you have finished it.[2]

Your's ever truly
C. Patmore

[1] A letter from GMH is missing between the letters of 26 July and 18 Aug. The 'little translation' was probably Patmore's second wife's *St. Bernard on the Love of God*, completed by himself (1881; new edn. 1884; the British Library copy was received on 2 Aug.). On the front cover it is described as a 'little' work by St Bernard.

[2] Not known.

21–4 August 1884 to Robert Bridges

LRB, no. CXVII, p. 195 Bodleian, Dep. Bridges, vol. 92, fos. 48–50v

University College, 85 & 86, Stephen's Green, Dublin. Aug. 21 1884 [*Printed address with date added by hand*]

Dearest Bridges, — I must let you have a line to acknowledge, with many thanks, the receipt of the MS book and two or three very kind letters. I guessed whose was the elegant and legible hand on two of the addresses. As for the piece of a new garment, I came to the conclusion it was put in to bigout the enclosure. I al~~ways~~^so^ concluded that that new garment was a pair of wedding trousers. Circumstances may drive me to use my piece as a penwiper.

It is so near your wedding that I do not know I ought to write of anything else. I could not ask to be present at it; and indeed, much as I desire to see you and your wife and her mother and Yattendon itself, perhaps that would not be ~~the best~~ ^so good a^ day for this after all as some other. Only unhappily I do not see when that other is to be. However it is a fine buoyant saying, Non omnium rerum sol occidit {*the sun has not set on all things*}.[1]

I had an interesting letter from Mr. Patmore all in praise of you.

Several things in your letters call for reply, but not now. If you do not like "I yield, you do come sometimes,"[2] (though I cannot myself feel the weakness you complain of it in it, and it has the advantage of being plain) will "I yield, you foot me sometimes" do? "Own my heart" is merely "my own heart", transposed for rhythm's sake and then tamquam exquisitius {*as if in a more exquisite/refined manner*}, as Hermann[3] would say. "Reave" is for rob, plunder, carry off.

I find that in correcting "Margaret" I wrote "world of wanwood" ~~for wo~~ by mistake for "worlds", as the sense requires.

Our society cannot be blamed for not valuing what it never knew of. The following are all the people I have let see my poems (not counting occasional pieces): some of them however, as you did, have shewn them to others. (1) The editor and subeditor of our Month had the Deutschland and later the Eurydice offered them — (2) My ~~m~~ father and mother and two sisters saw these, one or both of them, and I have ^sent^ them a few things besides in letters — (3) You — (4) Canon Dixon — (5) Mr. Patmore — (6) Something got out about the Deutschland and Fr. Cyprian Splaine,[4] now of Stonyhurst, ~~ask~~ wrote to me to send it him and perhaps other poems of mine: I did so and he shewed ~~them~~ ^it^ to others. They perhaps read it, but he afterwards acknowledged to me that in my handwriting he found it unreadable; I do not think he meant illegible — (7) On the other hand Fr. Francis Bacon,[5] a fellownovice of mine, and an admirer of my sermons saw all and expressed a strong admiration for them which was certainly sincere. They are therefore, one may say, unknown. It ~~d~~always seems to me that poetry is unprofessional, but that is what I have said to myself, not others to me. No doubt if I kept producing I should have to ask myself what ~~I mean to do with them, ?but~~[6] I meant to do with it all; but ~~things~~ have long been at a standstill, and so the~~y~~ ^things^ lie. It would be less tedious talking than writing~~;~~: now at all events I must stop.

I must tell you a humorous touch of Irish Malvolio or Bully Bottom,[7] so distinctively Irish that I ca~~m~~nnot rank it: it amuses me in bed. A Tipperary lad, one of our people, lately~~,~~ from his noviceship, was at the wicket and another bowling to him.[8] He thought there was no one within hearing, but from behind the wicket he was overheard after a good stroke to cry out "Arrah, sweet myself!"[9]

I must write once more against the 3rd.[10] Believe me always your affectionate friend Gerard M. Hopkins S.J.

Aug. 24 1884.

[1] A Latin tag adapted from Livy, bk. XXIX. 26. 9, where Philip says that 'nondum omnium dierum solem occidisse' {*the sun has not yet set on all his days*}; usually used in the form 'nondum omnium dierum sol occidit', meaning roughly 'it's not the end of the world', and so there may yet be another opportunity.

[2] 'Peace', l. 4 unchanged.

[3] Gottfried Hermann (1722–1848) was an influential Greek scholar who emphasized the importance of linguistic research in classical philology. He wrote books on Greek grammar and the teaching of metrics.

[4] Cyprian Splaine (1843–92) was born in Liverpool and educated at Stonyhurst. He entered the novitiate in 1863 but then taught at Stonyhurst before doing his moral theology at St Beuno's, where he was a fellow student of GMH's.

[5] Francis Edward Bacon (1839–1922) was born in London. After working in business, and teaching in England and Guiana, he converted to Catholicism (1866), spent a year in a seminary in Lisbon, and became a novice in 1867. Like Splaine he was at St Beuno's with GMH. Ordained in 1875, he spent most of his life working in Glasgow.

[6] The cancelled section was at the top of the next sheet and was part of, probably, four lines that were cut before the letter was continued.

[7] Malvolio, Olivia's Puritanical steward in Shakespeare's *Twelfth Night*. Bully {*a good person*} Bottom is how Peter Quince refers to the weaver in *A Midsummer Night's Dream*. Both characters wonder at themselves but lack awareness of how others see them.

[8] They were playing cricket.

[9] 'Arrah'. This was one of eighty-nine contributions GMH made to the *English Dialect Dictionary*. See N. White, 'G. M. Hopkins's Contributions to the EDD', *English Studies* (Aug. 1987), 325–35.

[10] i.e. for their wedding, which was to take place on the third of September; see his letter of the second.

25 August 1884 from Coventry Patmore to GMH

FL, no. CLXXVI H, p. 357 Campion Hall, P 25/8/84
Addressed to 'Reverend Gerard Hopkins, S.J. | University College | Stephen's Green | Dublin'. PM HASTINGS AU 26 84, H&K PACKET AU 27 84.

Hastings. August 25. 1884
My dear Mr. Hopkins,

Since receiving your last[1] I have read "Mano" again, in hopes of finding in it all that you seem to find; for I always suspect my own opinion when it is negative as against the positive impression of a reader like yourself. I have ended my reperusal with renewed admiration for what I saw in the poem before, — its depth of thought, tenderness of feeling, and gravity of manner, and its many memorable lines and passages. The Monk's "vision of hell" is one of these.[2] The souls leaping to & fro, from heat to cold, like a mist of shrimps, is fully worthy of Dante. But I fail altogether to catch the motif of the Poem. If it is simply an epic narrative, it is defective, I think, in naturalness and probability; and the hero's "point of honour" about restoring Diantha does not satisfy my sympathies for the sacrifices he makes for it. If, as I suppose, however, there is much more meant than meets the ear, and the primary interest is symbolic, then it seems to me that the veil under which the real significance is hidden is much too opaque. "Fit though few" readers[3] may be a good prayer for a Poet; but the Author of Mano will find very few indeed who are fit for his mystery — supposing there be a mystery.

Your's ever truly
Coventry Patmore

[1] Between the letters of 18 Aug. 1884 and 25 Aug. 1884 a letter from GMH is missing.
[2] Book II, Canto XII.
[3] An allusion to Milton's *Paradise Lost*, VII. 30: 'Still govern thou my song, | Urania, and fit audience find, though few.'

2 September 1884 to Robert Bridges

LRB, no. CXVIII, p. 197 Bodleian, Dep. Bridges, vol. 92, fo. 51

University College, 85 & 86, Stephen's Green, Dublin. Sept. 2 1884 [*Printed address with date added by hand*]

My dearest Bridges and my dear Mrs. Bridges, — This is to wish you the happiest of days tomorrow[1] and all the blessings of heaven on that and all the days of your wedded life. I did not consider the mails; the consequence is that these wishes must, like the old shoe, be sent after you;[2] but there is no harm in that if when they overtake you they ever after attend you. More than this there is no need to write now. I am affectionately yours both Gerard Manley Hopkins S.J.

[1] On 3 Sept. 1884, RB married M. Monica Waterhouse, daughter of Alfred Waterhouse the architect, of Yattendon Court.
[2] E. Cobham Brewer, in his *Dictionary of Phrase and Fable* (1894), records that 'It has long been a custom in England, Scotland, and elsewhere, to throw an old shoe, or several shoes, at the bride and bridegroom when they quit the bride's home, after the wedding breakfast, or when they go to church to get married. Some think this represents an assault and refers to the ancient notion that the bridegroom carried off the bride with force and violence. Others look upon it as a relic of an ancient law of exchange, implying that the parents of the bride give up henceforth all right of dominion over their daughter.'

8 September 1884 from Dr William J. Walsh[1] *to GMH*

FL, no. F1, pp. 424–5 Campion Hall, Misc. Walsh
Addressed to 'The Rev. G. M. Hopkins S.J. | University College | 85 & 86 Stephens Green | Dublin'. PM MAYNOOTH SE 8 84, DUBLIN SE 8 84.

St Patrick's College, | Maynooth. [*printed address*]
8th Sept 1884
My Dear Fr Hopkins

As your letter did not require an immediate answer I put off writing until we should have got through our Entrance Examinations — always a heavy piece of work.

I am glad you have come to satisfactory terms with Loisette.[2]

He has written to me asking me for a testimonial which he can publish.

I do not quite like the idea of writing one, but this does not come from my having in any way lost faith in his system.

I have had during the last few days a very satisfactory illustration of its use. The application of the system is one contemplated by Loisette himself. It was this. During the entrance examinations, in the hall in which I presided, about 50 students were examined. In about 30 of these cases, just as I happened to think of the matter, I applied Loisette's system to keep in my memory the name of each student — seeing them, as I did, then for the first time, and knowing nothing about them previously. Now I find that I have not had the least difficulty in remembering and identifying all whose names I thus learned.

I may add that I have always found it practically impossible to remember the names of the freshmen candidates merely from seeing them at the entrance examinations.

I am glad to hear that Fr Delany is getting all right again.

I have been unable to call, for I have not been able to go to Dublin, since I heard of his being ill.

I remain, my dear Fr Hopkins,
Sincerely yours
William J. Walsh

[1] Dr William J. Walsh (1841–1921; *ODNB*) was appointed Roman Catholic Archbishop of Dublin on 23 June 1885. He was on the Senate of the Royal University of Ireland in 1883–4. For details of why he resigned after GMH was given a fellowship, see the introduction to *CW* vii. Walsh's interest in Loisette accords with the note in *ODNB* that he 'mastered the Pitman script'. See GMH to his mother, 26 Nov., n. 4.

[2] William Walsh had written to William Delany on 9 Apr. 1884: 'I enclose two copies of Loisette's First lesson—one for you and one for Fr Murphy. I paid him for you 3 Guineas, one guinea for each, including Fr Hopkins.' (Copy in Bischoff collection at 36:20 in the Foley Centre, Gonzaga.) Abbott records on p. 451 of *FL* that he had been sent a letter from Professor E. Hughes Dowling, which said that he had known GMH 'rather well; he & I were students or practisers of "Loisette's" system of memory training, & had walks together to practise the art & to puzzle one another'. 'Professor' Alphonse Loisette (?1826–96, born Marcus Dwight Larrowe and also known as Silas Holmes) was a vendor of a mnemonic system and wrote *Assimilative Memory or How to Attend and Never Forget* (New York, 1896). He peddled his system in London, Washington, Melbourne, Auckland, and Dublin, though it was attacked as derivative and inferior.

30 September 1884 to Robert Bridges

LRB, no. CXIX, p. 198 Bodleian, Dep. Bridges, vol. 92, fo. 53[r–v]
Postcard addressed to 'Robert Bridges Esq. | Yattendon | Newbury | Berks | England' [*the last added as an afterthought*]. PM DUBLIN 11 A OC 1 84 and on the verso [C]HIEVELEY A ? 2.

~~St Ignatius'~~ University College ~~SJ~~, | ~~23, Upper Temple-street~~, Stephen's Green, | Dublin. [*printed address corrected*]
Sept. 30 1884

I am in the very thick of examination work and in danger of permanently injuring my eyes. I shall have no time at all till past the middle of next month and not ^much^ then, for I have to begin lecturing and cannot now prepare. I wd. ^then^ try to read N.,[1] but you see how things stand~~s~~ — it wd. not be a very satisfactory recension. Send nothing just now — i.e. not till October is past the full.

Your friend may do as she likes,[2] but I disavow those things. I believe I shd. not disavow but retouch "Elected silence" and ~~D~~St. Dorothy.[3]
G. M. H.

[1] RB's play, *Nero*.

[2] Evidently as to copying his early poems.

[3] See *CW* viii for 'The Habit of Perfection' (i.e. 'Elected silence') and 'St. Dorothea' (and 'Lines for a Picture of St. Dorothea').

30 [19] October 1884 to *Nature*[1]

Patricia M. Ball, *The Science of Aspects: The Changing Role of Fact in the Work of Coleridge, Ruskin and Hopkins* (London, 1971), 148–50 and *HRB* 2, pp. 5–7. Published in *Nature*, 30 (30 Oct. 1884), 633.

The Red Light round the Sun—The Sun Blue or Green at Setting

I can confirm Mr. Backhouse's and Mr. E. D. Archibald's impression about the colour now and for some time past seen round the sun; that it first appeared about November last and has been more or less visible ever since. The colour was then, and still is, sometimes rose, sometimes amber or buff. It is best observed, when the sun on bright days is behind a cloud, round that cloud, in the place where, at other times, broken beams of shadow, thrown out from the cloud like a row of irregular palings and deepening the blue of the sky, are to be seen. Towards sunset it becomes glaring, and white and sallow in hue. Something of a circular shape may then perhaps be made out on it, but it does not seem to me that it ought to be called a halo. A halo, as I understand, is a ring, or at least a round space inclosed by a ring. This appearance has no ring round it. Also in a halo (I have seen numbers) it is the ring that is coloured — either throughout, or at four places where the ends of the four arms of a cross would rest upon it; and the inclosed field is uncoloured or coloured like the red of the sky: here there is an uninclosed but singularly-coloured field.

But whether we call the appearance a halo or not is perhaps only a question of terms: to call it a corona, as Mr. Leslie does, is another, and, as it seems to me, a hazardous thing, because it would imply that what we are looking at is an appendage of the sun's own (and that too at a time when it is strongly doubted if the sun has a corona of any sort of all), instead of what is much easier to suppose, a terrestrial or atmospheric effect. If there is going on, as Mr. Leslie thinks, an "increase of sun power," this ought to be both felt and measured by exact instruments, not by the untrustworthy impressions of the eye. Now Prof. Piozzi-Smyth says that sunlight, as tested by the spectrocope, is weaker, not stronger, since the phenomena of last winter began. To set down variations in light and heat to changes in the sun when they may be explained by changes in our atmosphere, is like preferring the Ptolemaic to the Copernican system.

It is, however, right and important to distinguish phenomena really new from old ones first observed under new circumstances which make people unusually observant. A sun seen as green or blue for hours together is a phenomenon only witnessed after the late Krakatoa eruptions (barring some rare reports of like appearances after like outbreaks, and under other exceptional conditions); but a sun which turns green or blue just at setting is, I believe, an old and, we may say, ordinary one, little remarked till lately. I have a note of witnessing it, with other persons of a company, in North Wales on June 23, 1877, the sunset being very clear and bright. It is, possibly, an optical effect only, due to a reaction (from the red or yellow sunset light, to its complementary colour) taking place in the overstrained eye at the moment when the light is suddenly cut off, either by the sun's disappearance or by his entering a much thicker belt of vapour, which, foreshortened as the vapour is close to the horizon, may happen almost instantaneously. And this is confirmed by a kindred phenomenon of sunset. If a very clear, unclouded sun is then gazed at, it often appears not convex, but hollow; swimming — like looking down into a boiling pot or a swinging pail, or into a bowl of quicksilver shaken; and of a lustrous but indistinct blue. The sky about it appears to swell up all round into a lip or brim, and this brim is coloured pink. The colour of the light will at that time be (though the eye becomes deadened to it) between red and yellow. Now it may be noticed that when a candle-flame is looked at through coloured glass, though everything else behind the glass is strongly stained with the colour, the flame is often nearly white: I suppose the light direct from the sun's disk not only to master the red and yellow of the vapour medium, but even, to the eye, to take on something of the complementary blue.

Even since writing the above I have witnessed, though slightly, the phenomenon of a blue setting. The sunset was bright this evening, the sun of a ruddy gold, which colour it kept till nothing was left of it but a star-like spot; then this spot turned, for the twinkling of an eye, a leaden or watery blue, and vanished.

There followed a glow as bright almost as those of last year. Between 6.15 and 6.30 (Dublin time) it was intense: bronzy near the earth; above like peach, or of the blush colour on ripe hazels. It drew away southwards. It would seem as if the volcanic "wrack" had become a satellite to the earth, like Saturn's rings, and was subject to phases, of which we are now witnessing a vivid one. G. M. H.

Dublin, October 19

[1] One of a series of four letters to *Nature*: 16 Nov. 1882, 15 [12] Nov. 1883, 3 Jan. 1884 [21 Dec. 1883], and 30 [19] Oct. 1884. This letter shows GMH closely following the debate in *Nature* on sky effects, since it includes reference to letters from Professor C. Piozzi-Smyth in the issue of 11 Spet. 1884 (pp. 462–3); T. W. Backhouse on 'The Sky-Glows' in the issue of 25 Sept. 1884 (p. 511); E. Douglas Archibald on 'The Solar (Dust?) Halo' in the issue of 2 Oct. 1884 (pp. 559–60); and Robert Leslie on 'The Sky-Glows' in the issue of 16 Oct. 1884 (p. 583).

25 October 1884 to Richard Watson Dixon

CRWD, no. XXXII, p. 123

[*University College printed heading deleted*]
Milltown Park,
Milltown.
Oct. 25 1884.

My dear friend, — I am heartily ashamed of myself that I never answered your ~~very~~ ^most^ kind and comforting letter received on Galway Bay in the summer. Neither do I answer it now, but only say that I am, thank God, much better since then and now drowned in the last and worst of five examinations. I have 557 papers on hand: let those who have been thro' the like say what that means. At this most inopportune time Mr. Tom Arnold[1] has asked me to write a short notice of you for the forthcoming new edition of his handbook of English Literature and somehow or other I must do it. Therefore please fill up the following and send it me ~~here~~ without delay here (where I am come for quiet).[2]

*[*GMH footnote*: *Th~~ese~~is of course is a rough draft] Richard Watson Dixon now Rector of Warkworth and Hon. Canon of Carlisle was born . . . . at . . . . . . and is of a Northamptonshire family. He ~~gradu~~ matriculated at . . . . . . College, Oxford, ... where ~~he was became~~ and elsewhere ~~he becam~~ enjoyed the friendship of Mr. Burne Jones and ~~others of~~ others who wrote and illustrated the Germ. He is ~~the~~ engaged on a Hist. of the Church of England on a great scale, of which 3 vols. have appeared. He published in . . . . Christ's Company, in . . . . Historic Odes, in . . . . Mano and in 1884 Odes and Eclogues. Add any particulars you like, but I do not say they or even all the above can appear, so short is the space at my disposal.[3]

I am your affectionate friend Gerard M. Hopkins S.J.

[1] Thomas Arnold (1823–1900; *ODNB*) was the second son of Arnold of Rugby, younger brother of Matthew Arnold, and father of Mary Arnold Ward (Mrs Humphry Ward). Educated at Rugby and Oxford, he spent five years in New Zealand, then became Inspector of Schools in Tasmania before converting to Catholicism and returning to England in 1856. He held a variety of posts and for a time withdrew from the Catholic communion before returning and taking a post as examiner and in 1882 Fellow and Professor of English Literature at University College, Dublin. See his *Passages of a Wandering Life* (1900). His *Manual of English Literature* (1862) went through a number of editions.

[2] See RWD's reply in the next letter for corrections and dates.

[3] For GMH's several drafts of the biography, see *CW* vii. For his final version see below in letter to RWD of 24–7 Nov., n. 4.

27 October 1884 from Richard Watson Dixon to GMH

CRWD, no. XXXII A, p. 123 Campion Hall, D 27/10/84
Addressed to 'The Rev[d]. Gerard Hopkins S.J. | Milltown Park, | Milltown, | Dublin | Ireland'. PM ACKLINGTON OC 27 84, WARKWORTH OC 27 84, H&K PACKET OC 28 84, MILLTOWN OC 28 84.

Warkworth Vic. | 27 Oct. 1884

My dear Friend,

I am so glad to hear from you again, the news of your better health: of which I had heard from Bridges, but glad to be further confirmed. I write in haste, for I am like you nearly stiffled with with[1] work. I shall be all week writing against time: not for gain, for that I seldom do: but at my Bishop's command.

Curiously, I had a letter fr. Bridges by the post of yours, & also from Fr. Forbes: to whom you referred me.

He cannot help me: so I send the paper I sent him, to be filled by you, or some one you may perchance give it to, at y[r] leisure, with a few ordinary facts about the Mission of yr Society to Ireland. I only want to sketch it: but have not ordinary materials. He mentions Mac Arthy's ~~His~~ Collections in Irish Ch. Hist.[2] which I have not. You will see I want to make an ordinary paragraph to complete my Irish part. In utter haste

Your aff fr[d]
R W Dixon

Me.

Now Vicar of W & H. C. of C. born 1833, at Islington: son of Dr. Dixon a celebrated Wesleyan Minister, grandson of Rd. Watson author of the chief text books of the same body: (~~Leicestershire family.~~) educated at King Edw. Sch. Birmingham, & Pembroke Coll. Ox. friendship of B. Jones, W. Morris, & others with whom ^he was^ associated in ~~the~~ undertaking the Oxford & Cambridge Magazine, in 1856, of Præraphaelite principles: engaged on H. of C. of Eng. on a gt. scale, of wh. 3 vols have appeared: published in 1859[3] Christs Company, in 1863[4] Historical Odes, in 1883 Mano, in 1884 Odes & Eclogues.

[1] Thus in MS.

[2] Daniel McCarthy edited Laurence F. Renehan's *Collections on Irish Church History* (1861).

[3] An error for 1861.

[4] 1864 on title page.

2 November 1884 to Grace Hopkins

Published in *The Hopkins Quarterly*, IV/3–4, 177–83. HRHRC, Container 1.5

University College, Stephen's Green, Dublin. Nov. 2, 1884.

Dearest Grace, — Unless letters of yours to me have miscarried (which may have happened) I believe your reproaches are not just; rather it seems to me that I wrote last. However it may be, for some while past I have had no time for unnecessary letterwriting and am just over a bout of severe work, which leaves me jaded; but this will pass off, I hope~~,~~. Tomorrow I begin lectures (no more than lessons) and am not sorry for it: they say (indeed prove) that public speaking, acting, preaching, and so on prolongs life.

The weather with us is very mild; we have not needed fires and could sit in the open air. It is due, as I suspect, to the volcanic dust, which still floats and cannot come down; and for the same reason I believe the winter will be mild, not severe. I suppose your friend's reasoning was: the years ~~on~~ keep nearly to an average temperature; to ~~bala~~ do this a bitter winter must balance a hot summer; but this summer has been hot; therefore this winter will be cold. There is something in it, but it cannot be trusted.

I suppose you are very happy with the Webers and no doubt they love you, as indeed, my dear, you deserve to be beloved. And ^in^ the thought of your loss, mingled of sweet and bitter, ~~must~~ I should think the sweetness would by degre~~es~~es gain upon the bitterness.[1]

I must make, I suppose, some musical remarks. I enclose a concert bill with notes made on the spot as you say they interest you. I hope to hear some finer concerts soon. I have made the acquaintance of our two musical examiners — Sir Robert Stewart,[2] who has a pleasant hearty undisguised ~~snub~~snubbing way and has lent me his lectures; and Dr. Joseph Smith[3] (known quite simply as Joe), one of the most thorough "tykes" I ever met and an Englishman ~~but~~ ^yet^ not from Yorkshire, the land of tykes, but from Worcester. I made Sir Robert's acquaintance (we were intimate in about you could count forty) in the great hall of the Royal University as the degrees were being conferred, including nine lady bachelors, "girl-graduates," one of them also a bachelor in music, Miss Taylor by name, and her ~~piece~~ diploma-piece, melodious and correct, was performed, Sir Robert conducting. Sir Robert is a great admirer of Purcell* [*GMH footnote*: * and (very frankly) "thought at first there was something in me because I admired Purcell, but now" etc.]; a decrier of Arne[4] — "the pedantic and ungenial Arne" he said twice, out of some lecture, I shd. guess; as if it were some kind of Lord Chief Justice's sentence and no more to be said; does not believe in Greek music, nor in some other things that are good, let ~~he~~ un say ^what^ a will. But for all that I like him and hope to know more of him and the great Joe acknowledges (wonderful for a brother musician) that he makes the organ speak. I must hear him and it. I know also Dr. Cruise, a [5]

[1] See letter to Grace of 9–10 June 1883 and to RB of 5 Aug. 1883.

[2] Sir Robert Prescott Stewart (1825–94; *ODNB*), born in Dublin, educated at the Cathedral school of Christ Church; he became organist at Christ Church at the age of 19. He was Professor of Music at Dublin 1862–94, where Charles Villiers Stanford was one of his students and friends. He edited the *Irish Church Hymnal* (1876). He was knighted in 1872.

[3] Dr Joseph Smith was the other examiner (with Stewart) for Music at the Royal University of Ireland at this period.

[4] Thomas Arne (1710–78; *ODNB*), educated at Eton and intended to enter law but practised secretly the harpsichord and violin and persuaded his father to let him become a musician. He wrote operas, music for masques, twenty-five books of songs, masses, and motets, concertos for keyboard and violin, and was composer to Vauxhall Gardens, Drury Lane Theatre, and Covent Garden.

[5] The rest of the letter is missing. 'Dr. Cruise' is probably Sir Francis Richard Cruise (1834–1912), who pioneered endoscopy in Ireland. He was Senator of the Royal University of Ireland and of the Royal College of Physicians in Ireland in 1884–6, and was also a distinguished cellist, classical scholar, and author of a variety of musical settings, essays on medical matters, and a translation of Thomas à Kempis's *The Imitation of Christ* (1907, etc.).

11–12 November 1884 to Robert Bridges

LRB, no. CXX, p. 198 Bodleian, Dep. Bridges, vol. 92, fos. 54–6

University College, ~~85 & 86~~, Stephen's Green, Dublin. Nov. 11 1884 [*Printed address with date added by hand*]

Dearest Bridges, — My heavy examination work is now some ~~time~~ ^while^ over and I have begun to lecture: it is time therefore that I shd. write; indeed I have done so once, but the letter did not please and this is its recast.

I was very glad you gave me some word of your married life; I wish it had been more. I have a kind of spooniness and delight over married people, especially if they say "my wife", "my husband", or shew the wedding ring.

I shall read *Eros and Psyche*[1] with the greatest joy; so let civilisation execute its daily eggtrick over the book with the usual adroitness as far as the south side of Stephen's Green.

Mr. Tom Arnold (but I dreamt I told you this before) asked me to write a short notice of Canon Dixon for a new edition of his handbook of English literature.[2] I did it, but whether it was time enough (for he was in the press) and short enough (for he was under pressure) I have not heard.

I have some musical matters to speak of. Stainer has written a capital ~~t~~Treatise on Harmony which has earned him the heartfelt thanks of people as ignorant as myself[3] (I cannot say his Novello-Primer of the same earned them) and of others, I believe, not ignorant at all. For instance Sir Robert Stewart,[4] learned musician of this city, ^much^ given to ~~t~~ Purcell, Handel, and Bach, says it is the most scientific treatment he has seen. Though his theory is not final, it is a great step forward and has ^quite^ a daylight, a *grand jour*, of sense. I am sure Stainer must be very nice to know and meet.

I have a great light on the matter of harmony myself, new, I need not say (framed on the model of Mr. Pecksniff's "pagan, I regret to say");[5] true, I hope.

You saw and liked some music of mine to Mr. Patmore's *Crocus*.[6] The harmony came in the end to be very elaborate and difficult. I sent it through my cousin to Sir Frederick Gore Ousely[7] for censure and that censure I am awaiting.

Before leaving Stonyhurst I began some music, Gregorian, in the natural scale of A, to Collins' *Ode to Evening*.[8] ~~I grop~~ Quickened by the heavenly beauty of that poem I groped in my soul's very viscera for the tune and thrummed the sweetest and most secret catgut of the mind. What came out was very strange and wild and (I thought) very good. Here I began to harmonise it, and the effect of ^~~suitab~~^ harmony well in keeping upon that strange mode (which, though it is, as far as notes go, the same as the descending minor, has a character of which the word ~~mi~~ minor gives you little notion) was so delightful that it seems to me (and I think you would find the same) as near a new world of musical enjoyment as in this old world we could hope to ~~find~~ ^be^. To the novelty of effect the rhythm and a continued suspense natural to the mode and easy to carry further contribute too. It is meant ~~to be~~ for a solo and a double choir singing in unison, the organ or a string band bearing all the harmony. It is in three movements, something like a glee, the third returning to the first.

If this letter is dull the writer was so and wearifully tired. So good-night, and goodnight to Mrs. Bridges or (what is more beautiful) to your wife: I am your affectionate friend Gerard M. Hopkins S.J.

Nov. 12 — You asked me some time since if I would write you a short paper on English scanning. I should like to do this if you still want it, but all that we Jesuits publish ^(even anonymously)^ must be seen by censors and this is a barrier which I do not know how anything of mine on a large scale ~~e~~would ever pass. In this particular case no doubt there would be no difficulty.

[1] This poem was printed at the Chiswick Press, and published in 1885.

[2] This long footnote will be found in the 'fifth edition, revised', 1885, of *A Manual of English Literature Historical and Critical*. See *CW* vii.

[3] The third edition of Stainer's *Theory of Harmony* was published in 1876. For Stainer, see letter to RB of 19 Apr. 1883.

[4] See letter of 2 Nov. 1884 to Grace.

[5] Dickens, *Martin Chuzzlewit* (1843–4), ch. 4: 'The name of those fabulous animals (pagan, I regret to say) who used to sing in the water, has quite escaped me.'

[6] *The Year*, of which the first lines are:

> The crocus, while the days are dark,
> Unfolds its saffron sheen[.]
> (*Poems*, 1906, p. 428)

[7] The Revd Sir Frederick Arthur Gore Ouseley (1825–89; *ODNB*), from 1855 till his death Professor of Music at Oxford. He was known also as a composer, edited the church music of Orlando Gibbons, and published treatises on *Harmony, Counterpoint and Fugue, Form and General Composition*.

[8] That is, in the Aeolian mode, without the leading note. As John Stevens says in *J&P*, 475, 'There is no composition by GMH that one would more like to see'; but sadly no copy is extant. GMH mentions it again in letters to RB of 1 Jan. 1885, 24–5 Mar. 1885, and 1–2 Apr. 1885. GMH made a transcription of Collins's ode; see *CW* vii; and see *CW* vi for his music in general.

25 November 1884 to Robert Bridges

LRB, no. CXXI, p. 200 Bodleian, Dep. Bridges, vol. 92, fo. 57^{r-v}
Postcard addressed to 'Robert Bridges Esq. | Yattendon | Newbury | Berks | England'. PM DUBLIN 8A NO 26 84 and CHIEVELEY A NO 27

~~St. Ignatius'~~ University College ~~SJ~~, ~~23 Upper Temple-street~~, Stephen's Green, Dublin. [*printed heading corrected*]
Nov. 25 '84

P. F. came safe, and many thanks.[1] The form is in my eyes rather convenient than handsome. Some things struck me on reading aloud which I will mention hereafter. I have lent it to Mr. Tom Arnold. The notice of C. D.[2] will appear, with some omissions, needful but to be regretted, because they were calculated to whet the reader's appetite, send him for more. G. M. H.

[1] A new edition of *Prometheus the Firegiver* was published in this year by Bell: it was printed at the Chiswick Press.
[2] i.e. Canon Dixon.

26 November 1884 to his Mother

FL, no. XCIV, p. 163 Bodleian, MS Eng. lett. e. 41, fos. 79f–79h
Addressed to 'Mrs. Manley Hopkins | Oak Hill | Hampstead | London N.W.' PM DUBLIN NO 29 84 and LONDON N.W. NO 29 81.

University College, | ~~85 & 86,~~ Stephen's Green, | Dublin [*Printed letterhead*] Nov. 26 1884

My dearest mother, — It is very long since I wrote and ought not to be and I am ashamed of it, but yet . . . however no matter about excuses. Also tell Kate[1] I will write soon to her; I did to Grace, not that she had the first claim at all, but she made such a hullabaloo and said, what in her case was I believe unfounded, that it was like throwing letters to me into a well.

I do not seem to think it would be well for me to visit you at Christmas; better in the summer. You can easily understand reasons. If I came now I could not again so soon. Travelling long distances in winter is harder, more tiring, and the broken sleeps are a great trial to me. Then Grace is away. Then it is so soon after coming to Ireland; it does not look so well. Then the holidays are short and I have an examination at the end of them. Altogether I do not welcome it.

If I knew Milicent's[2] address I would write to her; I am sure I do not know what in the world, in which we scarcely ever meet, we gain by not writing. I might say the same of other people, but most of her. And I have never written to Lionel[3] since he has been out: it seems a misery. And yet letter writing, so pleasant in doing, is a most harassing duty to set to with other work on hand.

We have enemies here — indeed what is Ireland but an open or secret war of fierce enmities ~~?~~ of every sort? — and our College is really struggling for existence with difficulties within and without; which nevertheless I believe we shall weather, for no other reason than that Fr. Delany[4] has such a buoyant and unshaken trust in God and wholly lives for the success of the place. He is as generous, cheering, and open hearted a man as I ever lived with. ~~In other respects I have~~ And the rest of the community give me almost as much happiness, but in particular Robert Curtis,[5] elected ^Fellow^ with me, whom I wish that by some means you could some day see, for he is my comfort beyond what I can say and a kind of ~~unex~~ godsend ~~beyond~~ I never expected to have. His father Mr. Stephen Curtis Q.C. and mother live in town and I often see them and shd. more if I had time to go there. I lecture also and like it well enough, that is rather than not. But the ~~house~~ ^College^ is poor, all unprovided to a degree that outsiders wd. scarcely believe, and of course — I cannot go into details — it cannot be comfortable. It is, this comes nearest it, like ~~waiting a long while~~ ^living^ at a temporary Junction and everybody knowing and shewing as much. No more time now. With best love to all believe me your loving son Gerard M. Hopkins S.J.

[1] See Biographical Register.

[2] See Biographical Register.

[3] See Biographical Register.

[4] Fr William Delany (1835–1924) was educated at Stonyhurst and spent two years in Rome. He was a successful headmaster of Jesuit schools in Ireland and selected to be in charge of the refounded University College. He wanted to establish a Catholic rival to Trinity College Dublin and controversially gave one of two fellowships secured in opposition to the wishes of Dr William Walsh to GMH, who was resented because he was English and a convert. Walsh wanted an Irish scholar and would have liked one of the two fellowships to go to one of the other colleges of the Royal University of Ireland, of which University College was only one. See *WHALB*, 357–64, and Thomas J. Morrissey, *William J. Walsh, Archbishop of Dublin, 1841–1921: No Uncertain Voice* (Dublin, 2004).

[5] Robert Curtis, SJ, professor of Natural Science. An Irish Jesuit eight years GMH's junior, Curtis was not ordained because he suffered from epilepsy. An excellent mathematician, he had been a scholar of Trinity College Dublin. Curtis was known for his sense of humour and was keen on walking and swimming (Robert Bernard Martin, *Gerard Manley Hopkins: A Very Private Life* (London, 1991), 377–9).

24–7 November 1884 to Richard Watson Dixon

CRWD, no. XXXIII, p. 124 Bodleian, Dep. Bridges, vol. 92, fos. 124–7
Addressed to 'The Rev. | Canon Dixon | Warkworth Vicarage | Northumberland | England'. PM DUBLIN NO 29 84, NEWCASTLE-ON-TYNE NO30 84. One folded sheet with printed heading and a single sheet.

University College, | ~~85 & 86,~~ Stephen's Green. | Dublin. Nov. 24 1884 [*Printed address with date added by hand*]

My dear friend, — You may be delayed by the want of the information you asked for and I must not keep you longer waiting.[1] Fr. Edmund Hogan,[2] to whom I applied, was then suffering from ulcers of the cornea, a sad blow to a devoted student like him, suddenly and unexpectedly fallen: the evil was in process of cure, but he can scarcely expect the full use of his eyesight again. He answered my enquiries, by word of mouth, much as follows.

(1) John Codur's appointment was cancelled: the document cancelling it and appointing Brou~~t~~^e^ (or Broet) and Salmeron ~~exis~~ instead / exists.

(2) Brouet and Salmeron went, ~~Brouet~~ accompanied by Zapata (not Zapota); Brouet was to take the lead and be the spokesman with persons of consequence. (He was a Picard, remarkable for gentleness of disposition, perhaps of birth. Salmeron was a most able commentator on Scripture, as his rema~~n~~ins prove). Zapata was a novice. St. Ignatius ~~had~~ has assigned to the noviceship six experimenta, tests or ordeals of fitness — hospital-nursing, catechising or preaching, the Long Retreat (or making the full 30 days of the Spiritual Exercises), begging, pilgrimage, and I forget what else. Th~~is~~^e^ journey might be treated as involving two or three of these for Zapata. He was a man of position and means, had been Notary Apostolic, and bore the expense of the journey. But afterwards he said that it was unbecoming in a member of the Society to preach from a barrel in the streets, which coming to St. Ignatius' ears he dismissed him as unfit. He remained however on good terms with ours.

(3) They were forced to go by Scotland. James received them well and forwarded them, but it was ~~afterwa~~ thought that the information of them which reached ~~Eli~~ Henry came from him or his court.

(4) They were 42 days only in Ireland. Their mission was not a success: the chiefs or nobles were ^then^ in much the condition of the English nobility, trimming to the king.

(5) "Unlettered <I presume ^not absolutely ignorant but^ unlearned> clergy." Fr. Hogan thinks the bulk of the clergy were unlearned, the Tridentine reforms not having been carried out, but that there were some learned men.

Most of the above is to be found in Orlandini's ~~or~~ 'semi-official' or even Crétineau-Joly's semi-officious ~~life~~ Histories of the S.J.[3] and in lives of St. Ignatius: I knew a good deal of it myself. ~~For~~ Further information as to places and persons visited may be had, if you care for it, in Fr. Hogan's Hibernia Ignatiana (privately printed, but I cd. procure and lend you a copy) and in certain numbers of the Irish Ecclesiastical Record, which I could consult for you.

He further added this. In 1559 Fr. Wolfe ^S.J.^ came to Ireland with the powers but not the name of Apostolic Nuntius, and since that time there have always been Jesuits in Ireland.* [*GMH footnote*: * To the suppression 1771.] There was a working ~~p~~^P^rovince, with perhaps 15 houses, e.g. 3 at Kilkenny, by 1629, at which time they set up a University in Dublin and it flourished till Cromwell.

Let me know whether you will want the further researches I have mentioned. Fr. Hogan promised to look for some loose sheets he thought he had of his book containing the part wanted, but since his return to Limerick I have heard no more of it.

The notice of you is to appear in Mr. Arnold's book,[4] but with omissions, made necessary by want of room, of some of my references; for which I am sorry, for I had calculated them, as far as from memory I could, so as to whet the reader's appetite and send him to the spring for more. † [*GMH footnote*: † For extracts there was not room.]

I am your affectionate friend Gerard M. Hopkins S.J.
Nov. 27 1884.

You know that Prometheus is now published.[5]

[1] RWD's paper of questions with GMH's notes for reply is in Campion Hall. In the following transcription, we have distinguished by typeface between RWD's draft and questions and GMH's notes:

The Society of Jesus indeed, even from the year of their institution, had selected this neglected realm for one of the scenes of their operation. The first of this body who reached Ireland was John (1) Codur, who came in 1541. He was followed by Alphonso Salmeron, Pachuse Broet, and Francis Zapota (2); all of whom were of St. Ignatius's first company. They selected the districts of (3). . . . .

they were favoured by (4). . . . .

they were successful in (5). . . . .

in ten years they had acquired (6) ~~a firm hold~~ . . . .

This influence extended equally among the ~~wre~~ wretched people and the unlettered clergy (?):

(1) Was named, and alone, but never came; the other two substituted (Orlandini; life of St. Ignatius; see Hibernia Ignatiana ed. Ed. Hogan S.J. printed for priv. circ. Fr. Green has them; 12s.6d.)

(2) Zapata novice ^paid their expenses^ afterwards left for saying it was beneath dignity of a priest to preach from a barrel; had been notary apostolic. Not of the first company

(3) See the Hibernia

(4) James of Scotland . . . .

The chieftains betrayed the cause

See also Eccl. Record ~~vol~~ '71, '72 perhaps, where things which not in the Hibernia

(5) Very unsuccessful

(6) Only 42 days

In 1559 Fr. Wolfe ~~as~~ came as apostolic nuntio without the title. There was a working Province (with houses etc) by 1629, when they set up a University in Dublin and flourished till Cromwell's time (e.g. 3 houses in Kilkenny; some 15 or so altogether). There were always Jesuits in Ireland since 1559 till the suppression 1771.

[2] Edmund Ignatius Hogan, SJ (1831–1917) was Professor of Irish language and history at University College Dublin. He wrote, apart from the book mentioned and a book on *The Irish Wolfdog* (1897), *Distinguished Irishmen of the 16th Century* (1894), an *Irish Phrase Book* (1899), and his most important book *Onomasticon Goedelicum: An Index of Irish Names of Places and Tribes* (1910). His obituary is in *Studies: An Irish Quarterly Review* (Dec. 1917).

[3] Niccolò Orlandini (1554–1606) wrote a *Historia Societatis Jesu* (Rome, 1614, etc.), which was completed and published after his death by Francesco Sacchini. Jacques Crétineau-Joly (1803–75) published *Histoire Religieuse, politique, et pittéraire de la Compagnie de Jésus* (6 vols., Paris, 1844–6), of which an English version was published by R. J. McGhee in 1863.

[4] GMH's note on RWD is to be found on pp. 470–1 of *A Manual of English Literature Historical and Critical* by Thomas Arnold, M.A. of Univ. Coll. Oxford Fellow of the Royal University of Ireland, and Professor of English Language and Literature in the University College, Stephen's Green, Dublin, Fifth Edition, Revised 1885. Since it is part of GMH's writing of this period, and contains opinions of *Mano* which may well reproduce what he wrote in a missing letter, we quote it in full below:

'Richard Watson Dixon, now vicar of Warkworth and hon. canon of Carlisle, was born at Islington, near London, in 1833, and educated at King Edward's School, Birmingham, and Pembroke College, Oxford. At Oxford he became the friend and colleague of William Morris, Burne Jones, and others of the mediævalist school, to which, as a poet, he belongs. The chance reading of his earlier poems also won for him the friendship of D. G. Rossetti.

He is engaged on a history of the Church of England on a great scale; of this three volumes have appeared. In verse he has published—in 1859, *Christ's Company, and other Poems*; in 1863, *Historical Odes* (on Marlborough, Wellington, Sir John Franklin, &c.); in 1883, *Mano* (his greatest work, a romance-epic in *terza rima:* Mano is a Norman knight put to death A.D. 1000, and the story, darkly and affectingly tragical, turns upon the date); in 1884, *Odes and Eclogues.*

In his poems we find a deep thoughtfulness and earnestness, and a mind touched by the pathos of human life, of which *Mano* is, in a strange but a typical case, the likeness; noble but never highflown, sad without noise or straining—everything as it most reaches and comes home to man's heart. In particular he is a master of horror (see Mano's words about the nettles on his way to the stake) and pathos; of pathos so much that here it would be hard to name his rival. We find also the very rare gift of pure imagination, such as Coleridge had (see the song "Fallen Rain", and the one on the sky wooing the river). But he is likest and owes most to Keats, and his description and imagery are realised with a truth and splendour not less than Keats' own (see the scene of the nine lovers in *Love's Consolation*; the images of the quicksilver and of the heart fastened round with hair, *ibidem*). This richness of image, matched with the deep feeling which flushes his work throughout, gives rise to effects we look for rather from music than from verse. And there is, as in music, a sequence, seeming necessary and yet unforeseen, of feeling, acting often with magical strokes (see *e.g.*, in *Love's Consolation,* "Ah, God! Thy lightnings should have wakened me three days before they did;" in *Mano*, "She would have answered underneath the boughs").

He is faulty by a certain vagueness of form, some unpleasing rhymes, and most by an obscurity—partly of thought, partly of expression—suggesting a deeper meaning behind the text without leaving the reader any decisive clue to find it. This fault injures the general effect of *Mano.* He employs sometimes the archaic style now common, but with such a mastery and dramatic point as justify a practice otherwise vicious.' '(Notice by the Rev. G. Hopkins)'

[5] i.e. for general circulation, by Geo. Bell & Sons, 1884.

1 December 1884 from Richard Watson Dixon to GMH

CRWD, no. XXXIII A, p. 126 Campion Hall, D 1/12/84

Addressed to 'The Rev^d^. | Gerard Hopkins S.J. | University College, | Stephen's Green, | Dublin, Ireland'. PM ACKLINGTON DE 2 84, WARKWORTH DE 2 84, H&K PACKET AP 16 84. On the back of the envelope, probably in GMH's hand, is a diagram, which perhaps relates to canon or counterpoint.

Warkworth Vicarage. | Northumberland. 1884 | 1 Dec.
My dear Friend,

I have just received your Letter: how welcome it is I cannot say, nor how much I thank you for the information you give, tho still more for writing to me so kindly. I had heard the day before from Bridges, asking me to send you his poem of Eros and Psyche:[1] & wrote you a note to accompany it; but was too late for the post, ~~but sin~~ ^so now^ need not send it. I was afraid I had troubled you unduly with my inquiries: and am not sure now that I have not: I mean whether I might not have made out for myself enough from accessible sources. But I was ignorant what sources there were. I shall now go to work on what you have sent: and if I want to know more I will ask again: and perhaps ask the loan of Fr. Hogan's work: that is if I were allowed to make reference to it as my authority for anything I might say. Otherwise it would not be useful to me.

All that you tell me of the first Mission, of 1540, is highly interesting: but besides that I want to cover the whole period from 1540 to 1553 (death of Edward VI). Your Society must have returned within that period: because in 1553, or a little earlier, Browne, the Henrician Archb. of Dublin, preached a sermon against them, complaining of their activity and success.

Fr. Hogan, in your letter, seems to imply that they did not return till 1559, when Fr. Wolfe came.

If there were no Jesuits in Ireland between 1540 and 1559, Browne was unveracious: which I can readily suppose from his character.

Please thank Mr. Hogan for his kindness whenever you write to him.

I shall be interested to see Mr. Arnold's book: of which I shall hear probably whenever it comes out. It is a thing that I feel much that you have written about me. Perhaps some time you will kindly tell me the title of the work, and how to be had: or where to look for it.

You will find Eros & Psyche a beautiful poem. I have made a few notes on it & sent them to Bridges, at his request: I mean I made them at his request. Prometheus, as you say, is out, & will succeed. There was a very good review in the Academy.[2] Have you seen his Nero? It seemed very good when I read it: especially the metre. He is writing a great deal just now.

You do not say anything about yourself. Bridges told me you were through all that examination work, and ready to read anything. I hope the illness and prostration, of which you spoke before, is really passed.

I am, My dear Friend,
Yours affectionately
R. W. Dixon
Kindly let me know by a P.C of Psyche's safety.

[1] Published in 1885.
[2] The issue of 22 Nov. 1884.

9–13 December 1884 to his sister Kate

FL, no. XCV, p. 164 Bodleian, MS Eng. lett. e. 41, fos. 79k–80v

University College, | ~~85 & 86,~~ Stephen's Green. | Dublin. [*Printed heading*]

Dec. 9 1884

Me dear Miss Hopkins,[1] — Im intoirely ashamed o meself. Sure its a wonder I could lave your iligant corspondance so long onanswered. But now Im just afther conthroiving a jewl of a convaniance be way of a standhen desk and tis a moighty incurgement towards the writin of letters intoirelee. Tis whoy ye hear from me this evenin.

It bates me where to commince, the way Id say anything yed be interistud to hear of. More be token yell be plased tintimate to me mother Im intirely obleeged to her for her genteel offers. But as titchin warm clothen tis undher a misapprehinsion shes labourin. Sure twas not the inclimunsee of the saysons I was complainin of at all at all. Twas the povertee of books and such like educational convaniences.

And now, Miss Hopkins darlin, yell chartably exkees me writin more in the rale Irish be raison I ~~w~~ was never rared to ut and thats why I do be so slow with my pinmanship, bad luck to ut (savin your respects), but for ivery word I delineate I disremember two, and thats how ut is with me.

(The above very fair.)

The weather is wild and yet mild.

I have a kind of charge of a greenhouse.

I am hoping to hear Dvorak's Stabat Mater at Trinity College tomorrow. I think you heard it.

I have an invitation for Xmas to Lord Emly's.[2]

A dear old French Father, very clever and learned and a great photographer, ~~finding~~ who at first wanted me to take to photography with him, which indeed in summer would be pleasant enough, finding that once I used to draw, got me to bring him the few remains I still have, cows and horses in chalk done in Wales~~,~~ too long ago to think of, and admired them to that degree that he is urgent with me to go on drawing at all hazards; but I do not see how that could be now, so late: if anybody had said the same 10 years ago it might have been different.

You spoke in your last of meeting Baillie. He was al~~most~~^ways^ the kindest and best of friends and I always look upon myself in the light of a blackguard when I think of my behaviour to him and of his to me. In this case however he has not written since you met him and I hope to be beforehand with him.

Tis a quare thing I didn't finish this letter yet. Ill shlip me kyard in betune the sheets the way ye~~d~~ll know ~~I wasnt~~ ^Im not^ desaivin ye. Believe me your loving brother Gerard.

Dec. 13 1884.

[1] The first three and last paragraphs of this letter are in GMH's mock Irish ('very fair' as he says) and can best be understood by reading them out in a stage Irish accent.

[2] William Monsell, 1st Baron Emly (1812–94; *ODNB*), educated at Winchester and Oriel College, Oxford, which he left without a degree in 1831. He converted to Catholicism in 1850, and defended its interests in Parliament, where he was member for Limerick in the Liberal Party (till 1874). In the House of Commons he held a number of posts, including President of the Board of Health (1857), Vice-President of the Board of Trade (1866), Under-Secretary of State for the Colonies (1868–71), and Postmaster-General (1871–3). He became Vice-Chancellor of the Royal University of Ireland in 1885. His first wife, Lady Anna Maria Charlotte Wyndham-Quin (1814–55), bore two sons who died in infancy, and by his second wife, Bertha de Montigny (1835–90), he had a son, Gaston (b. 1858), and a daughter, Mary (b. 1860). He was knighted in 1874. His opposition to the Irish national Land League and the Home Rule movement lost him much of his former popularity in Ireland but would have accorded with GMH's views.

17 December 1884 to Robert Bridges

LRB, no. CXXII, p. 201 Bodleian, Dep. Bridges, vol. 92, fos. 58^{r-v}
Postcard addressed to 'Robert Bridges Esq. | Yattendon | Newbury | Berks England.' PM DUBLIN ? DEC 17 84

~~St. Ignatius'~~ University College ~~SJ~~, ~~23 Upper Temple-street~~, Stephen's Green, Dublin. [*printed heading corrected*]
Dec. 17 '84

I have been some days annotating as desired, either gilding or else refining gold.* [*GMH footnote*: *I shall not be long.]

I want to know in what Athenaeum, for I missed ~~a~~ it and must see it, there was, as I am told, a review of P. F.[1]

The book ~~the~~ ^my^ notice (almost entire) of C. D. is in is Thos. Arnold's Handbk. of English Literature, a wellknown work. G. M. H.

[1] This review, of the edition published by Bell, did not appear till 24 Jan. 1885. It begins: 'If this were a translation it would be a good one.' The 'parable of the plot' is sketched out and criticized for missing dramatic opportunities. However, the anonymous reviewer concludes that 'Mr. Bridges's use of the Promethean myth is subtle and suggestive. His parable is inexact . . . [but] worth the thinking out' (p. 115). GMH evidently refers to the enthusiastic review of nearly two columns by J. W. Mackail in the issue of the *Academy* for 22 Nov. 1884, who found 'the welcome fulfilment of a remarkable promise. . . . *Prometheus the Firegiver* comes nearer, perhaps, to the Greek spirit and tone than any English play that has been written since Milton'.

1885

1 January 1885 to Robert Bridges

LRB, no. CXXIII, p. 201 Bodleian, Dep. Bridges, vol. 92, fos. 59–61ᵛ

University College, | ~~85 & 86,~~ Stephen's Green, | Dublin. New Year's day 1885 [*Printed address with date added by hand*]

Dearest Bridges, — I wish you and your wife a very happy new year.

I believe it would have been better for me to have gone to Hampstead as they wanted me, ~~as~~ ^since^ it seems I need a change; at all events I am jaded. It would have been the world of pleasant to have seen you.

What a pleasure must that music have been! "Then what charm company"[1] etc. Now talking of music I must tell you I have a great matter on hand. It is music to the Battle of the Baltic, the tune made long ago and now I am harmonising it. My first attempt in harmony was "~~t~~^T^he Crocus.[2] I got it sent to Sir Frederick Gore Ouseley a good time ago and he has not returned it. The reason ~~will~~ ^must^ be that finding it will not do he cannot make up his mind to tell me so. Indeed the second and third verses were a kind of wilderness of unintelligible chords, but the first seemed to me very good. However this new thing will be intelligible,[3] and in a few days I am going to send you the first two ^ — ^ or two first ^ — ^ verses (I hold it is all the same) and then I want you, please, to get — [4] as before to pass judgment on them — this on~~c~~e ^time^ more, as children go on. There is a bold thing in it: in the second verse a long ground bass, ^a chime^ of fourteen notes, repeated ten times running, with the treble moving freely above it. It is to illustrate "It was ten of April morn by the chime". If — [4] should approve it I am made, musically, and Sir Frederick may ^wallow and^ choke in his own Oozeley Gore. Then I have in the background Collins' Ode to Evening I mentioned to you before, which is a new departure and more like volcanic sunsets or sunrises in the musical hemisphere than anythin ye can conçave.

One word on Psyche and volcanic sunsets. The description of ~~th~~ the one over the Cretan Sea[5] ~~is~~ so closely agrees with an account I wrote ^in

Nature^, even to details which were local only, that it is very extraordinary: you did not see my letter, did you?[6] Swinburn, perhaps you know, has ^also^ tried his hand — without success.[7] Either in fact he does not see nature ^at all^ or else he overlays the landscape with such phantasmata, secondary images, and what not of a ~~D.T.~~^delirium-tremendous^ imagination that the result is a kind of bloody broth: you know what I mean. At any rate there is no picture.

There is one stanza about Psyche ~~falling~~ 's ^sister^ falling like a stone.[8] In suggestion it is one of the most brilliant in the poem but in execution ~~of the most~~ ^very^ imperfect, and therefore I have been freer there than anywhere else.

I do not want to say more of Psyche now.

I shall be proud to send you the fragments, unhappily no more, of my St. Winefred. And I shd. independently be glad of your judgment of them.

I do not believe you will succeed in producing a 12 syll. or 6 foot line which shall not, as you say, be an Alexandrine. There is, ~~to~~ according to my experience, an insuperable tendency to the Alexandrine, so far, I mean, as this, that there is a break after the 3rd foot, cutting the line into equal halves. This is the ~~most~~ first feature of the measure and will assert itself. It has some advantages, but it makes it monotonous; and to vary the division, the phrasing, successfully, and for long, is a most difficult matter. Common blank verse on the other hand is in this respect selfacting, for 2 ft. + 3 or 3 ft. ~~2~~ + 2 or 2½ + 2½, one of which ^divisions^ almost every line ~~one~~ you ^can^ without thinking make is sure to have, are all good and even without attention they will vary one another; whereas the equal division of the Alexandrine is first poor ^and^ then nearly invariable. Nevertheless ~~you an~~ I have grappled with this^;^ ~~and~~ how far successfully you will judge.

In such a case, the invention of a new vehicle, nothing wiser certainly can be done than to concert action as you propose to do: it is the best substitute for a ~~histor~~ past experience and a tradition. — But it is strange that you should select for comedy what I ~~find~~ from its pathos chose for tragedy.[9]

I have found that this metre is smooth, natural, and easy to work in broken dialogue^,^ ~~and~~ so much so that it produces nearly the effect of 5 foot blank verse; but in continuous passages it is a very different thing. In passionate passages I employ sprung rhythm ^in it^ with good effect.

I am going, I am glad~~,~~ to say, for change to Clongowes Wood College, near Naas, tomorrow. I shall take Psyche with me and also try to copy ~~you~~ out and send you the passages from St. Winefred. I wish it might act as a stimulus to go on with it. At times I have been very much pleased with some things in them.

You will perhaps say that besides the Alexandrine, which is a dimeter, there might be a trimeter, like the Greek. But the trimeter arises by taking the stresses of the odd feet stronger than those of the even and so coupling the feet in pairs of stronger and weaker. With quantity this subordination and coupling is easy^,^ ~~and~~ but in English it is hard and cannot be continuously done. Mr. Patmore has pointed out the smooth musical effect of it where it occurs, ~~as he says~~ though better instances might, I believe, be quoted than the one he gives.[10] The ~~effect~~ ^impression^ of the Greek trimeter ^as a whole^ is very closely given by our ~~ex~~ ^5ft.^ blank verse, though the metres are different. I do not think that taking a 6 foot line would bring us any nearer the Greek trimeter than we are now, rather the reverse; probably you think the same.

I hear that in a nocturn of Field's[11] there is a chime as a ground bass. However I presume the treble is written to the bass; mine is not.

If —[4] will not do Stainer must: one of the two you must get for me. It is but a short little thing, two verses.

Believe me your affectionate friend Gerard Hopkins S.J.

[1] RB's poem, 'Spring', st. 4.

[2] GMH's music to 'The crocus' is no longer extant.

[3] See *J&P*, 477–82 and *CW* vi.

[4] Name cancelled by RB. See letter of 11 May 1883.

[5] *Eros and Psyche* (*P.W.*, i), March, stanzas 24–6. RB's note says that this description 'is a portrait of the phenomena which followed the great eruption of Krakatoa'. There is also a reference to 'the sunsets of five years ago' in *The Growth of Love*, 67.

[6] See letter of 21 Dec. 1883 above, published in the issue of 3 Jan. 1884.

[7] Perhaps *Evening on the Broads* (*Studies in Song*, 1880).

[8] *Eros and Psyche*, August, st. 27.

[9] GMH for 'St. Winefred's Well' and RB for *The Feast of Bacchus, A Comedy in the Latin Manner* (1889). See RB's Note I on this play for his account of the metre used.

[10] See *Prefatory Study on English Metrical Law*, 49–50, *Amelia*, *Tamerton Church-Tower*, etc., 1878, or the *Essay on English Metrical Law*, 245–6, vol. ii, *Poems*, Sixth Collective Edition, 1897.

[11] John Field (1782–1837), born in Dublin, pianist and composer. He made his debut as a pianist at the age of 9 and then studied with the pianist and piano maker Muzio Clementi in London. He wrote and performed the first of his seven piano concertos when he was 17. In 1801 he accompanied Clementi on tour to Paris and Vienna and then moved with Clementi to Russia, where he demonstrated his pianos. He married and settled as a concert pianist and piano teacher in St Petersburg in 1810. Contracting cancer in 1831, he returned to London and went to Italy for medical care. He spent his last months in Moscow. A small group of his Nocturnes is important not only for intrinsic merit, but historically because Chopin was influenced by them.

19 January 1885 from Richard Watson Dixon to GMH

CRWD, no. XXXIII B, p. 128 Campion Hall, D 19/1/85

Warkworth Vicarage. | 19 Jan. 1885
My dear friend,

Will you excuse a hasty note to ask you either to send me the Hibernia Ignatiana, or tell me out of it the places to which the first Irish Mission went, and any incidents related: with permission to refer to the book, and reference given.

The published books to which you referred me are defective in that, they say nothing of the localities.

I have been to London for four days, & rather hoped to have seen Bridges, but he decided not to come up. My 3^{d}. volume of Ch. hist.[1] is finished since last July, but still there are many holes to stop, such as this that I write about now.

Your affec^{te} Friend
R. W. Dixon

[1] Published 1885 (2nd edn. 1893).

24 January 1885 to his Mother

FL, no. XCVI, p. 166 Bodleian, MS Eng. lett. e. 41, fos. 81–85^{v}
Addressed to 'Mrs. Manley Hopkins | Oak Hill | Hampstead | London N.W.'
PM DUBLIN JA 26 85 and LONDON N.W. JA 26 85.

University College, | ~~85 & 86,~~ Stephen's Green, | Dublin. [*printed heading*] Jan. 24 1885

My dearest mother, — I am all going to pieces with a cold, but my heart is light because I have just got the Scholarship examination papers done.

The business in hand is this. To begin at the beginning, we are expecting as a student and boarder AN IMPERIAL PRINCE or at least a prince from the Austrian Empire. He has four names tied together with hyphens besides ~~those~~ Christian names.[1] Now these unspeakable nationalist papers, which call any man that shews common respect to authority, a flunkey and are ^ready^, none so ready, to play the flunkey themselves; one of these papers, I say, published the other day a flaming puff preliminary of the Prince. Of course we were vexed and of course everybody will think and say we did it, but there was nothing to be done but to do nothing.

However I do expect Fr. Delany will have been a little fluttered and the imperial sitting-and-bedroom-in-one ~~is~~ has been got up in a style gayer than the rest of this shabby and dingy establishment. (~~i~~If you could hear me sneeze you could think it a dynamite counterblast to the explosions at the Houses of Parliament and the Tower, the news of which is, while I write, being cried in the streets.[2]~~)~~ I reserve comments.) And as our windows, when they open at top at all, ~~b~~ as mine did not, till, by gentle but continued pressure, I got a carpenter to it, open by the pulling of a rope, the imperial ~~rope~~ ^tackle^ has been made of crimson ^cord^ ^like a^ girdle ~~stuff~~, with an acorn knop, the size of a big fircone, at each end, which is a thing of beauty and will be to the prince, a ~~thi~~ joy for ever till he pulls it off. Now I am getting nearer the point, but must begin a new paragraph.

I have spoken before this of ~~old~~ Fr. Mallac,[3] a delightful old gentleman hailing originally from the Mauritius but since then from most parts of Europe, who is a very learned man and a believer in a wonderful system of medicine discovered by a certain Italian nobleman, Duke or Count or something Mattei,[4] and made up into tiny ~~globules~~ ^pills, globules,^ drops, beads, like the homoeopathic ones just, and taken in water; I take ~~it~~ the~~ir~~^em^ for any ailment and am none the worse, but I must own that this cold does seem to be rather too many for Mattei. (Robert Curtis had a fit the very night after he took his first globule.) Now I am getting nearer.

It is due to Fr. Mallac that the Prince is coming. It further appears that ~~th~~ his sister the Countess Mary (but why not Princess Mary? however so I understood Fr. Mallac to call her) wants to read some good English story books. Accordingly Fr. Mallac went to his bookseller's, almost the only place he goes to out of the house, and got certain books ^which were^ recommended there to him. The~~re~~^y^ were Catholic tales and — but he took the precaution of reading them. Now it un~~t~~^f^ortunately happened that children were born in the first chapters of both of them. This is not a bad thing to do in fact and must be allowed also to the characters in fiction, but not under all circumstances; and in one of the two the child was stillborn. This, for a young countess of fifteen or eighteen, he found too strong. Something of the same sort occurred in the other book. He then appealed to me to ~~recommend him~~ ^name^ some books to him~~,~~ which shd. be interesting and in which the personages should have got their birth completely over before the story begins.

I named some — Alice in Wonderland[5] (a book I never admired, indeed never read much of; I hold it is not funny) of course; then Mrs. Molesworth's[6] and Mrs. Ewing's[7] tales, which I have not read, but ^I knew^ they ~~are~~ were highly praised; then Miss Thackeray's[8] fairy tales modernised; Ruth and her Friends,[9] which has been through 9 editions and is much praised — I never read it; the Heir of Redclyffe;[10] and perhaps I named others (well the Little Duke and Lances of Lynwood I named).

But here I must stop a bit. Fr. Mallac wants the books not to be lovestories. This is a great difficulty: the most highly proper English stories have love in them. Also since last night I have read some of one of Mrs. Molesworth's books, called Christmas-Tree-Land for him. I am not so very well pleased with it. It is not so particularly natural. I do not see that there is any humour in it. There is a kind of slobbery nice~~s~~ness and good humour all over it, very common in some books and very distasteful to me, ^when^ without the salt of humour. And it is illustrated by Walter Crane and the illustrations are sweetly pretty, but look at them twice and you see they are not well drawn; the squirrels are very good and Rollo the hero has a lovely curly highbred upper lip, but there is a good deal of deception and gilt gingerbread.

To come to it then. I want you and your accomplished daughters to name some good books (1) in good English (about that again more anon), (2) in which the characters shall be born ~~o~~^b^ehind the scenes and come on the stage alive, (3) with no or the least possible lovemaking in them, (4) if well illustrated so much the better. Expense no great object to the p~~i~~rincely exchequer.

About the good English, that is another thing. I presume ^that^ that Mrs. Molesworth is connected with our Mrs. Molesworth and that she comes from the North. Anyhow she writes provincial north country English. She says "should have done" for "should have", nay worse "would" and "will" for "should" and "shall" like any Irishwoman.

I named also the Princess of Thule[11] because it is mostly made up of repenting, not of lovemaking.

I believe this has been a lively letter, but how it can be with such a cold on the writer amazes me. With best love to Grace and all believe me your loving son Gerard.

[1] Count Maximilian Waldburg-Wolfegg-Waldsee (1863–1950). In April his brother, Count Joseph (1864–1922), joined him and the brothers stayed for two terms. Their

sister was Maria Leopoldine (1866–1905) (*WHALB*, 390–1). They were three of the seven children of Prince Franz Waldburg-Wolfegg-Waldsee (1833–1906).

[2] This was indeed up-to-the-minute news: that very day at two o'clock, Fenians in the 'dynamite war' had caused explosions in the Houses of Parliament and in the White Tower at the Tower of London. Two men, John Gilbert Cunningham and Harry Burton, were later tried and sentenced to penal servitude for life. See Lord Ronald Sutherland Gower's *The Tower of London* (1902).

[3] Fr Jacques Mallac taught philosophy at University College from 1884 to 1890, when he was recalled to France. He was a 'black-avised' man of striking appearance, 'fanatically Aristotelian', and had been till middle age a confirmed free-thinker. One writer (C. P. Curran) reports that GMH was mercilessly chaffed by him for his Englishness and regards this as part of 'the eternal feud between Platonist and Aristotelian'. However, the references that GMH makes to him in his letters suggest both a kindlier man and a more friendly relationship with Hopkins.

[4] See letter of 13 Jan. 1886 and its n. 3.

[5] First published in 1865.

[6] Mary Louisa Molesworth [née Stewart] (1839–1921; *ODNB*) was born of Scottish parents in Rotterdam but her family settled in Preston and then Manchester in 1841, where her father worked for Robert Barbour, a merchant and shipping agent. She was educated at home and in 1861 married Captain Richard Molesworth (1836–1900), who had a violent temper. The couple had five children and separated in 1879 while living in France. Mrs Molesworth returned to England in 1883. She wrote over 100 works of fiction, mostly for children, characterized by a sympathy for younger children's perspective but an outmoded attention to class.

[7] Juliana Horatia Ewing (1841–85; *ODNB*), daughter of Mrs Alfred Gatty, wrote many children's books such as *Jan of the Windmill* (1884), first printed as *The Miller's Thumb* (1873), *Jackanapes* (1884), and *The Story of a Short Life* (1885).

[8] Anne Isabella Thackeray, Lady Ritchie (1837–1919; *ODNB*), the eldest daughter of William Makepeace Thackeray, was a successful journalist and novelist whose works included *The Village on the Cliff* (1867), *Old Kensington* (1873), and *The Story of Elizabeth* (1863). Her sister Minnie married Leslie Stephen in 1867, dying of pre-eclampsia in 1875. In 1877 Annie married her cousin Richmond Thackeray W. Ritchie (1854–1912), ceased to write fiction, and edited her father's works.

[9] *Ruth and her Friends: A Story for Girls*. No author's name given: British Library, 1857.

[10] Charlotte Mary Yonge (1823–1901; *ODNB*) was educated by her father and a visiting tutor along the lines advocated by the Edgeworths. She became a prolific author of over 200 works of fiction and non-fiction, among them *The Heir of Redclyffe* in 1853, *The Little Duke* in 1854, and *The Lances of Lynwood* in 1855. She was a devout Tractarian and her works conveyed her religious ideals. She never married and devoted a large part of the money that her publications earned to missionary works abroad and to churches in England.

[11] By William Black (1841–98; *ODNB*): first published in 1874. Black was born in Glasgow and initially studied landscape painting at the Glasgow School of Art but then became a journalist. From 1864 he also wrote many successful novels that combined detailed background description gleaned from his travels on the Continent with fictional situations.

6 February 1885 to Robert Bridges

LRB, no. CXXIV, p. 204 Bodleian, Dep. Bridges, vol. 92, fos. 62–63^{v}

University College, | ~~85 & 86,~~ Stephen's Green, | Dublin. Feb. 6 1885. [*Printed address with date added by hand*]

Dearest Bridges, — I have much to write to you, but one thing presses and I have no time for more. I beg you will very carefully attend to what I say.

Some years, say five, ago there came out a tragedy, its name I do not remember but its subject was Nero's history.[1] Poppaea was in it. I read a review of it, in which was quoted a scene between Nero and Poppaea. She suggests to him the murder of Agrippina and the suggestion is of the shape "Pray, gentlem~~a~~en, do not nail his ears to the pump". In it were the words "No crimes, I beg, no crimes".[2]

About this much I am certain. I ~~have~~ ^was^ struck by the words, have often thought of them, and I believe have quoted them.

The following I am not quite sure about. When you told me of your designing a tragedy of Nero (it was by word of mouth, not letter) and said it was wonderful ~~it had not been~~ ^the^ the story had not been made use of or more use of before (though you knew better than I did that there was one or more plays called Britannicus), I told you of the play spoken of above, and I think, I am not certain but it is likely in itself, that I quoted to you the words "No crimes" etc.

It would be well if you could get to see that play, but ~~it~~ in any case you will see ~~that~~ how highly likely it is that I have here traced the history of the words "No crimes" in your play both to their source and ~~down~~ ^up^ their channel.

Now since I am certain about that other play and since it may very easily happen that its author or a friend or a reviewer may recall those words in it I earnestly hope it is not too late for you to strike them out of yours. Not only they are not original but an echo, but it would be almost impossible for you to give any explanation of their appearance, even the true one, which would not be lame and laughable. I read them first today and ~~strike~~ ^I act^ at once.

You are peculiarly liable to these echos. For instance in Octavia's second line in the <u>rosatio</u> you have "unblamed"[3] in the same place and cadence and with the same "affective" ~~as~~ effect as Milton in "Hail, holy light".[4] Another point is not an echo exactly but a commonplace, only ^one^ to which unhappily <u>pereant qui bona nostra</u> {*may they perish who (have said) our good things*}[5] applies: you make Nero say of his mother's attempted drowning what Macbeth or Lady Macbeth more tersely says of Duncan — "The attempt and not the deed Confounds us."[6] Playwrights however cannot escape this: where particular cases are pointed out they may be modified. The echos are a disease of education, literature is full of them; but they ~~are~~ remain a disease, an evil. The above case will open your eyes. I can write no more:

I have other faults and a world of praise to find. Gerard.

[1] Presumably *Nero: A Tragedy*. By Richard Comfort (Philadelphia), of which *The Academy* (6 Nov. 1880) says: 'The art of writing unreadable tragedies in tolerably polished verse has spread to America.' 'Richard Comfort' was the *nom de plume* of Richard Tapper Cadbury (1853–1929), BA Haverford College, Pennsylvania (1868), MA Harvard (1878). He was a teacher, businessman, writer, and art critic for *The Nation* (<http://www.swarthmore.edu/library/friends/ead/5025cadb.xml>).

[2] Here RB has written the following interlinear note:

> I never saw the book nor have seen it: but I remembered GMH quoting the expression, & it seemed to me as if P. had really said it. So when I wrote the play I took it as if I had found it in Tacitus. R B
>
> Also I was experimenting without any expectation of producing what might be worth publishing. When it came to publishing I saw (as here warned) that the only person who could possibly suffer by the theft was myself — & as I was quite indifferent about that I let the words stand.

[3] *Nero*, IV. iii. 1–2:

> Hang there, sweet roses, while your blooms are wet,
> Hang there and weep unblamed; . . .

[4] *Paradise Lost*, III. 1.

[5] St Jerome quotes his teacher Aelius Donatus (*fl.* mid-4th c. AD) in his commentary on Ecclesiastes 1, referring to the words of Terence: 'pereant qui ante nos nostra dixerunt' {*may they perish who have expressed our bright ideas before us*}.

[6] Lady Macbeth in Shakespeare's *Macbeth*, II. ii. 12.

8 February 1885 to Robert Bridges

LRB, no. CXXV, p. 206 Bodleian, Dep. Bridges, vol. 92, fos. 64–6

University College, | ~~85 & 86,~~ Stephen's Green, | Dublin. Feb. 8 1885 [*Printed address with date added by hand*]

Dearest Bridges, — I daresay I shall be able to send you your book[1] in a day or two now. I am in the last Measure.* [*GMH footnote*: *~~after~~ I resumed the work this morning after a long break.] The first Measure is perhaps the least satisfactory and it is only at the 5th or 6th that I have begun to revise carefully.

I admire the equable beauty of the work and the quaintness and freshness of the pictures. The ~~plo~~ story you have not elevated but confined yourself to making it please. ~~C~~Eros is little more than a winged Masher, but Psyche is a success, ^a sweet little “body”, rather than “soul”.^ The dramatic side of the poem is very good, the characters say all the right things, and so on. I should think it would be widely and lastingly admired. On particular points I do not further dwell.

I am now ready to send my piece of music, the two first verses of the Battle of the Baltic, set of course for the piano, for what else can ~~it~~I do? but really meant for an orchestra — if I cd. orchestrate. But this is indeed to fly before I can walk, as a severe musician told me~~,~~ (but I did not care) of something else. Any lights Mr. —[2] gives me, any remarks he makes I shall be very grateful indeed for. I hope of course he will not find the thing ‘impossible’~~,~~ not the first verse surely, which even on the piano sounds a success; but the ground bass in the second needs a body of easily distinguishable instruments to bring it out. My hope is that, however complicated the harmony, the whole wd. be quite intelligible with a choir (the bigger the better) and an orchestra. My poor Crocus went to Sir Fred~~r~~erick Gore Ouseley and has not been heard of since, I fear is hopelessly lost.

Remember me very kindly to Mrs. Bridges and believe me your affectionate friend Gerard M. Hopkins S.J.

The critical remarks above will strike you perhaps as faint praise, but take it for said that the beauties of the poem are extreme: the seagull under water[3] alone is immortal and so are lots of things, pretty well everything that amounts to a feature.

Try my music yourself, at all events the first verse, and say what you think.

[4]Composed, as here, for the piano, for which instrument it is unfitted, because the parts and particularly the ground bass in the second verse cannot properly be distinguished; but I can do no otherwise. I am sensible that the rhythms of the second verse are very confusing and see now how bars 1, 2 might be made more intelligible, but nevertheless prefer to send it off as it is and correct ~~afte~~ afterwards. There shd. be a great body of voices and the ground bass shd. be done by bells or something of the sort. The triplets shd. be taken as made with notes of the same length as the couplets, that is the quaver is the same in both and no shorter in the triplet than in the couplet.

[1] *Eros and Psyche*.
[2] Name deleted by RB. See letter of 11 May 1883.
[3] *Eros and Psyche*, September, stanzas 5–7.
[4] This leaf was placed by RB at the end of the letter of 6 Oct. 1886, but it seems more probable that it belongs here, and accompanied GMH's setting of the *Battle of the Baltic*. See *CW* vi.

27 February 1885 from John Henry Newman to GMH

FL, no. C27, p. 413 present location unknown

Febr. 27. 1885
My dear F[r] Hopkins,

Thank you for your very kind remembrance of my birthday. I am so sorry to say my hand is too weak now to enable me to write — and I fear the weakness is permanent. I grieve to find you corroborate from your own experience what other friends tell me about the state of Ireland. What are we coming to!

Yours affect[ly],
J. H. Card. Newman

2 March 1885 to his Mother

FL, no. XCVII, p. 169 Bodleian, MS Eng. lett. e. 41, fos. 86–88[v]
Addressed to 'Mrs. Manley Hopkins | Oak Hill | Hampstead | London N.W.' PM DUBLIN MR 3 85 and LONDON N.W. MR 3 85.

University College, | ~~85 & 86,~~ Stephen's Green, | Dublin. March 2 1885 [*printed heading with dated added by hand*]

My dearest mother, — I wish you many very happy returns of tomorrow and time scarcely allows of my saying more than that.

Yesterday Mr. O'Brien M.P.[1] held his monster meeting in the Phoenix Park to protest against his suspension. It was not so very monster, neither were the people excited. Boys on the skirt of the crowd made such a whistling and noise for their own amusement ~~that~~ as must have much interfered with the hearing of the speeches. Fr. Mallac and I went: I fancy it was rather compromising. The~~y~~re were bands — it gave them an outing — and banners, including the stars and stripes and the tricolour. The people going were in Sunday clothes when they had got any, otherwise in their only suit, which with some was ~~n~~^r^ags. They were quiet, ~~orderly~~ ^well behaved^, and not jocular (which the Irish in public are not, that I see) — "neither sad nor glad like a dog at his father's funeral".[2] Mr. O'Brien spoke ^bareheaded^ from a drag, the wind was (alas, it long will be) in the East, and today ^he^ must have a terrible cold. I looked at him through opera glasses and got near~~e~~ enough to hear hoarseness, but no words. Excitable as the Irish are they are far less so than from some things you would think and ever so much froths off in words. Fr. Mallac, who ^in Paris^ witnessed the revolution of '48, ~~in Pari~~ said that there the motions of the crowd were themselves majestic and that they organized themselves ^as^ with a military instinct.

Though this particular ^~~as~~^ matter did not disturb me, yet the grief of mind I go through over politics, over what I read and hear and see~~,~~ in Ireland about Ireland and about England, is such that I can neither express ^it^ nor bear to speak of it.

I should correct what I said above about the crowd, that it was neither sad nor glad: it was, I should say, cheerful but not merry (except some drunken fellows).

They are crying some bad news in the streets. All news is bad.

I have no more time.

I should like you to see Mr. Curtis some day~~,~~ — to see him (or know him) is to love him — but hitherto he has never been out of Ireland.

Believe me your loving son Gerard.

I enclose a programme for Grace. I have another somewhere mislaid for her.

~~I~~^D^id I tell you of our German count?[3] He is a ~~most~~ splendid sample of a young nobleman, especially on horseback.

[1] William O'Brien (1852–1928) was an MP 1883–1918, during which time he represented various constituencies. In 1883–5 he had represented Mallow but the constituency was abolished in 1885 and he then became MP for South Tyrone. O'Brien had been suspended for disregarding the Speaker and for obstructing the business of the House of Commons through his interruptions. He was also imprisoned a number of times because of his active campaigning for proper conditions both in housing and livelihood for tenant farmers, in which he ultimately succeeded. He pursued these aims both in his role as editor of a series of papers including the *United Irishman*, the *Irish People*, and the *Cork Free Press*, and in more active agitation such as the No rent manifesto written while he was imprisoned in 1882 and through negotiation for such legislation as the Land Act (1903) and the Labourers Ireland Act of 1906.

[2] An Irish phrase. P. W. Joyce in *English as We Speak It in Ireland* (1910) writes: 'If a person is indifferent about any occurrence—doesn't care one way or the other—he is "*neither glad nor sorry like a dog at his father's wake*"' (p. 118).

[3] See letter to his mother of 24 Jan. 1885.

19 March 1885 from Richard Watson Dixon to GMH

CRWD, no. XXXIII C, p. 128 Campion Hall, D 19/3/85
Addressed to 'The Rev[d] | Gerard Hopkins S.J. | University College, | Stephen's Green, | Dublin | Ireland'. PM ACKLINGTON MR 19 85, WARKWORTH MR 19 85, LIVERPOOL MR 20 85, H&K PACKET MR 20 85.

Warkworth North[d]. | 19 Mar | 1885.
My dear Friend,

I cannot say how much I thank you, or how valuable your help, or how I feel your goodness in bestowing so much labour. I have completed my account of the Mission: & the footnote with wh. it begins runs thus.

"The following account of the first Jesuit mission into Ireland is compiled from ~~a~~ ^the^ valuable volume entitled Ibernia Ign. printed by the Soc. Typogr. Dublin. The author is the Reverend Edmond Hogan S.J. who has drawn from materials that seem unknown to the historians of the Order that are generally read. For my knowledge of this & for other information I am indebted to my friend the Reverend Gerard Hopkins S.J."[1]

I have not read all Nero in print yet. It is magnificent

Yours aff. & gratefully
R W Dixon

[1] *The History of the Church of England*, iii, footnote pp. 418–19, where, in the last sentence, 'gifted' is inserted before 'friend', an epithet which GMH regarded wryly. See letter to RB of 14 Dec. 1885.

24–5 March 1885 to Robert Bridges

LRB, no. CXXVI, p. 208 Bodleian, Dep. Bridges, vol. 92, fos. 67–70[v]

University College, | ~~85 & 86,~~ Stephen's Green, | Dublin. March 24 1885 [*Printed address with date added by hand*]

Dearest Bridges, — You will have been expecting to hear from me about Nero, but now I cannot say much on that if I am to answer you at once. I am in a low way of health, indeed ~~now~~ I always ~~n~~ am, but especially now in Lent; not that I fast, but the restriction of diet makes a difference to me. The delightful old French Father[1] who teaches Logic here (in which subject he reads, in 5 or 6 languages, everything published in Europe this century, pretty ~~well~~ nearly) will have it that I am dying — of anaemia. I am not, except at the rate that we all are; still I could do (indeed ^how gladly^ I could) — as they say — with more life.

I do not remember the place about Hora.[2] I am sure I did not mean what you think. Rather it was some infelicity in feeling, some want of ~~want~~ ^point^, I ~~point.~~ think.

Nero is a great work, it appears to me, breathing a true dramatic life. As an acting play I fancy there would be found defects~~.~~ in it. There is plenty of story and action and you writing it and a reader reading it might overlook something and think that was enough. But for an acting play not only must there be the requisite stir of action but that action must be seen.[3] It is to the reader much the same to read a scene of Agrippina's murder with the stage directions ~~and~~ ^or to read^ a description of it by one of the characters. There is a difference ~~of~~ ^in^ perspective as in painting between the ~~bac~~ foreground and the background, but when all is done they are on the same level of canvas. On the stage itself it is otherwise. Agrippin~~'~~a's death is the climax of the story; it shd. then be the climax of the stage business. You wd. then lose the noble line about the indivisible point of time,[4] but if you have two thoroughbreds you cannot ride both at once: one must be in the stable. You will say on the Gk. stage the climax is told by ~~w~~ ^mouth of^ messenger. But first this is really a defect, a shrinking from the crowning tragic effect; next as the scene is mostly unchanged it is readily accepted by the audience as being natural and necessary, for how else are they to know of it? But with us if the scene may be changed why not change it?

Further — the play is a History, like Henry ~~V~~ IV etc etc. History plays are the dramatising of a string of events which did ^at all events^ really take place and so much unity is not looked for in them as in ~~another plot others~~ ^other tragedies^. But the history shd. be well known. There ~~are~~ ^is^ interesting dramatising of ~~much~~ ^many^ historical points in your play, but some of these look "off" or outside the play and are nevertheless not very well known, e.g. Poppaea's two Caesars, ~~Petronius' appointment~~ ^Lucan's suspension^, Pallas' dismissal. It is true you make them bear, but it seems they shd. bear harder. So that I fancy the business or action is ^both^ scattered and ravelled. If everybody knew the ~~eve~~ history minutely they wd. say: So the events were scattered and these were the ravellings of circumstance, but now being but ill informed they want you to ~~gather~~ unravel and to gather up. It strikes me that these two kinds of ~~dram~~ action and of drama thence arising are like two kinds of tracery, which have, I dare say, names; the one in which the tracery seems ~~cut~~ ^like^ so much of a pattern cut out bodily by the hood of the arch from an infinite pattern; the other in which it is sprung from the hood or arch itself and wd. fall to pieces without it. It is like tapestry and a picture, like a pageant and a scene. And I call the one kind of composition end-hung and the other centre-hung and say that your play is not centre-hung enough. Now you see.

Blamed bad pens.

There are inimitable touches, such as "The sleek extortionate Pallas! Do you defend the despicable Pallas?"[5] and Burrus's "I never blamed your supper"[6] and Agrippina turning with "Polla is ~~d~~killed" cum sqq.[7]

Every scene is good, every soliloquy beautiful to individuation. (By the by the Irish, among whom I live, have no conception of this quality: the~~y~~ir ambition is to say a thing as everybody says it, only louder.) And therefore your avowal of plagiarism is the more shameless and your disavowal of originality the more affected;[8] but I say no more of this, especially as it is useless to dwell ~~long~~ ^hard^ on the point of honour; if it does not prick at the first push it was blunt beforehand.

Flaws remarked — ~~Acc~~ Accerronea should, I suppose, be Acerronia. Chalcocondyles seems an anachronism: ^were^ compounds so cumbrous ~~were not~~ found in Gk. at that date ? There were others, forgotten.

The timing Petronius' words with Britannicus' poisoning is ^a^ very ~~pi~~ fine piece of workmanship, but I have some doubts about it on the stage[9] — whether τὸ τραγικόν {*the tragic*} or τὸ παθητικόν {*the pathetic*}[10] is clearly struck: it ~~must~~ might pass as some touch of a ghastly quaintness. Experience would shew.* [*GMH footnote*: * This scene wd. need good byplay, careful concerting. But there is no depth of stupidity and gape a race could not fall to on the stage that in real life gapes on while Gladstone negotiates his surrenders~~.~~ of the empire.][11]

"This much were all" is hard. I can give it a sense indeed, but one expects "This all were much".

No more, as I believe I maunder.

To go back and correct myself and you — Do and did are not the weak ^present and^ perfect. Weak perfects are like leaped, ~~and~~ dreamed, strong like leapt, dreamt; or in different instances loved, hated are weak, rode, thought strong. You meant that do and ~~weak~~ did were morally weak. But this is no discovery of yours; it is as old as Pope: ~~An~~ "Then expletives their feeble aid do join And ten dull words oft creep in one low line".[12] And no doubt they ^do^ for the most part, but not in the present sentence, have a weak effect — which wd. nevertheless have been better if I had said / They have for the most part. But Wordsworth revived them, using them with great delicacy of effect. I did not notice that you had not used them, nor indeed do I remember using them in my suggestions myself, but have no doubt you are correct about both ~~poins~~ points; nevertheless I might well suppose you had ~~used them~~, for they quite belong to that half archaic style you there employ.

Now then about Ulysses. I will do what I can, but cannot promise much, in my unsatisfactory condition, weak in body and harassed in mind.

I am going to send you in a few days from St. Winefred (1) the first lines of the first scene, a dozen lines of dialogue or less; (2) ~~a~~ ^the villain's^ soliloquy after the murder, 71 lines, a very great effort; ~~and~~ (3) a dozen lines or less, beginning another soliloquy. I shall be glad of your comments. The metrical ~~effort~~ ^work^ is laborious, yet it seems to me a success. The unit~~y~~ies ~~are~~ ^will be^ much closer than in modern plays.

—[13] has not written, but I am getting on with the Ode to Evening.[14] It seems to me like a new art, the ~~a~~ effect is so unlike anything I ever heard. The air is plain chant where plain chant ~~is~~ most departs from modern music; on the other hand the harmonies are a kind of advance on ^advanced^ modern music. The combination of the two things is most singular, but it is also most solemn, and I cannot but hope that I have something very good in hand. It is so very unlike everything else~~,~~ that I am independent of and do not hold myself in abeyance to the judgments of musicians here; for ~~inf~~ in fact they know no more than I do what right I have to employ such and such chords and such and such progressions.

Believe me your affectionate friend Gerard M. Hopkins S.J.
Lady Day 1885.

1 Fr Jacques Mallac. See letter of 24 Jan. 1885 to his mother.

2 *Eros and Psyche*, 'September', st. 8.

3 RB's note to this play begins: 'This play was not intended for the stage, as the rest of my plays are.'

4 In the lines that follow Agrippina's speech to her assassins (V. ii. 3199–201):

> None answered, and awhile
> as such delay as makes the indivisible
> and smallest point of time various and broad.

5 II. iv. 938–9.

6 IV. iv. 2215.

7 V. i. 2810 sqq.

8 This refers to remarks in RB's letter: there was no author's note to the original edition of *Nero*.

9 III. v. 1579–1650.

10 Aristotle's *Poetics*, *passim*.

11 GMH had resented the loss of the Transvaal (see letters of 1881). Gladstone, recently returned to power, was trying to bring about Home Rule for Ireland, about which GMH had deep and mixed feelings. Gladstone had also been blamed in the Press for not assisting Charles Gordon in his defence of Khartoum in Jan. 1885.

12 *An Essay on Criticism*, ll. 346–7: 'dull' and 'low' should be reversed.

13 Name deleted by RB. See letter of 11 May 1883.

14 A project begun at Stonyhurst late in 1883 or early in 1884 (see letter to RB of 11 Nov. 1884; mentioned in letter to RB of 1 Jan. 1885). Although he says he will send it to RB (see next letter), no music is extant, but see *CW* vii for GMH's transcription of William Collins's 'Ode to Evening'.

1–2 April 1885 to Robert Bridges

LRB, no. CXXVII, p. 212 Bodleian, Dep. Bridges, vol. 92, fos. 71–74v

University College, | ~~85 & 86,~~ Stephen's Green, | Dublin. April 1 1885 [*Printed address with date added by hand*]

Dearest Bridges, — Ulysses is safe, but I will not write of it now÷. I am afraid I cannot be of much service. Holidays are begun, but I am not in the frame of body or mind to avail myself of them for work, as I should wish.

I return your Alexandrines and enclose my own. Please return these, remarking what may strike you. Metrically they will save my commenting on yours. I daresay our theory is much the same. I hold that each half line is by nature a dimeter, two bars or four feet, of which commonly one foot is silent or lost at the pause. You will find it sometimes employed in full. The third sample is patchwork: I once thought well of the pieces, I do not know that I do now. But A and B please me ~~now~~ well enough.[1] I do not like "recĕnt enough".[2]

You will see that as the feeling rises the rhythm ~~beg~~ becomes freer and more sprung: I think I have written nothing stronger than some of those lines. In the passage following Caradoc is to die impenitent, struck by the finger of God.

Your ^self^ quotation "mortal overthrow" is from the sonnet "In all things beautiful"–, last line:

Unshaken by man's mortal overthrow.[3]

I remember it, for the book is not ~~here~~ here. It must be left in the sonnet and should therefore, I think, be changed in Psyche.

Do and did "weak" present and perfect — It is a question of usage of words. The usage I follow is, I suppose, taken from the German, but now it is established, ~~I believe,~~ and that is enough. I object myself to calling do come, did come tenses at all: do, did are tenses (of do); come is a tense (if you like) of another mood ~~and~~ ^of^ another verb~~:~~. ~~t~~Two tenses and two moods and two verbs do not make a tense nor a ~~verb~~ mood nor a verb. It is the same confusion to call of him the genitive case: it is a preposition and an accusative case. These things are obvious, but scarcely anybody sees them.

You do not seem quite to have followed my meaning about the supper. The scene was ghastly of course. I feared that your scene was not ghastly enough. The stress was on "quaintness", that the ghastly or the tragic was carried off in a quaint coincidence instead of being ~~enforced~~ ^driven home^. But you may be right and on the stage perhaps that treatment might be the most effective.[4]

I am thankful to —[5] and did not want him hurried, as it is plain from the Athenaeum itself how busy he must be kept: however that is done now. His remarks are to be sure not ^in my circumstances^ encouraging, but they are instructive and if I could manage it I should attend Sir Robert Stewart's[6] or somebody else's course, as he advises; ~~but~~ only that I seem more in the way to compose my own requiem, like Mozart, ~~and on~~ ^but in^ plain chant, than any other ^musical^ exercise. Still there is something I do not understand. My piece puzzled you. Why? —[5] found it so plain, far too plain. (By the by, he does not speak of nor mark any mistake: that is the main thing, to be correct; if I am that, that is the great point gained.) As for not modulating, that was deliberate: I look on modulation as a corruption, the undoing of the diatonic style. What they call the key of the dominant, viz. one in which the fourth of the tonic is sharpened, I ~~call the key of the tonic~~ say is not the key of the dominant (which ~~naturally~~ ^is in another mode^ than the key of the tonic and has no leading note) but the key of the tonic misplaced and transposed. ~~I hold that~~ I believe that —[5] and I ~~e~~ would give diametrically opposite names to the same things: what he calls variety I call sameness, because modulation reduces all the rich diatonic keyboard with its ^six or^ seven authentic, not to speak of plagal, modes, to one dead level of major; where he finds tameness I find variety, specific quality (not of key, which is not specific, but) of mode. Here however, I must allow, is the hitch. For if I am right in theory, in practice I am bound to give that variety by my own methods. I find a difficulty in doing so and I am obliged to resort to devices of counterpoint (would I knew more of them!). Still I do hear plenty of variety which pleases me in that piece, and I hoped others would: it seems not; there is the mischief. To me plain chant melody has an infinite ~~dram~~ expressiveness and dramatic richness. The ~~omission~~ ^putting^ in or leaving out of a single note in an "alphabetic" passage changes the emotional meaning: all we admirers of plain chant feel this, the rest of the world (and I expect this includes —[5]) do not; and it is the old story, Fieri non potest ut idem sentiant qui aquam et qui vinum bibunt {*it is impossible that those who drink water and those who drink wine should feel the same*};[7] we are sober, they intoxicated with rich harmonies cannot taste our fine differences. When I hear one of Chopin's fragmentary airs struggling and tossing on a surf of ~~harmonies~~ ^accompaniment^ what does it matter whether one or even half a dozen notes are left out of it~~,~~? its being and meaning lies outside itself in the harmonies; they ~~give~~ give the tonality, modality, feeling, and all. But I could write reams on this matter, which time does not allow my further running on about. When the Ode to Evening is done or well advanced I will send ~~it~~ you that; study it yourself till you see my meaning (it is slow and easy to play); it is a test too: if you do not like it it is because there is something you have not seen and ~~which~~ I see. That at least is my mind, and if the whole world agreed to condemn it or see nothing in it I should only tell them to take a generation and come to me again. But ~~I~~ as it is I am well contented with —'s[5] judgment of the other thing and thankful to him for it; if I were otherwise than I am it would brisk me up and set me to work, but in that coffin of weakness and dejection in which I live, without even the hope of change, I do not know that I can make or, making, could keep up the exertion of learning better.

By the by, the mark ┌───┐ in the verses means a sort of spondee, two long syllables equally accented or nearly so, though nominally one of the two has the stress. This is my difficulty, what marks to use ~~or~~ ^and^ when to use them: they are so much needed and yet so objectionable. About punctuation my mind is clear. I can give a rule for ~~a~~ everything I write myself and even for other people, though they ~~would~~ ^might^ not always agree with me perhaps.

Believe me your affectionate friend Gerard M. Hopkins S.J. Holy Thursday '85.

You once objected to the word fleeced, which you will find in sample B:[8] I mean the velvetiness of roseleaves, ~~and~~ flesh, and other things, duvet.

I had almost forgotten to say that Michael Field is the author of Callirrhoe, Fair Rosamund, and other plays one or all published very lately and much praised by the critics.[9] He is a dramatist: ~~nothing~~ nought which concerns the drama concerns not him, he thinks. It might indeed do him good to know that you had never heard of him, but I hope you will not ~~make~~ let him make up a trio of enemies (<u>spretae injuria formae</u> {*the affront offered to slighted beauty*}[10] you know) with Marzials[11] and Hall Caine. The last has just written a novel said to be very good indeed.[12] M. F. may perhaps be Irish: Field is a common, Michael a very common Irish name. Do be wise.

[1] The three fragments of 'St. Winefred's Well'.
[2] Not found in the printed fragments.
[3] *P.W.*, *G of L*, 31: the final version has 'unsullied' for 'unshaken'.
[4] *Nero*, III. v.
[5] Name deleted by RB. See letter of 11 May 1883.
[6] See Biographical Register.
[7] See letter of 19–24 Jan. 1879 and its n. 5.
[8]

> its rose, time's one rich rose, my hand
> By her bloom, fast by her fresh, her fleecèd bloom,
> Hideous dashed down, . . .

[9] Michael Field is the name under which Katharine Harris Bradley (1846–1914; *ODNB*) and her niece Edith Emma Cooper (1862–1913) wrote numerous verse dramas and lyrics which are enjoying a renewed reputation. The first work in which they collaborated under the name of Michael Field was *Callirrhoë and Fair Rosamond* (1884).
[10] Juno's displeasure at Paris having awarded the golden apple to Venus, *Aeneid* I. 27.
[11] See letter of 13–21 May 1878, n. 3.
[12] *The Shadow of a Crime*.

Easter Eve [4 April] 1885 to Coventry Patmore

FL, no. CLXXVII, p. 358 Durham

University College, | ~~85, 86,~~ Stephen's Green, | Dublin. [*printed heading*] Easter Eve, 1885.

My dear Mr. Patmore, — It is very long since I wrote to you: I now take the opportunity of holidays and wish you a very happy Easter. Some time back I wrote you a longish letter, but repented of it, as I often do, and did not send it.

Part of it was to spur you on with your poem,[1] and to that I return.[2] You will never be younger; if not done soon it will never be done, to the end of eternity. Looking back afterwards you may indeed excuse yourself and ~~shew~~ ^see^ reasons why the work should not have been done — but ^it^ will not have been done, what might have been will not exist. This is an obvious and a homely thought, but it is a good one to dwell on. You wait for ~~volunt~~ your thoughts voluntary to move harmonious numbers. That is nature's way; possibly (for I am not sure of it) the best for natural excellence; but this poem was to be an act of devotion, of religion: perhaps a strain against nature in the beginning will be the best prospered in the end.

You think, as I do, that our modern poets are too voluminous: time will mend this, their volumes will sink. Yet where there is high excellence in the work, labour in the execution, ^there^ volume, amount, quantity tells and ~~hel~~ helps to perpetuate all. If you wrote a considerable poem ^more^ it would not only add to your works and fame its own weight or its own buoyancy but it would bulk out and buoy ~~out~~ up all the rest. Are Virgil's Georgics and Bucolics read more or less for his having written the Aeneid? Much more. So of Shakspere's and Dante's sonnets. It was by providence designed for the education of ~~manki~~ ^the^ human race that great artists should leave ~~their~~ works not only of great excellence but also in very considerable bulk. Moreover you say in one of your odes that the Blessed Virgin seems to relent and promise her help to you to ~~wrte~~ write in her honour~~:~~. ~~i~~If this is not to be followed it is but a foolish scandalous saying. You will not venture to say heaven failed to do its part or expect others to say so; either then you deluded yourself with groundless hopes or else you did not take the pains of correspondence # with heaven's offers. Either way the words would better have been left unsaid. This is presumptuous language on my part, yet aimed at the Blessed Virgin's honour and at yours.

I have read Bridges' Psyche, his Nero, and now have Ulysses on the table. Perhaps you have seen them all, some I know you have. Psyche is ^to me^ full of beauty. It does not aim ^at^ and could not possibly attain the elevation of your ~~Th~~ Unknown Eros, which ~~is~~ ^Eros is^ quite unknown indeed to the author; but by popularising the story, if it should be popular, it would heighten the interest of your treatment of it too. Nero is a fine work, I think, and breathes an Elizabethan life; but as an acting play would have, I ~~th~~fancy, certain drawbacks. In Ulysses I am somewhat disappointed. I cannot take heathen gods ~~as serious~~ ^in earnest^; and want of earnest I take to be the deepest fault a work of art can have. It does not strike at first, but it withers them in the end. Goethe's Faust has this fault: it is really farce. Also ~~it~~ ^Ulysses^ is sicklied o'er too much with archaic diction. This too will wither.

He now wants to write a comedy[3] in Alexandrine blank verse and sent me a sample, being a translation of the opening of Terence's Heautontimorumenos, very well as far as the diction went but the verse not interesting — I will not say it was a failure, but no great success. ~~Ha~~ He knew that I ^had^ employed this measure in a tragedy[4] I had been long attempting and asked to see some samples; so I sent him three, which is indeed nearly all the play, something over ~~a~~ ^100^ lines. I find the metre difficult, but very flexible and full of capacity. My theory of it is yours, that ideally every line has 8 feet, 8 stres~~es~~ses; but not equal — 4 dimeters ~~of~~ or bars of ~~two~~ ^2^ feet each. Then at the pause in the middle of the line and at the end one of these ~~e~~8 feet may be and commonly is suppressed, so that 6 are [*page break*][5] are left. This gives boundless variety, all of which is needed however to control the deep natural monotony of the measure, with its middle pause and equal division. It is likely my experiments, which satisfy me metrically, will be of more use to Bridges than myself — if he likes them.

I believe you will have shared, you cannot have equalled, the mortification and grief the policy (or behaviour) of the government have been costing me. But it is better prayed over than talked about.

I now hope to hear from you matters of interest. I have even some hopes I might see you, for I think I may likely be in England this summer; but I cannot tell how it will shape.

Believe me, dear Mr. Patmore, very sincerely your friend Gerard M. Hopkins S.J.

1 The projected 'Marriage of the Blessed Virgin'. See Frederick Page, *Patmore: A Study in Poetry* (London, 1933), 129–46.

2 See letter to RB of 13 Oct. 1886.

3 *The Feast of Bacchus; a Comedy in the Latin Manner; partly Translated from Terence.*

4 'St. Winefred's Well'. See letters of 24–5 Mar., 1–2 Apr., and 17–29 May 1885.

5 GMH continues the letter on a sheet which began a letter dated 'Good Friday' to 'My dear Fr. Cu##', which he abandoned and deleted.

7 April 1885 from Coventry Patmore to GMH

FL, no. CLXXVII A, p. 361 Campion Hall, P 7/4/85
Addressed to 'Revd Gerard M. Hokpins [*sic*], S.J. | University College | Stephens Green, | Dublin'. PM HASTINGS AP 7 85, H&K PACKET AP 8 85.

Hastings. April 7. 1885.

My dear Mr. Hopkins,

I was very glad indeed to see your handwriting again, and still better pleased to hear that there is a chance of seeing you this Summer.

I believe that I have done all that it will be possible to me to do in the way of fulfilling the intention you speak of; ~~but~~ I do not think the work will ever take the form of a poem. I have written a series of notes wh. I purpose shall be published after my death, ~~until~~ ^under^ the title of "Sponsa Dei."[1] I do not think they would be more, or so impressive in verse. They lend themselves as little to verse as the Epistles of St. Paul would do — though there ends their likeness. I should much like you to read them, and hope that you will do so when I see you.

I agree with your opinion of "Nero". "Ulysses" I have not read. I wrote a notice (the only one I have written, with one exception, for more that[2] 25 years) on "Prometheus" in the St. James's Gazette,[3] and I hope it will bring this poem into wider notice than it has yet had — Bridges, however, professes to feel a profound indifference as to whether people read his poems or not. I cannot understand this. Every additional reader, to me, is an addition to the fulfilment of the purpose for which I write.

The new Ed^n of the "Angel"[4] comes out this or next week. I think I have adopted about two thirds of your suggestions. I agree with all, but I ~~had~~ have got too far away from my first feeling to dare any corrections wh. ~~involve~~ involve re-writing.

What you say about bulk in poetry being a good thing is quite true, I think; & I wish that I had had force enough in me to make mine more bulky. But I have written all that I had to say, and as well as I could; and I must rest content. I spend many hours a day in meditating on my own line, but that line has carried me and daily carries me further & further away from the thoughts that can or ought to be spoken. I do not think, however that I am uselessly employed. Dont you think that a soul wh. has filled itself very full of a great unspoken & unspeakable thought may, if it attains its last end, teach the world by uttering it into the hearts of men in some far more powerful way than words?

Let me hear from you as soon as there is any ~~th~~ chance of my seeing you anywhere. If it ~~could~~ ^can^ be here, you know how glad I shall be.

Your's ever truly
C. Patmore.

[1] See letter of 6–7 May 1888 and 11 May 1888 from Patmore; see also Champneys, i. 315–19, 373; ii. 249.

[2] Obviously 'than'.

[3] 'Prometheus the Firegiver', *St. James's Gazette*, 9 Mar. 1885. Reprinted in *Courage in Politics* (1921).

[4] The 6th edn., in one volume.

7 April 1885 from Mandell Creighton to GMH

FL, no. E5, p. 424 Campion Hall, C 7/4/85

Addressed to 'The Rev. G. M. Hopkins, S.J. | University College | Stephen's Green, | Dublin'. PM CAMBRIDGE AP 7 85, H&K PACKET AP 7.

Langdale Lodge, | The Avenue, | Cambridge. [*printed address*].
Ap: 7. 1885.

My dear Hopkins,

I am glad to hear that you [are] settled in Dublin about which I hear sometimes from Tom Arnold, who seems to enjoy his work on the whole. You say truly that the drudging of examinations is the thing which overwhelms one most. Lecturing is less wearisome: but why cannot one be left in peace without it?

As to your question, — I know of no book recently published about Merton. The last account of the origins of Merton which I know is in Mullinger's History of the University of Cambridge Vol I.[1] Of course you know Nelson's Life of Walter de Merton.[2] There is a good deal about Oxford in earlier times in Lechler's Johann Wiclif, more in Lorimer's English translation with notes.[3] An article on John Wiclif at Oxford in the Church Quarterly of October 1877, an article with a great deal of learning about University history.[4] The preface to Anstey's Monumenta Academia in the Rolls series of Chronicles[5] gathers together most that is known of University life. I think I have now given you all the authorities that I can think of. Anstey disposes of the 30,000 students: they cannot have exceeded 5000. I had occasion to consider the number of students at Prag in 1408. They were put down at 20000: their real number seems to have been 4000 — guesses at numbers are very vague.

I am pursuing the History of the Papacy in the sixteenth century. It is not a task which will interest you — It is certainly a very difficult one.

Yours very sincerely
M Creighton

[1] James Bass Mullinger (1834–1917), *The University of Cambridge*, i (1873). Creighton was later to edit this work.

[2] Edmund Hobhouse, Bishop of Nelson, *Sketch of the Life of Walter de Merton* (1859).

[3] Gotthard Victor Lechler (1811–88), *Johann von Wiclif* (Leipzig, 1873), trans. Peter Lorimer (1812–79) and published in London in 1878 and 1884.

[4] *Church Quarterly Review*, 5 (Oct. 1877–Jan. 1878), 119–41. The anonymous article includes consideration of '*Fasciculi Zizaniorum.* Edited by W. W. Shirley for the Master of the Rolls' Series of Chronicles (London, 1858), *Second and Fourth Reports of the Royal Historical Commission.* And *Johann von Wiclif.* By Von Gotthard Lechler. 2 vols. (Leipzig, 1873).'

[5] Henry Anstey's book was called *Munimenta Academica or Documents Illustrative of Academical Life and Studies at Oxford*, Rolls Series 50 (2 vols., 1868).

4 May 1885 to Robert Bridges

LRB, no. CXXVIII, p. 216 Bodleian, Dep. Bridges, vol. 92, fo. 75^{r-v}
Postcard addressed to 'Robert Bridges Esq. | Yattendon | Newbury | England Berks'. PM DUBLIN X M[A]Y 4 85

University College, | Stephen's Green. [*Printed heading*]

May 4 '85 — I return your book,[1] almost, I am sorry to say as if I had not read it. I could do no better. "Providentiae nostrae incertae et ~~saepe~~ non est in homine via ejus" {*our future is uncertain and the way of man is not in himself*}.[2] I will write when I can. G. M. H.

[1] Presumably *Ulysses*.
[2] GMH is combining Vulgate texts from Wisdom 9: 14 ('incertae providentiae nostrae') and Jeremiah 10: 23 ('non est hominis via eius').

14 May 1885 to Coventry Patmore

FL, no. CLXXVIII, p. 362 Durham University Library, Abbott MS 195
One folded sheet watermarked with monogram EN and EBLANA NOTE, written on two sides.

University College, | ~~65 & 86~~ Stephen's Green, | Dublin. [*printed address*]
May 14. 1885.

My dear Mr. Patmore, — Thank you very much for the Angel in the House, which reached me the night before last: to dip into it was like opening a basket of violets. To have criticised it looks now like meddling with the altar-vessels; yet they too are burnished with washleather.

I see that this is the 6th edition, which shews a steady popularity or a steadily reading public. But it is a popularity and a public rather below the surface. This may content you, in itself it is not satisfactory. A good book is to educate the world at large. The ~~teaching~~ Angel in the House is in the highest degree ^~~an~~^ instructive, it is a book of morals and in a field not before treated and yet loudly crying to be treated. It cannot indeed ever be popular quite with the general, but I want it to be popular as a classic is, read by many, recognised by all. And I am not satisfied because it is not enough recognised. I cannot now say more, but remain your very sincere friend Gerard M. Hopkins S.J.

24 April–17 May 1885 to Alexander William Mowbray Baillie

FL, no. CXL, p. 254 UCD L 49
Two folded sheets of headed paper; 8 sides.

University College, | ~~85/86~~, Stephen's Green, | Dublin. [*printed address*]
April 24 1885

My dearest Baillie, — I will this evening begin writing to you and God grant it may not be with this as it was with the last letter I wrote to an Oxford friend, that the should-be receiver was dead before it was ended. (There is no bad omen in this, as you will on reflexion — REMARK: REFLEXION: I USED TO WRITE REFLECTION TILL YOU POINTED OUT THE MISTAKE; YOU DID SO TWICE, FOR I HAD, THROUGH ^HUMAN^ FRAILTY AND INADVERTENCE, LAPSED — see.) I mean poor Geldart, whose death, as it was in Monday last's Pall Mall, you must have heard of. I suppose it was suicide, his mind, ~~havi~~ for he was a selftormentor, having been unhinged, as it had been once or twice before, by a struggle he had gone through. Poor Nash's[1] death, not long before, was certainly suicide and certainly too done in insanity, for he had been sleepless for ten nights: of this too you will have heard. It much comforts me ~~that~~ and seems providential that I had renewed my friendship with Geldart some weeks before it was too late. I yesterday wrote to his widow. Three of my intimate friends at Oxford have thus drowned themselves, a good many more of my acquaintances and contemporaries have died by their own hands in other ways: it must be, ~~b~~and the fact brings it home to me, a dreadful feature of our days. I should say that Geldart had lent me his autobiography called (I wish it had ~~a better~~ ^another^ name) A Son of Belial.[2] It is an amusing and a sad book — but perhaps you have seen it. I am in it and Addis, Coles, ^Jeune,^ MacInnon, Nash, Jowett, Liddon, and lots more thinly disguised, though some I do not recognise.[3] You are not there.

May 8 — For one thing I was sorry when I got your late delightful letter. Since my sister told me of her meeting you I had been meaning to write and be first with you — but now I am slow even in answering. Some time since, I began to overhaul my old letters, accumulations of actually ever since ~~scho~~ I was at school, destroying all but a very few, ~~but~~ ^and^ growing ever lo~~a~~ther to destroy, but also to read, so that at last I left off reading; and there they lie and my old notebooks and beginnings of things, ever so many, which it seems to me might well have been done, ~~Old~~ [*heavy deletion illegible*] ruins and wrecks; but on this theme I will not enlarge by pen and ink. However there were many of your~~s~~ letters among them and overflowing with kindness (but not towards Hannah[4] and MacFarlane; however you need not distress yourself so much about them; I agree with you in the main, and believe I used to remonstrate sometimes of old on their behalf, because they were good fellows and the persistency of their attentions was a most real compliment — a sort of compliment that as one gets older and writes the senile parenthetic style I am maundering in now one values a great deal higher — but still I can distinctly remember, though I shall not recall, real provocation they gave you; and you never did more than ~~half~~ have a humourous fling at them;[5] but to return) and for those letters I was deeply grateful and keep it constantly before me that I was undeserving of them; but still it was a cruel thing of you now to tell me that my own very first letter to you begins with "Yes, you are a fool". The context, I suppose, ~~or~~ the sequel, I mean, does something to mitigate, but mitigate as you may I wish it were not said. But I ^have to^ regret so much! and what is it to withdraw ^a thing^ long after the event? Almost meaningless.

As I have told you before, the first thing not that you said to me but that I can remember your saying was some joke about a watering hose which lay on the grass plot in the Outer Quad: a small spray was scattering from it. I stood watching it and you, coming in from a walk, waving your stick at it quoted or parodied either "Busy ~~thir~~ curious thirsting fly" or the Dying Christian to his Soul.[6] You never could remember ~~me~~ this after and IN FINE (an expression which, it has always appeared to me, could never take root in our garden and yet we could never make up our minds to throw back again over the wall into ~~France~~ ^the French one^ where it came from) I am more sure that it was said than that you said it.

I think this is from a literary point of view (not from a moral) the worst letter I ever wrote to you, and it shall not ~~be~~ ^run^ much longer. You will wonder I have been so long over it. This is part of my disease, so to call it. The melancholy I have all my life been subject to has become of late years not indeed more intense in its fits but rather more distributed, constant, and crippling. One, the lightest but a very inconvenient form of it, is daily anxiety about ~~the~~ work to be done, which makes me break off or never finish all that lies outside ~~it~~ that work. It is useless to write more on this: when I am at the worst, though my judgment is never affected, my state is much like madness. I see no ground for thinking I shall ever get over it or ever succeed in doing anything that is not forced on me to do of any consequence.

I forget what the verses were I shewed you and you 'did not criticise'. It is putting friendship unwisely to a strain to shew verses, neither did I do it much. Those verses were afterwards burnt and I wrote no more for seven years; then, it being suggested to write something I did so and have at intervals since, but the intervals are now long ones and the whole amount produced is small. And I make no attempt to publish.

You said, and it was profoundly true then, that Mr. Gladstone ought to be beheaded on Tower Hill and buried in Westminster Abbey. Ought he now to be buried in Westminster Abbey? As I am accustomed to speak too strongly of him I will not further commit myself in writing.

Much could be said about Ireland and my work and all, but it would be tedious; especially as I hope we may meet soon. I seem glad you keep up your Oriental studies. Believe me always your affectionate friend Gerard M. Hopkins S.J.

May 17 '85 and still winter.

[1] Thomas Nash (1845–85), Balliol 1863–7, graduating with a first in 1867; barrister.

[2] *A Son of Belial: Autobiographical Sketches*. By Nitram Tradleg, pp. vii + 250 (1882). It is an interesting, discursive book, revealing a strange, uneasy personality, and important to students of GMH for the chapters (7–9) that give some account of the Oxford of the day and its religious 'atmosphere'. Belial is Balliol. Jowett is 'a certain Mr. Jewell, Professor of Greek, who had written a dangerous book of Commentaries to St. Paul's Epistles'. GMH appears as Gerontius Manley, 'my ritualistic friend'; V. S. S. Coles as Vincentius Staccato (and, familiarly, 'Stuckey'); Liddon as Canon Parry. Of 'Stuckey' it is said: 'Nor was logic his strong point; gushing was his forte. Gerontius gushed as well, but then he meant it.' See also the posthumous *Echoes of Truth* (1886) for a photograph of Geldart, and a selection of sermons preached by him at the Hope Street Church, Liverpool, and the Free Christian Church, Croydon. Between 1881 and 1886 there are several publications by him, including sermons and a simplified grammar of modern Greek.

[3] Francis Henry Jeune, Baron St Helier (1843–1905; *ODNB*) figures as 'Young' in Geldart's book. In 1867 he went to Australia to find information for the Tichborne case.

[4] John Julius Hannah (1844–1931), Balliol 1862–6; 4 Cl. and BA 1866. He was vicar of St Nicholas, Brighton, 1874–88; like his father, vicar and rector of Brighton; rector of West Blatchington, 1888–1902; and Dean of Chichester from 1902 to 1929.

[5] 'them' is the first word on a page written on college notepaper which GMH has dated 'May 8 1885'.

[6] 'Busy curious thirsty fly' is the first line of 'On a Fly drinking out of his Cup' by William Oldys (1687–1761). 'The Dying Christian to his Soul' is by Alexander Pope. Perhaps the lines which Baillie parodied were lines 8–9 of Pope's poem: 'What is this absorbs me quite? | Steals my senses, shuts my sight', alluding to GMH's characteristic absorption in something he is looking at.

17 May 1885 from Coventry Patmore to GMH

FL, no. CLXXVIIIA, p. 363 Campion Hall, P 17/5/85
Addressed to 'Rev[d] Gerard M. Hopkins, S.J. | University College, | Stephens Green, | Dublin'. PM HASTINGS MY 17 85.

Hastings. May 17. 1885:
My dear Mr. Hopkins,

I think that the "Angel" is in a fair way to get the sort of recognition you desire for it. Six large editions (10,500 copies) in England and more than twice that number in America is quite as large a circulation as is safe. A great popularity always produces a reaction — such as is setting in now against Tennyson.

A very good critic assures me that your suggested corrections have had a very decided effect on the impression made by the whole poem. It is wonderful how two or three awkward & unfinished lines deteriorate from a whole volume. I think I may now safely [say] that the poem is as complete as I can make it. The reason it is not so popular as you think it ought to be is probably the apparent fluency wh. has been given to it by laborious finish. Pope says that "Easy writing's sometimes damned hard reading".[1] The public and especially the Critics do not know that "Easy reading's sometimes damned hard writing".

Your's ever truly
C. Patmore.

[1] You write with ease, to show your breeding,
But easy writing's vile hard reading.

'Clio's Protest' by Richard Brinsley Sheridan; written 1771, published 1819. Patmore was probably confusing this with Pope's *Essay on Criticism*, ll. 362–3.

17 May 1885 to his Mother

FL, no. XCVIII, p. 171 Bodleian, MS Eng.lett.e.40, fos. 89–91v
Addressed to 'Mrs. Manley Hopkins | Oak Hill | Hampstead | London N.W.'
PM DUBLIN MY 18 85 and LONDON N.W. MY 19 85.

University College, | ~~85 & 86,~~ Stephen's Green, | Dublin. [*printed heading*] May 17 1885

My dearest mother, — I send you a line now and will write more hereafter, to my father it shd. be, for I owe him a letter. I am glad your journey was a success. You have returned to winter: at least it is winter in Ireland. I still have a fire. The hail today lay long like pail~~s~~fuls of coarse rice.

Since I last wrote I believe the Prince and Princess of Wales have been and gone.[1] They were well received all things considered: most people wanted to be civil and respectful, on the other hand it was felt with ~~truth~~ ^reason^ that to the ~~R~~^r^oyal family Ireland owes little gratitude. The Queen, who spends months every year in Scotland, does she not? or did once, has only thrice in all her reign visited Ireland and never lived there. But do not let us talk ~~polit#ics~~ politics, it kills me, especially under the present Prime Minister.[2]

I am in a sort of languishing state of mind and body, but hobble on. I should like to go to sea for six months.

With best love to all believe me your loving son Gerard.

If I shd. be able to visit you this year there is one thing I am much set on seeing, Epping Forest: Everard[3] might go with me; but I will be bound he will not be at home. Indeed I shd. like to ^go^ further and see the New Forest.

[1] Prince Albert and his wife, Alexandra. See letter of 10–13 July 1863 to Baillie for GMH's interest in the Royal family.

[2] Gladstone.

[3] GMH's brother; see Biographical Register and letters of 5–8 Nov. and 23 Dec. 1885.

17–29 May 1885 to Robert Bridges

LRB, no. CXXIX, p. 216 Bodleian, Dep. Bridges, vol. 92, fos. 76–81

University College, | ~~85 & 86,~~ Stephen's Green, | Dublin. May 17 1885 [*Printed address with date added by hand*]

Dearest Bridges, — I must write someth#ing, though not so much as I have to say. The long delay was due to work, worry, and ~~long~~ languishment of ~~m~~ body and mind — which must be and will be; and indeed to diagnose my own case (for every man by forty is his own physician or a fool, they say; and yet again he who is his own physician has a fool for his patient — a form of epigram, by the bye, which, if you examine it, has a bad flaw), well then to judge of my case, I think that my fits of sadness, though they do not affect my judgment, resemble madness. Change is the only relief, and that I can seldom get.

I saw that Ulysses was a fine play, the action and interest well cent~~e~~red, the characters finely drawn and especially Penelope, the dialogue throughout good; nevertheless, ~~put~~ perhaps from my mood of mind, I could not take to it, ~~it~~ did not like it, beyond a dry admiration. Not however to remain in a bare Doctor Felldom[1] on the matter, I did find one fault in it which seems indeed to me to be the worst fault a thing can have, unreality. I hope other people will think otherwise, but the introduction ~~wh into the serious~~ in earnest of Athene gave me a distaste I could not recover from. With Prometheus it was not the same. Three kinds of departure from truth I understand and ~~allow~~ agree to in a play — first in a ~~h~~History those changes and conventions without which, ~~like~~ ^as in^ other works of art, the facts could not be presented at all; secondly ~~in a play~~ ^a plot^ of fiction: though the facts never actually happened they are a picture of ~~what does, life~~ life and a sample of the sort of facts that do — those ^also^ subject to their own changes and conventions; lastly an allegory, where things that neither do nor could be mask ^and mean^ something that is. To this last class Prometheus, as I take it, belongs; moreover it was modelled on the Greek and scarcely meant for acting. But Ulysses is to act; and in earnest, not alle~~le~~gorically, you bring in a goddess among the characters: it revolts me. Then, not unnaturally, as it seemed to me, her speech is the worst in the play: being an unreality she must talk unreal. Believe me, the Greek gods are a totally unworkable material; the merest frigidity, which must chill and kill every living work of art they are brought into.

Even if we put aside the hideous and, taken as they stand, unspeakable stories told of them, which stories nevertheless are as authentic as their names and personalities — both are equally imaginary; if you do not like that, both equally ~~alleg~~ symbolical —, putting these out of sight and looking only at their respectable side, they are ~~a~~ poor ignoble conceptions ennobled bodily only~~,~~ (as if they had bodies) by the ~~sculptor~~ artists, but once in motion and action worthless — not gentlemen or ladies, cowards, loungers, without majesty, without awe, antiquity, foresight, character; old bucks, young bucks, and Biddy Buckskins. What did Athene do after leaving Ulysses? Lounged back to Olympus to ~~eve~~ afternoon nectar. Nothing can be made of it. May 21, 1885. The background of distance and darkness and doom which a tragedy should always have is shut out by an Olympian drop-scene; the characters from men become puppets, their bloodshed becomes a leakage of bran. (This, upon my word, is to ply the lash and to be unpardonable~~:~~). I see the nobility of the rest, but this one touch to my eye spoils all; it looks to me like fine relief all daubed and creamed over with heavy whitewash.

I do not wonder at those ladies reading Nero through at a sitting. It is very interesting and I feel quite the same. You offer~~r~~ed to send me a correcter copy: I shd. be glad if you now would.

I must add there was another fault I had to find with Ulysses and it was to the same effect and same defect, of unreality; I mean the archaism of the language, which was to my mind overdone. I hold that by archaism a thing is sicklied o'er~~, bligh~~ as by blight. Some little flavours, but much spoils, and always for the same reason~~,~~ — it destroys earnest: we do not speak that way; therefore if a man speaks that way he is not serious, he is at something else than the seeming matter in hand, non hoc agit, aliud agit {*he is not doing this thing, he is doing something else*}.[2] I believe you agree with me in principle: if so I ~~hold~~ ^think^ that your practice in that play is beyond what your principle allows. But slight changes would satisfy me. The example of Shakspere (by a "corrupt following", for it is an absurd fallacy — like a child ^having to^ repeat~~ing~~ the substance of something it has been told and saying you and I wherever the speaker said you and I, whereas it should say I where he said you and so on) has done ever so much harm by his very genius, for ~~they~~ ^poets^ reproduce the diction which in him was modern and in them is obsolete. But you know all this.

How did Michael Field in the end go off?[3]

It is too bad that I shd. so abuse Ulysses after your encouragement of St. Winefred. But how cd. you think such a thing of me as that I shd.

in cold blood write "fragments of a dramatic poem"? — I of all men in the world. To me a ~~finished~~ completed fragment, above all of a play, is the same unreality as a prepared impromptu. No, but we compose fragmentarily and what I had here and there done I finished up and sent ^as samples^ to see if I cd. be encouraged to go on — and I was encouraged; that is by your last, for before I thought you thought they wd. not do. There is a point with ~~them~~ ^me^ in matters of any size when I must absolutely have encouragement as much as crops rain; afterwards I am independent. However I am in my ordinary circumstances unable, with whatever encouragement, to go on with Winefred or anything else. I have after long silence written two sonnets, which I am touching: if ever anything was written in blood one of these was.[4]

^Of^ ~~T~~two metrical criticisms you made on the fragments one I did not well understand, the other was a misunderstanding on your part.

About the music I shd. like to write at some length. But for the present I only say first, how could you think I shd. be offended at your criticism or remarks or want^ed^ you to express yourself so modestly? May 28, 1885. Next I am much obliged for the quotations from Purcell, but could not get my ~~domestic~~ household musician to play the one in open score nor have had time or opportunity of running after ~~musicians~~ ^professionals^, besides that for myself I have kept away some time now from the piano. Thirdly the bass solo you give me to shew the variety Purcell could command by the modern system — well of that beautiful passage I have to say that it illustrates the wellknown variety of the minor as we now understand ^it^, a variety for which Purcell particularly prized it, but that that variety I did not need ^the^ illustrating of and, ahem, I can send you an illustration of my own which as it seems to me is happy in that way — ~~written~~ made ~~not~~ ^long^ ago. Then of course I admire and surely I could produce ^~~modulation~~^ — it requires no more knowledge than I have already got for at least the simpler effects and in fact modulation even to remote keys and so on is not difficult to do; it may be to explain — could produce~~d~~ and have produced modulations, but in the two first verses of the Battle of the Baltic~~,~~ (which has some eleven) I wanted to see what could be done (and for how long I could go on) without them.[5] — [6] of course thought they cd. not be done without even for that length and I do not dispute the judgment; I scarcely had myself heard my second verse — for that is the great difficulty, in reality my only, and I fear my insuperable, one, that I cannot play. But nevertheless Palestrina and ^the^ old madrigal writers and others did produce masterpieces — and Hullah[7] says actually final in their kind, that is which you cannot develope by modern science; you can only change the school and kind — without modulations -^,^ but employing the modes; without even the authentic cadence: I wish I cd. study them. Then 'do I mean to rival Purcell and Mozart?' No. Even given the genius, a musician must be that and nothing else, as music now is; at least so it has been with all ^the^ great musicians. But I did aim at two things, not in themselves unattainable, if to me far easier things were not now unattainable. But of these, if ever, hereafter. Believe me Gerard M. Hopkins S.J.[8]

May 29 1885.

[1] As in the nursery rhyme: 'I do not like thee, Doctor Fell, | The reason why I cannot tell; | But this I know, and know full well, | I do not like thee, Doctor Fell.' The poem was written by the satirist Tom Brown (1663–1704) in imitation of an epigram of Martial, about the then Dean of Christ Church, Dr John Fell (1625–86; *ODNB*).

[2] Though not a direct quotation, parts of this phrase can be matched in Augustine and in Scotus.

[3] *Works and Days: From the Journal of Michael Field*, ed. T. and D. C. Sturge Moore (London, 1933), the first selection from the journals and papers of Michael Field, contains one direct reference (p. 128) to RB.

[4] Various suggestions have been made, with 'I wake and feel', 'No worst there is none', and 'Carrion Comfort' mentioned frequently, but neither sonnet can be identified with certainty.

[5] See *CW* vi.

[6] Name deleted by RB. See letter of 11 May 1883.

[7] John Pyke Hullah (1812–84) wrote several operas and numerous ballads but is best known for his educational activities. He was a conductor, an inspector of musical training schools, and taught singing. His *History of Modern Music*, based on a series of lectures given at the Royal Institution (1862, rev. 1875), may be the volume to which GMH refers. Hullah also produced a number of books on learning to sing.

[8] A sentence and a postscript have been cut out of the letter here.

11 June 1885 from Coventry Patmore to GMH

FL, no. CLXXVIII B, p. 363 Campion Hall, P 11/6/85

Addressed to 'Rev[d] Gerard Hopkins, S.J. | Stephens Green, | Dublin'. PM HASTINGS JU 11 85, H&K PACKET JU 12 85.

Hastings. June 11. 1885.

My dear M[r] Hopkins,

Is there any chance of our meeting this Summer? I propose going North with my wife for a fortnight in July, & if you should be at Stonyhurst then I would stop on my way to see you. But what of course would be the greatest pleasure to me would be a visit, if possible, from you here. I assure you that I shall always regard my having made your acquaintance as an important event of my life, and there are few things I desire more than a renewal of opportunity of personal intercourse with you.

Your's very truly
C. Patmore.

23 June 1885 to Coventry Patmore

FL, no. CLXXIX, p. 364 Durham University Library, Abbott MS 196
One folded sheet of headed paper, watermarked with shield, with the letters A. P. & S on a scroll below and the words Antique Parchment Note Paper. Written on two sides.

UNIVERSITY COLLEGE, | ST. STEPHEN'S GREEN, | DUBLIN. [*printed heading*]
June 23 1885

My dear Mr. Patmore, — I am very sorry to have so long neglected replying to your last kind letter, but my mind is harassed with the work before and upon me. I expect to go to England some time after the middle of next month and how long I may be there I do not know, but perhaps it might be possible to see you towards the end of it if you were then returned from the north. I have no thought of going to Stonyhurst but to my father's at Hampstead. Believe me very sincerely yours Gerard M. Hopkins S.J.

I heard ^yesterday^, amazing news, of an Irishman a great reader of you. I call it amazing, for the Irish have little feeling for poetry and least of all for modern poetry: they close the canon with Byron and Shelley and indeed most poets have never been admitted into it.

10 July 1885 from W. E. Addis to GMH

FL, no. G1, p. 425 Campion Hall, Misc. Addis
No envelope but an annotation on the letter reads: 'Addressed to H. | at Milltown Park | Postmark London | July 10 1885'.

My dearest Hopkins

I have been very tho' not seriously ill all week and the sight of your ~~le~~writing cheered me up. It is so tiresome lying on my back or sitting in an easy chair. A bed is at your service here and you will be most welcome.

Your affectionate friend
W E Addis

Kindly let me know as soon as possible when to expect you.

30 July 1885 from Coventry Patmore to GMH

FL, no. CLXXIX A, p. 364 Campion Hall, P 30/7/85
Addressed to 'Revd Gerard Hopkins, S.J. | Stephens Green, | Dublin'. 'Forward' written on top left of envelope. PM HASTINGS JY 31 85, H&K PACKET JY 31 85.

Hastings. July 30. 1885.
My dear Mr. Hopkins,

I returned yesterday from the North, and write at once in order that I may not miss any chance of seeing you either here or at Hampstead. Please let me know your whereabouts. Your last letter did not give me your Hampstead address, or I should have called there on my way home, on the chance of finding you there. I desire greatly to see more of you, and should be very sorry if you returned to Dublin or Stonyhurst without our meeting.

Your's ever truly
Coventry Patmore.

20 August 1885 to his Mother

FL, no. XCIX, p. 172 Bodleian, MS Eng. lett. e. 41, fos. 92–94v
Addressed to 'Mrs. Manley Hopkins | Woodlands | Easeb~~u~~^o^urn | Midhurst | Sussex'. PM DUBLIN AU 20 85 and MIDHURST AU 22 85.

UNIVERSITY COLLEGE, | ST. STEPHEN'S GREEN, | DUBLIN. [*printed heading*]
Aug. 20 '85.

My dearest mother, — I left Hastings yesterday evening and was here early. I am going tomorrow to Clongowes (address Clongowes Wood College, Naas, Co. Kildare) to make my retreat. The Patmores were very kind.[1] Mrs. Patmore[2] is a very sweet lady. There are two Miss Patmores, daughters I suppose of Mr. Patmore's first wife (he has had three), very nice, not handsome, one sadly lame since a child but a most gifted artist,[3] a true genius: she draws butterflies, birds, dormice, vegetation, in a truly marvellous manner; also illuminates. By his present wife Mr. Patmore has a very interesting and indeed alarming little ~~w~~boy "Piffy" or Epiphanius[4] (born on Twelfthnight), two and a half years old, of such a strange sensibility and imagination that it beats anything I ever saw or heard of. He treats flowers as animated things, animals as human, and cries~~,~~ — howls~~,~~ — if ^he thinks^ they are hurt or ~~he~~ even hears of their being hurt: I witnessed ~~a~~ ^some^ case^s^. I should not like it in a brother of mine. We went to see Battle, Winchilsea, Rye, and so on. East Sussex is all burnt up: they did not get our rain.

With best love to all and very many thanks for your kindness believe me your loving son Gerard.

I hear that the dulness of Sussex people has passed into a proverb and that it is called "dunny Sussex": I suppose dunny is something like duncish.

[1] After visiting his family at Midhurst, GMH spent 'a few days' with Patmore.

[2] Patmore had married his third wife Harriet Georgina Robson on 13 Sept. 1881.

[3] Bertha Patmore.

[4] Francis Joseph Mary Epiphanius. See GMH's letter to Patmore of 4–6 June 1886 and the letters from Patmore of 10 Nov. 1886, and 26 Oct. 1887.

21 August 1885 to Coventry Patmore

FL, no. CLXXX, p. 365 Princeton University Library, RTCO1

UNIVERSITY COLLEGE, | ST. STEPHEN'S GREEN, | DUBLIN. [*printed heading*]
Aug. 21 1885.

My dear Mr. Patmore, — Before going into retreat tonight I write to give you and Mrs. Patmore and the Miss Patmores ^my best thanks^ for your kindness to me during my happy stay at Hastings.

I am glad you let me read the autobiographical tract:[1] it will be a valuable testimony.

I do not know that you need trouble yourself about Denzinger: Dr. Rous's judgment will do.[2] After all, anything however high and innocent may happen to suggest anything however low and loathsome. But as I am upon this subject I may mention in proof of the abuses high contemplation is liable to three things which have come under my notice — (1) Molinos[3] was condemned for saying (and proving, as the unhappy man thought he did, from Scripture) that during contemplation acts of unnatural vice might take place without the subject's fault, being due to the malice of the devil and he innocent; (2) Fr. Gagliardi S.J.[4] (early in the history of our Society) found a congregation of nuns somewhere in Italy who imagined that such acts were acts of divine union; (3) such practices appear widely in the Brahmanic mystic literature, though naturally the admirers of the Vedas and their commentators have kept dark about it — but there ^(not in the Vedas)^, as we now learn, they are.[5] The Apostle St. Jude perhaps alludes to something of the sort also.[6] I am sorry to disgust you with ~~such~~ ^these^ horrors; but such is man and such is Satanic craft. I could not bring myself to speak by word of mouth.

Believe me very sincerely and gratefully yours Gerard M. Hopkins S.J.

[1] Champneys says that this is the only allusion in Patmore's correspondence to an account of his conversion to the Roman Catholic Church which Patmore's wife and GMH urged him to write, and of which Champneys prints a version in vol. ii, pp. 41–56, there dated Epiphany, 1888. In his printing of letters to Patmore from GMH, Champneys only reproduces the first two short paragraphs of the above letter (up to 'testimony'), and makes no mention of Patmore's problem; and nothing in the

'autobiographical tract' as we have it quite fits what seems to be worrying Patmore. As published, his autobiography mentions his mind being 'poisoned by positive infidel teaching' (p. 46), and how he would 'discern sexual impurity and virginal purity, the one as the tangible blackness and horror of hell, and the other as the very bliss of heaven, and the flower and consummation of love between man and woman' (p. 45), but these are not quite the difficulty one infers from the rest of the letter.

[2] Patmore obviously wished to go to the top for an opinion. Heinrich Joseph Dominicus Denzinger (1819–83) was a leading theologian of the modern Catholic German school, professor of dogmatic theology at Würzburg from 1854 till his death, and best known for his *Enchiridion Symbolorum et Definitionum* (Würzburg 1854, and often reprinted), commissioned by Pope Pius IX, which is a manual of basic Catholic doctrine, containing extracts of all major definitions and declarations on faith and morals. Dr Rous was Patmore's spiritual adviser.

[3] Miguel de Molinos (*c.*1628–97), founder of Quietism, was a Roman Catholic priest who published his *Guida Spirituale* in 1675, was accused by the Jesuits and Dominicans, and condemned for heresy by the Inquisition. The *Catholic Encyclopedia* records: 'He taught interior annihilation, asserting that this is the means of attaining purity of soul, perfect contemplation, and the rich treasure of interior peace: hence follows the licitness of impure carnal acts, inasmuch as only the lower, sensual man, instigated by the demon, is concerned in them. In the cases of seventeen penitents he excused their lascivious acts, and claimed that those committed by himself were not blameworthy, as free will had no part in them.'

[4] Achille Gagliardi, SJ (1537–1607), whose *Commentarii in Exercitia spiritualia S.P. Ignatii de Loyola* had recently been published in Bruges (1882), argued that union with God takes place in three ways, of which the first is by conformity, which is a complete subordination of our will to the Divine Will in all our actions, and in all occurrences and events, so that we will and accept all that God wills and sends, however painful and repulsive it may be.

[5] At Oxford, GMH read Max Müller's account of the *Rig-Veda*. See *CW* iv. 295–99.

[6] In the Epistle of St Jude, the Bible's penultimate book, the fourth verse reads in part: 'ungodly men, turning the grace of our Lord God into riotousness'. G. H. Boobyer, in *Peake's Commentary on the Bible*, ed. Matthew Black and H. H. Rowley (London and New York, 1962), speculates that these men 'claimed special revelations in dreams as the sanction of their ungodly behaviour' (p. 1042).

23 August 1885 from Coventry Patmore to GMH

FL, no. CLXXX A, p. 366 Campion Hall, P 23/8/85

Addressed to 'Rev[d] Gerard M. Hopkins, S.J. | University College, | St. Stephen's Green, | Dublin'. PM HASTINGS AU 24 85, H&K PACKET AU 25 85.

Hastings. Aug. 23. 1885.

My dear Mr. Hopkins,

I am glad to know that you did not pass your short visit here unpleasantly. It was a great pleasure, and much more, to me.

I had arrived at the same conclusion as you about my reading Denzi[n]ger.[1] If once one departs from the straight line of direction there is no safety from confusion.

Your's affectionately
Coventry Patmore.

[1] See letter of 21 Aug. 1885.

1–8 September 1885 to Robert Bridges

LRB, no. CXXX, p. 220 Bodleian, Dep. Bridges, vol. 92, fos. 82–83v

UNIVERSITY COLLEGE, | ST. STEPHEN'S GREEN, | DUBLIN. [*printed heading*] Sept. 1 1885.

Dearest Bridges, — I have just returned from an absurd adventure, which when I resigned myself to it I could not help enjoying. A hair-brained fellow took me down to Kingstown and on board his yacht and, whereas I meant to return to town by six that evening, would not let me go either that night or this morning till past midday. I was afraid it would be compromising, but it was fun while it lasted.

I have been in England. I was with my people first at Hampstead, then at Midhurst in Sussex in a lovely ~~land lan~~ landscape: they are there yet. And from there I went to Hastings to Mr. Patmore's for a few days. I managed to see several old friends and to make new ones, amongst which Mr. W. H. Cummings[1] the tenor singer and composer, who wrote the Life of Purcell: he shewed me some of his Purcell treasures and others and is going to send me several things. I liked him very much but the time of my being with him was cut short. I did not attempt to see you: I did not ~~think~~ ^know that^ visitors wd. at that time be very welcome and it wd. have been difficult ~~in~~ to me in any case to come. I am very sorry to hear of Mrs. Bridges' disappointment: somehow I had feared that would happen.[2]

I shall shortly have some sonnets to send you, five or more. ~~Three~~ ^Four^[3] of these came like inspirations unbidden and against my will. And in the life I lead now, which is one of a continually jaded and harassed mind, if in any leisure I try to do anything I make no way~~.~~ — nor with my work, alas! but so it must be.

Mr. Patmore lent me Barnes' poems[4] — 3 volumes, not all, for indeed he is prolific. I hold your contemptuous opinion an unhappy mistake: he is a perfect artist and of a most spontaneous inspiration; it is as if Dorset life and Dorset landscape had taken flesh and tongue in the man. I feel the defect or limitation or whatever we are to call it that offended you: ~~that~~ he lacks fire; but who is perfect all round? If ~~that~~ ^one defect^ is fatal what writer could we read?

An old question of yours I have hitherto neglected to answer, am I thinking of writing on metre?[5] I suppose thinking too much and doing too little. I do greatly desire to treat that subject; might perhaps get something together this year; but I can scarcely believe that on that or on anything else anything of mine will ever see the light — of publicity nor even of day. For it is widely true, the fine pleasure is not to do a thing but to feel that you ~~can~~ ^could^ and the mortification that goes to the heart is to feel ~~that~~ it is the power that fails you: qui occidere nolunt Posse volunt {*he who does not want to kill would like to be able to*};[6] ~~we like~~ ^it is^ the refusal of a thing ^that we like to have^. So with me, if I could but get on, if I could but produce work I should not mind its being buried, ^silenced,^ and going no further; but it kills me to be time's eunuch and never to beget.[7] After all I do not despair, things might change, anything may be; only there is no great appearance of it. Now because I have had a holiday though not strong I have some buoyancy; soon I am afraid I shall be ground down to a state like this last spring's and summer's, when my spirits were so crushed that madness seemed to be making approaches — and nobody was to blame, except myself partly for not managing myself better and contriving a change. Believe me, with kind wishes to Mrs. Bridges, your affectionate friend Gerard M. Hopkins S.J. Sept. 8 '85. This day 15 years ago I took my first vows.

I hope Mrs. Molesworth is well. Where is she now?

Is your brother John going to bring out a second volume?[8]

If I had not reread your letter I shd. have left it unanswered. The expression "The Mass is good" is, I feel sure, never used in these islands. But the meaning in the circumstances is pretty plain and must be just what you take it to be. To satisfy the obligation of hearing mass on Sundays and the 'Festivals of Obligation' one must be present from at least the Offertory to the Priest's Communion. The question is well threshed out: for laxer and for stricter opinions see the Moral Theologians passim; whose name is Legion, but St. Alphonsus Liguori[9] will do for all (Treatise de Praeceptis Ecclesiae or De Decem Praeceptis Decalogi {*Treatise on the teachings of the church or On the ten commandments*}). However the phrase would not easily be understood by your readers or hearers. I hope to see those plays. ~~Is~~^Are^ the choral parts written strictly to the music? I never saw good poetry ~~written~~ ^made^ to music unless that music itself had first been made to words.

[1] William Hayman Cummings (1831–1915; *ODNB*) was organist at Waltham Abbey and tenor. He founded the Purcell Society in 1876. In 1879–94 he was professor of singing at the Royal Academy of Music, and then became principal of the Guildhall School of Music.

[2] Monica had a miscarriage in August.

[3] It is not known exactly which sonnets GMH was referring to but the reference is generally thought to be to some of what W. H. Gardner called the sonnets of desolation. Sonnets usually included under this title are 'To seem the stranger', 'I wake and feel', 'No worst', '(Carrion Comfort)', 'Patience, hard thing!,' and 'My own heart'.

[4] Patmore wrote about William Barnes in a number of articles: see the *North British Review* for Nov. 1859, and *Macmillan's Magazine* for June 1862, the reprinted article contributed to the *Fortnightly Review* of Nov. 1886 in *Principle in Art, &c.* (1889), and two reviews contributed to the *St. James's Gazette* on 9 Oct. 1886 and 19 Dec. 1887, reprinted in *Courage in Politics and Other Essays* (1921), 118–26.

[5] See letter to RB of 11–12 Nov. 1884.

[6] Actually 'qui nolunt occidere quemquam | posse volunt' {*even those who do not want to kill someone would like to have the power [to do it]*}; Juvenal, *Satires*, x. 96–7.

[7] This phrase reappears in GMH's poem, 'Thou art indeed just, Lord', dated 17 Mar. 1889:

birds build — but not I build; no, but strain,
Time's eunuch, and not breed one work that wakes.

[8] John Bridges had published *Wet Days* in 1879. His other works of verse are *In a Village, Poems* (1898) and *The Lost Parson and Other Poems* (1902).

[9] St Alphonsus de Liguori (1696–1787), founder of the Redemptionists and author of *Theologia Moralis* {*Moral Theology*} (1753–5, etc.), of which the treatises mentioned form sections.

5–8 November 1885 to Everard Hopkins

TLS 8 Dec. 1972, p. 1511, ed. by Anthony Bischoff, SJ; in *HRB*, 4 (1973), 12–14, and in *SL*, 216 HRHRC, Container 1.5

Clongowes Wood College, | Naas | [*highly decorated printed heading*]: Nov. 5, 1885

Dear Everard, — I am taking a short rest after deadly work.

I have with me here Literature and Dogma and Ecce Homo that you lent me (I almost thought you might forget). My long spell of work, which allowed of no other reading, interrupted my study of L. and D. and Ecce Homo I have read but a little of. Had I better ~~sa~~ send them back without more delay? or finish them? And by the by after E. H.

I ought to read his later book called Natural Religion, on which I ~~t read~~ ^found^ an able review in Mallock's Atheism volume and I have another review of it by G. A. Simcox in the Nineteenth here in the room. These are very instructive books.[1]

I have not read Drummond's book that you praise. My father has it, I think: I saw it in his hands.

While on books let me recommend you a masterly one I have just made the acquaintance of — Moulton's Shakespeare as a Dramatic Artist (Clarendon Press, this year).

I have also Diana[2] by me. After all the difficult style, which can never never be simple, is very faulty.

I have seen your broadside in the Graphic.[3] I can well fancy that the drawing, the draught^s^manship, has been injured in engraving and was finer than now appears (as my father led me to expect to find), but, to tell you the truth, I am disappointed in it for faults which are not the engraver's. You did not, I believe, realise that so large a design can by no means be treated as differing from one ^a^ half, a quarter, or an eig[h]th the size in its size only. As difficulties of perspective increase greatly with the scale so do those of composition. ~~They It~~ ^The composition^ will not come right of itself, it must be calculated. I see no signs of such calculation. I find it scattered and without unity, it does not look to me like a scene and one ^dramatic^ moment, the action of the persons is independent and not mutual, the groups do not seem aware of one another. The two wrestlers do not struggle hard enough and in general there is a want of liveliness. Small, no Green,[4] had a last-century election scene, better composed and livelier than yours, but defective in those respects too: the fighting figures seemed not to have been fighting when the drawing was made but before it, to have been 'struck so' (as children fear to ~~me~~ ^be^ in making faces). And then drawn. I am glad therefore you ~~were~~ got the commission but not satisfied with yr. discharge of it. I do not expect you are yourself, are you? (I need scarcely say that as my bent is for glowing colours so it is for violent action, but here at least violent action was in place.) The subject I expect was not congenial. The crowd being an essential element of it more of the crowd shd. have been seen and it shd. have been more crowded. Crowds have perhaps not been mastered in art yet. Doré[5] (I do not like him, but we must admire his bucketfuls of talent) has ~~a~~ good simultaneous-acting crowds, e.g. in Christ coming down the steps of the judgment hall. I have seen a fine crowd by Rembrandt. I think there [are] a good few (~~and~~ ^or^ a few good) crowds to be seen in well known pictures.[6] What I have written appears discouraging as I read it. But necessity the mother of invention has been in your case her stepmother and starved her: what I mean is that this drawing was made I suppose to order on an uncongenial subject. Naturally you would like repose and long flowing lines, low colours, and the conditions of grace and ease.

To touch on the Eurydice etc again. The run-over rhymes were experimental, perhaps a mistake; I do not know that I shd. repeat them. But rhyme, you understand, is like an indelible process~~;~~: you cannot paint over it. Surely they can be recited but the effect must have been prepared, as many things must. I can only remember one, the rhyme to electric:[7] it must be read "startingly and rash". It is "an effect".

I am sweetly soothed by your saying that you cd. make any one understand ~~the~~ ^my^ poem by reciting it well. That is what I always hoped, thought, and said; it is my precise aim. And thereby hangs so considerable a tale, in fact the very thing I was going to write about Sprung Rhy[th]m in general (by the bye rhythm, not metre: metre is a matter of arranging lines, rhythm is one of arranging feet; anapaests are a rhythm, ~~a~~ ^the^ sonnet is a metre; and so you can write any metre in any rhythm and any rhythm to any metre — supposing of course that usage has not ~~fixed~~ ^tied^ the rhythm to the metre, as often or mostly it has), that I must for the present leave off, give o'ër, as they say in Lancashire.

Every art then and every work of art has its own play or performance. The play^~~ing~~^ or performance of a stageplay is ^the playing^ it on the boards, the stage: reading it, much more writing it, is not its performance. The performance of a symphony is not the scoring it however elaborate^ly^; it is in the concert room, ~~with~~ ^by^ the orchestra, and then ^and there^ only. A picture is performed, or performs, when anyone looks at it in the ~~inten~~ proper and intended light. A house performs when it is ^now^ built and lived in. To come nearer: books play, ~~or~~ perform, or are played and performed when they are read; and ordinarily by one reader, alone, to himself, with the eyes only. Now we are getting to it, George. Poetry was originally meant for either singing or reciting, a record was kept of it; the record could be, was, read, and that in time by one reader, alone, to himself, with the eyes only. This reacted on the art: what was to be performed under these conditions for these conditions ought to be and was composed and calculated. Sound-effects were intended, wonderful combinations even; but they bear the marks of having been meant for ~~that~~ ^the^ whispered, not even whispered, merely mental performance of the closet~~,~~ the study, and so on. You follow, ^Edward^ Joseph? You do: ^then^ We are there. This is not the true nature of poetry, ^the^ darling child of speech, of lips and

~~human~~ ^spoken^ utterance: it must be spoken; till it is spoken it is not performed, it does not perform, it is not itself. Sprung rhythm gives back to poetry its true soul and self. As poetry is emphatically speech, speech ~~re~~ purged ~~of all but~~ ^of dross^ like gold in the furnace, so it must have emphatically the essential elements of speech. Now emphasis itself, stress, is one of these: sprung rhythm makes verse stres~~y~~sy; it purges it to an emphasis as much brighter, livelier, more lustrous than the ^regular but^ commonplace emphasis of common rhythm as poetry in general is brighter than ~~prose~~ ^common^ speech. But this it does by a return from that regular emphasis~~, to~~ ^towards, not up to^ the more picturesque irregular emphasis of talk — ~~not~~ ^without^ however becoming itself lawlessly irregular; then it would not be art; but making up by regularity, equality, of a larger unit (the foot merely) for ^in^equality in the less, the syllable. There it wd. be necessary to come down to mathematics and technicalities which time does not allow of, so I forbear. For I believe you now understand. Perform the Eurydice, then see. I must however add that to perform it quite satisfactorily is not at all easy, I do not say I could do it; but this is ~~no hind~~ nothing against the truth of the principle maintained. A composer need not be able to play his ~~music~~ violin music or sing his songs. Indeed the higher wrought the art, clearly the wider severance between the parts of the author and the performer.

Neither of course do I mean my verse to be recited only. True poetry must be studied. As Shakespere and all great dramatists have their maximum effect on the stage but bear to be or must be studied at home before or after or both, so I shd. wish it to be with my lyric ~~ver~~ poetry. And in practice that will be enough by itself alone to any one who ~~can~~ ^has^ first realised the effect of reciting; for then, like a musician reading a score and supplying in thought the orchestra (as they can), no further performance is, substantially, needed. But you say you have not so realised it — or perhaps you have. Mr. Patmore never admired the Eurydice or any of my things, except some in common rhythm, for just this reason (I hope — and he himself suggested).

Much the same is the case with plain chant music. Many of those who ~~can~~ ^~~will~~ do^ not admire it have never heard it performed (or, worse, have heard it murdered) and cannot conceive the performance; for to read and even play it, without the secret, is no good.

On the other hand there is verse, very good of its rhetorical kind~~,~~ (for that is what it is, rhetoric in verse), such as Macaulay's Lays, Aytoun's[8] ditto, and ever so much that the Irish produce, flowing, stirring, and pointed, which recited seems first rate but studied at leisure, by the daylight, does not indeed turn out worthless but loses the name of genuine poetry.

I asked you, did ~~?~~I? to try and find me Campion, Thomas Campion,'s "Rose-cheeked Laura, come":[9] I had almost forgotten. He was an Elisabethan, nothing, that I know of, to Edmund Campion the Jesuit his contemporary~~, who~~ ∴. ^The latter^ wd. have been, I shd. think, a great poet if he had chosen or chance had served, to judge by the noble eloquence of passages in his History of Ireland, read and made use of, as Simpson in his Life of Campion[10] has shewn, by Shakespere. Thomas Campion's poem enquired for is an avowed experiment in rhythm and metre (rather metre) and bears the marks of so being; still it is beautiful and very striking. I have seen it in some handbook or collection of English poetry.

It seemed like death almost at first for us to leave Hampstead, but on the other hand Haslemere[11] ~~seems~~ ^is^ a delightful thought. We shd. not be far from Midhurst either. It is artists' country. There is a capital paper on Surrey in the Nineteenth for August, worth having. The same number contains a paper by Fr. Ryder of the Oratory on "A Jesuit Reformer and Poet," to wit Fr. Spee, whose efforts and sufferings put down the witch mania and its hideous prosecution and persecutions.[12]

By the bye, as prose, though commonly less beautiful than verse and debarred from its symmetrical beauties, has, at least possible to it, effects more beautiful than any verse can atta~~n~~in, so perhaps the inflections and intonations of the speaking voice may give effects more beautiful than any attainable by the fixed pitches of music. I look on this as an infinite field & very little worked. It has this great difficulty, that the art depends entirely on living tradition. The phonograph may give us ^one,^ but hitherto there ~~is~~^could be^ no record of fine ~~inflexions pronunciation~~ ^spoken utterance^. In drama the fine ~~pro~~ ^spoken^ utterance has been cultivated and ~~has~~ a tradition established, but everything is most highly wrought and furthest developed where it is cultivated by itself; fine utterance then will not be best developed in the drama, where gesture and action generally are to play a great part too; it must be developed in recited lyric. Now hitherto this has not been done. The Greeks carried lyric to its highest perfection in Pindar and the tragic choruses, but what was this lyric? not a spoken lyric at all, but song; poetry written neither to be recited nor chanted even nor ^even^ sung to a transferable tune but each piece ^of itself^ a song. The same remark then as above recurs: the natural performance and delivery belonging properly to lyric poetry, which is speech, has not been enough cultivated, and should be. When performers were trained to do it (it needs the rarest gifts) and audiences to appreciate it it would be, I am persuaded, a lovely art. Incalculable effect could be produced by the delivery of Wordsworth's Margaret ("Where art thou, my beloved son?" — do you know it?). With the aid of the phonograph each phrase could be fixed and learnt by heart like a song.

I am now back at Stephen's Green and must lecture tomorrow and tonight conclude this long letter. I am your loving brother Gerard.

I have seen none of those St. Stephen's (not Green) character-sketches;[13] cannot think what they can be like. I feel sure you have not found (at least for public purposes) your true vein yet, which I suppose to be something more refined than political drawing can allow of.

Nov. 8 1885.

[1] Matthew Arnold, *Literature and Dogma* (1873); John Seeley's *Ecce Homo* (1865) (see letter of 12 Feb. 1868) and *Natural Religion* (1882); William Mallock, *Atheism and the Value of Life* (1884); Henry Drummond, *Natural Law in the Spiritual World* (1883).

[2] George Meredith, *Diana of the Crossways* (1885).

[3] Everard's large picture (47 × 33 cm) 'Addressing the Free and Independent Electors' was published in *The Graphic* on 24 Oct. 1885 and is reproduced in *AMES*, 44.

[4] Benjamin Richard Green (1807/8–1876; *ODNB*), born in London, became a watercolour painter and author. He entered the Royal Academy Schools in 1826 and exhibited some forty portraits of public figures, mostly miniatures, at the Royal Academy between 1837 and 1858. He also exhibited with the Society of British Artists and the New Watercolour Society.

[5] Gustav Doré (1832–83) was a French artist, engraver, illustrator, and sculptor. He produced illustrations for an English Bible (1866), *London: A Pilgrimage* (1872), as well as the works of a number of poets including Milton, Tennyson, and Thomas Hood.

[6] Pictures such as Rembrandt's *The Night Watch*.

[7] 'The Loss of the Eurydice', ll. 23–4 rhyme 'he | Came . . . deadly-electric'.

[8] Thomas Babington Macaulay (1800–59; *ODNB*), *Lays of Ancient Rome* (1842); William Aytoun (1813–65), *Lays of the Scottish Cavaliers* (1849).

[9] Thomas Campion (1567–1620; *ODNB*), poet and musician, whose *Observations in the Art of English Poesie* (1602) was 'the last, and subtlest, of the forlorn Elizabethan attempts to regulate English verse by the rules of classical metrics' (*ODNB*). 'Rose-cheeked Laura, come' was written to illustrate his theories of versificaton.

[10] Richard Simpson (1820–76), *Edmund Campion* (1867).

[11] GMH uses very similar phrasing here to that in the following letter to his mother. This is the first mention of the move to Haslemere, which was made in the summer of 1886, first to Court's Hill Lodge, which did not seem satisfactory, and then to the Garth in High Lane, which remained the family home until the death of Lionel Charles Hopkins in 1952. GMH visited and wrote from Court's Hill Lodge in Aug. 1887. Haslemere, the most southerly town in Surrey, in attractive countryside about forty miles south-west of London, is a historic market town, its market confirmed by charter in 1394 and its right to elect two MPs granted by Elizabeth I. Its railway connection to the London–Portsmouth line in 1859 helped to make it a fashionable

place to live, particularly for artists and writers. Helen Allingham, who painted its cottages, Walter Tyndale, and Josiah Whymper lived and worked there; Tennyson lived at nearby Aldworth for twenty-five years until he died in 1892 and George Eliot wrote much of *Middlemarch* at Shottermill Common nearby. Midhurst, where there seems to be a family connection, is about eight miles south of Haslemere (see letter to his mother at Midhurst of 20 Aug. 1885 and to RB of 1–8 Sept. 1885).

[12] *The Nineteenth Century*, 18 (Aug. 1885) published Henry G. Hewlett's 'County characteristics: Surrey' on pp. 274–93, which followed H. I. D. Ryder's 'A Jesuit reformer and poet' on pp. 249–73 (reprinted in his *Essays*, 1911). See letter to Ryder of 2 July 1868. Friedrich von Spee (1591–1635).

[13] The *St. Stephen's Review* had Phil May (1864–1903) on its staff from spring to autumn 1885 and it is probably his drawings which had caught Everard's eye.

13 November 1885 to his Mother

FL, no. C, p. 173 Bodleian, MS Eng. lett. e. 41, fos. 95–98ᵛ
Addressed to 'Mrs. Manley Hopkins | Oak Hill | Hampstead | London N.W.' PM DUBLIN NO 14 85.

University College, | St. Stephen's Green, | Dublin. [*printed heading*]
Nov. 13 '85

My dearest mother, — I write at once for Mary's sake.[1] I have to say that one common cause ~~for~~ of toothache is an abscess at the root of the tooth. This can mostly be cured by putting le~~a~~^e^ches there. There is no pain nor, really, anything nasty: it is only bringing oneself to let them be put on. They must suck till they are tired and fall off. Then the place must be let bleed as long as it likes, which may be an hour or two. This relieves and cures.

That examination work is for this time over. I never was so spent with work before. And it was not work only but moral annoyance and the having to deal with officials whose ~~manner of dealing~~ ^behaviour^ was overbearing and ungentlemanly. However do not repeat this. Were I free to act I should have taken steps on my own and others' account, but this I could not do. One of my colleagues, a great scholar, one of the old school of fine and laborious scholars, was very ill treated. It was a painful scene; he was censured by the ~~s~~Standing Committee of the Senate and he replied fiercely and defiantly. It was a mistake on his part, but I sympathised with him. But I do not think the Royal University will live long: it will suffer a sea change ~~it~~ into something rich and strange.[2]

To tell the truth I am this very evening asked to take musical tea with one of those very ~~people~~ ^persons^ whom I have characterised above. But unofficially people can be amiable and in office otherwise.

I enclose a list to be filled in of English songs of the people. They must be (1) English, not Scotch~~,~~ or Welsh or Irish. (2) They must be really ~~good~~ ^fine^ music. (3) They must be people's songs, not by great composers nor from operas: however I wd. not ~~in^ex^clude~~ exclude Ford[3] and Dowling,[4] I am doubtful about Dibdin.[5] A hard and fast line cannot be drawn. But nothing well outside these rules is to be entered. Circulate in the family and return.

It seemed like death at first to leave Hampstead. But Haslemere is, it must be owned, a welcome thought. I gather the house has little to recommend it.[6] I understand it is to be kept dark from Arthur. But this seems great secrecy.

I hope to send my father some notes soon.

I have heard no more of that ill starred lawsuit.

I am your loving son Gerard.

Our weather has been as yours but worse. Nothing can be wretcheder than gloomy weather in Dublin.

Mr. Parnell finds he cannot shape the destinies of the country without my cooperation at the Pillar Room of the Rotunda on Monday.[7] Nevertheless I shall spend that evening in unsphering the spirit of Plato or something of the sort.

[1] See letter of 15 Aug. 1877, n. 4.

[2] Quoting from Ariel's song in Shakespeare's *The Tempest*, I. ii. 398–9.

[3] Thomas Ford (*c.*1580–1648; *ODNB*), one of the musicians of Prince Henry, son of James I, best known perhaps for his four-part songs, 'There is a ladie sweet and kind' and 'Since first I saw your face'.

[4] Presumably John Dowland (1563–1626; *ODNB*), one of the most famous lutenists, also known for such laments as 'I saw my Lady weepe', and 'In darkness let me dwell'. Most of his music was written before 1606 at the court of Christian IV of Denmark although he served in 1612–26 as lutenist at the court of James I.

[5] Charles Dibdin (1745–1814; *ODNB*), singer, composer of operas and music variety shows, best remembered for his sea-songs, such as 'Tom Bowling', which is still played on the Last Night of the Proms. He was employed by Pitt's government from 1803 to write and sing patriotic ballads to maintain patriotic fervour during the Napoleonic Wars. He composed over 1,400 songs.

[6] Court's Hill Lodge, Haslemere.

[7] Parnell was at the height of his unpopularity in England in the winter of 1885, but also at the height of his influence. He was preparing for the election of 24 Nov. 1885, at which the Irish Parliamentary party won eighty-six seats in Parliament (Liberal 319, Conservative 249 out of a total of 670) and thus held the balance of power, and could press for home rule.

14 December 1885 to Robert Bridges

LRB, no. CXXXI, p. 223 Bodleian, Dep. Bridges, vol. 92, fos. 84–85[v]

UNIVERSITY COLLEGE, | ST. STEPHEN'S GREEN, | DUBLIN. [*printed heading*]
Dec. 14 '85

Dearest Bridges, — The first of the Catholic periodicals is the Dublin Review, but I am altogether unknown to them and I think nothing whatever would be gained by my forwarding them the book.[1] Our magazine is the Month: I know the editor[2] of course and can and will recommend the book and though I do not want to have ^it^ to review (because, to speak the truth, it would take time, and that I can ill afford; that is the only reason; otherwise I shd. enjoy it), yet I believe he will at once ask me to do so. There is also the Tablet and to that I am unknown too and they do not like Jesuits, but I have always maintained the Tablet is a very good well conducted gentlemanly paper, unequal in ability, but some of its articles are very good and able; so that I think you shd. send them the book and Catholic households, finding a book of poetry decent and spoken ~~high^l^y~~ highly of (if it should), will be glad to get it. No people are so nice as the English Catholic gentry. (~~a~~As for the Irish Catholic gentry, by what I see, the country is going shortly to be made too hot to hold them~~;~~: a persecution of them, it is no less, headed by two Archbishops has begun. Only that those two Archbishops will, I expect, shortly have a crow to pick with the Holy See. By the by Leo XIII. has written a really beautiful letter to the English bishops, the most liberally worded in dealing with those outside the Church that ever Pope, I shd. fancy, ~~has~~ yet penned.)[3]

Alas! has "the gifted Hopkins" appeared in C.D's. "abrupt note"?[4] — too plainly the son and literary executor of Lang's Gifted Hopkins (the American) who "died of the consequences of his own jocosity". C. D. shd. remember: "surtout point de zèle" {*above all, no enthusiasm*}.[5] It can not help me, it may (if remarked, must) harm me. Praise of the unknown brings about the frame of mind with which one reads for the first time of the effects of Mother Seigel's Soothing Syrup,[6] which la~~s~~tely burst (or oozed) upon the universe.

Yr. affectionate friend Gerard.
Not a word to C. D.

[1] Presumably *Eros and Psyche*.

[2] Henry Coleridge, SJ (1846–1920), an old friend, who had rejected 'The Wreck of the Deutschland'.

[3] Leo XIII, *Spectata fides* (On Christian Education), Encyclical promulgated on 27 Nov.

[4] An acknowledgement by Canon Dixon of help received in writing his account of the Jesuit Mission in Ireland. The footnote ends: 'For my knowledge of this and for other information I am indebted to my gifted friend the Reverend Gerard Hopkins, S.J.'

[5] A phrase attributed to Charles Maurice de Talleyrand (1754–1838), advising the employees of the ministry of foreign affairs against precipitate action.

[6] Shaker Extract of Roots, or Mother Siegel's Curative Syrup, was a concoction which contained tincture of capsicum, dilute hydrochloric acid, aloe, and water. It was introduced in New York in 1876 by A. J. White, claiming to cure impurities of the blood, dyspepsia, and liver complaints, crossed the Atlantic, and was sold until the late 1950s. It was advertised with letters attesting its wonderful curative properties.

23 December 1885 to Everard Hopkins

Published in *TLS* 8 Dec. 1972, pp. 1511–12, ed. by Anthony Bischoff, SJ and *SL*, 221 HRHRC, Container 1.5

UNIVERSITY COLLEGE, | ST STEPHEN'S GREEN, | DUBLIN. [*printed heading*]
Dec. 23 '85

Dear Everard, — There are things in my last long letter that do not please me in the retrospect and I am afraid you are still less pleased with certain of them, the faults I found with your picture. ~~I hope that~~ ^Nevertheless I^ did not want to discourage, and ^I knew that^ Arthur takes criticism very peaceably always. Indeed I seem to think this is not really the reason why you have not answered.

But have you not been dunned for those books you lent me? I must send them you back now, for even holidays bring no holiday to me and I do not want to keep them longer in hope of more leisure. Of course if I had ~~b~~ ^not^ been a fool I could have had them read (Irish idiom and convenient) long since, in ~~by~~ spare spells; but with the hope of making anything out of them, which at one time I entertained, ~~went~~ ^vanished^ the desire ~~the desire~~ of reading them.

Did not Seeley write Ecce Homo? and since that Natural Religion, in which the supernatural element, the miracles, taken for granted in the former book, has disappeared. He is the author of the Expansion of England and has an article in the last Nineteenth which is worth reading. I think you shd. read both: he will hit it off with you. Alas, all the men that in better days one might build on for England's good, like him and Matthew Arnold and, I do believe, Bradlaugh,[1] drift or ride or scud upon the tide of atheism, ~~and loss~~ where all true guiding principle is lost. Unhappy country, its morals ministered to by Booth and Stead[2] (you know no doubt, better than I do, from the English papers, that the crimes the Pall Mall was so zealous over have immensely increased); its foreign policy by Gladstone; its speculation by Matthew Arnold — not to speak of what is to befall from Ireland. The Pope has written the most beautiful letter to the English bishops,[3] speaking in terms of such heartfelt affection for England that I kiss the words when I read them.

I enclose some Irish drawings ^(old ones)^. The National papers have a coloured cartoon every week and these pictures are a power. Is not Pat in the boat good? The artist is called O'Hea:[4] he has a powerful chromo of an Irish ~~rebel~~ ^peasant^ in the rebellion of 1798 ~~defending~~ ^at^ bay against an army of British redcoats, and this picture like everything said or done in Ireland will go to swell the gathering and insatiable flood of hatred.

Another thing you must read is Patmore's ode (in the Unknown Eros) "O England, how hast thou forgot?" By the bye, how do you like Bridges' Eros and Psyche?

I take it for granted you ~~be~~ will be tomorrow at Hampstead. My Christmas is much a clouded one, for I have suddenly to prepare papers for a supplementary matriculation examination to be held next month, as well as the Scholarship, which I knew of before. But it was to be. Give all my best Christmas wishes, thank Grace for her pretty card, and believe me your loving brother Gerard.

I have friends at Donnybrook, so hearty and kind that nothing can be more so and I think I shall go and see them tomorrow.[5]

Christmas Eve, 1885

I think if I find I am not in yr. black books I shall soon send you a black ^ms^ book of my own containing nearly all my poems, and see if you quite come round to Sprung Rhythm.

[1] Charles Bradlaugh (1833–91; *ODNB*) was a well-known advocate of free thought. Elected MP for Northampton in 1880, he had not been allowed to take his seat because he refused to swear on the Bible. Re-elected in 1881, the same argument started again and continued until 1886, when he finally received permission to join the House of Commons. GMH heard him speak with Mrs Annie Besant in 1879 and remarked to Baillie, 'To think I could ever have called myself a Liberal! "The Devil was the first Whig". These two are at large (I mean Bradlaugh and Besant) and the Government is arresting Irish agitators, that will do far more harm in prison than on the stump.'

[2] In 1885 William Bramwell Booth (1856–1929; *ODNB*)—son of William Booth (1829–1912), the outspoken founder of the Salvation Army—associated with William Thomas Stead (1849–1912; *ODNB*) in an attempt to combat the prostitution of young girls. Stead, who had become the editor of the *Pall Mall Gazette* in 1883, used his position to advocate social and political change, and published in June 1885 a series of articles under the title 'The Maiden Tribute of Modern Babylon', in which he gave an account of the purchase for immoral purposes of a 13-year-old virgin for £5. In response, the 1885 Criminal Law Amendment Act raised the age of consent to 16, but Booth, Stead, and others were arrested and tried. Though Booth was acquitted, Stead served three months in prison.

[3] *Spectata fides*: Leo XIII to the English bishops, dated 27 Nov. 1885: 'we love with a paternal charity that island, which was not undeservedly called the Mother of Saints, and we see in the disposition of mind of which we have spoken [fidelity to "the ancient faith"] the greatest hope and as it were a pledge, of the welfare and prosperity of the British people.'

[4] John Fergus O'Hea (1838–1922), from Cork, was an artist and cartoonist who worked for such papers as the *Dublin Weekly Freeman*, producing such political cartoons as 'Erin on the floor of a lion's cage with England about to devour her' (23 July 1887).

[5] The MacCabe family, Dr (later Sir) Francis MacCabe, his wife Margaret, and their children, John Francis (Jack), Freddy, Mary, Katherine Frances, and another girl and boy, who lived at Belleville on the Stillorgan Road, three doors from the church of the Sacred Heart, had an affection for GMH which was reciprocated. See Joseph J. Feeney, SJ, *The Playfulness of Gerard Manley Hopkins* (Aldershot, 2008), 34–6; 'Hopkins and the MacCabe Family: Three Children Who Knew Gerard Manley Hopkins', *Studies* (Dublin), 90 (2001), 299–307; and *WHALB*, 410–12.

1886

13 January 1886 to his Mother

FL, no. CI, p. 174 Bodleian, MS Eng.lett.e.40, fos. 99–101^{v}
Addressed to 'Mrs. Manley Hopkins | Oak Hill | Hampstead | London N.W.'
PM DUBLIN JA 13 86 and LONDON N.W. JA 14 86.

UNIVERSITY COLLEGE, | S^{T} STEPHEN'S GREEN, | DUBLIN. [*printed heading*]
Jan. 13 '86

My dearest mother, — I should like, very much indeed, to see those pictures, but I do not see how it can be at all. I shall for a few days be examinging the papers for the Scholarship and when those ~~wer~~ ^are^ done, later than, but for them, it would be and later than is desirable, begin my lectures with my pupils, which will last till the Easter holidays. Then I suppose I shall have some days free, but how could I propose to go to England? on what reasonable pretext? If I were writing a book on modern art (for I am taking notes for one on Homer's Art) I should have a plea. It is true I dare say I shall some time soon ask to go to Oxford to get information on matters of scholarship, but I do not need that at once. So that I cannot think I should do right to ask, or should be very likely to get leave if I did ask, to go to London to look at Millais' pictures,[1] so, seemingly at least, unprofessional a purpose. Everard's zeal, which is very kind, ~~has~~ ^will^ have had, I am afraid, no other effect than to make my mouth water. I am your loving son Gerard.

Many thanks to Grace for the kind trouble she has taken.

I am very glad to hear Mary is better.[2] I had thoughts of proposing another remedy, which learned people in this house ~~think~~ ^make^ much of, something electric, but I cannot persuade myself it is not quackery. However it is: Count Mattei's White Electricity[3] (there ~~is~~ ^are^ also other degrees or kinds distinguished as Red, Blue, Yellow, Green), a liquid to be applied on cotton wool to the parts affected, 2 francs a flask, at Mr. Emil Wüterich's, 43 Duke Street, Grosvenor Square. We have an electric battery with which extraordinary effects are produced and prodigious sparks drawn off you. It cured a chillblain of mine in a single go.

[1] The exhibition of Millais's collected works at the Grosvenor Gallery. It was first intended to hang the pictures chronologically and part of this intention was carried out; but Millais denounced the notion and insisted on a regrouping. The earlier works, except The Huguenot, were relegated to the small room of the gallery. See J. G. Millais, *The Life and Letters of Sir John Everett Millais* (London, 1899), ii. 195.

[2] See letter of 15 Aug. 1877, n. 4.

[3] Count Cesare Mattei (1809–96) was the inventor of electrohomeopathy, and marketed lotions and potions containing supposed bio-energy extracted from plants. The *British Medical Journal* in 'The Mattei Fable' (17 Jan. 1891) wrote that 'the "red electricity" and "white electricity" supposed to be "fixed" in these "vegetable compounds" are in their very nomenclature and suggestion poor and miserable fictions'.

11 February 1886 to Alexander William Mowbray Baillie

FL, no. CXLI, p. 257 UCD L 50

One folded sheet of headed paper with watermark 'EBLANA NOTE' and monogram; 4 sides

UNIVERSITY COLLEGE, | S$^{\underline{T}}$ STEPHEN'S GREEN, | DUBLIN. [*printed heading*]

Feb. 11 1886

Dearest Baillie, — Perhaps occasional letters are the best, as I believe. Newman says the best literature in general is occasional (probably this is not quite what he says:[1] at all events the Iliad and Odyssey, ^Aeneid,^ Divine Comedy, Paradise Lost and Regained, and in general more than half the great works in poetry; in prose most histories, philosophies, works of science — well, it is clear a great many ^fine^ things are not occasional; but) the present work is occasional and is to ask you two things. One is some~~tim~~ on-the-spot account of the late riots,[2] as witnessed by yourself or friends and informants, also London political gossip in general. The other is the following.

I am struggling to get together matter for a work on Homer's Art. I suppose like everything else ^of mine^ it will come to nothing in the end, but I cannot keep that likelihood always in view or I should do nothing at it at all. Many things crop up as you may suppose and the present point has.

I have found from Maspéro[3] (<u>Histoire des Peuples d'Orient</u> 1884: I mention the date because I saw the other day there was a new and enlarged edition: can there be later than '84?) that *Αἴγυπτος* {*Egypt*} comes from Ha-ka~~p~~-phtah | Abode of Phtah = Memphis, also that ~~He~~

Ἥφαιστος[4] is Phtah too. (Is Ha | the?) Now it has struck me that perhaps ~~Ἀφροδί~~ Ἀφροδίτη {*Aphrodite*} is from something like Ha — Phra (or Pira or Pra or what not) — D . . . and I want to know if among Egyptologists this is either agreed or suspected and if so ^I want^ to be oriented on the matter; and, if neither, ~~if~~ ^whether^ anything occurs to you as possible. Does not the second syllable as I have put it ~~mean~~ occur in Pharaoh and mean House? I make no account of ~~the~~ Liddell and Scott[5] deriving it from ἀφρός: it is such an easy afterthought.[6] They did not know about Αἴγυπτος* [*GMH footnote*: * nor about Ἥφαιστος {*Hephaistos*} — suggest it is from √ ΑΦ | kindle.]

I saw something about the origin of Semele[7] the other day but have missed it.

I may say that we have the second vol. of Rawlinson's Hist. of Egypt[8] in the house; why not the first I do not know.

I hope you are well, happy, and pleasantly employed. I am not markedly any of these things, but shall be bettered all round by a letter from you answering the above and conveying countless more points of interest. Till when I am your affectionate friend Gerard M. Hopkins S.J.

[1] At all events, Newman's writings are themselves predominantly occasional.

[2] On 8 Feb. 1886 a meeting of the Fair Trade League in Trafalgar Square was disrupted by several thousand supporters of the Marxist Social Democratic Federation, though policed by 563 policemen. Allegedly taunted by members of private clubs in Pall Mall, the SDF mob broke windows and looted along the major West End thoroughfares, destroying property worth more than £50,000. See 'Report of the Committee on the Origin and Character of the Disturbances which took place in the Metropolis on Monday, the 8th of February' (Select Committee, House of Commons, 'London Riots' 1886 [c. 4665] v. 34).

[3] Gaston Maspero, *Histoire ancienne des peuples d'Orient* (1875 etc.; 4th edn. 'entièrement refondue' 1886), 24. Brugsch's derivation from Ḥat-ka-Ptaḥ is quoted in Pauly-Wissowa-Kroll, *Real-Encyclopädie*, s.v. Aigyptos. See pp. 113, 116.

[4] Maspero, *Histoire ancienne*, 55. S.vv. Hephaestos, Athena: no mention of Egyptian derivations. This is the beginning of a series of proposed Egyptian-Greek derivations in which GMH wishes to show that 'Egyptian civilisation may well have rocked the cradle of Greek' (6 Apr.). He himself looked on his enquiries as 'perilous and conjectural' (10 Apr. 1886), 'not to be taken too seriously' (26 Mar. 1886) and on 20 Feb. 1887 said: 'My Egyptian guesses were wild and the children of ignorance.' He is doing it out of playful enquiry: 'we must start a hypothesis, enquire, test, verify; nothing venture nothing win' (27 Mar. 1886). We have therefore not commented on individual conjectures except when there was something particular to note.

[5] The great *English–Greek Lexicon* by Henry George Liddell and Robert Scott (1st edn. 1843). Liddell was Dean of Christ Church and Scott was Master of Balliol when GMH was at Oxford.

[6] This etiological myth was already known to Hesiod in the 8th c. BC; there is still much speculation about the origin.

[7] In Greek myth, Semele was the daughter of Cadmus and Harmonia, and mother of Dionysus.
[8] George Rawlinson, *History of Ancient Egypt*, 2 vols. (1881).

25 February 1886 from John Henry Newman to GMH

FL, no. C28, p. 413 Campion Hall and MS copy in Birmingham Oratory, N 25/2/86

Addressed to 'The Rev F^r^ Hopkins SJ | University College | Stephen's Green | Dublin'. PM BIRMINGHAM FE 25 86, H&K PACKET FE 26 86. Pencil drawing of beetles on envelope, probably by GMH.

The Oratory | Febr 25. 1886
My dear F^r^ Hopkins

I have read your letter with much interest, both the sad part and the reference to your intended analysis of old Homer. Alas, I cannot send you more than a few lines in answer, for I am losing the use of my fingers and do not write except with difficulty. My birthday, then, I fear is more clouded in prospect of the future to me than my doctor will allow on his own part

Anyhow, I want your good prayers and I am sure I shall have them in my necessity

Very sincerely yours
John H Card. Newman

23 March 1886 to Alexander William Mowbray Baillie

FL, no. CXLIII, p. 259 UCD L 52

One folded sheet of headed notepaper watermarked 'Antique Parchment Notepaper'; 4 sides.

UNIVERSITY COLLEGE, | S^T^ STEPHEN'S GREEN, | DUBLIN. [*printed heading*]
March 23 '86

Dearest Baillie, — I am very much obliged to you for your enquiries. I agree to your principles of etymology and shd. have said the same, though I might not have chosen such good examples. But I was deceived by Maspero, I ~~trusted him~~ thought he was to be trusted. I felt, it is true, a difficulty about *Αἴγυπτος* coming not from the name of Memphis[1] (that is Mannouwer or something like it) but from ~~such~~ ^some^ complimentary title, which Greek merchants or sailors were not very likely to hear — but then I thought Maspero must know. But if the word does not even occur, if it is his own coinage, that is very unjustifiable indeed.

But when you ask why Aphrodite shd. not be a Persian or an Indian name you seem to me less reasonable. If you were a Zend or Sanskrit scholar I might apply to you for a Persian or Indian origin for the name~~,~~. Now you are an Egyptologist and I ask for what you can give. But in any case it wd. be right to begin with Egypt, for Egypt was known to the Greeks long before Persia and India. The history of heathen religions is the history of ~~po~~ foreign worships introduced and ~~popularised~~ ^adopted^, sometimes with resistance at first. We have traces of great struggles ~~against~~ against the worship of Dionysus. Even so Greek a god as Apollo seems foreign. He was Delius et Patareus Apollo[2] and was a late tenant (see Aeschylus' Eumenides) of the oracle at Delphi. To Homer he is not thoroughly naturalised; he favours the Trojans and seems to be at home at places in Asia. It seems likely that there was a Greek Trinity of ^the same ~~as~~^ gods ~~like~~ ^as^ the Trinity of the Capitol at Rome, which was of Jove, Juno, and Minerva; only by Homer's time it had begun to vary and Homer's people pray to *Ζεῦ τε πάτερ καὶ Ἀθηναίη καὶ Ἄπολλον* {*father Zeus and Athena and Apollo*}, not *Ἥρη* {*Hera*}.[3] Besides I think some plausible identifications have been made; as of Semele.

I seem somewhere to have read that some legends represented Epaphus[4] son of Zeus and Io as a being with serpent legs, but I cannot verify it. But if it were verified, then I cd. make an interesting identification. It is not mentioned in Smith's great dictionary nor in Keightley's ~~m~~^M^ythology.[5]

I have a murderous cold and rheumatism and write with labour, but perhaps if I had not the cold I shd. not be writing at all. That is why the hand is so bad.

I have bought a book about Rome ^by^ Middleton.[6] It is now known there are extensive Etruscan remains at Rome. This overthrows the traditional account more than ever. It is not easy to understand how a language so pure as Latin cd. have been at home at a city ~~made~~ largely Etruscan. One wd. think the Etruscans must have been quite got rid of.

I have written a song in four parts. They are all quite tuneful, but whether they are right, that is another matter.

Since politics disquiet me and make me speak impatiently I will not enter on them, but I am your affectionate friend Gerard M. Hopkins S.J.

[1] Current scholarship says that the name is a Greek corruption of the Egyptian name of Pepi I's pyramid Mennufer (or Men-nefer—it is variously spelled, meaning 'the good place'), which in Coptic was *Menfe*.

[2] 'The Apollo of Delos and of Patara'; Horace, *Odes* iii. 4. 64.

[3] A frequently recurring prayerful invocation, used in the *Iliad* (four times) and the *Odyssey* (four times) giving solemn emphasis to what is said: e.g. *Iliad* ii. 371, *Odyssey* iv. 341.

[4] See Herodotus ii. 38 and the note on the passage in W. W. How and J. Wells, *A Commentary on Herodotus* (1912, rev. 1928).

[5] William Smith published several dictionaries of classical subjects. GMH's copy of his *Dictionary of Greek and Roman Biography and Mythology* (1853; 3 vols.) is mysteriously inscribed 'G. M. J. F. Hopkins / 1866' (see Madeline House, 'Books Belonging to Hopkins and his Family', *HRB*, 5 (1974), 31). Thomas Keightley published *The Mythologies of Ancient Greece and Italy* (4th edn. 1883).

[6] John Henry Middleton's *The Remains of Ancient Rome* appeared in 1892, but was enlarged from *Ancient Rome in 1885* and *Ancient Rome in 1888*, of which GMH had bought the former.

26 March 1886 to Alexander William Mowbray Baillie

FL, no. CXLIV, p. 261 UCD L 53
Postcard addressed to 'A. W. Mowbray Baillie Esq. | 22 Sackville Street | London W.' PM DUBLIN MR 27 86 186

University College, | Stephen's Green. [*printed heading*]
March 26 '86

About Dyaus, Ζεύς, Jovis, Tiu (in Tuesday), and perhaps a Celtic word found in Teutoboduus[1] etc there is no doubt. It is perhaps the only case. And remark that even here it is the word that is common, not the thing; for Tiu was not the supreme being: "maximum deorum Mercurium <Woden> colunt" {*of all the gods, Mercury [Woden] is the one they worship most*}.[2] Ahana is no better than Ha-ka-Ptah. The word is found only once; its meaning disputed, it is not clear a person is meant at all (I read abt. it lately, but cannot verify); the identification with Athene very, very doubtful. I believe you like others have been imposed on by the Sanskritists. In the vast ~~liter~~ vocabulary of the vast literature of India it is ^generally^ easy to find a word something like a Greek one. Sanskrit was necessary at the beginning of scientific philology; now it is a stumbling-block, a delusion~~,~~ and a snare. Look at the etymologies in e.g. Lewis and Short's Latin Dictionary:[3] they are the pretence of knowledge, without the reality. Language throws little light on the hist. of religion. See how like are Latin and Gk.; the religions of the ~~true~~ ^two^ races (the original ones, before the fusion) how unlike. I am sure Egypt is a likelier field for explanations of early Gk. religious thought etc than India or Persia.[4] It is solid ground, not guesswork like "The highlands of Pamir".[5] More anon or on next card, q.v.

[1] Teutobod (or Theudobod) was king of the Teutons, defeated in the battle of Aquae Sextiae in 102 BC. He is mentioned in Mommsen's *History of Rome* (see n. 9 of the letter to Patmore of 24 Sept. 1883), but the Latin ending suggests that GMH met him in a Latin account of the battle.

[2] Tacitus, *Germania* 9, has 'deorum maxime Mercurium colunt'.

[3] The *Latin Dictionary* of Charlton T. Lewis and Charles Short (revised edition 1873).

[4] GMH read Max Müller's speculations about Sanskrit in *Chips from a German Workshop* (vol. i, 1867) while at Oxford. See Cary H. Plotkin, *The Tenth Muse: Victorian Philology and the Genesis of the Poetic Language of GMH* (1989).

[5] According to Müller's theories, which were widely questioned and in part recanted, what he termed the 'Aryan' races and languages of mankind descended from the highlands of Pamir in central Asia to spread across Russia and Europe, to lay the foundations of future civilizations. Thomas Huxley in his essay on 'The Aryan Question' in 1890 wrote: 'Professor Max Müller, to whom Aryan philology owes so much, will not say more now, than that he holds by the conviction that the seat of the primitive Aryans was "somewhere in Asia"'.

[27 March 1886] to Alexander William Mowbray Baillie[1]

FL, no. CXLII, p. 258 UCD L 51
Postcard addressed to 'A. W. Mowbray Baillie Esq. | 22 Sackville Street | London W.' PM DUBLIN MR 27 86 186

University College, | Stephen's Green. [*printed address*]

I have a light. When the Gks. reached the Mediterranean they found older civilisations, and soon came to know the Phoenicians, whose civilisation was not native but borrowed, and chiefly from Egypt. It was they who taught the Gks. letters. Their intercourse with them was commercial chiefly. They wd. say of a little bronze image "(so to speak): "C'est le Ptah: ça vient de l'Égypte", putting in their own Semitic definite article. This became em~~o~~bodied in the Gk. name: Ἡ — φαιστος, Αἴ — γυπτος (from Caphtor perhaps). I grant this is guesswork, but it suggest[s] enquiries. After all perhaps Aphrodite might be

Ha-<Semitic definite article> + P <Egyptian ditto> + Ra <Sun> + one of his attitudes or positions, and the Gks. mistake it for a goddess. Why not the Rising Sun, *ἀναδυόμενος* {*rising from the waves*}? You say there is no legend of an Egyptian origin for ~~the~~ ^her^ worship. But Aphrodite is the consort of Hephaestus, who after all very probably is Ptah. I am afraid you will be put out by my persistency. I am quite alive to the hazard of all this; but we must start a hypothesis, enquire, test, verify; nothing venture nothing win. By the by the identification of Melicertes with Melkarth is certain. G. M. H.

[1] This postcard is in small writing. Across it, in a much larger hand, were first written the following words, which are cancelled: 'March 22 '86. By all means come tomorrow I too am perishing of a cold, let us call it a catarrh. I left sundry cards at both clubs, sundry times: I suppose they were not delivered.' This was probably not written to Baillie.

28 March 1886 to Alexander William Mowbray Baillie

FL, no. CXLV, p. 262 UCD L 54

Postcard addressed to 'A. W. Mowbray Baillie Esq. | 22 Sackville Street | London W.' PM DUBLIN MR 29 86 186

University College, | Stephen's Green. [*printed heading*]
March 28 '86

Those cards, that diptych, not to be taken too seriously. I dare say you are now writing to say Caphtor never meant Egypt. Say it soft. And that the article in Egyptian is never put before proper names; that possibility was before my mind. But the Semitic Article is good, it is a real workable light.

G. M. H.

28 March 1886 to Alexander William Mowbray Baillie

FL, no. CXLVI, p. 262 UCD L 55

Postcard addressed to 'A. W. Mowbray Baillie Esq. | 22 Sackville Street | London ~~N~~ W.' PM DUBLIN MR 29 86 186

University College, | Stephen's Green. [*printed heading*]
March 28 '86

I have it.

Information, lore, earnestly requested on "Neprat, divinité des grains",[1] ἀναδυόμενος {*rising from the waves*} of course from the inundations. G.

My last card.

[1] From Maspero, *Histoire ancienne*.

29 March 1886 to Alexander William Mowbray Baillie

FL, no. CXLVII, p. 262 UCD L 56

One folded headed sheet, watermarked with monogram and 'EBLANA NOTE'; 4 pages.

UNIVERSITY COLLEGE, | S^T STEPHEN'S GREEN. | DUBLIN. [*printed heading*]
March 29 '86

Dearest Baillie, — I am downcast about those ungentlemanly postcards, the two last at all events, as I am afraid you must have thought them.

I have thought of some more etymologies from the Sanskrit #given by Max Müller[1] or others, viz. ~~ο~~ *Οὐρανός* {*Ouranos, Uranus*} | varunas, ^Varuna,^ the nightly heaven~~;~~ (but what does this prove? only that two kindred languages had kindred words for heaven and divinised ^or ~~def~~ deified^ heaven, as where do men not?); *Προμηθεύς* {*Prometheus*} | pramanthas, kindlingstick for the "needfire" (not certain and, if certain, only shews that Prometheus meant as well as was the bestower of fire on man; besides that the Greek treatment of the myth due to the mistaken, if mistaken, etymology from προμηθής {*forethinking*}, which brings in Ἐπιμηθεύς {*Epimetheus, Afterthought*}, is its most interesting ~~me~~, ethical, and religious part); Ἐρινύς | Saraṇyû "a mythical being in the Veda" as per M.M. (whom I have not got and therefore cannot ~~ge~~ ^say^ if the two mythical beings have anything in common beyond the name and the never having existed); Ἑρμείας, Ἑρμῆς | Sarameya (spelling, especially dots etc, not further known), a heavenly greyhound, hound of dawn (I have, in spite of Lang, a considerable belief in the Solar myth and especially in these "hounds of ~~dau~~ dawn", which are really very widespread and found in Greek, Irish, Egyptian — ? the "divine jackals" — as well as Indian mythology; but all that does not shew that Hermes, afterwards identified with Mercury, god of wages, was in Gk. religious history a hound of dawn: in fact he never was): I ~~nev~~remember no more.

I do not dispute these etymologies nor deny they throw light on the past history of Greek mythology, but I do say they do not throw much light and that what they throw is prehistoric, so to call it, and not part of the history ^proper^ of Greece and Greek religion, about which I believe Phoenicia and Egypt have more to say than India and the Pamir.[2] And, though I do not maintain it, yet I believe it might ^be^ as easily maintained, that Ἀθήνη comes from Aten or Athen the disk of the sun as from Ahana the pretended dawn goddess. We do know the one was worshipped (furiously) and we do not the other. And I will risk it that Ῥαδάμανθυς {*Rhadamanthys*} is Ra-Ament or something like that, if Ament means infernal.

You will find about Ha-ka-~~p~~^ph^tah in "Brugsch G. Insch., t. 1, p. 83".[3] It is then Brugsch's conjecture adopted by Maspero.

I am afraid the effect of all this will be to make you say "A firm foot must be put down on ~~all~~ this sort of thing AT ONCE", but if it makes you write so much the better. It is a great help to me to have someone interested in something (that will answer my letters), and ^it^ supplies some sort of intellectual stimulus. I sadly need that and a general stimulus to being, so ~~ha~~ dull and yet harassed is my life.

Believe me your affectionate friend Gerard Hopkins S.J.

(If you dash Neprat I will "run" Khepra, which please explain.)
I think proper names may have the article: e.g. T'ape | Thebes.

1 (Friedrich) Max Müller (1823–1900; *ODNB*) was a noted Sanskrit scholar and founder of the study of comparative religion. He had a long-running dispute with Andrew Lang on the origins of myth and folk beliefs, which polarized into the 'solar mythology' school of Müller, which argued that ancient myths are anthropomorphic explanations of natural phenomena, and the 'polygenesis' school of Lang, for whom myths were preserved tradition. For Lang's extensive criticism of Müller's theories, see his article on 'Mythology' in the ninth edition of the *Encylopaedia Britannica* (vol. xvii, 1884), which GMH made a note to read in late Oct. 1884 (see *CW* vii). Lang (1844–1912: *ODNB*), fellow student at Balliol 1865–8, prolific poet, journalist, translator of Homer, was well known for his work on folklore (*Custom and Myth*, 1884; *Myth, Ritual and Religion*, 1883), and his fairy tales.

2 In denying the importance of Pamir (see postcard of 26 Mar. 1886, n. 5), GMH is beginning to question Max Müller's theories.

3 Heinrich Karl Brugsch (1827–94), *Geographische Inschriften altägyptischer Denkmäler* (1857–60). Brugsch was a pioneer in deciphering Egyptian demotic script.

3 April 1886 to Alexander William Mowbray Baillie

FL, no. CXLVIII, p. 264 UCD L 57

Postcard addressed to 'A. W. Mowbray Baillie Esq. | 22 Sackville Street | London W.' PM DUBLIN 19A AP 4 86 186

University College, | Stephen's Green. [*printed heading*]
~~M~~ April 3 '86

I am greatly obliged as well as gratified by your letters and will write more fully. I always treated and still treat Ra-t'Amenti (~~as~~ happily emended) as a guess only and ~~do not~~ ^give it no absolute^ assent, but it is a helpful guess and I now supplement and support it. I suppose an Egyptian occupation of Crete or early intercourse with Crete (which, by the by, is commonly said to be the Caphtor of the Sep.). The point about his father Hephaestus had not escaped me. His brother Sarpedon I wd. try as something like Osar-pi-Toum. (For the loss of O cp. Sarapis = Osar-Hapi.) Minos and the Minotaur, one or both, are perhaps connected with the Bull Mnevis (for the variation ω and ευ cp. Θώθ and Θεύθ and for the termination ως I find ~~other~~ parallels in Maspero, e.g. shou = Σῶς.) Then Εὐρώπη {*Europa*, *Europe*} is perhaps Har-Hapi. I find that Pausanias[1] has a tradition of Hephaestus being the son of Cres, eponymous hero of Crete. There was a Cretan ~~(besides others)~~ town Phaestus (the same name occurs elsewhere), founded by a hero Phaestus (observe no He-). The degradation of gods to heros and kings is familiar and the Egyptian gods were especially liable to it, because the Egyptians themselves treated their gods (did they not?) as matter of fact kings of Egypt and told of their wars. G. M. H.

[1] Pausanias, a Greek traveller who flourished AD 150, wrote a *Description of Greece.*

6 April 1886 to Alexander William Mowbray Baillie

FL, no. CXLIX, p. 264 UCD L 58
Three folded sheets of 'EBLANA NOTE' watermarked and headed paper; 12 sides.

UNIVERSITY COLLEGE, | ST. STEPHEN'S GREEN, | DUBLIN. [*printed heading on all three double sheets*]
April 6 1886

Dearest Baillie, — I have first some detached remarks to make.

(1) The variation t | th etc is surely not peculiar to the later stages of the language. What you are thinking of in Hebrew (I never knew ~~of~~ ^of^ it but the most elementary part — learnt ~~I~~ or studied or spelled at, I mean, for know it I never did; and what I learnt I have forgotten, but I remembered that this) is called Daghesh.[1] It is written by a dot in the midst of a letter. It means for t, k, p that they are t, k, p; its omission leaves them th, kh, ph — or something like. It answered exactly to nothing Greek: hence the variants *Ματθαῖος* and *Μαθθαῖος* {*Matthias*} — the *Τ* or *Θ* or combination of them must have the Daghesh. In l, m, n (if I remember) it is expressed by doubling the letter. There is something answerable in Arabic. Daghesh I think means stab; like drive home, insist. But the same principle exists widely — that letters are weakened or ^strengthened,^ emphasised, by position.

(2) The rules for transliterating Egyptian into Greek I have not seen stated. They ought to be. But I will observe that such rigid laws cannot be looked for in the representation of foreign words ^by foreigners^, an instantaneous change, so to call it, as ^in^ the correlating of parallel forms variants from a common original form, where the change is long and gradual. One Greek sailor heard one thing, another another, and so on. I remark that some of the Egyptian names seem fairly well represented by the Greek, others ill, and others differ so much that they seem to bear witness to some other name or form of the name. For instance some names beginning Ouser are Hellenised ~~Se~~ *Σεσω*: is it not from some form Shesou? There are others ^again^, some royal names,

^~~in Greek~~^ which ^in Greek^ clearly do not represent the existing Egyptian ones. There is something odd about the Greek terminations in is: either they bear witness to some other pronunciation than a, eh etc or else perhaps they are a kind of instinctive effort to make a name outlandish.

(3) You ask, is not ~~all~~ ^the greater part of^ Greek religion prehistoric? If you like, but not equally~~,~~. ~~not~~ Part is as far back as the common life of the Aryan race, and this part I think is not much, or it may be great in importance but ~~not~~ ^is not^ extensive in names and legends. Most of the vast Greek mythology is localised in Greece itself and was invented or developed therefore there. The following case is curious. It is said that at Dodona, the oldest known sanctuary of the race, Zeus or Jove's consort was not Hera but Dione, which seems to be the feminine of Zeus as Juno~~,~~^(^Joveno~~,~~^)^ of Jove. Her worship ~~has~~ disappeared before that of Hera. Now, as you say, there is reason to suspect Hera of an Eastern ^(indeed Egyptian)^ origin. The first Greeks found her worship established, I suppose, at Argos ~~I~~ and elsewhere (for there were older inhabitants) and adopted it. It is this development of the Greek religion prehistorically, as you say, but in Greece that I am concerned with.

And here consider that in religion more than in language a thing may have no one origin, it may ~~have~~ ^be at^ the meeting point of many influences. Even words (as they say is shewn in Murray of allow)* [*GMH footnote:* * Mérimée, I remember, held this of French words.] are sometimes two words rolled into one, approximated till they blend their meanings.[2] As soon for instance as the Romans settled that Mercury was Hermes, everything told of Hermes was true of Mercury, and so on. I will apply this to Aphrodite.

Homer is ~~her~~ ^our^ earliest authority. He makes her daughter of Dione. This is (as suggested above) thoroughly, patriarchally Greek. But if my suspicion is right that Aphrodite is a foreign word it ^~~s~~^may have been identified with some earlier Greek divinity and one title have supplanted the other. Or thus: the worship may have been altogether foreign and the identification may have been of Aphrodite's foreign mother with the Gk. Dione — perhaps before the worship of Hera was established.

Next, the Eastern Aphrodite (strongly ~~connected~~ ^identified^ with the planet Venus) is well known. She is Ashtoreth. Astaroth. Astarte. The Phoenicians established her worship at Cyprus, Cythera. and other places; not only so but the Greeks knew this and it seems, for I have not got it, there is a ~~P~~Homeric hymn about ~~her~~ ^it^.[3] (It has struck me that *Κύθηρα* or *Κυθήρα* = *Κήθυρα* {*Cythera*}, as *Μιτυλήνη* and

Μυτιλήνη {*Mytilene*} are both found, may further = *Κίθυρα* = *Κίνυρα*, as *κιθάρα* = kinnor: now Cinyras is a legendary personage in some way connected with Aphrodite.) But the name Aphrodite does not seem Phoenician. Consequently ~~I~~ whoever Aphrodite was she has been ^first brought into being, then^ identified with the Eastern Astarte afterwards. So I come back to the question of the etymology of that name, which seems not Greek and not Phoenician: may it not be Egyptian? And that although the ~~goddess (or~~ ^Egyptian^ divinity who bore it may have small claims to be identified with the Syrian or the old Greek one. Some slight circumstance may have served ^for this identification^ and some advantage in the sound may have perpetuated, perhaps, the name of the personage whose personality, so to speak, contributed the least of three or more to the Greek Aphrodite. Now I do not assert, I only enquire; and it seems to me this line of thought is scientific enough in an enquiry. In the enquiry I start two possible veins — Khepra and Nepra or Neprat (Maspero gives both forms) ~~(~~ for that about the two articles was a mere freak.~~)~~ It is not quite certain it might not be both. For the thought has struck me that perhaps Phtah became Hephaestus ^(if he did)^ through some confusion with Pasht, a confusion of thought or merely of sound. (But I cannot find about Pasht in Maspero.)

But there was an Egyptian Aphrodite, from whom ^Aphroditopolis and^ the Aphroditic name ~~was~~ ^were^ called. ~~s~~So far as I can make out she is Nebtep~~;~~. ~~a~~And is not this Nephthys? But if so Nebteb seems as if it must have to do with Nept, who, as you tell me, ~~as~~ ^is^ the ~~a~~ goddess of corn. Here is more confusion, but also room for enquiry.

And here two parentheses: 1. please to not sit up so late on my account;

2. What book on Egypt wd. you recommend me? — not in 5 volumes; still a good one.

So much on Aphrodite.

(4) My light on Crete I have great hopes of. It is generally agreed that Crete played some great part in early Greek civilisation: ancients and moderns say so. In particular the Zeus and Cronos legends are localised there, ~~which~~ ^and these^, I presume, next to the name and conception of Zeus himself, which is Aryan, are the most important in Greek mythology. Now if I can shew a ~~great~~ likelihood of there having been at some time an Egyptian civilisation in Crete (as the batch of names Rhadamanthys, * [*GMH footnote*: * So in Plato, as I remembered. Rhadamanthos is also found][4] Sarpedon, Minos, Minotaur, Europe, Phaestus, Labyrinth makes likely~~,~~ — subject to your treatment of them) I do shew

that Egyptian civilisation may ~~ha~~ well have rocked the cradle of Greek, quod erat demonstrandum {*which was to be demonstrated*}.

There is a connection between Crete first and the Troad (e.g. the two Mount Idas) and here the Trojan Θήβη {*Thebes*} is worth noticing, secondly and Boeotia: I have forgotten the link~~.~~; ~~But~~^but^ I wd. suggest Egyptian traces in Thebes; in the Sphinx legend; perhaps in the Minyae; possibly in Oropus ~~(~~| another Har-Hapi; ^lastly in the early civilisation of Boeotia, exceeding the rest of G.^

I suspect therefore an early Egyptian colonisation. There are, as you know, some legends carrying ^Sesostris and^ Egyptians even to Colchis ^and beyond^ (and there is the odd cock-and-a-bull, bull by all means, story in Tacitus and elsewhere of the fetching of Sarapis ~~S~~from Sinope.[5] There was a σινωπεῖον {*temple or sanctuary of Serapis*} near Memphis; which does not in my opinion explain the story by a confusion ^of places^ but makes it more likely that Sinope is really an Egyptian word and contains Hapi~~)~~: afterwards, or at some time, Sinope is said to have been Phoenician and ~~afterwards~~ ^later still^ certainly Greek). There are a lot of Minoas on the ^A^Egean coasts: they must be connected with Minos and more likely with some divinity than with a historical man. If so, I still suggest my Mnevis.

Which leads me to beg for information on Mnevis, which in Maspero I cannot get.

~~Then of course there is the legend of Sesostris' campaigns~~ Whoever the Pelasgians were I find it mentioned of them that they introduced Egyptian rites (Herod. ii 51:[6] I cannot verify it in my room.)

Altogether I think the enquiry into the early influence of Egypt on Greece promising and important. I need not, I suppose, tell you that the decoration of the palaces at Tiryns and elsewhere is bastard Egyptian. Indeed this rather shews the builders had been to Egypt than the Egyptians to Greece, or that there was some gobetween: if so the Phoenicians perhaps.

But the ~~legen~~ tradition is strong that Minos put down piracy and demanded tribute. Now this may have been an Egyptian occupation and expulsion of Phoenicians and others. May it have taken place after that strange invasion of the Delta by a motley ~~European~~ ^northern^ host, among whom there are Akaiusha, not after all unplausibly identified with the Achaeans, since ~~the~~ Ach[a]eans was the most general name for the Greeks in Greece before the Dorian conquest — ? But then there ought to be some trace of ~~it~~ ^all this^ in Egyptian monuments.

I had forgotten the legend of ~~the~~ Aegyptus, the Danaids, and Argos.

I am very long and must conclude. Please inform me on Sarpedon and Mnevis. By pi in Osar-pi-Toum I did not mean the article, but the word (what does it mean?) in Pi-Toum the city now exploring.[7]

Believe me affectionately yours
Gerard Hopkins.

P.S. If there was any contact between early Greece and Egypt how cd. it help having great results? The Gks. were materially uncivilised, the most intelligent of men but in their mental childhood; the Egyptian civilisation was mature and brilliant: it must have dazzled them entirely.

PPS. The Egyptian ~~of~~ occupation of Crete may have had to do with the expulsion of the Philistines, if Caphtor is Crete.

[1] In the *OED* 'dagesh' is defined as 'A point or dot placed within a Hebrew letter denoting either that it is doubled (*dagesh forte*), or that it is not aspirated (*dagesh lene*).' It is derived from the Syriac word for 'to prick'.

[2] Prosper Mérimée (1803–70). Sir James Augustus Henry Murray (1837–1915) had published on 1 Feb. 1884 the first fascicle, *A–Ant*, of what would become the *OED*. The entry for 'allow' still notes the double derivation from *allaudare*, 'to praise' and *allocare*, 'to bestow'.

[3] Three of the *Homeric Hymns*, V, VI, and X, are hymns to Aphrodite.

[4] In the *Gorgias*, 424A.

[5] This story is now believed by most authorities. See Tacitus *Histories*, IV. 83–4 and Plutarch, *De Iside at Osiride* c. 28 (from Manetho).

[6] On Herodotus, see W. W. How and J. Wells, *A Commentary on Herodotus* (Oxford, 1912), and Alfred Wiedemann, *Herodots zweites Buch mit sachlichen Bemerkungen*, 2 vols. (Leipzig, 1890).

[7] The city is variously known as Pithom, Per-Atum, Heroöpolis and Heroönopolis. In the spring of 1883 Edouard Naville believed he had identified its location as the archaeological site Tell-el-Mashkuta, east of Wadi Tumilat and south-west of Ismalia. The identification has since been disputed.

6–10 April 1886[1] to Alexander William Mowbray Baillie

FL, no. CL, p. 270 UCD L 59
Postcard addressed to 'A. W. Mowbray Baillie Esq. | 22 Sackville Street | London W.' PM DUBLIN 6A AP 10 86 186

University College, | Stephen's Green. [*printed heading*]
April 6 '86

I have found abt. Pasht or Bast. She = Sekhet.

I find an old form *ΗΕΦΑΣΤΟΣ* {*Hephaistos*}. The h of Phtah was a difficulty to the Greeks: for its representation by i cp. coelum or caelum = cailum = cohilum (acc. to late lights). I had other instances.

What you say abt. the Thebeses is possible. But remark. Homer speaks of Thebe in the Troad;[2] (2) Egyptian Thebes with 100 gates; and (3) in the Catalogue, now said to be later than the rest, (but this is uncertain and irrelevant), of Ὑποθῆβαι {*Hupothebai*}[3] in Boeotia. The prep. ὑπό with a proper name of place is, so far as I remember, unique. The plural is like Athens, Erythrae, Clazomenae. I understand it to mean the upper and lower towns. The upper was the Acropolis, (here the Cadmea). The unusual form Ὑποθῆβαι suggests to me T' Ape peh'ou (or something like that); for I find a coupling of AB khent and AB peh'ow common.

What do you think of the Home Rule Bill?[4]

[1] Abbott dated this series of postcards to the 'April 6' written on this card, but the postmarks, though a little confusing, are unequivocally the 10th.

[2] In the *Iliad* 1, l. 366, Homer calls Thebe the city of Eëtion, which is in the Troad, the historical name of the Biga peninsula in the north-western part of Anatolia, Turkey.

[3] See *Iliad* 2, l. 505.

[4] Gladstone brought in his Home Rule Bill on 8 Apr. 1886, and it was read a first time without a division. See letter to AWMB of 1 June 1886.

10 April 1886 to Alexander William Mowbray Baillie

FL, no. CLI, p. 270 UCD L 60

Postcard addressed to 'A. W. Mowbray Baillie Esq. | 22 Sackville Street | London W.' PM DUBLIN AP 10 86

University College, | Stephen's Green. [*printed heading*]

(T'Ape or T'Apu is said to mean the Head, Capital; if so it is a title, not a proper name, and applicable to many places.) The plural in the name of the Egyptian Thebes is due to the Boeotian.

The tradition of a Phoenician foundation of Thebes was strong. And there was a tradn. of a second founding and in fact the Upper and Lower Cities were said to have distinct founders. I suspect the names Labdacus, Laius, and Oedipus to be historical and to = Ra-ptah, Ra+something, Hoteb — uas (?). And Athene Onca, said to be Phoenician, is perhaps Egyptian. What does Ankh mean?

The enquiry that ought to be made is when did this Egyptian colonisation of Crete etc take place. It seems to be mixed with the Phoenician, not altogether opposed to it. This wd. seem ^then^ to be at the Hyksos[1] period. (I remark also that the legend of Isis connects her with Phoenicia.)

I find Nefert in a female proper name and now suggest Aphrodite = ~~Nefert Nefr~~ Nefrat-isi.

I hope to be in London after Easter and to see you. Three cheers. G. M. H.

[1] See letter to AWMB of 20 Feb. 1887.

10 April 1886 to Alexander William Mowbray Baillie

FL, no. CLII, p. 271 UCD L 61

Postcard addressed to 'A. W. Mowbray Baillie Esq. | 22 Sackville Street | London W.' PM DUBLIN AP 10 86

University College, | Stephen's Green. [*printed heading*]
April 10 '86.

Omissions and amendments.

I have two bks. on Egypt — Rawlinson's History, vol. 2 (the first is missing), and Sayce's Herodotus, vol. 1 (now withdrawn from publication in consequence of blunders found in it, esp. by Trinity Dublin scholars. A whole number of Hermathena was devoted to the attack and defence. The historical essays are useful however.)[1]

Cohilum was illogical. I shd. have said coh-lum. It is connected, they say, with the word ^cohum^ meaning ~~that~~ part of a plough~~, into which the~~, and cohum itself is said to have meant coelum.

It has also struck me, why shd. not *Βοιωτία* ~~itself~~ be peh'ou | lowlands? Perhaps the same word occurs in *Εὔβοια*. The change of p into b occurs in *Βουτώ* = *Pα*-outs, that of e into oi in Meri | *Μοῖρις*.

It seems there was a sacred bull in Rhodes in early times; ~~G.M.H.~~ another (well known) at Lemnos, which was famous for Hephaestus-worship.

Perilous and conjectural as all this enquiry is I find it very interesting and suggestive. And if it throws light on Greek history it must also on Egyptian and kill two birds with one stone. G.H.

[1] See above (11 February 1886) for Rawlinson. The Revd Archibald Henry Sayce (1846–1933) published *The Ancient Empires of the East. Herodotus I–III* in 1883.

19 April 1886 to Alexander William Mowbray Baillie

FL, no. CLIII, p. 272 UCD L 62
Postcard addressed to 'A. W. Mowbray Baillie Esq. | 22 Sackville Street | London W.' PM DUBLIN AP 20 86

University College, | Stephen's Green. [*printed heading*]
April 19 '86

Very many thanks for your two letters. I make no further answer, as I hope I may see you this week on Thursday or Saturday; for I expect to be in London by Wednesday morning. G. M. H.

By the by, Caphtor is said to be Kepht-ur, ~~and~~ Greater Phoenicia, and to mean the Delta, where at one time numbers of Phoenicians were settled. Kepht is said to mean[1] palm tree, palmland, Phoenicia. There are traces also of a word Fenekh, meaning either Phoenicia or palm and in any case the immediate origin of the Gk. φοῖνιξ.

[1] MS 'to be mean'.

24 April 1886 from John Rhys[1] to GMH

FL, no. D4, pp. 416–19 Campion Hall, R 24/4/86
Addressed to 'The Rev[d] | Gerard M. Hopkins | University College | St. Stephen's Green | Dublin' and readdressed to 'Jesuit Church | Farm Str. | London'. PM Oxford AP 25 86, H&K PACKET AP 26 86, DUBLIN AP 27 86, LONDON AP 27 86.

Ap. 24. 1886

43 Banbury Road, Oxford. [*on paper with Jesus College embossed crest*]
My dear Hopkins

I was very glad to have a word from you and at such a length as I had completely lost sight of you. I am sorry you are so over worked but let us hope that better things are in store for you, and that you will have time to write on Homer and also return to Celtic studies. If I had known of your being in Dublin when I was over there about 2 years ago looking up Irish Ogams[2] in the company (at any rate for some time) of Father Barry of Youghal:[3] I should then have looked you up and possibly inspired you with some zeal for Ogamic research. I have however left it off myself for a while but I am going to return to it ere long I think. I have lately been getting ready 8 lectures for the Hibbert Trust to be delivered next month on Celtic Heathendom, which I have just got into some sort of shape for delivery but not yet for publication.[4] They will interest you greatly I think as they will not be lacking in new ideas (and doubtless very many new blunders). I have come pretty nearly spoiling them by trying to cram into them all I thought I had to say on the subject: I find that however out of the question and I now think~~ing~~ I shall go on with the subject and devote the rest of ^my^ time to it. The Welsh texts ~~are~~ ^scheme is^ really due to a Welshman[5] whom I have inoculated here with a taste for such things: he has by infinite perseverance made himself the only Welsh palaeographer living. He does all the copying work and I revise; but alas! his health is very bad and we may lose him any time and then I fear the scheme would be done for but I must say his health is much better since he has begun this definite work. But if we only do a part of what we propose that will have been done well. — I asked him to send you a prospectus, which I expect he has done long ago — I shall now probably be much occupied the rest of this year in getting the Hibbert Lectures ready for the press. My next job will be 6 lectures for the Rhind people at Edinburgh in 1889[6] on the early inhabitants of Britain and Ireland (they call it Scotland ~~and~~ but that explanation is in confidence): I mean there to be no more than 6 lectures and to do duty as prolegomena to the Celtic inscriptions of the British Islands which I want to publish in some form or other. I have already seen nearly all of them; but I must make some more visits to Ireland before that is done. If you ever take a holiday let me direct you to some of the old stones — I will give you full directions topographic and other, if you will only let me know, and for studying Ogams there is no place like Dublin especially the cellar of the Irish Academy where I spent two whole days when I was last there without emerging even to lunch. Cork is also a good place for the purpose especially now that Dr. Sullivan has got most of the Ogam stones at the Queen's College taken excellent care of. There is my programme — Celtic Heathendom as a standing study, revision of of my friend's work in issuing Welsh texts, the early inhabitants & the inscriptions: I had almost forgotten the critical edition of the Mabinogion &c but they would form almost a part of my studies of Celtic Heathendom. I have talked so much of myself in this letter that your sentence will be "plein de lui." {*full of himself*}

You mention the derivation of the Englyn from the rhymed elegiac: I have never heard the suggestion but I should be very glad if you would work it out, or at least indicate the sort of connection that has struck you.[7] I have never published anything but the lectures and Celtic Britain of which a second edition ^is^ in the publishers hands and ought to be in the market. But now and then I have written in the Revue Celtique and you will find rather an elaborate article of mine in the last volume on the Welsh of our old poetry, pointing out some interesting things in old Welsh grammar. I wish you could return to your idea of editing the Confessio of S. Patrick: I have read most of Fr. Shearman's Loca Patric.[8] What you say about the perverse ideas entertained about S. Patrick's origin has often presented itself to my mind too in much the same way: my only doubts being what part exactly of the Brythonic domain he set out from, and that doubt is probably owing ^only^ to my not having systematically studied the documents and especially the Confessio with care enough. * [*footnote:* *Stokes[9] has spotted the old names of Érinn and of its people in the Confessio, and elsewhere he gets Evernili patriâ. I think it occurs àpropos of S. Columba somewhere.] Partizanship prevails very much with Welshmen as it does with Irishmen, but it ought not in the case of men who have had a sound historical training; but it is rather fostered by the writings of men who eternally harp on the Anglo-Saxon race as they call it. There is unfortunately no such book as you want to throw ~~much~~ light on the Gaulish gods: the Revue Celtique contains some articles in point and M. Gaidoz has written some articles here and there. With regard to Lucan's Gaulish gods you should I am told consult Usener's scholiast.[10] I think Esus was a kind of Celtic Saturn or farmers' god; Teutates was a Mars, but the Celtic Mars was Mars and Jupiter in one — the chief Gaulish & Celtic god being the war god or vice versa (in spite of Caesar ^who^ gives a Mars and a Jupiter, a small Jupiter as he comes low in the list, a weather god just begun to be departmentalized) who was perhaps no other than ^the^ Taranucnus of the inscriptions), and lastly I want very much to prove that Taranis was a goddess but I doubt that I can.

My wife wishes to be very kindly remembered to you: she is in much better health than she has been.

Yours very truly
J. Rhys

[1] See letter to Rhys of 23 June 1877, n. 1.

[2] Oghams were the twenty (later expanded to twenty-five) characters in an ancient Irish alphabet, mostly found on monuments and boundary markers; also inscriptions in these characters.

[3] The Revd Patrick Power, MRIA, in his *Prehistoric Ireland* (1925), writes of the Revd Edmund Barry, PP of Rathgormac, County Cork, who began a study of Oghams late in life, made important discoveries, and published many articles but no book on the topic.

[4] The Hibbert lectures were an annual series of non-sectarian lectures (still being given) founded in 1847 by Robert Hibbert. Rhys gave the lectures in 1886 on 'The Origin and growth of religion as illustrated by Celtic heathendom' (published in 1888). Rhys also published a number of essays on the subject of Celtic inscriptions, and with J. Gwenogvryn Evans published *The Text of the Mabinogion* (1887).

5 John Gwenogvryn Evans (1852–1930, *ODNB*), an important palaeographer and printer of Welsh texts.

6 A series of lectures to the Society of Antiquaries of Scotland, funded by the bequest of Alexander Henry Rhind (1833–63). Rhys gave the 1889 lectures on 'The early ethnology of the British Isles'.

7 See *Cymmrodor*, 18 (1905), for Rhys's 'The origin of the Welsh Englyn'. It seems possible that Rhys developed GMH's suggestion.

8 John Francis Shearman, *Loca Patriciana* (1879).

9 Whitley Stokes (1830–1909; *ODNB*), Celtic scholar; in the Rolls Series (London, 1887), he published the text and translation of the *Vita Tripartita*, together with many original documents from the *Book of Armagh* and other sources.

10 Hermann Karl Usener (1834–1905), *Scholia in Lucani bellum civili* (1869).

28–9 April 1886 to Alexander William Mowbray Baillie

FL, no. CLIV, p. 272 UCD L 63

One folded sheet of 'W T & Co' watermarked paper with embossed address; 4 sides.

Oak Hill, | Hampstead, N.W. [*embossed heading*]
April 28 '86.

My dear Baillie, — I use such buttons and drop them down my back, but none seems to be missing now. I hereby entitle you to make what use of it you like, even to give it (in indivisible moieties, say) to your friends, to bring it into hotchpot,[1] sell it and invest it in ~~el~~ consols, or have an auction of it giving the proceeds to the unemployed. Other methods will suggest themselves to you.

Curtius[2] and others do hold that θ, ϕ, χ were all t+h, p+h, k+h. I am not ~~on~~ posted in the controversy. In modern Greek they are th (as in English th proper: Geldart told me he went out to Greece believing there was a difference but found none), ph or f, and ch as in German etc. Curtius knows this, but says the change took place later than classical times, later than the Christian era I think. The evidence available on this and like heads is difficult to deal with and seems at first sight to prove more than it does. For instance Tahuti | *Θεύθ* or *Θώθ* {*Thoth*} seems conclusive that θ was t+h. But it is not. For what the first θ appears to prove the second as much appears to disprove. It does rather more, for an initial θ and especially in the name of a god was very congenial to a Greek tongue but a final θ quite the contrary. It may therefore be (and, I think myself, was) the case that the Egyptian t here sounded to the Greeks like their θ and that the h was omitted (for the Greeks did not write it in the body of a word, excepting certain grammarians, and especially in the word ταῶς | peacock; but there it was, ~~pr~~ I think, rather a w than an h) and then the two vowels became the diphthong ευ or (in the form T'huti) ω. ~~This ^It^ is har~~

It is hard for us to conceive that t+h cd. become th and in English they scarcely could, because the position of the organs has to be changed so much; but I find in myself a tendency to ~~mak~~ turn make haste into ma-khaste, the change of position being slighter.

Your affectionate friend Gerard M. Hopkins.
April 29.

[1] A legal method by which things are gathered together so that they can be divided equally.
[2] Ernst Curtius (1814–96), *History of Greece* (1857–67, translated A. W. Ward, 1869–73).

4 May 1886 to Robert Bridges

LRB, no. CXXXII, p. 224 Bodleian, Dep. Bridges, vol. 92, fos. 86–7

~~UNIVERSITY COLLEGE, | ST. STEPHEN'S GREEN, | DUBLIN~~. [*printed heading*] | St. Aloysius' Church, St. Giles's, Oxford. May 4 '86

My dear Bridges, — Thursday May 6 is the day I must come.

You say I am to come to Hampstead Norris. So let it be, but the earliest train I cd. come by gets there at 10.57, that is, nearly 11, whereas if I went to Pangbourn I cd. be there at 10.11 and possibly by 9.7. But this last ^and first^ would involve ~~great struggling~~ ^going without breakfast^; and though the later train (10.11) is 46 minutes earlier than the one to Hampstead Norris, yet I suppose the difference is more than made up for in the drive.* [*GMH footnote:* * This will not do either, for it is incredible that either place shd. be so distant from you as to make a difference of 46 minutes and more in driving.] Even so . . . but perhaps it is the horse you are thinking of or ~~s~~there is some other point to be considered. However it may be, to Hampstead Norris at

10.57 I go, — unless, which perhaps posts make impossible, I hear from you to the contrary.

I must be back here at night.

Yours ever Gerard Hopkins.

And I must wait at Didcot 50 minutes for that local train, O dear O dear. But you wd. have it so.

10 May 1886 from Mrs. Elizabeth Waterhouse[1] *to GMH*

FL, no. H1, p. 426 Campion Hall, Misc. Waterhouse

Addressed to 'The Rev[d] | Gerard M. Hopkins. S.J. | University College | St. Stephens Green | Dublin'. PM NEWBURY MY 10 86, H&K PACKET MY 1? 86, C . . . VELEY MY 10 86.

Yattendon, near Newbury [*printed heading with the extra information*: 'Station—Pangbourne. G. W. R.' *and* 'Telegrams—Bradfield. 4 miles'.]

10 May. 86

Dear Father Hopkins,

I am sending you the little book[2] as you were kind enough to say that you would care for it — you will think it sadly undogmatic and perhaps when I was gathering it together I was a little too much afraid of dogma — as life goes on every year leads one to be more sure that one need be afraid of nothing through wh. the pure in heart have at any time seen their Lord — unless it has come to be in any way a cloud between them and Him — it also leads one to believe that any words of ours are so infinitely far from saying anything about Him as he is, that the difference between one set of words and another is but little — and that what is spoken in silence between Him and the Soul is the closest approach we can make to an utterance — and that in that language there is the <u>answer</u> too, which is the highest joy.

It was so nice to me to see you the other day only it seemed but a very little time — and I should have liked to know so much of your thoughts and of your life — it was very sad to me to hear that you were "worried" with work — because I had fancied you quite otherwise — and free to lead the hidden life — away from the world and its cares — but such freedom though one of the things I always delight in picturing, is not like the Master — one forgets this at times — though now and then the "no leisure, so much as to eat" is a comforting thought in days busy for others.[3] As for myself, I should be afraid that my rest here was almost too pleasant to be right — except that it seems so like the Best Giver that I think it must be given by Him & so a blessed thing — Please excuse my going on chatting as if you were here — & believe me — yours sincerely

E Waterhouse

[1] Elizabeth Waterhouse was a Quaker who converted to the Church of England. She was the wife of Alfred Waterhouse and their daughter Mary Monica married RB in 1884.

[2] Probably Elizabeth Waterhouse's *Book of Simple Prayers*. See letter to RB of 26 July 1883.

[3] Quoting Mark 6: 31.

22 May [1886] from Sir Robert Stewart[1] to GMH

FL, no. I1, pp. 426–7 Campion Hall, Stewart 1

Saturday Evening 22[d] May

My Dear Padre — It is not likely the DMS[2] will send me(!) admission for their Concert, & I don't buy tickets — "clericus Clericum non decimat" {*one churchman does not make another pay*}[3] on principle, so you wont have my society — to bore, or instruct you I fear. Now d[r] Padre. Does it not strike you as unnatural to invite me to hear the Mass in C, & yet to say you "cannot" come to our little Concert the other night? I send you ^— as a proof of our orthodoxy as Catholics! —^ the programme, by which you will see that that very motet of J S Bach you invite me to hear along with you, was to be heard with me the other Evening — It is likely we did it better (with our picked choir of 25 or 30) than your "tag-rag-&-bobtail" levies will do it.

Indeed my dear Padre I cannot follow you through your maze of words in your letter of last week. I saw, ere we had conversed ten minutes on our first meeting, that you are one of those special pleaders who never believe yourself wrong in any respect. You always excuse yourself for anything I object to in your writing or music so I think it a pity to disturb you in your happy dreams of perfectability — nearly everything in your music was wrong[4] — but you will not admit that to be the case — What does it matter? It will all be the same 100 Years hence — There's one thing I do admire — your hand-writing! I wish I could equal that, it is so scholarlike!

R P S

[1] See Biographical Register and letter to Grace Hopkins of 2 Nov. 1884 n. 2.

[2] Dublin Music Society.

[3] A medieval saying.

[4] Refers to GMH's setting of 'Who is Sylvia', as he reports to RB on 28 Oct. 1886. See *CW* vi.

1 June 1886 to Robert Bridges

LRB, no. CXXXIII, p. 225 Bodleian, Dep. Bridges, vol. 92, fos. 87–89v

UNIVERSITY COLLEGE, | ST. STEPHEN'S GREEN, | DUBLIN. [*printed heading*] June 1 '86.

Dearest Bridges, — I ought to have ^written^ "hot foot" on my return from Yattendon, when the memory was quite fresh. It is however and will ~~contin~~ ^continue^ fragrant. That was a delightful day.

Mrs. Bridges was not as fancy painted her (indeed fancy painted her very faintly, in watered sepia), but by no means the worse for that.

I was improved by my holiday. My anxiety mostly disappeared, though there is more reason than ever for it now, for I am terribly behindhand and cannot make up. But no more of that — nor now of anything further. (A lie: look on.)

By the bye the Paravicinis gave me Richard Crawley's Venus and Psyche,[1] which I had long wanted to see. Did not like it. He is a true poet, but this poem is no success or at least it does not please. It is in the metre and manner markedly of Don Juan,[2] mocking and discursive about modern life and so on. The verse very flowing and, where he took any pains, finely phrased. It is not serious; the scenes are scarcely realised; the story treated as a theme for trying style on. There is not the slightest symbolism.

This leads me to say that a kind of touchstone[3] of the highest or most living art is seriousness; ~~t~~not gravity but the being in earnest with your subject — reality. It seems to me that some of the greatest and most famous works are not taken in earnest enough, are farce (where you ask the spectator to grant you something not only conventional but monstrous). I have this feeling about Faust and even about the Divine Comedy, whereas Paradise Lost is most seriously taken. It is the weakness of the whole Roman literature.

Give my best love to Mrs. Bridges and Mrs. Molesworth[4] and believe me your affectionate friend Gerard Hopkins S.J.

I shd. add that Crawley is loose and makes his looseness much worse by quoting his original in the notes. And amazing to say, he is so when addressing his sister.

[1] *Venus and Psyche, with Other Poems* (1871). The title poem runs to three cantos, 164 pages in all.

[2] Lord Byron's satiric and irreverent poem in sixteen cantos (1819–24), written in *ottava rima*.

[3] Matthew Arnold (1822–88; *ODNB*), Professor of Poetry at Oxford when GMH was a student, introduced his theory of literary and cultural 'touchstones' or standards in 'The Study of Poetry' (1880).

[4] Mrs Molesworth, RB's mother, who lived with him from 1877.

1 June 1886 to Alexander William Mowbray Baillie

FL, no. CLV, p. 273 UCD L 64

One folded sheet of 'EBLANA NOTE' watermarked paper with printed address; 4 sides.

UNIVERSITY COLLEGE, | ST. STEPHEN'S GREEN, | DUBLIN. [*printed heading*]

June 1 '86.

Dearest Baillie, — You must have given me up. I am very much obliged for your last letter and that and further forthcoming information, but just at present Egypt is off, because examination work is on, that is setting, comparing, revising, and correcting proof of, papers, and the examinations themselves will follow. I have remarked a few points about the Egyptians in Boeotia, small but significant. One is | the scholiast on the Seven agst. Thebes[1] (474. Ὄγκας Ἀθάνας {*Onca Athena*}) tells a story about Cadmus being guided by a cow to that city, the cow stumbling, his sacrificing it to Athene, and worshipping her there under the Egyptian name of Ὄγκα. Another is that somebody I forget who (in the scholia on Pindar), somebody connected with Thebes, made one of the Muses Νειλώ {*Neilo*}. Herodotus[2] often talks of Egyptian rites and so forth in Greece: these places I must look up. I shall, I hope, be able to make out some case and that is enough.

Matthew Arnold has a fine paper in the Nineteenth[3] on the Home Rule bill, a temperate but strong condemnation of the G.O.M.[4] It might with truth be much stronger. Not but what I wish Home Rule to be: it is a blow at England and may be followed by more, but it is better that shd. be by peaceful and honourable means with at least the possibility of a successful working which otherwise may come by rebellion, bloodshed, and dishonour and be a greater and irretrievable blow — or have to be re~~sisted~~fused at a cost it is not worth. How sad and humbling it shd. have come to such a choice!

I suppose now the bill will not pass.[5] Gladstone will then go to the country and to pass this bill (for his Messiahship requires success to justify it) will, I daresay, offer other bribes, as abolition of the Church of England, and more "in the dim and distant future".[6]

The weather is such one wd. gladly have a fire. In Ireland, thank goodness, "it is not always May"[7] nor June.

Yours affectionately Gerard Hopkins.

[1] Aeschylus, *Seven against Thebes*, 487 (A. Sidgwick, *Oxford Classical Texts*): cf. vv. 164, 501.

[2] See letter to AWMB of 6 Apr. 1886, where GMH says he cannot check up this reference in his room. Herodotus (484–*c*.425 BC).

[3] *The Nineteenth Century*, 19 (May 1886), 645–63, 'The Nadir of Liberalism'.

[4] The Grand Old Man, i.e. Gladstone.

[5] See note to postcard of 6–10 Apr. 1886. At the second reading, after a long debate, it was rejected (on 7 June) by a majority of thirty (343 to 313).

[6] Gladstone used this phrase in a Nov. 1885 speech; it reappeared in H. Rider Haggard's *She*, which was serialized in *The Graphic*, Oct. 1886–Jan. 1887.

[7] GMH is quoting a line from 'It is not always May', which appeared in *Ballads and Other Poems* (1842) by the American poet Henry Wadsworth Longfellow (1807–82).

4–6 June 1886 to Coventry Patmore

FL, no. CLXXXI, p. 366 Durham University Library, Abbott MS 197
Two folded sheets, one embossed with the stamp of the Royal University of Ireland, and the other with the printed address of University College and with the watermark EBLANA NOTE. Eight sides.

[*Embossed with the Royal University of Ireland stamp*]
June 4 1886

My dear Mr. Patmore, — I have been meaning and meaning to write to you, to return the volumes of Barnes' poems[1] you lent me and for other reasons, and partly my approaching examination work restrained me, when last night there reached me from Bell's[2] the beautiful ^new^ edition of your works. I call it beautiful and think it is the best form upon the whole for poetry and works of pure literature that I know of and I thank you for your kindness in sending it. And I hope the bush or the bottle may do what little in a bush or bottle lies to recommend the liquor to the born and the unborn. But how slowly does the fame of excellence spread! And crooked eclipses and other obscure causes ~~act upon it in ^endanger^~~ ^fight against^ its rise and progress.

Your poems are a good deed done for the Catholic Church and another for England, for the British Empire,[3] which now trembles in the balance held in the hand of unwisdom. I remark that those Englishmen ~~not all Englishmen,~~ who wish prosperity to the Empire (which is not all Englishmen or Britons, strange to say) speak of the Empire's mission ~~of civ~~ ^to extend^ freedom and civilisation in India and elsewhere. The greater the scale of politics the weightier the influence of a great name and a high ideal. It is a terrible element of weakness that now we are not well provided with the name and ideal which would recommend and justify our Empire. "Freedom": it is perfectly true that British freedom is the best, the only successful ~~one~~ ^freedom^, but that is because, with whatever drawbacks, those who have ~~realised~~ ^developed^ that freedom have done so with the aid of law and obedience to law. ~~But the~~ The cry then shd. be Law and Freedom, Freedom and Law. But that does not please: it must be Freedom only. And to that cry there is the telling answer: No freedom you can give us is equal to the freedom of letting us alone: take yourselves out of India, let us first be free of you. Then there is civilisation. It shd. have been ~~the~~ Catholic truth. That is the great end of Empires before God, to be Catholic and draw nations into their Catholicism. But our Empire is less and less Christian as it grows. There remains that part of civilisation which is outside Christianity or which is not essentially Christian. The best is gone, still something worth having ~~remains~~ is left. How far can the civilisation England offers be attractive ^and valuable^ and be offered and insisted on as an attraction and a thing of value to India for instance? Of course those who live in our civilisation and belong to it praise it:~~;~~ it is not hard, as Socrates said, among the Athenians to praise the Athenians;[4] but how will it ~~appear~~ ^be^ represented by critics bent on making the worst of it or even not bent on making the best of it? It is good to be in Ireland to hear how enemies, and those rhetoricians, can treat the things that are unquestioned at home. I know that ~~against~~ ^to^ mere injustice and slander innocence and excellence themselves stand condemned, but since there is always in mankind some love of truth and admiration for good (~~but~~ ^only that^ the truth must be striking and the good on a great scale) what marked and striking excellence has England to shew to ~~draw~~ make her civilisation attractive? Her literature is one of her ~~att~~ excellences and attractions and I believe that criticism will tend to make this more and more felt; but there must be more of that literature, a continued supply and ~~of~~ in quality excellent. This is why I hold that fine works of art, and especially if, like yours, that are not only ideal in form but deal with high matter as well, are really a great power in the world, an element of strength even to an empire. But now time and tediousness forbid me to write more on this.

It has struck me since I was at Hastings that, if it is not impertinent of me to say it, Miss Patmore might gain by taking some lessons from some painter.[5] It is true she does what no painter can either do or teach but it is also true there are ^other^ things she might with advantage learn. For in fact everyone is the better for teaching: it is universally true. It struck me that she was hampered by want of some mechanical knowledge, as in the ~~tr~~ use of washes for background, and she tends, I think, to use bodycolour in a way which would be considered vicious. This has naturally arisen from her circumstances; for in the delicate detail in which she so wonderfully excells the use of bodycolour is legitimate and even necessary and naturally she extended a practice with which she was familiar to a ^new^ field. ~~she was ne~~

I will send Barnes's poems back in a few days.

Believe me your sincere friend Gerard M. Hopkins S.J.

Please give my kindest remembrances to Mrs. Patmore and the Miss Patmores. I hope all are well and Piff[6] is not killing himself with his sensibilities.

June 6.

[1] For a list of Patmore's critical writings on William Barnes, see note to letter of 1–8 Sept. 1885. Barnes had written an article, 'Coventry Patmore's Poetry', which appeared in *Fraser's Magazine*, July 1863.

[2] The firm of George Bell (1814–90), the publisher.

[3] A similar thought is expressed in the letter to RB of 13 Oct. 1886.

[4] Near the beginning of his *Menexenus*, Socrates says that 'Had the orator to praise Athenians among Peloponnesians, or Peloponnesians among Athenians, he must be a good rhetorician who could succeed and gain credit. But there is no difficulty in a man's winning applause when he is contending for fame among the persons whom he is praising' (*The Dialogues of Plato*, trans. Benjamin Jowett, 1892), vol. ii.

[5] For Bertha Patmore as artist, Ruskin's opinion of her work, and three examples of it, see Champneys, *passim*.

[6] Francis Joseph Mary Epiphanius, affectionately known as Piffie, born Jan. 1883, the only child of Patmore's third marriage. See *Champneys*; and *The Friends and Other Verses*, by F. J. Coventry Patmore (1904). The rest of the sentence from this point is written at the head of the letter.

[*June 1886*][1] *from Sir Robert Stewart to GMH*

FL, no. I2, pp. 427–8 — Campion Hall, Stewart 3

[*No date or address*.]

Darling Padre! I never said anything "outrageous" to you. Dont think so, pray! but you are impatient of correction, when you have previously made up your mind on any point, & I R.S. being an "Expert", you seem to me to err, often times, very much.

Thus, you will not like to be told, that 𝄽 𝄽 𝄽 𝄽 4 crotchet rests, are not used, but one bar rest (semibreve) 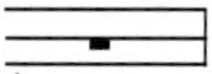 nor will you be pleased to hear that the Violin always plays from the 𝄞 clef which is often called the "Violin clef" indeed, <soprano chorus ought to use this 𝄡 and does use it, too.>

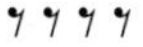

Your viol. <q^{y} "Viol<u>a</u>", or German "Bratsche"?> never plays from C clef on 4th line, but on the 3rd 𝄡. A pause on "<u>did</u>" is absurd, & on "<u>ad</u>-mired be" too — in bar 6 of page 2, G♯ & E♭ won't work together. I don't quite know what "8^{ve}" means in this 2^{d} page, if 8va <u>alta</u> (upper 8^{ve}) you should say so, 8va <u>bassa</u> is also used, you know — The 1st Vio. part will, I fear be here too far above the tenor voice, more than 2 8^{ves} away! 8^{ves} on the Vcello would be difficult to play unless in the case of 𝄢 or 𝄢 where one note is an "open note" or an unstopped string, — In 3rd page you have many such 8^{ves}. Is your music ^a duet^ for 2 tenors? or is it a 4 voice (SATB)[2] piece, as in ending verse? This latter form is much the best, most accurate, most rational, most in the proper compass of your voices — but to accompany a tenor duet first, & then drop all accompt & end with a new, choral setting, is wanting in coherent plan. In fine, excuse delay, I had a very important work by Dvorak to direct,[3] this took up all my time. Vale! Vale!

[1] No date, but presumably part of the 'mauling' of GMH's setting of 'Who is Sylvia', of which he writes in the next letter to his mother.

[2] Soprano, alto, tenor, bass.

[3] Stewart conducted the University of Dublin Choral Society in the first performance in Ireland of Dvořák's 1884 piece *The Spectre's Bride* (Op. 69). See Lisa Parker, 'Robert Prescott Stewart (1825–1894): A Victorian Musician in Dublin' (Ph.D. thesis, National University of Ireland, Maynooth, 2009), 54, 76.

11 June 1886 to his Mother

FL, no. CII, p. 176 Bodleian, MS Eng. lett. e. 41, fos. 102–3

UNIVERSITY COLLEGE, | ST. STEPHEN'S GREEN, | DUBLIN. [*printed heading*]
June 11 '86

My dearest mother, — I am or am going to be very hard at work, for I have got my first batch of answer books from the Royal University.

I ought to have written before. I was greatly improved by my holiday: Sweetman (the irrepressible, the ~~yachs~~ yachtsman)[1] said he never saw anyone so changed ~~by~~ ^in^ so short a ~~holiday~~ ^time^. My spirits rose fifty per cent. I am not quite so well now: I have been troubled with sleeplessness.

Perhaps this is the last letter I shall write to Hampstead.[2]

My Sylvia,[3] after being mauled by Sir Robert Stewart, corrected and simplified for convenience, is to be performed at a concert or speechday at Belvidere House,[4] a school of ours here in Dublin.

I hope my father's influenza is going or gone.

I am your loving son Gerard.

[1] This may well be the 'hairbrained fellow' who took GMH on an 'absurd adventure' overnight on his yacht sailing to Kingstown; mentioned in the letter to RB of 1–8 Sept. 1885.

[2] See letter to Everard Hopkins of 5–8 Nov. 1885, n. 11.

[3] 'Who is Sylvia', for which two melodies and several accompaniments are extant. See *J&P*, 492–3, *CW* vi and Stewart's letter of [June 1886] above.

[4] It became Belevedere College and was where James Joyce, Austin Clarke, and Joseph Plunkett were educated.

17 June 1886 from Coventry Patmore to GMH

FL, no. CLXXXI A, p. 369 Campion Hall, P 17/6/86
Addressed to 'Rev[d] Gerard Hopkins, S.J. | University College, | St. Stephen's Green, | Dublin'. PM HASTINGS JU 17 86, H&K PACKET JU 18 86.

Hastings. June 17. 1886
My dear Mr. Hopkins,

I was very glad to see your handwriting again. Your letters are always very encouraging, and really I sometimes require a little encouragement, considering the way I get treated by the fashionable Critics. Mr F. Harrison, in a book just published on Books & Reading, speaks of my poetry as "good-goody muddle",[1] and in last Saturday's Athenæum, in a notice evidently meant to be generally favourable, "Honoria" and "Amelia" are described as "girls smelling of bread-and-butter".[2]

My new ed[n] owes very much to you. "It is the last rub that polishes the mirror"[3] (a proverb by the way of my own making & of which I am very proud) and your suggestions have enabled me to give my poems that final rub. I think I have acted on at least two-thirds of your hints, and have only not acted on the other third because they involved an amount of re-writing of wh. I am not now capable. You will find that I have altogether overcome the "thou" & "you" difficulty in "De Natura Deorum", & that the poem is immensely improved thereby.

I of course entirely agree with all you say about politics. As I have come to an end of ^my^ poetry, I have taken up the cudgels in a lower arena, & am writing regularly (about two papers a week) in the St. James's Gazette — political leaders, criticisms, essays on art, farming, etc.

I will send you, in a few days, a series of these papers wh. are being reprinted.[4]
Bertha is much out of health and not up to any work. Your advice is excellent.

Your's ever truly
Coventry Patmore

[1] *The Choice of Books* (1886), by Frederic Harrison (1831–1923), ch. 4, p. 74: 'Mr. Ruskin, I suppose, is answerable for the taste of this one-sided and spasmodic criticism; he asks readers to cast aside Coleridge, Shelley, and Byron, and to stick to—such goody-goody dribble as *Evangeline* and the *Angel in the House*.'

[2] The issue of 12 June 1886, where the collected edition of Patmore's *Poems*, 2 vols. (1886), is reviewed by Edmund Gosse, who also wrote articles on the same subject for the *St. James's Gazette* (13 June) and the *Saturday Review* (19 June). For a letter from Patmore to Gosse on the article in the *Athenaeum*, see Champneys, ii. 257. Abbott gives an extract from this not unkind but devastatingly accurate review in *FL*, 450, in which the salient sentence reads: 'This laureate of the tea-table, with his humdrum

stories of girls that smell of bread and butter, is in his inmost heart the most arrogant and visionary of mystics.'

[3] 'De Natura Deorum', *Poems* (1906), 344.

[4] A series of eight papers, running from 20 May to 9 June 1886, on 'How I managed and improved my Estate', reprinted in book form in 1886.

21 June 1886 from Richard Watson Dixon to GMH

CRWD, no. XXXIII D, p. 130 Campion Hall, D 21/6/86

Addressed to 'The Rev[d]. | Gerard Hopkins S.J. | S. Stephen's Green, | Dublin | Ireland'. PM ACKLINGTON JU 22 86, WARKWORTH JU 22 86, H&K PACKET JU 23 86.

Warkworth Vicarage, | Acklington. 21 June 1886
My dear friend,

I am employed by Mess[rs]. Routledge the Publishers to edit a Bible Birthday Book: a collection of texts & verses of poetry.[1] I want to include at least one of yours. Bridges gave me the following out of his MS of your poems.

The dappled die-away
Cheek, & wimpled lip,
The gold-wisp, the aery-grey
Eye, all in fellowship —
This, all this, beauty blooming,
This, all this, freshness fuming,
Give God, while worth consuming.[2]

May I take it? & if so can you put a text before it?

I have been down at Yattendon with Mrs Dixon, & greatly enjoyed my visit. We talked of you several times. I am inserting several pieces from Bridges.[3] What a fine thing his classic Comedy is.[4]

I feel as if I ought to write you a long letter, & would fain do so: but have little to say that you would care to hear. I have been in London a few days, & saw the Colonial Exhibition without caring for it, and the pictures of the year without caring for them. Burne Jones seemed to me still to stand topmost: but I am out of sympathy with him. His great work the Depths of the Sea is very fine, & stood forth as the only serious thing in the Academy.[5] But beyond feeling that, the sort of passionate grandeur, & the powerful drawing, I did not feel that it carried weight or delight. All the other ambitious pictures seemed unendurably bad to me.

I was truly glad & happy to hear from Bridges of the restoration of your health, and of the affection with which all there regarded you.

I shall be bringing out some time this year a small Daniel of lyrics.[6] You know most of them. Will you accept the dedication of them?

Have you ever seen Whistler's works?[7] I saw his little gallery in Bond St. He is a man of great genius, but eccentric. He puzzles me. Ruskin was wrong about him, & did him great injustice. Ruskin is publishing a sort of penitential edition of Modern Painters. He should take the opportunity of repenting about Whistler.

Ever, my dear Friend,
Your affec. friend
R. W. Dixon

Can you send me anything else for the Birthday Book?

[1] Published in 1887. Routledge published *Mano* and vols. 2 and 3 of his *History*. RWD's second wife was Matilda, eldest daughter of this George Routledge.

[2] Printed, with minor changes, under 25 May, with the text: 'As for the oblation of the first-fruits, ye shall offer them unto the Lord. Leviticus ii. 12.' See Norman H. MacKenzie, *GMH: The Later Manuscripts* (New York, 1991), plate 374b.

[3] There are six extracts from RB's poetry (13 Jan., 27 Mar., 11 May, 26 Aug., 7 Sept., 8 Oct.), and one from Coventry Patmore (13 Feb.).

[4] The second draft of *The Feast of Bacchus* was finished on 5 Aug. 1886; RWD therefore probably saw this play in its first draft on his visit to Yattendon.

[5] Burne-Jones was chosen ARA in 1885, but this was the only picture he exhibited at Burlington House.

[6] *Lyrical Poems*, Richard Watson Dixon, printed by H. Daniel in an edition of 105 copies (Oxford, 1887).

[7] James Abbott McNeill Whistler (1834–1903). See next letter.

30 June–3 July 1886 to Richard Watson Dixon

CRWD, no. XXXIV, p. 132 Bodleian, Dep. Bridges, vol. 93, fos. 131–137v
Addressed to 'The Rev. Canon Dixon | Warkworth Vicarage | Acklington | Northumberland | England'. PM DUBLIN JY 5 86. Three folded sheets with printed heading, or four if one includes the undated fragment (see n. 18).

University College, St. Stephen's Green, Dublin. [*printed heading*]
June 30 '86

My dear Friend, — I am in the midst of my heaviest work of the year, the summer examinations, and not at all fit for them. This is why I delay writing and is some excuse for not earlier answering your former letter; which was however a fault.

There are first two points of what we may call business. The dedication: this is a great honour, which on the one hand I do not like to decline but which nevertheless I have some dread of, for I do not want my name to be before the public. It is true your poems do not command a large public, unhappily; but then the small one might contain enemies, so to call people, of mine. So do which you think best: if you dedicate I am flattered, if you do not I am reassured.[1]

I think there could be no objection to my lines appearing in the Birthday Book, ~~but~~ especially anonymously (as I should wish),[2] but I ought to get a formal leave and will. However I should tell you that the poem in question is in three stanzas#: did you know that?[3] Nevertheless the first, the one you quote, might stand by itself. If so the text should be something about First fruits: there must be several that would do, but I think of none just now. The second line had better be "Cheek and the wimpled lip"[4] and the count made up to six. And the stopping "This, all this, beauty" etc is cumbrous: it is better "This, all this beauty".[5] I have nothing else to send, but something ^new^ might strike me. There is a 3-stanza piece made at a wedding that possibly might do,[6] but I rather think not: it is too personal and, I believe, too plainspoken.

I saw the Academy. There was one thing, not a picture, which I much preferred to everything else there — Hamo Thornycroft's statue of the Sower,[7] a truly noble work and to me a new light. It was like Frederick Walker's pictures put into stone and indeed was no doubt partly due to his influence. The genius of that man, poor Walker, was amazing: he was cut off by death like Keats and his promise and performance were in painting as brilliant as Keats's in poetry; in fact I doubt if a man with purer genius for painting ever lived. The sense of beauty was so exquisite; it was to other painters' work as poetry is to prose: his loss was irretrievable.[8] Now no one admires more keenly than I do the gifts that go into Burne Jones's works, the fine genius, the spirituality, the invention; but they leave me deeply dissatisfied as well, where Walker's works more than satisfy. It is their technical imperfection I can not ~~bear~~ ^get over^, the bad, the unmasterly drawing — as it appears to me ^to be^. They are not masterly. Now this is the artist's most essential quality, masterly execution: it is a kind of male gift and especially marks off men from women, the begetting one's thought on paper, on verse, on whatever the matter is; the life must be conveyed into the work and ~~be th~~ ^be^ displayed there, not suggested as having been in the artist's mind: otherwise the product is one of those hen's-eggs that are good to eat and look just like live ones but never hatch~~:~~ (I think they are called wind eggs: I believe most eggs for breakfast <u>are</u> wind eggs and none the worse for it,). — Now it is too bad of me to have compared Burne Jones's[9] beautiful and original works to wind-eggs; moreover on better consideration it strikes me that the mastery I speak of is not so much the male quality ^in the mind^ as a puberty in the life of that quality~~,t~~^.T^he male quality is the creative gift, which he markedly has. But plainly, while artists may differ indefinitely in the degree and kind or variety of their natural gifts, all shd. ~~have~~, as artists, ^have^ come, at all events shd. in time come, to the puberty, the manhood of those gifts: that should be common to all, above it the~~y~~ ^gifts^ may differ.

It may be remarked that some men exercise a deep influence on their own age in virtue of certain powers at that time original, new, and stimulating, which afterwards ceasing to stimulate their fame declines; because it was not supported by an execution, an achievement equal to the power. For nothing but fine execution survives long. This was something of Rossetti's case perhaps.

There is a Scotch painter Macbeth whom I much admire.[10] My brother Arthur, who is a ~~pan~~ painter too, took me to Macbeth's studio when I was last in town. There happened to be little of Macbeth's own there then, but he was employed on an etching of Walker's *Fisherman's Shop* for Messrs. Agnew and the original was of course with him. It is not a work that I care for very much except so far as I revere everything that Walker did (I remember the news of his death gave me a shock as if it had been a near friend's), though artists greatly admire the technic of it; but there were ^other^ etchings by Macbeth and other reproductions of Walker's ~~works~~ ^pieces^ and most of them new to me, the *Ferry* I think it is called (an upper-Thames riverside scene), ~~and~~ the *Plough* (a divine work),[11] the *Mushroom-gatherers*,[12] and others. If you have not yet studied Walker's work you have a new world of beauty to ~~look into ^enter^~~ open and go in. You shd. also study where you can *North's*[13] things. It was my brother drew my attention to him. It seems Walker — I do not know that he studied under North but he learnt methods from him: "North" said someone in vulgar phrase to my brother "learnt", that is taught, "Walker to paint". He survived his pupil, if Walker was that. His landscapes are of a beautiful and ~~lifelike~~ poetical delicacy and truth at once~~,~~^.^ ~~b~~^.B^ut I have seen very little of his.

I agree to Whistler's striking genius~~,~~ — feeling for what I call *inscape* (the very soul of art); but then his execution is ~~no~~ ^so^ negligent, unpardonably so sometimes (that was, I suppose, what Ruskin particularly meant by 'throwing the pot of paint ~~at~~ ^in the face of^ the public'): *his* genius certainly has not come to puberty.[14]

Now something on music. A piece of mine, called, not by my wish, a madrigal in the programme, is to be performed at a school-concert in

Dublin tomorrow. It is Who is Sylvia? set as a duet and chorus, the tune made very long ago, the harmonies lately set (and very great fears about their puberty entertained). I made it for a string orchestra. And I am very slowly but very elaborately ~~at wor getting on with~~ ^working at^ "Does the South Wind" for solos, chorus, and strings. Some years ago I went from Glasgow, where I was, one day to Loch Lomond and landed at Inversnaid (famous through Wordsworth and Matthew Arnold)[15] for some hours. There I had an inspiration of a tune. The disproportion is wonderful between the momentary conception of ~~a tune~~ ^an air^ and the long long gestation of its setting. I endeavour to make ~~all~~ the under parts each a flowing and independent melody and they cannot be independently invented, they must be felt for along ^a few^ certain necessary lines enforced by the harmony. It is astonishing to see them come; but in reality they are in nature bound up (besides many others) with the tune of the principal part and there is, I am persuaded, a world of profound mathematics in this matter of music: indeed no one could doubt that.

I have written a few sonnets: that is all I have done in poetry for some years.

I have not seen Bridges' comedy.

Swinburne has written for the Times an ode on the crisis,[16] Somebody called it a rigmarole and I cd. not say it was not: on the contrary everything he writes is rigmarole. But I wonder how he finds it suits him to be clerical, as this ode with appeals to conscience and declaiming against assassination is. Moreover there was an earlier ode of his in honour of the "Manchester Martyrs",[17] as the Irish call them: so then he has changed as much as Gladstone. As they neither of them have any principles it is no wonder. But the passage about Gordon and so on is to the point.[18] It seems to me ~~now~~ that "bad is the best" that can happen now. With this sad thought I must conclude and am your affectionate friend Gerard M. Hopkins S.J.

Some hindrance happened and the madrigal was not sung. If it had been I could not have heard ^it^, for I was helping to save and damn the studious youth of Ireland.

July 3 1886.

You speak of "powerful drawing" in Burne Jones's picture. I recognise it in the mermaid's face and in the treatment of her fishments ^and fishmanship^, the tailfin turning short and flattening to save striking the ground — a stroke of truly artistic genius; but the drowned youth's knees and feet are very crude and unsatisfactory in drawing, as it seemed to me.

[19] I have found your former letter, as old as December last,[20] and must add a little more.

The sonnet of Gray's that you ask about is the well known one (the only one, I daresay) "In vain to me": I remarked on its ~~metrical b~~ rhythmical beauty, due partly to the accent being rather trochaic than iambic. Wordsworth says somewhere of it that it is 'evident' the only valuable part of it ^is^ (I believe) "~~A diffe~~ For other notes" and the quatrain that follows.[21] Such a criticism is rude at best, since in a work of art having so strong a unity as a sonnet one ~~part~~ part which singly is less beautiful ~~then~~ than another part may be as necessary to the whole effect, like the plain shaft in a column and so on. But besides what he calls evident is not so, nor true.

You make a criticism on Handel. I have the very same feeling about him and you 'tell me my own dream',[22] that "one can never hear five bars of him without feeling that something great is beginning, something full of li~~v~~^f^e". A piece of his at a concert seems to flutter the dovecot of the rest of them, to be a hawk among poultry. The immediateness of the impression must be due, I suppose, to his power being ~~carried~~ ^conveyed^ into smaller sections ^of his work^ than other men's and not needing accumulation for its effect.

I was glad of an appreciative review of your third volume in the <u>Academy</u> (I think) and much interested.[23] Would I could read ~~it~~ ^the work^! but I cannot under present, which are permanent, circumstances do that.

I could wish you had been elected to that Chair.[24] But "life is a short blanket"[25] — profoun^d^est of homely sayings: great gifts and great opportunities are more than life spares to one man. It is much if ~~they~~ ^we^ get something, a spell, an innings at all. See how the great conquerors were cut short, Alexander, Caesar just seen. Above all Christ our Lord: his career was cut short and, whereas he would have wished to succeed by success — for it is insane to lay yourself out for failure, prudence is the first of the cardinal virtues, and he was the most prudent of men — nevertheless he was doomed to succeed by failure; his plans were baffled, his hopes dashed, and his work was done by being broken off undone. However much he understood all this he found it an intolerable grief to submit to it. He left the example: it is very strengthening, but except in that sense it is not consoling.

I passed a delightful day at Yattendon. Mrs. Bridges not as I had fancied her (which was but faintly), but none the worse for that.[26]

[1] The book is 'Dedicated to the Reverend Gerard Hopkins by the Author'.

[2] The stanza is signed simply *Hopkins*. As he goes on to remark, he would need to get permission from his Jesuit superiors to publish.

[3] 'Morning, Midday, and Evening Sacrifice'.

[4] This change was not made by RWD, though GMH kept the change.

[5] This change was made.

[6] 'At the Wedding March'.

[7] Sir (William) Hamo Thornycroft (1850–1925; *ODNB*). One version of *The Sower* is now in Kew Gardens. There are illustrations of the statue in *AMES*, 103 and in *VVW*, 241.

[8] Frederick Walker (1840–75; *ODNB*) was mainly self-trained, and known as an illustrator before he began exhibiting both watercolours and oils at the Academy in 1863. See J. G. Marks, *Life and Letters of Frederick Walker, A.R.A.* (London, 1896). The Tate Gallery has sixteen works by Walker including *The Plough* and a study for *Marlow Ferry*.

[9] See letter from RWD of 8 June 1878 for RWD's friend, the painter Burne-Jones.

[10] Robert Walker Macbeth (1848–1910; *ODNB*), painter and later etcher of others' works. GMH saw his *Phillis in the New-Mown Hay* at the Academy in 1874 (see *CW* iii).

[11] Exhibited at the Academy in 1870. See Marks, *Life and Letters*, 193–4 for Walker's description, in a letter, of what he intended to do in this picture.

[12] Unfinished: the artist was working on it towards the end of his life.

[13] John William North (1842–1924; *ODNB*) was a painter of genre and landscape, an illustrator, and wood-engraver. He was friendly with R. W. Macbeth and Frederick Walker, with whom he travelled in Algiers and who sometimes added the figures to his landscape paintings.

[14] Whistler gives a full account of the story in *The Gentle Art of Making Enemies* (1890). Ruskin had published in *Fors Clavigera* on 2 July 1877 a review of an exhibition including Whistler's *Nocturne in Black and Gold: The Falling Rocket* (now in Detroit Institute of the Arts) saying that he 'had never expected to hear a coxcomb ask two hundred guineas for flinging a pot of paint in the public's face'. Whistler brought a suit for libel, which was tried on 25–6 Nov. 1878. He won the case, but was awarded only a farthing damages and had to pay a share of the costs, which bankrupted him.

[15] See letter to RWD of 26–30 Sept. 1881.

[16] 'The Commonweal, a Song for Unionists', printed in the issue of 1 July 1886, and published in *A Channel Passage and Other Poems*. It contains bitter lines on Gladstone.

[17] 'An Appeal to England' [for the condemned Fenian prisoners], first published in *The Morning Star* of Friday, 22 Nov. 1867 and reprinted in *Songs before Sunrise* (1870). William O'Mera Allen, Michael Larkin, and William O'Brien were hanged in Manchester on 23 Nov. 1867 for their part in the killing of a policeman during an escape from a police vehicle. The policeman had been inadvertently killed when the attackers attempted to blast open a lock on the carriage while he was looking out through the keyhole.

[18] 'Far and near the world bears witness of our wisdom, courage, honour;
Egypt knows if there our fame burns bright or dim.
Let but England trust as Gordon trusted, soon shall come upon her
Such deliverance as our daring brought on him.'

[19] What follows is marked by RB 'Undated fragment', and was placed here by him. Whether it formed part of this letter or another is not certain. The visit mentioned at the end was made on 6 May 1886 (see letters to RB of 4 May and 1 June 1886).

[20] This letter is not known to be extant.

[21] Preface to the 2nd ed. (1800) of *Lyrical Ballads*.

[22] Callimachus, *Epigrams* 32.2.

[23] In the issue of 27 Feb. 1886: a very complimentary review by Mandell Creighton, which begins with a long paragraph praising the style and temper of the work.

[24] In 1885 RWD stood for the professorship of Poetry at Oxford, but withdrew his candidature before the election.

[25] Proverbial paraphrase of Isaiah 28: 20.

[26] These are the words he used in a letter to RB of 1 June 1886, and may indicate an earlier date for this fragment.

28 July 1886 from Richard Watson Dixon to GMH

CRWD, no. XXXIV A, p. 138 Campion Hall, D 28/7/86

Addressed to 'The Rev. | G. Hopkins S.J. | S. Stephen's Green | Dublin | Ireland'. PM ACKLINGTON AU 7 86, WARKWORTH AU 7 86, LIVERPOOL AU 8 86, H&K PACKET AU 8 86.

[*Dixon has annotated the front of the envelope*:] I have now found, & send, the letter I wrote first.

Warkworth | 28 July 1886

My dear, dear Friend,

I cannot now answer your precious Letter: but must thank you for it.

I have inserted your "first fruits" piece, & propose, if you do not forbid, to put your name to it thus, G. (or else Gerard) Hopkins S.J.[1]

I have heard from Bridges to-day.

I dedicate to you my Lyrical Poems: but have not heard of them since I sent them to Daniel months ago. His health prevents, I fear, the immediate publication.

Your aff. friend

R. W. Dixon

[1] See letter of 30 June–3 July 1886.

7–9 August 1886 to Richard Watson Dixon

CRWD, no. XXXV, p. 138 Bodleian, Dep. Bridges, vol. 93, fos. 138–142v
Addressed to 'The Rev. Canon Dixon | Warkworth Vicarage | Acklington | Northumberland | England'. PM DUBLIN AUG 9 86. Two folded sheets.

University College, Stephen's Green, Dublin. Aug. 7 '86.

My dear Friend, — The note you speak of did not reach ^me^ and no doubt was never posted, for the post never misses (if there is a never in human things) and every alternative should be exhausted before we come to that. (And therefore I say that the number of the Academy which shd. have ~~reached me~~ ^come to hand^ this morning was also not posted or, what is more likely, has gone astray in the house.)

If the poem is printed it may rest, but I am going to see the Provincial tomorrow or next day and will ask him about it. I ought to have settled this before; but since I last wrote I have been altogether overwhelmed with examination-work, six or seven weeks of it without any break, Sundays and weekdays. Even now — but it is no use talking of it.

Mr. Rawnsley's name is quite unknown to me.[4]

It is not possible for me ~~to have~~ to do anything, unless a sonnet, and that rarely, in poetry with a fagged mind and a continual anxiety; but there are things at which I can, so far as time serves, work, if it were only by snatches. For instance I am writing (but I am almost sure I never shall have written) a sort of popular account of Light and the Ether. Popular is not quite the word; it is not meant to be easy reading, for such a difficult subject can only be made easy by a very summary and sketchy treatment; rather it is meant ~~la~~ for the lay or unprofessional student~~,~~ who will read carefully so long as there are no mathematics and all technicalities are explained; and my hope is to explain ^things^ thoroughly and make the matter ^to ~~hi~~ such a reader^, as far as I go in it, perfectly intelligible. No such account exists and scientific books, especially in English, are ~~quite~~ very unsatisfactory. The study of physical science has, ^~~for those who write for it~~^ unless corrected in some way, an effect the very opposite of what one would suppose. One would think it ^might^ materialise~~d~~ ~~them~~ ^people^ (no doubt it does make them or, rather I shd. say, they become materialists; but that is not the same thing: they ~~may~~ do not believe in Matter more but in God less); but in fact they seem to end in conceiving ^only^ of a world of formulas, ^with its being^ properly speaking. ~~a world of~~ ^in^ thought, ~~to~~ ^towards^ which the outer world acts as a sort of feeder, supplying examples for literary purposes. And they go so far as to think the rest of ~~the~~ mankind are in the same state of mind as themselves. I daresay I may ~~assemple~~ ^gather together^ some illustrations of this: one will serve now. “It is very remarkable” says Tait[2] on Light “how slowly the human race has reached some even of the simplest, facts of optics <he rather means laws>. We can easily understand how constant experience must have forced on men the conviction <as if they were resisting it: the force would have been to make them think the contrary> that light usually moves in straight lines — i.e. that we see an object in the direction in which it really lies.” ^<^Where else shd. one expect to see it?> But” etc.

It ~~is~~ will in any case be a pity for S.J. to have been added to my name in the book, for ~~it~~ ^the letters^ acts like italics, asterisks, or ~~rub~~ rubric.

Some learned lady having shewn ^by the flora^ that the season of the action in Hamlet is from March to May, a difficulty is raised about the glowworm’s ineffectual fire ~~at th~~ in the first act, since glowworms glow chiefly from May to September. Mr. Furnival[3] having consulted an authority learns that the grub, though not so easily found, shines nearly as bright as the fullgrown worm, that is beetle, and begins in March, and so all is saved. Does not this strike you as great trifling? Shakspere had the finest faculty of observation of all men that ever breathed, but it is ordinary untechnical observation, neither scientific nor even, like a farmer’s professional, and he might overlook that point of season. But if he knew it he would likely enough neglect it. There are some errors you must not make, as an ~~el~~ eclipse at the halfmoon or a lobster “the Cardinal of the seas”,[4] but others do not matter and convention varies with regard to them. If I am not mistaken, there are notorious and insoluble inconsistencies in Hamlet, due to Shakspere’s having recast the play expressly for Burbage, who was elderly, “short, stout, and scant of breath” (or something of the sort),[5] without taking the trouble to correct throughout accordingly — not ^even^ wishing I dare say; for no one can ^so^ conceive of Hamlet’s person. Besides there are inconsistencies in the Iliad, Aeneid, Don Quixote, Three Musketeers, and so on; it is a ~~disease~~ frailty of literature. And indeed on reflection the defence makes the matter worse. For few of the audience could know that glowworms do shine, if you ~~can~~ look well for them, in March. So that Shakspere would have been breaking Aristotle’s rule, that in art ~~a~~ likely seeming fiction is better than unlikely seeming fact.[6]

By the by, why should Wordsworth-worship be “a difficult thing”? It is a common one now, is it not? Not the common, but like soldiers in a crowd, ^not a numerous but a^ notabl~~y~~e fact. Did you see what Lord Selborne[7] lately said? What I suppose grows on people is that

Wordsworth's particular grace, his charisma, as theologians say, ~~was~~ has been granted in equal measure to so very few men since time was — to Plato and who else? I mean his spiritual insight into nature; and this they perhaps think is above all the poet's gift? It is true, if we sort things, ~~and~~ ^so that^ art is art and philosophy philosophy, it seems rather the philosopher's than the poet's: at any rate he had it in a sovereign degree. He had a "divine philosophy" and a lovely gift of verse; but in his work there is nevertheless beaucoup à redire {*much to find fault with*}: it is due to the universal fault of our literature, its weakness is rhetoric. The ~~ins~~ strictly poetical insight and inspiration of our poetry seems to me to ^be^ of the very finest, finer perhaps than the Greek; but ~~the~~ ^its^ rhetoric is inadequate ~~to~~ ^ — ^ seldom first rate, mostly only just sufficient, sometimes even below par. By rhetoric I mean all the common and teachable element in literature, what grammar is to speech, what thoroughbass is to music, what theatrical experience gives to playwrights. If you leave out the embroidery (to be sure the principal thing) of for instance the Excursion ~~is it r~~ and look only at the groundwork and stuff of the web is it not fairly true to say "This will never do"? There does seem to be a great deal of dulness, superfluity, aimlessness, poverty of plan. I remember noticing as a boy, ~~(~~it was ~~a~~ ^the^ discovery of a trade secret, how our poets treat spirit and its compounds as one syllable: it is, though founded really on ^a mistake, — the^ mere change of pronunciation, a beautiful tradition of the poets. Wordsworth had told himself or been told this trifle: why did he not learn or someone tell him that sonnets have ~~an essential~~ ^a natural^ charpente {*underlying framework*} and structure never, ~~to~~ or at least seldom, to be broken through? For want of knowing this his inspired sonnets, εὔμορφοι κολοσσοί {*beautiful statues*},[8] suffer from "hernia", and combine the tiro's blunder with the master's perfection.

Believe me your affectionate friend Gerard Hopkins. Aug. 9.

[1] The Revd Hardwicke Drummond Rawnsley (1851–1920; *ODNB*), whose name and work are intimately associated with the Lake District, was a Balliol man, Honorary canon of Carlisle from 1891, founder of the National Trust, and an indefatigable sonneteer.

[2] *Light*, by Peter Guthrie Tait (1884). Tait (1831–1901; *ODNB*) was a physicist and mathematician.

[3] Frederick James Furnivall (1825–1910; *ODNB*), editor and textual scholar.

[4] Jules Janin (1804–74), French writer and critic, made an infamous error in calling the lobster the 'Cardinal de la mer'. Alfred Delvau records in his *Dictionnaire de la langue verte* (1866, etc.) that the word is 'dans l'argot ironique des gens de lettres, par allusion à la bévue de Jules Janin'; Marx alludes to it in a letter to Engels of 15 Apr. 1869, and Henley and Farmer in *Slang and its Analogues* (1890) record under 'cardinal'

that 'Jules Janin once made a curious blunder and called the lobster *le cardinal de la mer*.'

[5] GMH is slightly misremembering Gertrude's line in *Hamlet*, V. ii. 301: 'He's fat, and scant of breath.'

[6] 'A likely impossibility is always preferable to an unconvincing possibility'; Aristotle, *Poetics*, 24.1460[a].

[7] Lord Selborne delivered the Presidential Address at the final meeting of the Wordsworth Society on 9 July 1886, collected in *Wordsworthiana*, ed. William Angus Knight (London and New York, 1889), 277–88.

[8] Aeschylus, *Agamemnon*, 416.

25 September 1886 from Richard Watson Dixon to GMH

CRWD, no. XXXV A, p. 142 Campion Hall, D 25/9/86

Warkworth Vic. | Northumberland | 25 Sept. 1886

My dear Friend,

Would you mind looking over the enclosed,[1] & making any suggestion or objection or correction.

I am in no hurry for a week or so. You will perhaps not have the time or inclination. If so do not, please, force yourself. I am sorry to leave no time to write, but will soon, I hope, more fully.

Your affc friend
R W Dixon

[1] The proofs of 'Ulysses and Calypso', afterwards the first of *Lyrical Poems* (1887).

30 September 1886 to Richard Watson Dixon

CRWD, no. XXXVI, p. 142 Bodleian, Dep. Bridges, vol. 93, fos. 143–145a[v]
Addressed to 'The Rev. R. W. Dixon | Warkworth Vicarage | Acklington | Northumberland'. No readable PM. One folded sheet with printed heading 'Carnarvon' deleted.

11 Church Street, Tremadoc, North Wales. Sept. 30 1886.

My dear Friend, — Your enclosure very opportunely reached me this morning in this remote and beautiful spot, where I am bringing a pleasant holiday to an end. My companion and colleague left me last night, being called to Dublin on University business more pressing than mine. The weather is quite broken and the soldier in Mrs. Evans's weatherclock stands out of his box with a dismal effrontery, while the maiden sulks, like Weeping Winefred, indoors.[1]

My situation is that Wild Wales breathes poetry on the one hand and that my landlady gives me the heartiest breakfasts on the other; it is indigenous to this part of the country, for the Rev. P. B. Williams A.B. Rector of Llanrwg and Llanberis in his Tourist's Guide through the County of Caernarvon ibid. 1821 says of Snowdon "It was then that the thought of the great Creator . . . at whose nod they shall crumble into dust!

These are thy glorious works,
Parent of good . . . .
. . how wondrous then!

Parties generally take cold meat with them, and a bottle either of Wine, or Spirits, and dine" etc, p. 122.

I have read your beautiful poem and will shortly return you the proofs with such slight comments as may occur. At present I have a difficulty about "Whence in her secret cave".[2] Parallels I daresay may be found and, if not, the expression may be innovated; but in itself it appears incorrect, for "whence" would seem to mean ^only^ from which place, but you mean from a place at which.

In the meantime guided by the Rector of Llanruy and Llanberis I am thinking of taking a hard-boiled egg with me and rhapsodising either the Vale of Ffestiniog or for a second time Pont Aberglaslyn, which not to have seen, as till a few days ago I never had, is a dreadful underbred ignorance.

I am your affectionate friend Gerard M. Hopkins.

I have long wished to write a tragedy ~~on~~^f^ St. Winefred and had some fragments of it done, and since I have been here I have got on ^with it^ a little, with promise of more. It is in an alexandrine verse,[3] which I sometimes expand to 7 or 8 feet, very hard to manage but very effective when well used: I think I mentioned this point before.

I have a few odd sonnets accumulated over some time which I must try and let you have.

I have the Castle of Otranto[4] ^here^ and incline to think it is great rubbish. In one place a hollow groan ~~was~~ ^is^ heard, which both Theodore and Matilda conclude "to be the effect of pent-up vapours".

[1] 'Weeping Winefred' was a favourite tune of GMH's, referred to in his journal for 8 Aug. 1874 and in a letter of 14–21 Aug. 1879. 'I looked into a lovely comb which gave me the instress of Weeping Winefred'. Franz Joseph Haydn's opus Hob. XXXIb/31, composed in 1804, is 'Mwynen Cynwyd' ('The Song of Cynwyd'), which begins 'What weeping Winefred for shame'. GMH may have found this, as other songs he knew like 'Polly Oliver' and 'Poor Mary Ann', in his aunt's copy of William Chappell, *Popular Music of the Olden Time* (1856–9). See also diary for Sept. 1864.

[2] RWD changed this to 'From where in secret cave', l. 7.

[3] See letter of 3 Dec. 1872 and *CW* viii.

[4] Horace Walpole, *The Castle of Otranto* (1764). In ch. 3 occurs the passage GMH refers to:

> A deep and hollow groan, which seemed to come from above, startled the Princess and Theodore.
>
> "Good heaven! we are overheard!" said the Princess. They listened; but perceiving no further noise, they both concluded it the effect of pent-up vapours. And the Princess, preceding Theodore softly, carried him to her father's armoury, where, equipping him with a complete suit, he was conducted by Matilda to the postern-gate.

2–4 October 1886 to Robert Bridges

LRB, no. CXXXIV, p. 226 Bodleian, Dep. Bridges, vol. 92, fos. 90–93v

11 Church Street, Tremadoc, North Wales. Oct. 2 1886.

Dearest Bridges, — Your letter, you see, written from South Wales reaches me in Gwynedd after making a long elbow at Dublin. A delightful holiday comes to an end to-day, but I am going to take duty at Pwllheli tomorrow and start for Holyhead in the evening.

I will back Tremadoc for beauty against Fishguard. There are no myrtles, at least I have seen none, but right over the village (clean, modern, solidly built, spacious, and somewhat picturesque) rises a cliff of massive selfhewn rock, all overrun with a riot of vegetation which the rainy climate seems to breathe here. Tremadoc is said to take its name from some Mr. Madox and is in the parish of Ynys Cynhaiarn. Portmadoc half a mile off is still more modern: my landlord remembers when there were only three houses there. It is rising, but fashion has not found it. Bretons come here in jerseys, earrings, and wooden shoes to sell vegetables, and Portmadoc and all N. Wales seem to live upon slate, to get which they are quarrying away great mountains: nowhere I suppose in Europe is such a subjection of nature to man to be witnessed. The end is that the mountains vanish, but ^in^ the process they take a certain beauty midway between ~~n~~ wildness and art. Mountains are all round. The feature of the coast are the great traethau or tracts of sand — seasand, links, and reclaimed land; two estuaries, at the meeting point of which ~~Pyn~~ Penrhyn Deudraeth~~,~~ (two tracts) stands, reach the sea hereabouts; they are commanded by Moelwyn and other mountains and by Criccieth and Harlech Castles. A long walk skirting one of these and ~~commanding~~ ^discovering Snowdon and other^ grand mountain views leads to Pont Aberglaslyn and ^into^ the Pass which from that leads to the valley where Beddgelert is. The beauty of this Pass is extreme. The Glaslyn, a torrent of notably green water, runs through it and thereby hangs a sad tale. I made a drawing (its ruins enclosed)[1] of one fall of it over a rock, not at all so good as I could have wished, for water in motion, highly difficult at best (I need not say), needs the most sympathetic pencils, and this ~~had~~ was done with an unsatisfactory HB and touched, not for the better, with a better at home; but however I thought well enough of it to mean to "set" it and send it to you. I used milk in a saucer and put the saucer by the fire, where the gluey milk stuck it so fast to the earthenware that it could not be got off without grievous tearing. Still such as it now is I send it.

I am now at Pwllheli: a young Irish exciseman is my host.

How voluminous you are getting! I will do what I can with the "Feast of Bacchus".[2] Examination work is in my foreground, but that will not altogether hinder. I have just at present got Canon Dixon's proofs to a poem ~~called~~ on Calypso.[3]

Some scenes of my Winefred have been taking shape here in Wales, always to me a mother of Muses. It is a drama of passion more than of character and not at all of manners, something in what I understand to be Marlowe's treatment (I could flog myself for being so ignorant as to say "I understand to be"). You have seen fragments, I now definitely hope to finish ^it,^ but I cannot say when.

Also other things have got on a little, as my ode on Campion.[4]

I think Fishguard must be a purely English name. If ~~it~~ ^the place^ has a Welsh name it will have only one and Fiscard is no doubt the phonetic spelling of the Welsh attempt at Fishguard. It is odd how much mispronunciation lies in imaginary difficulties. Sh is a Welsh sound, but occurs always before vowels and ~~a~~ is written si (e.g. Siabod pronounced Shabod and siop = shop), even between words, as Lewis Evans pronounced Le-wish Eevanss. But there was the analogy of Pyscod/Fish and the Welsh mould everything into a false Welsh form. Then you see Newport is English and Goodwic English or Norse, and is it Dinas or Pinas? Dinas is pure Welsh. Pinas wd. probably be Pinnace.

~~My~~ ^Our^ Welsh holiday came ~~as~~ on me and my companion as a happy surprise. And though we had much rain we did Snowdon to admiration. We walked much. We fell upon honest people and lived cheap, too cheap, so that nearly £8 is left out of £20, and that is mismanagement; but my companion had to return before me. I had at first set my heart on Yorkshire and Fountains,[5] but to save ^journey^ money we went to Wales: why do I complain, when I have seen such lovely things and met such good people, unless that I always complain? But if you have not seen Pont Aberglaslyn in sunlight you have something to live for. But then we ought to have seen Bettws y Coed. We had money to see anything.

And I have read the Castle of Otranto and find it to be rubbish. Yet it was epoch-making, was it not? But some of these epoch-making books succeeded by virtue of new and interesting matter in spite of a poor form, for instance Ossian and in the main the Waverleys; of which ^last^ I hold, subject to wider reading and ^your^ better judgment, that, though they contain a mass of good reading and scattered literary excellences, yet as wholes they are scarcely to be called works of art and have been and are overrated.[6] They seem to be the products of a fine and gentle character, a fertile memory, and a flowing talent and to have even touches of genius in certain incidents, strokes of true invention; but ^in^ the general texture of them genius seems to me to be quite wanting. I think Robert Lewis Stevenson[7] ~~has~~ ^shews^ more genius in a page than Scott in a volume. Tell me what you think.

I have made a great and solid discovery about Pindar or rather about ~~his~~ the Dorian and Aeolian ~~Mae~~ Measures or Rhythms and hope to publish something when I have read some more.[8] But all my world is scaffolding.

With best love to Mrs. Bridges, believe me your affectionate friend Gerard M. Hopkins.

University College, Stephen's Green, Dublin. Oct. 4 1886.

Talking of counterpoint, good Sir Robert Stewart of this city has offered to correct me exercises in it if I wd. send some: I have sent one batch.

[1] This drawing was extant when Abbott commented that 'To reproduce this drawing in its present state would be unfair to GMH', but it is not in the Bodleian collection. However, a version of the drawing, dated 'Above Pont Aberglaslyn | Sept. 30 1886', has been obtained from a rotograph (negative image) in the Abbott collection in Durham University Library (draft for *Letters of GMH to Robert Bridges*, fo. 532), and is reproduced in *CW* vi.

[2] Privately printed, Oxford, 1889.

[3] *Ulysses and Calypso*: the first of *Lyrical Poems*, 1887.

[4] GMH's ode on Campion is no longer extant.

[5] Fountains Abbey, the magnificent Cistercian ruin about five miles from Ripon.

[6] *Castle of Otranto* (1764) by Horace Walpole (1736–96; *ODNB*) was influential in establishing the fashion for Gothic fiction. Ossian was the supposed author of a series of poems that James Macpherson said he had translated from Scots Gaelic based on stories of the Irish mythical hero Oisin, published in 1760 as *Fragments of Ancient Poetry collected in the Highlands of Scotland*; this was widely influential on Romantic writers. The Waverley novels were the long series of novels by Walter Scott (1771–1832; *ODNB*), beginning with *Waverley* in 1814, which for much of the century were the most widely read in Europe. Scott did not publicly acknowledge authorship until 1827.

[7] Robert Louis Stevenson (1850–94; *ODNB*), a Scottish novelist, poet, and writer of essays and travel books. Plagued by ill health for most of his short life, he had by 1886 published many travel essays and poems, *The New Arabian Nights* (1882), *Treasure Island* (1883), *The Strange Case of Dr Jekyll and Mr Hyde* (1886), and *Kidnapped* (1886).

[8] This is one of his long-term projects on Greek lyric, choruses, the Pindaric, and the Dorian measure, which he agreed in discussion with Fr Purbrick; see letters of 26–7 Sept. and 18–19 Oct. 1882 to RB, 14 Jan. 1883 to AMWB, 21–2 and 28 Oct. 1886 to RB, 7 Nov. 1886 to Patmore, 11 Dec. 1886 to RB, 23 Dec. 1886 to AMWB, 20 Jan. 1887 to Patmore, and 1 May and 30 July–1 Aug. 1887 to RB.

5 October 1886 to his Mother

FL, no. CIII, p. 176 Bodleian, MS Eng. lett. e. 41, fos. 104–107[v]
Addressed to 'Mrs. Manley Hopkins | Court's Hill Lodge | Haslemere | Surrey | England'. PM DUBLIN OC 5 86 and HASLEMERE OC 6 86. 'Carnarvon' is printed on the back of the envelope in fancy lettering.

UNIVERSITY COLLEGE, | ST. STEPHEN'S GREEN, | DUBLIN. [*printed heading*]
Oct. 5 1886.

My dearest mother, — Our holiday was most pleasant and serviceable — at least to me; but poor Robert Curtis was dogged from the University with letters (including his own returned from the dead letter office; for he sent off four without addresses, besides other feats) and with telegrams. One batch of papers had to be set thrice over and that in Wild Wales and on a holiday: it was of some one else's first setting, for which he had to draw up two distinct subs^t^itutes. When day after day these afflictions fell in I used to do the cursing; he bore all with the greatest meekness. Our landlady at Carnarvon a Cheshire woman, who knew Vale Royal and Tarporley and all, some distant cousin of ours if all were known, gave me instructions on patience: she had, poor soul, had great ~~afflictions~~ ^troubles^, as by her history appeared.

We were a week at Carnarvon and another at Tremadoc,[1] but Robert had to go away before the end to conduct an o~~r~~^r^al examination here.

We had to deal with very honest people and lived very cheap, too much so; we might have done much more than we did if we had known ~~or rather~~ ^and also^ if weather and other things had permitted;[2] on my return I gave back not much less than half the money we had been furnished with.[3] However this will encourage Fr. Delany for the future, as he said himself.

We ascended Snowdon and had a beautiful day. We walked ever so much. We went up the toy railway to Blaenau Ffestiniog and enjoyed it, in spite of heavy clouds and of the disgusting sulphur smoke and jolting, which almost made me sick that never suffer at sea. We saw Pont Aberglaslyn, the beauty of which is unsurpassed, and I saw the Pass of Llanberis and Beddgelert. We did not go near Bettws y Coed. We had much rain, but did well nevertheless. We got no seabathing. I preached two little sermons. The holiday has been a new life to me — I am even getting on with my play of St. Winefred's Well.

Did you send on the letter I enclosed to Watson?[4] I shd. like to hear that he got it.

Monsignor Carter sent me some more minute information about Liphook.[5]

^The^ Bridges's have been at Fishguard in South Wales and will I believe be home the day after tomorrow.

By the by^e^ I saw a bard in the flesh. I made also the acquaintance of the genial and learned antiquary Mr. Howel Lloyd.[6]

With love to all, I am your loving son Gerard.

[1] Carnarvon (Caernarfon) is a town on the north-west coast of Wales with a 13th-c. stone castle constructed by Edward I; Tremadoc lies south on the other side of the Lleyn Peninisula and Mount Snowdon. It had been constructed between 1800 and 1811 on land reclaimed from marshes. It is set back from the coast, north of Portmadog and off Traeth estuary.

[2] For a fuller account of this holiday see the letter to RB of 2–4 Oct. 1886.

[3] 'Nearly £8 is left out of £20, and that is mismanagement.'

[4] Will Watson, Shooter's Hill. See letters of 10 June 1875 to his mother and 6 Feb. 1887.

[5] Liphook, a large village established in Norman times, 6 km west of Haslemere. It was on the London to Portsmouth railroad.

[6] Howel William Lloyd (1816–93), antiquary. Educated at Rugby and Balliol and a scholar of Jesus College, he was ordained as an Anglican, but was received into the Roman Catholic Church at Oscott in 1846, with the intention of becoming a priest. Ill health precluded that course. He took a post in Manning's Catholic University College in Kensington in 1874 but it closed after four years. He wrote many pamphlets and a *History of the Parish of Llangurig* with Edward Hamer (1875). See *A Literary and Biographical History . . . of the English Catholics from the Breach with Rome, in 1534, to the Present Time*, by Joseph Gillow, iv (1893).

6 October 1886 to Robert Bridges

LRB, no. CXXXV, p. 229 Bodleian, Dep. Bridges, vol. 92, fos. 94–95^{v}

UNIVERSITY COLLEGE, | ST. STEPHEN'S GREEN, | DUBLIN. [*printed heading*] Oct. ~~5~~ 6 1886.

~~My dear Mrs. More Madden~~, Dearest Bridges, — I forgot to speak of the copies of Prometheus and Odes and Eclogues[1] (but whose? for I do not remember that any publication of yours had that title). I could make, I think, good use of them: I should give one copy to Mr. Tyrrell[2] of Trinity and get Prometheus known among Trinity men if I could.

But in general Irishmen are no ^poets nor^ critics of poetry, though much alive to what we vaguely called poetry in nature and language and very capable of expressing it in a vague, ~~and~~ ^a^ rhetorical way. They always mistake the matter of poetry for poetry. However education goes for much in such a case.

A consignment of 331 examination papers tonight, I [am sorry] to say, and more will come.

Yours Gerard Hopkins.

I no[w se]e my time will be so short that it will go hard with the Feast of Bacchus.

You are quite wrong about Barnes's poems — not to admire them ever so much more. I have two good tunes to two of them.[3] I had one played this afternoon, but as the pianist said: Your music dates from a time before the piano was. The parts are independent in form and phrasing and are lost on that instrument. Two ~~si~~ choristers, who were at hand, sang the tune, which to its fond father sounded very flowing and a string accompaniment would have set it off, I do believe. By the bye, I will send you this thing as a sample and if it does not suit the piano you will at least see what is meant. Consider it and return it. The harmonies are not commonplace, with leave of Mr. — [4] and there is plenty of modulation. (I told you I am acting on Mr. — [4] advice.)

[1] By R. W. Dixon.

[2] Robert Yelverton Tyrrell (1844–1914; *ODNB*), a classical scholar, at this time Regius Professor of Greek in the University of Dublin. See *CW* vii.

[3] No longer extant.

[4] Name cut out by RB. See letter of 11 May 1883.

6 October 1886 to Coventry Patmore

FL, no. CLXXXII, p. 370 Durham University Library, Abbott MS 198
One folded sheet of headed paper. Four sides.

~~St. Ignatius'~~ University College, ~~S.J., | 23, Upper Temple-street,~~ | Stephen's Green, | Dublin. [*Address altered in MS from printed address*]
Oct. 6 1886

My dear Mr. Patmore, — I have just returned from a very reviving fortnight or so of North Wales, the true Arcadia of wild beauty.

I have a long letter somewhere to you, but shall never send it. I read with pleasure the account of you in the *World*, but you have not sent the papers from the *St. James's*.

You are not to think I now begin to admire Barnes: I always did so, but it was long since I had read him. (Bridges is quite wrong about him and off his orthodoxy.) I scarcely understand you about reflected light: every true poet, I thought, must be original and originality a condition of poetic genius; so that each poet ~~was~~ ^is^ like a species in nature ~~and~~ (not an *individuum genericum* or *specificum*) and can never recur. That nothing shd. be old or borrowed however cannot be, and that I am sure you never meant.

~~Sti~~ Still I grant in Barnes an unusual independence and originality, due partly to his circumstances. It is his naturalness that strikes me most; he is like an embodiment or incarnation or manmuse of the country, of Dorset, of rustic life and humanity. He comes, like Homer and all ^poets of^ native epic, ~~poets~~, provided with epithets, images, and so on which seem to have ^been^ tested and digested for a long age in their native air and circumstances and to have a *keeping* which nothing else ~~can~~ ^could^ give; but in fact they are rather all of his own finding and ^first^ throwing off ^~~first by him~~^. This seems to me very high praise. It is true they are not farfetched or exquisite (I mean for instance his mentions of rooks or of brooks) but they are straight from nature and quite fresh. His rhythms are charming and most characteristic: these too smack of the soil. However his employment of the Welsh *cynghanedd* or chime I do not look on as quite successful. To tell the truth, I think I could do that better, and it is an artificial thing and not much in his line. (I mean like *Paladore* and *Polly dear*,[1] which is in my judgment more of a miss than a hit.) I have set tunes to two of them[2] which appear to me very suitable to the words and as if drawn out of them, and one I have harmonised and got today played; but I can never succeed with piano music, for the piano cannot really execute independent parts, as I make mine; indeed my pianist said to me, Your music dates from a time before the piano was invented. However two schoolboys sang the air; which went well. But now no more of Barnes or of music, for I have overhanging me 500 examination papers and that only one batch out of three.

With the kindest remembrances to Mrs. Patmore and the Miss Patmores, I am your sincere friend Gerard M. Hopkins S.J.

Before I went to Wales I was much pulled down: that was why I did not[3] sooner write. Bridges says Barnes has no fire, and this I think we must grant.

[1] See 'Shaftesbury Feäir', from the Third Collection of *Poems of Rural Life in the Dorset Dialect* (1863).

[2] No MS known.

[3] From here onwards written above the address.

10 October 1886 to Father Matthew Russell, SJ

'Four Newfound Letters: An Annotated Edition, with a Fragment of Another Letter', ed. Joseph J. Feeney, SJ, *HQ* 23/1–2 (1996), 18–23 Gonzaga 1: 2

UNIVERSITY COLLEGE, | ST STEPHEN'S GREEN, | DUBLIN. [*printed heading*]
Oct. 10 1886

My dear Father Mat, Pax Christi — Great haste, as I have an invoice of 331 papers from the R.U.I.

Please do not communicate my judgment, much less ~~my~~ ^the^ giver's name.

I think the piece a poor thing.

It is plain that a "Jew de spree"[1] like this (which is now no new joke too but a well thumbed one) is in itself the most trifling thing in the world and ~~depends~~ to be justified at all and have a reason for being must exhibit some notable happiness of rendering, e.g. a burlesque of elegant Latin or a parody of Virgil or some great writer or ~~a great~~ some metrical excellence, and so on.

I think this example is wanting in such features.

First it is not a faithful translation. To write nonsense in Latin because some one else has written nonsense in English is not enough, it is not the game: the game is to put that English nonsense into Latin.

One of these trifles, the only one I just now recollect, a version of “Hey diddle diddle, the cat and the fiddle” begins “Hei didulum atque iterum didulum fel~~e~~isque fidesque”: this is capital. “~~Iterum~~ ^Didulum^ atque iterum~~” is i~~ didulum” is idiomatic; “fel~~e~~isque fidesque” is Virgilian mock-heroic; it sounds as if it meant something and means nothing; but it faithfully translates. But the third stanza of the piece before us means nothing and does not represent the original. “In aulis” seems to me to be nothing at all; at any rate it is not “in the parlour” or, as it shd. be, “in his counting house”. “Cellis” (besides that the omission of in is violent and perhaps impossible) means nothing either and certainly neither “^the^ kitchen” nor, as that should be, “her parlour”. What then is “pandit vestem”? Nothing like “~~ha is~~ ^was^ hanging out the clothes”. It is quite pointless. And the last line, which shd. be the best, is the worst: one cannot gather whose nose. The English has a sort of ridiculous climax: here there is no climax, indeed no meaning.

Metrically the third line, the hard ~~line~~ ^one^ of the Alcaic stanza, is nowhere good. I cannot ~~s~~now search Horace to find how often he allows a pause after the 4th syllable, certainly not in two stanzas running. And the remaining 3rd line is not good either.

I do not say there are no good touches, but there are not enough to redeem it.

Besides all this, line 5 does not scan. The word vas or some other must be supplied to fill it out.

This is what I think and I believe you will think much the same. I am yours very sincerely Gerard M. Hopkins S.J

[1] GMH had obviously been asked by Matthew Russell, SJ, for many years editor of the *Irish Monthly*, for an opinion on a translation into Latin Alcaics of ‘Sing a song of sixpence’. GMH punned on ‘Jew d’esprit’ and other phrases in his letter of 14 May 1881 to AWMB, adding, ‘If you put your head aside at the proper angle these are good jokes’, yet though willing to call Disraeli a ‘Jew’, he opposed Coventry Patmore’s prejudice and argued that to be Jewish by race ‘is no reproach but a glory, for Christ was a Jew’ (6–7 Dec. 1883).

10 October 1886 from Coventry Patmore to GMH

FL, no. CLXXXII A, p. 37 Campion Hall, P 10/10/86
Addressed to 'Rev. Gerard Hopkins, S.J. | University College | St. Stephen's Green, | Dublin'. PM HASTINGS OC 10 86, H&K PACKET OC 11 86.

Hastings. Oct. 10.
My dear Mr. Hopkins,

Pray send me the "long letter" when you find it, for your letters are quite events in my life of a hermit.

I dont remember what it was I said about reflected light, but I am sure that I could never have meant that the very best of Poets was such by reflected light.

The Papers from the St. James's are in a little book called "How I managed & improved my estate". It is without my name so that, if it reached you, you may not have recognised me. If it has not reached you I will send you another copy.

I should much like to hear your music to Barnes, but as we have only a piano and my daughter Bertha is too ill to be likely to sing part songs with her sister for a long while, I suppose it is of no use asking for the notes.

I am writing very hard for the St. James's and shall probably write for the "Fortnightly",[1] as the editor has asked me to become a contributor. I have written all that I can or at least all that I ought to say, in the way of poetry; and I begin to think that I may do a little good, on a lower level, before I die.

Your's affectionately
C. Patmore

[1] For Patmore's contributions to the *Fortnightly Review* see Frederick Page's Appendix II (p. 210) to *Courage in Politics, &c.* (1921).

13 October 1886 to Robert Bridges

LRB, no. CXXXVI, p. 230 Bodleian, Dep. Bridges, vol. 92, fos. 96–98^{v}

University College, Stephen's Green, Dublin. Oct. 13 1886.

Dearest Bridges, — Fr. Mat~~.~~ Russell of ours (he is Sir Charles Russell's brother), who edits a little half-religious publication the Irish Monthly, wrote to me lately for an opinion of some Latin verses furnished him; and ~~my reply led to~~ this led to two things. The first was my suddenly turning a lot of Shakspere's songs[1] into elegiacs and hendecasyllables (my Latin muse having been wholly mum for years) and sending him one copy (and the rest I believe I can and shall get published in the Trinity Hermathena[2] by means of Mr. Tyrrell)~~,~~. The other was that he proposed to me to introduce your poems to the few^ish^ but not despicable readers of his little periodical.[3] Now this I must do, as soon as it shall become possible; but you must therefore send me (not for this purpose Prometheus, which ~~here~~ I have, but) those pamphlets ^copies of^ which I think I left at Stonyhurst. It is no doubt wasteful work giving me presentation copies; but the ~~present~~ ^above^ is my most permanent abode~~,~~ and the nest likely to be best feathered. Yours Gerard M. Hopkins S.J.

By the bye, I say it deliberately and before God, I would have you and Canon Dixon and all true poets remember that fame, the being known, though in itself one of the most dangerous things to man, is nevertheless the ~~necessary~~ true and appointed air, element, and setting of genius and its works. What are works of art for? To educate, to be standards. Education is meant for the many, standards are for public use. To produce then is of little use unless what we produce is known, if known widely known, the wider known the better, for it is by being known ~~they~~ ^it^ ~~acts~~ ^works^, ~~they~~ it influences, it does its duty, it does good. We must then try to be known, aim at it, take means to it. And this without puffing in the process or pride in the success. ~~b~~^B^ut still. Besides, we are Englishm~~a~~en. A great work by an Englishman is like a great battle won by England.[4] It is an unfading ~~by~~ bay tree. It ~~is~~ will even be admired by ^and praised by and^ do good to those who hate England (as England is most perilously hated), who do not wish even to be benefited by her. It is then even a patriotic duty ~~to~~ τῇ ποιήσει ἐνεργεῖν {*to be active in producing poetry*}[5] and to secure the fame and permanence of the work. Art and its fame do not really matter, spiritually they are nothing, virtue is the only good; but it is only by bringing in the infinite that to a just judgment they can be made to look infinitesimal or small or less than vastly great; and in this ordinary view of them I apply to them, and it is the~~ir~~ true rule for dealing with them, what Christ our Lord said of virtue, Let your light shine before men that they may see your good works (say, of ~~work~~ ^art^) and glorify yr. ~~f~~Father in heaven[6] (~~say~~ ^that is^, acknowledge ^that^ they have an absolute excellence in them and are steps in a scale of infinite and inexhaustible excellence).

Let me hear ^that^ you got all my letters. One, begun I think in Wales and sent from here, was addressed to Judge Fry's[7] at Bristol, the next to Yattendon and had (I believe it was that one) a torn drawing in it.

Well of course you must have got that one, but the one to Bristol with the long address you may not. Earlier ones are I think accounted for.

Did I ever send you St. Patrick's "Breastplate" or prayer?[8] I do now at all events. Read it and say if it is not one of the most remarkable compositions of man.

[1] GMH wrote (i) a Latin version of 'Come unto these yellow sands', (ii) two Greek versions of 'Tell me where is Fancy bred', (iii) a Latin version of 'Full fathom five', (iv) a Latin version of 'Tell me where is Fancy bred', (v) a Greek version of 'Orpheus with his lute made trees' (with a prosodic scheme), (vi) a Latin version of 'Orpheus with his lute made trees', and (vii) a Latin version of 'When icicles hang by the wall'.

[2] *Hermathena* (A Series of Papers on Literature, Science and Philosophy by Members of Trinity College, Dublin) contains nothing by GMH.

[3] The *Irish Monthly* contains no review of RB's poetry by GMH, but two Latin versions by him from Shakespeare were printed in vol. 14 (1886), 628 and vol. 15 (1887), 92.

[4] The same thought is expressed in the letter to Coventry Patmore of 4–6 June 1886.

[5] Presumably a phrase coined by GMH.

[6] GMH is quoting from Matthew 5: 16.

[7] Judge Fry. Elizabeth Waterhouse's brother's family.

[8] St Patrick's 'Breastplate' or prayer dates from the 8th c. It asks for God's protection on a journey (or the journey of life). Its style is a Christianized version of pagan Irish protection charms. The popular Victorian hymn 'I bind unto myself to-day' is a translation of it.

18 October 1886 from Richard Watson Dixon

CRWD, no. XXXVI A, p. 144 Campion Hall, D 18/10/86
Addressed to 'The Rev[d]. | Gerard Hopkins S.J. | Stephen's Green, | Dublin | Ireland'. PM ACKLINGTON OC 18 86, WARKWORTH OC 18 86, LIVERPOOL OC 19 86, H&K PACKET OC 19 86.

Warkworth | 18 Oct. 1886.
My dear Friend,

I am greatly obliged by your kindness in criticising Ulysses & Calypso in the midst of so much work of your own. I have benefited much by what you say about it: making several important alterations.

I do not altogether understand your opinions about mythology, of which I have heard through Bridges, who shewed me a letter about it.[1] I think the Greek mythology very beautiful; most beautiful in the hands of the dramatists, more than in Homer: and probably the dramatists looked on it in somewhat the way that

English poets have, as a storehouse. Bridges in his Prometheus treats it finely: indicating at the same time (I think) that there are heights above it: in the passages about primordial fire, & fate. It has been a source of beauty to all poetry.

You spoke of Wordsworth. I quite agree as to his healing power: which is perhaps the best quality of poetry. In my opinion his finest poem is The Old Cumberland Beggar. [*illegible deletion of a line*] ^He is very great in that function of the seer's healing & consolation.^ Unfortunately there is so often a sense of baulk, in his lyrics particularly. The image is conveyed, but with a kind of unhappiness: "Lord of the vale, astounding flood."[2] "Little cyclops with one eye,"[3] of the daisy. "He was a lovely youth I guess" &c.[4] In fact nearly all his best known lyrics have that misfortune. This has kept me from being "a Wordsworthian", in the full sense. On the other hand, in metres that suit him, he is almost ~~ml~~ ^sometimes^ matchlessly vivid: e.g.

> While a dark storm before my sight
> Was yielding, on the mountain hight
> Loose vapours have I watched, that won
> Prismatic colours from the sun.[5]

And this not for the sake of the picture, but in the midst of a lot of consolation.

I am very much pressed with work, or I should like to go on talking with you. Thank you very much for your former delightful letter. One thing that has stood in the way of Wordsworth with me is the extravagan~~t~~^ce^ ~~cla~~ ^of^ some of the claims made for him. Pattison[6] said the Ode about Immortality was the second poem in the language, Lycidas being the first. It is constantly called the Great Ode. I do not see that it is particularly good (for Wordsworth, or as Wordsworth), much less great. But Wordsworth was a great poet.

Thank you again for the valuable services you have done to U. & C.

I wish you would send me some of your own: you spoke of some sonnets &c.

Your affecte friend
R. W. Dixon

The short piece (perhaps a sonnet?) called 'Sky prospect' is worth any number of ~~the~~ Great Odes.[7] It is as good as a tour to read his memorials of Tours: how fine are the lines on Trajan's Column. e g.[8]

[1] The letter of 17–29 May 1885.

[2] 'Memorials of a Tour in Scotland, II. Composed at Cora Linn, in sight of Wallace's Tower', l. 1.

[3] 'To the Daisy' (second poem, 1802), l. 25.

[4] 'Ruth', ll. 37 sqq.

[5] 'Written in a Blank Leaf of Macpherson's Ossian', ll. 5–8, with 'the' for 'a' in l. 6.

[6] Mark Pattison (1813–84; *ODNB*) wrote in ch. 2 of his *Milton* (1879) that 'In

Lycidas we have reached the high-water mark of English Poetry and of Milton's own production. A period of a century and a half was to elapse before poetry in England seemed, in Wordsworth's *Ode on Immortality* (1807) to be rising again towards the level of inspiration which it had once attained in *Lycidas*'.

7 'Sky-Prospect—From the Plain of France' (no. xxxiii of *Memorials of a Tour on the Continent*, 1820).

8 'The Pillar of Trajan' (1826).

21–2 October 1886 to Robert Bridges

LRB, no. CXXXVII, p. 232 Bodleian, Dep. Bridges, vol. 92, fos. 99–102v

UNIVERSITY COLLEGE, | ST. STEPHEN'S GREEN, | DUBLIN. [*printed heading*]
Oct. 21 1886

(I was received into the Catholic Church this day 20 years hence.)

Dearest Bridges, — Here follows the remainder, the Burden, of Yellow sands. You may copy it in, but you will say it is only a curiosity.

Ariel. Hark, hark.
Burden (dispersedly). Bow wow.
Ariel. The watchdogs bark.
Burden. Bow wow. ~~B~~
Ariel. Hark, hark. I hear
The strain of strutting chanticleer
Cry Cock a diddle dow.[1]

Lascivae latrare; ita plaudere. At hoc juvat: ergo
~~Et~~ ^Nos^ Hecuba et Hecubae ~~nunc chorus~~ ^nos canes^
Adlatre^n^t. ~~hos~~. Gallus sed enim occinit, occinat: ~~hora~~ aequumst
Cantare gallos ~~aequum erat~~ ^temperi^.

You will have seen that in one of the pieces were some phrases borrowed from Horace and Virgil. In original composition this is most objectionable, but in translation it is lawful, I think, and may be happy, since there it is question of matching the best of one language with the best, not the newest, of another.

These verses cannot appear in Hermathena, which admits no translations. Mr. Tyrrell said he liked them very much, but he did not himself approve of my Catullian rhythms. I employ them of choice, taking Catullus[2] for my warrant only, not my standard, for metrically Catullus was very unsure. In my judgment his Atys, though (just like Tennyson's imitation) it shows ~~his~~ ^the poet's^ genius, is metrically and even in other respects an unsuccessful experiment.

You would like Mr. Tyrrell. He is a fine scholar and an amiable man, free from every touch of pedantry.

I added two metrical schemes to my Greek verses for you.[3] They are inconsistent; that is to say, one is fuller than the other. I have made what I think is a great discovery; it is of ^a^ fundamental point~~.~~; and I hope to publish something on it. It is shortly this~~,~~. ~~that~~ ~~t~~^T^he Dorian rhythm, the most used of the lyric rhythms, arises from the Dorian measure or bar.[4] The Dorian bar is originally <u>a march step in three-time ~~and~~ executed in four steps to the bar</u>. Out of this simple combination of numbers, three and four, simple to state but a good deal more complicated than any rhythm we have, arose the structure of most of Pindar's odes and most of the choral odes in the drama. In strict rhythm every bar must have four steps. Now since four were to be taken to three-time, say three crotchets, ^(1)^ one crotchet had to be resolved, ^(2)^ only one~~,~~ at a time, and that ^(3)^ never the last. Hence the two legitimate figures of the Dorian bar were these: ∪ ∪ – – (the rising Ionic) and – ∪ ∪ – (the choriambus). But the following irregularities were allowed: ∪ ∪ – ∪ (the ~~Th~~ third paeon), either by prolonging the third syllable (∪ ∪ ≥ ∪) or by irrationally lengthening the last (∪ ∪ – ∪͐); – ∪ – – (the second epitrite), (which is not~~,~~ as Schmidt[5] th~~us~~inks ≥ ∪ – –, ~~bu~~ for that wd. destroy the three-time, but –∪ – –), by resolving the first long into three instead of two, exactly as we employ triplets in music and write 3 over them~~)~~; lastly the very irregular but important combination of these two licences – –∪ ≥ ∪ or –∪ – ∪͐ (the double trochee). The beautiful figure ∪– – – is the ^one^ most characteristic of the rhythm: Hephaestion calls it the Carian foot.

When the measure is more loosely used two new licences appear — syncopation, by which syllables are lengthened so ~~as to~~ ^that three^ fill a bar and so that the last of one bar becomes the first of the next; and triple resolution, so that a bar can have five syllables. By means of syncopation the measure can be made dactylic and practically brought into common time. The strict Dorian can only be found in odes meant to be marched to.

I shd. say a word of the accentuation ~~of~~ or stressing. Naturally the strongest place in the Dorian bar is the second ^crotchet^, not the first, and I have so marked it in the schemes I sent, but perhaps it would be best to mark the first as strongest: it is made so, so to speak, by a correction, to redress the heaviness of the second crotchet. Pindar and all the poets continually pass from heavier feet, like –∪ – – or

∪∪ – – , to lighter, – ∪ ∪ –, where by the stress falling sometimes on a long or crotchet, sometimes on a short or quaver, a beautiful variety is given and the variety is further enhanced by ~~foll~~ making an imperfect Ionic follow a choriambus, thus: – ∪ ∪ – | ∪ ∪ –, by which a dactylic cadence is given but with the stress falling on different syllables of the dactyls. With all this the rhythm ~~has~~ ^came to have^ an infinite flexibility, of which the Greeks seem never to have tired.

Thus you are not to mark *ἔρως ἀνί|κατε μάχαν, || ἔρως ὃς ~~ἔρως ἀνίκατε μάχαν~~ ἐν | κτήμασι πίπτεις*, as here, but as here: *ἔ|ρως ἀνίκα|τε μάχαν, || ἔ|ρως ὃς ἐν κτή|μασι πίπτεις* {*Eros, unconquered in the fight, Eros who makes havoc of wealth*}.[6] However the musicians no doubt took their own way with these things. By the bye, I will send you my plain chant notes to this: it greatly brings out the nature of the rhythm. Good night.

Oct. 22 — Tufts of thyme from Bumpus's Helicon[7] are to hand and I have sent three copies to Mr. Tyrrell and shall consider ~~how~~ where ~~else~~ to bestow the others.

I enclose the music to *ἔρως ἀνί|κατε μάχαν*. Ahem, study it. You will find that it is (but not designedly) composed, though it contains octaves, in the older # heptachord scale~~,~~ having ~~a~~ ^the^ lower keynote on La (here E) and the higher on ~~Sol~~ ^its seventh Sol (here D)^ — as we should speak. The music therefore is neither major nor minor, or is both and fluctuates between them, settling at last on the minor keynote. The two modes ~~ag~~ are connected by Mi which is the fifth of La and the Third of Do; and as the fifth is more important in a scale, being with us the dominant, than the third, so the minor mode predominates over the major. They are also connected by ~~th~~ Sol, which is the upper extremity or keynote (not the octave) of ^the^ La-mode and the fifth or dominant of the Do-mode, and here again the upper keynote is more important than the fifth. This old heptachord scale is founded deeply in nature; it can never perish; and it is it which compels us to use and to find so much pleasure in the dominant seventh, in other words in a chord having for its two extrem~~ities~~^e^ ~~the~~ notes the extremities of the heptachord scale. ~~Both t~~The octave and the heptachord scales ^both^ arise from doubl~~ing~~^ed^ tetrachords, overlapping, ^conjunct^ or closed in the one case; free, disjunct, or open in the other. The ~~line~~ ^vein^ I am working in is the application of this double system, the heptachord and the octave, in a new ~~paper~~ ^way^, by founding the ~~sevenths~~ ^heptachord^ on La, not on Sol.

The above is not lucid nor perhaps all true. Perhaps the major and minor modes ^in the heptachord^ best communicate by means of the note between ~~them~~ ^their keynotes^, Ti (about which much might be said), flattened at option as in Greek and medieval music.

I have much more to answer in yr. letter, but want now to send this. I can also let you see some other settings of Greek ^to^ music as curiosities and some of them (as indeed the enclosed piece seems to me) as good in themselves.

With best love, your affectionate friend Gerard.

[1] This quotation from *The Tempest*, I. ii. 380–5, is followed by the Latin which offers a rendering of it; this forms lines 9–12 of his 'Come unto these yellow sands'. See *CW* viii.

[2] Gaius Valerius Catullus (*c*.84 BC–*c*.54 BC) was a Latin poet, something of a revolutionary in writing very personal poems, and the rhythm of his 'Atys' is distinctive and idiosyncratic. In *Enoch Arden* (1864) Tennyson wrote one of his 'Experiments', 'Boädicea', in galliambics (lines made of two iambic dimeters) in imitation of Catullus.

[3] 'Tell me where is fancy bred' and 'Orpheus with his lute'. Preserved in MS A. See N. H. MacKenzie, *LPM*, 294 and 296.

[4] See *CW* vii for GMH's initial notes on this project; and *CW* vi; and for the progress of these unfinished projects see also letters of 18–19 Oct. 1882 to RB, 14 Jan. 1883 to AMWB, 2–4 and 28 Oct. 1886 to RB, 7 Nov. 1886 to Patmore, 11 Dec. 1886 to RB, 23 Dec. 1886 to AMWB, 20 Jan. 1887 to Patmore, and 1 May and 30 July 1887 to RB.

[5] See the *TLS*, Correspondence, 16 Feb. 1933 and next three issues.

[6] Sophocles, *Antigone*, 781 sqq.

[7] A joking reference to *England's Helicon: A Collection of Lyrical and Pastoral Poems*, published in 1600; actually RB's *Eros and Psyche*, *Prometheus the Firegiver*, *Nero*, and perhaps *The Growth of Love*.

23–4 October 1886 to Richard Watson Dixon

CRWD, no. XXXVII, p. 145 Bodleian, Dep. Bridges, vol. 93, fos. 146–51
Three folded sheets, each with printed letterhead.

University College, | St. Stephen's Green, | Dublin. [*printed heading*]
Oct. 23 1886

My dear Friend, — There are some points in your letter I have to reply to. First of the Greek mythology. Of course I agree with the rest of the world in admiring its beauty. Above everything else the Greeks excelled in art: now ^their^ mythology was the earliest of their arts that have in any way survived, older in the main than Homer's poems, and is I daresay as much more beautiful than ~~any~~ other mythologies as Homer's epic is than other epics; speaking of epic proper. It is free from that cumber of meaningless and childish rubbish which interrupts and annoys one even in the midst of fine invention ^in^ for instance the Irish legends.

~~But this~~ ^This however^ is to speak of it as stories, as fairy tales, well invented well told fairy tales. But mythology is something else besides fairy tale: it is religion, the historical part of religion. It must have been this side of the Greek mythology I was speaking of in that letter; and could I speak too severely of it? First it is as history untrue. What is untrue history? Nothing and worse than nothing. And that history religion? Still worse. I cannot enter on this consideration without being brought face to face with the great fact of heathenism. Now we mostly pass heathenism by as a thing utterly departed, which indeed it is not but in India rank and flourishing; but if for once ^we^ face it what are we to say of it? For myself literally ~~would~~ words would fail me to express the loathing and horror with which I think of it and of man setting up the work of his own hands, o~~f~~^r^ that hand within the mind the imagination, for God Almighty who made heaven and earth.[1] Still he might set up beings perfect in their kind. But the Greek gods are rakes, and unnatural rakes. Put that ~~asd~~ aside too; put yourself in the position of a man who like Homer first believes in them, next forgets or passes over their wickedness: even so are the Greek gods ~~brave~~ majestic, awe inspiring, as Homer that great Greek genius represents them? They are not. The Indian gods are imposing, the Greek are not. Indeed they are not brave, not selfcontrolled, they have no manners, they are not gentlemen and ladies. They clout one another's ears and blubber and bellow. You will say this is Homer's fun, like the miracle-plays of Christendom.[2] Then where is his earnest about them? At their best they remind me of some company of beaux and fashionable world at Bath in its palmy days or Tunbridge Wells or what not. Zeus is like the Major in Pendennis[3] handsomer and better preserved sitting on ~~P~~^O^lympus as behind a club-window and watching Danae and other pretty seamstresses cross the street — not to go farther. You will think this is very Philistine and vulgar and be pained. But I am pained: this is the light in which the matter strikes me, the only one in which it will; and I do think it is the true light.

But I grant that the Greek ~~my~~ mythology is very susceptible of fine treatment, allegorical treatment for instance, and so treated gives rise to the most beautiful results. No wonder: the moral evil is got rid of and the pure art, morally neutral and artistically so rich, remains and can be even turned to moral uses.

The letter you saw must have been in criticism of Bridges' Ulysses. I was set against that play by the appearance of Athene in the prologue or opening. Bridges took her almost seriously: so then did I, and was disgusted. But I hold it was a false step of his: the heathen gods cannot be taken seriously on our stage; nowadays they cannot even be taken humorously; and it would ~~have~~ ^tell^ against the play's success. I know that was a noble play; but I had another objection besides to it, the great severity, the aridity even and joylessness of the lyrics. So I damped and damned and must have hurt Bridges.

I feel now I am warm and my hand is in for my greater task, Wordsworth's ode;[4] and here, my dear friend, I must earnestly remonstrate with you; must have it out with you. Is it possible that — but it is in black and white: you say the ~~ode~~ ode is not, for Wordsworth, good; and much less great.

To say it was the second ode in the language was after all only a comparative remark: one might maintain, though I daresay you will not, that English is not rich in odes. The remark therefore is not of itself extravagant. But if the speaker had said that it was one of the dozen or of the half dozen finest odes of the world I must own that to me there would ^have^ seemed no extravagance. There have been in all history a few, a very few men, whom common repute, even where it did not trust them, has treated as having had something happen to them that does not happen to other men, as having seen something, whatever that really was. Plato is the most famous of these. Or to put it~~,~~ as it seems to me I must somewhere have written to you or to somebody, human nature in these men saw something, got a shock; wavers in opinion, looking back, whether ~~that~~ there was anything in it or no; but is in a tremble ever since. Now what Wordsworthians mean is, what would seem to be the growing mind of the English speaking world~~,~~ and may perhaps come to be that of the world at large/ is that in Wordsworth when he wrote that ode human nature got another of those shocks, and the tremble from it is spreading. This opinion I do strongly share; I am, ever since I knew the ode, in that tremble. You know what happened to crazy Blake, himself a most poetically electrical subject both active and passive, at his first hearing: when the reader came to "The pansy at my feet" he fell into a hysterical excitement. Now commonsense forbid we should take on like these unstrung hysterical creatures: still it was a proof of the power of the shock.

The ode itself seems to me better than anything else I know of Wordsworth's, so much as to equal or outweigh everything else he wrote: to me it appears so. For Wordsworth was an imperfect artist, as you say: as his matter varied in importance and as he varied in insight (for he had a profound insight of some things and little of others) so does the value of his work vary. Now the interest and importance of the matter were here of the highest, his insight was at its very deepest, and hence to my mind the extreme value of the poem.

His powers rose, I ~~say~~ ^hold^, with the subject: the execution is so fine. The rhymes are so musically interlaced, the rhythms so happily succeed (surely it is a magical change "O joy that in our embers"), the diction throughout is so charged and ~~bathed~~ steeped in beauty and yearning (what a stroke "The moon doth with delight" !). It is not a bit of good my going on if, which is to me so strange in you and disconcerting, ^you do not^ feel anything of this. But I do hope you will reconsider it. For my part I shd. think St. George and St. Thomas of Canterbury[5] wore roses in heaven for England's sake on the day ~~when~~ that ode, not without their intercession, was penned; for, to better a little the good humoured old cynical proverb, "When grace of God is gone and spent Then learning is most excellent" and goes to make the greatness of a nation — which is what I urge on Bridges and now on you, to get yourselves known and be up betimes on our Parnassus.

Now no more. I will copy you soon some odd ends, sonnets. Have you my song for my play of St. Winefred called The Leaden Echo and the Golden Echo? If not I will try and copy it as time serves: I never did anything more musical.

May the Muses bring you to a better mind. May God Almighty, and this without reserve. I am your affectionate friend Gerard M. Hopkins S.J.

Oct. 24. Examinations over and I begin lecturing tomorrow.

[1] See Psalm 115: 15.

[2] English miracle plays, though solidly Christian in inspiration and purpose, contain broad and sometimes coarse humour. GMH had begun work on a study of Homer and many of the letters to Baillie in 1886 sprung from his efforts to trace what he thought were the Egyptian origins of the mythology found in Homer. See letters to his mother of 13 Jan. 1886; to Baillie of 11 Feb., 22 Mar., 23 Mar., 26 Mar., 28 Mar., 29 Mar., 3 Apr., 6 Apr., 10 Apr., 19 Apr., 28 Apr. 1886, and 1 June 1886; see too 20 Feb. 1887; from Newman 25 Feb. 1886; from J. Rhys 24 Apr. 1886.

[3] William Makepeace Thackeray, *The History of Pendennis* (published serially 1848–50).

[4] 'Intimations of Immortality'.

[5] St George and St Thomas represent a focus for English patriotism. It was to St Thomas's shrine in Canterbury that Chaucer's Canterbury pilgrims were going, while Henry V in Shakespeare's play rouses his men with the battle cry, 'God for Harry! England and St George!' (III. i. 34).

25 October 1886 from Richard Watson Dixon to GMH

CRWD, no. XXXVII A, p. 149 Campion Hall, D 25/10/86
Addressed to 'The Rev[d] | Gerard Hopkins S.J. | University College, | Stephen's Green, | Dublin | Ireland'. PM ACKLINGTON OC 26 86, WARKWORTH OC 26 86, H&K PACKET OC 27 86.

Warkworth | 25 Oct. 1886.
My dear Friend,

I can only write to thank you for your Letter: I go tomorrow to Newcastle to the Diocesan Conference, where I have to read a paper, which now occupies me. I am much touched by your letter, & will certainly give all attention to Wordsworth's Ode. Indeed after what you say I feel certain I must be mistaken about it. Pattison said it was the second poem, not ode, in the language.

This is to acknowledge your letter and thank you for it. ^It was the letter on Ulysses.^

Yes, I read your two Voices at Bridges' once: but I have no copy. They produced in me secretly some slight approach to what you say of Blake

Your affec[te] Friend
R. W. Dixon

[?Late October 1886 to Richard Watson Dixon]

CRWD, p. 129 *LPM* p. 452 Bodleian, Dep. Bridges, vol. 93, fo. 128
The sonnet that follows, written out by GMH, is on a piece of paper, alone. GMH always dated copies of his poems to their inception. This copy would seem from the paper, ink, and handwriting to belong to late October 1886.

To what serves mortal beauty?

(sonnet: alexandrines: the mark ⌐¬ over two neighbouring syllables means that, though one has and the other has not the metrical stress, in the recitation-stress they are to be about equal)

To what serves mortal beauty — | dangerous; does set danc-
Ing blood — the O-seal-that-so | feature, flung prouder form
Than Purcell tune lets tread to? | See: it does this: keeps warm
Men's wits to the things that are; | what good means — where a glance
Master more may than gaze, | gaze out of countenance.
Those lovely lads once, wetfresh | windfalls of war's storm,
How then should Gregory, father, | have gleanèd else from throng-
Èd Rome? But God to a nation | dealt that day's dear chance.
To man, that needs would worship | block or barren stone,
Our law says Love what are | love's worthiest, were all known;
World's loveliest — men's selves. Self | flashes off frame and face.
What do then? how meet beauty? | Merely meet it; own,
Home at heart, heaven's sweet gift; | then leave, let ~~it~~ ^that^ alone.
Yea, wish that though, wish all, | God's better beauty, grace.

Aug. 23 1885

28 October 1886 to Robert Bridges[1]

LRB, no. CXXXVIII, p. 235 Bodleian, Dep. Bridges, vol. 92, fos. 103–10

University College, Stephen's Green, Dublin. Oct. 28 '86.

Dearest Bridges, — To't again; for though my last was long and tedious and the one before that, if I remember, a literary budget, I have not yet dealt with your last.

My examinations are over till the next attack of the plague. My lectures, to call them by that grand name, are begun: vae unum abiit et vae alterum venit {*one woe goes and another woe comes*}.[2] I was I cannot tell when in such health and spirits as on my return from Cadwalader and all his goats but 331 accounts of the First Punic War with trimmings, have sweated me down to nearer my lees and usual alluvial low water mudflats, groans[2], despair[4], and[3] yearnings[1].

Now I have at much length remonstrated with Canon Dixon for slighting Wordsworth's Ode on the Intimations, at which he might have taken offence but on the contrary he took it with his usual sweetness;[3] and I beg you will my remonstrances ~~to~~ ^with^ you about Barnes and Stephenson;[4] ~~about~~ of both of whom, but especially S., you speak with a sourness which[5] tinges your judgment.

It is commonly thought of Barnes that "local colour" is just what he excells in and this is my own opinion. A fine and remarkable instance (a case of ~~p~~ colour proper) was quoted by the Saturday in the article on him which followed the news of his death.[6] But of him another time or never; no more now. (The expressions "the ^supposed^ emotions of peasants" grates on me, but let it pass.)

I have not read Treasure Island.[7] When I do, as I hope to, ~~T~~I will bear your ~~cor~~ criticisms in mind. (By the bye, I am sorry those poor boys lost the book because you found ~~a~~ consecutive fifths somewhere. However give 'em Rider Haggard's King Solomon's Mines.[8] They certainly will enjoy it; anyone would; and the author is not a highflier.) Nevertheless I mean to deal with two of these criticisms now, for it is easy to do so~~,~~ on the face of them.

One is that a boy capable of a brave deed ~~is~~ would be incapable of writing ^it^ down — well that boy. Granting this, still to make him tell ^it^ is no fault or a trifling one.[9] And the criticism, which ignores a common convention of romance or literature in general, is surely then some ἀγροικία {*boorishness*} on your part. Autobiography in fiction is commonly held a ~~d~~hazardous thing and few are thought to have succeeded in it on any great scale: Thackeray in Esmond[10] is I believe held ^for^ one of the exceptions. It is one of the things which 'O Lord, sir, we must ~~wink a~~ connive at'.[11] ~~You are~~ ^The reader is^ somehow to be informed of the facts. And in any case the fault is removeable without convulsing the structure of the whole: like a bellglass or glass frame over cucumbers or flowers it may be taken ^off^, cleansed, and replaced without touching them. So this criticism I look on as trifling.

The other criticism is ~~on~~ the discovery of a fault of plot about the whereabouts of some schooner:[12] I take your word for it. One blot is no great matter, I mean not a damning matter.[13] One blot may be found in the works of very learned clerks indeed. Measure for Measure is a lovely piece of work, but it was a blot, as Swinburne raving was overheard for hours to say, to make Isabella marry the old Duke. Volpone is one of the richest and most powerful plays ever written, but a writer in a late Academy points out a fault of construction[14] (want of motive, I think, for Bonario's being at Volpone's house when Celia was brought there): it will stand that one fault. True you say that in Stevenson's book there are many such: but I do not altogether believe there are.

This sour severity blinds you to his great genius. Jekyll and Hyde[15] I have read. You speak of "the gross absurdity" of the interchange.[16] Enough that it is impossible and might perhaps ^have^ been a little better masked: it must be connived at, and it gives rise to a fine situation. It is not more impossible than fairies, giants, heathen gods, and lots of things that literature teems with — and none more than yours.[17] You are certainly wrong about Hyde being overdrawn: my Hyde is worse. The trampling scene is perhaps a convention: he was thinking of something unsuitable for fiction.

I can by no means grant ^that^ the characters are not characterised, though how ~~far~~ deep the springs of their surface action are I am not yet clear ~~about~~. But the superficial touches of character are admirable: how can you be so blind as not to see them? e.g. Utterson frowning, biting the end of his finger, and saying to the butler "This is a strange tale you ~~are~~ tell me, my man, a very strange tale". And Dr. Lanyon: "I used to like it, sir <life>; yes, sir, I liked it. Sometimes I think if we knew all" etc. These are worthy of Shakespeare. Have you read the Pavilion on the Links in the volume of Arabian Nights (not one of them)?[18] The absconding banker is admirably characterised, the horror is nature itself, and the whole piece is genius from beginning to end.

In my judgment the amount of gift and genius which goes into novels in the English literature of this generation is perhaps not much inferior to what made the Elizabethan drama, and unhappily it is in great part wasted. How admirable are Blackmore and Hardy![19] Their merits are much eclipsed by the overdone reputation ^of^ the Evans-Eliot-Lewis-Cross woman (poor creature! one ought not to speak slightingly, I know), half real power, half imposition. Do you know the bonfire scenes ^in the Return of the Native^ and still better the sword-exercise scene in the ~~Madding Crowd~~ Madding Crowd, breathing epic ? or the wife-sale in the Mayor of Casterbridge (read by chance)? But these writers only rise to their great strokes~~:~~; they do not write continuously well: now Stevenson is master of a consummate style and each phrase is finished as in poetry. It will not do at all, your treatment of him.

(Today is Degree-day ~~th~~ at the R.U. and a holiday.)

I have some odds to say still.

I enclose, or shall send soon after, music to Sappho's ode to Aphrodite, more curious than beautiful, but very flowing in a strange kind.[20] It seems to be in the heptachord scale.

I also send something ~~not~~ meant quite in earnest which I do hope you will like — music to a song of Barnes's. If you ~~find~~ or anyone staying with you, as Mr. — [21], or anyone that knows the science ~~can point out~~ ^~~has~~^ ^any downright blunder (like consecutives) or has^ any contrapuntal criticisms to make on it I shall be very glad to hear and correct. It is a first draft. But I want you [to] study it, with the following points understood: (1) the parts are distinctly composed and phrased (for a first draft); ~~they are~~ ^it is^ really polyphonic, and cannot therefore be played properly on the piano: still try it there. (The ~~tenor~~ ^middle part^ is in red.)

(2) The 'dry fifths' are of course intentional and necessary. For since it is the very office of the third to fix the modality (not the tonality, as they confusedly write), the omission of it may be necessary to unsettle that or to allow ~~of~~, as at bar 12, of another one: there the middle part softly asserts the natural minor by the, to my ear, delicious rise of a tone. (If there were four parts I cd. use the third ^(mi)^ there, but not in three.)

I am also going to send with it or soon my Who is Sylvia? This tune is very old, almost boyish; the setting done lately, and some faults corrected by Sir Robert Stewart (though in the end he said almost everything was wrong: perhaps he would not allow in such a composition the use of the $^{6}_{4}$ chord, and I am ready to rewrite it and make it stricter; nevertheless you look at it and say what you think~~.~~). It was to have been performed (and Sylvia was turned into Erin, for reasons) but miscarried at the last moment, the bass fighting shy of his part. These two things wd. not be at all my best, but if you shd. find anything you think well of in them it wd. be encouraging and stimulating to me. I think now it was unlucky [I] shewed Mr. — [22] the Battle of the Baltic, for my purp[os]es: his criticism was just upon the piece as submitted, [bu]t the ~~h~~timidity in harmony would not have ♯ struck him if he had seen, I suppose, succeeding verses; but never mind that now.

I shewed my Greek verses to my colleague old Mr. Ornsby,[23] most modest and estimable of men. He praised them and wanted me to make a little volume. After some of his criticisms I altered Tell me where and enclose a corrected copy.

I hope I may be able some day to let you have a better waterscape from the Dargle or somewhere near Dublin. (By the bye I did soak the other in hot water, perhaps not long enough: the tenacity of the glue in milk is wonderful.)

I think I have little more to learn about the Dorian ~~Mo~~ Measure[24] now, but before writing a paper (and still more a book) on it I must have read ^for illustration and authority^ a good deal, all the poetry in it and Hephaestion[25] and the Metricists, also the Musical writers: it is ^a^ tedious and formidable task.

Upon my word that is all, three sheets, and I am, with best love to Mrs. Bridges and Mrs. Molesworth~~,~~ and kind remembrances to Mrs. Waterhouse, your affectionate friend Gerard.

I may be able to take the Feast of Bacchus, but not quite yet.

P.S. The ceremony is over. We gave an honorary degree to Fr. Perry S.J.[26] of Stonyhurst, the astronomer who conducts transit and ~~el~~ eclipse expeditions to Kerguelen Island and elsewhere. We made a lady Mistress of Arts and Hearts.[27] Ladies, girl graduates, look very nice in gowns. The Lord Lieutenant was better received than might have been expected by the (by ticket admitted) mob, considering that a harebrained pupil of mine (he got the Gulf[28]) was there to lead the hissing.

I am going to send this tonight and pack the music tomorrow. Keep the music as long as you like, but return it. Even get opinions, competent and incompetent; if it can in any [way] be performed so that opinions can be formed.

I shall shortly be writing a review of you, and juiced dispassionate.[29]

[1] At the end of this letter RB has written the following note:

'Wishing to keep this letter I have made a few notes in justification of my criticisms, which were no doubt ill expressed—to give rise to such misrepresentation.

The letter gives a true picture of GMH's views of English literature, & his judgt of modern writers. RB

About Louis Stevenson I may add that my chief "objection" to his works is merely a want of sympathy. I admire his art much, but he is constantly offending my feelings.'

RB also made certain interlinear comments, which are printed as footnotes in their place.

[2] Although not quite a quotation, this uses the language of Revelation 9: 12: 'vae unum abiit ecce veniunt adhuc duo vae post haec' [*one woe is past and then come yet two woes more thereafter* (Douay-Reims)] and the commentary of Hieronymus on Ezekiel 26: 'vae unum abiit, et vae alterum veniet cito' [*one woe goes and another woe comes quickly*]. See also Revelation 11: 14.

[3] See letters of 18 and 25 Oct. 1886 from RWD and 23–4 Oct. 1886 by GMH.

[4] Spelt thus.

[5] MS 'with'.

[6] In the issue of 16 Oct. 1886: an appreciative, well-informed, unsigned review. The quotation referred to is the first stanza of *Went Hwome* (*Poems of Rural Life* . . . (London, 1887), 362).

[7] Published in 1882. First printed as a serial in *Young Folks*, starting in the issue of 1 Oct. 1881.

[8] Published in 1886.

[9] 'My objection was not to his telling, but to his narration being sometimes in a vein untrue to his character as required by his actions, the two being incompatible & bad as art. RB'

[10] William Makepeace Thackeray (1811–63; *ODNB*) published *The History of Henry Esmond* in1852. Henry Esmond himself is the narrator.

[11] Sheridan, *The Rivals*, III. iii.

[12] 'This I gave as an instance of the author's art [wh. is not disguised] breaking down. RB'.

[13] 'There are others in plenty—RB'.

[14] A review, on 16 Oct. 1886, by H. C. Beeching of J. A. Symonds's *Ben Jonson*. Here is quoted from the book: 'the heaviest blot upon Jonson's construction' is that 'he

has suggested no adequate motive for Mosca's introduction of Bonario into Volpone's palace at the moment when Corbaccio is coming to execute his will, and Celia is being brought by her unworthy husband'.

[15] Published in 1886.

[16] 'No—of the means employed, wh. is physical & shd have been magical. RB'.

[17] '[but does not make chemistry of]' RB.

[18] 'The Pavilion on the Links' was a short story published in the *Cornhill Magazine* (Sept.–Oct. 1880). A revised version was included in *The New Arabian Nights* (1882).

[19] Richard Doddridge Blackmore (1825–1900; *ODNB*), novelist (*Lorna Doone*, 1869) and fruit farmer. Thomas Hardy (1840–1928; *ODNB*), novelist and poet. Both, like William Barnes, featured local dialect in their texts. Marian Evans [pseud. George Eliot] (1819–80; *ODNB*), novelist and scholar, lived with George Henry Lewes (1817–78; *ODNB*) from 1853 until his death, and married John Walton Cross (1840–1920) in 1880.

[20] *Sappho's Ode to Aphrodite* (barred as for Dorian Rhythm).

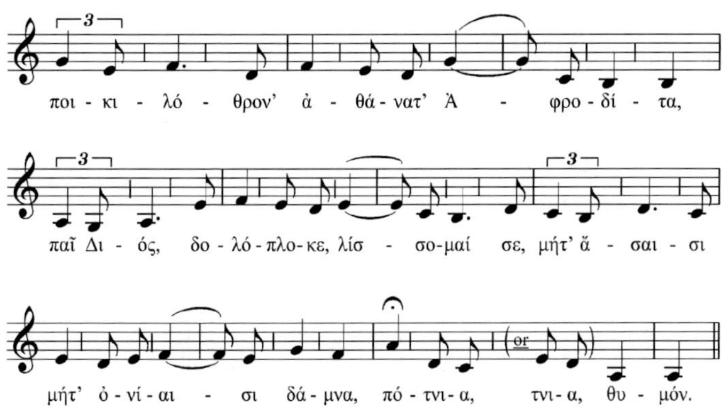

[21] Name cut out by RB.

[22] Name cut out by RB; see letter of 11 May 1883.

[23] Robert Ornsby (1820–89), 1st Lit. Hum. 1840, fellow of Trinity College, Oxford; converted to Catholicism 1847; helped to edit *The Tablet*; Professor of Greek and Latin Literature at the Catholic University, Dublin 1854. After a period as private tutor to the future Duke of Norfolk, with whom he travelled in southern and eastern Europe, he returned to the Catholic University in 1874; became Fellow in Classics at the Royal University of Ireland and examiner in Greek in 1882. He published a life of St Francis (1856), an annotated edition of the Greek Testament (1860), and two volumes of *Memoirs of Robert Hope-Scott, QC* (1884).

[24] See *CW* vi and vii.

[25] Hephaistion, a grammarian of Alexandria of the 2nd c. AD, wrote a manual on Greek metres, the only complete one to survive. Rudolf Westphal edited a text in *Scriptores metrici Graeci* in 1866.

[26] Stephen Joseph Perry, SJ (1833–89; *ODNB*), who observed several transits and solar eclipses, and caught dysentery while photographing the eclipsed sun of Dec. 1889 in a French convict settlement off Guiana.

[27] The Mistress of Arts was Letitia A. Walkington, who had prepared for the MA examination by 'Private tuition' rather than attending one of the colleges of the Royal University.

[28] 'To get the Gulf' was Oxford university slang for failing to get honours but to get a pass degree.

[29] If this review were written, it was not published.

29 October 1886 to Robert Bridges (Postcard)

LRB, no. *CXXXIX, p. 241 Bodleian, Dep. Bridges, vol. 92, fo. 111[r–v]
Postcard addressed to 'Robert Bridges Esq. | Yattendon | Newbury | England Berks'. PM DUBLIN 3 9 1 OC 29 86 186

University College, Stephen's Green, Dublin. Oct. 29 '86.

I send those two pieces. Of Who is Sylvia?[1] observe that it is not as I wish it done, for the accompaniment to the second verse ^should be^ ~~as~~ quite different from that to the first, but as it was necessary to simplify it for that performance which miscarried. But ~~as~~ ^since^ the true version wd. need recopying ~~it~~ I send this one just as it went to the nonperformers. G. M. H.

[1] The postcard accompanied the setting of 'Who is Sylvia', for which two melodies and several accompaniments are extant. See *J&P*, 492–3, *CW* vi, and letter to his mother of 11 June 1886. The other of the two pieces is probably the music to Sappho's ode to Aphrodite, but might also be a setting of poems by Barnes (not extant), since both were promised in the letter to RB of 28 Oct. 1886.

30 October[?] 1886[?] from Sir Robert Stewart to GMH

FL, no. I3, pp. 428–9 Campion Hall, S/4
No envelope, date or address.

D[r] Father! I have not forgotten your Theses,[1] but I have not had the time to look at them till now (30th). Last night I ^tired &^ went to bed (!) 10/40, but had to get up, dress(!) & go down to work, & sat up till 3 am! Today (God forgive me!) I had also to see to printers! I mark all I dislike, you are very much improved, I rejoice to say. Dont choose a tune again with long skips, rather read your definition of the essence of a C.F.[2] Avoid two difft scales—a cadence in G & a tune in F is bad; don't separate Alto & Tenor: This is bad

Gaps — rests of 2 bars are an error — as in No. 5. Keep Chappell[3] till you are done with him. I'll look up those Naumann Numbers[4] for you.

3 — Why didn't you come hear Haydn's work? It is very fine C^pt altho' too free for modern taste (nello stilo Palestrina) {*in the style of Palestrina*} a renaissance of stiff rules like the Cecilian Music School.

Ever yours truly
R P S

Can you play Pfte[5] at all? If so get Bach's 48 P & F,[6] they are "A 1 at Lloyds"[7] — If you were my son instead of my Father I could give you no better advice than to study & play this truly incomp^ble work!

[1] See *CW* vi. Stewart was looking at GMH's exercises in music. See letter to RB of 4 Oct. 1886: 'Talking of counterpoint, good Sir Robert Stewart of this city has offered to correct me exercises in it if I wd. send some: I have sent one batch.'

[2] *Canto Fermo*.

[3] Perhaps a *History of Music* (one vol. only, 1874), by William Chappell (1809–88), or another of his editions.

[4] Probably some piece(s) by the prolific Johann Gottlieb Naumann (1741–1801).

[5] Pianoforte.

[6] *Preludes and Fugues* (the Well-Tempered Clavier, 2 vols.).

[7] Classified as a vessel of the best standard of maintenance in Lloyd's Register of Shipping; thus 'of the highest quality'.

31 October 1886 to Robert Bridges

LRB, no. CXL, p. 242 Bodleian, Dep. Bridges, vol. 92, fo. 112^r–v

In all things beautiful, I cannot see[1]
(first draught)

Nempe ea formosa est: Adeo omne quod aut facit aut fit
Cynthia continuo fomes amoris adest.
Stat, sedet, incedit: quantum^st^ ~~haec est~~ ^modo^ pulchra quod instat,
Haec modo res! sequitur pulchrior illa tamen.

Nec mora nec modus est: nam quod mihi saepe negavi
  Suavius illam unquam posse placere placet.
Quid? tacet. At taceat. Jam vera fatebor:[2] ut illud,
  Ut vincit vestros, musa, tacere choros!
Si quis in ulla volet perpellere verba silentem
  Vexet marmoreos improbus ille deos.
Hunc in Olympiaca post tot fore saecla sereno
  Intempestivum non pudet aede Jovi.

<Here follow the first three lines of the sextet, which I do not correctly remember: please send me them.>

Postremo si qui~~s~~a jam de re disputat, his et
  Ipsa velit Virtus dicere et ipsa Fides;
Aurea non alio sunt saecula more locuta;
  Astraeam his usam vocibus esse reor.

They are not satisfactory, I feel.

I want you to tell me about Gosse. I am concerned about him. You know of course of the attack made on him in the current Quarterly and I hope he will be ~~ma~~ able to make a good defence in the main, but I have not yet seen the article myself.[3] Gerard Hopkins. University College, Dublin. Oct. 31 1886. You need not in writing join issue about Stevenson any more: instead of that you can read a book or two more of his and ripen a while.

In the above the line "'Tis joy the folding of her robe <?> to view" does not appear. I can expand it into a couplet, but you know I have always felt that to be the weak line in a masterpiece and have wished for something like

'Tis joy to watch her folds fall where they do,
And all that comes is past expectancy.[4]

And here I take the opportunity of renewing my protest against the first line of Prometheus. Nothing can reconcile me to "domeless". You yourself never offered any defence or explanation of it. It has two independent faults, either of which would condemn it: courts are unco~~n~~vered spaces in their nature; all then are roofless, a fortiori domeless; so that the word is without point. And next domes were not used by the Greeks, the keepings of whose art and architecture you are to keep to: so then again of course the buildings of Olympus, let alone the courts, are domeless. And there remains an infelicity still. For when anything, as a court, is uncovered and roofless strictly speaking, ~~it~~ a dome is just the one kind of roof it may ^still^ be said to have and especially in a clear sky and on a mountain, namely the spherical vault or dome of heaven. What can you say?

P.S. And I may even add that domeless is a heavy sink-rhythm word there. You want a lifting word — aerial.[5]

[1] *Growth of Love*, Daniel Press Edition (1889), 32: final form, *P.W.*, i. 31.

[2] MS 'fabebor'.

[3] A prolonged bludgeoning of Gosse's lapses from scholarship, an unsigned article by Churton Collins entitled 'English Literature at the Universities', which runs to forty pages and pulverizes *From Shakespeare to Pope: An Inquiry into the Causes and Phenomena of the Rise of Classical Poetry in England* (1885), the book form of the Clark lectures Gosse had delivered at Cambridge. Its violence produced a reaction: irony would have been a better weapon. See also 'Our Literary Guides' in *Ephemera Critica, or Plain Truths about Current Literature*, by John Churton Collins (1901).

[4] These lines have been in question before; they ran originally:

'Tis joy the foldings of her dress to view,
And all she doth is past expectancy.

The final form is:

'Tis joy to watch the folds fall as they do,
And all that comes is past expectancy.

[5] See letter to RB 04.11.1882: finally 'aetherial' was used.

6 November 1886 from Katharine Tynan[1] to GMH

FL, no. J1, p. 430 Campion Hall, Misc. Tynan

Addressed to 'Rev. Gerard Hopkins, S.J. | University College, | Stephen's Green, | Dublin'. PM DUBLIN NO 7 86.

Whitehall, | Clondalkin. | Nov. 6th. 1886.

Dear Father Hopkins,

The books came safely this morning. You are abundantly generous in giving me three books instead of one; I suppose I have all Mr Bridges' work now.[2] I wish you had written in them; it would have given them double value in my eyes, but some day perhaps you will do that too for me. I have had only time to peep into Eros and Psyche but I can see from that glimpse that it is very fine. Thank you so much for the beautiful gift.

I wonder how you and Mr Yeats finished the discussion on finish or non-finish. I hope you like Mr Yeats, because I like him so much and think him so true an artist.

It has been a real pleasure to me to meet you; I hope I may have that pleasure again.

With kindest regard, and thanks,
I am, dear Father Hopkins,
Ever sincerely yours
Katharine Tynan
Rev. Gerard Hopkins. S.J.

[1] Katharine Tynan (Mrs Hinkson, 1859–1931; *ODNB*). See Biographical Register.
[2] See card of 28 Nov. 1886 and letter of 11 Dec. 1886 to RB.

7 November [1886] to Coventry Patmore

FL, no. CLXXXIII, p. 372 Durham

Nov. 7. 1886. University College, Stephen's Green, Dublin.

My dear Mr. Patmore, — Your pamphlet must, I think, have miscarried: the name How I managed my Estate or to that effect is familiar but I believe from a review in the Academy. It is like a dream to me that I saw such a pamphlet lying about, but at any rate I did not recognise it as belonging to me, much less read it. And therefore I shd. be glad if you wd. be so kind as to send another copy.

The long letter I spoke of was cancelled, as it often happens to me to cancel letters and it would be better if it happened oftener still; best of all would be never to write anything that could need cancelling.

I seem to have been among odds and ends of poets and poetesses of late. One poetess was Miss Kate Tynan,[1] who lately published a volume of chiefly devotional poems, highly spoken of by reviews. She is a simpele bright-looking Biddy with glossy very pretty red hair, a farmer's daughter in the County Dublin. She knows and deeply admires your Muse and said this, which appears in some way noteworthy — complaining that you are sometimes austere or bare or something like that: 'How is it, Fr. Hopkins, that however bare it is it is always poetry?' I am at present Bridges' Muse-broker and had to send Miss Tynan an invoice of him. I am to read Miss Tynan herself when she comes, that is, as many pages as she has walked ~~up~~ ^to^ and ~~do~~ fro over — to say of her what one might say of any writer. Then there is a young Mr. Yeats[2] who has written in a Trinity College publication some striking verses and who has been perhaps unduly pushed by the late Sir Samuel Ferguson[3] (I do not know if you have read or heard of him: he was a learned antiquary, a Protestant but once an ally of Thomas Davis and the Young Ireland Party, but he withdrew from them and even suppressed ~~p~~some of his best poems for fear they, or he, shd. be claimed by the Nationalists of later days; for he was a poet; the Forging of the Anchor is, I believe, his most famous poem; he was a poet as the Irish are — to judge by the little of his I have seen — full of feeling, high thoughts, flow~~ing~~ ^of^ verse, ~~often~~ point, often fine imagery and other virtues, but the essential and ~~oft~~only lasting thing left out — what I call inscape, that is species or individually-distinctive ~~style~~ beauty of style: on this point I believe we quite agree, as on most: but this is a serious parenthesis). I called on his, young Yeats's, father by desire lately; he is a ~~pan~~painter; and with some emphasis of manner he presented me with Mosada: a Dramatic Poem by W. B. Yeats,[4] with a portrait of the author by J. B. Yeats,[5] himself; the young man having ~~striking~~ finely cut intellectual features and his father being a fine draughtsman. For a young man's pamphlet this was something too much; but you will understand a father's feeling. Now this Mosada I cannot think highly of, but I was happily not required then to praise what presumably I had not then read, and ~~happily~~ I had read and could praise another piece. It was a strained and unworkable allegory about a young man and a sphinx on a rock in the sea (how did they get there? what did they eat? and so on: people think such criticisms very prosaic; but commonsense is never out of place anywhere, neither on Parnassus nor on Tabor nor on the Mount where our Lord preached;[6] and, not to quote Christ's parables all taken from real life but in the frankly impossible, as in the Tempest, with what consummate and penetrating imagination is Ariel's 'spiriting' put before us! all that le~~a~~d~~s~~ up and that must follow the scenes ~~before yo~~ in the play is realised and suggested and you cannot lay your finger on the point where it breaks down), but still containing fine lines and vivid imagery.

I find that Miss Tynan has a great admirer in Lord Lytton who writes to her at length and has invited her to visit him.

By the bye I saw a letter of yours to the Times written as a rally against Mr. Gladstone, not however proposing any alternative policy.

This is a foolish letter of gossip, I must bring it to an end. Since I returned from Wales I have been in better health than usual, ~~more~~ fitter for work; and very much better spirits. And I am hoping to write (if not this year a book, yet) this year a paper for the Society of Hellenic Studies, to which I belong, (or some other quarter) on the Dorian Measure,[7] the true scansion of perhaps half or more than half of the

Greek and Latin lyric verse: I do believe it is a great and it is an unsuspected discovery. Give my kind regards to your circle and believe me your sincere friend Gerard Hopkins, S.J.

[1] See previous letter.

[2] Most of what was published in the *Dublin University Review* in 1885 and 1886 was reprinted in *The Wanderings of Oisin* (1889).

[3] Ferguson (1810–86) took his degree at Trinity College Dublin, and became keeper of the records of Ireland. His most important historical work was *Ogham Inscriptions in Ireland, Wales, and Scotland* (published posthumously 1887). He also wrote poems on Irish mythological and historical characters.

[4] His first separate publication. *Mosada* originally appeared in *The Dublin University Review* for June, 1886.

[5] John Butler Yeats, RHA (1839–1922).

[6] Three mountains: Parnassus in central Greece, sacred to Apollo, and the home of the Muses; Mount Tabor, a hill in Israel near Nazareth believed by many to be the site of the Transfiguration of Christ; and the location of the Sermon on the Mount.

[7] Neither paper nor book was printed, though GMH wrote a good deal of it but never completed it. Further moments in this long and unfinished work can be found in letters 18–19 Oct. 1882 to RB, 14 Jan. 1883 to AMWB, 2–4, 21–2, and 28 Oct. 1886 to RB, 11 Dec. 1886 to RB, 23 Dec. 1886 to AMWB, 20 Jan. 1887 to Patmore, 1 May and 30 July 1887 to RB.

10 November 1886 from Coventry Patmore to GMH

FL, no. CLXXXIII A, p. 375 Campion Hall, P 10/11/86
Addressed to 'Rev[d] Gerard Hopkins, S.J. | University College | Stephen's Green, | Dublin'. PM HASTINGS NO 10 86, H&K PACKET NO 11 86.

Hastings. Nov. 10. 1886
My dear M[r] Hopkins,

I am always raised in spirits by the sight of your handwriting, and I thank you much for sometimes sending me such full & lively letters in reply to my brief & dull ones. But my brain is very sluggish, and is becoming more & more so.

I have told Bell[1] to send you another copy of the St. James's articles. I am still writing for that Journal as hard as I can, i.e. at the average rate of two articles a week.[2] The Editor[3] has taken a fancy to my writing and lets me say what I like — allowing me to say & still oftener to hint things a good deal above the religious level of modern journalism. And I [*illegible word*] believe that this is all the good that is now left for me to do, in the way of writing.

Your friend Miss Tynan's criticism was striking. I hope it's true that it is poetry even when bare.

I have just come home from a visit to Cambridge, where I find that everybody knows and a good many like my poetry. I confess, however, that I am very glad to live in a place where I am only looked up to because I live in a big house. In that simple sort of flattery I do not feel that there is any danger.

I think I remember to have read "The Forging of the Anchor"[4] & to have been struck by it. I am amused by your account of his literary "mise en scène".

You have Coleridge's authority for requiring good-sense in every kind of poetry. "A palace" he says "should at least be a house." [5]

I look forward to reading about your metrical discovery. I dare say I shall be able to understand it partially, though I dont know Greek.

Piffie is more and more engrossingly charming. He is stronger than when you were here, but as Raffaelesque as ever, and as much absorbed by flowers.

Your's ever truly

C. Patmore.

You need not return the inclosed.[6]

[1] George Bell, publisher of the volume.

[2] Patmore's connection with the *St James's Gazette* lasted until 10 Aug. 1888. See Appendix II, pp. 208–11, of Frederick Page, *Patmore: A Study in Poetry* (London, 1933).

[3] See the letter from Patmore to RB of 12 Aug. 1889 below, for Patmore's praise of Greenwood.

[4] See previous letter.

[5] *Specimens of the Table Talk of S. T. Coleridge* (1835) by Henry N. Coleridge contains the entry for 9 May 1830: 'Poetry is certainly something more than good sense, but it must be good sense at all events; just as a palace is more than a house, but it must be a house, at least.'

[6] There is no enclosure.

14 November 1886 to Katharine Tynan

Published in *Studies: An Irish Quarterly Review*, 63/252 (Winter 1974), 389–96, ed. David J. DeLaura, and in *The Month*, NS 19/5 (May 1958), 266–7 HRHRC, Container 1.5

UNIVERSITY COLLEGE, | ST STEPHEN'S GREEN, | DUBLIN. [*printed heading*]

Nov. 14 1886

My dear Miss Tynan, — This is to tell you that Bridges has published some other things besides those you have,[1] namely a set of Sonnets called The Growth of Love and some lyrics and miscellaneous pieces. These were published in pamphlet form, not even sent to the reviews, and are now withdrawn or not to be had: some were printed at Mr. Daniel's fancy press.[2] They will no doubt be republished in due time and then, I hope, you will read them, for he has done nothing better. Some of the sonnets are as beautiful as anything of that kind in English next to Shakespeare and Milton. I wd. send you one sample,[3] the best perhaps of all, but I cannot remember it in one place, and having asked Bridges to send me the missing lines, for I am turning it into Latin, I have had no ~~a~~ answer yet. Some of the short lyrics have the exquisiteness of Herrick[4] and more of earnest feeling. I send one favourite.[5]

Fr. Russell has not hitherto sent either your poems or his own.[6]

I am, my dear Miss Tynan, yours very truly Gerard M. Hopkins S.J.

Song

Thou didst delight my eyes.
Yet who am I? Nor first
Nor last nor best that durst
Once dream of thee for prize;
Nor this the only time
Thou shalt set love to rhyme.

Thou didst delight my ear.
Ah, little praise! Thy voice
Made other ears rejoice,
Makes all hearts glad that hear;
And short my joy; but yet,
O song, do not forget.

For what wert thou to me
How shall I say? The moon
That shed her midnight noon
Across his wrecking sea;
A sail that for a day
Hath cheered the castaway.

Robert Bridges

[1] The three books for which Katharine Tynan had thanked GMH on 6 Nov. were *Prometheus the Firegiver* (Daniel Press, Oxford, 1883), *Nero*, Pt. I (1885), and *Eros and Psyche* (1885). *The Growth of Love*, A Poem in Twenty-four Sonnets (1876), was reviewed with high praise in the *Academy*, 17 June 1876, as an "unobtrusive pamphlet",

but otherwise passed unnoticed. RB's other anonymous pamphlets were: (i) *Poems*, 1873 (suppressed by the author); (ii) *Carmen Elegiacum de Nosocomio Sti. Bartolomaei Londiniensi*, 1876; (iii) *Poems by the Author of the Growth of Love*, First Series (2nd edn.), 1880; Second Series, 1879; Third Series, 1880.

[2] H. V. O. Daniel (1836–1919; later Provost of Worcester College; *ODNB*) included seventeen poems from the three series cited above in his *Poems* by Robert Bridges (Daniel Press, 1884). The remainder of the twenty-four shorter poems, selected by RB, came from a Fourth Series, written *c.*1882, but not published before. Most of these were included in *Shorter Poems* (1890).

[3] "In all things beautiful, I cannot see" (No. V, 'Love Strengthened', in *The Growth of Love*, 1876); final form, *Poetical Works* (1898), no. 31. GMH had sent RB the first draft of his Latin version on 31 Oct. 1886 and asked him to send the lines he had forgotten (9–11); but there is no evidence that he did so, before arranging for the new Daniel Press edition (1889) to be sent to GMH in May 1889 (see RB's letter of 18 May 1889).

[4] Robert Herrick (1591–1674; *ODNB*), a master of the graceful, playful lyric.

[5] The song "Thou didst delight my eyes", first published in *Poems*, Third Series (1880), no. II. The copy enclosed with the letter is almost identical with the new version in *Poetical Works*, ii (1899), 106, incorporating the major change in ll. 2–4 made as a result of GMH's criticism (letter of 1 Feb. 1882), but has these variants: 'made' for 'make' in l. 9; transposition of 'hearts' and 'ears' in ll. 9 and 10; and 'shed' for 'poured' in l. 15.

[6] Fr Russell had published two books of religious verse in 1880: *Emmanuel* and *Madonna*. Selections from these were reprinted in his *Idylls of Killowen* (1899) and *Vespers and Compline* (1900).

26 November 1886 to Robert Bridges

LRB, no. CXLI, p. 244 Bodleian, Dep. Bridges, vol. 92, fos. 113–114v

UNIVERSITY COLLEGE, | ST STEPHEN'S GREEN, | DUBLIN. [*printed heading*]
Nov. 26 1886

Dearest Bridges, — Act promptly on the following, though promptitude, I am aware, withers ~~i~~on Berkshire soil.

Miss Taylor of 1 Sandford Parade, Ranelagh, Dublin, last year took her degree of Bachelor of Music at the Royal University: her diploma piece, a Magnificat, was then performed and sounded learned and melodious. I was introduced to her and call on her; ~~I~~ ^she^ lend^s^ me Blow[1] and I lend her Purcell. She is a nice unassuming girl. She is now going to take her Doctor's degree and consulted me on the subject ^matter^ of the ~~piece~~ diploma work. On consideration I saw I cd. kill two birds, a dove and an eagle, with one stone. I have advised the Elegy on one whom grief for the loss of her beloved killed. I added what could interest her, and she warmly welcomed the proposal. (Objections on your part, if any, are now too late and will be "taken as read".) I want you to send her the text ~~or~~; if necessary, even copied in MS: it is not too much to ask, the circumstances considered. You will appear to full orchestral accompaniment.

I have been disposing of Bridges' works as I thought best. I have a Prometheus and a Nero left and am minded to bestow them on Professor Dowden.[2]

I have improved the Latin of "~~i~~^I^n all things beautiful". I asked you to send me three missing lines and you have not done so.

My marketing of your books brought in admiration everywhere; but publicity, fame, notoriety, and an American sale are ~~wanting~~ wanted. I enclose the gentle poetess Miss Tynan's second letter.[3]

I have at last ~~ended~~ ^completed^ but not quite finished the longest sonnet ever made and no doubt the longest making.[4] It is in 8-foot lines and essays effects almost musical. Otherwise I am recovering from the effects of my Welsh holiday and returning to helplessness. Your affectionate friend Gerard Hopkins.

Sputters of poetry by Michael Field appear now in every week's Academy, vastly clever, pointed, and flowing, but serving in the end to shew Coventry Patmore was right in his opinion[5] of woma~~a~~^e^n's poetry.

[1] John Blow (1649–1708; *ODNB*), the eminent composer of church music, overshadowed by his pupil Purcell.

[2] Edward Dowden (1843–1913; *ODNB*), a graduate of Trinity College Dublin in 1863, became Professor of English Literature at Trinity in 1867. He published on Shakespeare and other poets, but his largest work, and the one he was working on while GMH was in Dublin, was his biography of Shelley (2 vols., 1886). He was an outspoken critic of Home Rule and might well have found GMH congenial had he known him better. But see letter of 11 Dec. 1886, n. 8.

[3] The letter of 6 Nov. 1886.

[4] 'Spelt from Sibyl's Leaves' (undated in 'MS A').

[5] These views can best be gathered from the essay called *Mrs. Meynell* (*Fortnightly Review*, Dec. 1892; reprinted in *Religio Poetae, etc.*, 1893; and in *Principle in Art, etc.*, 1907).

28 November 1886 to Robert Bridges

LRB, no. CXLII, p. 245 Bodleian, Dep. Bridges, vol. 92, fo. 115r–v
Postcard addressed to 'Robert Bridges Esq. | Yattendon | Newbury | England Berks.' PM DUBLIN 20 NO 28 86 186

University College, Stephen's Green, Dublin. Nov. 28 '86.

Did you get from Mr. Cummings the Prospectus of the Purcell Society?[1] And do you belong?

Books all disposed of thus: (1) Mr. Tyrrell all; (2) Miss Tynan all; (3) a young Mr. Gregg, sometime my pupil, <u>E. and P.</u>; (4) Prof. Dowden the other two. G. M. H.

[1] W. H. Cummings edited many of Purcell's works and wrote a life of him that GMH read and recommended to RB. See letter to RB of 1–8 Sept. 1885.

11 December 1886 to Robert Bridges

LRB, no. CXLIII, p. 245 Bodleian, Dep. Bridges, vol. 92, fos. 116–119v

UNIVERSITY COLLEGE, | S<u>T</u> STEPHEN'S GREEN, | DUBLIN. [*printed heading*]

~~Nov.~~ ^Dec.^ 11 1886

Dearest Bridges, — Miss Taylor is full of gratitude to you for the book and of admiration at you for the poems. 'She is dreadfully afraid though that she will ~~be~~ not be able to write anything that will do the Elegy the barest justice.' Thereupon she does me the honour of asking my advice on the allotment of ~~it in~~ ^the^ numbers. Having lights I communicated them, they agreed with her own, and the work is now in hand. In the course of examining the ~~work~~ poem for this purpose I was more than ever convinced of its extreme and classical beauty. I think however the line "The pale indifferent ghosts wander and catch" etc[1] has a somewhat modern and vulgar <u>prétiosité</u>[2] in the rhythm ^etc^. It irks me to think that my own ~~poe~~ lines are faulty in this way and, if one, almost all, ~~every one,~~ I am afraid. We agreed to leave out the second verse. There is no doubt that it is a splendid subject.

I mean to enclose my long sonnet, the longest, I still say, ever made;[3] longest by its own proper length, namely by the length of its lines; for anything can be made long by eking, by tacking, by trains, ~~tack~~ tails, and flounces. I shd. be glad however if you wd. explain what a coda is and how employed. Perhaps I shall enclose other sonnets. Of this long sonnet above all remember what applies to all my verse, that it is, as living art~~,~~ should be, made for performance and that its performance is not reading with the eye but loud, leisurely, poetical (not rhetorical) recitation, with long ~~pauses~~ ^rests^, long dwells on the rhyme and other marked syllables, and so on. This sonnet shd. be almost sung: it is most carefully timed in tempo rubato.

In sending the music to Wooldridge there was of course no harm done, but it is not worth his while (and so, with other things, I am telling him; but please card me his initials, for otherwise I cannot address the letter; or else I shall enclose it): Who is Sylvia? is tuneful (I hope) only, not experimental (at least as I sent it) and, what is more, not strict nor correct. The other piece is experimental, but it is slight.

My book on the Dorian ~~Rh~~ Measure is going on,[4] but may ~~easly~~ easily either wreck (by external difficulties, examinations and other ones) or founder (of its own). For in fact it needs mathematics, but how can I make them up? Yet I hope, I do hope, to get out something: ~~its~~ ^my^ purpose is, in explaining the Dorian Measure, to bring in the most fundamental principles of art, to write almost a philosophy of art~~,~~ ^and^ illustrat~~inge~~ ~~it~~ ^that^ by the Dorian Measure. If I shd. be able to publish one edition I cd. in a second ^edition^ or in a second volume add much more. I propose to print the Greek in ~~Engli~~ ^Ro^man type, so that no scholarship shall be required, only study (which must be close) of the book, for it will be thoroughgoing.

Why shd. you leave Yattendon? Do not leave it. Listen to what the wise say. *Σπάρτην ἔλαχες, ταύτην κόσμει* {*Sparta is your portion; do your best for her*}.[5] And A Kempis says Imaginatio locorum et mutatio fefellit multos {*the idea that we make of places and the desire to change them has deceived many*}.[6]

I am sorry for poor Lang, if his dejection is so deep as you describe (only that, since you speak of me, I may say that I must conceal myself or it, which it seems he does neither of). But I cannot think the political danger so great. In the meantime he writes very amusing verses in the Saturday, if those are his;[7] but we know people can joke in the deepest gloom. I sometimes think Lang may be the writer too of some articles dealing with Ireland. If so I wish he could find it in him to speak ~~with~~ more gently and with more sympathy, as they call it, I mean the other-man's-point-of-viewishness. The Saturday does sneer, and a sneer drives the Irish to madness. (They continually do it with all their might themselves and do not even know they are doing it, do not understand what you have to complain of and so on.)

I am your affectionate friend Gerard M. Hopkins S.J.

Mr. Tyrrell expresses his deep admiration of your muse, his conversion, so to speak. So too young Mr. Gregg. So too Miss Tynan. But perhaps these two are "fry". But ~~Pro~~ Mr. Dowden I have not heard from. I told him not to acknowledge the books, but I also told him to read them and I by no means told him when he had ~~done~~ ^read^ them not to write to you and thank you.[8]

I send tonight only one sonnet.[9]

[1] The last stanza of the *Elegy* (*P.W.*, ii, book i, 14).

[2] Perhaps Latin influenced this unusual but not unknown spelling of *préciosité*, or affectation.

[3] 'Spelt from Sibyl's Leaves'.

[4] A further stage in the sad history of his unfinished projects. See letter to Patmore of 7 Nov., n. 7.

[5] Euripides, fragment 722 (Nauck). The correct reading is *κείνην* for *ταύτην*, but the proverb is usually found with the Doric form *ταύταν*, which is how Cicero quotes it (*ad Atticum* 4. 6. 2). The Latin translation is also often found: 'Spartam nactus es; hanc orna' {*Sparta is your portion; do your best for her*}.

[6] i.e. the grass is greener on the other side of the fence. In *De Imitatione Christi*, 1. 9. 6.

[7] Humorous verses, political in bent, not characteristic of Lang.

[8] The matter did not end here. Dowden's article, 'The Poetry of Robert Bridges' (*Fortnightly Review*, July 1894), begins thus: 'Father Gerard Hopkins, an English priest of the Society of Jesus, died young, and one of his good deeds remains to the present time unrecorded. We were strangers to each other, and might have been friends. I took for granted that he belonged to the other camp in Irish politics . . . Father Hopkins was a lover of literature, and himself a poet. Perhaps he did in many quarters missionary work on behalf of the poetry of his favourite, Robert Bridges. He certainly left, a good many years since, at my door two volumes by Mr. Bridges, and with them a note begging that I would make no acknowledgement of the gift. I did not acknowledge it then; but, with sorrow for a fine spirit lost, I acknowledge it now.'

[9] i.e. 'Spelt from Sibyl's Leaves', as mentioned above.

23 December 1886 to Alexander William Mowbray Baillie

FL, no. CLVI, p. 274 UCD L 65

UNIVERSITY COLLEGE, | ST. STEPHEN'S GREEN, | DUBLIN. [*printed heading*]
Dec. 23 '86

Dearest Baillie, — This is to renew communications and to wish you a very merry ~~X~~ ^Christ^mas and happy New Year and to tell you that I have made by letter the acquaintance of D'Arcy Thom^p^son,[1] to whom I introduced myself by you. (I addressed him sadly: Darcy, not D'Arcy; Thomson, not Thompson.) Mr. Davies of the Queen's College, Galway, having res~~e~~igned his Fellowship at the Royal University, D'Arcy Thompson of the same College was elected in his place and I wrote on ^University^ business. We shall meet of course in the summer. He says it is many years since he saw you, but he has later than that met and dined with Pearson,[2] who was your class fellow. He says you were seven years running head of your class at his school.[3]

Maspero is soon to bring out something new about Egypt. Egypt is off with me just now and very serious work ~~on~~ ^touching^ Pindar and the theory of rhythm and the "Dorian Measure" is on, but I cannot do what I would for want of mathematics. Our College is at a crisis to end or mend. I am your affectionate friend Gerard M. Hopkins S.J.

[1] D'Arcy Wentworth Thompson (1829–1902; *ODNB*). After graduating (Pembroke College, Cambridge) in 1852, he became classical master at Edinburgh Academy where he taught till 1863, while Baillie and Robert Louis Stevenson were students there. He left to become professor of Greek at Queen's College, Galway, where he died. He is now perhaps best known for his *Day Dreams of a Schoolmaster* and his rhymes for children.

[2] Sir Charles Pearson, Lord Pearson (1843–1910; *ODNB*), lawyer and judge. See letter of 7 Sept. 1887.

[3] Edinburgh Academy, where Baillie was head of his class right through the school.

23 December [1886] from Sir Robert Stewart to GMH

FL, no. I 4, p. 429 Campion Hall, Stewart 2
No envelope, year, or address.

Dear Father Hopkins, I mark alphabetical references to y^{r} work (a) it is not according to rule to begin y^{r} Counterpoint on the 5th when your C. F. is above it (read Bridge)[1] I see a doubtful tonality as the result, for the key of C is not established for 4 bars. The 4th and all diminished intervals are forbidden (see b) and we must neither quit or approach a discord "by Skip" (see c) at d you use augmented intervals  at "e" you use a diminished interval & quit it by a skip — at f the "implied harmony" is  and therefore the E (last crotchet only) is a discord, although being ^only^ a 6 to the bass, it ought not to be one, at "g" an augmented interval is found  at 'h' you skip to 4th! (8^{ve} jump). The skip of an 8^{ve} is little harm and as B says often gives vigour, but dont keep skipping sixths (see i) — at j you have 2 distinct chords (harmonies) in one bar which in this species, is illegal — at k false relations: why use flats at all, save ^for^ a simple modulation to F?

At l, I dont like yr Chromatics nor your $^{6}_{4}$ & skips — at m a diminished 4th is inadmissible, & of no force or power, omit <♭> and you improve it.

At 'n' don't pass into, and out of a note see Bridge. At o, six-four chord! Q^{y}? are your crotchets sung by the same class of voice as in 1 & 2? The alto is a soprano some bars. ^in^ this is nothing gained. I am going to London on Monday night to get rid of a bad cough.

Adieu, padre mio!
RS
23 Dec

[1] Sir (John) Frederick Bridge (1844–1924; *ODNB*), author of several of Novello's Music Primers on counterpoint, canon, and organ accompaniment, including *Counterpoint* (1878).

27 December 1886 from Katharine Tynan to GMH

FL, J2, pp. 430–1 Foley Centre Bischoff Collection at Gonzaga, 25:44

Whitehall. | Clondalkin, | Dec 27th. 1886.
Dear Father Hopkins,[1]

I did not answer your last letter because I thought it would be kinder to a busy man like you to spare you a correspondence, and I was not sure that your courtesy would permit me to have the last word. Now I am writing to wish you tardily the compliments of the season, and also to say that I hope sometime to see you again. I enjoyed my one talk with you genuinely, and it would be a real pleasure to me if I thought I might hope for a repetition. Perhaps when the Spring makes my cottage lovely, you would come with Father Russell to see me? I know I am presuming on precious time, but nevertheless I dare.

I have taken a great fancy to the beautiful way in which Mr Bridges' books are bound. I should like my next book bound like his "Prometheus." I hope he and his are well. His work has given me real pleasure: it seems so very perfect of its kind.

I have seen a clever letter from that Mr Paravicini (of whom you spoke) in The Spectator; it was about Mr Shorthouse's "Sir Perceval".[2] Did you see it?

Mr Yeats has not yet returned; he seems to be getting a good deal to do in London, I am glad to say. I don't know if he has seen your brother.

I hope you may have found something to interest you in my book[3] — something of promise perhaps. I think now that it is coloured too much with other people's performance to have any of its own. It was handled with extreme kindness by the Press, as you will see from the enclosed booklet of reviews. Pray pardon my egotism in sending it.

Believe me, dear Father Hopkins,
with all kind regards and wishes,
Ever faithfully yours
Katharine Tynan.

[1] First published by Fr Matthew Russell, SJ, in 'Poets I have known', *Donahoe's Magazine* (Boston, Mass.), 48/4 (Apr. 1902), 401.

[2] The letter (in the issue of 13 Nov. 1886, p. 1526) was in fact from Frances de Paravicini, not Francis, and was titled '"Sir Percival" as an allegory'. It was a response to a review on pp. 1483–5 in the issue of 6 Nov. 1886 of *Sir Percival: A Story of the Past and of the Present* by Joseph Henry Shorthouse (Macmillan, 1886).

[3] Her first collection, *Louise de la Vallière and Other Poems* (1885).

1887

2 January 1887 to Robert Bridges

LRB, no. CXLIV, p. 248 Bodleian, Dep. Bridges, vol. 92, fos. 120–1

UNIVERSITY COLLEGE, | S^T^ STEPHEN'S GREEN, | DUBLIN. [*printed heading*]
Monasterevan,[1] Co. Kildare,
Jan. 2 1887.

Dearest Bridges, — It was (but first I wish you all a very happy new year) quite right to tell me what Wooldridge thought — ^that is what^ I wanted to know — and to use it as a dissuasive, if you liked; but not as a discouragement (yr. own word): discouragement is not what my complaint, in my opinion, needs. Our institute provides ^us^ means of discouragement, and on me at all events they have had all the effect that could be expected or wished and rather more. However Wooldridge and I are now in correspondence: he writes ^a^ very fine thoughtful letter. He has lately had from me a prodigious treatise of remarks and enquiries about the false fifth. Do you know what and where the false fifth is? If not, "blush and retire".

I am staying (till tomorrow morning, alas) with kind people at a nice place. I have had a bright light, and begun a poem in Gray's elegy metre, severe, no experiments.[2] I am pleased with it and hope you will be and also Mrs. Waterhouse, for I want her to see it. I therefore enclose ~~it~~ what there is of it and write no more now, but am your affectionate friend Gerard M. Hopkins S.J.

[1] GMH was visiting the Cassidys, to whom he had been introduced by Fr Delany. The Cassidys owned a distillery in Monasterevan, the town's chief employer. The family were Catholic but loyal to the British government and served as magistrates, insisting on adherence to British law. Mary, known as Miss Cassidy, and Eleanor, widow of Daniel O'Connell Wheble, then in their late fifties or early sixties, were the sisters of the current owner of the distillery, James Cassidy. The cousins whom GMH met there were relatives of Mrs Wheble's late husband. GMH's duties at Monasterevan were to say mass for the family and to assist at Sts Peter and Paul, the local Catholic church opened in 1847. See *WHI*, 114–19.

[2] 'On the Portrait of Two Beautiful Young People'. See also letters to RWD of 27–9 Jan. 1887, to RB of 29 Mar. 1887, from RWD of 7 July 1887, to RWD 22–3 Dec. 1887, to his mother of 25 Dec. 1887, to RWD of 29–30 July 1888.The portrait of Leo and Ursula Wheble is now housed at Gonzaga University (Gonzaga 12:41) and see *WHI*, 119 ff.

5 January 1887 to Robert Bridges

LRB, no. CXLV, p. 249 Bodleian, Dep. Bridges, vol. 92, fos. 122–3

UNIVERSITY COLLEGE, | S^T STEPHEN'S GREEN, | DUBLIN. [*printed heading*]
Jan. 5 1887

Dearest Bridges, — If you will more curiously consider you will see it was not exactly the word I complained of. I quoted the word.

In any case I must ^get to^ know something of counterpoint. ~~It~~ ^It^ ~~m~~ is the ~~most~~ ~~best~~ most scientific part of the science of ^one of^ the only two arts that have any science to speak of, music and architecture. And theoretically I have real lights upon it. Unhappily I can never have much literary knowledge, knowledge got from the texts of great masters.

The ~~imperfect~~ false ~~fith~~ fifth is not the imperfect fifth (though ^that is^ sometimes called so, but musical terminology is full of confusion): it is a fifth less than the true (which has the ratio $\frac{3}{2}$) by the interval called Didymus' comma.[1] The difference is not so small as might be thought and has sufficed, I am inclined to believe, twice over to work a slow but complete revolution in music, first between the Periclean and the Augustan ages, next between the early Middle Ages and the Renaissance or the present time. It occurs in our diatonic scale on ~~tu~~ truly tuned instruments between Re and La,[2] in the scale of C between D and A. Its incorrectness appears to me to make the First Mode, what Wooldridge, Rockstro[3] etc, call the Dorian, now inadmissable (if that is how the word should be spelt). I am your affectionate friend Gerard Hopkins.

[1] The *OED* describes 'the comma of Didymus or common comma, which is the difference between four perfect fifths, and two octaves and a major third, from a given note (ratio 80: 81)'.

[2] GMH refers to equal temperament. In the Middle Ages and Renaissance the fifths would be pure in Pythagorean intonation except on keyboard instruments, which were in meantone temperament.

[3] William Smith Rockstro (1823–95; *ODNB*), an important influence in the musical life of his day as teacher and writer, and an instigator of the study of modal music. He wrote well-known textbooks on harmony (1881) and counterpoint (1882), and was the 'first authority of his time in England' on ancient music. He became a Roman Catholic in 1876.

20 January 1887 to Coventry Patmore

FL, no. CLXXXIV, p. 376 Durham University Library, Abbott MS 199
One folded sheet of paper with watermark BROWN & NOLAN DUBLIN round a circle with monogram of B&N. Four sides.

UNIVERSITY COLLEGE, | S$^{\underline{\text{T}}}$ STEPHEN'S GREEN, | DUBLIN. [*printed heading*]
Jan. 20 1887

My dear Mr. Patmore, — I am ashamed of myself for not sooner writing to thank you both for the book (How I managed my Estate) and the paper in the St. James's.[1]

The book is interesting and instructive and would be more so still if I ~~were goin~~ ^had an^ estate myself.

The paper is probably clearer to me on the contrary than to those who may not have read your poems and so got the clue to your line of thought. Also it strikes me as written in the ~~manner~~ way of one who thinking long on one subject till ~~they are~~ ^it is^ very familiar to him does not communicate ~~his on it~~ with others and learn where it is dark to them. To him one word calls up a world of things, not so to them; he needs no long explanations, they do. It also gave me the impression of using up all a philosophy in ~~an~~ ^one^ article. It is well, ~~it~~ I believe, to have a kindness for that large class of people ~~who have~~ ^with^ plenty of intelligence and ~~who~~ plenty of moral teachableness who cannot take a hint but yet will follow, study, master, and put in practice a clear and patient explanation. It is the class I should like to [be] useful to. It has none of the knowing ^in it^ but many of the young.

I think I told you how I was writing ~~a~~ on the Dorian Measure, the first instalment of a work on Greek metre and metre in general. Coming to the point where I must go deep into scientific first principles I had a happy thought of ~~wri~~ putting my ideas for the purpose into the shape of a Paper to be read before a physical and mathematical science club which meets at the Royal Dublin Society once a month.[2] It struck me when ^I was^ present as a stranger at ~~a~~ ^one of its^ meetings to hear a paper by a colleague ~~, and they have given me leave to~~ who belongs to it.

I have asked and obtained leave to read my paper at the next meeting and have written most of it. Writing it has naturally cleared my mind and indeed opened out a sort of new world. I believe that I can now set ~~rhythm~~ metre and music both of them on a scientific footing which will be final like the law of gravitation. This is a great boast, God grant it may not be an empty one.

Though I may get to read my paper I fear I shall after that be unable for long to go on with my book.

With kind regards to all, I am, my dear Mr. Patmore, your sincere friend Gerard M. Hopkins, S.J.

[3]If I send you the paper after its hearing by the club shall you have leisure and will to read it?

"The only use of natural science"![4] It is a hard saying, who can hear it?

[1] 'Love and Poetry', *St James's Gazette*, 31 Dec. 1886.

[2] Abbott noted that he could trace neither club nor paper, but on pp. 450–1 of *FL* quotes from a letter from Professor E. Hughes Dowling, which says of a mathematical society in University College that 'it was mooted by J. H. Stewart but I think it never was really formed . . . Apropos of Father Hopkins I remember that Stewart invited him to one lecture at least of the Society known as the *Social* Science Club. . . . The lecture was interesting but Fr. Hopkins did not take much interest in things scientific. By the way I knew him rather well; he & I were students or practisers of "Loisette's" system of memory training, & had walks together to practise the art & to puzzle one another.' See GMH's letter to Patmore of 12 May 1887 for a report that 'I have now no paper on metre on hand but a good deal written of a sizeable book on that subject'.

[3] From here onwards is written above the address.

[4] 'Love and Poetry' (*Principle in Art, Religio Poetae, &c.* (1913), 336): 'The greatest and perhaps the only real use of Natural science is to supply similes and parables for poets and theologians.'

24 January 1887 to his Mother

FL, no. CIV, p. 178 Bodleian, MS Eng. lett. e. 41, fos. 108–110^{v}
Addressed to 'Mrs. Manley Hopkins | Court's Hill Lodge | Haslemere | Surrey | England'. PM DUBLIN JA 25 87 and HASLEMERE JA 26.

UNIVERSITY COLLEGE, | S$^{\underline{\mathrm{T}}}$ STEPHEN'S GREEN, | DUBLIN. [*printed heading*]
Jan. 24 '87

My dearest mother, — Your letter has just come and I will begin answering it now, as my evening pupil, a young Scotch Protestant, the

~~cleverest~~ ^best^ and brightest of all my pupils, who takes ~~the~~ ^a^ most visible pleasure in learning and being taught and whom ^therefore^ to teach is correspondingly a pleasure, does not tonight appear to be coming.

We had in Ireland little snow and no con~~i~~tinuance of frost, so little skating. But still I found the weather very trying, more than I ever did. Not that I took a cold, I never do to speak of in winter (I am too cold for it), but it exhausted me every morning and I felt as if kept on long it would kill me. One thing I am afraid it has done, ruined the good sight of my eyes and I shall have to get glasses. The focus is unchanged and objects at all distances as clear as ever, but they ache at any exertion. And any want of sleep makes havoc of them.

I had, in spite of the severe cold, some very pleasant days down at Monasterevan[1] in Co. Kildare at Xmas and again at New Year and it was a happy acquaintance to make, for they made no secret of liking me and want me to go down again.

Robertson, who is punctual, has not come and therefore will not come.

Was it you who recommended me to read the Trumpet Major?[2] Well I am reading it with pleasure.

With best love to all, I am your loving son Gerard.

[1] Where he stayed with Miss Cassidy; see letter to RB of 2 Jan. 1887 and to his mother of 25 Dec. 1887.

[2] By Thomas Hardy. First published in book form (three vols.) on 23 Oct. 1880.

27–9 January 1887 to Richard Watson Dixon

CRWD, no. XXXVIII, p. 149 Bodleian, Dep. Bridges, vol. 93, fos. 152–156^{v}
Addressed to 'Canon Dixon | Warkworth Vicarage | Acklington | Northumberland | England'. PM DUBLIN JA 29 87. Two folded sheets of different sizes with printed address.

UNIVERSITY COLLEGE, | S^{T} STEPHEN'S GREEN, | DUBLIN. [*printed heading*]
Jan. 27 '87

My dear Friend, — It is long since I heard from you. You sent me no more of your proofs; of which, if I could be of any use, I am sorry on the one hand and yet I own that in school time I can scarcely undertake anything.

The winter, though much less severe in Ireland than in England, ~~has left~~ tried me more than any yet; half killed me; and leaves me languishing. Especially it has attacked my eyes, but perhaps this effect will pass off. The weather is now of a summer mildness.

I have done some part of a book on Pindar's metres and Greek metres ^in general^ and metre in general and almost on art in general and wider still, but that I shall ever get far on with it or, if I ~~did~~ do, sail ~~over~~ ^through^ all the rocks and ~~quicksands~~ shoals that lie before me I scarcely dare to hope and yet I do greatly desire, since the thoughts are well worth preserving: ~~T~~ they are a solid foundation for criticism. What becomes of my verses I care little, but about things like this, what I write or could write on philosophical matters, I do; and the reason of the difference is that the verses stand or fall by their simple selves and, though by being read they might do good, by being unread they do no harm; but ~~about~~ if the other things are unsaid right they will be said by somebody else wrong, and that is what will not ~~re~~ let me rest.

I was at Xmas and New Year down with some kind people in Co. Kildare,[1] where I happened to see the portrait of two beautiful young persons, a brother and sister, living in the neighbourhood. It so much struck me that I began an elegy in Gray's metre,[2] but being back here I cannot go ^on^ with it. However I must see if I can enclose you a copy of the part done.

Have you heard of any great admirers of Mano or your other poems since Mano came out, by letter or otherwise? I set up a little Propaganda[3] for Bridges' muse here lately, distributing, with commendations, the copies he sent me; also I ^have^ got a lady to compose her Doctor^ate^-of-Music diploma work to his Elegy on a Lady whom Grief etc; and I tell people of you when I can put in a word. But it seems one can do little in this distracted globe and ^one^ is inclined to let things alone.

I have made the acquaintance of the young and ingenuous poetess Miss Kate Tynan,[4] a good creature and very graceful writer, highly and indeed somewhat too highly praised by a wonderful, perhaps alarming, unanimity of the critics; for the truth is she is not exactly an original "fountain ~~but~~ in a shady grove"[5] (the critics would not be standing all round her so soon if she were), but rather a sparkling townfountain in public gardens and draws her water from other sources. She half knows this herself and lately wrote me a letter which for various reasons I am slow to answer and as long as I do not I cannot help telling myself very barbarously that I have stopped her jaw at any rate.

Jan. 29 – Bridges says he has three works on hand. Like "Young Copperfield" (according to Steerforth), he is going it.[6]

Believe me your affectionate friend Gerard M. Hopkins S.J.

[1] The Cassidys, of Monasterevan.

[2] 'On the Portrait of Two Beautiful Young People'. See also letters to RB of 2 Jan. and 29 Mar. 1887, from RWD 7 July 1887, to RWD 22–3 Dec. 1887, to his mother 25 Dec. 1887, to RWD of 29–30 July 1888.

[3] A jocular reference to the Congregatio de Propaganda Fide.

[4] See letter of 6 Nov. 1886 and Biographical Register.

[5] Wordsworth's 'A Poet's Epitaph' has 'a fountain in a noonday grove' at l. 42.

[6] In ch. 6 of Dickens's *David Copperfield* (1849–50), where Steerforth advises on the lavish spending of all of David's money.

6 February 1887 to his Mother

FL, no. CV, p. 179 Bodleian, MS Eng. lett. e. 41, fos. 111–112v

UNIVERSITY COLLEGE, ST STEPHEN'S GREEN, DUBLIN. [*printed heading*]
Feb. 6 '87

My dearest mother, — I wished I had never written that silly letter about the people at Monasterevan liking me: it reminds me of Mr. Durdles (is it?)[1] in Edwin Drood and his tombstone to his wife and how in the course of a life of 50 years[2] he had not met a woman who appreciated ^him^ ~~like~~ as she did. However at any rate I appreciated them. Since then Miss Cassidy has asked when I am going down again, and if I could it would be a good thing to go, for I feel I want it. But I am better than when I wrote last. I got codliver oil, but after one bottle I think I can take no more. It is revolting (I take it neat). I think there was nothing the matter with my eyes but general weakness. They are right again now. I am your loving son Gerard.

How is Will Watson?[3]

[1] No, Mr Thomas Sapsea, Auctioneer, the 'purest Jackass in Cloisterham'. For the inscription to Ethelinda, his 'reverential wife', and her capacity for 'looking up to him', see ch. 4.

[2] 'Much nearer sixty years of age than fifty, with a flowing outline of stomach, and horizontal creases in his waistcoat.'

[3] William Watson. See letters to his mother of 10 June 1875 and 5 Oct. 1886.

17–18 February 1887 to Robert Bridges

LRB, no. CXLVI, p. 250 Bodleian, Dep. Bridges, vol. 92, fos. 124–130^{v}

UNIVERSITY COLLEGE, | S^{T} STEPHEN'S GREEN, | DUBLIN. [*printed heading*]
Feb. 17 '87

Dearest Bridges, — I am joyed to see your hand again and delighted to hear your praise of the Canon's book.[1] I too have thought there is in him a vein of truly matchless beauty: it is not ^always^ the whole ~~ex~~ texture but a thread in it and sometimes the whole web is of that. But till you spoke I had almost despaired of my judgment and quite of publishing it. The pathetic imagination of Sky that rollest ever[2] seems to me to have nothing like it but ^some of^ Coleridge in our literature.

Mrs. Waterhouse has not written: it never indeed entered my head that she would, the piece being a fragment too. But I wanted to pay her a compliment and conceived she would like this particular poem.[3] It is in a commoner and smoother style than I mostly write in, but that is no harm: I am sure I have gone far enough in oddities and running rhymes (as even in some late sonnets you have not seen) into the next line.[4] I sent a later and longer version to C. D., who much admired and urged me to ~~wr wrt~~ write lots of it. It should run to about twice the present length and when complete I daresay you will like it. I am amused and pleased at ~~Mau~~ Maurice W.[5] expounding it: it is not at all what I wanted to happen, but after all if I send verse to Mrs. Waterhouse I cannot suppose no one else in the house will see it.

Tomorrow morning I shall have been three years in Ireland, three hard wearying wasting wasted years. (I met the blooming Miss Tynan again this afternoon. She told me ^that^ when she first saw me she took me for 20 and some friend of hers for 15; but it won't do: they should see my heart and vitals, all shaggy with the whitest hair.) In those I have done God's will (in the main) and many many examination papers. I am in a position which makes it befitting and almost a duty to write anything (bearing on classical study) which I may feel that I could treat well and advance learning by: there is such a subject; I do try to write at it; but I see that I cannot get on, that I shall be even less able hereafter than ~~you~~ ^now^. And of course if ~~I can do no~~ ^I cannot do^ what even my appliances make best and easiest, far less can I anything else. Still I could throw myself cheerfully into my day's work? I cannot, I am in a prostration. Wales set me up for a while, but the effect is now past. But out of Ireland I shd. be no better, rather worse probably. I only need one thing — ^a^ working health, a working strength: with that, any employment is tolerable or pleasant, enough for human nature; without it, things are liable to go very hardly with it.

Now come on Mrs. Gaskell. What ails poor Mrs. Gaskell?[6] One book of hers I have read through, Wives and Daughters: if that is not a good book I do not know what a good book is. Perhaps you are so barbarous as not to admire Thomas Hardy — as you do not Stevenson;[7] both, I must maintain, men of pure ~~genius~~ and direct genius.

Have you followed the course of late Homeric criticism?[8] The pendulum is swinging heavily towards the old view of a whole original Iliad. In the track of the recent dialectic investigations I have made out, I think, a small but ^(as a style-test)^ important point; but my induction is not yet complete.

I will bear in mind to send for the Feast of Bacchus at an early opportunity, if (but that is not certain) one should occur.

I am almost afraid I have offended, not offended but not pleased, Mr. Patmore by a late letter:[9] I hope it is not so bad. I hope you will enjoy yourselves there: let me see, do you know Mrs. Patmore? If you do you cannot help liking her. With best love to Mrs. Bridges I am your affectionate friend Gerard.

Yesterday ~~Arch~~ ~~(Feb.~~ Archbishop Walsh[10] had a letter in the Freeman enclosing a subscription to the defence of Dillon and the other traversers on trial for preaching the Plan of Campaign and saying that the jury was packed and a fair trial impossible. The latter was his contribution to the cause of concord and civil order. Today Archbp. Croke[11] has one ~~tell~~ proposing to pay no taxes. One archbishop backs robbery, the other rebellion; the people in good faith believe and will follow them. You will see, it is the beginning of the end: Home Rule or separation is near. Let them come: anything is better than the attempt to rule a people who own no principle of civil obedience at all, not only to the existing government but to none at all. I shd. be glad to see Ireland happy, even though it involved the fall of England, if that could come about without shame and guilt. But Ireland will not be happy: a people without a principle of allegiance cannot be; moreover this movement has throughout been promoted by crime. Something like what happened in the last century between '82 and 1800 will happen in this: now as then one class has ~~got~~ passed off its class-interests as the interests of the nation and so got itself ~~supported~~ ^upheld^ by the support of the ~~most~~ nation; now as then it will legislate in its own interest and the rest will languish; distress will bring on some fresh convulsion; beyond that I cannot guess.

The ship I am sailing in may perhaps go down in the ~~pres~~ approaching gale: if so I shall probably be cast up on the English coast.

After all I have written above my trouble is not the not being able to write a book; it is the not being fit for my work and the struggling vainly to make myself fitter.

Feb. 18 1887.

[1] RWD's *Lyrical Poems* (1887). Dedicated to the Reverend Gerard Hopkins by the Author.

[2] The first line of the last Song in *Lyrical Poems*: reprinted in *Selected Poems*, 143–4, with the title 'Wayward Water'.

[3] 'On the Portrait of Two Beautiful Young People'.

[4] As, for example, in 'To seem the stranger', ll. 6–8 ' . . . hear | Me . . . wear- | Y of . . . '.

[5] Maurice Waterhouse (1868–90), one of Alfred Waterhouse's sons. He died at the age of 22 after a brief illness. The family's grief is expressed in RB's poem 'I never shall love the snow again' (*P.W.*, 309).

[6] Elizabeth Cleghorn Gaskell (1810–65; *ODNB*), whose unfinished *Wives and Daughters* appeared in the *Cornhill* in 1864–6.

[7] See letter to RB of 28 Oct. 1886.

[8] R. C. Jebb in his *Homer: An Introduction to the Iliad and the Odyssey* (1887), which GMH was reading (see letter of 20 Feb. 1887), says that 'Everything tends to show that the *Iliad* was planned by one great poet who also executed the most essential parts of it. By the "primary" *Iliad* we shall here denote the first form which the poet gave to his work, as distinguished from the enlarged form afterwards given to it, partly (perhaps) by himself, partly by others' (4th edn., p. 157).

[9] See letter to Patmore of 20 Jan. 1887.

[10] William J. Walsh (1831–1921) had been appointed Archbishop of Dublin in 1885, despite protests by the English government. His hostility to the English had helped to drive his attempt in Jan. 1884 to prevent GMH's appointment (see *WHALB*, 460 ff.). He had been president of Maynooth College. In 1881 he supported Gladstone's Land Bill, and in 1883 had challenged public attention with 'The Queen's Colleges and the Royal University of Ireland'. He supported the Plan of Campaign led by Timothy Harrington, William O'Brien, and John Dillon urging tenants not to pay exorbitant rents during times of bad harvest but negotiate for a reduction of 25 per cent. If a landlord refused, the rents were not paid but banked to assist those evicted. See GMH's letter to his mother of 26 Nov. 1884 and to Baillie of 20 Feb. 1887.

[11] Thomas William Croke (1824–1902), from 1875 Roman Catholic Archbishop of Cashel, perhaps the most notable figure of his day in the Irish R. C. church. He ardently supported the land agitation that started in 1878 and gave his powerful support to the Irish Nationalist party. He disagreed, however, with some of the Land League's actions and strongly objected to the no-rent manifesto of 1881. He had similar sympathies to Archbishop Walsh.

19 February 1887 from Coventry Patmore to GMH

FL, no. CLXXXIV A, p. 377 Campion Hall, P 19/2/87
Addressed to 'Rev[d] Gerard Hopkins, S.J. | University college, | St. Stephens Green, | Dublin'. PM HASTINGS FE 19 87, H&K PACKET FE 20 87.

Hastings. February 19. 1887
My dear M[r] Hopkins,

What you say about the paper in the St. James's is quite true,[1] but I have no faculty for saying things of that sort in a generally intelligible way, and rely upon finding here & there a reader who will do the necessary diluting in some way of his own. I find that there are not a few Protestants who jump at such hints; but ^that^ Catholics, as a rule, can make nothing of them.

Should your paper on metre be printed I hope you will let me see it. I dont suppose that I have knowledge enough to understand all you have to say; but I may get glimpses.

For the past 15 months I have been writing in the St. James's at the rate of about 2 columns a week — on all sorts of subjects. I am surprised to find that the Editor lets me write all sorts of Catholic ideas, and I do not know of any journal which would disseminate them among a better class of readers.

It is of no use writing for "Catholics". I have turned myself to the Gentiles.[2]

Bridges and his wife have just been staying here; & it was very pleasant.

You will be sorry to hear that Bertha[3] has for many months ~~being~~ ^been^ suffering from dreadful religious depression — so bad that the Doctors wont let her be in the same house with her sister.

Your's affectionately
Coventry Patmore

[1] See letter to Patmore of 20 Jan. 1887.
[2] A reference to Acts 13: 44–48, specifically verse 46.
[3] Patmore's daughter (b. 1856) by his first wife Emily.

20 February 1887 to Alexander William Mowbray Baillie

FL, no. CLVII, p. 275 UCD L 66
One folded sheet + three half sheets + a folded sheet + a half sheet + a folded sheet; 20 sides of paper watermarked with monogram and 'BROWNE & NOLAN DUBLIN' and printed with university address.

UNIVERSITY COLLEGE, | S$^{\underline{\text{T}}}$ STEPHEN'S GREEN, | DUBLIN. [*printed heading*]
Feb. 20 1887

Dearest Baillie, — Thank you very much for your kind letters and for the trouble you are so good as to take. The list is valuable, but what I still more wish for is the transliteration of Egyptian ~~an~~ into Greek (and perhaps vice versa) words. Only remark.

I do not want you to trouble about it; I am afraid it will be no good. I shd. like it, but I shd. be sorry that you shd. have been throwing pains and time away. It is so doubtful, so very doubtful, that I shall be able to pursue any study except the needs of the day (and those not enough) at all. I have tried and failed so often and my strength serves me less.

I do something, what I can, but I cannot believe it will come to anything. What I want if possible to get done first is a book on the Dorian Measure,[1] one of the rhythms employed by Pindar and the other lyric poets, the most important and the least understood; nominally on this but with an introduction on the philosophy (for the speculation goes pretty deep) of rhythm in general. I have written some way ~~on~~' ^on^ at two places, and shall ~~go on~~ ^continue^ as best I can. I had some hope of bringing out somewhere — in the Society for Hellenic Studies or ~~the~~ Hermathena or the new Classical Review — this year a preliminary paper not on the profounder matter of course but on the Dorian Measure itself; but I fear I shall not.

Meantime my Homeric studies are postponed. But they are not altogether dropped. And now I must say that I have Jebb's good little book[2] and am reading it. Yesterday I read in the Journal of the Soc. Hell. S. a paper by Jevons of Durham[3] (who lately wrote a good handbook of Greek Literature) on the Rhapsodists and Homeric question. His point is shortly this: that the Iliad as we have ^it^ is ^~~it,~~^ probably, from beginning to end, Homer, the original work; that the com~~b~~^p^~~in~~^l^ation and expansion theories in every shape and form are good for nothing; that the dialect however has been changed from Achaean, that is

Aeolian, to Ionian, as proved by Fick,[4] and this by Ionian rhapsodists; and that the inconsistencies are all due to rhapsodists, who altered or added a line or so to round off for the time being the fit ~~or~~ they were declaiming — and this he calls a vera causa {*true cause*}, saying "Diaskeuasts" are not ^one^, Rhapsodists are.

The closer examination of Homer's dialect and scansion is clearly the line of the day. I have not at present at all the knowledge to pronounce ^on this^. I have however made a little discovery of my own, which I am ~~testing~~ ^trying,^ ^proving.^ If correct it may serve as a good test. It is this.

Taking as true that the diphthongs *ει* and *ου* ~~may~~ ^shd.^ wherever the line allows be resolved into *εϊ* and *οο*, as Fick has made likely, I think I have found the following law of Homeric scansion.[5] When the fourth foot is undivided and ends (without el~~s~~ision) with the 'bucolic caesura' (between ~~fif~~ fourth and fifth foot, pause or no pause in sense) it must be a dactyl. Exceptions are allowed in proper names and probably some stock phrases closely bound together, like *ποδαρκὴς δῖος Ἀχιλλεύς* {*the swift-footed noble Achilles*}.

Of course the seeming breaches are numerous and on the treatment of these my discovery depends both for its ~~truth and~~ establishment and its value. Most yield to ~~the~~ simple resolution or slight change~~s~~, as *ὁμίλει* (imperfect) | *ὁμίλεε*, *κελεύθου* | *κελεύθοο*, *ἀφ' ἵππων* | *ἀφ' ἵπποϊν* ~~Others introduce new~~ or *ἵπποφιν*. Others introduce new resolutions, such as *αὐτῶϊ* for *αὐτῷ*.[6] I feel uncertain about them and must have a fuller induction of cases than I have now. Since I began my observation I have found that Monro remarks on the rareness of three long syllables before the bucolic caesura, but quotes *ὑσμίνῃ μίμνε φίλον κῆρ* {*their hearts abode not steadfast in close fight*}[7] and *Θηβαίου Τειρεσίαο* {*Theban Teiresias*}.[8] These shd. probably ~~by~~ ^be^ *ὑσμίνηϊ* and *Θηβαίοο*. He adds "The rarity of ~~the~~ verses with this rhythm may be judged from the fact that it is never found with the oblique cases of *ἄνθρωπος* (*ἀνθρώπων* etc.) <but is it found with the singular, as *ἀνθρώπου* and *ἀνθρώπῳ*, I wonder>, although these occur about 150 times, and in every other part of the verse: or with *ἀλλήλων* etc., which occur about 100 times". Prof. Seymour also is quoted (in Jebb's appendices) as remarking on the rarity of spondees before the bucolic caesura. ~~F~~Perhaps they may turn out to be like the spondaic hexameter, a rare form, but employed.

My Egyptian guesses were wild and the children of ignorance, which opens ^up those^ possibilities that knowledge wd. close. Still three deserve ~~d~~ consideration — Rhadamanthys, Sarpedon, and Aphrodite.[9] Oedipus is the mere suggestion of a possibility. The name may, as you say, be foreign and yet not Egyptian. I did not however overlook this. I knew that much in Greek religion and civilisation came from Asia Minor, ~~(~~a ~~great~~ ^wide^ region and hitherto little explored. But of two doors, one open, the other locked, we ~~try~~ go in by the open one; if inside that we find what we want we leave the locked-up room alone. So of Egypt and Asia. Besides there were grounds of expectation. The worship of Apollo and of Dionysus ~~seems~~ ^bears^ marks of coming from Asia: one wd. not then look to Egypt for that. But for Aphrodite one might take a rise off the Nile waters. And so for Oedipus. I cannot however agree with you that ~~be traceable~~ ^such names as his are^ "archaic, ~~or~~ ^i.e.^ older than Greek as an independent language". Every Greek word, so to say, is that; or all but those that have been compounded (or borrowed) in historical times. And if it has borne ~~like~~ ^with^ the rest the weathering effects of time why is it not shaped as Greekish as the rest, why should it be more outlandish~~?~~ than other words?

In the case of Oedipus the "accommodation"[10] has gone so far as to add a new ^though^ unimportant incident to the story, # in which the Sphinx and the riddle were older incidents. The story of the Sphinx may be compared with that of the Minotaur and the yearly sacrifice, which Curtius says arose from the worship of Moloch with human sacrifices in Crete. And it is to be remarked that the common legend coupled Thebes with Phoenicia too. I think this confusion of Phoenicians with Egyptians may perhaps be accounted for. It arose from the time when the Hyksos[11] in Egypt spoke Egyptian and adopted Egyptian customs and in part religion, but did not to foreigners call themselves Egyptians. After all we do not for certain know the ~~meaning~~ ^origin^ of the word *Φοῖνιξ*. It came to mean Phoenician, that is ~~men~~ man from Sidon, Tyre, etc, ~~and~~ but ~~orig~~ earlier it may have meant southerner of any sort. It is commonly taken to come from the name Pount or Phount or whatever that is. But possibly it may be connected with *φοίνος* and mean Red Man.

The Egyptians were not much of colonists themselves, were they? ~~But~~ Though there are ^Greek^ legends of ^their^ coloni~~e~~sing Attica and Argos. In any case it is remarkable the Greeks in Homer's time know so little of so ancient and famous a race. *Αἴγυπτος* is the name for the Nile, only that Thebes in Egypt is called Egyptian; but even that might mean Thebes-upon-Nile. But again it is remarkable that other foreigners were reduced to call^ing^ Egypt Mizraim,[12] which I understand means the Two Fortresses, that is the ~~fronti~~ fortresses on the Syrian and Sinaitic frontier. ~~Th~~ What do the Egyptians call themselves? Egypt they call Kem or Kem^i^t,[13] do they not?

In Homer's time the day when either Egypt or Phoenicia cd. make or hold settlements on Greek ground had passed and was little remembered. The towns with their temples and worships had become Greek; the ^local^ histories had been absorbed, embodied, and Hellenised; and there was no first hand knowledge of Egypt, and little of Phoenicians but as traders. Such is the Greek world in which I shd. like, if I could, to trace the survival of Egyptian words and ideas.

You ask who knows what Greek was in, say, 2000 B.C. Of the Greek language at that time we can scarcely hope ever to know more than by a better knowledge of two extremes, which may be put together — historical Greek and the form of the original Aryan language. ~~But~~ ^It^ must be a mean term between those two. But more may be learnt by closer study of those extremes, the one known positively and minutely, the other pieced together by guesswork from scattered but considerable bodies of knowledge. But of the Greek race at such a time perhaps some further positive knowledge may be gained by archaeology not only in Greece but in the earlier abodes of the race in its movement towards Greece. You are aware that it is now the fashion to say the Aryan races or languages arose in Europe and worked eastwards, not in Asia westwards. But I do not believe it.

On the list of ~~w~~accommodations I have some remarks to make. I find myself very sceptical ~~e~~about the first of them, acorn. Does Skeat prove his point? According to him it shd. have meant fieldgrowth.[14] This seems a very unlikely name. First acre means arable or cultivated ground, not wild or forest land. Then I presume ~~acor~~ the original word wd. be collective, like mast, hay, corn itself; but acorn is individual. We ^say^ "eating acorns", not "acorn". (You will say pease from collective has become individual — pea.) ~~Why after~~ How has so vague and inappropriate a word superseded a proper ~~name~~ ^one^? For of course people had some word for the fruit of the oak. Why is it not after all ake, that is oak, corn (as in barleycorn, peppercorn) or kern (in kernel)? In Lancashire they call it akkern.

Ferrule — I have heard this pronounced (by an Irishman) furl. This wd. be a fresh accommodation, for a ferrule (on a stick) does furl the wood.

Jaunty — But jaunty now means "on the jaunt". Either then Skeat is mistaken or it is an interesting case of a word passing from one root to another.

Lapwing, which I do not dispute, is another and striking ~~one~~ ^case^. It appears that it now ^has come to^ mean~~s~~ in another and inverted shape ~~wh~~ much the same as it did in the beginning and ~~not~~ to express its meaning not less happily.[15]

So also _stark naked_: we certainly understand and convey the same thought as in "stark mad" — stiffly, uncompromisingly so and so.

In like manner _touchy_, _uproar_, _upside down_ now mean what they seem to mean.

Wiseacre I cannot understand. Does Skeat mean it is really _derived_ from the German _Weissager_?

Counterpane is perhaps a complicated matter. If I am not mistaken old writers call pieces of cloth (and not ~~onl~~ only of glass) _panes_. _Counterpane_ wd. then be perfectly regular. Still it may be like _lapwing_ above.

I have had no more dealings with D'Arcy Thompson.[16] I shall see him in the summer, and then you shall hear.

There remains a word about Home Rule and so on. In general I am sure we agree on this as on most matters, but particular conclusions vary with particular facts. Home Rule of itself is a blow for England and will do no good to Ireland. But it is better than worse things. You would understand that if you lived in Ireland. My position is not at all a favourable one for observing the country, still it is much better than people in England can have and they in fact do not at all realise the situation. People think that Ireland was always a "distressful country", ~~turbulent~~ ^troubled^ and hard to rule at the best, and they do not see that things are worse than or so bad as they have read of their being~~,~~ before. I do not say things are as bad as they were during ~~Iri~~ the horrors of Irish rebellions or the greater horrors of their putting down. I only say that we are approaching a state of things which must be put an end to either by the sword or by Home Rule. It is, if people would see it, high praise of our constitution that it sh~~d~~ould enable us to pass through a crisis of which the natural end is war / without war; for now for the first time the Irish are using the constitution against England. But the country is in a peaceful rebellion, if you can understand what that is, and the rebellion is becoming more serious. Every step which has been taken since, say, the Land Act of 1881 (I cd. go much further back, but that is enough), to satisfy — satisfy it could not, but let us say to better the condition of Ireland, has made things worse. The Irish had and have deep wrongs to complain of in the past and wrongs and abuses to amend which are still felt in the present. But the strange and alarming thing is that the removal of and the wish to remove these has not conciliated them, it has inflamed them. For these steps have ~~ndone~~ nothing to give them, but have nevertheless done much to bring them nearer getting, the object of their undying desire and now of their flaming passion. This is what they call Nationhood. The passion for it is of its nature insatiable and Home Rule will not satisfy it; it will be a disappointment too like the rest; but it will have some good effects and it will deliver England from the strain of an odious and impossible task, the task of attempting to govern a people who own no principle of civil allegiance (only religious, and that one is now strained), not only not to the existing government, in which they share, but to none at all; and of enforcing a law which the people wish to set at nought and to defeat. For such a complexion ^of things^ no constitution was made: absolute monarchy with strong forces at command alone could deal with it, and that miserably. Things will not mend: if they would mend now they would have mended before. Consider. There was a feud between the two most prominent classes in the country, landlords and tenants. The position of the landlords was superior; they oppressed the tenants. The position of the tenants was bettered till it became more favourable than that of any other tenant farmers. And the feud increased. Agriculture ^happened then to^ suffer~~ed~~, the prosperity of England and Ireland declined, all classes ~~suffered~~ ^were strained^; the tenants combined to ask reductions of rent: the landlords mostly gave those reductions. And the feud increased. The landlords, once able to evict at will, try to evict for non-payment, of three, four, five, six, seven years' rent: sometimes they cannot, at other times three kingdoms and two continents are set on fire by it. The feud fills the world. Not content with a court for reducing the rents of the unwilling landlord, not appeased by the willing reductions of others, the Plan of Campaign is invented. Mostly it succeeds, and with it the feud increases. The judges with one mouth pronounce it against the law: members of parliament all the more boldly promote it and the feud, now a struggle with the law, increases. I have said nothing of the sieges and battles, a miniature war, which has meanwhile gone on. The traversers are put on their trial: an Archbishop, the people's nominee, who has already approved of the Plan of Campaign, now attacks the justice of the court which is to try its promoters. Another Archbishop proposes to refuse taxes. The trial will end, I suppose, today either in some miscarriage, which will be a victory for the traversers, or perhaps in a verdict~~,~~ which the people will with indignation disregard. For they allow neither the justice of the law nor the honesty of its administrators. Be assured of this, that the mass of the Irish people own no allegiance to any existing law or government. And yet they are not a worthless people; they have many true and winning virtues. But their virtues do not promote civil order and it has become impossible to govern them. Cost what it may, what wise man would try or wish to govern a people that own no duty to any law he can enforce? It is a hopeless task: they must have Home Rule with all that it may cost both them and us. You would say so if you lived here. Gladstone is a traitor. But still they must have Home Rule.

Do not believe this is only a struggle for land. I will explain that point (if I may speak so boldly) another time. ~~That~~ ^This^ is really an old story, an altes stück {*old piece of news*}: everything, if we look in the right quarter, is known. What is happening now happened in the last century and so, I suppose, what happened ~~w~~then will happen now. Proportions and features no doubt differ, but the main thing is the same. Hullabaloo, long letter!

Your affectionate friend Gerard M. Hopkins S.J.

[1] See letters of 18–19 Oct. 1882 to RB, 14 Jan. 1883 to AMWB, 2–4, 21–2 , and 28 Oct. 1886 to RB, 7 Nov. 1886 to Patmore, 11 Dec. 1886 to RB, 23 Dec. 1886 to AMWB, 20 Jan. 1887 to Patmore, 1 May and 30 July 1887 to RB.

[2] See letter of 17–18 Feb. 1887, n. 8.

[3] *Journal of Hellenic Studies*, 7 (1886), 291–308, 'The Rhapsodising of the *Iliad*', by Frank Byron Jevons, whose *History of Greek Literature* came out in 1886.

[4] August Fick (1833–1916), the German comparative philologist, whose *Die homerische Ilias* was published in 1886.

[5] See Walter Leaf, *The Iliad*, ii (London, 1902), Appendix N: 'The Fourth Foot of the Hexameter and "Wernicke's Law"'.

[6] GMH is speculating on different forms of words meaning 'associate with', 'path', 'horseless', and 'just so'.

[7] Homer, *Iliad*, xiii. 713. David Binning Monro (1836–1905; *ODNB*) was an Oxford scholar who wrote a *Grammar of Homeric Dialect* (1882). GMH obviously has the text in front of him since he quotes verbatim (with his own parenthesis on forms of the word for 'man') from the text (p. 341 in the second edition of 1891). ἀλλήλων means 'to one another'

[8] Homer, *Odyssey*, x. 492.

[9] See his letters to Baillie of 11 Feb., 29 Mar., 3 Apr., and 6 Apr. 1886.

[10] GMH is responding to an extensive letter from Baillie concerning various 'accommodations', i.e. adaptations of words, expressions, systems, or practices to something different from their original purpose (as in the possible connection of Moloch, Minotaur, Sphinx, for example). This gives rise to cultural, historical, and linguistic speculations in the style of the modern scholars, philologists, and archaeologists (like Ernst Curtius) attempting to envisage the Greek world in Homer's day and how it showed traces of the connection with Egypt only in the survival of certain Egyptian words and ideas.

[11] Hyksos were a group of mixed Semitic-Asiatics who settled in northern Egypt in the 18th c. BC, seized power in 1630 BC, and ruled Egypt as the 15th dynasty (*c.*1630–1521 BC). The name Hyksos was used by Manetho, and Josephus identified the Hyksos (probably wrongly) as the Hebrews of the Old Testament. See letter to AWMB of 10 Apr. 1886.

[12] Mizraim is the son of Ham, grandson of Noah (Genesis 10: 6). As the Hebrew name for 'Egypt', the dual form of the word is explained as referring to Lower and Upper Egypt, or to the two great walled enclosures of Northern Egypt and Southern Egypt (E. A. Wallis Budge, *Cook's Handbook for Egypt and the Egyptian Sudan* (4th edn., London, 1921), 52).

[13] Kamt, 'the black land' (describing the alluvial soil of the Delta): see ibid. 53.

[14] Skeat's *Principles of English Etymology* was published in 1887, collecting material from many smaller articles; it includes notes on most, though not all, of the words mentioned. He says that 'oak-corn' is impossible and the *OED* still insists on the derivation from *akran*, 'fruit of the unenclosed land', explaining that 'The formal history of this word has been much perverted by "popular etymology"' of the sort which GMH favours.

[15] Lexicographers derive the name from a description of the flight of the bird, combining words for 'leap' and 'waver' (compare 'wink'). Again, popular etymology tells a different story.

[16] See letter to Baillie of 23 Dec. 1886.

2 March 1887 to his Mother

FL, no. CVI, p. 179 Bodleian, MS Eng. lett. e. 41, fos. 113–16

UNIVERSITY COLLEGE, | ST STEPHEN'S GREEN, | DUBLIN. [*printed heading*]

March 2 '87

My dearest mother, — I wish you many very happy returns of tomorrow. It is your first birthday at Haslemere,[1] which soon will begin to put on, I suppose, those bright looks which you can ~~as yet~~ never have seen yet.

Dublin is very dull and ~~m~~one of my best friends, an old Stonyhurst pupil, Bernard O'Flaherty,[2] is going to leave it and live in the country. He has constantly called on me and taken walks with me ever since I have been here, which is the highest compliment he could pay me, and now I am every minute expecting him for a last one. He passed his final law examination with great honour the other day, ~~and~~ being head of the list, and will now set up as an attorney.

I have another great friend Terence ~~Flana~~ Woulfe-Flanagan,[3] who was an undergraduate at Oxford when I was curate there. His father is a judge lately retired and he is studying medicine. These two young men are not Nationalists at all, which, as things go, is a relief.

I hope the government are not going to prosecute Archbishop Croke[4] for his no-tax manifesto: it will be a great mistake. It shd. be let drop. It has commonly been the custom of English statesmen to take no notice of wild words if they were not likely to lead to deeds and not to give them needless importance by taking them up. Now I daresay Dr. Croke has seen by this time that what he wrote was — not wrong, for he will never think that, but foolish. For what could people do? Most of the taxes are indirect: how could they get their tea without paying the duty on it? And the income tax does not weigh much on the only class that he thinks about, the tenant farmers. Besides to get a conviction against him is not possible with ^~~the~~ Irish^ juries: then why try and fail? And probably the words themselves would not so easily support a prosecution. But the attempt would make him doubly a hero.

Ireland is outwardly pretty quiet, except where evictions are attempted. This is because the people have beaten the government and the law. There is no government and the law cannot be carried out. What is to be done? Only one thing now: give them Home Rule. It will not end all our troubles, but at any rate they will be much worse without it.

With best love to all, I am your loving son Gerard.

[1] See letter to Everard Hopkins of 5–8 Nov. 1885, n. 11.

[2] Bernard O'Flaherty entered Stonyhurst in Sept. 1874 and spent over nine years there. 'From Hodder to Philosophy his career was one of unbroken success, and few have had such a record' (Obituary, *Stonyhurst Magazine*, June 1929). After qualifying in 1887 he went into partnership with his father, a well-known Wexford solicitor, and continued in this profession till his death in Mar. 1929.

[3] Terence Woulfe-Flanagan (1859–1914), Balliol 1877–82; 2 Cl. Mods. 1879; BA 1882. Of Ballyrach, Co. Dublin. He qualified in medicine at Dublin and practised in Chelsea.

[4] See letter of of 17–18 Feb. 1887.

3 March 1887 from John Henry Newman to GMH

FL, no. C29, p. 413 Birmingham Oratory

March 3. 1887.
Dear Fr Hopkins

Your letter is an appalling one — but not on that account untrustworthy. There is one consideration however, which you omit. The Irish Patriots hold that they never have yielded themselves to the sway ^sway^[1] of England and therefore have never been under her laws, and have never been rebels ^rebels^.[2]

This does not diminish the force of your picture, but it suggests that there is no help, no remedy. If I were an Irishman, I should be (in heart) a rebel. Moreover, to clinch the difficulty the Irish character and ~~tate~~ ^tastes^ is very different from the English.

My fingers will not let me write more.

Very truly yr
J H Card Newman

[1] Newman adds another attempt at a word over the first to try to write more clearly.

[2] Newman had explored this position in a letter to William Walsh of 19 Dec. 1881. See *LDJHN*, xxx. 32–3.

10–11 March 1887 to Alexander William Mowbray Baillie

FL, no. CLVIII, p. 283 UCD L 67
Two folded sheets of paper watermarked 'BROWNE & NOLAN DUBLIN' and with university printed heading; 8 sides.

UNIVERSITY COLLEGE, | ST STEPHEN'S GREEN, | DUBLIN. [*printed heading*]
March 10 '87

My dear Baillie, — I think the most convenient plan would be to give conventional values as [illegible] always = a and so on: it ~~wd~~. would be easy to make the necessary allowance. You could of course treat the vowels as semivowels, í as y, u as w, and a as some guttural — ‘ or ’.

It is quite like^ly^ Aelfric[1] ~~was translating from~~ used the older version of the Scripture, the Itala or whatever it was, for controversy about it is endless. The Vulgate (St. Jerome's edition, consisting of (a) St. Jerome's ~~origin~~ own translation; (b) his revision of an older version, viz. the whole NT. and some part of the Old; (c) the unrevised old ~~version of the~~ Psalter) was never formally adopted till the Council of Trent nor consequently the older version formally disallowed: indeed the last was never done. Portions of this older version are embedded in the Breviary ^and^ missal, and Church writers long after St. Jerome quote it.

Will you look up scope in Skeat for me?[2] As an English word it is primarily nautical and means the play of a vessel at anchor, as the wind, tide, or current may carry her east, west, or all round it; hence "at a short scope", "a long scope", that is play or range. And the usual literary sense ~~is~~ agrees strictly with this — freedom of action or play. But I have remarked in Newman and I find the Imperial Dict. quotes

^from^ much older writers, Hooker I think, a usage evidently mistaken and got from thinking of σκοπός and the School-Latin scopus | mark, aim. There even seems a fusion (a real and unfortunate confusion) of these two meanings. The Imp. Dict. as above (it is no authority and therefore I ask for Skeat) indeed recognises no etymology ~~or~~ but σκοπός (remarking however that there is nothing corresponding in French and so our writers took it direct) nor meaning but mark (nevertheless quoting instances of the other and truer one).

No time now for more, but I am very glad my long letter did not annoy you. Your affectionate friend Gerard M. Hopkins.

March 11 — I shd. be glad to hear if there is any other word scape than escape abridged. I think Skeat says landscape is Dutch: the English form wd. have been landship.[3]

[1] GMH is putting the picture as it was understood in his time. Ælfric (*c.*950–*c.*1010; *ODNB*), Benedictine abbot of Eynsham, near Oxford, may well have used for his translations from the Bible those texts which had been translated from the Greek into Latin before St Jerome (*c.*340–420), and were known as the Itala. It was their variable quality which spurred Jerome to try to make a more authoritative text, which he put together from those elements GMH describes. His Bible became, not the only, but the common Bible, the 'Vulgate', whose authority was affirmed at the Council of Trent (1545–63), but elements of the original versions remained in some places. Perhaps Baillie had been reading Aelfric in Skeat's edition of *Ælfric's Lives of the Saints*, which the Early English Text Society had begun to publish in 1881.

[2] See letter of W. W. Skeat to GMH, 27 Feb. 1888.

[3] Baillie's pencilled notes on 'scope' and 'scape', evidently derived from dictionaries, are on the blank leaf of the letter.

25–6 March 1887 to Michael F. Cox[1]

SL, p. 253 Irish Jesuit Archives, 35 Lower Leeson St., Dublin
Published in *Studies: An Irish Quarterly Review*, 59/233 (Spring 1970), 19–25, ed. Peter M. Troddyn, SJ, and in *HRB* 3 (1972), 3–9.

Monasterevan, | Ireland. | Lady Day[2] 1887
My dear Dr. Cox,

— I have had a book of yours[3] too long and ought to have returned it. This was brought to my mind in setting my things to rights yesterday. I will bring it you on getting back.

I am led to make some remarks on the matter. Irish writers on their own history are naturally led to dwell on what in history is most honourable to Ireland: every patriotic spirit would feel itself so led.

They are also led to dwell on what in history is most dishonourable to England: this also is natural, and there is plenty of room for doing it. Still it is the way with passion to exceed; and the passion here in question is often said, by Irishmen themselves, to be the deepest feeling of an Irish heart. Now since the object of history is truth and truth is likely to suffer from the play of passion, it is desirable that Irish writers on Irish history should be on their guard especially on this matter, and, failing that, it is left for Englishmen like myself to do what we can (which is almost, under the circumstances, nothing at all) to point out untruths and overstatements and understatements due to passion and correct them. The devil is not so black, the saying is, as he is painted.

There are in perhaps all the heaviest charges of accusation by Ireland against England certain circumstances not justifying indeed but mitigating and essentially modifying the nature of the wrong done. These circumstances are always unknown to or forgotten or wilfully suppressed by popular writers and speakers. Even those that lie on the surface of history are so treated; how much more then those that appear on research. And this my position has brought me to feel not only with sorrow but with the deepest indignation and bitterness. The late Mr. Maguire M.P. in his book on the Irish in America,[4] the purpose of which was to warn English statesmen of the danger of not listening to the claims of Ireland, mentions that he once had to set right an Irish American who supposed there to be duties imposed by England on Irish exports: when he informed him that all such duties had long since been removed the man's countenance fell and betrayed his disappointment. This man did not care that Ireland should prosper; he cared only for the food of his hatred against England. This no doubt is not the mind of the lady who writes on Irish Woollens; still I should like her to have known and knowing to have mentioned certain points, one of which at least is very material. I learnt them from a paper in last April's number of the English Historical Review by the Rev. W. Cunningham,[5] and perhaps it might have been expected that a lady of so much research as that pamphlet shows her to be and who was only restrained by insuperable difficulties from verifying a single mention of Irish goods in the old poet Fazio degli Uberti should have found out this important fact.[6]

This is that the most extensive (and in the 17th century seemingly the only) Irish woollen industry was frieze,[7] that this was never checked by English legislation (but on the contrary expressly excepted in the acts), and nevertheless that it is now not far from dead. And indeed I gather from her own paper some such process with regard to the Irish woollen industries in general. In the 14th century we hear from Dante's contemporary Fazio degli Uberti of certain fine Irish serges as being exported as far as Florence; one or two centuries later we hear of certain coarse stuffs as selling at Antwerp (if I remember); and later than that, though my authority for this is Cunningham's paper, quoting Sir Wm. Pettie,[8] it seems that nothing but frieze was exported and little of that and that little mostly to England. The reason I presume is that Ireland was early in the field with woollen goods, but other nations learnt to make as good or better or at all events goods which what with the cost of freight and, maybe, import duties, foreign goods could not compete with. This then was not England's doing.

And in fact why do at least the plainer people not wear more frieze? The reasons, whatever they are, are to be sought in some principle of wider reach than acts of parliament.

In Cunningham's paper you will find other points which deserve to be borne in mind (I might more sadly say, which deserve suppression); as that the party injured by the legislation of 1699 and thereafter was the Protestant party (though of course in the end the prosperity of the whole country was affected); that this party themselves wanted to keep the cloth manufacture out of Catholic hands; that the outcry from England was made only by the west-country weavers and clothiers and not from anticipation only of rivalry but from serious and actual loss by emigration to Ireland of their workpeople (a selfish spirit no doubt but one scarcely to be got rid of in commerce and the same by which Swift[9] and those who thought with him were actuated in the way of retaliation); that parliament did not do all that these people wanted nor from their self-interested motives but from political ones; that they meant to save the English manufacturers from serious loss and no more, not to ruin the Irish one, though it is true the measures they took had that effect, being excessive and, to a rising trade, ruinous; and lastly that the actual evil done was small and rather the prevention of wealth that might have come than the destruction of what was.

I am yours very truly Gerard M. Hopkins.
March 26.

[1] Michael F. Cox (b. 1852) was a distinguished physician in Dublin, lecturer in the Medical School of the Catholic University of Dublin, and, as an examiner of the Royal University of Ireland, a colleague of GMH's.

[2] In GMH's day, as in ours, Lady Day (the Feast of the Annunciation of the Virgin Mary) was 25 Mar.

[3] Identified by N. H. MacKenzie as *Arts and Industries in Ireland* by S[arah] A[tkinson] (1882). It is the second of the book's two essays, 'Irish Wool and Woollens: Passages from the History of the Staple Trade', that GMH discusses.

[4] John Francis Maguire (1815–72; *ODNB*), *The Irish in America* (1868).

[5] William Cunningham (1849–1919; *ODNB*) was a distinguished economic historian.

[6] Fazio (Bonifacio) degli Uberti (1305/9–post 1367), imitator of Dante and author of *Dittamondo* (Venice, 1474), an account in *terza rima* of a journey round the known world. Sarah Atkinson had written that the need to have the librarian in attendance when using the Trinity College Library's copy deterred her from consulting it. She probably got her information, and the bias of her opinion, from Lord Charlemont, who had written a paper on 'The antiquity of the woollen manufacture in Ireland, proved from a passage of an antient Florentine poet', *Transactions of the Royal Irish Academy*, 1 (1787), 3.

[7] Coarse woollen cloth with a nap, usually only on one side.

[8] Sir William Petty (1623–87) was Surveyor-General of Ireland. His *Maps of Ireland* (1685) and *Political Anatomy of Ireland* (1691) give very detailed accounts of the country.

[9] Jonathan Swift (1667–1745; *ODNB*) the great satirist and Dean of St Patrick's, Dublin, was fiercely indignant on behalf of the Irish, and his 'retaliation' can be judged from the title of his pamphlet of 1720: *A Proposal for the universal use of Irish manufacture, in clothes and furniture of houses, &c., utterly rejecting and renouncing everything wearable that comes from England.*

29 March 1887 to Robert Bridges

LRB, no. CXLVII, p. 253 Bodleian, Dep. Bridges, vol. 92, fos. 131–133v

UNIVERSITY COLLEGE, | ST STEPHEN'S GREEN, | DUBLIN. [*printed heading*]
March 29 '87

Dear Bridges, — I found your letter on coming back to town ^last night^ from Monasterevan, quite too late for return of post. However for ^the^ curiosity of the thing I answer your queries.

The ^irises of the^ present writer's ^~~irises of the~~^ eyes are small and dull, of a greenish brown; hazel I suppose; slightly darker at the outer rims.

His hair (see enclosed sample, carriage ~~f~~paid) is lightish brown, but not equable nor the same in all lights; being quite fair near the roots and upon the temples, elsewhere darker (the very short bits are from the temple next the ear, the longer snip from the forehead), and shewing quite fair in the sun and even, a little tawny. It has a gloss. On the temples it sometimes appears to me white. I have a few white hairs, but not there.

It is a very pleasant and flattering thought that Wooldridge is painting my portrait,[4] but is it (and was yours) wholly from memory? I am of late become much wrinkled round the eyes and generally haggard-looking, and if my counterfeit presentment is to be I shd. be glad it were of my youth.

And if Wooldridge is still with you tell him not to ^trouble to^ answer that letter at all nor to make the enquiries, which I have made elsewhere (besides which I feel pretty sure the matter never struck Rockstro[2] nor perhaps anyone else and that I have the key to the history of modern music in what my enquiry points to, viz. that modern harmony could not arise till the old system and its tuning was got rid of and that it was goodness, not dulness, of ~~our~~ ear which delayed its growth). Presently I hope to write to him again, not lengthily, and may enclose something.

I shd. have felt better for the delicious bog air of Monasterevan were it not that I had a sleepless night of it last night.

The young lady of my Elegy[3] was tossed in the earthquake. She and her mother ran down lightly clad and spent the next day under an umbrella (against sun, not rain). She was greatly terrified and begged and prayed her father to fetch her home, which I fancy he has not yet done.

I am yours affectionately Gerard M. Hopkins S.J.

If I can manage to read the Feast of Bacchus it must be in the ensuing Easter holidays. You shall hear in a day or two.

1 This is in the possession of the Bridges family: it was done from a photograph, and was meant to be finished from life. The picture was used on the dustjacket of both the White and the Martin biographies.

2 See letter to RB of 5 Jan. 1887.

3 Ursula Wheble of 'On the Portrait of Two Beautiful Young People'. The earthquake occurred on 23 Feb. off the coast of southern France and Italy, destroying villages and killing some 2,000 people.

31 March 1887 to Michael F. Cox[1]

Published in *Studies: An Irish Quarterly Review*, 59/233 (Spring 1970), 19–25, ed. Peter M. Troddyn, SJ, and in *HRB* 3 (1972), 3–9 Irish Jesuit Archives, 35 Lower Leeson St., Dublin

UNIVERSITY COLLEGE, | S$^{\underline{T}}$ STEPHEN'S GREEN, | DUBLIN.
March 31 '87

My dear Dr Cox,

I now return your pamphlet with thanks: since coming back I have studied it again. I more than ever note the selfishness of the legislation of 1699 etc., but I also more clearly see that it goes but a very little way to explaining the poverty of Ireland.

I wish I could lend you Cunningham's paper. But from it I extract the following relevant facts.

1672 The Irish peasantry better clothed than the French, or indeed most of the world, in home-manufactured cloth — frieze (Sir Wm. Petty). Little frieze exported (the same) 1687 (the year before the Revolution) maximum manufacture of frieze, which was in 1665 more than four times what it was in 1696 and in 1687 therefore still higher (Report of Commissioners of Trade).

1665 'New drapery' begins to rise by immigration from West of England, Holland, and France to Dublin, Cork, Kinsale, Waterford, Limerick, and Clonmel. But whole quantity exported not equal to half the exports of one English clothing county (as, say, Devonshire?) (Report of Commissioners and a private letter quoted in Smith's Memoirs of Wool). It increases rapidly till 1687 and declines, but again more slowly increases till 1696, when it affects the W. country English trade, who petition for its restriction (but no other parts of England). The petitioners fix a duty (one petition says 20 per cent), shewing they do not mean to destroy it, but only to protect themselves (Commons Journals). The Commissioners of Trade fix 20 per cent on the 'Old Drapery' (= broad cloth) and 10 on the 'New' (mixed woollens), saying that a higher duty wd. be prohibitive, which shews that was not their purpose. But the House of Lords, though taking no measures, shew signs of wishing altogether to kill the Irish export trade.

1698 The Protestant woollen manufacturers of Dublin petition the Irish Parliament for an act disabling Papists[2] from the woollen manufacture, of which a third, they say, is in their hands. They plead the inferiority of the goods made as an injury to themselves (Irish Commons Journal). Remark here who the parties are in this commercial struggle, viz., English Protestants jealous for English commercial ascendence versus Irish Protestants jealous for their own commercial (and religious, as elsewhere, more fully expressed) ascendency.

1699 The act of the English Parliament restricting the Irish export trade in woollens. The trade declines, emigration of Protestants engaged in the trade.

1703 The Irish Parlt. addresses the Crown in vain, representing that 'the number and power of Papists is very formidable' (Irish Commons Journals).

However the linen trade, which was in some small way encouraged in the act of 1699, was by the immigration of Huguenots increasing and by 1710 the trade of Ireland was greater than in 1698 (Dobbs).

The above shews a picture of selfishness and shortsighted folly, but it also fails to shew the cause of Ireland's want of commercial prosperity. So far as there is blame Irishmen must be in great part to blame for that. It is to be desired, but it has not yet been seen, that some statesman both powerful and unselfish shd. apply himself to this matter. There is not a breath stirring to do it now: what little has been done in the recent past is the work of such people as Fr Davis, Baroness Burdett-Coutts, and Mitchell-Henry.[3]

I am, sincerely yours, Gerard M. Hopkins.

[1] See letter of 25–6 Mar. 1887.

[2] A term for Roman Catholics or adherents to the Pope, usually used disparagingly by opponents.

[3] Fr. Davis was the parish priest of Baltimore, Co. Cork who, helped by the wealthy philanthropist Baroness Burdett-Coutts (1814–1906; *ODNB*), worked to establish a well-equipped fishing industry and to create in England a demand for Irish embroidery and the products of other cottage industries. The Baroness had been enthusiastically received in Baltimore on her first visit there only three years before the date of this letter. Mitchell Henry (1826–1910; *ODNB*) was an English industrialist who bought an estate at Kylemore, Co. Galway and became MP for the county. He built and lived in Kylemore castle and his reclamation of thousands of acres of bogland brought money into the district.

6 April–Maundy Thursday[1] 1887 to Alexander William Mowbray Baillie

FL, no. CLIX, p. 284 UCD L 68
Three folded sheets of paper watermarked 'BROWNE & NOLAN DUBLIN' and with university printed heading; 12 sides.

UNIVERSITY COLLEGE, | S^T STEPHEN'S GREEN, | DUBLIN. [*printed heading*]
April 6 '87

Dearest Baillie, — I ought to have written before to acknowledge and warmly to thank you for the very valuable tables you send. I am going more closely to study them and tabulate some results. My first impression however is that Greek and Egyptian must be languages very unlike and 'disparate' (a rare word for a common thought: how is it there is not a better one?) in their systems of sounds, as appears by the inconsistency and fluctuation with which one letter is put for another, especially vowels. I do not enter into details today.

Clearly the vowels in Egyptian cannot have been distinctively important: I mean they cannot have served to distinguish (for instance) roots. But there may have been laws regulating their use which depended on the consonants they accompanied, the accent, the construction, and so on: these laws may have been complex and as impossible now to discover as the Greek accent would have been if it had not been ~~re~~ put on record.

Thoth is written *Θευθ* in Plato somewhere; [2] I have not the place. It must somewhere else be *Θωθ* I think.

I know now where to find Skeat's dictionary and Murray's.[3] I am going to write to Skeat about scope. My informant was a commander R.N. and positively knew.[4] I have doubts about Skeat's ~~wh~~ treatment of a whole class of words like scope, cope, scoop, scape, cap. Though some of these words as they stand (not scope) may have come to English from French or low Latin, yet they must ~~have~~ before that have got into those same languages from English or some Teutonic one. Escape comes from cape, but cape cannot come from cope the Church vestment: cope the vestment must come from cape or from an older unecclesiastical sense of the word cope. Cope probably is a popular or slang word: even now the ritual term in Latin is (in the Roman missal) ^not cappa but^ ~~pl~~ pluviale, and ~~even~~ that is itself a slang word; for this very solemn vestment, used in processions and so forth, cannot really have been a 'topcoat': that must be an altarboys' term. Clearly casula | hut, ~~the~~ from which chasuble, is popular or altarboys' slang. Rochet is from rock — German, ^and cotta I suppose from coat.^ I suspect that cope then comes from the root of coop in hencoop | and of shop (= scop).

There is a word scape which is another form of skep or skip | basket or cage (see Jam~~i~~eson). So that perhaps even landscape may be a genuine English formation. For in Milton it appears landskip, already ~~abraded and~~ worn down from the form it must have borne at the time of borrowing from the Dutch — if it was borrowed: now that time must have been recent. However this is not *πρὸς Διόνυσον* {*to do with Dionysos*}.[5]

Holidays have begun and I am very tired and unable to do the work which I have to wait for holidays to do: it is a vicious circle. However I am going down to the country for a few days in Easter Week, I hope.

Believe me your affectionate friend Gerard M. Hopkins.

Have you got Maspéro's Archéologie égyptienne?[6] If so, is it good ?

Have you seen about Petrie's interesting discoveries at Thebes (is it?)?[7]

I have a few words on politics to add. I do not think that my mind is one altogether of despair. Of one course, the refusal of Home Rule to Ireland, I despair; of the other, ^the granting it,^ though it is dangerous, I do not despair: there is, as often, a choice of evils and one is much worse than the other. It is good to recognise the facts. In some cases there is [a] kind of longsighted wisdom in a stubborn refusal to see them when they are adverse, in not knowing when you are beaten: there might be, putting the question of justice aside, something of the sort here if the English nation, if its public men, were agreed; but the fatal, the traitorous, spirit of party has paralysed ~~the~~ ^its^ strength and resolution ~~of action.~~

You say the legislation of the century, of the last half and the last quarter of a century, has been more and more favourable and advantageous to Ireland (or to that effect). So it has, ~~but s~~ and the Irish tenant farmers, who are the representative class, are now the most favourably placed of all tenant farmers in Europe; but look for yourself, see the effect: is Ireland, are the tenant-farmers satisfied? They are less so than ever before; their spokesmen in and out of parliament more violent, their champions in Ireland and America more bent on outrage, as dynamite and laying London in ruins,[8] than when the Irish were without power and without redress. I state the facts, however baffling.

National recognition, national aggrandisement, glory as a nation, is the passion of the Irish and the condition for that, the first at least, they consider to be Home Rule. ~~Now~~ And Home Rule they think within reach. Now the nearer passion is to its attainment the fiercer it is.

Besides this one class, not the whole nation, as speakers and newspapers would represent, but still the most important class want land for nothing if possible; if not ~~for~~ ^at a price^ the least possible. But for this, some of them (as a friend who travels and hears from themselves tells me) ~~some of them~~ do not want Home Rule: they fear heavy taxation. As things are however, the material self interest of a great class and the national self assertion, ~~of~~ or patriotism, of the people in general run the same way and work together and together are irresistible. They might once have been parted and made to balance one another, and this might have been done both wisely and justly. But now it is too late — not too late even now perhaps if some statesman of real genius arose; but where is he? Meanwhile I say what is.

~~I am~~ Maunday Thursday 1887.

[1] Maundy Thursday, Holy Thursday, the feast recalling the Last Supper, was on 7 Apr. in 1887. See letter of 16 June 1882.

[2] *Phaedrus*, 274C.

[3] Walter William Skeat's *Etymological English Dictionary* appeared in four volumes in 1879–82, and the first fascicle of the *New English Dictionary* (now the *OED*), which James Murray was editing, had appeared in 1884.

[4] One assumes this was Henry Schomberg Kerr (1838–95).

[5] A proverb, οὐδεν πρὸς τὸν Διόνυσον {*nothing to do with Dionysos*}, applied to innovations in drama, here means 'this digresses from my main theme'. See the Suda, s.v. *Lexicon*; Zenobius, s.v.

[6] Gaston Maspéro's *Archéologie égyptienne* (1887) was translated this same year into English as *Egyptian Archæology*.

[7] Sir William Matthew Flinders Petrie (1853–1942; *ODNB*), English Egyptologist, was working in 1887 at Aswan, Thebes (Luxor) West Bank (in the 'Valley of the Kings' the major discoveries of the tombs of the pharaohs were beginning), and Dahshur.

[8] See letter to his mother of 24 Jan. 1885 and *CW* vii.

n.d. ? Spring/Summer 1887 to his Father

The following account of a letter from GMH to his father occurs in Manley Hopkins's *The Cardinal Numbers* (London, 1887), 20–2 when he is writing of 'spectral images' and 'the power or condition of *seeing* numbers': 'What is now being described, and has been exemplified by plates in Mr. Francis Galton's volume [*Inquiries into Human Faculty*, 1883],[1] is the mental visibility of figures, or, as we might name them, *spectral numbers*' (pp. 18–19). We simply quote the whole passage as the least distorting way of including this letter. Since there is no date and there is no reference to the subject in other letters before the publication, one simply guesses at a date in 1887, some time before the examination period began to occupy all his time: but April is merely a conjecture, and the subject of Welsh numbers could have come at any time after the publication of Galton's book.

I cannot explain and illustrate spectral numbers better than by quoting a letter from the relation whom I have already mentioned. He writes the following as his own personal experience. After alluding to Galton's engraved specimens as being "very fantastic and interesting," he goes on to say, "I have such a pattern. From No. 1, which as scarcely seen, to 12, the numbers rise either uprightly, or leaning a little to the right, in a gloomy light. From 12 to 20, they run to the right, rising a little, and are in a cheerful daylight. From 20 to 100, the numbers are as if far away to my right, and seem as if I must go towards them, to see them properly. They are not very bright. From 100 to 1000 the figures are in another 'reach' – distant and indefinite. They appear to be returning to the left. A million is in a clear light, far off, on the left. Still farther, and behind, scattered over a sort of vague landscape, are billions, trillions, and the rest — all to the left; in blocks, not in lines. On the left of number *one* are a few minus numbers, and below it, swarms of fractions. The place where these appear is gloomy grass. Backgrounds of rooms and remembered open-air scenes appear in different parts of this picture or world." He adds, "It is remarkable that so many people make 12, and not 10, the turning point in their patterns."

Before returning to my point of departure in this digression, I may add some observations on numbers, which the same correspondent, my relative, makes.

He says that the Welsh are clumsy reckoners, or, rather, that they employ clumsy methods for reckoning, such as, commonly, the use of *five*, as being *half ten*, instead of using *ten* for counting. They often count and reckon in English; but, when counting aloud, they prefer the sort of symmetry which they conceive to exist in their habitual manner, and which to them is found convenient. Instead of naming *sixteen* or *seventeen*, they say *one upon fifteen*, or *two upon fifteen*. *Eighteen* is spoken of as "*two nines*" *nineteen* as "*four on fifteen*." This audible way of reckoning produces a sort of jingle; useful, for instance, to shepherds in telling the tale of sheep, and to others. From Wales, this kind of counting has spread into parts of England; it has been carried to America, and has even been adopted by Indians, having been lately found in use among them.

There are many forms of number jingles. One of them was given in the *Athenæum* (Sept. 22, 1877), and may be taken as a specimen. It runs as follows. The numbers are from *one* to *twenty*. *Iny*, *tiny*, *tethery*, *fethery*, *phips*, *ither*, *lather*, *cother*, *quather*, *dix*, *iny-dix*, *tiny-dix*, *tethery-dix*, *fethery-dix*, *bumfit*, *iny-bumfit*, *tiny-bumfit*, *tethery-bumfit*, *fethery-bumfit*, *jigget*. This form of jingle, used for counting stitches, scoring sheep, &c, prevails in the north of England, Scotland, and the Isle of Man. To us lowlanders it sounds as if it were the cant or slang of thieves. In Wales, the names of the first twenty numbers are as follows, their termination being mostly masculine, but a smaller number feminine. *Un*, *dau*, *tri*, *pedwar*, *pump*, *chwêch*, *saith*, *wyth*, *naw*, *dêg*, *arddeg*, *deuddeg*, *tri-ar-ddeg*, *pedwar-ar-ddeg*, *pymtheg*, *un-ar-bymtheg*, *dau-ar-bymtheg*, *deunaw*, *pedwar-ar-bymtheg*, *hugain*.

1 Francis Galton (1822–1911; *ODNB*) had written of visualized numbers in *Nature* (e.g. in his article on the subject in the issue of 15 Jan. 1880) and gathered his observations in this popular book.

26 April 1887 to his Mother

FL, no. CVII, p. 181 Bodleian, MS Eng. lett. e. 41, fos. 117–119v
Addressed to 'Mrs. Manley Hopkins | Court's Hill Lodge | Haslemere | Surrey | England'. PM DUBLIN AP 27 87 and HASLEMERE AP 28 87.

UNIVERSITY COLLEGE, | ST STEPHEN'S GREEN, | DUBLIN. [*Printed heading*]
April ~~25~~ ^26^ '87

My dearest mother, — I ought certainly to ^have^ answered your enquiries about the summer sooner. My holidays, that is the available ones, for all July no doubt will be littered with papers ~~and one examination, for B.A., ^and^ does not even begin till~~ and I am afraid more than July, will be in August and September. I do not anticipate much difficulty in getting leave. But I foresee that getting to chapel will be inconvenient: going to Guilford or elsewhere once in a way, as on Sundays, is all very well, but every day is another thing. And the train to those nearer places, as Liphook, is scarcely any convenience. No, it wd. be better and pleasanter to walk (all the way; that is ~~I~~ ^after all^ only a third or a quarter more than I should still have to walk if I took the train) or else find some ~~convenience~~ ^handy service^ of a butcher's cart or what not and so manage between one thing and another. Never mind about that now.

I have much more to say of Romola Tynte[1] besides what I wrote to Kate. First remark the spelling — Tynte, not Tint. But alas! now we must brush the bloom: ~~her na~~ ^she^ is not of the Tyntes of County Wicklow, ^Tyntes will fade,^ her name is not Tynte ~~to s~~ at all, ~~Tyntes will fade, and~~ (I blush to write it) ~~she~~ her name is Potter. Her father is a clergyman of some sort. He is a stern parent, and here romance comes in again. He wanted her to marry against her will; she refused; and he told her to shift for herself. So the poor thing had to take to dramatic recitals. She works hard. Her costume (what I described) was designed by Oscar Wilde.[2] She wore it yesterday at Mrs. More Madden's.[3] If she has only one costume she must indeed be poor: ~~I~~^i^t is true she could not easily ~~have~~ ^find^ another so becoming. ~~(~~But some of the young men there said she had inadvertently come in her night-gown.~~)~~ They also said she "made up well". I hope the poor thing will "make up well" for her hard usage by success. She was introduced to Fr. Delany, who found her frank and unassuming. Everybody is talking of her now. She is going to give a farewell recital at the Antient Concert Rooms tomorrow and I am going. There is a portrait of her in the Hibernian Academy and three in the music shop windows, one after Sant.[4] I am every moment afraid to hear that her Christian name is not Romola either. I suppose she will break upon London now.

With best love to all, I am your loving son Gerard.

In Easter week I was down with my old pupil Bernard O'Flaherty at Enniscorthy in Co. Wexford. Weather cold but bright, country beautiful, and the people very ~~ho~~ kind and homely.

Miss Cassidy has given me two more invitations to Monasterevan, but it cannot be.

[1] Katharine Tynan in her *Twenty-five Years: Reminiscences* (1912) recounts how she came across Romola Tynte at Lady Wilde's and she 'struck me dumb with admiration. She was a Miss Mary Potter, who afterwards was a public reciter under the name of Romola Tynte. She was very beautiful, and her straight, falling cloak of black plush, her wide black hat with a rose in it, seemed to me a garb for an æsthetic princess' (p. 130). The 'farewell recital' was reviewed in the *Irish Times* (Thursday, 28 Apr. 1887). The room was packed and Miss Tynte recited 'Out of work' and 'Late for dinner' (G. R. Sims), 'The legend of Provence' (Adelaide Procter) with musical effects, 'The Spanish mother' (Sir F. Doyle), 'The deadly weapon' (G. R. Sims), 'Not in the programme' (Collier), a scene from *Macbeth*, 'The captive' and 'Aux Italiens', again accompanied. Interspersed with the spoken items were songs: Theo. Marzial's 'River of years' (sung by Mrs Standish Rowley), 'La dove prende' (Mrs Rowley and Mr E. Wolseley), 'Tell her I love her so' (sung by Mr Wolseley), and 'The Devout Lover' (sung by Lieutenant H. H. Butterworth). An enthusiastic opinion of her recitation and a sonnet to her, which had appeared in the *Dublin Evening Mail* in 1887, were reprinted in Ramsay Colles's *In Castle and Court House* (1911). See also *The*

Complete Letters of Oscar Wilde, ed. Merlin Holland and Rupert Hart-Davis (2000), 292, where she is identified as Helen Potter, author of *Impersonations* (1891). She was still reciting in 1894, when the *New York Times* for 3 Jan. 1894 reports a 'tragic little rendition'.

[2] Oscar Wilde was entering his most productive and important period of writing, and had just agreed to edit and reshape *Woman's World*, but he had been lecturing on dress both in England and America for some time.

[3] Dr More Madden was a prominent doctor in Dublin, listed with Michael Cox and Frs. Delany and Conmee in the party that met Queen Victoria for her visit in Apr. 1900.

[4] James Sant (1820–1916; *ODNB*), a prolific British portraitist, member of the Royal Academy and from 1872 'Principal Painter in Ordinary' (official portrait painter) to Queen Victoria and her family.

1 May 1887 to Robert Bridges

LRB, no. CXLVIII, p. 254 Bodleian, Dep. Bridges, vol. 92, fos. 134–135[v]

University College, Stephen's Green, Dublin. Mayday 1887.

Dearest Bridges, — Perhaps if you sent yr. Bacchus now I could make some suggestions. It is true I am beginning my sets of papers, but it will be not so easy later, and later still might be too late. But perhaps now is too late. The truth is I ought to have written for it before going down to Enniscorthy on ~~M~~ Easter Monday: I had then till Saturday down in the country.

You too spoke of answering some ~~le~~ letter of mine "and that soon". I do not remember what needed answering, but the words themselves are such as lead the prudent reader to prepare for the worst. He sees that you are getting leave for more delay. A promise is a kind of fulfilment; it is interest on capital; it is a [*a new page starts here*] a light meal in the afternoon, that "spoils dinner" and leads to that being put off two hours longer.

A beautiful Sappho has broken on Dublin, Miss Romola Tynte: she gives dramatic recitals. Oscar Wylde designed her very becoming costume and she herself, I suppose, her equally becoming name. The Muse of History in reply to correspondents calls her Mary Potter.[1]

I have written a good deal of my book on the Dorian Measure or on Rhythm in general. Indeed it is on almost everything elementary and is much of it physics and metaphysics. It is full of new words, without which there can be no new science. Would it were done: but I hope it will have been done once for all.[2]

With best love to Mrs. Bridges and Mrs. Molesworth AND FOR THE MATTER OF THAT (Mr. Parnell's words)[3] Mrs. Waterhouse, I am your affectionate friend Gerard. Or rather to Mrs. Waterhouse kind regards.

[1] See previous letter.

[2] It never was finished. See letters 18–19 Oct. 1882 to RB, 14 Jan. 1883 to AMWB, 2–4, 21–2, and 28 Oct. 1886 to RB, 7 Nov. 1886 to Patmore, 11 Dec. 1886 to RB, 23 Dec. 1886 to AMWB, 20 Jan. 1887 to Patmore, 30 July 1887 to RB.

[3] From March of 1887, *The Times* ran a series of articles on 'Parnellism and Crime', culminating in an article on 18 Apr. 1887 linking Charles Stewart Parnell (1846–91; *ODNB*) with the Phoenix Park murders of 6 May 1882, and quoting the following letter sympathizing with the murders, which it was claimed he had written under the date 15 May 1882: 'Dear Sir,—I am not surprised at your friend's anger, but he and you should know that to denounce the murders was the only course open to us. To do that promptly was plainly our best policy. But you can tell him, and all others concerned, that, though I regret the accident of Lord Frederick Cavendish's death, I cannot refuse to admit that Burke got no more than his deserts. You are at liberty to show him this, and others whom you can trust also, but let not my address be known. He can write to House of Commons. | Yours very truly, | Charles S. Parnell.' Publication was obviously designed to sway opinion on the Perpetual Crimes Act, due for its second reading that day. Parnell delivered a speech in the House of Commons 'On the Forged Letter printed in the London "Times"', during which he said: 'It is no exaggeration to say that if I had been in the park that day I would gladly have stood between Lord Frederick Cavendish and the daggers of his assassins, and, for the matter of that, between the daggers and Mr. Burke, too.' He recovered £5,000 in damages from the newspaper in 1889. See also *CW* vii. The Irish journalist and blackmailer Richard Pigott (1838–89; *ODNB*), who later admitted the forgery, fled to Madrid, and committed suicide. See letters of 10–11 Nov. 1888, 1 Mar. 1889.

12 May 1887 to Coventry Patmore (part only)

FL, no. CLXXXV, p. 378 Durham University Library, Abbott MS 200

From a copy, probably made by a member of Patmore's family, of an untraced original, and following its layout; 'is private' marks an omission of unknown length.

University College, | Dublin. | May 12, 1887.

Dear Mr. Patmore,—I have to acknowledge with thanks the National Library Edition of the Angel[1] and am delighted with the News of its sale. (These cheap issues are a great boon: indeed it was time they came, if literature was not to be buried under litter). It would seem that there is some kind of smoldering fame a writer may have, which on being fuelled with a cheap supply breaks into flame. That at least accounts for a part; the other part must be readers to whom you have hitherto been a name only or not even that. But every way it is truly good news. But now does it not show that I have some reason for wishing you not to aim at the few only? Here you see are the many. A friend said to me that the success of 'Called Back'[2] was greatly due to the size and price, by means of which publishers ["]tapped a stratum", so he said, of almost untouched reading or ready-to-read public. Now it seems that your Angel has tapped this same level — no but a lower and larger one the threepennies.

is private . . . .

I have now no paper on metre on hand but a good deal written of ^a^ sizeable book on that subject. For the purpose of grounding the matter thoroughly I am subjecting the terms of geometry, line, surface, and solid and so on, many others to a searching examination. Most therefore of what I have written is metaphysics and stiff reading, though written by me with a flowing pen (which you will say is just as it should not be). It must be rewritten for I see my ground clearer as I go on and so can recast the past matter to its advantage. This I do not mind, if only I have time, for I find writing prose easy and pleasant. Not so verse (though indeed such verse as I do compose is oral, made away from paper, and I put it down with repugnance). I have invented a number of new words; I cannot do without them. Still I have great doubts whether I shall be able to get on. It can only be done in spare time, and what is far harder, spare strength, so to speak. Believe me very sincerely yours,

Gerard M. Hopkins, S.J.

[1] No. 70 in Cassell's National Library (1886). *The Victories of Love and Other Poems* was added to the same series, No. 122, in 1888. In the 1880s this series, edited by Henry Morley, issued 209 volumes at weekly intervals at threepence (paperbound) and sixpence (clothbound).

[2] *Called Back* (1883) by Hugh F. Conway (pseudonym of Frederick John Fargus, 1847–85), sold 350,000 copies in four years. Fargus died of typhoid.

2 June 1887 to Katharine Tynan

Published in *Studies: An Irish Quarterly Review*, 63/252 (Winter 1974), 389–96, ed. David J. DeLaura; and *The Month*, NS 19/5 (May 1958), 268
HRHRC, Container 1.5

UNIVERSITY COLLEGE, | ST STEPHEN'S GREEN, | DUBLIN. [*printed heading*]
June 2 1887

My dear Miss Tynan, — Thank you very much for yr. elegant new volume,[1] which I hope more inwardly to value when I have read it all. The reading of the earlier pages gives me the impression of a freer and surer hand than before. You seem also to employ more sparingly the form characteristic of our time which consists in two short epithets like "gold soft hair," "warm wet cheek," and so on. This being my busiest time of year or at least the most anxious, when I prepare my examination papers, I ~~can~~ cannot now write more; but when I meet you there is a metrical point I should like to remonstrate with you upon. Meantime I remain yours sincerely Gerard M. Hopkins S.J.

P.S. I wrote a longish letter yesterday on the metrical matter, but have destroyed it, and think it better to deal with it by word of mouth.

[1] *Shamrocks* (Kegan, Paul, Trench, 1887).

18 June 1887 to Richard Watson Dixon

CRWD, no. XXXIX, p. 151 Bodleian, Dep. Bridges, vol. 93, fos. 157–159[v]
Addressed to 'The Rev. Canon Dixon | Warkworth Vicarage | Acklington | Northumberland.' PM DUBLIN JU 19 87. One folded sheet with printed address.

UNIVERSITY COLLEGE, | ST STEPHEN'S GREEN, | DUBLIN. [*printed address*]
June 18 1887

My dear Friend, — I have just begun my examining and shall be hard at it for weeks, a weary task indeed, but I must just let you know of (~~but~~ ^though^ that you ^perhaps^ will already; at any rate I wish to speak of it) an admiring notice of ~~Songs~~ ^your^ Lyrical Poems in today's

Academy.[1] It quotes all the Spirit Wooed and says it is "an ode which takes rank with the finest in English". After that he <the critic> makes further discoveries. There is an 'Ode to Fancy' which haunts him; there are songs which sing themselves; there are lines scattered all about which seem to interpret theories he once read about the province of the 'imagination' in poetry.

"'Morning . . . claspèd hands'.

Indeed, he would not like to be asked too suddenly why this is all only minor poetry, as it must be since he is writing only a minor review of it". (The ~~lin~~ couplet "Morning' etc seems to be quoted in illustration of what goes just before.)

I was down at Monasterevan lately and managed to see the young lady of the Elegy,[2] which however I have had no chance of continuing ~~it~~. She was in the earthquake on the Riviera and was much frightened.

Believe me your affectionate friend Gerard M. Hopkins.

[1] About a column (mainly quotation) is given to the book. GMH gives the gist of it. RB added a footnote to this letter: 'The Academy Rev. mentd in this letter was by H. Beeching Rector of Yattendon who knew of the poems thro' me.' Henry Charles Beeching (1859–1919; *ODNB*) was a Balliol man, who became Rector of Yattendon from 1885 to 1900. He married RB's niece, Mary Plow, daughter of Harriett Louisa Bridges and Anthony John Plow; he was later Dean of Norwich.

[2] See letter of 29 Mar. 1887 and n. 3.

7 July 1887 from Richard Watson Dixon to GMH

CRWD, no. XXXIX A, p. 152 Campion Hall, D 7/7/87

Addressed to 'The Rev[d] Gerard Hopkins S.J. | University College, | Stephen's Green, | Dublin | Ireland'. PM ACKLINGTON JY 7 87, WARKWORTH JY 7 87, H&K PACKET JY 8 87.

Warkworth Vicarage, | Northumberland. | 7 July 1887

My dear Friend,

I have been long in acknowledging your kindness in writing to tell me of the Academy review. Thank you indeed. It was a pleasing incident.

You will now be in the midst, I suppose, of your Examination work: which is no doubt very severe & wearisome. Bridges has mentioned something of your music work, besides what you have told me yourself. How is that getting on? And do finish that Elegy.[1]

Have you happened to see anything of the controversy on Gosse's book "From Shakespeare to Pope", which shook the literary world (i.e. about half a dozen periodicals) some months ago?[2] I happen to have been reading the book. It is not good: but has some interesting points. Gosse is such a poor writer. If it were entirely rewritten, it might be made something of.

Some time or other I sd. be glad to have your opinion of a narrative poem in couplets, of the Byzantine times, that I have.[3] I will say more about it when I send it: which may not be for months.

I expect Bridges here this month, perhaps next week.

I am your affec^te^ friend
R. W. Dixon

[1] 'On the Portrait of Two Beautiful Young People'; see also letters to RB of 2 Jan. 1887, to RWD of 27–9 Jan. 1887, to RB of 29 Mar. 1887, to RWD of 22–3 Dec. 1887, to his mother of 25 Dec. 1887, to RWD 29–30 July 1888.

[2] See letter of 31 Oct. 1886.

[3] 'The Story of Eudocia', subsequently printed by Daniel in 1888.

8 July 1887 to Katharine Tynan

Published in *Studies: An Irish Quarterly Review*, 63/252 (Winter 1974), 389–96, ed. David J. DeLaura; and in *The Month*, NS 19/5 (May 1958), 268–9
HRHRC, Container 1.5

UNIVERSITY COLLEGE, | S^T^ STEPHEN'S GREEN, | DUBLIN. [*printed heading*]

July ~~7~~8 1887 My dear Miss Tynan, — In replying to your kind bidding I have to say what you must bear in mind about everything, that this is with me the busiest time of the year and ~~leaves~~ ^that^ the work of examination leaves ~~time~~ ^leisure^ and strength (of mind at all events) for no other thing. During it all is haste and pressure, ~~af~~ before it ^all^ anxiety and worry. The Spring therefore went by and I did not attempt to visit you. And now the only chance would be a day stolen from the Papers. This is of itself desirable and even necessary, but I have promised if possible to visit a sick man at Howth and that is what I must first do. If later I should find an evening I will try and reach Whitehall.[1] I do not think it well to concert anything with Fr. Russell: our conveniences would then have to wait ~~one~~ ^on^ each other and this would be changing the difficult into the im~~practicable~~possible. I expect in August to go to England for a short ~~whle~~while[2] and if I do not see you before then still I might after. I ought to let you know the day I am coming, but I do not want to be met, thank you: it would not suit me. I now see what an ungraciously worded note I am writing, which yet I must send and make things better (or worse) by word of mouth. I am sincerely yours Gerard M. Hopkins.

[1] Katharine Tynan's farmhouse in Clondalkin near Dublin. GMH visited her there once with Fr Russell; Katharine Tynan, *Memories* (London, 1924), 155.
[2] GMH was on holiday in England for two to three weeks that August.

30 July–1 August 1887 to Robert Bridges[1]

LRB, no. CXLHX, p. 255 Bodleian, Dep. Bridges, vol. 92, fos. 136–139ᵛ

UNIVERSITY COLLEGE, | S$^{\underline{T}}$ STEPHEN'S GREEN, | DUBLIN. [*printed heading*]

July 30 1887
Prof. J. E.
lately publ
will be goo
of learning
book which
Also if
tor's name
get him to c
an I forget
It is an ex
the fundamen
paradoxical
but the anal
fine observa
the Caskets
I think

The drama ought ~~not~~ to grow up with its audience; but now the audience is, so to say, jaded and senile and an excellence it ~~has seen~~ ^knows of already^ cannot move it. Where a real novelty is presented to it, like Gilbert's and Sullivan's operas,[2] which are a ~~real~~ genuine creation of a type, it responds. However I cannot write more now and I have not the proper knowledge of the subject.

I have been reading the Choephoroi[3] carefully and believe I have restored the text and sense almost completely in the corrupted choral odes. Much has been done in this way by dint of successive effort; the recovery, from the "pie" of the MSS, of for instance the last antistrophe of the last ode is a beautiful thing to see and almost certain; but both [*GMH footnote, though the thing it refers to is missing*: *he always presents his ~~au~~ ~~hearers~~ θεαταί {*audience*}with new types (ἰδέας) or ideas, καὶ πάσας δεξιάς, all new hits.][4] in this and the others much mere pie remains and it seems to me I have recovered nearly all. Perhaps I might get a paper on it into the <u>Classical Review</u> or <u>Hermathena</u>:[5] otherwise they must wait to be put into a book; but when will that book or any book of mine be? Though I have written a good deal of my book on Metre. But it is a great pity for Aeschylus' choruses to remain misunderstood, for it is his own interpretation of the play and his own moral to the story.

What a noble genius Aeschylus had! ~~And~~ Besides the swell and pomp of words for which he is famous there is in him a touching consideration and manly tenderness~~, and~~ ^; also^ an earnestness of spirit and would-be piety by which the man makes himself felt through the ~~dramatist~~ ^playwright^. This is not so with Sophocles, who is only the learned and sympathetic dramatist; and much less Euripides.

On Irish politics I had something to say, but there is little time. "It only needs the will," ^you say^: it is an unwise word. It is true, it (that is, to govern Ireland) does 'only need the will'; but Douglas Jerrold's[6] joke is in place, ~~of~~ ^about^ Wordsworth (or whoever it was) that could write plays as good as Shakespeare's 'if he had the mind', and 'only needed the mind'. It is a just reproach to any man not to do what lies in his own power and he could do if he would: to such a man you may ^well^ say that the task in question only needs the will. But where ~~action~~ a decision does <u>not</u> depend on us and we cannot even influence it, then it is only wisdom to recognize the ~~want of will in~~ ^facts — the will or want of will in those, not us, who have control of the^ question; and that is the case now. The will of the nation is divided and distracted. Its judgment is uninformed and misinformed, divided and distracted, and its action must be corresponding to its knowledge. It has always been the fault of the mass of Englishman[7] to know and care nothing about Ireland, to let be what would ^there^ (which, as it happened, was ^persecution,^ avarice, and oppression): ^and^ now, as fast as these people wake up and hear what ^wrong^ England has done~~,~~ ^(^and has long ceased doing~~,~~^)^ to Ireland, they, like that woman in Mark Twain, "burst into tears and rushing upstairs send a pink silk parasol and a box of hairpins to the seat of war".[8] If you in your limited but appreciable ~~e~~sphere of influence can bring people to a just mind and a proper resolution about Ireland (as you did, you told me, take part in your local elections) do so: you will then be contributing to that will which 'only is wanting'; but do not reproach me, who on this matter have perhaps both more knowledge and more will than most men. If however you think you could do but little and are unwill~~n~~ing even to do that (for I suppose while you are writing plays you cannot be canvassing electors), then recognise with me that with an unwavering will ~~on o~~^,^ or at least a flood of passion, on one, the Irish, side and a wavering one or indifference on the other, the English, and the Grand Old Mischief-maker loose,[9] like the Devil, for a little while and meddling and marring all the fiercer for his hurry, Home Rule is ^in fact^ likely to come and ^even,^ in spite of the crime, slander, and folly with which its advance is attended, may perhaps in itself be a measure of a sort of equity and, considering that worse might be, of a kind of prudence.

I am not a judge of the best way to publish. Though double columns are generally and with reason objected to yet ~~I thou~~ I thought Nero looked and read well with them.[10] (I am convinced it is one of the finest plays ever written.) I have not seen Miss Taylor[11] for long: I half fear she has given up the Elegy.

I know scarcely anything of American literature and if I knew much I could not now write about it.

I hope soon to write to Canon Dixon. Give him my best love~~;~~. I am happy to think of your being together.

I daresay I shall be at Haslemere within the week. Court's Hill Lodge is the name of the house and is probably now not necessary.

Monsignor Persico[12] is going about. His coming will certainly do good. I should like to talk to him, perhaps may. I have met him at a great dinner.

Your affectionate friend Gerard.

Aug. ~~2~~ 1 1887. "Getting old"—you should never say it. But I was fortythree on the 28th of last month and already half a week has gone.

[1] RB evidently wished to destroy the first leaf of this letter, and of it kept only the address and date. There is, therefore, a considerable hiatus between the date and what has perforce become the beginning. The beginnings of lines are on the verso, which is usually p. 3 of GMH's letters.

[2] The collaboration of William Schwenck Gilbert (1836–1911; *ODNB*) and Arthur Seymour Sullivan (1842–1900; *ODNB*) in the writing of comic operas was at its peak of quality and popularity. Beginning in 1874 with *Trial by Jury*, it continued through

H. M. S. Pinafore (1878), *The Pirates of Penzance* (1879), *Patience* (1881), *Iolanthe* (1882), *Princess Ida* (1884), to *The Mikado* (1885). *The Yeomen of the Guard* (1888) and *The Gondoliers* (1889) were yet to come.

[3] The *Choephoroi* (*The Libation Bearers*) is the second part of Aeschylus' trilogy, the *Oresteia*. The copy of the play, in the version edited by Arthur Sidgwick (1840–1920: *ODNB*) in 1884, which GMH used and annotated, is in the Irish Jesuit Archives, Dublin, and has extensive annotation on many pages, including that on which the last antistrophe occurs at lines 965–72. Sidgwick's notes say that these lines are 'Very corrupt and difficult' and GMH's suggestions invite further study. (Many thanks to Damian Burke of the Irish Jesuit Archives for making available images from this text.)

[4] GMH's footnote refers to Aristophanes, whose play *The Clouds* he is quoting and translating here. In the passage from which he quotes, ll. 547–8, the chorus speaks for the author and harangues the audience for a poor response to the play, comparing his writing to that of others: 'but I am always clever at introducing new fashions, not at all resembling each other, and all of them clever' (William James Hickie's translation, *Aristophanes's Birds, Frogs and Clouds* (1899)).

[5] There is no contribution by GMH in either review.

[6] Douglas Jerrold might have said this, but the story seems to originate with Charles Lamb, who wrote to Manning, 26 Feb. 1808: 'He [Wordsworth] says he does not see much difficulty in writing like Shakspeare, if he had a mind to try it. It is clear, then, nothing is wanting but the mind.' *The Letters of Charles Lamb* . . . , ed. E. V. Lucas (1935), ii. 51.

[7] Thus in MS.

[8] This has the appearance of a quotation, but from which of Twain's writings we do not know.

[9] W. E. Gladstone, playing with his nickname, the G.O.M. (Grand Old Man).

[10] Between 1885 and 1894, eight plays by RB (issued separately but with continuous pagination) were printed, all, except *The Feast of Bacchus*, in double columns.

[11] Miss Charlotte Mary Taylor (BA and BMus 1884 Royal University) was encouraged by GMH to write her Doctorate of Music diploma on RB's 'Elegy on a Lady whom Grief for the death of her betrothed killed'. See letter to RWD of 27–9 Jan. 1887.

[12] Ignatius Persico (1823–96) was in Mar. 1887 promoted to the titular archbishopric of Tamiatha and sent as Apostolic delegate to Ireland to report upon the relations of the clergy with the nationalist political movement. But before his final report had been delivered the Holy See condemned the Plan of Campaign (see letter to RB of 17–18 Feb. 1887, n. 10).

11 August 1887 to Robert Bridges

LRB, no. CL, p. 258 Bodleian, Dep. Bridges, vol. 92, fos. 140–1

On black-edged mourning paper.[1]

Court's Hill Lodge, Haslemere. [*printed heading*]
Aug. 11 1887

Dearest Bridges, — If you will come here, which will be delightful, we cannot, I am sorry to say, give you a bed, for the house will be full, but you can lodge either at the Railway inn almost next door or[2] at Mrs. Bush's at the Gables, ~~and we~~ which is perhaps preferable, and we will find what is possible and best (for Haslemere is sought after and full of visitors). In the meantime I am studying your essay, truly an admirable piece of work.[3] I think however that if space allows some things should be expanded. I am making considerable notes (not of course on your paper or vellum). I have also found some oversights. The observation about l̲ is new to me. No more now. Yours Gerard.

[1] GMH's maiden aunt, Ann Eleanor Hopkins, who had lived with GMH's family for large parts of her adult life, had died on 18 May 1887, though that may be too long ago to explain the mourning paper. For Haslemere, see the letter to Everard Hopkins of 5 Nov. 1885, n. 11.

[2] MS 'at'.

[3] The MS form of the essay, 'On the Elements of Milton's Blank Verse in *Paradise Lost*', contributed (pp. 19–37) to the edition of *Paradise Lost*, Book I, edited by the Revd H. C. Beeching, and published by the Clarendon Press in 1887. This essay grew eventually into a book, *Milton's Prosody* (1889, 1893, 1901, revised edn. 1921).

25 August 1887 to Robert Bridges

LRB, no. CLI, p. 258   Bodleian, Dep. Bridges, vol. 92, fos. 142–143[v]

Court's Hill Lodge, Haslemere. Aug. 25 1887.

Dearest Bridges, — First I want to thank you, Mrs. Bridges, Mrs. Molesworth, Miss Plow, Mrs. Waterhouse, Mr. Beeching,[1] and everybody concerned for the delightful visit (would it could have been longer) I paid to Yattendon.

Then I have to say that I must have left Miss Tynan behind:[2] did I not? If so please send her to Dublin and if you found anything complimentary to ~~say~~ ^remark^ it would be of service to me.

I must write to Mrs. Waterhouse about her little book.[3] It is charmingly written and we have all read it with great interest, but are divided as to whether it describes a fancy or a fact. I say a fact; but then ought not the place to be made known, that it may save more men?

I enclose for greater clearness on a slip what I suppose the paraphrase of "Fallen cherub, to be weak" is.[4]

I cannot but hope that in your metrical ~~pa~~ Paper you will somewhere distinctly state the principle of Equivalence and that it was quite unrecognised in Milton's and still more in Shakespeare's time. All, but especially young students, need to [be] made clearly to understand what metrical Equivalence is, that it is in use in English now, and that it was not then — and that it was Milton's artifices, as you explain them, that helped to introduce it. Now not to say this, when the context cries for it, is . . is . . I can find nothing ~~but~~ to call it but blasted nonsense. It is like the tedious and distracting keeping-up of mystification in a comedy; which brings me happily to the Feast of Bacchus.

The Menandr~~e~~ian period[5] appears to me the dullest and narrowest world that one could choose to lay an action in, a jaded and faded civilisation; moreover I have a craving for more brilliancy, more picturesque, more local colour: however you austerely set these things aside and I am to take the play for what it is. In its kind then, which has ^for me^ no attraction, and in its metre, which has to me no beauty, I think it a masterpiece. The language is a strong and chaste English; it is, I suppose, for us much what the French admire in Télemaque and in Racine's plays.[6] The dialogue is everywhere nature, than which more cannot be said: I like no touch better, though there are plenty, than Menedemus's saying that Antiphila drinks and Clinia's "Oh, father!" and what follows.[7] I daresay the metre will serve its purpose,[8] which is, I suppose, to give a slight form and pressure to the language and a corresponding degree of ~~I~~ idealisation, and it may work well on the stage: in itself I do not admire it. The only particular fault I find is that there are many lines in which the pause in the middle, without which, as it seems to me, it is merely prose rhythm and not verse at all, is wanting. I may add that the continual determination to be smooth and lucid ^in style^ gives upon the whole a sort of childish effect. I have only read it once through and therefore add no more now. I do not however think that I shall have much more to say. I could not recommend you to write more Menandrian plays. The going to a book of astrology for gibberish, as if one sent to the Azores for hay or salt or brown paper, is a strange freak.[9]

I am going away tomorrow and expect to be in Dublin by Saturday or Sunday.

I hope Mrs. Bridges is better and, with the kindest remembrances, remain your affectionate friend Gerard Hopkins.

[1] See letter to RWD of 18 June 1887, n. 1.

[2] Probably the book of verses called *Shamrocks*, published in 1887. See letter to Tynan of 2 June 1887 and Biographical Register.

[3] *The Brotherhood of Rest*: it described an imaginary place.

[4] Fall'n Cherube, to be weak is miserable
Doing or Suffering: . . .
Paradise Lost, I. 157 sqq.

[5] RB's note says: 'This attempt to give Menander to the English stage is based upon his "Heautontimorumenos" as we know it through Terence.'

[6] *Télémaque* was written by Fénelon (1651–1715) in the middle of the 1690s for the teenage Duke of Burgundy, second in line to the French throne, and was one of the most popular works of the 18th c. The tragedies of Jean Racine (1639–99), such as *Phèdre* (1677) and *Andromaque* (1667), are of a classic simplicity of style.

[7] *The Feast of Bacchus*, V, ll. 1380 sqq.

[8] See RB's n. 1 to this play for an account of the metre used.

[9] A reference to the pseudo-Persian spoken in the play.

7 September 1887 to Alexander William Mowbray Baillie

FL, no. CLX, p. 287 UCD L 69
One folded sheet of paper watermarked 'BROWNE & NOLAN DUBLIN' and with university printed heading and one folded sheet; 8 sides.

UNIVERSITY COLLEGE, | S$^{\underline{T}}$ STEPHEN'S GREEN, | DUBLIN. [*printed heading*]
Sept. 7 1887

Dearest Baillie, — It was not D'Arcy Thompson himself,[1] but the next worst thing, his son, who with two companions was boating on Lough Corrib near Galway, where Thompson lives. They landed on an island, I am told, where an old man begged them not again to put out, foreseeing, I suppose, a squall. But they would not heed him, not realising, no doubt, the danger, and were all drowned: their watches were found stopped at about ten minutes after the man's warning. I will give you more particulars when I learn them, viz. the young man's Christian name and anything else. "Professor" is probably a confusion with his father; but however Thompson has a son, his eldest I think, who is Professor of Biology or Physics at (if I mistake not) Durham.[2]

In our too short meeting I forgot to speak of D'Arcy Thompson and will only say now that I took to him strongly and felt much at my ease with him.

~~After~~ ^On^ leaving town I went down to Haslemere in Surrey and spent a fortnight in a very beautiful country. I also had a glimpse of the Manchester Exhibition on my way back: it is worth your while to see.[3] I had to take to setting fresh examination-papers on my return and am still so engaged and scarcely feel any better for my holiday unhappily and am attacked with eczema, a fashionable complaint — to use a consideration which is like the flower upon the nettle. For this and other reasons I could wish I were in the Highlands. I never had more than a glimpse of their skirts. I hurried from Glasgow one day to Loch Lomond. The day was dark and partly hid the lake, yet it did not altogether disfigure it but gave a pensive or solemn beauty ~~to it~~ which left a deep impression on me. I landed at Inversnaid (of Wordsworth and Matthew Arnold)[4] for a few hours and had an inspiration of a very good tune to some lovely words by Canon Dixon, of whose poems (almost unknown) I am a ~~most~~ ^very^ earnest admirer.

Remember me to Sir Charles Pearson[5] if he ^will^ remember~~s~~ on being reminded. I am your~~s~~ affectionate friend Gerard M. Hopkins.

[1] See letter of 23 Dec. 1886 to Baillie.

[2] Sir D'Arcy Wentworth Thompson (1860–1948; *ODNB*), Professor of Natural History, St Andrews University, 1884–1948.

[3] The Manchester Royal Jubilee Exhibition was opened by the Prince of Wales in May 1887. It was very much on the model of the Great Exhibition of 1851.

[4] See Wordsworth's 'To the Highland Girl of Inversnaid'. See letter to RWD of 30 June–3 July 1886.

[5] Sir Charles John Pearson, Lord Pearson (1843–1910; *ODNB*), judge, was at Edinburgh Academy in Baillie's time there, proceeded to the University of St Andrews, and then to Corpus Christi College, Oxford, where he distinguished himself in classics, winning the Gaisford Greek prizes for prose (1862) and verse (1863). He graduated BA with a first class in the final classical school in 1865.

28 September 1887 to Robert Bridges

LRB, no. CLII, p. 260 Bodleian, Dep. Bridges, vol. 92, fos. 144–145[v]

THE MOURNE HOTEL | ROSTREVOR, | Co. DOWN. [*printed heading*] On my way back to Dublin Eve of Michaelmas '87

Dearest Bridges, — I will see what I can do for ~~me~~ ^you^ while my eggs are boiling (hard by express instructions). This, let me tell, you is a beautiful spot; but to business. Where is the Feast of Bacchus? In my box, which will go to Dublin by goods train from Dromore, from a house once Bishop Percy's,[1] and grounds ^and groves^ by him very tastily planted then and haunted now. The book is there and I hope safe; the sense of it, with judgment thereupon, is in my head. My judgment is in substance the same as at the first reading, but my feeling is changed: I enjoy it more. It is "an excellent piece of work: would 'twere done"[2] — on the stage. In its own kind I believe it could not be bettered. ~~The~~ I have made no notes and offer no verbal criticisms but one, that to repeat a question as Chremes somewhere does, If I have been to town? = Si je suis allé à la ville? appears to me not English: there is, ~~I~~ ~~if I am~~ unless I mistake, no such idiom.[3] The rhythm wd. I ~~im~~ believe have an excellent effect in performance~~:~~. I will not now say it has no beauty of itself: as verse it has to my ear none; but as a form, as a simple rhythm given to diction, and making such diction intermediate between ~~prose and~~ verse and prose it is elegant. The value of the play is, like Terence's, as a study of human nature and in that it is firstrate; in vis comica {*comic power*}, ^in fun,^ like Terence too, it is not strong: still there is enough to make me laugh aloud sometimes. Th~~e~~is is, I believe, all I have to say and shall say~~.~~ on this subject and I will send the book from Dublin. Yes, I may add that, so far as I can see, nothing is gained by those amorphous lines without a ^middle^ pause (like 4 + 4 + 4): however it does not matter much (for I look on the rhythm as a rule, not as a law; as a convention, not as a nature) and I do not say they should be changed.

My broken ~~ho~~ holidays are coming to an end (now holidays and work, like sleep and waking, are dead opposite and ~~gain~~ both lose sadly by combination and enlacement) and I do not feel well: however I am in pretty good spirits. I read at Dromore another excellent romance, Christie Johnstone by Charles Reade: it chanced to be in the room. It seems to have been written in 1850;[4] contains some nonsense but more sense; ~~and a b~~ ~~plenty of wit, an ^too^ excess of rollick,~~ enough wit, too much rollick; a somewhat slipshod brilliancy; ^an overboisterous manliness;^ but a true mastery of the proper gifts of a romancer and especially of the natural-unfor~~e~~seen, which there should be in all good romance. The abundance of genius in ^English^ romance in this age appears to me comparable with its abunda~~nce~~nce in drama in the Elizabethan: but ^here^ I am afraid I speak to deaf ears. It would be worth while reading all that Charles Reade has written~~:~~. ~~w~~Was he a Scotchman?[5] this story is Scotch.

With other things I have not got on, but I have been touching up some old sonnets you have never seen and have within a few days done the whole of one, I hope, very good one and most of another; the one finished is a ^direct^ picture of ~~the~~ ^a^ ploughman, without afterthought.[6] But when you read it let me know if there is anything like it in Walt Whitman, as perhaps there may be, and I should be sorry for that. I am your affectionate friend Gerard. The eyes are almost out of my head.

Also I am at a fugue, of which I have great hopes. — vocal of course.

[1] Thomas Percy (1729–1811) was Bishop of Dromore from 1782 till his death.

[2] Sly's comment in Shakespeare's *The Taming of the Shrew*, I. i. 256–7: ''Tis an excellent piece of work, madam lady: would 'twere done.'

[3] *The Feast of Bacchus*, IV, l. 1071: *Pamphilius*. Have you not found them, father? *Chremes*. If I have found them?

[4] Published in 1853.

[5] Charles Reade (1814–84; *ODNB*) was born in Oxfordshire and educated at Oxford, where he became a fellow of Magdalen College and vice-president. He was called to the bar in 1843, Doctor of Civil Law (1847), and subsequently lived in London. He was a dramatist, but primarily a novelist of sixteen books, a number with social concerns (trade unions, lunatic asylums, etc.).

[6] 'Harry Ploughman'. The other one was probably 'Tom's Garland'.

11 October 1887 to Robert Bridges

LRB, no. CLIII, p. 262 Bodleian, Dep. Bridges, vol. 92, fos. 146–7

UNIVERSITY COLLEGE, | S^T STEPHEN'S GREEN, | DUBLIN. [*printed heading*]
Oct. 11 1887

Dear Bridges, — I will now return you Bacchus, with only one more remark, that so famous a text as Homo sum {*I am a man*}[1] deserves a more studied rendering. I am not at all contented with yours. It seems to me it should be something like: I am a man, and one ~~who~~ that thinks ~~that~~ he has ^everything^ to do with ^what has^ anything ~~that has~~ to do with man. I mean, it seems to me that having to do with is what has to be expressed. ~~B~~ Otherwise there is the proverb What is everybody's business is nobody's business, (the contrary of which Chremes holds) and it might be utilised.

I will enclose the sonnet on Harry Ploughman, in which burden-lines[2] (they might be recited by a chorus) are freely used: there is in this very heavily loaded sprung rhythm ~~a g~~ a call for their employment. The rhythm of this sonnet, which is altogether for recital, not for perusal, ^(^as by nature verse should be,^)^ is very highly studied:. From much considering it I can no longer gather any impression of it: perhaps it will strike you as intolerably violent and artificial.

I am your affectionate friend Gerard Hopkins.

[1] The famous line 'Homo sum: humani nil a me alienum puto' occurs in Terence's Menandrian *Heautontimorumenos*, and RB's final version of the line in *The Feast of Bacchus* for the character Chremes to speak is: 'I am a man. | Nought which concerns mankind concerns not me, I think'; *P. W.*, vi (1905), ll. 47–8.

[2] Refrain, chorus, or intercalary lines.

22 October 1887 to Alexander William Mowbray Baillie

FL, no. CLXI, p. 289 UCD L 70
One half sheet; 2 sides.

Oct. 22 1887

Dearest Baillie, — I saw D'Arcy Thompson once at our autumn examinations (just over: today the first free day; first lecture the day after tomorrow). Between two minds whether I should or should not allude to his loss, I decided to say "You have suffered a great affliction since ~~I saw~~ ^we^ last met" and told him of your letter of enquiry and that I had seen you.[1] He gave a kind of brokenhearted look but only said "How is Baillie?"

To tell you this is one purpose of this short letter, the other is to ask you to ascertain for me the address of a Mr. Drummond[2] a barrister of I rather think but do not swear Lincoln's Inn. He is, as you see (or "it goes without saying": how our civilisation is blistered with that phrase now! and with the word <u>grandiose</u>, which is my daily indigestion), though remotely, your countryman. He lives or lived at Hampstead, where I might have made his acquaintance years ago, but never did till this year in this country. He is a very charming fellow; ten years I dare say younger than us or more; fair haired, inclining to be stout, an aquiline nose, a buoyant manner. You may recognise him by these marks; for there will probably be several Drummonds at the bar. I want to write to him and cannot get his address. Thumb then your Register or whatever it is and oblige your affectionate friend Gerard M. Hopkins.

But in replying on no account confine yourself to the Head "Drummond, Henry" (or William: by the bye ascertain his Christian name). Wave your pen over the paper and call down on it the locusts of Egypt.

[1] See letter to Baillie of 7 Sept. 1887.

[2] This may be Lister Maurice Drummond (1856–1916), a Roman Catholic who was Secretary to the Evicted Tenants' Commission.

20–4 October 1887 to Coventry Patmore

FL, no. CLXXXVI, p. 379 Durham

UNIVERSITY COLLEGE, | S$^{\underline{T}}$ STEPHEN'S GREEN, | DUBLIN. [*printed heading*]
Oct. 20 1887

My dear Mr. Patmore, — I find I began writing to you a fortnight since. I was then examining: I am still, but am nearly at an end. I enclose the Paper[1] you sent, supposing that you could not wait for it longer. I had meant to write some remarks on it, but I cannot delay the Paper for them. I may send them afterwards.

But I make one now which will amaze you and, except that you are very patient of my criticisms, may incense you. It is that when I read yr. prose and when I read Newman's and some other modern writers' the same impression is borne in on me: no matter how beautiful the thought, nor, taken singly, with what happiness expressed, you do not know what writing prose is. At bottom what you do and what Cardinal Newman does is to think aloud, to think with pen to paper. In this process there are certain advantages; they may outweigh those of a perfect technic; but at any rate they exclude that; they exclude the belonging technic, the belonging rhetoric, the own proper eloquence of written prose. Each thought is told off singly and there follows a pause and this breaks the continuity, the contentio, the strain of address, which writing should usually have.

The beauty, the eloquence, of good prose cannot come wholly from the thought. With Burke[2] it does and varies with the thought; when therefore the thought is sublime so does the style appear to be. But in fact Burke had no style properly so called: his style was colourlessly to transmit his thought. Still he was an orator in form and followed the common oratorical tradition, so that his writing has the strain of address I speak of above.

But Newman does not follow the common tradition — of writing. His tradition is that of cultured, the most highly educated, conversation; it is the flower of the best Oxford life. Perhaps this gives it a charm of unaffected and personal sincerity that nothing else could. Still he shirks the technic of written prose and shuns the tradition of written English. He seems to be thinking 'Gibbon[3] is the last great master of traditional English prose; he is its perfection: I do not propose to emulate him; I begin all over again from the language of conversation, of common life'.

You too seem to me to be saying to yourself 'I am writing prose, not poetry; it is bad taste and a confusion of kinds to employ the style of poetry in prose: the style of prose is to shun the style of poetry and to express one's thoughts with point'. But the style of prose is a positive thing and not the absence of verse-forms and pointedly expressed thoughts are single hits and give no continuity of style.

After all the very Paper which leads me to make these remarks is entitled 'Thoughts on Knowledge etc', so that I am blaming you for not doing what you do not attempt to do. Perhaps then I ought to blame you for not attempting and doing. However I have said my say and feel inclined to burn it.

In the Paper itself there are some things I feel hard but do not speak of now. The parable of the carcase is in the highest degree illustrative and ghastly-vivid: it ought to be everywhere known.[4]

During the summer examinations one of my colleagues brought in one day a St. James's Gazette[5] with a piece of criticism he said it was a rare pleasure to read. It proved to be a review by you of Colvin's book on Keats. Still, enlightening as the review was, I did not think it really just. You classed Keats with the feminine geniuses among men and you would have it that he was not the likest but rather the unlikest of our poets to Shakspere. His poems, I know, are very sensuous and indeed they are sensual. This sensuality is their fault, but I do not see that it makes them feminine. But at any rate (and the second point includes the first) in this fault he resembles, not differs from Shakspere. For Keats died very young and we have only the work of his first youth. Now if we compare that with Shakspere's early work, written at an age considerably more than Keats's, was it not? such as Venus and Adonis and Lucrece,[6] it is, as far as the work of two very original minds ever can be, greatly like in its virtues and its vices; more like, I do think, than that of any writer you could quote after the Elizabethan age; which is what the common opinion asserts. It may be that Keats was no dramatist (his Otho I have not seen); but it is not for that, I think, that people have made the comparison. The Cap and Bells is an unhappy performance, so bad that I could not get through it; senselessly planned to have no plan and doomed to fail: but Keats would have found out that. He was young; his genius intense in its quality; his feeling for beauty, for perfection intense; he had found his way right in his Odes; he would find his way right at last to the true functions of his mind. And he was at a great disadvantage in point of education compared with

Shakspere. Their classical attainments may have been much of a muchness, but Shakespere had the school of his age. It was the Renaissance: the ancient Classics were deeply and enthusiastically studied and influenced directly or indirectly all, and the new learning had entered into a fleeting but brilliant combination with the medieval tradition. All then used the same forms and keepings. But in Keats's time, and worst in England, there was no one school; but experiment, division, and uncertainty. He was one of the beginners of the Romantic movement, with the extravagance and ignorance of his youth. After all is there anything in Endymion worse than the passage in Romeo and Juliet about the County Paris as a book of love that must be bound and I can't tell what?[7] It has some kind of fantastic beauty, like an arabesque; but in the main it is nonsense. And about the true masculine fibre in Keats's mind Matthew Arnold has written something good lately.[8]

My brother also sent me a paper of yours on Women's Rights,[9] very, perhaps cruelly, plainspoken.

The night, I think, before I began this letter I had a dream touching you which raises a point of interest. I thought I was at a station where cheap trips were advertised. I went to the bookingoffice and pulling out what I had in my purse, about three and sixpence, said 'I don't care where I go: put me down as near the sea as you can'. The clerk gave me a ticket for Lewes. I rejoiced and said to myself that I should now be able to get over to you at Hastings for a night. I think I have never been near Lewes these twenty years but in passing it to and from Hastings on my visit to you. So then, though I felt surprised at the Lewes ticket, it would seem that in my dream it was really Hastings suggested Lewes, not Lewes Hastings, and that I was really constructing the plot which should bring Hastings about, unknown to myself, all the time.

Believe me very sincerely yours Gerard M. Hopkins.
Oct. 24, 1887.

In reality I was in August in England at Haslemere, where my family now live, and had thoughts of trying to get over to see you, but time (principally) did not serve. Remember me kindly to all.

After rereading your letter — I can by no means remember, when I was enjoying your hospitality, that it was give on my part and take on yours; and if it was, it seems to me I must have babbled greatly.

[1] 'Thoughts on Knowledge, Opinion, and Inequality.' *Fortnightly Review*, Aug. 1887. Reprinted in *Religio Poetae* (1893). A letter from Patmore seems to be missing.

[2] Edmund Burke (1729–97; *ODNB*), influential Anglo-Irish orator, writer, and politician, best known for his *Reflections on the French Revolution* (1790).

[3] The energetic narrative, fluid prose, and persuasive arguments of *The Decline and Fall of the Roman Empire* (6 vols., 1776–89) by Edward Gibbon (1737–94; *ODNB*) have made it a classic in historical literature.

[4] Patmore sees a sheep's carcass moving with white grubs and contrasts their self-interested activity with the harmonious parts of the living animal; he then applies this to the ordered state of England contrasted with 'the sort of democracy to which we are fast drifting' (*Religio Poetae*, uniform edn., 1907, pp. 135–6).

[5] The issue of 28 June 1887, reviewing Sidney Colvin's *Keats*, English Men of Letters series (1887). The criticism is reprinted in *Principle in Art, &c.*

[6] William Shakespeare (1564–1616; *ODNB*) published the narrative poems 'Venus and Adonis' and 'The Rape of Lucrece' in 1593 and 1594, when he was nearly 30. John Keats (1795–1821; *ODNB*) wrote his Byronic poem 'The Cap and Bells' and his unsuccessful tragedy *Otho the Great* (with Charles Armitage Brown) in 1819–20, and died in 1821 at the age of 25.

[7] Lady Capulet in I. iii. 81 ff.

[8] The Preface to the selection from Keats in Ward's *English Poets*, iv (1880); and reprinted in *Essays in Criticism*, 2nd ser., 1888.

[9] Probably 'Why Women are Dissatisfied' (*St James's Gazette*, 29 Sept. 1887), the latter half of an essay 'The Weaker Vessel', begun on 7 Jan. 1887.

26 October 1887 from Coventry Patmore to GMH

FL, no. CLXXXVI A, p. 383 Campion Hall, P 26/10/87
Addressed to 'Rev[d] Gerard Hopkins, S.J. | University College, | St. Stephen's Green, | Dublin'. PM HASTINGS OC 26 87, H&K PAC OC 27 1887.

Hastings. Oct. 26. 1887.
My dear M[r] Hopkins,

Whenever I get a letter from you about anything I have written it makes me feel a little ashamed of myself; you give my words so much more attention than it seems to me they deserve, and I feel that I ought to have written so much better for such a reader.

I am quite of your mind about modern prose, including ~~your~~ ^my^ own, and I have said as much, in a paper I wrote in the St. James's some time ago,[1] I think, on Sir Thomas Browne. There are two reasons for my not attempting to make my prose what I know that prose might, and, on certain subjects, should be. First there is no audience for such writing; secondly, I could ~~do the~~ work in verse, with little more difficulty, and much more effect.

I cannot agree with your comparison of the early works of Shakespeare and those of Keats. In "Venus and Adonis" there is plenty of sensuality, but the intellect is immensely predominant, — more predominant, even, than it is in his later and greater works. In Shakespeare the sensuality seems the accident, in Keats the essence. Your remark on the real difference between the educational influences wh. operated on the two poets is I think very striking and true: but I do not think that it accounts for what seems to me to be their opposition of character. I have not seen M. Arnold's words on your side of the question. Surely also Keats' letters aid my view.

Your dream must have arisen from a lingering, imperceptible remorse at not having run over here from Haslemere, or, at least, not having given me the word that would have taken me to Haslemere.

I am considering whether it will be well to reprint the best of my papers in Quarterlies, Magazines, & St. James's. If I dont somebody, without any idea of selection, will probably do it when I am dead. Otherwise I should probably not entertain the idea.

We are all fairly well. Bertha is restored to perfect health — better, I think, than she has ever had. Piffie[2] is more delightful than ever, and I am learning a great deal from him — not only of the oracular knowledge of which he is naturally a professor, but of "science". I was pointing out to him the beauty of the "horns" of a silk-worm moth, the other day: "Piffie calls them antennæ, Papa."

Your's ever affectionately
C. Patmore

[1] The issue of 1 Apr. 1886, 'Sir Thomas Browne'. Reprinted in *Courage in Politics, &c* (1921), 54–9.
[2] Patmore's son; see letter to Patmore of 4–6 June 1886, n. 6.

2 November 1887 to Robert Bridges

LRB, no. CLIV, p. 263 Bodleian, Dep. Bridges, vol. 92, fos. 148–9

UNIVERSITY COLLEGE, | ST STEPHEN'S GREEN, | DUBLIN. [*printed heading*]
Nov. 2 1887

My dear Bridges, — You owe me a letter, but as I might wait longer and still want I write myself and ask you two things. I enclose a song ^turned up from a drawer to-day^ (if I ever gave you a copy before send this one back), which try, and try if you can like it, as I do greatly; but I am biassed: if you approve of it I sh~~ould~~^all^ be gladder than if it were mine.

Next please tell me how correctly to make codas to sonnets; with the most approved order of rhymes and so on. And do not say that I know and that I can find for myself and that there is one in Milton (that one is not enough), but do what I ask you. And soon: a sonnet is hot on the anvil and wants the coda.[1] It is the only time I have felt forced to exceed the ~~tim~~ beaten bounds.[2] I hope Mrs. Bridges is well and that nothing in the way of ill health has kept you from writing. I do not know whether I told you at the time, but, for fear it should never have been said, I may ~~tell~~ write now that when I was last at Yattendon I had the impression I had never in my life met a sweeter lady than Mrs. Bridges. ~~One~~ ^You^ may wear a diamond on your finger and yet never have seen it in a side light, so I tell you.

I hope soon to enter a batch of sonnets in my book and when I do that I can send you copies. They are the thin gleanings of a long weary while, but singly good.

I am your affectionate friend Gerard M. Hopkins.

[1] Probably 'Tom's Garland'.

[2] To 'beat the bounds' is to mark out the boundaries of a parish by striking significant points with a rod, so that observers can see where the territory lies; hence to indicate the limits.

6 November 1887 to Robert Bridges

LRB, no. CLV, p. 264 Bodleian, Dep. Bridges, vol. 92, fos. 150–153[v]

UNIVERSITY COLLEGE, | S[T] STEPHEN'S GREEN, | DUBLIN. [*printed heading*]
Nov. 6 1887

Dearest Bridges, — I must write at once, to save you the trouble of copying that music: I reproduced it by a jelly-process[1] at Stonyhurst ^on purpose^ and only wanted the copy back ~~if~~ in case you had one already. I do not remember anything about the harmony: it is the tune I think so good, and this I revived my memory of before I sent it you. I cannot at all make out the meaning of "If your sister has learnt harmony I can't understand what the moderns mean". Grace did learn harmony, but girls are apt not to study things thoroughly and perhaps she has not kept it up as she should. I remember years ago that the organist at Liverpool found fault with a hymn of hers, in four parts, very regular, for hidden fifths in the inner parts. But he was an ignoramus: I did not know then but I know now that hidden fifths must be and are freely used in the inner parts and are only faintly kept out of the outer ones. And see what became of him: he got drunk at the organ~~. (it is the~~ (I have now twice had this experience: it is distressing, alarming, agitating, but above all delicately comic; it brings together the bestial and the angelic elements in such a quaint entanglement as nothing else can; for ~~they~~ ^musicians^ never play such clever descants as under those circumstances and in an instant everybody is thrilled with the insight of the situation~~)~~)) and was dismissed. He was a clever young fellow and thoroughly understood the properties of narrow-necked tubes.

I am thankful to you for the account of the Coda, ^over^ which you gave yourself even unnecessary trouble. You say the subject is treated in many books. That was just it. I had not got those books and the ~~simplest~~ ^readiest^ source of information was you. It seems they are formed on ~~a uniform~~ ^an invariable^ plan and that Milton's sonnet gives an example.[2] Of course one example was enough if there is but one type; but you should have said so.

I want Harry Ploughman to be a vivid ~~pi~~ figure before the mind's eye; if he is not that the sonnet fails. The difficulties are of syntax no doubt. Dividing a compound word by a clause sandwiched in^to it^ was a desperate deed, I feel, and I do not feel that it was an unquestionable success.[3] But which is the line you do not understand? I do myself think, I may say, that it would be an immense advance in notation~~,~~ ^(^so to call it~~,~~^)^ in writing as the record of speech, to distinguish the subject, verb, object, and in general to express the construction to the eye; as i~~n~~^s^ done already partly ~~by~~ ^in^ ~~puc~~ ^punc^tuation by everybody, partly in capitals by the Germans, more fully in accentuation by the Hebrews. And I daresay it will come. But it would, I think, not do for me: it ~~seen~~ ^~~sem~~^ seems a confession of unintelligibility. And yet I don't know. At all events there is a difference. My meaning surely ought to appear of itself; but ~~in~~ ^in^ a language ^like English, and in^ ~~and~~ an age of it like the present, ~~is~~ ^written words are^ really matter open and indifferent to ^the receiving of^ different and alternative verse-forms, some of which the reader cannot possibly be sure are meant unless they are marked ~~out~~ for him. Besides metrical marks are for the performer and ~~those~~ ^such marks^ are proper in every art. Though indeed one might say syntactical marks are for the performer too. But however that reminds me that one thing I am now resolved on, it is to prefix short prose arguments to some ^of my pieces^. These too ^will^ expose me to carping, but I do not mind. Epic and drama and ballad and many, most, things should be at once intelligible; but everything need not and cannot be. Plainly if it is possible to express a sub[t]le and recondite thought on a subtle and recondite subject in a subtle and recondite way and with great felicity and perfection, in the end, something must be sacrificed, ~~in~~ ^with^ so trying a task, ^in the process,^ and this may be the being at once, nay perhaps even the being ~~at all~~ without explanation at all, intelligible. Neither, in the same light, does it seem to be to me a real objection (though this ^one^ I hope not to lay myself open to) that the argument should be even longer tha[n] the piece; for the merit of the work may lie for one thing in its terseness. It is like a mate which may be given, one way only, in three moves; otherwise, various ways, in many.

There is some kind of instinct in these things. I want^ed^ the coda for a sonnet which is in some sort "nello stilo satirico o bernesco" {*in a satiric or burlesque style*}.[4] It has a kind of rollic at all events. ~~It~~ ^The coda^ is an immense resource to have. This sonnet, I hope, very shortly.

In glancing over the Paper[5] I am ^much^ pleased with the additions and final treatment. (I remark various faults of punctuation.) I shall nudge the professors of English about this book and paper. Just now something catches my eye, p. viii. — "a pronunciation eale".[6] Better write eel: ~~It~~ ^that^ is a word. Now eale is not strictly "a pronunciation" but ^is^ the actual ^printed^ word of the passage in Shakspere about the "dram of eale", to which if you use this form you should certainly refer. Otherwise why that fantastic spelling? I am afraid it is however too late.

Mr. Tyrrell[7] (a ^devout^ convert) sets you to Trinity men to turn "into the original Greek".* [*GMH footnote*: * I do not mean literally that he says that.] More, more by token! The wreck of me that remains to study anything is studying Aeschylus, chiefly the lyrics, for a book (or set of Papers ~~there~~ in the Classical Review perhaps) thereon. He has made a number of happy conjectures, though I say it that know him too well, and yesterday a very happy one, Seven against Thebes 424–434, which redispose thus:[8] ET. *θεοὺς ἀτίζων . . Ζηνὶ κυμαίνοντ' ἔπη* (42~~7~~8–430.) . | *Ζεὺς δ' οὐκ ἀπειλεῖ* (for *Καπανεὺς δ' ἀπειλεῖ*), *δρᾶν παρεσκευασμένος* (427.). | *καὶ τῷδε κέρδει* (viz. the having heaven on our side) *κέρδος ἄλλο τίκτεται* (viz. that his boastful words ~~are~~ ^will prove^ to the enemy an omen of his defeat). | *τῶν τοι ματαίων . . κατήγορς* (424–426.) | *ἀνὴρ δ' ἐπ' αὐτῷ* (contrasted with *Ζεύς* above), *κεὶ στόμαργός ἐστ' ἄγαν* etc (434 sqq.). The source of all the confusion was ~~in~~ reading *ΖΕΥΣ* | *ΝΕΥΣ*, and then supplying *ΚΑΠΑ* and of course striking out *οὐκ*. But see how Aeschylus has borrowed your "And him Zeus stayed not to deride". Misplacing of lines in Aeschylus is almost certain.

Your affectionate friend Gerard M. Hopkins S.J.

No, I do not ask "enthusiastic praise". But is it not the case that the day when you could give enthusiastic praise to anything is passing or past? As for modern novels I will only say one thing now. ~~In~~ ^It is in^ modern novels ^that^ wordpainting most abounds and now the fashion is to be so very subtle and advanced as to despise wordpainting and to say that old masters were not wordpainters. Just so. ~~It~~ ^Wordpainting^ is, ~~the~~ in ^the verbal^ arts, the great success of our day. Every age ~~of~~ ^in^ art has its secret and its success, whe~~n~~^re^ even second rate men are masters. Second rate, third rate men are fine designers in Japan; second rate men were masters of painting in Raphael's time;[9] second rate men were masters of sculpture in Phidias' time; ^second rate men of oratory in Cicero's;^ and so of many things. These successes are due to ~~the~~ steady practice, to the continued action of a school: one man cannot compass them. And wordpainting is in our age a real mastery and the second rate men of this age often beat at it the first rate of past ages. And this I shall not be bullied out of.

For my case I shd. also remark that we turned up a difference of taste and judgment, if you remember, about Dryden.[10] I can scarcely think of you not admiring Dryden without, I may say, exasperation. And my style tends always ^more^ towards Dryden. What is there in Dryden? Much, but above all this: he is the most masculine of our poets; his ~~won~~ ~~language~~ ^style^ and his rhythms lay the strongest stress of all our literature on the naked thew and sinew of the English language. It is the praise that with certain qualifications one would give in Greek to Demosthenes,[11] ^to be^ the greatest master of bare Greek.

I am driven to the blackguard device of a palimpsest envelope.

[1] The hectograph or gelatin duplicator is a printing process which involves the transfer of an original, prepared in a special ink, onto a pan of gelatin in a metal tray, and taking copies by pressing paper on the reversed image. It was probably used in the school at Stonyhurst but has long fallen out of use, except, it is said, by tattooists.

[2] Milton's sonnet 'On the New Forces of Conscience under the Long Parliament' has two codas of a half line and a couplet, as does GMH's 'Tom's Garland'.

[3] Perhaps l.17, 'broad in bluff hide his frowning feet lashed'.

[4] The Italian satirists, especially the followers of Francesco Berni (1496–1535), had often used the caudated sonnet.

[5] On Milton's prosody.

[6] Milton: *Paradise Lost, Book I*, ed. Rev. H. C. Beeching (Oxford, 1887), p. 26 under 'Note on the word evil'.

[7] See letter to RB of 6 Oct. 1886.

[8] The usual modern numbering of the lines 424–38 discussed by GMH (e.g. in the Clarendon Press edition of G. O. Hutchinson, 1985) is 437–51. GMH's numbering agrees with that of editions of his day, such as *The Seven against Thebes of Aeschylus, with an Introduction, Commentary, and Translation* by A. W. Verrall (London, 1887). Verrall comments on p. 44 in a note to line 425 (modern 438) that 'There seems no reason to suspect any fault in these lines', although emendations have been proposed, for example by Keck, Brunck and Verrall himself.

We are grateful to Alistair Elliot for the following comment and translation: 'The Tyrrell conjecture for *Seven Against Thebes* line 427 (modern 440) which GMH admired involves more changes to the one line than could be accounted for palaeographically; it borders on rewriting Aeschylus's speech rather than correcting a scribe's faulty handiwork.

The best way to appreciate GMH's admiration of the conjecture and rearrangement of lines is to compare the two full trains of thought in a line-by-line translation. The speech responds to the messenger's alarm at the boasting of Capaneus. First, the original arrangement of lines (numbering as in GMH):

Messenger: Send against such a man – well, who will stand up to him?
Who without shaking can face a man shouting boasts?
Eteocles: And to this advantage another advantage is born: 424
The man's thoughts being empty – to other men – 425
The truthful tongue can condemn them [– to other men]. 426
Capaneus threatens, while quite ready to act; 427
Mocking the gods, giving his mouth a work-out, 428
In empty delight, a mortal, he throws to heaven 429
His swelling words into the ears of Zeus. 430
And I'm sure that down on him will justly come 431
That fire-bringer, lightning, real, not pictured like 432
The sun's warm rays at midday [on his shield]. 433
Against him, even if he's such a mouthman, 434
A shining warrior's posted, strong Polyphontes . . . etc. 435

Tyrrell and GMH amend and rearrange Eteocles' reply as they thought it might have been written by Aeschylus:

Eteocles: Mocking the gods, giving his mouth a work-out, 428
In empty delight, a mortal, he throws to heaven 429
His swelling words into the ears of Zeus. 430
But Zeus does not threaten, while quite ready to act; 427
And to this advantage another advantage is born: 424
The man's thoughts being empty – to other men – 425
The truthful tongue can condemn them [– to other men]. 426
And I'm sure that down on him will justly come 431
That fire-bringer, etc.

The new Tyrrell/GMH first line follows awkwardly from the last lines of the previous speaker. To start the next speech without a connecting word is unusual for Greek, which customarily begins sentences with "and" or some other conjunction. Moreover, the messenger's "person shouting boasts" is in the accusative case, and Eteocles immediately has him in the nominative. These are serious objections to the proposed changes, perhaps balanced by the obvious improvement in the line of thought. Finally, line 424 (as GMH knew it) is perfectly normal Greek but the phrase "to this advantage" does not seem to fit the context (what *is* this advantage?) and Keck's emendation "to this boasting" seems to have been accepted since GMH's time. GMH's feeling that "to this advantage" can be made to mean the advantage of having Zeus annoyed with Capaneus and therefore "on our side" (in Eteocles's mind) would seem to press the words rather hard, for the understanding of an audience in the theatre. Perhaps "to this boasting" would be better then even in the revision.'

[9] Three great figures: Raffaele Sanzio da Urbino (1483–1520), Renaissance painter; Phidias (*c*.480–430 BC), Greek sculptor whose work graced Athens, though little now can be ascribed to him with certainty; and Marcus Tullius Cicero (106–43 BC), philosopher and statesman of ancient Rome.

[10] John Dryden (1631–1700; *ODNB*), poet, playwright, and critic. For RB's views on Dryden see his *Collected Essays*, v. 123, note, and x, especially pp. 274 and 279.

[11] Demosthenes (384–322 BC), the greatest of the Greek orators, with a simple, pithy, and effective style.

21 December 1887 to Robert Bridges

LRB, no. CLVI, p. 268 Bodleian, Dep. Bridges, vol. 92, fos. 154–155v

UNIVERSITY COLLEGE, | ST STEPHEN'S GREEN, | DUBLIN. [*printed heading*]
Dec. 21 1887

Dearest Bridges, — I am (humbly I mean was) truly delighted to hear of your daughter's birth,[1] though I have left the news so long unacknowledged, and hope the little nymph and her mother are doing better and better. I mean to be of no length now; but, to shew you that the world marries and is given in marriage generally, ~~and~~ you are to know that my brother Everard is deeply in love with and properly betrothed to a Jessica, a sweet Jewess (by the nose, not by the faith and gaberdine: the~~y~~ whole family are of the Chris~~t~~htian pershuashionsh ash Chrishtianity goesh – I am afraid I have been profane, but I did not think of it till it was down), Miss Amy Sichel (WHY NOT SHEKEL? she has some). Nothing could aqual the hoigth of the pothry in which he announced the fact to me. But what are the prospects to English art? Disquieting: he will people the illustrated papers with lovely Rebe~~kka~~^ccas^ and Rachels and Esthers and Shumanites and Aholibamahs.[2] As for peopling the world, that in a match between ~~a~~ Christian and ~~a fa~~ Jewish blood, is quite another thing. If they have issue, then, when I consider that my father's and my mother's family have both an aquiline bent, I see ^in thought^ a procession of white elephants, of toucans, of something very gibbous and preposterous and obuncous. A TRUCE TO THIS BUFFOONERY.

Touching Aeschylus, if you wish to translate Prometheus do so and the choruses with the rest: I cannot undertake ~~it~~ ^them^. It would not be much to my purpose~~,~~: I do not care for a verse translation, but textual criticism, interpretation, and a prose paraphrase.

At Christmas if you write address Miss Cassidy, Monasterevan, Co. Kildare.

Please give my very best wishes to Mrs. Bridges and believe me your affectionate friend Gerard Hopkins.

What is she called?

[1] Elizabeth (1887–1977) was born on 6 Dec.

[2] Beautiful Jewish women of the Old Testament: Rebecca, Isaac's wife (Genesis 25: 20); Rachel, Jacob's wife (Genesis 29, 30); Esther, Ahasuerus's queen (Esther 2: 17); Shumanite, i.e. Abishag, a companion of David (1 Kings 1: 3); Aholibamah, a name given to Judith, wife of Esau (Ezekiel 28).

22–3 December 1887 to Richard Watson Dixon

CRWD, no. XL, p. 153
Addressed to 'The Rev. Canon Dixon | Warkworth Vicarage | Acklington | Northumberland | England'. PM DUBLIN 3 DE 23 87.

UNIVERSITY COLLEGE, | ST STEPHEN'S GREEN, | DUBLIN. [*printed address*]
Dec. 22 1887

My dear Friend, — It is long since I wrote to you, and I wonder why I should stint myself in one of the best pleasures of life. Bridges has a little daughter, I dare say you have heard; born on the 6th, I think. The weather, which has been wild but not dark or cold with us, has now turned to a sharp bright frost: I hope you do not find this, as you used to do at Carlisle, too searching. Tomorrow I am going down to my friends at Monasterevan in Co. Kildare, the scene of many misadventures (not to me) and now of the poisoning of the hounds, which threatens to put an end altogether to hunting in ^all^ that ~~part of the country~~ neighbourhood and with it to Punchestown races,[1] — what ~~altoge~~ ^would^ mean on the whole the ~~drainin~~ withdrawal of a great deal of money from the country. But that is how we live ^now^ and with fervour cut off our nose to revenge ourselves on our face.

I enclose two sonnets,[2] works of infinite, ^of^ over great contrivance, I am afraid, to the annulling ^in the end^ of the right effect. They have also too much resemblance to each other; but they were conceived at the same time. They are of a "robustious" sort and perhaps "Tom's Garland" approaches bluster and ^will remind you of^ Mr. Podsnap with his back to the fire.[3] They are meant for, and cannot properly be taken in without, emphatic recitation; which nevertheless is not an easy ~~feat~~ performance.

I have Blake's poems by me.[4] Some of them much remind me of yours. The best are of an exquisite ~~fre~~ freshness and lyrical inspiration, ~~the~~ but there is ~~mixed~~ mingled with the good work a great deal of rubbish, want of sense, and some touches of ribaldry and wickedness.

I cannot find your last letter, in which I think you spoke of shewing me some new poems. I should greatly like to read them; but I could not do so, I am afraid, with the closeness which is needed for ~~any much~~ serviceable criticism. I ought to have written about this before.

I thought I might copy some more sonnets, but they seem not quite ready and time runs. I cannot get my Elegy[5] finished, but I hope in a few days to see the hero and heroine of it, which may enable me (or quite the reverse; perhaps that: it is not well to come too near things).

Believe me your affectionate friend Gerard M. Hopkins.

Dec. 23 1887. The post is gone. I wish you a very happy Christmas and new year.

I am at work on a great choral fugue! I can hardly believe it.

[1] Punchestown racecourse at Naas in Co. Kildare is not far from Clongowes, Monasterevan and the Cassidys. The Kildare hunt sponsored Punchestown races, and had experienced disruptions for some years in the Land War. Charles H. E. Philpin (ed.), *Nationalism and Popular Protest in Ireland* (Cambridge, 1987), an essay on 'Stopping the Hunt, 1881–1882: An Aspect of the Irish Land War' by L. P. Curtis Jr. (pp. 349–402) describes an enthusiastic hunt supporter, Harry Sargent, writing in 1881 as 'The Fox': 'Running true to form after several Kildare hounds had been poisoned, "the Fox" declared that Punchestown races would be doomed if its sponsors the Kildare hunt, ceased operations. And if that happened, then the county stood to lose at least £100,000 through the cancellation of contracts to build a branch railway line that would take passengers to and from Punchestown' (p. 377). Sargent may have exaggerated, but Punchestown races were immensely popular, drawing a crowd of 150,000 on the first day of its 1868 meeting.

[2] Versions of 'Tom's Garland: on the Unemployed' and 'Harry Ploughman' were enclosed: now BL Add. MS 42711, fos. 153 and 154.

[3] A type of self-satisfaction and self-importance in Dickens's *Our Mutual Friend* (1864–5).

[4] William Blake (1757–1827; *ODNB*) achieved new popularity in the mid-19th c. with Alexander Gilchrist's *Life of William Blake* (1863), Algernon Swinburne's

first book-length study of the poetry in 1868, and enthusiastic praise from the Pre-raphaelites. GMH could well have been using Richard Herne Shepherd's new edition of *The Poems of William Blake* (1887) or even Henry Daniel's edition of Blake's *Songs* (1885).

[5] 'On the Portrait of Two Beautiful Young People'; see also letters to RB of 2 Jan. 1887, to RWD of 27–9 Jan. 1887, to RB of 29 Mar. 1887, from RWD 7 July 1887, to his mother of 25 Dec. 1887, to RWD of 29–30 July 1888.

25 December 1887 to his Mother

FL, no. CVIII, p. 182 Bodleian, MS Eng. lett. e. 41, fos. 120–1

Monasterevan [*printed heading on banner*]

My dearest mother, — I wish you a very merry Christmas season and happy new year and thank you for your kind gift, which I found waiting for me. Thank the girls for their letters. I hope Grace duly got the music: she does not mention its arrival, but I think she should have had it before the date of her letter.

You will see that I am staying with my kind friend Miss Cassidy and her sister Mrs. Wheble, and three younger Whebles are also in the house, cousins.[1]

I assisted the parish priest, who is recovering from a dangerous sickness, in giving communion this morning. Many hundreds came to the rail, with the unfailing devotion of the Irish; whose religion hangs suspended over their politics as the blue sky over the earth, both in one landscape but immeasurably remote and without ~~any~~ contact~~,~~ or interference. This ^phenomenon^ happens to be particularly marked at Monasterevan.

With best love to all, I am your loving son Gerard.
Christmas Day 1887.

These three young Whebles rejoice in the names of Tristram, Ursula, and Leo. They are half English, half Irish, and their nationality is thus divided: outwardly or in the body they are almost pure Paddy and Biddy, inwardly and in the mind mainly John Bull.[2] The youngest boy Leo is a remarkably winning sweetmannered young fellow.

[1] See letter to RB of 2 Jan. 1887, n. 1.The Cassidys owned a distillery in Monasterevan, the town's chief employer. The family were Catholic but loyal to the British government and served as magistrates, insisting on adherence to British law.

Miss Cassidy and Mrs Wheble, then in their late fifties or early sixties, were the sisters of the current owner of the distillery, James Cassidy. Mrs Wheble was widowed and the cousins were relatives of her late husband. GMH's duties at Monasterevan were to say mass for the family and to assist at Sts Peter and Paul, the local Catholic church opened in 1847. See *WHI*, 114–19.

[2] i.e. Irish in appearance but English in manner and thought.

1888

12–13 January 1888 to Robert Bridges

LRB, no. CLVII, p. 268 Bodleian, Dep. Bridges, vol. 92, fos. 156–159v

UNIVERSITY COLLEGE, | ST STEPHEN'S GREEN, | DUBLIN. [*printed heading*]
Jan. 12 1888

My dear Bridges, — I am glad that you will be back at pastoral Yattendon, but do not understand why you should be unhappy in London. Unless indeed one thing explains it, the new enemies you have made (for so of course you meant to write; but what you have written is "new ones", that is "friends", which word occurs just before). I am sorry, I must say, for the tussle with Patmore.[1] The cynical remark about forgetting that people believed in their own theories does not please me. ~~The~~ ^As far as I am concerned in that matter, the^ additions that I wanted you to make to the essay[2] were for the essay's sake, to make it ^historically and logically^ complete; and the reader's, to put him in possession of all the necessary facts or principles — not to leave him in the dark, in that "superior" style; mystify him — a thing I cannot abide. However the essay is^, I believe,^ pretty nearly complete within its limits and is first rate work. I do not, so far as I remember, really think that Coventry Patmore's doctrines needed mentioning at any rate there:[3] they are mostly ~~of general~~ ^of wider scope^ and would be introduced best into a paper on English versification as a whole or on versification simply.

Yes, I shall be very glad of some copies of it. I lent my one to a young man who teaches English ~~in~~ ^for^ the Royal University curriculum ^and^ in Mr. Tom Arnold's absence[4] takes his class: now he can keep it. He said he wanted it in order "to come at Saintsbury"; I warrant it is not for ~~verse he~~ rhyme or rhythm he wants to come at Saintsbury, though he may stalk ^him^ behind them: no, Saintsbury writes in the Saturday the great enemy and writes anti Irish verse and jokes in it too. Hinc illae lacrimae {*hence these tears*}.[5] Never make an enemy, except for duty's sake; try not, even then.

My remark about my brother Everard[6] and English art was not to be taken with such great seriousness. It is true people who constantly illustrate the Papers, like Tenniel[7] and the rest in Punch,[8] having a vogue and being seen by ~~so~~ millions, must exercise an influence for good or bad; but my brother has no such position. However painting, drawing, pictorial art of some sort is his profession, and as you know him I thought you were aware of that.

At Monasterevan I tried to get some outstanding and accumulated sonnets ready for hanging on the line, that is in my book of MS, the one you wrote most of,[9] and so for sending to you. All however are not ready yet, but they will soon be. I could send one tonight if time served, but if possible I should like to ~~fini~~ despatch this letter. It is now years that I have had no inspiration of longer jet than makes a sonnet, except only in that fortnight in Wales: it is what, far more than direct want of time, I find most against ~~me~~ ^poetry and production^ in the life I lead. ~~Only unh u~~Unhappily I cannot produce anything at all, not only the luxuries like poetry, but the duties almost of my position, its natural outcome~~.~~ — like scientific works. I am now writing a quasi-philosophical paper on the Greek Negatives:[10] but when shall I finish it? or if finished ~~wl~~ will it pass the censors? or if it does will ^the Classical Review or^ any magazine take it? All impulse fails me: I can give myself no sufficient reason for going on. Nothing comes: — I am a eunuch — but it is for the kingdom of heaven's sake.

Did you see Wooldridge in town? No doubt. And how is ^he^ getting on~~,~~? painting, music, and all~~?~~. I am sure he is right in the advice he gave me, to be very contrapuntal, to learn ~~it~~ ^that^ well. I want to do ~~that~~ ^so^ if I can; it is the only way. I have fooled at it too much. I have found a thing that, if I had my counterpoint well at my fingers' ends, wd. be most valuable: it is that the tunes I make are very apt to ~~make~~ ^fall into^ fugues and canons, the second strain being easy counterpoint to the first or ^to^ its fugal answer. E.g. my Crocus, which you once expressed an admiration for, makes a canon with itself at the octave two bars off and, as far as I have found, at one bar off too. This is a splendid opening for choral treatment. And I have a fine fugue on hand to "Orpheus with his lute";[11] but I shall not hurry with it, but keep the counterpoint correct. There ~~is~~ ^seems to be^, I may remark, no book that bridges the gap between double counterpoint and fugue. For instance, I have Ouseley ^on both^ and Higgs on Fugue and neither breathes a word on so simple a point as this,[12] that the answer in Bach and Handel enters, that is that the counterpoint begins, freely on an unprepared discord. But this is contrary to the elements of counterpoint proper. What I ^ought to do,^ or somebody else rather to have done, is to tabulate Bach's practice and principles.

We are suffering from the region-fog, as it seems to be. I have been a little ill and am still a little pulled down; however I am in good spirits. Term has begun.

There was more to say, I ~~for~~ forget what. It seems this will not go tonight. Did you go to see Jem Smith[13] and his mates#?

There, I have copied one — Tom's Garland. It has many resemblances to Harry Ploughman, a fault in me ^the sonnetteer,^ but not a fault that can be traced home to either of the sonnets. They were conceived at the same time: that is how it is. But I have too much tendency to do it, I find. "There is authority for it~~,~~" — not the lady of the strachey,[14] but Aeschylus: he is always forgetting he said a thing before. Indeed he never did, but tried to say it ~~too~~ two or three ~~things~~ ^times^ — something rich and profound but not by him distinctly apprehended; so he goes at it again and again like a canary trying to learn the Bluebells of Scotland.[15] To bed, to bed: my eyes are almost bleeding.

With best wishes to Mrs. Bridges, I am your affectionate friend Gerard M. Hopkins.

By saying you ~~have~~ ^are going to^ register~~ed~~ your little daughter as an Elizabeth I take you to signify that you reserve her for Mr. Beeching to christen at Yattendon.[16]

Jan. 13 1888. What, by the bye, is that new departure in yr. poetry which 'it was high time' you made? — Talking of this, Hall Caine, that poor Deiphobus[17] of yours, said in some review lately that whether a good book shall be a hit and live, or no, appears to him, from literary history, to be as purely a matter of chance as anything he knows of. And if, as I ~~dare say~~ ^suppose^, he is speaking with consideration, ~~it~~ ^what he says^ sounds to me sense and I daresay he is right.

[1] The details are unknown but the dispute was evidently over prosody. RB suggested that Milton's *Paradise Lost* had a syllabic metre, based on Chaucer, with a variable iambic pentameter rhythm superimposed. The suggestion was made to instil more sensitive reading of *PL*.

[2] 'On the Elements of Milton's Blank Verse in Paradise Lost' (privately printed, then included in H. C. Beeching's edition of the *Paradise Lost, Book I* (Oxford, 1887)).

[3] Coventry Patmore's *Essay on English Metrical Law* was first printed in the *North British Review* of Aug. 1857 as *English Metrical Critics*. There is no mention of his doctrine in the first printed form of RB's essay.

[4] See letter to RWD of 25 Oct. 1884. Thomas Arnold's wife Julia died of cancer in 1888.

[5] Terence, *Andria*, l. 126.

[6] Everard Hopkins (1860–1928), GMH's younger brother. See Biographical Register.

[7] Sir John Tenniel (1820–1914; *ODNB*), the English illustrator who worked on *Punch*'s small team from 1850 and designed the woodcut engravings to Lewis Carroll's *Alice's Adventures in Wonderland* (1865) and *Through the Looking-Glass* (1870). He was knighted in 1893.

[8] *Punch* was a satirical paper published from 1841 to 2002. It included articles and drawings on contemporary society and politics, varying in tone from recognizing the slightly eccentric to acerbic. Tenniel was one of the best known of its illustrators.

[9] MS 'B'. In 1883 RB began to transcribe GMH's poems from his holograph collection (MS 'A') into a second album. The immediate reason for doing so was to show GMH's poetry to Coventry Patmore, though RB evidently expected that there would be others interested to whom he might post the collection. Knowing that he had sometimes the only copy of particular poems, GMH not keeping copies himself, he did not want to risk losing MS 'A'. It was also a less tidy collection since the poems had been written over some sixteen years on a variety of pieces of paper, which had had to be cut and rearranged in order to fit on to the album's pages.

[10] No paper by GMH on the Greek negatives is known.

[11] GMH's music to 'The crocus while the days are dark' and 'Orpheus with his lute' has disappeared. See *CW* vi.

[12] The Revd F. A. Ouseley, *A Treatise on Counterpoint, Canon and Fugue* (1880); James Higgs, *Fugue* (1878).

[13] Jem Smith (1863–1931), a bare-knuckle English pugilist from 1881, who won the last international bare-knuckle prizefight (Bruges, 1889). He then fought as a British Heavyweight until 1891.

[14] Malvolio soliloquizing: 'There is example for't: the lady of the Strachy married the yeoman of the wardrobe.' *Twelfth Night*, II. v. 44–5.

[15] 'The Bluebells of Scotland' is a traditional folk song, number 13849 in Steve Roud's Folk Song index, <http://library.efdss.org/cgi-bin/home.cgi>. GMH follows this with an allusion to the nursery rhyme 'To bed, to bed, said Sleepy Head, | Tarry a while said Slow'.

[16] She was christened at Yattendon on 29 Jan. 1888 by the rector, the Revd H. C. Beeching, and Dr Sanday was her godfather by proxy.

[17] In Greek mythology, Deiphobus was Hector's brother. Athena (the goddess of wisdom, who supported the Greeks) took his shape to lure Hector to his death at Achilles' hands, after which Deiphobus became the leader of the Trojan army. After his brother Paris was killed, he was married to Helen but she left him for Menelaus, king of Sparta. In the *Aeneid* (Book VI) Aeneas meets him in the Underworld.

18 January 1888 to Robert Bridges

LRB, no. CLVIII, p. 272 Bodleian, Dep. Bridges, vol. 92, fo. 160[r–v]
Postcard addressed to 'Robert Bridges Esq. | Yattendon | Newbury | England Berks'. PM DUBLIN 12A JAN 19 186

Jan. 18 1888. Univ. Coll., Stephen's Green, Dublin.

My young friend wants to know if Mr. Beeching's book, Paradise Lost Bk. the First, in the Clarendon Press, is out yet.[1]

I have the first vol. of your Malory:[2] I think I had better send it back, as I seldom read it. Indeed if I # often read it I shd. have done it by this time and have sent it back. G. M. H.

[1] See previous letter, nn. 1 and 2.

[2] The only multiple-volume edition of the works of Sir Thomas Malory (1415/18–1471; *ODNB*) in the decades before this letter was Thomas Wright's edition, *La Mort d'Arthure: The History of King Arthur and the Knights of the Round Table*, complete in three volumes (1858 and 1866).

10 February 1888 from Coventry Patmore to GMH

FL, no. CLXXXVI B, p. 385 Campion Hall, P 10/2/88

Addressed to 'Rev[d] Gerard Hopkins, S.J. | University College, | St. Stephen's Green, | Dublin'. PM HASTINGS FE 10 88, H&K PACKET FE 11 88.

Hastings. Feb. 10. 1888.

My dear M[r] Hopkins,

I send you a St. James's which contains an article[1] which I hope may please you.

Much-meditating on the effect which my M.S. "Sponsa Dei" had upon you, when you read it while staying here, I concluded that I would not take the responsibility of being the first to expound the truths therein contained: so, on Xmas Day, I committed the work to the flames without reserve of a single paragraph.[2]

Since I wrote my last letter ^to you^ I have felt some compunction on the matter. I confess it was no real answer to what you said about prose style.

Yours ever truly

C. Patmore.

[1] 'Real Apprehension', 20 Jan. 1888. Reprinted in *Religio Poetae, &c* (1893).

[2] In the letter to RB of 12 Aug. 1889 (see below) Patmore repeats his claim: 'The authority of his goodness was so great with me that I threw the manuscript of a little book – a sort of "Religio Poetae" – into the fire, simply because, when he had read it, he said with a grave look, "That's telling secrets"'. Champneys gives an account of the composition and content of the work, saying that he 'cannot believe that it has wholly perished' since he finds similar ideas in others of Patmore's works. See Champneys, i. 315–19 and ii. 249. Subsequent letters show that the truth was not quite so simple as Patmore maintains.

10 February 1888 to Robert Bridges

LRB, no. CLIX, p. 272 Bodleian, Dep. Bridges, vol. 92, fos. 161–162^{v}

UNIVERSITY COLLEGE, | $\mathrm{S}^{\underline{\mathrm{T}}}$ STEPHEN'S GREEN, | DUBLIN. [*printed heading*]
Feb. 10 1888

Dearest Bridges, — know that the copy of your Paper[1] never came, so that I have none at all, and you said I might have several: I am content with one and please send one; if two, I can do better still.

I laughed outright and often, but very sardonically, to think you and the Canon could not construe my last sonnet;[2] that he had to write to you for a crib. It is plain I must go no farther on this road: if you and he cannot understand me who will? Yet, declaimed, the strange constructions would be dramatic and effective. Must I interpret it? It means then that, as St. Paul and Plato and Hobbes and everybody says, the commonmonwealth[3] or well ordered human society is like one man; a body with many members and each its function; some higher, some lower, but all honourable, from the honour which belongs to the whole. The head is the sovereign, who has no superior but ~~g~~God and from heaven receives his or her authority: we must then ~~conceive~~ ^imagine^ this head as bare (see St. Paul much on this)[4] and ~~crowned~~ ^covered^, so to say, only with the sun and stars, of which the crown is a symbol, which is an ornament but not a covering; it has an enormous hat or skull cap, the vault of heaven. The foot is the daylabourer, and this is armed with hobnail boots, because it has to wear ^and be worn by^ the ground; which again is symbolical; for it is navvies or daylabourers who, on the great scale or in gangs and millions, mainly trench, tunnel, blast, and in others ways disfigure, "mammock" the earth ~~as~~ ^and^, on a small scale, ~~their~~ ^singly,^ and superficially ^stamp it with^ their foot prints. And the "garlands" of nails they wear are therefore the visible badge of the~~ir~~ place~~,~~ ^they fill,^ the lowest~~,~~ in the commonwealth~~, but~~. ^But this place still^ shar~~ing~~^es^ the common honour~~.~~, and if it wants one advantage, glory or public fame, makes up for it by another, ease of mind, absence of care; and these things are symbolized by the gold and the iron garlands. (O, once explained, how clear it all is!) Therefore the scene of the poem is laid at evening, when they are giving over work and one after another pile their picks, with which they earn their living, and swing off home, knocking sparks ~~out~~ ^out^ of mother earth not now by labour and of choice but by the mere footing, being strong~~hod~~^shod^ and making no hardship of hardness, ^taking all easy.^ And so to supper and bed. Here comes a violent but effective hyperbaton or suspension, in which the action of the mind mimics that of the labourer — surveys his lot, low but ~~without~~ ^free^ from care; then ~~sud~~ by a sudden strong act throws it over the shoulder or tosses it away as a light matter. The witnessing of which lightheartedness makes me indignant with the fools of Radical Levellers.[5] But presently I remember that this is all very well for those who are in, however low in, the Commonwealth and share in any way the Common weal; but that the curse of our times is that many do not ^share it^, that they are outcasts from it and have neither security nor ~~glory~~ splendour; that they share ~~the~~ care ~~of~~ with the high and obscurity with the low, but wealth ~~an~~ or comfort with neither. And this ^state of things^, I say, is the origin of Loafers, Tramps, Cornerboys, ~~R~~ Roughs, Socialists and other pests of society. And I think that it is a very pregnant sonnet and in point of execution very highly wrought. Too much so, I am afraid.

I have more, not so hard and done before, but I am not prepared . . . [6]

On referring to yr. letter I see you speak of modern music, not music of this century. It is, I suppose, as you say.[7]

I hope your rheumatism is abated, is gone: why not gone? But I have a poor ~~fr~~, very charming friend~~,~~ on his back with spinal ~~complaint~~ ^disease^: when he complains of rheumatic pains his doctor rubs his hands with joy and says nothing cd. be better.[8]

[1] On Milton's prosody. See letter of 12–13 Jan. 1888.

[2] 'Tom's Garland'.

[3] Error introduced by page turn in the middle of 'commonwealth'.

[4] For example in 1 Corinthians 11: 7: 'The man indeed ought not to cover his head, because he is the image and glory of God.'

[5] The name Levellers was first applied in the reign (1625–49) of Charles I to a political party that wished to level all differences in position or rank, and emphasized equality before the law, religious tolerance, and popular power. Their influence waned in the 1650s, but the name has since been taken up from time to time by or to label factions with similar ideals. GMH sees dangerous socialist, communist, and iconoclastic movements in the world about him.

[6] The end of the letter is missing: what follows is a postscript written at the head of the first leaf.

[7] On 10 Feb. 1893 RB wrote to his friend Lionel Muirhead that 'the new concerted vocal music, part-songs by Brahms and Henschel, is extraordinary stuff, in my humble and stiffening opinion just intellectual rot' (Stanford, i. 236). He later thought rather better of it. During the 1890s and the first two decades of the 20th c. RB played an important part in the English musical renaissance, collaborating with Charles Hubert Parry several times and with Charles Villiers Stanford. He also worked with

Wooldridge and Monica on a new hymnal and a number of the settings they produced for hymns have become well known. Gustav Holst and Gerald Finzi both set suites of poems by Bridges in the early 20th c.

[8] Probably George Teeling; see next letter to Newman.

20 February 1888 to John Henry Newman

'Four Newfound Letters: An Annotated Edition, with a Fragment of Another Letter', ed. Joseph J. Feeney, SJ, *HQ*, 23/1–2 (Winter–Spring 1996), 23–8 Gonzaga 1:3, annotated 'Ans' in top left

UNIVERSITY COLLEGE, | S^T STEPHEN'S GREEN, | DUBLIN. [*printed heading*]
Feb. 20 1888

Your Eminence and dearest Father, Pax Christi – I wish you a very happy eighty-eigth[1] birthday and year and as many more as God shall send. It seems that you still enjoy the blessing granted Moses.[2]

This poor University College, the somehow-or-other manned wreck of the Catholic University, is afloat and not sinking; rather making a very little way than losing any. There is scarcely any ^public^ interest in the University question in this country. Nay, there is none. But this does not prevent good and really patriotic people in a quiet but not ineffective way doing what can be done to advance it.

We sustained a loss by the resignation (~~and then~~ ^followed by^ the withdrawal from our Society) of Fr. Martial Klein,[3] Fellow of the Royal University and professor here of Biology; an able, learned, and amiable man; who nevertheless took ~~a~~ ^this^ step to ours and his own injury. But the money loss of his salary[4] was almost at once made up ^for the time^ by the appointment of a learned Father of our Community[5] not indeed to a permanent Fellowship but to a Fellow's duties of examining and teaching for a year with the same salary. In this and in other respects the Senate of the Royal University is very friendly to us and to Catholic interests, thank God.

Politically, the times are most troubled. There is a great strain of feeling. I live, I may say, in an air most painful to breathe and this comes home to me more, not less, with time. There is to my mind only one break in the sky, but it is a notable one; it is from Rome. The Pope is acting very much as I thought he would and the effect of what he does, though slow^ly^ and guarded^ly^, is likely to be powerful.

A great good fortune has happened to me, if it is not cruel to say it, in George Teeling's's[6] sickness: he is lodged a few doors down on our side of the Green and I see him almost every day. His doctor now operates on him by ~~burning~~ cauterising the spine and today he was lifted higher on his couch than before and that without bad effect or pain, so that a gradual recovery may be hoped for. He is as winning as ever. I commonly find him in good spirits, neither buoyant nor dejected.

I am your Eminence's affectionate son in Christ Gerard M. Hopkins.

[1] GMH is doubly inaccurate: he has the spelling wrong; and Newman was celebrating his 87th birthday but entering his 88th year, as Joseph Feeney, SJ, points out in his article in *HQ*, to which the following notes are heavily indebted.

[2] i.e. the blessing of a long and fruitful life.

[3] Leopold Martial Klein, SJ, later known as de Beaumont (1849–1934). Alsatian by birth and trained in medicine, he entered the English Province in 1878, was ordained in 1884, and went to teach in Ireland in 1885. He troubled his superiors and muddied the relations of the English and Irish Provinces by his machinations and lack of Jesuit obedience, problems which came to a head in relation to a garden party in 1887, attendance at which had political implications. He did not well explain his situation, was recalled to England by his provincial, and (later arguing that he was never baptized and therefore never validly ordained) left the Jesuits on 8 Nov. 1887. In 1897, having become a Unitarian, he married the young Kathleen O'Hagan of the distinguished Dublin family. Fredric W. Schlatter gives a full account of Klein and the background in his 'Martial Klein, Hopkins's Dublin Colleague', *HQ*, 29/3–4 (2002), 69–105.

[4] An examining fellow (FRUI) received £400 yearly; except for gifts or stipends, FRUI salaries were the Jesuits' sole support.

[5] John J. O'Carroll, SJ (1837–89). Master of some fourteen languages and enthusiast for Irish, he was 'entirely of the old school' with 'strong views on many subjects', yet he taught well, inspired students with his 'delightful personality', and published in the *Gaelic Journal* ('Account Book', Irish Province archives; *A Page of Irish History: Story of University College, Dublin, 1883–1909*, compiled by Fathers of the Society of Jesus (Dublin, 1930), 100–1, 125, 127–8; Matthew Russell, SJ, "The Late Father O'Carroll", *Irish Monthly*, 17 (1889), 209–10).

[6] George Luke Teeling (1847–92). Nephew by marriage to Thomas, Baron O'Hagan (1812–85; Lord Chancellor of Ireland, 1868–74, 1880–1), he went to the Birmingham Oratory in 1875 as a novice, never became an Oratorian, worked in the Oratory School for some years, then taught in the Benedictine school at Fort Augustus Abbey in Scotland; later Private Secretary to his uncle, he edited O'Hagan's speeches (1885) and died at the O'Hagan House in Howth. Newman knew him at the Oratory; GMH would have known him through the O'Hagans, and mentions helping him with a poem in the letter to Fr Ignatius Ryder of 14 Nov. 1888. See 'Four Newfound Letters' for further bibliography.

24 February 1888 from John Henry Newman to GMH

FL, no. C30, p. 414 — Campion Hall, 24/2/88, and MS copy in Birmingham Oratory

Addressed to 'Rev^{d} F^{r}. G. M. Hopkins | University College | Stephens Green | Dublin'. PM BIRMINGHAM FE 22 88, H&K PACKET FE 23 88. A lithographically reproduced general letter of thanks with only the date correction, blessing, and signature in JHN's autograph.

You are one of those friends and well wishers, who have so kindly addressed to me letters of congratulation on my birthday, — letters which touched me much, and for your share in which I hereby offer you my sincere thanks.

With my Blessing

Febr. 24 188~~5~~^8^ J H N

27 February 1888 to Dr Francis MacCabe[1]

FL, no. XXXVI, p. 64 — Gonzaga 1:5

One folded sheet, four sides of which two only are used.

UNIVERSITY COLLEGE, | S$^{\underline{T}}$ STEPHEN'S GREEN, | DUBLIN. [*printed heading*]

Feb. 27 '88

Dear Dr. MacCabe, — You are right. At the San José you meant is a new College quite distinct from and independent of San Francisco. It must be small as yet: there are 3 masters. No names are given me, but there is no harm in that: address the Rector. It belongs to the Turin Province.

I am yours very sincerely Gerard M. Hopkins.

By the bye, it is called St. Joseph's College~~,~~[2] — San José, California, U.S.A.

[1] [Sir] Francis Xavier Frederick MacCabe (1833–1914), Medical Commissioner, Local Government Board for Ireland (1888–98). The MacCabes were GMH's closest friends in Dublin. He had taught one of their sons at Stonyhurst.

[2] Now Bellarmine College Preparatory, a Jesuit secondary school in San José, California.

27 February 1888 from Professor Walter William Skeat[1] *to GMH*

FL, no. K1, pp. 431–2 Campion Hall, Misc. Skeat
Addressed to 'Revd Gerard S. Hopkins | University College | St Stephen's Green | Dublin'. PM CAMBRIDGE FE 27 88, H&K PACKET FE 28 1888.

From Rev. Prof. Skeat | 2. Salisbury Villas | Cambridge. Feb. 27/88.

Dear Sir,

I'm very sorry. I received your former letter. But I have not the physical strength to answer all letters. It is more toil than all my other work. —

I can't discuss. I'm much obliged. And I regret to say I'm not convinced abt. scope. All my experience tells ~~me~~ the other way. There is no French form: so it's all the more likely that we took it from Greek. Sorry I'm so stupid. —

No one knows the etym[y] of cap & cape. Dr Murray[2] gives it up. Not Gothic. —

I know keeve: quite common. — I take it to answer to an A.S. *cêfe, variant of cýfe, which is merely Lat. cupa with mutation, just as our coop is Lat. cūpa without mutation. —

As to hullicinari, you may be quite right. I don't know. —

Of course my Dict[y] requires much amendment. But I've no time to do it now. I can't get through ordinary work.

As to Irish-English.

Dr A. Hume[3] made a complete MS Dict[y] of it, nearly half as big as Jamieson's Scottish Dict[y].[4] And he offered it to us to print. And I said no. A worse performance I never saw. He had included thousands of common literary & slang words, &c — that were not provincial a bit — he had included thousands of quotations from Middle-English authors of perfectly common words, which cd. be found in existing dictionaries, & which we all knew before: — & he had jammed the whole full of elaborate & ridiculous etymologies, all valueless. A part of a life-time wasted, because he did not know his business.

But the E.D. Soc[y] has printed a very fair collection of "Down & Antrim" words by Mr. Patterson, published separately (Trübner & Co) at 7 shillings.[5] It includes keeve, & other useful words. — That shd be taken ~~more~~ ^as^ the collection to which to add.

Please excuse more
Yrs in great haste
W. W. Skeat.

[1] Walter William Skeat (1835–1912; *ODNB*), philologist, had attended Sir Roger Cholmeley's School, Highgate, before he went to Christ's College, Cambridge in 1854. He was a prodigious and meticulous editor of Early English material, collaborated in the *OED*, and was a founder of the English Dialect Society. His *Etymological Dictionary* (1879–82, revised and enlarged 1910) would have been of particular interest to GMH.

[2] Sir James Augustus Henry Murray (1837–1915; *ODNB*), lexicographer, editor of the *Oxford English Dictionary* from 1879.

[3] Sir Abraham Hume (1814–84; *ODNB*), Doctor of Civil Law, whose *Remarks on the Irish Dialect of the English Language* (1878) is identified in Joseph Ronsley's entertaining *Myth and Reality in Irish Literature* (1977).

[4] John Jamieson (1759–1838; *ODNB*) published his *Etymological Dictionary of the Scottish Language* in 2 vols. in 1808.

[5] William Hugh Patterson (1835–1918), *A Glossary of Words in Use in the Counties of Antrim and Down*, English Dialect Society (1880).

7 March 1888 to Robert Bridges

LRB, no. *CLX, p. 274 Bodleian, Dep. Bridges, vol. 92, fo. 163[r–v]
Postcard addressed to 'Robert Bridges Esq. | Yattendon | Newbury | England Berks'. PM DUBLIN 2A MR 7 88 186 and CHIEVELEY A MR 8 88

EVEN NOW I'VE NOT GOT THAT PAPER WHEN ARE[1]

[1] On Milton's Prosody. See letter of 12–13 Jan. 1888.

13 March 1888 to his Mother

FL, no. CIX, p. 183 Bodleian, MS Eng. lett. e. 41, fos. 122–124[v]
Addressed to 'Mrs. Manley Hopkins | Court's Hill Lodge | Haslemere | Surrey | England'. PM DUBLIN MR 14 88.

UNIVERSITY COLLEGE, | S[T] STEPHEN'S GREEN, | DUBLIN. [*printed heading*]
March 13 '88

My dearest mother, — I am very glad to hear that ^there is news of^ Lionel and that he is coming.

Your winter may be ~~over~~ over but ours is begun and is nasty. We had none of your severe frosts and deep snows, but ~~things are~~ ^the weather is^ "slavish", as we say, just now.

I have an inward fire far worse than frost. It is an artificial toothache produced by my dentist, who put in drugs to kill a nerve (though he might have left the poor thing what little life it had), told me to come again next day, then when I called had gone out of town and will not be back till tomorrow, Wednesday~~,~~ — from Friday. So for four days I have been ~~suffering pain~~ ^aching^ without a moment's intermission day and # night, which with a natural toothache could scarcely be; and it is very wearing. And the continued aching shews the nerve cannot yet be dead.

I am making a collection of Irish words and phrases for the great English Dialect Dictionary[1] and am in correspondence with the editor.

I am your loving son Gerard.

Is Mary well now?

I want the enclosed to be ~~sent~~ ^conveyed^ to Mr. Cornelius van Eeghen:[2] you sometimes see his brother, do you not?

[1] The dictionary of Joseph Wright. See Norman White, 'G. M. Hopkins's Contributions to the English Dialect Dictionary', *English Studies*, 68 (1987), 325–35.

[2] As yet unidentified unequivocally. The van Eeghens (various spellings) were an old Dutch family and on 20 Sept. 1888 a Cornelis van Eeghen (1861–1940) married Maria Boissevain at the English Church in Amsterdam. One might hypothesize wedding wishes or presents, but in truth we have no detail of the nature of the association; GMH may well have met the van Eeghens during his trip with his family to Holland in late Aug. 1883, when he read *Mano*; see letters to RB of 5–6 Aug. 1883; to Patmore of 22 Aug. 1883; and to RWD of 11–14 Oct. 1883. This Cornelis van Eeghen had three brothers: Tijo Hendrik (1856–1930), Jacob Abraham (1859–1901), and David (1864–1909). Information from family history website <http://gw1.geneanet.org>.

1 May 1888 to Alexander William Mowbray Baillie

FL, no. CLXII, p. 290 UCD L 71

Three folded sheets of paper watermarked 'BROWNE & NOLAN DUBLIN' and with university printed heading; 12 sides.

UNIVERSITY COLLEGE, | ST STEPHEN'S GREEN, | DUBLIN. [*printed heading*]

Mayday, a stormy one, 1888.

Dearest Baillie, — Your letter has just come in. To the stormy weather it has made little difference, though just now the sun is out, but it helps to cheer my very gloomy mind. I answer it at once, that counsel of perfection which I so seldom follow and now follow from inclination, not principle.

You told me that about Hannah[1] before, in much the same words; but I am not displeased to hear it again. It gives me joy — subdued, for ~~it~~ I knew ^him little^ and cared for him no more — I never disliked him; still it gives me some joy. First I am glad ^that^ anything, any department of things, should be in good order and trim (and in case this, as said of a Protestant clergyman, should sound unprofessional on my part, I would ask the critic — but who would that be? not you — still I would ask him whether the world would be rel^i^giously better if Hannah mismanaged the Rectory of Brighton and its twelve preferments). Next, though otherwise he fills a small place in my affections, yet if he is ~~g~~ doing good he is a good fellow for doing it and so I wish "more power to his elbow", and in general I am so constituted (and it is a good feature in me, though I say it that should not, and not at all a common one) ^as^ to like people directly for their goodness: of course I like them for other things as well and dislike them for ~~their~~ other defects than downright badness. Thirdly I like Hannah because he sincerely (but ~~it~~ in a sort of blundering way) liked you (no doubt does so still more now; but I speak of what I remember). I may say the same of Macfarlane; and I think, and may have said before, that you did not always fully appreciate their merit in this regard; but now at your present age, much the same as mine, you are aware that affection, no matter from whom it comes, is a precious thing and not to be ~~had~~ ^found^ at random. So much on that theme.

Thank you for your photograph. It is not altogether as I should wish it either as a portrait or as a — for I am getting knowledgable in this matter, being amongst people who photograph — as a photograph, photogram, photographeme, *φωτογράφημα*, a work of the photographic ca~~me~~mera. Still it is a likeness and I am very glad to have it. I think presently I may be able to send you one of me, not shopdone but artistically better (untouched: photography ^proper^ now is mere scaffolding, rough-hewing; painting, stippling, "touching", a poor bastard art succeeds the lens-work and disguises what ~~it~~ ^that^ gives). The other ^day^ as I was walking in our backyard or catswing, little weeting,[2] somebody did me instantaneous; for the laboratory, now used for photography, is convanient. It will not be this however.

I have that book on Epigraphy, but have read little yet. Do not trouble yourself about knowing little of that. Consider how little Scaliger,[3] Bentley,[4] or even[5] Hermann[6] knew of it and if this consideration seems to you out of place, for we must have the knowledge of our times, remember that it can scarcely ^ever^ be more than an appliance or supplement to certain other studies; that with those it is easily mastered and without them of little use and less educational value. And so of some other supplementary studies required now. Mr. Tyrrell[7] has a little precipitated my judgment on these matters: he has a great admiration and even affection for the ^old^ scholarship of Oxford and Cambridge; says English scholars have really done more for the classics than German (if so, the quality of ~~the~~ our scholarship must surely be very fine to weigh against all that bulk); and laments to see our Universities gone after epigraphy, excavation, and so on, mere handmaids, to the neglect of ^the mistress^ scholarship itself. Do you agree?

Egyptology continues to be full of interest. The discovery about Ra-ian or Ian-ra[8] promises to be important. But I am reading nothing of it now except notices in the papers. What a woman Miss Edwards[9] is, to be sure! Next thing to Queen Hatasu,[10] I think she was ~~quall~~ called, that tomboy of the Nile. I suppose you meet her at learned gatherings, not the ~~mu~~ mummy woman but the living blue.

The Pope has just dealt us a stunning blow.[11] We attribute it to the unscrupulous wirepulling of English intriguers: this or nearly this is the idiom, but I do not understand it. The Pope condemns certain practices as sinful: he is right or wrong. We do not say he is wrong, it seems we allow he is right. If so, the practices <u>are</u> sinful, and they have been and are widely practised; they must then need to be forbidden. If then the Pope ought to forbid them it is not unscrupulous for those concerned to ask him to do so. What is unscrupulous is to practise them, defend, support, ^or^ conceal them. It would be unscrupulous of the Pope not to condemn them.

However this action of his is no doubt taken ~~about~~ ^upon^ his own visitor's report.

Whirligig of time! The body by which the Pope acts so much to the advantage (in effect) of ~~the the~~ British government is the Holy Office of the Inquisition.[12]

On the whole I believe the decision will be obeyed and things pass off quietly, here in Ireland.

I have just reread your last but one letter. It has nearly the same matter as this morning's. This for instance is in both, that life in London is intolerable. I find this difficult to follow. ~~I~~ Like you I love country life and dislike any town and that especially for its bad and smokefoul air. Still I prefer London to any large town in these islands (as for little ones they are for many purposes merely a block of houses in the fields, combining country air with certain postal conveniences and so on). ~~It~~ In fog it is dreadful, but it has many fine days, and ~~in~~ in summer — now I ~~know~~ ^see^ you will scout this and fling yourself about

~~it~~, but I know it to be true — in summer its air is ^a^ balmy ^air^, certainly in the West End. Then it — well the West End — is cheerful and quietly handsome, with many fine trees, and then there are so many resources, things to go to and hear and see and do. Everything is there. No, I think that very much may be said for life in London; though my dream is a farm in the Western counties, glowworms, new milk . . . but in fact I live in Dublin.

What I most dislike in towns and in London in particular is the misery of the poor; the dirt, squalor, and the illshapen degraded physical (putting aside moral) type of so many of the people, with the deeply dejecting, unbearable thought that by degrees almost all ~~the~~ our population will become a town population and a puny unhealthy and cowardly one. Yes, cowardly. Do you know and realise what happened at Majuba Hill? 500 British troops after 8 hours' firing, on the Dutch reaching the top, ran without ~~resistance~~ offering hand to hand resistance before, it is said, 80 men.[13] Such a thing was never heard in history. The disgrace in itself is unspeakable. Still it might have been slurred over by pushing on the campaign. But Gladstone was equal to himself and the occasion. He professed that the Queen's honour was by this dishonour vindicated, made the convention, and stamped the memory of Majuba in the minds of all African colonists for ever. What one man could do to throw away a continent and weaken the bonds of a world wide empire he did. He may do more ^in that kind^ yet. I therefore agree with you that the duty of keeping this fatal and baleful ~~power~~ ^influence^, spirit, or personality or whatever word one is to use out of political power is a duty paramount to ^that of forwarding^ any particular measure of Irish or other politics that[14] he can, for whatever reason, espouse and advance. Strange being! He is, ~~the~~ without foresight, insight, or resolution himself, the bright focus of the thoughts and wishes of the Liberal masses. Their views supply him with his, but he ~~concentrates~~ ^defines^ their ~~inconsistency on~~ ^uncertainty into^ one doctrine ~~for the~~ ^at a^ time; their wishes inspire his, but he concentrates ~~them~~ ^their^ fluctuation ^first on^ one attainable object, then on another.

Believe me your affectionate friend Gerard M. Hopkins.

[1] See letters of 4 May 1863, 24 Apr.–17 May 1885.

[2] Knowing or suspecting.

[3] Joseph Justus Scaliger (1540–1609), the foremost scholar of his age.

[4] Richard Bentley (1662–1742; *ODNB*), Master of Trinity College, Cambridge, and the greatest name in classical scholarship during the first half of the 18th c.

[5] MS 'ever'.

[6] Gottfried Hermann (1772–1848), famous as a textual critic, especially for his editions of the Greek tragic poets.

[7] See letters of 6, 13, and 21–22 Oct. 1886.

[8] GMH is keeping up with the most recent discoveries in Egypt. *The Times* for 6 Apr. 1888 reported on excavations at Bubastis (near Zagazig, near Cairo), which had just been resumed by the Swiss archaeologist Henri Édouard Naville (1844–1926), working for the Egypt Exploration Fund, for whom most of his excavations were carried out. The writer was excited to report the discovery of the site of an unsuspected Hyksos settlement, where a statue had been unearthed (found 'only ten days ago') on which were two cartouches. *The Times* quotes Naville's letter of 18 Mar., which reports: 'One cartouche contains a sign which is quite new to me, and which I therefore cannot decipher. The other reads "Ian-Ra" or "Ra-ian"—a name unlike any I have ever seen.' The local expert, Ahmed Kemal-ed-Deen-Effendi, 'said at once "That is the Pharaoh of Joseph."' This seemed to offer important evidence for establishing dates in biblical history, as one can see in the letter from F. D. Griffiths (a student at the site) to the *Times* of 22 May 1888, where he asserts that the statue does indicate that Joseph 'ruled Egypt under one or more of the Hyksos Pharaohs'. See also *The Academy* for 28 Apr. 1888; and the Revd Charles D. Bell, DD, *A Winter on the Nile, in Egypt and in Nubia* (London, 1888), 305.

[9] Amelia B. Edwards, novelist (1831–92; *ODNB*), author of *A Thousand Miles up the Nile* (1876), founded the Egypt Exploration Fund (now Society) in 1883. She described the recent excavations at a fund-raising meeting reported in *The Times* for 11 May 1888.

[10] Hatshepsut, the famous Queen of the 18th Dynasty (early in the 15th c. BC), built the temple at Deir el-Bahari on the west bank of the Nile opposite Luxor (Thebes), which Naville began to excavate in 1890.

[11] The visit of Monsignor Ignatius Persico (1823–96) as Apostolic delegate to Ireland in 1887 was not complete before the Pope issued a rescript on 20 Apr. 1888 condemning the Plan of Campaign and boycotting as immoral, a decree which was widely neglected. See letter of 30 July–1 Aug. 1887.

[12] The *Catholic Encyclopedia* explains that 'The great apostasy of the sixteenth century, the filtration of heresy into Catholic lands, and the progress of heterodox teachings everywhere, prompted Paul III to establish the "Sacra Congregatio Romanae et universalis Inquisitionis seu sancti officii" by the Constitution "Licet ab initio" of 21 July, 1542. This inquisitional tribunal, composed of six cardinals, was to be at once the final court of appeal for trials concerning faith, and the court of first instance for cases reserved to the pope.' Subject to certain refinements, this remains the first among Roman congregations.

[13] Although the exact story of Majuba Hill, South Africa, is disputed, what remains evident is that a British force of about 500 men, ineptly led in an ill-conceived occupation of Majuba Hill on 27 Feb. 1887, succumbed to Boer attacks and, the British leader Gen. George Colley having been shot and little command remaining, many fled. The casualties—on the British side 92 dead, 134 wounded, and 59 captured; on the Boer side one man killed and five injured—indicate graphically that there was no fierce resistance to the Boer attack. The Boer force is said to have been about 350.

[14] MS 'than'.

6–7 May 1888 to Coventry Patmore

FL, no. CLXXXVII, p. 385 Durham University Library, Abbott MS 201
The first two folded sheets of this letter are on paper embossed with the Milltown Park address; the last two half sheets are on paper printed with the address of University College, St. Stephen's Green and watermarked with BROWNE & NOLAN DUBLIN and monogram. Twelve sides.

Milltown Park, | Milltown, | Dublin [*embossed address*]
May 6 1888

My dear Mr. Patmore, — I have ~~much~~ ^greatly^ to beg your pardon for leaving you so long unanswered. This however is the second letter begun, and the other ran some length, but is cancelled.

Your news was that you had burnt the book called Sponsa Dei, and that on reflexion upon remarks of mine. I wish I had been more guarded in making them. When we take a step like this we are forced to condemn ourselves: either our work shd. never have been done or never undone, and either ~~de~~ way our time and toil are wasted — a sad thought; though the intention may at both times have been good. My objections were not final, they were but considerations (I forget now, with one exception, what they were); even if they were valid, still if you had kept to yr. custom of consulting your director, as you said you should, the book might have appeared with no change or with slight ones. But now regret is useless.[1]

Since I last wrote I have ^re^read Keats a little and the force of your criticism on him has struck me more than it did. It is impossible not to feel with weariness how his verse is at every turn abandoning itself to an unmanly and enervating luxury. It appears too that he said something like "O for a life of impressions instead of thoughts!"[2] It was, I suppose, the life he tried to lead. The impressions are not likely to have been all innocent and they soon ceased in death. His contemporaries, as Wordsworth, Byron, Shelley, and even Leigh Hunt, right or wrong, still concerned themselves with great causes, as liberty and religion; but he lived in mythology and fairyland the life of a dreamer.[3] ~~But still~~ ^Nevertheless^ I feel and see in him the beginnings of something opposite to this, of an interest in higher things and of powerful and active thought. On this point you shd. if possible read what Matthew Arnold wrote.[4] His mind had, as it seems to me, the distinctively masculine powers in abundance, his character the manly virtues, but while he ^gave himself up to^ dream~~ed and~~ing and self indulgence of course they were in abeyance. Nor do I mean that he wd. have turned to a life of virtue — only God can know that — , but that his genius wd. have taken to an austerer ~~art. His reason; the~~ ^utterance in art. Reason,^ thought, ^what^ he did not want to live by, would have asserted itself presently and perhaps have been as much more powerful than that of his contemporaries as his sensibility or impressionableness, by which he did want to live, was keener and richer than theirs. His defects were due to youth — the self indulgence of his youth; ~~the~~ its ill-education; and also, as it seems to me, to its breadth and pregnancy, which, by virtue of a fine judgment already able to restrain but unable to ~~g~~ direct, kept him from flinging himself blindly on the specious Liberal stuff that crazed Shelley and indeed, in their youth, Wordsworth and Coleridge. His mind played over life as a whole, so far as he a boy, without (seemingly) a dramatic but still with a deeply observant turn ~~cd. at that time see it~~ and also without any noble motive, ^felt^ at first hand, impelling him to look below ~~the~~ ^its^ surface, cd. at that time see it. He was, in my opinion, made to be a thinker, a critic, as much as a singer or artist of words. This can be seen in certain reflective passages, as the opening to Endymion and others in his poems. These passages are ~~those~~ ^the thoughts^ of a mind very ill instructed and in opposition; keenly sensible of wrongness in things established but unprovided with the principles ~~that should~~ to correct that by. Both his principles ^of art^ and his practice were in many things vicious, but he was correcting them, even eagerly; for Lamia one of his last works shews a deliberate change ~~of~~ ~~in style~~ ^in manner^ from the style of Endymion and ~~ev~~ in fact goes too far in change and sacrifices things that had better have been kept. Of construction he knew nothing to the last: in this same Lamia he has a long introduction about Mercury, who is only brought in to disenchant Lamia and ought not to ~~be~~ ^have been^ employed or else ^ought^ to be employed again. The story has a moral element or interest; ~~he~~ ^Keats^ was aware of this and touches on it at times, but could make nothing of it; in fact the situation at the end is that the sage Apollo~~n~~nius does more harm than the witch herself had done — kills the hero; and Keats does not see that this implies one of two things, either ~~the~~ ^some^ lesson of the terrible malice of evil which ~~can only be~~ ^when it is^ checked ~~by a~~ drags down innocence in its own ~~wreck~~ ruin or else the exposure of Pharisaic[5] pretence in ~~Apollonius~~ the wouldbe moralist. But then if I could have said this to Keats I feel sure he wd. have seen it. In due time he wd. have seen these things himself. Even when he is misconstructing one can remark certain instinctive turns of construction in his style, shewing his latent power — for instance the way the vision is introduced in Isabella. Far too much now of Keats.

You sent me also a paper of yours in the St. James's.[6] But I did not like the text of it, from Newman, and so I could not like the discourse founded on that. This was a paradox, that man is not a rational or reasoning animal. The use of a paradox is to awake the hearer's attention; then, when it has served that end, if, as mostly happens, it is not only unexpected but properly speaking untrue, it can be, expressly or silently, waived or dropped. But this you do not do with the paradox in question; you appear to take it in earnest. I always felt that Newman made too much of that text; it is still worse that you should build upon it. In what sense is man contemplative, or active, and not rational? In what sense may ~~it~~ ^man^ be said not to be rational and it might not as truly be said he was not active or was not contemplative? He does not always reason; neither does he always contemplate or always act — of course human action, not merely ^so through^ animal or vegetable functions. Everyone sometimes reasons; for everyone, arrived at the age of reason, sometimes asks Why and sometimes says Because or Although. Now whenever we use one of these three words we reason. ~~N~~ Longer trains of reasoning are rarer, ~~but as soon~~ because common life does not present the need or opportunity for them; but as soon as the matter requires them they are forthcoming. Nor are blunders in reasoning any proof ^that^ man is not a ^rational or^ reasoning being, rather the contrary: we are rational ^and reasoners^ by our ~~blun~~ ^false^ reasoning as we are moral ^agents^ by our sins. — I cannot follow you in your passion for paradox: more than a little of it tortures.

[*Change of ink*] Now, since writing the above, I have read the paper again, but indeed I cannot like it at all. The comment makes the text worse: for you say contemplation is in this age very rare indeed: is then reasoning in this age very rare indeed or none? ~~at all?~~ Other paradoxes follow; as that "persons like General Gordon or Sir Thomas More would stare if you called anything they did or suffered by the name of sacrifice".[7] ~~W~~ Did they then make no sacrifices? And if their modesty shrank from that word (I do not feel sure that it would) is the word not true? And do we not speak of Christ's sacrifice? and they were following him.

Also the "truly sensible man never opines", though "many things may be dubious to him". But the definition of opinion is belief accompanied by doubt, ~~or~~ ^by^ fear of the opposite being true; for, since many things are likely only but not certain, he who feels them to be most likely true ~~feels~~ knows also that ~~it~~ they may possibly be untrue, and that is to opine them — though in English the word opine is little used except jocularly. Here no doubt you did not want to speak with philosophic precision (and in the same way say that "to see rightly is the first of human qualities": I suppose it is the rightness or clearness or clearsightedness of the seeing that is the quality, for surely seeing is an act); but then the matter is philosophical, the title is so, the reference is to a philosophical work, and therefore philosophical precision would be in place and I in reading crave for it. But you know best what comes home to the readers you are aiming at. ~~But~~ ^Yet^ after all there is nothing like the plain truth: paradox persisted in is not the plain truth and ought not to satisfy a reader. The conclusion, about the unpardonable sin, is on dangerous ground: but I do not understand it and few readers, I think, will. You see, dear Mr. Patmore, that I am altogether discontented with this paper and can do nothing but find fault.

I saw somewhere (I do not think you told me) that the Second Part of the Angel is to appear or has appeared in ^the same^ cheap form as the First and I am glad.[8] Also having been asked to write a paper for a review I said I would write on your poems, but I am not sure I shall be able to carry this out,[9] for work presses and I am in a languishing state of body.

And now, with kind regards to all your circle, I am, my dear Mr. Patmore, yours very sincerely Gerard M. Hopkins.

May 7 1888. Yesterday was the anniversary of the Phoenix Park murders. The present also is a crisis, owing to the Pope's late action.[10] I have not time now to speak of matters political, but they must engross the mind of people living ~~here~~ ^where I do^ and would do so even if I were in England.

I lately read Blackmore's last book Springhaven:[11] perhaps you have. I am a devoted admirer of his descriptions, his word-painting, which is really Shaksperian. Otherwise this book is disappointing. The construction is clumsy, the character drawing superficial and sometimes melodramatic, and there is a vein of stupid jocularity all about "nose" and "stomach" and "breeches" and "find[12] feeding" which downright disgusts me. Hardy is a finer man.

[1] Champneys could 'not believe that it has wholly perished' (i. 319) and suggests places where the material might have been used.

[2] 'However it may be, O for a Life of Sensations rather than of Thoughts!' Keats, letter to Bailey of 22 Nov. 1817.

[3] Arnold's essay, and indeed what GMH himself goes on to say, seriously qualify the picture of Keats as dreamer. Certainly Keats was never as committed as Shelley,

Byron, Wordsworth, Coleridge, and Leigh Hunt were to political causes, but his poetry, though often sensual, is always thoughtful, and, if it is imaginative, is usually symbolically concerned with real and major questions (like life, death, loss, art, for example). His early and ambitious but immature poem *Endymion* (begun in 1817, published 1818) was soon superseded by poems like 'The Eve of St Agnes', his series of great odes, and *Lamia*, published only a year before he died in 1821.

[4] In his essay on Keats, which Arnold wrote as an introduction to his selection for T. H. Ward's anthology *The English Poets* (4 vols., London, 1880; iv. 427–37), he wrote the passage to which GMH perhaps refers: 'Signs of virtue, in the true and large sense of the word, the instinct for virtue passing into the life of Keats and strengthening it, I find in the admirable wisdom and temper of what he says to his friend Bailey on the occasion of a quarrel between Reynolds and Haydon.'

[5] Hypocritically self-righteous and condemnatory.

[6] See letter of 10 Feb. 1888. The text is: 'Man is not a reasoning animal; he is a seeing, feeling, contemplating, acting animal.' For a discussion of GMH's disagreements with Newman see Fredric W. Schlatter, 'Hopkins and Newman: Two Disagreements', *Christianity and Literature*, 27 (2008), 401–18.

[7] GMH seems to have the stronger case: it seems unlikely that the fanatical Gen. Charles George Gordon (1833–85; *ODNB*), a man of alarming chastity and self-denial, who had sensationally recently lost his life in Khartoum, and Sir Thomas More (1478–1535; *ODNB*), whose *The Sadness of Christ* reflects on his situation as the fearful martyr comforted by Christ's example, would not have recognized their sacrifice.

[8] See n. 1 of the letter to Patmore of 12 May 1887.

[9] As with many of his projects there is no evidence that this was ever carried out.

[10] Lord Frederick Cavendish, the newly appointed Chief Secretary for Ireland, and Thomas Henry Burke, the Permanent Undersecretary, were murdered by the 'Irish National Invincibles' in Phoenix Park, Dublin, on 6 May 1882. The reference to the Pope is to the decree of the Holy Office of 20 Apr. 1888 on the Plan of Campaign and boycotting, which was issued prior to the encyclical of 24 June.

[11] Richard Doddridge Blackmore (1825–1900; *ODNB*), author of *Lorna Doone* (1869), published *Springhaven* in three volumes in 1887.

[12] Mistake for 'fine'.

11 May 1888 from Coventry Patmore to GMH

FL, no. CLXXXVII A, p. 390 Campion Hall, P 11/5/88
Addressed to 'Rev[d] Gerard Hopkins, S.J. | Milltown Park, | Milltown, | Dublin'. PM HASTINGS MY 11 88, MILLTOWN MY 12 88.

Hastings. May 11. 1888
My dear M[r] Hopkins,

I am confined to my room by a bad attack of Quinsey[1] which has reduced me to a state of the greatest weakness, both of mind & body. This will be my excuse to you for not writing so fully as I otherwise ought, in reply to your kindness in writing me such a long & careful letter. I agree with most, perhaps all of what you say in objection to that article in the St. James's. Its drift, however, was not so much to expound Newman's "text", as to make an indirect attack upon the great popular fallacy that a thing must be "understood" in order to be a discernible reality.

You once told me that I had less in me of the "tyke" than any man you knew, & your smile told me that you meant I had not enough gall in me to make correction bitter. It is quite true. I have little or no paternal affection for the disorderly children of my brain, and am, and always have been, even thankful to any one who has had the goodness and courage to knock them on the head. I have a "real apprehension" that this is not quite as it should be, though I do not yet quite "understand" my defect.

I did not burn "Sponsa Dei" altogether without the further consultation you mentioned. After what you had said, I talked [to] my Dr Rouse[2] about it, and he seemed to ^have^ no strong opinion one way or another, but said he thought that all the substance of the work was already published in my poems & in one or two of my papers in the St. James's. So I felt free to do what your condemnation of the little book inclined me to do.[3]

Of course what I said in that article about "Sacrifice" is not theologically accurate; but it is accurate, I think, taking the sense of sacrifice as it would be understood by nearly all the readers of the "St. James's". What I intended to convey was that in the sacrifices made by such men as Gordon & Sir Thomas More there is none of the misery & reluctance which common men attach to the idea. If I have any power of guessing how it is with such men, the only real misery of ^their^ life lies in the doubt of what it is right to do in great crises, not in doing it when the right is clearly known.

I shall be sorry if you altogether abandon the idea which you tell me you had of writing that review. *You* know that what I have written has neither been [*illegible word deleted*] lightly conceived nor ~~carele~~ lightly executed. But even those who have intended to be most laudatory have given my work an entirely superficial consideration; and all the fashionable critics have utterly ignored it, mainly I believe because it has none of those airs of profundity which those poets who are not profound so easily assume. Every one knows that "Easy writing's sometimes d—d hard reading";[4] but few know that easy reading's sometimes d—d hard writing; and with the ^present^ arbiters of poetic fashion the "Angel in the House" is looked upon as unworthy of serious notice because all mere pretence of profundity has been so carefully avoided, and the truths that form the granite foundations of life are expressed with such clear simplicity and polish that the profundity & the labour are both obscured by their completeness.

I quite agree with all you say about "Springhaven"; but have not strength enough at present to go into my reasons for differing from you in thinking that Keats, had he lived, would ever have done much better than his last little volume.

Yours affectionately
C. Patmore

[1] Quinsey or quinsy is inflammation of the throat, or tonsillitis.

[2] See letter of 21 Aug. 1885.

[3] See below: letter of Patmore to RB of 12 Aug. 1889. Abbott discusses this in his introduction to *FL*, pp. xxxiv–xxxix.

[4] See his letter of 17 May 1885.

Whitsunday (20 May) 1888 to Coventry Patmore

FL, no. CLXXXVIII, p. 392 Durham University Library, Abbott MS 202
Folded sheet with printed heading and watermark of shield with rampant lion above a banner with A P & S above the words Antique Parchment Note Paper. Four sides.

GLENAVEENA, | HOWTH. [*printed address*]
Whitsunday 1888

Dear Mr. Patmore, — This is to express the hope that your attack of quinsy ^has passed or^ is passing off and to say that my paper on the Angel is really in hand and when finished will be printed without difficulty: there is more difficulty about getting it finished. If it is to be printed at all however it is a pity it cannot be somewhere where it would have more readers. It treats of the matters your letter touches on. But about the "tyke" you did not altogether understand me. If I had said you had less than anyone else of the Bohemian, though that is not the same thing, ~~my~~ ^the^ meaning would have been plainer. ^As^ there is something of the "old Adam" in all but the holiest men and in them at least enough to make them understand it in others, so there is an old Adam of barbarism, boyishness, wildness, rawness, rankness, the disreputable, the unrefined in the refined and educated. It is that that I meant by tykishness (a tyke is a stray sly unowned dog) and said you have none of; and I did also think that you were without all sympathy for it and ^must^ surveye~~d~~ it ^when you met with it^ wholly from without. Ancient Pistol is the typical tyke, he and all his crew ~~were~~ ^are^ tykes, and the tykish element undergoing dilution in Falstaff and Prince Hall appears to vanish, but of course really exists, in Henry V as king.[1] I thought it was well to have ever so little of it and therefore it was perhaps a happy thing that you were entrapped into the vice of immoderate smoking, ~~it tends~~ ^for to know one yields to a vice must help^ to humanise and make tolerant.

Since I wrote last I have had a piece of good luck which ^also^ has something to do with you. I made another attempt ~~of~~ on my tune to the

Crocus.[2] I set it in strict counterpoint (or as strict as the ~~c~~case allowed of) as a ^madrigal in^ canon at the octave, a most difficult task, and after much labour sent it to my friend Sir Robert Stewart to correct. ~~It g~~ He gave it a very good mark, but suggested some changes in the rhythm chiefly. I have made them, but to touch a composition of this sort is like touching a house of cards: one piece pulls down another, so the alterations cost a good deal of trouble more. And this is only the first verse: the two others are still to do. When all is done it ought to be sung by an unaccompanied choir. I hope in the end it may be: the attempt was daring (like verse in intricate metre) and Sir Robert's verdict amounted to saying that it was successful.

I am very sincerely yours Gerard M. Hopkins.

[1] In Shakespeare's *Henry* plays.

[2] See letters to RB of 11–12 Nov. 1884, 1 Jan. 1885, 8 Feb. 1885, 12–13 Jan. 1888, and 25–6 May 1888; and see *CW* vi.

25–6 May 1888 to Robert Bridges

LRB, no. CLXI, p. 274 Bodleian, Dep. Bridges, vol. 92, fos. 164–169ᵛ

UNIVERSITY COLLEGE, | S$^{\underline{T}}$ STEPHEN'S GREEN, | DUBLIN. [*printed heading*]
May 25 1888

Bridges, have at you. Not a low, not a crow, not a bark, not a bray from either of us ha~~ve~~^s^ crossed the Channel this long while. I am presently going gently to crow, but first I want you to send <u>Nero</u> (and anything else you like, but I recommend that) to Judge O'Hagan,[1] Glenaveena, Howth, Co. Dublin, and, if you can spare one, a copy of the paper on Milton's verse; else I shall have to give him one of mine and, what is worse, to get leave to do so. He is an interesting and able man, but old fashioned in notions of poetry, especially rhythm; ^he^ thought, without a suspicion, that Shakespeare's verse was often very rough, had never heard of the doctrine of equivalence, and so on. (And there it is, I understand these things so much better than you: we should explain things, plainly state them, ~~explain,~~ clear them up, explain them; explanation ~~(~~ — except personal — is always pure good; without explanation people go on misunderstanding; being ^once^ explained they thenceforward understand ^~~them~~ things^; therefore always explain: but I have the passion for explanation and you have not.)

Whenever I read the abovementioned Nero I am more struck by its mastery and perfect nature (for instance Burrus's saying "Well, well" to Seneca's pretended ignorance of his drift is a trifling but admirable touch); but in my opinion, though not archaic compared with Swinburne, Morris, and so on, it is sicklied o'er[2] a little with an Elizabethan diction, and this is its defect.

Canon Dixon says your Achilles[3] is very beautiful. He ~~only~~ ^also^ says you 'hate' his Eudocia~~:~~.[4] I have not seen it yet, but I have the Saturday's disagreeable review.[5] If anything made me think the age Alexandrine (as they say), ~~one~~ ^an age^ of decadence (a criticism that they sling about between the ~~emphatic~~ ^bursting^ Yes and blustering No, for want of more things to say, as ^also^ that the Academy is or is not "above the average" — ~~and~~ ^for^ what does it matter? — but it reminds me of my aunt's question when she went shopping with her mother as a child, "Is goose a poultry?" — not an unreasonable question in itself and even philosophical, for strictly speaking everything either is or is not poultry, but for the purposes of criticism not enough) well, it would be to see how secondrate poetry (and what I mean is, not poetry at all) gets itself put about for ^great^ poetry, and that too when the[re] are plenty of real, however faulty, poets living. I am thinking of people like Alfred Austin and Edwin Arnold and Austin Dobson ^and Lewis Morris[6]^, who have merits of course I know, but . . . you can finish up and I know you will think harder than anything I am likely to write. I must copy it for you, more by token: Mr. Skeat has written, out of pure gall (facit indignatio versum {*indignation produces the poem*}),[7] a down~~n~~right good villanelle in mockery of villanelle-writing.[8] If I were Russian censor of the press it would be my joy to force rondeliers to print this piece on the titlepage of each ^new^ volume of roundels. There is one of that crew[9] has written (did I tell you before?) the very worst line I ever remember to have read in English. It is from a villanelle in praise of the villanelle and says it, the kickshaw in question, cannot reach the roll and swell

Of organs grandiose and sublime~~,~~
(A dainty thing's the Villanelle).

An effeminate thing: I wish we were rid of them.

I wrote a paper of Readings and Renderings of Sophocles this year and sent it to the Classical Review. The passages commented on were strung together so as to illustrate a principle of lyrical construction: it was a critical essay. After a while the editor wrote to say they had little room for original essays, but that if I liked that two of the passages, which he named, shd. appear in the form of Notes, such as scholars send to every number, they could. To this I agreed, but that was some time ago and I see no sign of their appearing; so I am afraid the whole will come to nought.[10] However, to me, to finish a thing and that it shd. ~~owe its~~ ^be out of hand and^ owe its failure to somebody else is nearly the same thing as success.

For instance I began an Epithalamion on my brother's wedding: it had some bright lines, but I could not get it done.[11] That is worse. ^(^This wedding was last month. The honeymoon was in Paris; they wrote ^thence^ in ecstacy; but had not been home long when the bride's mother died. But perhaps an affliction endears husband and wife.^)^

But I have had one hit. Of this I meekly bray and mildly crow. In counterpoint. I wrote a complicated canon: it was the air to Coventry Patmore's "The crocus while the days are dark"[12] and I made it serve as ~~a~~ counterpoint exercise (they say canon is the best), keeping all rules as strictly as such a composition allows. At last I sent it, the first verse rather of three, ~~making~~ ^which are to make^ a madrigal, to Sir Robert Stewart; who gave it a very good mark (and he does not flatter), suggesting amendments ^however^, which I have since made. It was laborious, but I now can do canon easily and hope to have the two other verses ready soon. Success in canon beats the other successes of art: it ~~is~~ ^comes^ like ^a^ miracle, even to the inventor. It does seem as if the canon discovered the musician and not he it. But the truth is that in a really ~~g~~ organic tune the second ~~str~~ or third strain or both tend to be good counterpoint (with or even without bass) to the first. And then fugue is really canon at the fifth (or twelfth). So that I see a world of canon and fugue before me. I do not say I am going there. But one ~~canon~~ madrigal in canon I will finish and then I hope one in fugue. No accompaniments; and the human voice is immortal. You said nothing would come: I hope you may have been wrong.

With kind remembrance to Mrs. Bridges, Mrs. Molesworth, and Mrs. Waterhouse, I am your affectionate friend Gerard M. Hopkins. May 26 1888.

Villanelle.

How to compose a villanelle, which is said to require "an elaborate amount of care in production, which those who read only would hardly suspect existed".[13]

It's all a trick, quite easy when you know it,
As easy as reciting ABC;
You # need not be an atom of a poet.

If you've a grain of wit, and want to show it,
Writing a villanelle — take this from ~~any~~ ^me^ —
It's all a trick, quite easy when you know it.

You start a pair of rimes, and then you "go it"
With rapid-running pen and fancy free;
You need not be an atom of a poet.

[turn over

Take any thought, write round it or below it;,
Above or near it, as it liketh thee;
It's all a trick, quite easy when you know it.

Pursue your task, till, like a shrub, you grow it,
Up to the standard size it ought to be;
You need not be an atom of a poet.

Clear it of weeds, and water it, and hoe it,
Then watch it blossom with triumphant glee.
It's all a trick, quite easy when you know it;
You need not be an atom of a poet.

Walter W. Skeat
(Academy 19 May 1888)[14]

This has the inspiration of annoyance, a very much more vital and spontaneous thing than the pieces it satirises have.

I do not like the sour unspiritual tone of this letter; but if I were not like that I should not have written it and there it is. now.[15]

[1] At whose country house GMH occasionally stayed for a few days.

[2] Ironically using Shakespearean diction himself, quoting from Hamlet's 'the native hue of resolution | Is sicklied o'er with the pale cast of thought' (*Hamlet* III. i. 84–5).

[3] *Achilles in Scyros*, A Drama in a Mixed Manner; published by Bumpus in 1890.

[4] *The Story of Eudocia and her Brothers*; published by H. Daniel in 1888. See RB's letter to RWD of 16 Aug. 1888, Stanford, 179–80.

[5] In the issue of 12 May 1888. For example, 'It is needless to say that there are good things in *Eudocia*. Canon Dixon is too well equipped with learning and sympathy and feeling, and has in times past shown himself too good a metrist, to fail entirely.'

[6] Alfred Austin (1835–1913; *ODNB*) was born near Leeds and educated at Stonyhurst College. He became a barrister in 1857, edited the *National Review*, whose politically conservative views accorded with his own. He was appointed Poet Laureate in 1896, succeeding Tennyson but only after four years during which no suitable

candidate was found. Edwin Arnold (1832–1904; *ODNB*) was born in Kent, attended King's College, London and University College, Oxford. He taught at King Edward's School, Birmingham until 1856, when he became Principal of the Government Sanskrit College at Poona, returning to England in 1861. He joined the staff of the *Daily Telegraph* as a journalist, eventually becoming editor-in-chief. He was involved in the setting up of H. M. Stanley's expedition to find the source of the Congo River. His main literary work is *The Light of Asia* (1879), an Indian epic setting out the teaching of Buddha. It was very popular, much more so than later volumes of poetry. He later settled in Japan. Henry Austin Dobson (1840–1921; *ODNB*) was born at Plymouth, educated at Beaumaris, Anglesey, where his family moved when he was 8, and at Strasbourg. He worked for the Board of Trade 1856–1901, becoming principal of the harbour department. He produced a number of volumes of poetry, experimenting with rondels, rondeaus, and villanelles, and the biographies of several 18th-c. literary figures including Henry Fielding (1883), Richard Steele (1886), Oliver Goldsmith (1888), and Horace Walpole (1890). Sir Lewis Morris (1833–1907; *ODNB*), born in Carmarthen, belongs to the Anglo-Welsh school of poetry. After graduating from Oxford (Lit. Hum. 1856, Jesus College), he became a lawyer. He published eleven volumes of poetry and drama and was considered for the post of Poet Laureate in 1892.

[7] Juvenal *Satires* 1. 79.

[8] This villanelle accompanies the letter, and is here printed from GMH's copy, with his comment below.

[9] *Ballades and Rondeaus, etc.*, ed. J. Gleeson White ('Canterbury Poets', 1887) included examples of ballades, chants royales, kyrielles, pantoums, rondeaux redoublés, rondels, rondeaus, roundels, sestinas, triolets, and villanelles, with 'notes on the early use of the various forms and rules for their construction'. The poets included Edmund Gosse, Andrew Lang, Austin Dobson, A. C. Swinburne, Oscar Wilde, Robert Bridges, and the little-known W. E. Henley, whose poem on the villanelle which GMH so dislikes is on p. 252. See letter to RB of 24–5 Oct. 1883 for GMH's parody of a Dobson triolet (incomplete).

[10] These notes were not printed in the *Classical Review*, and no copy has been found of the work GMH submitted.

[11] The uncompleted 'Epithalamion'; written for the marriage of Everard to Amy Caroline Sichel, which took place at St Peter's Church, Crawley Gardens, on 12 Apr. 1888.

[12] Not extant. See *CW* vi.

[13] The quotation is from *Ballades and Rondeaus* (see n. 9), p. lxxiii.

[14] Originally 'May 19 – 1888'.

[15] This sentence is written above the salutation on the first page. The letter may have come close to joining the list of those GMH destroyed instead of sending.

5 July 1888 to his Mother

FL, no. CX, p. 184 Bodleian, MS Eng. lett. e. 41, fos. 125–127^{v}
Addressed to 'Mrs. Manley Hopkins | Court's Hill Lodge | Haslemere | Surrey | England'. PM DUBLIN JY 6 88 and [PETER]SFIELD JY 7 88.

UNIVERSITY COLLEGE, | S$^{\underline{\text{T}}}$ STEPHEN'S GREEN, | DUBLIN. [*printed heading*]
July 5 1888

My dearest mother, — I am now working at examination-papers all day and this work began last month and will outlast this one. It is great, very great drudgery. I can not of course say it is wholly useless, but I believe that most of it is and that I bear a burden which crushes me and does little to help any good end. It is impossible to say what a mess Ireland is and how everything enters into that mess. The Royal University is in the main, like the London University, an examining board. It does the work of examining well; but the work is not worth much. This is the first end I labour for and see little good in. Next my salary helps to support this College. The College is very moderately successful, rather a failure than a success, and there is less prospect of success now than before. Here too, unless things are to change, I labour for what is worth little. And in doing this ^almost^ fruitless work I ~~l~~ use up all opportunity of doing any other.

About my holiday I have no plan and know nothing.

We no longer take the Times now, so whenever you like to post a number it will be welcome.

The weather has been wet and cold, so that yesterday, after leaving off winter clothing for less than a week, I returned to it again.

I spent a few days lately at Judge O'Hagan's at Howth — the kindest people; and their house is beautifully but somewhat bleakly situated, overlooking the ~~b~~Bay of Dublin southwards.

I owe my father a letter, but it is no time to write now. I am your loving son Gerard.

29–30 July 1888 to Richard Watson Dixon

CRWD, no. XLI, p. 154 Bodleian, Dep. Bridges, vol. 93, fos. 161–165ᵛ
Addressed to 'The Rev. Canon Dixon | Warkworth Vicarage | Acklington | Northumberland | England'. No legible PM. Two folded sheets.

UNIVERSITY COLLEGE, | S<u>T</u> STEPHEN'S GREEN, | DUBLIN. [*printed heading*]
July 29 1888

My dear Friend, — It is now weeks since your poem of Eudocia[4] was sent to me and I thank you very much for it. But it found me (as I still am, but see daylight) very very busy. (It is killing work to examine a nation.) At first I thought only to acknowledge it; then I began a longer letter of criticism, but it miscarried and then I could not begin again. The present must be betwixt the too little and the too much.

I admired it, as I need scarcely say, throughout, but still, I can hardly tell why, read it with less of a distinct relish than I ~~can~~ commonly read you — either the subject seemed somewhat chosen at haphazard and so to have been worked at with less enthusiasm, or that I felt more sympathy for Pulcheria than you do, or whatever the reason. I think it would be caviare to the general and the mastery of ~~it~~ the style would be easily missed even by critics (as by the <u>Saturday</u>[2] it was).

I can only mention a few points ~~of~~ at random (~~and~~ I am writing from Milltown Park and the book is at the Green[3]) which I especially admire or which I demur to. I am struck for instance by the feeling for the tragedy that is kneaded up in human life ~~of~~ which your ~~writing is always so conscious o ^<u>Muse</u>^~~ writing always displays, without effort and in any natural incident of the story. I admire the portrait of Theodosius drawn with disapproval but without any satire and appearing in the dialogue advantageously as a dignified gentleman and a fine mind, ~~the~~ ^his^ weakness being then thrown into the background. The scene between him and ~~hi~~ the empress is a beautiful and subtle conception, it seems to me, and the waywardness of "Or ate it — as thou wilt"[4] a great and melancholy stroke. The scarcely perceptible touch of vanity in reminding Pulcheria that ~~she~~ he had had to point a detail out to her is interesting.[5] I much admire the thoroughly illustrative image of the fountain with half diverted source[6] and the picture of ^Eu^docia ~~and~~ ^white as^ her tablets;[7] also her answer "Sir, I have thought of this" as delicately hitting ~~a~~ ^the^ position of one who consents to a sort of intrigue without loss of candour or dignity.[8] Also the incident of the desperate return to the river growing louder and louder in its bed, and of the two arrows.[9] Also Eudocia declaiming to the air.[10] You will I hope see that ~~I do not mi~~ your strokes do not miss, or not all of them.

I feel a certain fault of construction (in a drama none, but less defensible in a narrative) in making Theodosius give the apple to Eudocia's brother ~~in~~ in the forest and make all his appointments ^then and there^ and then ~~die, and~~ ^be killed next minute,^ this being an unlikely concentration of events,[11] and on the other hand that the news of it should not have reached Eudocia till her brother came with the apple. Can this be in the history?

Metrically I find some fault. I see no ~~g~~ good in dropping a syllable (that is in giving a superfluous syllable) a few times at a stop. It is lawful and even effective in dramatic verse, and of course I know I often do it myself, but then on a very different ^rhythm and^ scheme of scanning; but in smooth narrative, in couplets, that highly polished metre, and for private reading I think it needless and faulty and that it puts the reader out. However it is a very small matter.

Making *apple* and *arrow* in Chaucerian style one syllable has a quaint charm, the charm of learned archaism; still I think it wrong, and inconsistent with the rest of the scansion. In no modern pronunciation of English could *apple*, I think, be monosyllab~~l~~ic (except of course if a vowel ~~vow~~ followed and ^the *e* were^ swallowed — like *appl' and pear*). *Arrow* on the other hand might here in ~~En~~ Ireland become a diphthong, the *r* ^before a vowel^ being not trilled or rolled as in England but burred or "furred" and half lost, so that the sound is like *ah-~~oo~~* and almost *ow* (they say "the marge and buryal of an Ornge ~~m~~ barster in Meryon Square", that is, *the marriage and burial* etc); and nearly this, no doubt, was Chaucer's sound; but you cannot well take your ground on that. And then, as above, the rest is not of a piece.

I make the same objection of inconsistency to a remarkable condensation or hurrying of syllables in "to have avoided" somewhere:[12] the line is, to be sure, to me who have the key, pleasing; but ^to others^ it will appear ever ~~lo~~ so much too long and you have scarcely prepared the reader for it. Instead of an instance it is an exception and instead of a last flourish an abrupt freak.

Lastly to touch on what is universal and woven into the whole, though I always hold that your archaism is the most beautiful ~~an~~ (as also I believe the most learned) archaism of any modern poet's, the only one that is of itself a ^living^ beauty in the style, still I cannot think even so that it is right: I look on the whole *genus* as vicious.

Which reminds me of ^Swinburne's^ Locrine.[13] I rēad very little modern poetry, however I rēad that. ~~As~~ It is scarcely to be called a play and the characterisation is youthful (Madan for instance is quite cousu avec de fil blanc {*roughly put together*}; he makes his points like the Governor of ~~Sir~~ Tilbury ^Fort^ or Sir Christopher Hatton in the Critic[14]); but for music of words and the mastery and employment of a consistent and ~~specialised~~ distinctive ^poetic^ diction, a style properly so called, it is extraordinary. But the diction is Elisabethan or nearly: not one sentence is properly modern, except where there could in no case be any difference to be made. I shd. think it could only be in Persian or some other eastern language that a poetical dialect so ornate and continuously beautiful could be found. But words only are only words.

What a preposterous summer! It is raining now: when is it not? However there was one windy bright day between floods last week: fearing for my eyes, with my other rain of papers, I put work aside and went out for the day, and conceived a sonnet.[15] Otherwise my muse has long put down her carriage[16] and now for years "takes in washing". The laundry is driving a great trade now.[17]

I hope your health is restored.

Believe me your affectionate friend Gerard M. Hopkins.

Please write more odes. The ode "Thou goest more and more"[18] seems to me one of the very grandest ever written in anything.

July 30 1888.

I have done some more of my elegy and hope to finish it.[19]

[1] *The Story of Eudocia & her Brothers.* By Richard Watson Dixon, Printed by H. Daniel, Fellow of Worcester College: Oxford, 1888. Pp. vi. 35. 50 copies printed. A poem of some 756 unnumbered lines in iambic pentameter couplets.

[2] The issue of 12 May 1888. It is quoted in *LRB*, note Y.

[3] i.e. from the Society's House at Milltown rather than from the University at St Stephen's Green.

[4] l. 287.

[5] l. 316.

[6] l. 58.

[7] l. 105.

[8] ll. 113–14.

[9] ll. 553–4 and 589 sqq. respectively.

[10] l. 420.

[11] ll. 686–714.

[12] l. 269: 'Well had it been to have avoided the first sign.'

[13] Published in 1887.

[14] Both characters appear in Richard Brinsley Sheridan's *The Critic* (1781) and are extremely verbose. The comparison with Madan's speeches is just. GMH may have remembered the play partly because it features Hopkins the under-prompter.

[15] 'That Nature is a Heraclitean Fire', which is dated in 'MS A': 'July 26 1888 | Co. Dublin'.

[16] i.e. unpacked her travelling bags and settled down (as opposed to 'took up our carriages' in Acts 21: 15).

[17] i.e. is employed in cleaning up other people's work, as GMH was doing energetically for RWD, RB, and Patmore.

[18] 'Ode on Advancing Age', *Lyrical Poems*, 1887 (*S.P.*, 132–5).

[19] 'On the Portrait of Two Beautiful Young People'; see also letters to RB of 2 Jan. 1887, to RWD of 27–9 Jan. 1887, to RB of 29 Mar. 1887, from RWD of 7 July 1887, to RWD of 22–3 Dec. 1887, to his mother of 25 Dec. 1887.

18–19 August 1888 to Robert Bridges

LRB, no. CLXII, p. 278 Bodleian, Dep. Bridges, vol. 92, fos. 170–173^{v}

~~UNIVERSITY COLLEGE, | S^T STEPHEN'S GREEN, | DUBLIN~~. [*printed heading*]

Monzie Villa, Fort William, North Britain. Aug. 18 1888

Dearest Bridges, — I am much in your debt for a letter, but at this time of the year you must not be surprised at that. Six weeks of examination are lately over and I am now bringing a fortnight's holiday to an end. I have leave to prolong it, but it is not very convenient to do so and I scarcely care. It appears I want not scenery but friends. My companion[1] is not quite himself or he verges towards his duller self and ^so^ no doubt ~~I~~ do ^I too^, and we have met few people to ~~welcome us much.~~ ^be pleasant^ with. We ~~hav~~ ^are^ in Lochaber (and are happily pestered with no sentiment) and have been to the top of Ben Nevis and up Glencoe[2] on the most brilliant days, but in spite of the exertions or because of them I cannot sleep (which is the very mischief) and we have got no bathing (it is close at hand but close also to the highroad) nor boating and I am feeling very old and looking very wrinkled and altogether . . . . Besides we have no books ~~(~~except the farce of the fellow reading Minchin's Kinematics:[3] he is doing so n~~w~~ow and dozing and shd. be in bed; this book I ~~do not~~ leave to him entirely, you may suppose, and have bought Dana's Two Years Before the Mast,[4] a thoroughly good one and all true, but bristling with technicality~~,~~ — seamanship — which I most carefully go over ~~b~~ and even enjoy but cannot understand: there are other things ^though^, as a flogging, which is terrible and instructive and it happened — ah, that is the charm and the main ~~thi~~ point. With the other half of the same shilling I bought The Old Curiosity Shop;[5] never read it before, am not going to give in to any nonsense about Little Nell (like, I believe, Lang[6] I cannot stand Dickens's ~~sentiment~~ pathos; or rather I can stand it, keep a thoroughly dry eye and unwavering waistcoat), but ~~like~~ admire Dick Swiveller and Kit and ~~the~~ Quilp and that old couple with the pony.

But business first. Your last little letter to me I never read. I never got it. I think perhaps Mrs. Bambury[7] did and hope there was nothing in it which shd. call a blush onto her cheek as, I will say, there was nothing in ~~the~~ ^Mrs. Bridges's^ beautifully written note of acceptance to Mrs. Bambury to cause a pang to me except of course that it was not what the envelope purported. This note I enclose.

I greatly admired the hand in which you wrote from Seaford and hope you will continue to employ it.

I will now go to bed, the more so as I am going to preach tomorrow and put plainly to ~~the~~ ^a^ Highland congregation of MacDonalds, MacIntoshes, MacKillops, and the rest what I am ~~giving~~ putting not at all so plainly to the rest of the world, or rather to you and Canon Dixon, in a sonnet in sprung rhythm with two codas.[8]

Aug. 19. That is done. — I am unfortunate in the time of my letters reaching you. The last contained mockery at the Rondeliers, of whom Lang is ringleader, is he not? and you read it seated next him on your trap in the extreme confidence of a country drive; so that, too probably, you let him know what I said and he will never forgive me. You should be very discreet about such matters.

Canon Dixon sent me his Eudocia. I admired it, but found it not particularly interesting as a story. It was all over genius not remarkably well employed. I did not agree with some metrical peculiari~~a~~ties.

I think you were not quite correct in your paraphrase of the passage in Galatians. I will say what I think it means, but perhaps not in this letter.

I was asked to my friends at Howth to meet Aubrey de Vere.[9] However ~~we~~ ^he^ was called away to London and when I came was gone. I was disappointed, till it was mentioned that he did not think Dryden a poet. Then, I thought and perhaps said, I have not missed much. And yet you share this opinion or something like it with him. Such are the loutish falls and hideous vagaries of the human mind.

Of Handel, by the bye. If it was only recitative[10] of his you did not like and 'wavered in your allegiance' never mind. The recitative which arose in the Renaissance at Florence, artificially and by a sort of pedantry, was ~~always~~ ^to begin with^ bad, and Handel's employment of it always appeared to me to be his poorest part: the thing is so spiritless and mean, with vulgar falls and floundering to and from the dominant and leading note. The only good and truly beautiful recitative is that of plain chant; which indeed culminates in that. It is a natural development of the speaking, reading, or declaiming voice, and has the richness of nature; the other is a confinement of the voice to certain prominent intervals and has the poverty of an artifice. But Handel is Handel. I was at the Glasgow Exhibition[11] (a very fine one) and heard a piece of an organ-recital ending with a chorus by Handel: it was as if a mighty besom swept away so much dust and chaff. But when you speak of sighing for Bellini and Palestrina, who is that Bellini? I only know of the modern Bellini.[12]

I agree about cricket and Darwinism and that "everything is Darwinism". But especially a ship. However the honeycomb is not quite so plain a matter as you think. The learned, I believe, are divided on the question whether the shape of the cell is really to be called a matter of mechanics. For observe: the cell can only be symmetrical, ^with^ a true hexagonal section and so on, by the bees being stationed ^at^ equal distances, working equally, and so on; in fact there is a considerable table of caetera paria {*other things that are equal*}. But this implies something more than mechanical to begin with. Otherwise the hexagonal ^etc^ cell wd. be the type tended to only and ~~som~~ seldom or never arrived at; the comb wd. be like the irregular figures of bubbles in the froth of beer or in soapsuds. Wild bees do, I believe, build something like that. But grant in the honey bee some principle of symmetry and uniformity and you have passed beyond mechanical necessity; and it is not clear that there may not be some special instinct determined to that shape of cell after all and ^which has^ at the present stage of the bee's condition, nothing to do with mechanics;, but ^is^ like the specific songs of cuckoos and thrush. Now to bed or rather to pack. I will therefore conclude, though there must have been more to say. With kindest remembrances to Mrs. Bridges and Mrs. Molesworth, believe me your affectionate friend Gerard M. Hopkins.

Send the letter that went to Mrs. Bambury. Address Dublin, though possibly I may not ^go^ there for a few days more. Do not write here.

[1] The Revd Robert Curtis, SJ, whose appointment—to the chair of Natural Science—was made on the same day as that of GMH. See introduction to *CW* vii.

[2] Sir Walter Scott's *A Legend of Montrose* tells of the battle of Lochaber in which the Campbells were defeated by Montrose on behalf of King Charles II. Ben Nevis (1344 metres) is the highest mountain in the British Isles, at the western end of the Grampian Mountains, close to the town of Fort William. Glencoe is a narrow and rugged glen, the site of a massacre in 1692 of the MacDonald clan under pretence for being slow in pledging allegiance to William of Orange.

[3] *Uniplanar Kinematics of Solids and Fluids*, by George Minchin Minchin (1882).

[4] Richard Dana (1815–82) was an American lawyer and politician who served aboard a ship in the Pacific in 1834–6 and published his experience in the book *Two Years before the Mast* (1840).

[5] Charles Dickens's *The Old Curiosity Shop* was first serialized in 1840 and published in book form in 1841. Dick Swiveller, Christopher Nubbles ('Kit'), the obnoxious Daniel Quilp, and the old couple (Mr and Mrs Garland) with their wilful pony Whisker are central figures. GMH shared the unsentimental response of Lang and Oscar Wilde, who famously remarked to Ada Leverson that 'One must have a heart of stone to read the death of Little Nell without laughing'.

[6] Andrew Lang (1844–1912; *ODNB*) was an astonishingly prolific writer of novels, poetry, history, anthropology, journalism, and folklore. He was born in Selkirk and overlapped with GMH at Balliol (Lit. Hum. First 1868) and became a fellow of Merton College, Oxford. He was the founder of the Society for Psychical Research.

[7] It seems that the same situation has occurred as mentioned in the letter to E. H. Coleridge of 2 Mar. 1863; the letters have been put in the wrong envelopes. He has received Monica Bridges's acceptance of an invitation from Mrs Bambury and she has been sent the letter meant for him.

[8] 'That Nature is a Heraclitean Fire and of the comfort of the Resurrection'.

[9] Aubrey Thomas de Vere (1814–1902; *ODNB*) was born at Adare in Co. Limerick to Sir Aubrey De Vere, second Baronet. He was educated privately, later attending Trinity College Dublin (1832–7) where his father hoped, in vain, that he would enter the Church. He spent time in England at Cambridge, Oxford, London, and the Lake District, meeting many of the literary figures of the time, including Carlyle and Wordsworth. In 1851 he converted to Catholicism in Rome (received on 15 Nov. 1851), and in 1854 was appointed by Newman to be the first Professor of political and social science in the Catholic University of Ireland because of the efforts that he had made to organize relief and longer-term strategies for dealing with the crop failures and famine in Ireland in the 1840s. De Vere did no teaching in the university and instead wrote volumes of poetry on the Virgin Mary and various saints, plays on Alexander the Great (1874) and St Thomas of Canterbury (1876), and political and philosophical essays.

[10] The form between singing and ordinary speech commonly employed in the dialogue and narrative parts of operas and oratorios.

[11] See *A Century of Artists* (by W. E. Henley and R. Walker), a Memorial of the Glasgow International Exhibition, 1888.

[12] Vincenzo Bellini (1801–35), born in Sicily, was a child prodigy who studied in Naples. He rapidly became a successful composer of opera, working in Milan, Parma, and Venice. His operas include *La sonnambula*, *Norma*, and *I Puritani*. It seems likely that RB was simply mentioning two composers whose work he liked without attention to their period. Abbott notes that 'The curious collocation is perhaps explained by the fact that RB was at this time very fond of an Aria di Chiesa, *Pieta! Signor!*, usually attributed wrongly to Stradella. RB thought it should be given to Bellini. Grove says: "the composer of that beautiful composition is generally believed to be Fétis, Niedermeyer, or Rossini".'

7–8 September 1888 to Robert Bridges

LRB, no. CLXIII, p. 282 Bodleian, Dep. Bridges, vol. 92, fos. 174–177^{v}

University College, | *Stephen's Green,* | *Dublin.* [*printed heading*] Sept. 7 1888

Dearest Bridges, — I believe I wrote to you last from Fort William. I went thence to Whitby, to be with my brothers, and returned here after being 3 weeks away. Since, I have been trying to set a discursive MA. Examination Paper, in a distress of mind difficult ~~either~~ ^both^ to understand ~~or~~ ^and to^ explain. It seems to me I can not always last like this: in mind or body or both I shall give way — and all I really need is a certain degree of relief~~, but I shall~~ and change; but I do not think that what I need I shall get in time to save me. This reminds me of a shocking thing that has just happened to a young man well known to some of our community. He put his eyes out. He was a medical student and probably understood how to proceed, which was nevertheless barbarously done with a stick and some wire. The eyes were found among nettles in a field. ~~He was taken~~ After the deed he ~~found~~ made his way to a cottage and said "I am blind: please let me rest for an hour". He was taken to hospital and lay in some danger — from shock, I suppose, or inflammation — , ~~or~~ but is recovering. He will not say what was the reason, and this and other circumstances wear ~~a~~ ^the^ look of sanity; but it is said he was lately subject to delusions. I mention the case because it is extraordinary: suicide is common.

It is not good to be a medical man in the making. It is a fire in which clay splits. There was a young man in this house in my first year, an Englishman, manly and winning too, the sweetest mannered boy. After he left us he went astray. I tried to call on him, but after many trials, finding he shunned me, I gave up trying. I hear he has made a mess of it and is going to make a new beginning in Australia

There are as many doctors as patients at Dublin, a'most.[1]

~~Not being~~ ^Feeling^ the need of something I spent the afternoon in the Phoenix Park, which is lar[2]ge, beau[1]tiful, and lonely. It did me good, but my eyes are very, very sore. Also there goes ten. Goodnight. Sept. 8 (it is now 20 years to a day since I began my noviceship). Well and I had a great light. I had in my mind the first verse of a patriotic ^song for^ soldiers, the words I mean: heaven knows it is needed. I hope to make some 5 verses, but 3 would do for singing: perhaps you will contribute a verse. In the Park I hit on a tune, very flowing and spirited. I enclose the present form of this, just the tune, for I cannot set a bass till I have an instrument. I believe however that you can make nothing of a bare tune; at which I am surprised. — I find I have made 4 verses, rough~~t~~ at present, but I send them:[2] do you like them and could you add one? I hope you may approve what I have done, for it is worth doing and ^yet is^ a task of great delicacy ~~to~~ and hazard to write a patriotic song that shall breathe true feeling without spoon or brag. How I hate both! and yet feel myself half blundering or ~~lurch~~^sink^ing into them in several of my pieces, a thought that makes me not greatly regret their likelihood of perishing.

By the bye you misquote ~~a~~ ^the same^ modern author in writing "airy between towers": what is not ^so^? it should be "branchy between towers".[3]

I enclose by the same ^hand^ a sonnet of some standing which Canon Dixon has had and you have not. I have also several more, done at long intervals. ^Also another.^[4]

You asked if you might use a thought of mine about the work~~,~~ (~~as~~ ^it was said of^ a canon in music) finding the man and not the man the work: by all means; you will execute it in chryselephantine.[5]

Can there be gout or rheumatism in the eyes? If there can I have it. I am a gouty piece now.

Gouty rhymes to Doughty. Since you speak so highly of his book I must try to see it: to read 1200 pages I do not promise.[6] But I have read several reviews of it, with extracts.[7] You say it is free from the taint of ~~El~~ Victorian English. H'm. Is it free from the taint of Elizabethan English? Does it not stink of that? for the sweetest flesh turns to corruption. Is not Elizabethan English a corpse these centuries? No one admires, regrets, despairs over the death of the style, ~~and~~ the living masculine native rhetoric of that age, more than I do; but "'tis gone, 'tis gone, 'tis gone".[8] He writes in it, I understand, because it is manly. At any rate affectation is not manly, and to write in an obsolete style is affectation. As for the extracts I saw they were not good ~~at~~ ^even as^ th~~is~~at — wrong as English, for instance calling a <u>man</u> a jade; and crammed with Latin words, a fault, let do it who will.

But it is true this Victorian English is a bad business. They say 'It goes without saying' (and I wish it did) and instead of 'There is no such thing' they say a thing 'is non-existent' and <u>in</u> for <u>at</u> and <u>altruistic</u> and a lot more.

Here is the tune:

What shall I do for the land that bred me, Her
homes and fields that fold - ed and fed me? Be
un - der her ban-ner and live for her hon-our:
Un - der her ban - ner I'll live for her hon-our,
CHORUS.
Un - der her ban - ner I live for her hon-our.

This is not final of course. Perhaps the name of England is too exclusive. I am [9]Your affectionate friend Gerard M. Hopkins.

Where is the letter that went to Mrs. Bambury?

By the bye, Doughty wd. not after all be grateful to you; for this is what you say: "Monica . . suspects that I must be drivelling and reminds me to tell you of a very remarkable book" etc

[1] It is curious that RB never told GMH that he had himself worked as a doctor in Dublin in 1873.

[2] 'What shall I do for the land that bred me'. See *J&P*, 491–2 and *CW* vi.

[3] 'Duns Scotus's Oxford', l. 1.

[4] 'That Nature is a Heraclitean Fire and of the comfort of the Resurrection' and 'To what serves Mortal Beauty'.

[5] GMH described Tennyson's poetry as '"chryselephantine"; always of precious mental material and each verse a work of art, no botchy places, not only so but no half wrought or low-toned ones, no drab, no brown-holland; but the form, though fine, not the perfect artist's form, not equal to the material' (letter to RWD of 27 Feb.–13 Mar. 1879).

[6] *Travels in Arabia Deserta* (2 vols., 1888), by Charles M. Doughty (1843–1926; *ODNB*) a travel book which, though it had little immediate impact, slowly became a touchstone for ambitious travel writing, valued as much for its language as for its content. RB was much taken with the book and recommended it to most of his correspondents.

[7] Among them one in the *Athenaeum* (17 Mar. 1888), 334, and one by Sir Richard Burton in the *Academy* (28 July 1888), 47–8, who mentioned the archaism of Doughty's diction. GMH seems to have been drawing on the article in the *Saturday Review* (31 Mar. 1888), 391–2, which included, as an example of the book's 'extraordinary' style, 'it seemed the jade might have been if great had been his chance, another Tiberius Senex'.

[8] Tongue in cheek, GMH bemoans the loss of Elizabethan English with a quotation from Shakespeare's *Romeo and Juliet*. Capulet reminisces that:

> I have seen the day
> That I have worn a visor and could tell
> A whispering tale in a fair lady's ear,
> Such as would please: 'tis gone, 'tis gone, 'tis gone (I. v. 639–42).

[9] From here to the end is written above the salutation.

10–11 September 1888 to Robert Bridges

LRB, no. CLXIV, p. 285 Bodleian, Dep. Bridges, vol. 92, fos. 178–181[v]

University College, Stephen's Green, Dublin. [*printed heading*] Sept. 10 1888

Dearest Bridges, — Though you have a good deal of pleasing modern author to comment on I add a post~~card~~^script^ more. You must have been surprised at ~~my~~ ^his^ saying on ~~my~~ ^his^ return from a 3-weeks' holiday that he ^could^ get no relief and so on. But what he ~~meant~~ ^wishes^ to be understood ~~was~~ ^is^ that his work, ^which^ is so harassing to his mind, was only suspended for that time (which of itself was most helpful and quite necessary) and not ~~thrown~~ ^for the time^ finished and done; so that there is no ~~rest from~~ ^end to^ anxiety and care, but only an interruption of it, and the effect accumulates on the whole. No doubt many people are in the same anxiety about money. Also I feel ~~rather~~ lighterhearted now. (In fact we must never mind what the modern author said.)

Are you going on with your garland of English music?[1] It might be useful to you to read three (numbered as four) Papers on the ~~music~~ ^~~Engli~~ subject^ by ~~Mr.~~ A. M. Wakefield in Murray's for July, August, and September.[2] He ~~says~~ ^puts^ Wilbye's two madrigals "Stay, Corydon" and "Sweet Honey-sucking Bees", he says, above all madrigals ever written;[3] next to those he puts Orlando Gibbons's Silver Swan and "Oh that the learned Poets".[4] Would that I could hear some madrigals. He says there is an English "composer, Robert Whyte,[5] whose works are on a level with those of Palestrina, whom he preceded." . . . A good collection of his MSS. are to be found in the Christ

Church library at Oxford, from whence no enterprising national feeling has ever cared to unearth them."

There is a poem on the Armada ~~on~~ by Lewis Morris in the same magazine which contains no. 1 of these Papers.[6] It is of an amazing flatness. Though constructed on patriotic and Protestant principles St. George is invoked, "by request"~~. The~~ ^and the^ Spaniards are allowed to invoke (or else Morris does it for them) St. James also, "positively for this time only". He says it makes little difference: the victory was really due to ~~the~~ our seamen.

> "Now St. George for merry England, and St. James for Papal Spain,
> Our seamen are our chiefest hope, nor shall we trust in vain".

However he principally puts his trust in princes, at least Queen Elizabeth.

> "Then came Lord Henry Seymour, with a letter from Her Grace,
> And Sir Francis read the missive with grave triumph on his face

<to let you know at once, it was to the effect to use fireships, and Drake "saw it" and entered into the fun; gravely however>,

> And he sware an oath

<let Morris be communicated with and be got to say plainly, in prose if necessary, though I believe he could get it in with verse, what the exact oath was>,

> that come what would,
> her orders should be ~~o~~ done
> Before the early rose of dawn[7] <here the poetry comes in, in spite of exhausting self restraint> proclaimed the coming sun".

The fireships were a great success. The Spanish ships

> "drift into the night,
> And many are crushed, and many burn, and some are sunk outright."

May I say that the last words have just a touch of me? But you must send for it.

Now for the passage in Galatians, which, as you say, is hard. [8]

The epistle is written to reproach the Galatians for listening to those who wd. have them be circumcised and keep the law of Moses and recalls them to their allegiance to the Gospel, which St. Paul had preached to them. St. Paul has occasion often to employ the following familiar images — of life or conduct as a journey made or race run, of sins as a fall, and of law and hard duty as burdens borne.

This premised, in chapter v. he says the Law was made to control passion and ~~fo~~ check sin and he enumerates the works of the flesh, that is the acts of sin ~~that~~ ^which^ passion prompts to. The Gospel or the Spirit~~,~~ as he calls it, that is Christianity, is quite another thing — an inspiration to do all good, and accordingly he enumerates here too the acts of virtue it prompts and inspires. People prompted by such an inspiration will do nothing but good and Christians therefore need no law (23.). Their flesh, their bad passions, have been disposed of ~~at~~ ^in^ Christ's crucifixion; they do not live for ~~them~~ them but for and by the Spirit, the inspirations of Christianity.

Now, says he~~,~~ (v 25.), if the spirit is our ^source of^ life, as we profess by being Christians, we ought to ('live up to it' or, as he puts it,) walk by it. It is no use to be vainglorious and challenge one another to races not enjoined us, seeing who can go furthest and do most, ~~by adding to~~ "handicapping himself" with the old Law. The meaning of this is really envy ~~and the wi~~ (26.) and ~~worldliness~~ ^~~cowardly~~^ ~~(vi~~ cowardice (vi 12.) and the desire to lead (ib. 13.).

~~But~~ ^Now^ (vi 1.) ~~you will say~~ ^of course I remember that^ the flesh, that is passion, is not physically dead: ~~people~~ ^Christians^ are tempted and ^do^ fall. But, brethren, if a brother does ~~on~~ ^so fall,^ the spiritual ones ^of you^, that is the unfallen, who live by the inspirations of Christianity, shd. help him to rise; kindly and humbly, remembering, every man of you, that you might do the same. Bear the weight of one another in ^thus^ uplifting one another: that weight and not the ^burdens of the^ old Law, will fill out, if it is question of that, the law of Christ.

Sept. 11 — What follows is so much conde~~m~~nsed that it cannot be understood without much expansion: if I am right, the sense is as follows. 3. However men may deceive themselves, of themselves they are nothing and nothing they do has any moral goodness from their doing it. It is then useless for a man to compare himself, who keeps the Mosaic law, with another, who does not, or himself, who set the example of keeping it, with another, who followed his example, to his own advantage: there is no such advantage. ^4.^ But the work or deeds done may have a goodness ^or badness^ of their own; they may, like the works of the flesh, be bad; like those of the spirit, be good; or, like those of the now abrogated ~~l~~Law, be meaningless and indifferent: this point is well worth men's examining themselves on. If they once did the works of the flesh and now do those of the spirit or if they once did a little of these good works and now do a great deal, then there is a positive gain, an advantage <u>of themselves over themselves</u>, and of this may be proud,

~~or~~ that is they may ~~be~~ exult at it; but always within the world of their own beings. ^5.^ Then each will be bearing his own burden, that is himself, his flesh with its trials and burdens, ~~in~~ ^on^ the road, or in the race, of life; as he has to do. In this sense each man is to keep to himself. 6. But in another way ~~inter~~^ex^change, ~~and~~ intercourse, commerce of good with good, ~~does~~ is quite right; if for instance the spiritual impart their greater spiritual knowledge to the ~~un~~^less^spiritual and these in return do them what service ~~they can~~ ^is in their power^. Let them by all means do as much good ^work^ this way as they can; for 7. behind all this outward shew of Jewish ceremonies and what not which men see ^is^ God ^who^ sees the heart and cannot be ~~defrauded~~ imposed upon. Before him it is certain ^all^ works bear their own fruit and as men sow they will reap — 8. from the works of the flesh (and here St. Paul throws in the discarded works of the law; for they are not spiritual, therefore they are carnal) corruption (that is either something dreadful or at least something barren), from the works of the spirit life everlasting. 9. ~~t~~To these last then let us apply ourselves, never minding how things look now. 10. If we have the choice it is better, as said above (6.~~)~~, also 1.), to let our good works be of service to Christians.

I have written the above without ~~consulting~~ ^looking at^ books, of which we are not well provided. However if you wish I will consult commentators.

I find there is gout or rheumatism of the eyes. It will, I hope, soon pass away from mine.

Your affectionate friend Gerard M. Hopkins.

I have reread your interpretation of Gal. vi 1 sqq. It partly agrees with what I give below,[9] partly disagrees; but the passage cannot be understood without the expansion I have given it. I think you will see I have made it intelligible.

You are three deep with me now.

[1] Probably a reference to a private collection that RB made of the best English motets, madrigals, and part-songs, of various dates, procurable in Novello's octavo editions. He had them bound in one volume, arranged according to 'schools', with a short MS account of each musician.

[2] *Foundation Stones of English Music*: six articles, July–Dec. 1888, written to call 'the attention of the general reader to forgotten and unappreciated music'.

[3] John Wilbye (1574–1638; *ODNB*) in the service of the Lady Kytson and then her daughter: these madrigals are from the *Second Set of Madrigales To 3. 4. 5, and 6. Parts: apt both for Viols and Voices* (1609), which contains Wilbye's most enduring work

including 'Sweet honey-sucking bees' and 'Draw on sweet night'. For the texts see *English Madrigal Verse, 1588–1632*, ed. E. H. Fellowes (Oxford, 1920), nos. xvii–xviii and xxxii.

[4] Orlando Gibbons (1583–1625; *ODNB*), court musician: these madrigals are from *The First Set of Madrigals and Mottets of 5. Parts: apt for Viols and Voyces* (1612), and are his masterpieces. See *English Madrigal Verse*, nos. i and ii.

[5] Robert Whyte (*c.*1532–74; *ODNB*). After taking his BMus at Cambridge (1560), he became master of choristers at Ely Cathedral and later at Chester and Westminster Abbey. He set Lamentations and various Latin texts and wrote music for viols.

[6] *Murray's Magazine*, July 1888, pp. 30–4, 'The Invincible Armada, 1588': a 'patriotic' ballad of the worst type. See *The Works of Lewis Morris* (London, 1890), 491–4. For Morris, see letter to RB of 25–6 May 1888, n. 6.

[7] From Tennyson: 'God made himself an awful rose of dawn' ('Vision of Sin').

[8] GMH's discussion centres on Galatians 5: 22 to 6: 10. He is not here addressing himself to the Douay–Rheims version (see his explanation of 6: 7).

[9] This postscript is written at the head of the letter.

13–14 September 1888 to Robert Bridges

LRB, no. CLXV, p. 289 — Bodleian, Dep. Bridges, vol. 92, fos. 182–183v

UNIVERSITY COLLEGE, | ST STEPHEN'S GREEN, | DUBLIN. [*printed heading*]
Sept. 13, 14 '88

Dearest Bridges, — I am interested to hear Mr. Rockstro is staying with you. It must be through Wooldridge that you know him. I know of him through George Fitzpatrick,[1] a dear young friend of mine but now not seen for 5 years.

I am very glad you like the tune and greatly honoured by Mr. Rockstro's setting an accompaniment,[2] which nevertheless can scarcely be read and as yet we have no piano in the house to try it by. I believe, in spite of what he says, that it allows of contrapuntal treatment; indeed, with some improvements I have since yesterday made, it ~~ma~~ may be accompanied in canon at the octave two bars off. Nor does it strike me as unlike modal music, but quite the contrary; so that I am surprised at that criticism. I will transpose it to F of course: all keys are the same to me and to every one who thinks that music was before instruments and angels before tortoises and cats. I should like you to tell me what are the ~~practical~~ ^ordinary^ limits to voices, that I may act accordingly.

If there is good in Doughty[3] no doubt I shall find it out (here there seems ~~so~~ ^some^ kind of jingling and punning, not meant, but may serve for future use) and no doubt there is good as you say so. But come, is it not affectation to write obsolete English? You know it is.

I have nothing now the matter with me but gout in the eyes, which is unpleasant and disquieting. The feeling is like soap or lemons.

I heard a goodish concert this afternoon. A Herr Slapoffski (real name) played Handel's violin ~~s~~Sonata in A:[4] what a genius! What a native language music was to him; such sense, such fluency, such idiom, and such beauty!

Yours ever Gerard M. Hopkins.

My stars! will my song be performed? But if so why not perform my madrigal in canon~~,~~? a most ambitious ~~pe~~ piece and hitherto successful but suspended for want of a piano this long while. You could not help liking it if even Sir Robert Stewart unbent to praise it (the most genial of old gentlemen, but an offhand critic of music and me).[5] I can send you the first verse to see~~.~~—four parts; of course no instrumental accompaniment; the canon is exact, at the octave, 4 bars off, between treble and tenor, and runs in the first verse to 44 bars, I think.

[1] See letter to RB of early Oct. 1882.

[2] This evidently refers to 'What shall I do for the land that bred me'; there is a copy, with a piano accompaniment by Rockstro, in RB's hand. For Rockstro see letter of 5 Jan. 1887, n. 3.

[3] See letter to RB of 7–8 Sept. 1888.

[4] Joseph Gustave Slapoffski (1862–1951) was born in London of a Russian father and Australian mother. He was educated at Christ Church Cathedral School and the Royal Academy of Music (1876–9). He became a violinist and conductor with the Carl Rosa Opera Company and made a number of tours with them. He was a founder member of the New South Wales State Conservatorium and conducted numerous opera and concert performances in Australia and New Zealand. For GMH's admiration of Handel see letter to RB of 18–19 Aug. 1888.

[5] 'The Crocus', not extant. See *CW* vi.

15 September 1888 to Katharine Tynan

Published in *Studies*, 63/252 (Winter 1974), 389–96, ed. David J. DeLaura, and in *The Month*, NS 19/5 (May 1958), 268–9 HRHRC, Container 1.5

UNIVERSITY COLLEGE, | St STEPHEN'S GREEN, | DUBLIN. [*printed heading*]
Sept. 15 1888.

My dear Miss Tynan,—Thank you kindly for the elegant photograph you have sent me. It does not represent you quite as I think of you

(Mr. Yeates' portrait[1] does that: I do not agree with his slight method of execution in that work or in others, but his portraits are nevertheless strikingly artistic; works of genius, I believe): it is however both a faithful likeness and a pleasing picture. Willie Coyne[2] agrees: he says it is like, but would not give a true impression to a stranger.

I have never written to you about your last volume, as I ought to have done, nor can I now say more than a word. In this volume the first poem[3] and the longest is also the best in my judgment. You there seize your subject with ease, zest, and mastery. It appears to me that a set story, a matter already made (as the ~~story~~ ^matter^ commonly is for the dramatist) best suits your powers and that you must have felt that yourself. You strike your effect without hesitation, your metres vary with unfailing aptness to the incident or feeling, you even treat your characters like creatures, as one who works in a world of his very own.[4] In the smaller poems of impression and feeling you linger on a thought as if uncertain how far the stroke has gone home. And then the ^rich and^ decorative style of diction which you, like the Rossettis, Swinburne, and the mode^r^n school in general, employ is never so advantageous and in place as where applied to matter which may be taken ~~to lie~~ ^as^ lying at a certain distance from you rather than ~~as~~ ^when it comes as if^ embodied in the thought from the first. This last ^manner^ (which ^was^ Wordsworth's manner for instance) is more spontaneous, it is true, but it is not compatible with a formed style and the free use of a style: we want matter to treat and it is fresher when it is not of our own making. I cannot help thinking that your own experience will respond to what I am saying. I should myself prefer to think your next ~~wor~~ volume[5] was ^to be^ some story or other theme ^on a considerable scale^ with plenty of features of its own independent of any impressions we may have about ~~it~~ ^them^ and that your achievement was to be the brilliant treatment of those features [rather] than a number of impression-pieces however rich in which a vague and evanescent state of mind is covered with a great deal of concrete imagery.

It is natural for you to choose subjects from Irish legend. They have their features of interest and beauty, but they have one great drawback: it is the intermixture of monstrosities (as of a man ~~lifting~~ ^throwing^ a stone one hundred others could not lift~~,~~ ^or^ a man ^with a^ leaping pole over-vaulting an army),* [*GMH footnote*: *You have evaded the difficulty by lightness of touch.] for these things are deeply inartistic and destroy all seriousness and verisimilitude.

Believe me yours sincerely Gerard M. Hopkins.

[1] The portrait of Katharine Tynan, painted in 1886 and exhibited at the Royal Hibernian Academy, 1887 (now in Dublin City Art Gallery, The Hugh Lane Collection) was by John Butler Yeats (1839–1922), father of William Butler Yeats, the poet, and Jack Butler Yeats, the painter. Reproduced as frontispiece to her *Twenty-five Years: Reminiscences* (1913).

[2] Probably William Patrick Coyne (1867–1904), then in his final year as a resident student at University College. He was an active contributor to the *Lyceum*, a monthly educational and literary magazine and review, which ran from Sept. 1887 to Feb. 1894. One of his first articles was a severe review of *Shamrocks.* The periodical contains no contribution from GMH. Coyne was fellow of the Royal University, 1897, and Professor of Political Economy, University College, 1899, before becoming the first Director of Statistics in the Government's new Department of Agriculture, 1900. His early death was mourned in the Irish Parliament as a national loss. See *A Page of Irish History: The Story of University College, Dublin, 1883–1909* (1930).

[3] 'The Pursuit of Diarmuid and Grainne'.

[4] W. B. Yeats had written of Katharine Tynan's Celtic romances in the *Gael*: 'I find, also, no imitation—a rare spontaneity, once or twice marred by an overweighting of picturesque detail, an originality without caprice or any pride of strangeness' (quoted in Matthew Russell, 'Two Irish Triumphs', *Irish Monthly*, 16 (Feb. 1888), 109–15.

[5] Her next volume was *Ballads and Lyrics* (1891).

17 September 1888 to John Gerard, SJ[1] (*Stonyhurst Magazine*)

From the *Stonyhurst Magazine*, 3, no. 40 (Nov. 1888), 236–7

FOOTBALL BAREFOOT

To the Editor of the Stonyhurst Magazine.

Sir, — Football is sometimes played barefoot in Ireland. A friend tells me that the club he belongs to challenged some village clubs in his neighbourhood; when the game came to be played their opponents stripped their feet and took the field barefoot. He and his company were surprised, and thought the bare feet would need to be tenderly dealt with, both by their wearers and by those who, like him, had reared three storeys of wool, leather, and iron between themselves and the county Tipperary; but the countrymen told them they could not play with any ease, unless unshod. And the event proved they had no need for apprehension. The barefooted men played as boldly as they did. The ball did not seem to be kicked with the end of the toe, but it was kicked strongly. In point of strength no loss could be seen, and in point of activity the lightness of the foot may have made a good deal of difference.

It is likely that those who are accustomed often to go barefoot feel this difference in nimbleness and fleetness keenly. In the old ballad of the Death of Parcy Reed[2] the hind who finds the hero dying, having to fetch water, casts off his clouted, that is heavily-nailed, shoon; it is implied that the gain in time would be notable.

I should add that Hurley[3] ought in strictness to be played with the feet bare, and that in the games played in the Phoenix Park many of the players may be seen barefoot. Indeed, since this game is in some sort a revival, perhaps as antiquaries discover more and more, advanced players will wear less and less.

If at Stonyhurst you would try playing football and other games barefoot you would find it an advantage on many grounds. Gravel however is not one of these grounds; you must play on grass.

And now, Sir, though I am pleading for barefootedness, barefacedness I cannot approve of. Iron on my heels I may wear, but brass upon my brow I will not. I therefore, with all respect for Mr Arthur Chilton Thomas,[4] sign myself yours,

GYMNOSOPHIST
Sept 17, 1888.

<The Maori football team now in England play barefoot.[5] Ed. *S. M.*>

[1] Letter to the editor, John Gerard, SJ (1840–1912). Eldest son of Col. Archibald Gerard, born in Edinburgh 30 May 1840, brother of the novelists Emily Gerard Laszowska and Dorothea Gerard Longard. Educated Stonyhurst, BA London University. Entered Society 1856, bequeathing his inheritance, the Rochsoles estates, etc. to his brother, Montague. Taught at Beaumont and Stonyhurst Colleges. Ordained 1873. Prefect of Studies at St Francis Xavier's, Liverpool, 1875–9, and at Stonyhurst, 1879–93. In charge of organization of classes when GMH taught classics to the Stonyhurst lay Philosophers 1882–4. Editor of *The Month*, 1893–7 and again 1900–12. Provincial of English Jesuits 1897–1900. Died at Farm Street Church, London, 13 Dec. 1912.

[2]
There's some will ca' me Parcy Reed,
And a' my virtues say and sing;
I would much rather have just now
A draught o' water frae the spring.

The herd flung aff his clouted shoon
And to the nearest fountain ran;
He made his bonnet serve a cup,
And wan the blessing o' the dying man.

193B.36 and 37 of Francis James Child's collection of *The English and Scottish Popular Ballads* (1882–98).

[3] In the Apr. 1887 issue of the *S. M.* there is an essay on Hurley in which it is said that both sides are 'usually barefoot', and mention is made of a historic match between Munster and Leinster in Phoenix Park.

[4] In the *S. M.* issue 38 of June 1888, a letter from Arthur Chilton Thomas deplores the use of pseudonyms.

[5] The Maori football team, supposedly renamed by this time the New Zealand Native football team, toured Britain, Australia, and New Zealand in 1888–9, usually (but not invariably) playing rugby football. They arrived in London on 27 Sept. 1888 and played seventy-four matches, leaving on 30 Mar. 1889. The detailed reports of their first four matches, against Surrey, Northamptonshire, Kent, and Middlesex (reported in *The Times* of 4, 8, 11, and 23 Oct. 1888 respectively), of which they won the first three, make no mention of playing barefoot. Their captain, Joe Warbrick, however, was reputedly able to kick drop goals from the half-way line in bare feet, but photographs of the team show them wearing boots.

20 September 1888 to Father Francis Goldie, SJ[1]

>'Four Newfound Letters: An Annotated Edition, with a Fragment of Another Letter', ed. Joseph J. Feeney, SJ, *HQ*, 23/1–2 (Winter–Spring 1996), 28–32

Gonzaga 1: 4

One folded sheet, four sides, of which three are used.

UNIVERSITY COLLEGE, | S$^{\underline{T}}$ STEPHEN'S GREEN, | DUBLIN. [*printed heading*]

My dear Father Goldie, Pax Christi — Your application comes at an untoward time,[2] for next month will be employed in the close work of examination and before that my retreat must be[3] made and other things done. Promise I cannot, but I will try something, and I must say that I have one consideration on the other side. It is that this evening I am going to ~~spen~~ Howth to spend a day or two with a friend[4] who, as it happens, has visited the Balearic Isles and has the greatest interest in them, has made a hobby of them; so that I may get something ^of^ local colour or point from him. I am sorry to say that the writers of saints' lives are not always or often desirous of giving local colour to their subject, rather they suppress it and clothe all their heroes in drab uniform. There is another extreme, more modern, of making the saint the vanishing point in a vast gallery of previous and contemporary history. Believe me yours affectionately in Christ Gerard M. Hopkins.

Sept. 20 1888.

You say nothing of the language: I suppose any that I possess.

[1] See letter to Goldie, de Lapasture, and Shapter of 17 Aug. 1882.

[2] The request, from Goldie, who had spent time in the Balearics (i.e. Mallorca, Minorca, Ibiza, and Formentera in the Mediterranean off the east coast of Spain) gathering material for his *Life of St. Alphonsus Rodriguez* (1889), is the stimulus for GMH's poem on that saint, who had been canonized on 6 Sept. 1887.

[3] MS 'me'.

[4] Probably Judge John O'Hagan (1822–90). Jurist, essayist, and poet, he toured Italy in 1856 and 1890 and may well have visited Spain and the Balearic Isles on these or other trips. GMH often visited Glenaveena, O'Hagan's home on the south side of Howth Hill overlooking Dublin Bay, and sometimes stayed for a few days (see *WHALB*, 442).

25 September 1888 to Robert Bridges

LRB, no. CLXVI, p. 291 Bodleian, Dep. Bridges, vol. 92, fos. 184–187

UNIVERSITY COLLEGE, | ST STEPHEN'S GREEN, | DUBLIN. [*printed heading*]
Sept. 25 1888

Dearest Bridges, — I am sorry to hear of our differing so much in taste: I was hardly aware of it. (It is not nearly so sad as differing in religion). I feel how great the loss is of not reading, as you say~~:~~; but if I did read I do not much think the effect of it would be what you seem to expect, on either my compositions or my judgments.

I must read something of Greek and Latin letters and lately I sent you a sonnet, on the Heraclitean Fire, in which a great deal of early Greek ~~speculati~~ philosophical thought was distilled; but the liquor of the distillation did not taste very Greek, did it? The effect of studying masterpieces is to make me admire and do otherwise. So it must be on every original artist to some degree, ~~to~~ ^on^ me to a marked degree. Perhaps then more reading would only refine my singularity, which is not what you want.

(While I remember it, in the ~~compo~~ ^other^ sonnet that went with ~~it~~ ^that^ was a false rhyme you overlooked — thronged instead of swarmed: please make the correction.)[1]

But not on my criticisms either, I suspect. Wide~~r~~ reading does two things — it extends knowledge and it adjusts the judgment. Now it is mostly found that a learned judgment is less singular than an unlearned one and oftener agrees with the common and popular judgment, with which it coincides as a fine balance ~~doe~~ or other measure does with the rule of thumb. ~~Now~~ But, so far as I see, where we differ in judgment, ~~my~~ ~~mine~~ ^my judgments are^ less singular than yours; I agree more than you do with the mob and with the communis criticorum {*critical community*}. Presumably I shd. ~~d~~ agree with these still more if I read more and so differ still more from you than now. Who for instance is singular about Dryden, you or I? These considerations are very general, but so far as they go they appear to be reasonable.

To return to composition for a moment: what I want there, to be more intelligible, smoother, and less singular, is an audience. I think the fragments I wrote of St. Winefred, which was meant to be played, were not hard to understand. My prose I am sure is clear and even flowing. This reminds me that I have written a paper for an Irish magazine the Lyceum,[2] organ of this College, one may say. I was asked and I ~~furnish~~ rewrote something I had by me and it is to appear next month. And yet I bet you it will not: my luck will not allow it. But if it does, I then bet you it is intelligible, though on an obstruse subject, Statistics and Free Will — and I mean very intelligible. (This, by the bye, is a badly made logical bed; ~~but no~~ for I can only win one wager by losing the other. But never mind.)

I send an improved version of my war-song, less open to the objections made, and am your affectionate friend Gerard Hopkins.

What shall I__ do for the land__ that__ bred me, Her__
homes and__ fields__ that__ fold - ed and fed me? Be
un- der her ban-ner and_ live__ for her hon- our:
Un-der her__ ban - ner I'll live__ for her hon- our.
CHORUS.
Un-der her__ ban - ner we† live__ for her hon- our.
* corrected from
fold - ed and__
† corrrected from 'I'll'

[1] 'To what serves Mortal Beauty', ll. 7–8. Presumably this was a new draft, or copy. RB has corrected the word mentioned in GMH's own copy of 23 Aug. 1885, which is pasted into 'MS A'.

[2] See letter to Katharine Tynan of 15 Sept. 1888, n. 2.

28 September 1888 from D. B. Dunne to GMH[1]

Unpublished Bodleian, Eng.Poet.c.48

ROYAL UNIVERSITY OF IRELAND, | EARLSPORT TERRACE, | DUBLIN. [*printed heading*]

28 Sept. 1888.

^My^ Dear F. Hoopkins[2]

If you have not destroyed yet the M.A. originals, please note all the references of passages for translation, so that we need not have a hunt for them when preparing for the Calendar.

Yours sincerely
D. B. Dunne
Rev. G. M. Hopkins MA

[1] D. B. Dunne, DD, D.Ph., had been lecturer in Logic at the Catholic University since Newman's time there, and was now Secretary of the Royal University of Ireland. See *CW* vii. The verso of the letter was used to compose lines for 'St. Alphonsus Rodriguez'.

[2] Perhaps Dunne's mistake here encouraged him to repeat the name correctly at the foot of the letter.

3 October 1888 to Robert Bridges

LRB, no. CLXVII, p. 292 Bodleian, Dep. Bridges, vol. 92, fos. 188–189v

Univ. Coll., Stephen's Green, Dublin. Oct. 3 1888.

Dearest Bridges, — In spite of matter in your last for which presently, when time allows (for I ~~have~~ ^shall^ tomorrow begin examining), you will, I assure you, "be handled without gloves." I ask your opinion of a sonnet[1] written to order on the occasion of the first feast ^since his canonisation proper^ of St. Alphonsus Rodriguez, a laybrother of our Order, who for 40 years acted as hall-porter to the College of Palma in Majorca: he was, it is believed, much favoured by God with heavenly lights and much persecuted by evil spirits. The sonnet (I say it snorting) aims at being intelligible.

~~Hon~~
[2]Honour~~s~~ should flash from exploit, so we say;
Strokes once that gashed the flesh, that galled the shield,
~~Now~~ ^Should^ tongue that time ~~and~~ ^now,^ trumpet ~~of~~ ^now^ that field
And, on the fighter, forge his glorious day.
On Christ they do; on martyr well they may:
But, ~~where the~~ ^be that^ war~~’s~~ within, the sword we ~~y~~^w^ield
Unseen, the heroic breast not outward-steeled,
Earth hears no hurtle then from fiercest fray.
Yet God the mountain-mason, continent-
Quarrier, earthwright; ~~he~~ who, with trickling increment,
Veins violets and tall trees makes more and more,
Could crowd career with conquest while there went
Those years on years ~~of~~ by of world without event
That in Majorca Alfonso watched the door.

And I am your affectionate friend Gerard M. Hopkins.

And please do not put it aside “for ~~future~~ ^further^ neglect” but answer smart. It has to go to Majorca.

Call in the Canon,[3] have a consultation, sit, and send result by return — or soon.

Tell him I lately passed Warkworth on my way from Glasgow to Whitby, but there was no stopping. I looked out at the station.

Or, against singularity, we may try this:

~~But~~
Yet God that mountain, and that continent,
Earth, all, builds; ~~who,~~ ^~~then,~~ or,^ with trickling increment,
Veins violets, etc.

No, this:

Yet God that hews mountain and continent,
Earth, all; that else, with trickling increment
Veins violets etc.

[1] The version given below differs considerably from that in MS ‘B’. See the letter of 19–20 Oct. 1888.

[2] Above the first line, RB has written: Glory is the flame of exploit.

[3] i.e. RWD.

19–20 October 1888 to Robert Bridges

LRB, no. CLXVIII, p. 294 Bodleian, Dep. Bridges, vol. 92, fos. 190–194v

~~Catholic Union of Ireland,. 75, MARLBORO' STREET, DUBLIN,~~ [*printed heading*]
Univ. Coll., Stephen's Green, Dublin. Oct. 1~~8~~9 '88

Dearest Bridges, — You remark, I am glad to ~~think~~ ^find^, a "lambness" in my last letter: now in the present I shall have somewhat as schoolboys say, to "lamb in". But first of various matters.

My little Paper on Statistics and Free Will obeyed the general law and did not appear; so I win that wager, if you remember. The editor made some objections which involved recasting it: I have partly done so, and when it is all recast he will no doubt find others. But meantime I get into print in a way I would not. My father wrote a little book on Numbers, the numbers One to Ten, a sketchy thing, raising points of interest in a vast, an infinite subject: the Saturday lately had a paper on this book, making great game of it from end to end (of it and the article), including something I had contributed to it; however I was not named.[1] Last week[2] same Review has an article "The American Poet", ~~in~~ ^a^ comment on Gosse, who lately said, it seems, there is no American poet — great poet, he means, or poet proper perhaps. It ends "After all, the whole affair is a fluke. Great poets are the results of exquisitely rare and incalculable combinations of causes, and nobody would be to blame if there were not a great poet for another century. This country does not seem likely to have another in a hurry <take that>, nor have we observed him mewing his mighty youth in France, Germany, Italy, or Spain. Perhaps he is at school in Bolivia at this moment, or he may be at Johns Hopkins University, Baltimore, and his Christian name may be 'Gifted'".[3] It is an allusion to that same "Gifted Hopkins" the humourist "who died of his own jocosity" that, if you remember, was meant the time before. But if Lang wrote this paper too, then, putting ^together^ that very fact that he ~~did~~ then did not mean me ~~and~~ with the fact that Gosse (you told me) admires my muse and the one that ~~he is~~ ^being^ imprudent ~~and~~ ^he^ may have said so and others, I do not know ~~wh~~ but I may say to myself, O my soul, perhaps This Is Fame. But I don't want it and beg you will not expose me to it; which you can easily forbear from doing now that you disapprove of my *γένος* {*kind*} as vicious, and surely you shd. not vitiate taste. And at any rate I shall never cease to deplore that unhappy letter of mine you read sitting leagues and parasangs of country lanes next to Lang that morning: how could I foresee it was so dangerous to write to a remote world's-end place like Yattendon?[4] But indeed you have told me there is plenty of intellectual life there.

Next, music. I am glad to find it is only there we are so far apart. But the contrary is true: there we agree well enough and the rift is elsewhere. I agree to your musical strictures and almost invite your rebukes and if I do not ^do so^ heartily it is because a perfect organisation for crippling me exists and the one for "encourag~~ing~~emental purposes" (modern English) is not laid down yet. I agree that for contrapuntal writing we shd. read the great masters and study the rules, both. The great masters unhappily I cannot read (unless very little), but the rules I do carefully study, and ^just^ on account of the great formality of the art of music it happens that mere adherence to them, without study of examples from the masters, produces — given ~~a~~ faculty — results of some interest and value. (I like not that last sentence: it is too much in the manner of the magazines I read and too far entirely from Doughty and the Mighty Dead.[5]) ~~But~~ And ~~the~~ ^my^ madrigal in canon, so far as it has gone, is strict and Sir Robert Stewar~~d~~t (a demon for rule) says it is correct and that it might even have been freer. But, as you say, you have not seen it and now that I have no piano I cannot go on with it. ~~Last~~ This morning I gave ~~him~~ ^in^ what I believe is the last batch of examination-work for this autumn (and if all were seen, ^fallen^ leaves of my poor life between all the leaves of ~~them),~~ it), and but for ~~this~~ ^that want^ I might prance on ivory this very afternoon. I have had to get glasses, by the bye: just now I cannot be happy either with or without them. The oculist says my sight is very good and my eye perfectly healthy but that like Jane Nightwork[6] I am old. And, strange to say, I have taken to drawing again. Perverse Fortune or something perverse~~,~~ (try me~~,~~): why did I not take to it before? And now enough, for I must whet myself, strop myself, be very bitter, and will secrete and distil a good deal beforehand.

However with no more stropping than the palm of my hand and chopping at a hair, no but at the "broth of goldish flue"[7] (how well now does the pleasing modern author come in in his own illustration and support!), I can deal with one matter, the sonnet on St. Alphonsus.[8] I am obliged for your criticisms, "contents of which noted", indeed acted on. I have improved the sestet (in itself I do not call the first version "cheeky", the imagery as applied to God Almighty being so familiar in the Scripture and the Fathers: however I have not kept it). But now I cannot quite understand nor so far as I understand agree with the difficulty you raise about the continents and so on. It is true continents ~~and so on~~ are partly made by "trickling increment"; but what is on the whole truest and most ~~st~~ strikes us about them and mountains is that they are made what now ~~they are~~ ^we see them^ by trickling decrements, by detrition, weathering, and the like.* [*GMH footnote*: * By the bye, some geologists say the last end of all continents and dry land altogether is to be washed into the sea and that when all are gone ~~the~~ 'water will be the world', as in the Flood, and will still be deep and have to spare.] And at any rate whatever is markedly featured in stone or what is like stone is most naturally said to be hewn, and to shape, itself; means ^in old English^ to hew and the Hebrew bara / to create, even, properly means to hew. But life and living things are not naturally said to be hewn: they grow, and their growth is by trickling increment.

I will not ~~k~~now interpret the thought of the sestet. It is~~,~~ however, so far as I can see, both exact and pregnant.

I am altogether at a loss to see your objection to exploit and to so we say. You will allow — would, I shd. think, urge on me — that where the *ὄνομα κύριον* {*proper word*}[9] ~~is itself itself ^where there is^ a handsome word~~ ^has nothing flat or poor about it^ it is the best word to use in poetry as in prose, better I mean than[10] ~~a~~ ^its^ paraphrase. Now exploit is the right word, it is *κύριον* {*proper*}, there is no other ^for the thing meant^ but achievement, which is not better, and it is a handsome word in itself: why then should I not say it? Surely I should. By "regular indoors work" I understand you to mean a ~~th~~ drawing finished at home with the eye no longer on the object, ^something^ poorly thrown in to fill up a blank the right filling of which is forgotten. But "so we say" is just what I have to say and want to say (it was made out of doors in the Phoenix Park with my mind's eye on the first presentment of the thought): I mean "This is what we commonly say, but we are wrong". The line now stands "Glory is a flame off exploit, so we say" and I think it must so stand.

I am warming myself at the flame of a little exploit of my own done last night. I could not have believed in such a success nor that life had this pleasure to bestow. Somebody had tried to take me in and I warned him I wd. take him in at our next meeting. Accordingly I wrote him a letter from "the son of a respected livery and bait stables in Parteen <suburb of Limerick> oftentimes employed by your Honoured Father" asking for an introduction to one of the Dublin newspapers "as Reporter, occasional paregraphs or sporting intelligence". The sentence I think best of was one in which I said I (or he) could "give any color which may be desired to reports of speeches or Proceedings subject to the Interests of truth which must always be the paremount consideration". It succeeded beyond my wildest hopes and action is going to be taken. The letter is ~~going~~ ^even^ to be printed in the Nation as a warning to those who are continually applying in the like strain; but before this takes place I must step in.

It is as you say about Addis.[11] But why should you be glad? Why at any rate ~~y~~ should you burst upon me that you are glad, when you know that I cannot be glad?

It seems there is something in you interposed between what shall we say? the Christian and the man of the world which hurts, which is ^to me^ like biting on a cinder in bread. Take the simplest view of this matter: he has made shipwreck, I am afraid he must even be in straits: he cannot support himself by his learned writings; I suppose he will have to teach. But this is the least. I hope at all events he will not pretend to marry~~.~~, ~~Marriage is h~~ and especially no one he has known in his ~~min~~ priestly life. Marriage is honourable and so is the courtship that leads to marriage, but the philanderings of men vowed to God are not honourable nor the marriages they end in. I feel the same deep affection for him as ever, but the respect is gone. I would write to him if I had his address, which, I am sorry to say, is still ^or was lately^ somewhere at Sydenham; for after bidding farewell to his flock he had not the grace to go away.

This is enough for the time and I will put off the lambing to another season. With kindest remembrances to Mrs. Bridges and Mrs. Molesworth, I am your affectionate friend Gerard M. Hopkins.

Oct. 20 '88.

[1] A review of a column and a half (22 Sept. 1888) of *The Cardinal Numbers*, by Manley Hopkins (1887), a 'little tract' which is treated throughout with an air of amused superiority that aims at irony.

[2] 13 Oct. 1888.

[3] Gosse had replied to a question from the editor of *The Forum*, 'Has America produced a Poet?'; his remarks are discussed, and the writer ends by suggesting names of poets of all nations, and asks whether America has produced a poet on their level. He proceeds: 'These are questions which Mr. Gosse may have the temerity to answer; we prefer to leave the reply to the American conscience.' Then follows the passage GMH quotes above. For 'Gifted' see the letters of 16 Oct. 1882 to RB, 19 Mar. 1885 from RWD, and 14 Dec. 1885 to RB.

[4] See letter to RB of 18–19 Aug. 1888.

[5] For Doughty see letters to RB of 7–8 Sept. 1888, nn. 6 and 7, and 13–14 Sept. 1888. GMH justifiably feels his sentence lacks the gravitas of Doughty and of the great authors of the past.

[6] In Shakespeare's *2 Henry IV*.

[7] 'Harry Ploughman', l. 1.
[8] 'St Alphonsus Rodriguez'.
[9] A term from Aristotle's *Poetics*, the exact word, the proper term.
[10] MS 'that'.
[11] See Biographical Register. RB wrote to Lionel Muirhead: 'Did you hear of Addis's leaving the R.C. Communion? I wrote to him and met him in London, and had a long talk with him. It is a great delight to me that he should have relinquished the untenable. He is as zealous as ever but now very much on my lines, but would not come under any formularies—so is not a member of our communion. He saw the reasonableness of becoming one, but could not after his experience burden his conscience again and I think he was wise' (13 Dec. 1888, Stanford, 182).

10–11 November 1888 to his Mother

FL, no. CXI, p. 185 Bodleian, MS Eng. lett. e. 41, fo. 128[r–v]

~~Catholic Union of Ireland, | 75, Marlboro' Street, Dublin~~ [*printed address*]

Univ. Coll., Stephen's Green, Dublin. Nov. 10 1888.

My dearest mother, — It is not convenient to my time or eyesight or memory or anything to read the long reports of the Parnell trial[1] at breakfast and nevertheless I ought to read them; now could you not stead me a little by sending me the weekly Times, if they are in that? If that will not suit I must try and get the whole at the end when it no doubt will be published together; but even that will not be easy for me.

You spoke of ~~b~~ Aubrey de Vere's book of criticism[2] and expressed the pleasure it gave you. I have only seen a little of it. He has a beautiful mind and is all full of noble and slightly vaporous thought. I have often been promised to meet him, but it ends in a miss. Like all that is best in Ireland he is entirely on the shelf and as ineffective as if he were not. I could tell you more about him.

I wrote to Lionel meaning to tap hi~~m~~^s liquor^. I am afraid my letter, which had a certain soreness, has only screwed him more up, and this is unfortunate. I suppose Everard and wife are at home. We have only 3 boarder-students now: one is a great singer, but as he ~~can~~ cannot play, nor the other two, we have no piano; so my music is at a stand still or going back. I shd. like Grace to know this.

I wish to be kindly remembered to that good Mrs. Pratt.[3]

Fr. Fowler's sister, a bright lady, much like him, is on a visit in this country.

With best love to all, I am your affectionate son Gerard.
Where is Milicent? At Leeds?
~~Feb.~~ Nov. 11 1888, Martinmas.[4]

[1] Accused by the *Times* in Apr. 1887 (see letter to RB of 1 May 1887, n. 3) of complicity in the Phoenix Park murders in May 1882, and referring to the incriminating letter which they printed and claimed was his, Parnell denounced it as a forgery, and on 9 July 1888 asked parliament for a special committee of the house to enquire into the matter; a special commission of three judges was set up. In Feb. 1889, Richard Pigott confessed to the forgery, and subsequently fled to Spain, where he committed suicide. See also *CW* vii and letters of 1 May 1887, 1 Mar. 1889.

[2] *Essays, chiefly on Poetry*, 2 vols. (1887). See letter to RB of 18–19 Aug. 1888, n. 9.

[3] Mrs Pratt and Father Fowler's sister are unidentified.

[4] The feast of St Martin, 11 Nov., traditionally a time for hiring servants, often at hiring fairs.

14 November 1888 to Fr Ignatius Ryder[1]

FL, no. XXXVII, p. 64 Birmingham Oratory

Univ Coll., Stephen's Green, Dublin. Nov. 14 1888.

My dear Fr. Ignatius, Pax Christi — Thank you for your prompt kindness and the Cardinal for his. One remark you make calls for reply. "Surely" you say "there must be" a copy of that Gazette "at the Catholic University". I daresay there is, but the difficulty is to find the Catholic University.[2] This house is its empty birds nest. For the books, it is true, I can answer: <u>they</u> at least are not at the Catholic University. The Bishops of Ireland decreed that the Jesuits should be asked to work this college; a committee of them was appointed to carry out the necessary arrangements; pursuant to the object of their appointment the committee, as the Jesuits came in, carried ~~the~~ out — it seems I ought to go on some other way, but they carried out the library; they disembar[r]assed the workmen of their tedious tools, and removed the books to the Diocesan Seminary at Clonliffe, where now they lie, acquiring antiquity and the interest of "worming". After a while our then Rector made an appeal to the Bishops. The Bishops, some of whom absolutely refused to believe the books had been taken away (<u>sed non in hoc justificatus sum</u> {*yet I am not hereby justified*}[3]; but <u>that</u> did not bring them back), passed a resolution they shd. be restored. Then all the more they rested at Clonliffe. Presently Mr. Tom Arnold[4] of the old staff wrote to the Archbishop for them. Diplomatic answer;

^and^ the books drove another root into Clonliffe parish. Now the students are petitioning: I shall be curious to see what becomes of their petition. But can these things be? Ay and worse things. As the old song used to say "This is the way we put on our close" and "so we go round the mulberry bush all on a Monday morning" or to that effect — or ineffectiveness.

I do think you need not trouble about George Teeling's sonnet.[5] To my certain knowledge that sonnet is the Syrophenician woman[6] of these parts, the Haemorrhoissa[7] of the nineteenth century: it has suffered many things of many physicians and is none the better but rather worse. I have myself performed some very trying operations on it and been positively assured that no more of the faculty should now be called in; yet I believe it has more cork and leather and splints and guttapercha about it now by a great deal than ever I left on it.[8] And really it was a graceful buxom young woman when I can remember. I would advise you to retire from the case.

I am yours very sincerely in Christ Gerard Hopkins.

[1] See letter of 2 July 1868.

[2] The tortuous history of the establishment of UCD and the squabbles over its library are laid out in *A Page of Irish History: Story of University College, Dublin* (Dublin, 1930) and in *WHALB*, 357 ff. See also introduction to *CW* vii.

[3] GMH is quoting the Vulgate, 1 Corinthians 4: 4. The whole verse reads: 'nihil enim mihi conscius sum sed non in hoc iustificatus sum qui autem iudicat me Dominus est' {*For I am not conscious to myself of any thing, yet am I not hereby justified; but he that judgeth me, is the Lord*}.

[4] Thomas Arnold (1823–1900; *ODNB*). See letter to RWD of 25 Oct. 1884 and to RB of 11–12 Nov. 1884.

[5] See letter to Newman of 20 Feb. 1888, n. 6.

[6] The woman from Syrophoenicia (a Roman province of western Asia which included Phoenicia and the territories of Damascus and Palmyra) whose story is told in Mark 7: 25–30 and in Matthew 15: 21–8. She pestered Christ for the cure of her offspring.

[7] The woman with the issue of blood, who touches Christ's robe to be healed in Mark 5: 25–43, Matthew 9: 20–2, and Luke 8: 43–56. GMH obviously refers primarily to Mark, where in verse 26 we read that she 'had suffered many things of many physicians'.

[8] GMH is comically elaborating his medical metaphor and imagining the ailing poem to be patched up with surgical appliances made of cork, leather, splints, and the recently introduced gutta-percha. This last, revealed to the West in 1843, is a tree sap rather like rubber, but its bio-inert quality made it ideal for insulating marine cables and for surgical devices. It also revolutionized the golf ball in 1848.

26–30 November 1888 to his brother Arthur[1]

FL, no. CXII, p. 186 Balliol College Library
Addressed to 'Arthur Hopkins Esq. | Tre Vean | 80 Finchley Road | London | N.W.' with PM DUBLIN NO 30 88. On two sheets of paper.

~~Catholic Union of Ireland, | 75, MARLBORO' STREET, DUBLIN | . . . . 187. .~~ [*printed heading*]
Univ. Coll., Stephen's Green, Dublin. Nov. 26 1888.

Dear Arthur, — I hope your exhibition has turned out a great success and sold your pictures and led to commissions.

You have sent me nothing of yours since those Atalanta[2] children, but some kind person has just this minute ~~sent~~ ^posted^ me your "no. 18".[3] Not that this is my first sight of it by a great deal. The resident students hung it in their reading-room and I have ~~obser~~ studied it and heard it discussed. It is admired, and it is a ^sweet and^ pretty face; but now~~,~~ I am sorry to say, that is all that I can write in its favour. I have to remonstrate with you about it.

In the first place it has to me the look of a sketch enlarged. A picture of that size~~d~~ whether engraved from ~~a~~ drawing or painting ought to be a picture, not a sketch. The enlargement of a sketch will not make a picture. This was Doré's weakness:[4] he was a sketcher only; his large drawings and the engravings after his paintings (for the paintings themselves I have never seen) are the works of a sketcher sketching on a great scale; the limbs, the draperies, the buildings have the outlines, contours, folds, shading, everything of a sketch; ~~a~~ ^the^ suggestion of things, not their representation. Or to speak more precisely, this head looks as if it had been ^first^ a picture proper, ^then^ a sketch on a small scale made from that, and then this sketch enlarged to the original size, the execution proper to ~~be~~ a picture being in the meantime lost. This appears in the hair, but flagrantly in the drapery of the breast: ~~The line of the nose which~~ there is no searchingness in the drawing of these ~~word~~ things. Then the line of the nose, which in a sketch might be ~~graceful~~ ^well^ enough, is not subtle enough for the size. There the engraver however may have injured you.

You came very near producing a very beautiful thing: the face has a Madonna-like ~~pen~~ pensiveness and sweetness; but there is also a certain foolishness in the expression and the updrawn upper lip is ~~not~~ too much of ~~a thing~~ ^an upper lip^, it is not successful.

Fr. Mallac[5] also makes the following criticisms. He says you are not strong in your perspective and that the off-side of the face is out of drawing and has the distortion given by some lenses to photographs. Also he says the back of the head is suppressed. I do not feel sure of this but about the side of the face I think he is right, though it is difficult to point out where the fault is. But his greatest complaint on the score of drawing is about the dwarfing of the breasts, which are altogether much too high up and probably too flat. It is generally agreed that a finely proportioned figure is divided in half exactly at the groin and into quarters at the nipples and lowest point of the kneecap respectively. These proportions will not suit your girl at all.

He complains also of the intense shadow between the lips, which makes the upper lip stand up from the paper. This also comes from carrying the methods of sketching into ^a^ finished picture, for in a sketch exaggeration of shadow to indicate certain things is necessary and suppression of it for others.

In conception this is a beautiful head and grows on one, as people have said ^of it^ to me; ~~N~~ and the beauty is regular. Now the number of really and regularly beautiful faces ~~in art ^and on a large scale^ is quite~~ (on a considerable scale and not the simple repetition of a type, as in allegorical figures) is quite small in art; for ancient works, which are perfectly regular, are mostly much wanting in grace, so much so that those Venuses of Cnidus and Milo[6] and what not can scarcely be said to be beautiful in face at all; while modern ~~works~~ ^ones^, which have plenty of charms, are often irregular: I think Leonardo's La Gioconda[7] even, perhaps the greatest achievement of modern art in the ideal ~~drawing~~ ^treatment^ of the human face, is not quite regular in the conformation of the cheeks. If I were you then I would keep this type by me, correct its drawing, carefully compose in life and then from life draw the draperies, and work at it till I had made the most perfect thing of it I could. That scrawl of folds on the breast "must come out, Bishop", as Mrs. Proudie said;[8] and the breasts must go down lower ~~and~~ vertically and come up horizontally. The hair and ear and all must be thoroughly done. And for the drawing of the face, here is a diagram which will shew you what I suppose to be the matter with it. It is a ~~vertica~~ bird's eye view. (Never mind my bad drawing: mind yours.) I believe it will carry conviction.

I am afraid this ballyragging will make you gloomy; I hope not angry. For then I shall not be able to ask you, as I do, if you have such a thing by you as a portecrayon[9] and some drawing chalk or charcoal, for there is nothing like it, and I want to be able to draw with it again; and I am obliged to husband my seldom seen pocketmoney. I enclose some trifles,

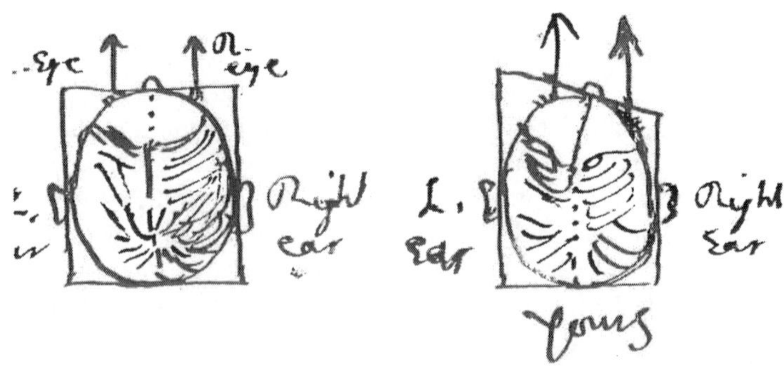

which please return, only to shew you how far my hand is in. Could you tell of a way of bringing out high lights in a drawing better than the watery Chinese-white I have employed on the ox in the Phoenix Park? The unintelligible Roebuck sketch was a brilliant autumn sunset effect in a lovely lane.

That drawing of the copse at Shanklin (in what year could it have been? I have supposed 1866)[10] has gone to be photographed, that it may not perish; but the photographs will be smaller. I will send you one when they come they are a precious time doing. That drawing appears to me unique in its kind: it is a pity it is not finished, which was only a few days' more work.

With best love to the vine and olives,[11] I am your affectionate brother Gerard.

Nov. 30 1888.

[1] Arthur Hopkins (1848–1930), GMH's painter brother. See Biographical Register.

[2] *Atalanta* (ed. L. T. Meade) ran from Oct. 1887 to 1898. The frontispiece to the number for Feb. 1888 ('The Valentine': two children, boy and girl, running towards the spectator through a garden) is by Arthur Hopkins.

[3] Type of Beauty no. xviii, published as a double spread in the *Graphic* of 24 Nov. 1888.

[4] Gustav Doré (1832–83; *ODNB*), born in Strasbourg, was a child prodigy. He had little formal artistic training and produced both enormous sculptures and paintings that were not well received; he is best known for his illustrations, among the most successful of which are to editions of Dante, Rabelais, and Cervantes. From 1856 he produced as much for English publishers as for French and often visited London, although he never settled there and learnt no English. His illustrations to Blanchard Jerrold's *London: A Pilgrimage* (1872) were admired for their contrasts between the lives of the wealthy and the misery of the poor. He also illustrated Tennyson's *Idylls of the King* (1867) and worked for the *Illustrated London News*.

[5] See GMH's letter to his mother of 24 Jan. 1885.

[6] The Aphrodite of Cnidus (often known as the Venus Pudica because her hand covers her groin) and the Aphrodite of Milos (the Venus de Milo) are among the most celebrated statues of Ancient Greece. Both have been attributed to Praxiteles of Athens (4th c. BC), but the Venus de Milo is almost certainly by Alexandros of Antioch. Only copies of the first survive, but the Venus de Milo is in the Louvre in Paris.

[7] La Gioconda is Leonardo's famous Mona Lisa, the portrait of Lisa Gherardini, wife of Francesco del Giocondo, now in the Louvre in Paris.

[8] Trollope's *Last Chronicle of Barset* (1867), ch. 11.

[9] An instrument used to hold a crayon, piece of chalk, or pencil; usually made of a metal tube, split at the end, into which the crayon is inserted and with a sliding ring to grasp the crayon. The point here is that it allows one to use the smallest ends of pencils and chalks, and so ekes out GMH's meagre supplies.

[10] See *CW* vi. The drawing is the one which he sends to his mother with the letter of 2 Mar. 1889 (Bodleian, MS Eng.misc.a.8, fo. 104). 1866 may well be the wrong year; it was more probably drawn in the summer of 1863.

[11] GMH's reference is to Psalm 127:3 (Vulgate): 'Thy wife as a fruitful vine, on the sides of thy house. Thy children as olive plants, round about thy table.'

24 December 1888 to his Mother

FL, no. CXIII, p. 189 — Bodleian, MS Eng. lett. e. 41, fos. 129–130v

UNIVERSITY COLLEGE, | DUBLIN. [*embossed heading*]
Christmas Eve
1888

My dearest mother, — Thank you very much for the truly beautiful Japanese pocketbook and the picture you send. I seem to be altogether in Japan: a generous doctor of this ~~ct~~ city lent me four or five splendid volumes, ~~of~~ Aud^s^ley's Ornamental Arts of Japan,[1] and I have them yet; further two other books on Japan; and another doctor, my great friend Dr. MacCabe,[2] two little Japanese fairytales: the humour and life likeness of the illustrations beats everything that was ever done for fairytales. So that I am or am becoming a little knowledg^e^able in things Japanese.

In an hour or so I shall start for Monasterevan, where I may be addressed at Miss Cassidy's. It is in the ~~Kings~~ Co. Kildare, but Monasterevan is enough. The parish priest ^Dr. Comerford[3]^ has just been made Coadjutor Bishop, with right of succession, of Kildare and has asked me to his consecration; but that I can hardly ~~do~~ ^go to^. His appointment is of some importance: he is no Campaigner, would take no part in the League[4] (presided over by his hot headed curates), and had the unusual courage, before the rescripts (and indeed it requires courage still), to forbid boycotting. But even he did not then dare to speak against[5] it by name: he described the thing. He is a learned antiquary and remarkably silent for anywhere, portentously for an Irishman; so that it is hard talking to him, but he is nevertheless very amiable.

Unhappily I have to make my yearly retreat (for the past year). I say unhappily, not that I dislike a retreat, but it is a severe tax on my short holidays. I could not make it in the summer, because the Royal University kept me in attendance correcting proofs and ^in^ other trifling things. This will be at St. Stanislaus' College, Rahan, Tullamore.[6]

The weather is unseasonable; pleasant to the feel by day, but by night it robs me of sleep, which has happened so often that I am spent with it and look forward to the country for more ~~h~~ chance of sleeping. Man like vegetation needs cold and a close season once a year.

With very best Christmas wishes to all, I am your loving son Gerard.
I enclose a Christmas card for Lionel, the only one suitable.[7]

[1] *The Ornamental Arts of Japan*, by George Ashdown Audsley, 2 vols. fol. with plates (1882–5).

[2] See letter to Dr MacCabe of 27 Feb. 1888.

[3] Bishop Michael Comerford (1830–95) was born in Carlow Town, attended St Patrick's College as a seminarian (1848–55), ordained May 1856; curate at Kill (1856–7), Maryborough (1857–61), Arles (1861–2), Naas (1862–3), and Monasterevan (1863–78), where he became parish priest 1878–95. Named Coadjutor Bishop of Kildare and Leighlin in 1888, his consecration was on 1 Jan. 1889. He published numerous scholarly historical articles, *Collections relating to the Dioceses of Kildare and Leighlin* (3 vols., 1883–6), as well as several devotional books and pamphlets.

[4] The Irish National Land League was founded in Castlebar, Co. Mayo on 21 Oct. 1879, with Charles Stewart Parnell as its president. Its aims were to reduce unfair rents and to make it possible for the peasant to own the land he worked. The struggle to bring this about developed into the 'Land War' of 1880–92 and the Plan of Campaign (1886–92), in which the League decided on a fair rent and encouraged its members to pay only that; if it was not accepted, it would be paid to the League to negotiate. The dispute cut across class and religious lines, with 'Dr Comerford forbidding his parishioners to take part in the activities of the Land League presided over by his own curates' (*WHI*, 131).

[5] From here to 'nevertheless' written to avoid the embossed heading of the notepaper.

[6] GMH kept MS notes of this retreat on four double sheets of notepaper very closely written on both sides, headed 'January 1st 1888 [*should be 1889*], St. Stanislaus's College, Tullabeg'. This MS was kept by RB in an envelope marked 'GMH private' in MS Book 'H'. It is now in the Bodleian, MS Eng.misc.a.8. With it are the notes of a retreat at Beaumont Lodge, 3–10 Sept. 1883. See *CW* v.

[7] Not present and not known to exist.

1889

21 January 1889 to Harry Bellamy[1]

FL, no. XXXVIII1, p. 66 Campion Hall, O

UNIVERSITY COLLEGE, | DUBLIN. [*embossed heading*]
Jan. 21 1889.

Dear Harry, — All is hurry. By the bye I do not believe I was in your debt when you last wrote. If you visit Ireland in June come to see me, but the ~~m#~~ time is crowded: I shall be either examining then or on the point of it; so that we should not be able, I am afraid, to go anywhere together, as I shd. like to do. Also I do not anticipate leaving Ireland so soon ^or perhaps ever^; but all is uncertain both on my part and that of this College, which may come to grief, as well as of Irish education and Ireland itself.

Cheer up about Oxford. I have no reason to think things are going badly there. ^A^ Mistake~~s~~ may have been made in the management of the church-services, but Father Strappini[2] is a clever as well as virtuous man and ~~he is~~ not likely to do harm but the contrary. I heard he was winning golden opinions.

Sullivan[3] is a highly talented composer, I know; brilliant; but seems to me wanting in genius. Orchestration! Can 'a write ~~counter~~ canons? does 'a know counterpoint? If 'a can tell un 'a shd. do it, not that there dratted modern stuff as I can't abide.[4] Believe me yours affectionately Gerard M. Hopkins.

The only great ~~composer~~ ^English^ musician of our times was Sterndale Bennett.[5] He had the divine fire. Unhappily he had to earn his bread and could not spare time for what wd. have [done] his genius justice. Bishop[6] had genius too, but was wanting in greatness; had an element of ~~smallness or triviali~~ pettiness or vulgarity. The very first and after all the most important element of musical composition is melody: in this we excel and for tune, both stately and sweet, original tune, and ~~yet~~ ^that^ directly and without chromatism fetched out of the major or minor scale, I never heard any ^national^ airs equal to the English: if ~~to~~ ^with^ the English you throw in the Scotch, Irish, and Welsh, I am sure they will not be matched. And for concerted voice music (finer than any orchestra) we had in the Elizabethan and succeeding age the greatest ~~ma~~ madrigal school in the world. Carl Rosa[7] in a paper I lately read remarks on the fine ear of English audiences and English ~~amateur~~ performers as compared with German. Come then, Britons, strike home.[8]

[1] See letter of 17 Aug. 1882, n. 24.

[2] Fr Walter Diver Strappini, SJ (1849–1914), author of *Meditations without Method* (1913) and *The Inward Gospel* (1909, enlarged edn. 1917). He was a colleague of GMH at Stonyhurst. GMH mentions walking on the fells with him in his journal for 16 June 1873.

[3] Sir Arthur Seymour Sullivan (1842–1900; *ODNB*), musician and author of the music for the Gilbert and Sullivan operas.

[4] GMH's comic dialect: 'Can he write canons? Does he know counterpoint? If he can make (?recognize) one, he should do it, not that cursed modern stuff which I can't abide.'

[5] Sir William Sterndale Bennett (1816–75; *ODNB*), composer and pianist, Professor of Music at Cambridge in 1856 and principal of the Royal Academy of Music from 1866. He was given an honorary Doctorate of Civil Law by Oxford in 1870.

[6] Sir Henry Rowley Bishop (1786–1855; *ODNB*), composer, briefly Professor at Edinburgh in 1841, appointed to the Chair of Music at Oxford in 1848.

[7] Carl August Nicholas Rosa (1842–89; *ODNB*) was German by birth and started his well-known opera company in 1875, campaigning for operas to be performed in English. For a contemporary view of him and his opera company and a comment soon after his death on 30 Apr. 1889, see *London Music in 1888–89 as Heard by Corno di Bassetto (Later Known as Bernard Shaw)* (London, 1937), 104–6, 353.

[8] The last five words are the title of a song from Purcell's opera *Bonduca* (1695), which became a popular rallying song of the British Navy.

23 February 1889 to Robert Bridges

LRB, no. CLXIX, p. 298 Bodleian, Dep. Bridges, vol. 92, fos. 195–8

UNIVERSITY COLLEGE, | DUBLIN. [*embossed heading*]

Feb. 23 1889

Dearest Bridges, — I enclose something and shall not write much. I feel inclined to send another copy to Wooldridge and then again I do not; at any rate I send none now.

The Italian tour must have been very nice and I am very glad you took Mary Plow.[1] I am sorry the monks were dirty and the extreme poverty ~~doe~~ they have been reduced to does not excuse them; but I offer the following remarks. Shaving is conventional cleanliness: if it were otherwise, the longer the beard the dirtier wd. the wearer be, 'which' (in the language of St. Thomas) 'is inconvenient.' Next your countrymen at Cambridge keep their rooms, you told me, "dirty, yea filthy", and they are not poor. Next spitting in the North of England is very, very common with the lower classes: as I went up Brunswick Road (or any street)~~,~~ ^at^ Liverpool~~,~~ on a frosty morning it used to disgust me to see the pavement regularly starred with the spit of the workmen going to their work; and they do not turn aside, but spit straight before them as you approach, as a Frenchman remarked to me with abhorrence and I cd. only blush. And in general we cannot call ours a cleanly or a clean people: they are not at all the dirtiest and they know what cleanliness means, as ^they know the^ moral virtues, but ^they^ do not always practise it. We deceive ourselves if we think ~~so~~ otherwise. And our whole civilisation is dirty, yea filthy, and especially in the north; for is ^it^ not dirty, yea filthy, to pollute the air as Blackburn and Widnes and St. Helen's are polluted and the water~~,~~ as the Thames and the Clyde and the Irwell are polluted? The ancients with their immense public baths would have thought even our cleanest towns dirty.

About singing out of tune, I am not altogether displeased to hear the Italians do it, as the Germans do. Carl Rosa in an article on English Opera[2] (= opera by anybody you like with the words in English, translated of course; <u>not</u> opera by English composers) remarks on the good ear of English audiences and amateur performers and says that he has witnessed ~~Gem~~ Germans at a concert listen undisconcerted to a singer out of tune ~~at~~ where in England ha^l^f the audience would manifest signs of distress; and to the same effect of performers. ~~A good~~

Also a good musical shrill bell at mass is pleasing and effective enough.

"The first touch of decadence destroys all merit whatever": this is a hard saying. What, all technical merit — as chiaroscuro, anatomical knowledge, expression, feeling, colouring, drama? It is plainly not true. And, come to that, the age of Raphael and Michelangelo was ~~an age of~~ ^in a^ decadence and its excellence is technical. Everything after Giotto is decadent in form, ~~but~~ though advancing in execution.[3] Go to.

You return home to see your country in a pretty mess — to speak jokingly of matter for tears. And the ~~great~~ ^grand^ old traitor must have come home almost or quite in the same boat with you.[4] And ~~O~~ what boobies your countrymen are! They sit in court at the Commission[5] giggling, yea guffawing, at ^the wretched^ Pigot's ~~floundering;~~ ^mess;^ making merry because a traitor to government and then a ~~trea~~ traitor to rebellion, both in a small way, has not succeeded[6] in injuring an enemy of their own who is a traitor to government in a great way and ^~~on~~ a danger on^ an imperial scale; and that after a trial which has at least shewn the greatness and the blackness of the crime ~~g~~ lawful government and the welfare of the empire have to contend with. And this I say as if Pigot were ^or employed^ the forger of those letters. For in my judgment, unless further evidence is forthcoming, ~~I believe~~ those letters ~~to be~~ ^are^ genuine. But no more of this misery. With kindest remembrances to Mrs. Bridges and Mrs. Molesworth I am your affectionate friend Gerard M. Hopkins.

Do pray return to your Seaford hand, a thing of beauty and a joy for ever.[7] For a little more after the manner of your last and I shall not be able to read you at all.

[1] RB and his wife (with Mary Plow, his niece, afterwards Mrs H. C. Beeching) spent about a month (Jan. 1889) abroad. They went to Italy (Genoa, Pisa, Florence, Rome) by way of Arles, the Riviera, and thence by the Corniche.

[2] Carl Rosa contributed an article on 'English Opera' to *Murray's Magazine*, 1/4 (Apr. 1887), 460–70, which was widely noticed. It voiced his familiar cry for opera in English, which his practice supported.

[3] For a context for these remarks, see Matthew Plampin, 'A Stern and Just Respect for Truth: John Ruskin, Giotto and the Arundel Society', *Visual Culture in Britain*, 6/1 (Summer 2005), 59–78. In his account of the growth of a taste for earlier painting, he points to works of Ruskin, Lord Lindsay, and Anna Jameson and indicates that a 'key text in this development in British taste was the French critic Alexis François Rio's *De la Poésie Chrétienne* (or *Poetry of Christian Art*) of 1836. In this volume, Rio crafted a simple but powerful polemical discourse based on the appreciation of a perceived moral or "religious" content in works of art over their technical accomplishments. He essentially identifies the Renaissance as the death of art, describing a loss of unity in the Florentine school of the mid fifteenth century, due to the revived influence of paganism, which would eventually overwhelm all worthy artistic endeavour. Not only did painting become "subservient to all the profane tendencies of the period", but certain artists began to strive for naturalism in their work, which Rio terms the "great element of decadence"' (pp. 61–2).

[4] Gladstone had been resting at Naples, much concerned with Italian policy; and, on account of the difficult political situation, he had given up the thought of visiting the marquess of Dufferin and Ava, the English ambassador at Rome.

[5] The special commission appointed to report to the House of Commons on the charges brought by *The Times* against Parnell and other Irish MPs. See letter of 1 Mar. 1889 and its n. 15.

[6] MS 'succeeding'.

[7] RB employed a range of handwriting from the legible and attractive script in which he transcribed GMH's poems in MS B to a typical doctor's hand, difficult to the point of illegibility, which he combined with an idiosyncratic system of punctuation that made his letters the jotted version of his thoughts. Writing on 18–19 Aug. 1888, GMH expressed admiration for the style RB had used when on seaside holiday in Seaford (east Sussex) in Feb. 1887 and hoped for its continuance. Its

description alludes to the first line of Keats's 'Endymion'. Monica Bridges had an interest in handwriting (she became an expert calligrapher, publishing *A New Handwriting for Teachers* in 1899) and in 1925 the Bridges collaborated with Roger Fry and E. A. Lowe on a tract for the Society for Pure English devoted to the subject.

1 March 1889 to his brother Lionel

FL, no. CXIV, p. 191 Bodleian, MS Eng. lett. e. 41, fos. 135–139^{v}
Addressed to 'Lionel Hopkins Esq. | Court's Hill Lodge | Haslemere | Surrey | England' and readdressed to him at '4 St Georges Terrace | Gloucester Road | London S W.' PM DUBLIN MR 3 89 and HASLEMERE MR 4 89.

University College, Dublin. (*embossed heading*)
March 1 1889

Dear Lionel, — Off "the peg of" no particular "circumstance" I ~~le~~ lift "the coat of correspondence" and struggle one arm into my sleeve of it. First I answer your questions.

Of good histories of Greece there are plenty. But I shall assume that you put aside Grote's,[1] not as altogether antiquated, for so able, learned, and earnest a study can hardly ever be that, ~~a~~but as not new enough; for of course much has been learnt since. I know Curtius's[2] only a little: I think it is very good, but it too is now far from new. Two volumes of Duncker's History of Antiquity[3] are a history of Greece and can be got (as every volume of that work can) separately, translated by Alleyne, but I have only the first and am not sure if the second has appeared. It is good and of course supplements Curtius; but the reasoning or proof of the views maintained is both loose in itself and certainly difficult to follow. Since Duncker two German histories, the names of the authors of which I do not at present remember, have (wholly or rather, I believe, partly) appeared, but I do not think they are translated. I should on any ground recommend Evelyn Abbot's history,[4] which has ^just^ lately ~~ap~~ been published — ^I mean the first volume.^ I have not seen it, but it is well spoken of, is by a competent man, and contains the latest information. It is not to be carried down far, which is a pity.

Dictionary of Classical Antiquities — Smith's well known volume[5] published in Murray's course when it appeared was neither bad nor ^yet^ first rate (except that the law part was bad, I believe)~~:~~ ^and now^ of course it is behind the age ~~now~~ and till ~~now~~ ^this date it^ was never made up, whatever may be said on titlepages about new editions or revisions. But it is ^soon^ to ~~be~~ appear recast, as I know, for some of the Trinity scholars ~~have~~ ^are^ furnishing the articles on the Theatre, the

Army, and other things. I should recommend ~~a~~ French books and at a guess Salomon Reinach's (for he is a learned man) Manuel de Philologie Classique,[6] two vols., the second an appendix, each 7 fr. 50. But besides there is a splendid work by Daremberg and Saglio,[7] which I would get if I dared, on a great scale: it is appearing, illustrated galore, but each fascicule is 5 francs and the whole is calculated to consist of about 20 of these. For Roman antiquities I use Bouché-Leclercq's Manuel des Institutions Romaines,[8] a first rate book. I can give you more information on more particular data of enquiry.

The great authority on Indoeuropean Philology (in the English sense) is Brugmann, fugleman[9] of the Young Grammarian school, who after costing the Old Lights half hour after half hour of increasingly severe pain have succeeded in ousting them from their stools, to be themselves shortly, perhaps[10] very shortly (for philological views chase one another like ~~mountain~~ ^cloud^ shadows among mountains~~,~~) ousted by still younger men; for youth is a very very bad horse to back in the race for permanence. (with this image I am not altogether satisfied, nor yet with my present handwriting.) I have the first volume, translated badly, of Brugmann's Comparative Philology and he who loves the nine-days' captain's biscuit of Crewe Junction,[11] he may love Brugmann.

As a tooth ceases aching so ~~have~~ ^will^ my lectures intermit after tomorrow for Shrovetide.[12] I shall be able, I hope, to fettle my Paper on the Argei.[13] I went yesterday to a public library to verify texts, but Varro, one of the principle,[14] happened to be out. This Paper will now be in two parts — the Argei and the Pontifices; for the Luperci have no necessary connexion with the rest and shall be put aside. The part on the Pontiffs is only half written and the subject touched on is vast, and difficult therefore to treat sufficiently and yet so as to bear on the Bridge-ceremony of the Argei and no further.

I also am greatly interested in Chaldaea and Egypt, but can read little about them. What books do you read?

My Nationalist~~s~~ friends are wild with triumph and joy over Pigott[15] (one of themselves and ^sometime^ editor of their most advanced organ, the paper which under a slight change of name[16] is now United Ireland). Pigott has confessed to making, by forgery, the charge against Mr. Parnell of, after the event, faintly approving or not disapproving of ~~a~~ ^the^ murder ^of ~~Lord Frederick~~^ ^Mr. Tom Burke^[17] and I want to know when his successor O'Brien is going to confess to the falsehood of his charge against Mr. Balfour of planning in general and then carrying out in particular[10] the murder of John Mandeville.[18] The charge is far more ~~de~~ hideous. I do not ask the Irish to see this, but I should like the English dupes and dullards to see it. If you knew the world I live in! Yet I continue to be a Home Ruler:[19] I say it ~~mu~~ must be, and let it be.

I am not convinced ^however that^ the Facsimile letter,[20] the one about the Phoenix Park, is not genuine after all.

I am your affectionate brother Gerard.

All but these words has been written with a narrowminded steel pen. You cannot overrule their vicious dispositions.

P.S. ~~The~~ Smith's Dictionary of Antiquities is of antiquities only: persons, ~~and~~ ^places,^ and peoples are provided for in ~~those of~~ the Classical Dictionary ^of Mythology and Biography^ and the Dictionary of ~~Ge~~ Classical Geography. But Reinach's book includes history; not so seemingly ~~does~~ ^do^ Daremberg and Saglio unless indirectly.

[1] George Grote, *A History of Greece*, 12 vols. (London, 1846–56); it went through numerous editions and was widely used in British schools and universities. The incomplete library lender's register at Highgate shows that GMH borrowed vols. 1, 2, 9, 10, 11 between Mar. 1860 and Nov. 1862. The page covering loans between Dec. 1862 and June 1863 is missing. The length of these loans varies from weeks over vacations to overnight, suggesting that his use was both for quick reference and more extended reading. He also used it as an undergraduate; see *CW* iv.

[2] *History of Greece* by Ernst Curtius, trans. A. W. Ward, 5 vols. (1868–73).

[3] *History of Antiquity* by Maximilian W. Duncker, trans. Evelyn Abbott, 6 vols. (1877–82); *History of Greece*, trans. S. F. Alleyne and E. Abbott, 2 vols. (1883–6).

[4] *History of Greece*, i (1888).

[5] First published in 1842. The 3rd edn. (ed. William Smith, William Wayte, and G. E. Marinder), in 2 vols., published 1890–1.

[6] 1883–4.

[7] *Dictionaire des antiquités grecques et romaines*, by Charles V. Daremberg and E. Saglio (1877–1911).

[8] 1886.

[9] A fugleman was an exemplary soldier placed at the front of troops as a model in their exercises. Karl Brugmann (1849–1919) was a central figure of the revolutionary Neogrammarians. He was from 1887 professor of Sanskrit and comparative linguistics at Leipzig, and his fame rests on his contribution to the monumental *Grundriss der vergleichenden Grammatik der indogermanischen Sprachen (Outline of the Comparative Grammar of the Indo-Germanic Languages)* (1886–93), which was almost immediately translated into English (1888–95). His method of presenting data rather than discursive argument is still found challenging.

[10] The words 'perhaps very' and 'particular' to 'see it' are spaced to avoid the notepaper's embossed letterhead.

[11] GMH's metaphor here is a compound of three elements to indicate that Brugmann's book is dry and unpalatable: the 'nine days' is perhaps remembering the 'nine days' wonder' of the impermanent philologists, but here indicates length of storage; the 'captain's biscuit' was, like the ordinary ship's biscuit but of finer flour, made hard

and dry to last on the voyage; and one can only presume that (compare the modern—now perhaps unfair—reputation of British Rail sandwiches) the famous railway junction at Crewe (the town named after the station) was known for rather dry provisions.

[12] Shrovetide strictly comprises Quinquagesima Sunday (the fiftieth day, counting inclusively, before Easter Sunday) and 'Shrove' Monday and Tuesday, when the faithful would be shriven before Ash Wednesday, the first day of the fasting season of Lent.

[13] According to William Smith's *Dictionary of Greek and Roman Antiquities* (1875) Argei had two principal meanings: consecrated places of worship in each district of Rome (perhaps twenty-seven of them), and thirty straw effigies of bound men that were thrown into the Tiber in a ceremony carried out by the pontifices, praetors, Vestals, and certain citizens on the ides of May (14 May). Smith refers to Varro, Livy, Ovid, Plutarch, etc. and concludes that the ceremony was to propitiate the gods and that the effigies may well have replaced human sacrifice. Pontifices were 'the most illustrious among the colleges of priests' with an extensive set of religious and judicial duties (Smith's *Dictionary*). Luperci were the priests of the Roman god Lupercus, the god of fertility (Smith's *Dictionary*). There is no paper by GMH on the Argei extant; see *CW* vii.

[14] Thus in MS. Varro is Marcus Terentius Varro (116–27 BC) to whose *De lingua Latina* all those who write on the Argei refer.

[15] The Irish journalist and blackmailer Richard Pigott (1838–89; *ODNB*), on whose forged documents the charges against Parnell of approving of the murder of Lord Frederick Cavendish and Mr T. H. Burke had been based. See letter to RB of 1 May 1887, n. 3. He committed suicide on this very day.

[16] *United Ireland* was founded in 1880 by William O'Brien. The *United Irishman* was published in Liverpool 1876–7.

[17] See n. 15.

[18] John Mandeville (1849–88) was a Munsterman imprisoned with William O'Brien (1852–1928; *ODNB*) on 31 Oct. 1887. He was released on 24 Dec. 1887 and died at Mitchelstown on 8 July 1888, owing, it was alleged, to ill treatment in Tullamore jail. An inquest (fully reported in *The Times* 13–30 July 1888) was held to investigate the charge, and O'Brien gave evidence in support of the allegation. Arthur Balfour, first earl of Balfour (1848–1930; *ODNB*), then Chief Secretary for Ireland (1887–91), was British prime minister 1902–5.

[19] Gladstone's Home Rule bill had been rejected on 8 July 1886 by thirty votes.

[20] See letter to RB of 1 May 1887.

2 March 1889 to his Mother

FL, no. CXV, p. 195 Bodleian, MS Eng. lett. e. 41, fos. 131–2

UNIVERSITY COLLEGE, | DUBLIN. [*embossed heading*]
March 2 1889

My dearest mother, — I wish you a very happy birthday tomorrow and many happy returns. I enclose an old sketch of mine, rather drawing, for it is in high finish, but unhappily ^it^ was never completed.[1] It lay so long in drawers and so on that it has grown dirty, as you see, beyond what can be safely touched and is sadly rubbed too. Seeing this I thought I would get it photographed by a friend, which has been done. I now send you therefore the original, disreputable as it looks, but it is the best of my drawings. It might, I believe, ~~me~~ ^be^ "set" by isinglass,[2] but I do not know who here could do it.

The weather is wintry. It is now steadily snowing. But the political weather is beyond measure severer to me.

I will write to my father soon and with best love to all (and grief to hear casually Kate has been so unwell) I am your loving son Gerard.

I enclose one of the photographic copies.

[1] The drawing made at Shanklin, Isle of Wight, dated 1866 [probably 1863], now in the Bodleian, MS Eng.misc.a.8, fo. 104. See *CW* vi.

[2] A transparent, almost pure gelatin prepared from the air bladders of fish, particularly the sturgeon, used as an adhesive and a clarifying agent and, as here, to preserve drawings.

20–4 March 1889 to Robert Bridges

LRB, no. CLXX, p. 301 Bodleian, Dep. Bridges, vol. 92, fos. 199–201v

Univ. Coll., Stephen's Green, Dublin. March 20 188~~1~~^9^.

Dearest Bridges, — I write you a few lines tonight for an ungracious reason, because I cannot do anything needing a greater effort.

I have been thinking what a fine subject you chose in <u>Achilles in Scyros</u>. Achilles is such a brilliant figure: Shakspere ~~could~~ ^did^ not read Homer, otherwise ~~how~~ ^he ~~w~~^ could ~~he~~ ^not have^ been guilty of that hideous and perverse freak of a cowardly Achilles in <u>Troilus and Cressida</u>. I hope you do him justice. I should like to see the play, but I do not ask to, no; I could not read it.

Mr. Jevons sent me his pamphlet.[1] I had already seen and agreed with it. I read it again and wrote to thank him and say so. I asked him to correct two references or rather give me the correct form and the references, if he knew them, of two stories, but he did not reply.

I am both flattered and dismayed about my song. It was only a sketch, a rough-hew of a song. I have been at it since and the task I have undertaken is so extremely difficult that I have not yet succeeded in it and have to put it aside at intervals, especially as I am languishing. First it is in canon at the octave at two bars: but I think scorn of such an achievement as that. But in the next verse it has to be in canon at the third above and third below at ~~the second~~ two and four bars ^off^ respectively — or to speak more precisely, the ~~bass – which is instrumental —~~ ^alto^ begins, at the ~~third below~~ ^sixth above^; the treble, after two bars, follows, with the original tune; and the bass — which is instrumental — after four bars, brings up the rear at the sixth below. Now this requires the tune to be capable of counterpoint at the octave, or with itself unchanged, and also with two other transpositions, all exact. It is, — I assure ^you^, very baffling; but I hope to do it. It almost comes of itself; so that I am persuaded by coaxing I can make it quite. Besides this I insert a firm chant. I see that the composers of canons besides the Muses and Graces should sacrifice, ~~t~~ like Timoleon, to Fortune.[2]

Is not Nero to be continued?[3] It is such a rich picture of life, indeed of our life as it would be without Christianity. Only on the other hand a Second Part would have to bring in the loathsome character of Sporus,[4] which is not desirable to put on the stage. (I read yesterday that Nero choked the oracular chasm at Delphi with carcases because the oracle rebuked him for killing his mother and did literally for some time ~~sp~~ stop the mouth of the god.)

By the bye, as you are a reader of Menander, you may like to know that Dr. Theodore Kock's Comicorum Atticorum Fragmenta {*Fragments of Athenian Comedy*}, vol. 3 containing Menander, price 16 marks, Teubner, is now out.

I shall be delighted to have the new issue of the Growth of Love[5] and think it well that some pruning has been practised; for on so dark and mystical a matter one may be~~come~~ glutted with the best of poetry. Neither should you grudge giving me a copy that will be after my time unread. For consider: you aim at oblivion; for that you descend into Daniel's den;[6] for that you print 24 copies (so that the College of Apostles[7] on parting could have ~~left~~ ^taken^ two copies only for the needs of all Scythia, suppose, all Parthia, all India, and so on). Now, as ~~one~~ ^some^ philosopher Cicero quotes[8] said, ^undique^ tantundem viae ad inferos est {*all places are at an equal distance from the infernal regions*} (Anax~~o~~^a^goras, by George)~~:~~; that is you can be forgotten "as hard" at Dublin as anywhere else, at ~~Las~~ Lampsacus as at Clazomenae: what do you want more?

I have from henceforth till the beginning of May to prepare examination-papers.

I have been drawing up a Paper, not for examination, you understand, on the Argei,[9] a curious subject, interesting by dint of study; but it is not corrected or copied or indeed all written. If I can get it done I shall try to publish it.

I enclose a sonnet[10] and am your affectionate friend Gerard M. Hopkins. March 21 1889.

I have a good few sonnets more you have never seen.

Monasterevan, March 24 — The sonnet will, I am afraid, fade: Miss Cassidy's ink is, I must say, shocking. Observe, it must be read <u>adagio molto</u> {*very slowly*} and with great stress.[11]

[1] Possibly *The Development of the Athenian Democracy*, by Frank Byron Jevons, formerly of Wadham College, Oxford, a pamphlet of 38 pp., printed in 1886.

[2] Plutarch's 'Life of Timoleon' in his *Parallel Lives* (16. 10) recounts how Timoleon was saved from assassination and how bystanders wondered 'at the dexterity of Fortune, seeing how she makes some things lead up to others, brings all things together from afar, weaves together incidents which seem to be most divergent and to have nothing in common with one another, and so makes use of their reciprocal beginnings and endings' (Loeb translation).

[3] *Nero*, Part II, was published in 1894.

[4] He is not one of the characters.

[5] *LXXIX Sonnets* (Daniel, Oxford; 1889): twenty-two copies were printed.

[6] (Charles) Henry Daniel (1836–1919; *ODNB*), a Fellow of Worcester College, Oxford as of 1863, became an influential private printer and publisher. He printed fifteen works by RB between 1883 and 1903. In the Bible (Daniel 6) it is Daniel who descends into the lions' den.

[7] i.e. the twelve apostles who were to spread the word; Andrew preached in Scythia, Matthew in Parthia, Thomas in Parthia and India, and Bartholomew in India.

[8] Cicero, *Tusculan Disputations*, 1. 43. 104, with slight variation in the word order. The whole passage is helpful (here in the translation of C. D. Yonge, 1877): 'Anaxagoras, when he was at the point of death at Lampsacus, and was asked by his friends, whether, if anything should happen to him, he would not choose to be carried to Clazomenae, his country, made the excellent answer, "There is," says he, "no occasion for that, for all places are at an equal distance from the infernal regions".'

[9] See letter of 1 Mar. 1889, n. 13. Apparently never completed and not known to be extant.

[10] 'Thou art indeed just, Lord'.

[11] From 'Monasterevan' is in ink that has faded to pale brown. A note by RB at the end of the next (and last) letter reads: 'The two letters preceding this one were destroyed RB.'

29 April 1889 to Robert Bridges

LRB, no. CLXXI, p. 303 — Bodleian, Dep. Bridges, vol. 92, fos. 202–5

Univ. Coll., Stephen's Green, Dublin. April 29 1889.

Dearest Bridges, — I am ill to-day, but no matter for that as my spirits are good. And I want you too to "buck up", as we used to say at school, about those jokes over which you write in so dudgeonous a spirit. I have it now down in my ~~tate~~ tablets that a man may joke and joke and be offensive; ~~and~~ I have had several warnings lately leading me to make the entry, tho' goodness knows the ~~one~~ ^joke^ that gave most offence was harmless enough and even kind. You I treated to the same sort of irony as I do myself; but it is true it ~~matt~~ makes all the world of difference whose hand administers. About Daniel I see I was mistaken: if he pays you more ^than^ and sells you as much as other publishers (which however is saddening to think of: how many copies ~~it~~ is it? five and twenty?)[1] my objections do not apply. Then you ought to remember that I did try to make you known in Dublin and had some little success. (Dowden I will never forgive:[2] could you not kill ~~your~~ Mrs. Bridges? then he might take an interest in you). Nay I had great success and placed you on the pinnacle of fame; for it is the pinnacle of fame to become educational and be set for translation into Gk. iambics, as you are at Trinity: this is to be a classic; "this", as Lord Beaconsfield[3] said to a friend who told him he found his young daughter reading Lothair, "O this is fame indeed". And Horace and Juvenal say the same thing. And here I stop, for fear of it ripening into some kind of joke.

I believe I enclose a new sonnet. But we greatly differ in feeling about copying one's verses out: I find it repulsive, and let them lie months and years in rough copy untransferred to my book. Still I hope soon to send you my accumulation. This one is addressed to you.[4]

Swinburne has a new volume out,[5] which is reviewed in its own style: "The rush and the rampage, the pause and the pull-up~~, th~~ of these lustrous and lumpophorous lines". It is all now a "self-drawing web"; a perpetual functioning of genius without truth, feeling, or any adequate matter to be at function on. There is some heavydom, in long water-logged lines (he has no real understanding of rhythm, and though~~e~~ he sometimes hits brilliantly at other times he misses badly) about the Armada,[6] that pitfall of the patriotic muse; and rot about babies,[7] a ~~bottomless~~ ^blethery^ bathos into which Hugo and he from opposite coasts have ~~been~~ long driven ~~e~~Channel-tunnels. I am afraid I am going too ^far^ with the poor fellow. Enough now, but his babies make a Herodian of me.[8]

My song will be a very highly wrought work and I do hope a fine one. Do you think canon wd. spoil the tune? I hope not, but the contrary. But if the worst came to the worst, I could, since a solo voice ~~can~~ holds its own again^s^t instruments, give the canon-following to a violin. I shall hear what Sir Robert Stewart says about it. This is how it now stands. I tried at first to make the air such that it shd. be rigidly the same in every note and rhythm (always excepting the alterations to save the tritone) in all its shifts; but I found that impracticable and that I had reached the point where art calls for loosing, not for lacing. I now make the canon strict in each verse, but allow a change, which indeed ~~of itself is~~ ^is^ besides called for by the change of words, from verse to verse. Indeed the air becomes a generic form which is specified newly in each verse, with excellent effect. It is like a new art this. I allow no modulation: the result is that the tune is shifted into modes, viz. those of La, Mi, and Sol[9] (this is the only way I can speak of them, and they have a character of their own which is neither that of modern major and minor music nor yet of the plain chant ~~tones~~ ^modes^, so far as I can make out). The first shift i~~n~~s into the mode of La: this shd. be minor, but the effect is not exactly that; rather the feeling is that Do is still the keynote, but has shifted its place in the scale. This impression is helped by the harmony, for as the ~~t~~Third is not flattened the chords appear major. The chord at the beginning of every bar is the common chord or first inversion; the $^{6}_{4}$ may appear in course of the bar and discords are ^in^ passing or prepared. Perhaps the harmony may be heavy, but I work according to the only rules I know. I can only get on slowly with it and must hope to be rewarded in the end. Now I must lie down.

Who is Miss Cassidy? She is an elderly lady who by often asking me down to Monasterevan and by the change and holiday her kind hospitality provides is become one of the props and struts of my existence. St. Emin[10] founded the monastery: a singular story is told of him. Henry VIII confiscated it and it became the property of Lord Drogheda. The usual curse on ~~A~~abbey lands attends it and it never passes down in the direct line. The present Lord and Lady Drogheda have no issue. Outside Moore Abbey, which is a beautiful park, the country is flat, bogs and river and canals. The river is the Barrow, which the old Irish poets call the dumb Barrow. I call it the burling Barrow Brown.[11] Both descriptions are true. The country has nevertheless a charm. The two beautiful young people live within an easy drive.

~~I~~^W^ith kind love to Mrs. Bridges and Mrs. Molesworth, I am your affectionate friend Gerard.

[1] See previous letter to RB.

[2] See letter to RB of 11 Dec. 1886.

[3] i.e. Benjamin Disraeli. We have as yet failed to find a reference to Disraeli's comment, but it recalls that recorded by William Hazlitt of Coleridge in his essay 'Coleridge (II)' in *Political Essays* (1819), 133: 'We well remember a friend of his and ours saying, many years ago, on seeing a little shabby volume of *Thomson's Seasons* lying in the window of a solitary ale-house, at the top of a rock hanging over the British Channel – "*That is true fame!*"'

[4] 'To R.B.'

[5] *Poems and Ballads*, Third Series (1889) was published in April. GMH may have been referring to a review in the *Academy* (27 Apr. 1889, pp. 279–80) by George Cotterell, who describes Swinburne's 'The Armada' in something like Swinburne's style: 'Doom gathers, and grows, and falls upon the swaggering captains and their galleons; glory waits upon "the men" that were "stout of spirit and stark / As rocks that repel the tide, / As day that repels the dark"'. There are places where the quotations from Swinburne's 'Armada' call to mind lines from GMH's 'Wreck of the Deutschland'. Cotterell describes Swinburne's patriotic faith that the superiority of the English was responsible for their victory over the Spanish and GMH may well have found this a provoking contrast to his own belief in his 'Wreck of the Deutschland' that it is God who is in control. Cotterell quotes extensively from Swinburne's poems about babies and regards 'In a Garden' as 'one of the gems of the book:

> Baby, see the flowers!
> — Baby sees
> Fairer things than these,
> Fairer though they be than dreams of ours.' Etc

The book was also reviewed in the *Times*, 10 Apr. 1889, but not in this way nor quoting all the poems mentioned. Advertisements in the *Athenaeum* in April also mention a review in the *Globe*, but the *Athenaeum* did not review it until 25 May 1889. GMH's language sounds more like Edward Lear in the story GMH enthuses about to his mother in the letter of 2 Mar. 1873, 'The Story of Four Little Children who went round the World': there one reads of a 'plumdomphious manner' and how 'all the Blue-Bottle-Flies began to buzz at once in a sumptuous and sonorous manner, the melodious and mucilaginous sounds echoing all over the waters, and resounding across the tumultuous tops of the transitory Titmice upon the intervening and verdant mountains, with a serene and sickly suavity only known to the truly virtuous'. The 'self-drawing web' comes from Shakespeare's *Life of King Henry VIII*, I. i. 65.

> but, spider-like,
> Out of his self-drawing web, he gives us note,
> The force of his own merit makes his way.

[6] *The Armada, 1588–1888*: a wordy rhapsody, 24 pp.

[7] 'In a Garden', 'A Rhyme', and 'Baby-Bird'.

[8] Matthew 2: 16–18 records how Herod the Great, king of Judaea, ordered that all children under 2 should be killed. This is the 'Slaughter of the Innocents', the term GMH used of the burning of his own verse in his journal on 11 May 1868.

[9] GMH uses the 'tonic sol-fa' system; see letter to RWD of 29 Oct.–2 Nov. 1881, n. 20.

[10] Monasterevan gets its name from from St Eimhin's (Evin) Monastery, which was built in the 6th c. St Eimhin was said to be the author of a life of St Patrick, the *Vita Tripartita*, which was translated by Whitley Stokes in 1887 as *The Tripartite Life of Patrick*.

[11] In 'On the Portrait of Two Beautiful Young People'.

1 May 1889 to his Mother

FL, no. CXVI, p. 195 Bodleian, MS Eng. lett. e. 41, fos. 133–134^{v}
Addressed to 'Mrs. Manley Hopkins | Court's Hill Lodge | Haslemere | Surrey | England'. PM DUBLIN MY 2 89 and HASLEMERE MY 3 89.

Univ. Coll., Stephen's Green, Dublin. May 1 1889

My dearest mother, — You have not heard from me for very long and now before going early to bed I write a line to say I am in some rheumatic fever, which comes very inconveniently when I shd. be and am setting my Papers for the examinations. I hope to be better tomorrow. If I am worse I may see the doctor. I am your loving son Gerard.

3 May 1889 to his Father

FL, no. CXVII, p. 196 Bodleian, MS Eng. lett. e. 41, fos. 140–142^{v}
In an unaddressed envelope annotated in ink [by his father?] 'Gerard's last letter. 3^{d}. May 1889.' with an addition in pencil in a different hand 'To his Father'

UNIVERSITY COLLEGE, | S^{T} STEPHEN'S GREEN, | DUBLIN. [*printed heading*]
May 3 1889

My dearest father, — I am laid up in bed with some fever, rheumatic fever I suppose, but I am getting round. This is the first day I took to bed altogether: it would have been better to do so before. The pains are only slight, but I wish that Charlton Scott and Isidore de Lara would agree to plant~~,~~ a garden, a garden of sleep in my bed,[1] as I am sleepy by day and sleepless by night and do not rightly sleep at all. I saw a doctor yesterday, who treated my complaint as a fleabite, a treatment which begets confidence but not gratitude.

I hope to hear better news of Mary,[2] whose complaint, I am afraid, is far more obstinate than mine. I suppose it is neuralgia and a general nervous sinking. Give her my best love and wishes.

With best love to all, I am your affectionate son Gerard.

[1] 'The Garden of Sleep', a song that won great popularity: words by Clement Scott (1841–1904; *ODNB*), music by Isidore de Lara (1858–1935; *ODNB*), whose opening

lines are: 'On the grass of the cliff, at the edge of the steep, | God planted a garden—a garden of sleep!' See the letter of 8 May 1889.

[2] See letter of 15 Aug. 1877, n. 4.

5 May 1889 to his Mother

FL, no. CXVIII, p. 196 Bodleian, MS Eng. lett. e. 41, fos. 143–145[v]
Addressed to 'Mrs. Manley Hopkins | Court's Hill Lodge | Haslemere | Surrey | England'. PM DUBLIN MY 5 89 and HASLEMERE MY 6 89.

UNIVERSITY COLLEGE, | DUBLIN. [*printed heading*]
May 5 1889

My dearest mother, — I am grieved that you should be in such anxiety about me and I am afraid my letter to my father, which you must now have seen and ought, it seems to me, to have had before this morning's letter was sent, can not much have relieved you. I am now in careful hands. The doctor thoroughly examined me yesterday. I have some fever; what, has not declared itself. I am to ~~take~~ ^have^ perfect rest and to take only liquid food. My ^pains and^ sleeplessness ~~was~~ ^were^ due to suspended digestion, which ~~was~~ ^has^ now been almost cured, but with much distress. There is no hesitation or difficulty about the nurses, ~~wh~~ with which Dublin is provided, I dare say, better than any place, but Dr. Redmond this morning said he must wait further to see the need; for today there is no real difference; only that I feel better.

You do not mention how Mary is.[1]

I am and I long have been sad about Lionel, feeling that his visit^s^ must be few and far between and that I had so little good of this one, though he and I have so many interests in common and shd. find many more in company. I cd. not send him my Paper,[2] for it had to be put aside.

It is an ill wind that blows nobody good. My sickness falling at the most pressing time of the University Work, there will be the devil to pay. Only there is no harm in saying, that gives <u>me</u> no trouble but an unlooked for relief. At many such a time I have been in a sort of extremity of mind, now I am the placidest soul in the world. And you will see, when I come round, I shall be the better for this.

I am writing uncomfortably and this is enough for a sick man. I am your loving son Gerard. Best love to all.

[1] See previous letter and letter of 15 Aug. 1877, n. 4.

[2] On the Argei; see letter to Lionel Hopkins of 1 Mar. 1889.

8 May 1889 to his Mother (dictated)

FL, no. CXIX, p. 197 Bodleian, MS Eng. lett. e. 41, fos. 146–147v

Written at F. Gerard's dictation.[1]
UNIVERSITY COLLEGE, | ST STEPHEN'S GREEN, | DUBLIN. [*printed heading*]
May 8. 89

My dearest Mother,

My fever is a sort of typhoid:[2] it is not severe, and my mind has never for a moment wandered. It would give me little pain were it not that while it was incubating I exposed my head to a cold wind, and took neuralgia which torments me now. Thank you for your letters & the flowers which duly revived in water: they are on my table now.

I wonder that none of you understood the allusion to the Garden of Sleep. It is a sentimental song which I thought you must be sick and tired of in England as it has now come over to us. Charlton or Clement Scott is the Author of the words. By every post he receives inquiries as to his meaning which he cannot give except that the Garden of Sleep is a poppygrown churchyard in the Corner of the Cliff. He gives a text from Ruskin to the effect that all pure natures admire bright colours, referring to the poppies.[3] Accordingly with his genius & his purity he must be a good catch. The Composer is Isidore de Lara who is represented with Byronic look heavy mustaches & furred cloak. He sings his own songs. The piece is not without merit; but when you have heard it as often as I have taken beef tea & chicken jelly, you will have had enough of it.

I had a good deal of sleep last night. The nurse is first rate and every condition is present that could make a serious thing trifling. The only complaint I have to make is that food and medicine keep coming in like cricket balls. I have in fact every attention possible.

Best love to all.
I am your affectionate son
Gerard.
per T. W.[4]

[1] This letter is written in Fr Wheeler's hand. See next letter.

[2] Typhoid is a highly infectious fever which affects the intestines and is caused by bacteria (usually *salmonella typhi*) that live in human faeces. The infection is spread by

contaminated food or water. The bad drains of 85/6 St Stephen's Green have conventionally been blamed for GMH's illness, though nobody else in the house became ill. His prolonged fever (5–6 weeks), the digestive problems, and the relapse after seeming better are all characteristic of typhoid.

[3] GMH must have seen the sheet music, where the tune is prefaced by a quotation from the last paragraphs of ch. 4 of Ruskin's *Proserpina* (1879): 'Whenever men are noble they love bright colour; and wherever they can live healthily, bright colour is given them—in sky, sea, flowers, and living creatures.'

[4] These initials stand for Fr Thomas Wheeler, SJ, vice-president and minister of University College, who had superintended the nursing of GMH with affectionate care and was later to be responsible for the first inspection of his papers.

14 May 1889 from Father Wheeler to Mrs Hopkins

Bodleian, Eng.misc.a.8, fos. 34–5

Addressed to 'Mrs Hopkins | Court's Hill Lodge | Haslemere | Surrey'. PM DUBLIN MY 15 89 and HASLEMERE MY 16 89.

UNIVERSITY COLLEGE, | DUBLIN. [*printed heading*] May 14

My dear Madam,

Many thanks for your letter of this morning and your too kind appreciation of any little thing we try to do to pilot dear Gerard through his straights. You will be glad to hear that he still is keeping up his strength admirably and if I, as non-professional may judge, I think he's now well round the corner and on the high road to mending. Still of course extreme care is required while he is regaining his lost strength to guard against a relapse. This evg. he is brighter than he has been anytime this past week, although he is generally less well in the evenings after, I suppose, the burden of the day. The Drs are quite pleased with him, and the nurses cannot look at the possibility of his being anything but quite well in a short time now. He would like to dictate his letters to you — but I think it far safer to spare him that pleasure, and do it myself. Many prayers have been offered to heaven for him and I feel that they have been heard.

Believe me dear Madam,
Yours very faithfully
T. Wheeler

18 May 1889 from Robert Bridges to GMH

FL, no. M 1, p. 433 Bodleian, Dep. Bridges, vol. 92, fos. 32–3

Yattendon.
Dearest Gerard.

I am so sorry to get a letter from one of your people telling me that you ~~we~~are ill with fever. And yesterday I sent you off a budget of notes on Milton's prosody. and when I last wrote I never mentioned your ailing tho' you told me in your letter that you interrupted it to lie down. . What is this fever? F. Wheeler says that you are mending. I hope you are recovering properly. let me have a line — I wish I c^{d} look in on you and see for myself. You must send me a card now and then, and one as soon as possible to let me know about you.[1]

Meanwhile I must be patient.

I think that if you are really mending Miltonic prosody will be just the sort of light amusement for your mind — I hope you are well enough already — and will make a quick recovery and complete for wh I pray. Yr affc.

RB.
May ~~9~~ 18. 89

5 minutes before the letter came I was writing your name for the binder of the "Growth of Love" to send you a copy. .

[1] This is the last letter we have either from or to GMH. During the night of Wednesday, 5 June, a serious change for the worse took place in his condition. His mother and father were summoned and were present when he died at half past one p.m. on Saturday, 8 June 1889. His funeral took place on Tuesday, 11 June 1889, in the Jesuit Church, St Francis Xavier's, on Upper Gardiner Street, where High Mass and the Office for the Dead were celebrated, with 'Seventy ecclesiastics & an immense congregation' (see letter of 15 June 1889 from Manley Hopkins to E. H. Coleridge below). He was buried in the Prospect Cemetery, Glasnevin, in the Jesuits' crowded burial plot. See *WHALB*, 455–6, and Martin, 413–14. His mother reports in her letter of 13 June 1889 that 'Before leaving Dublin all the letters Gerard received during his illness—(& which he read & re-read) were brought to me to look over & destroy'.

LETTERS ON THE DEATH OF GMH, 1889–1890

10 June 1889 from Arthur Hopkins to Mrs Hopkins

Bodleian, MS Misc. a. 8, fos. 37–38v

Mourning paper

Tre Vean: 10th June '89

My dearest Mother

I cannot write you many lines just now, but must at least thank you for your sad letter received this morning.

Some day, not now, I shall hope you will be able to write us some details — any little thing you can find to tell.

Everard came over to us this morning — we were very glad to see him. He was anxious to know what I thought about our own going to Dublin in the hopes of seeing Gerard's face once more.

Seeing the time that had already elapsed I thought it too unlikely that we should see him. He also seemed to think it might be some satisfaction to you & my father if we were at the funeral, but seeing that that will be in the hands of the College probably, I did not think we could be much comfort to you. I am going to write a line to Dr Bridges, & to Edward Bond.

I had a feeling that not having been able to see ~~h~~Gerard during his illness I hardly was very anxious to see what change it had effected, preferring to retain the recollection of him at Whitby last summer, and the vision in my memory of the marvellously beautiful expression that was in his face as he bid us Goodbye when he left us. It brought tears into our eyes then, and in some distant way I felt that I should see his face no more.

I hope your health will be spared in this blow.

With love ~~to~~^very^ much to you both
Ever your loving son
Arthur

10 June 1889 from Everard Hopkins to Mr and Mrs Hopkins

Bodleian, MS Eng. misc. a. 8, fos. 54–5
Mourning paper. Probably in same envelope as Amy's note below, which is on identical paper.

13, Barkston Mansions, | Barkston Gardens, | South Kensington. [*printed heading*]

My dearest Mother & Father

I must write just to let ~~to~~you feel I am with you by the grave of my dear dead brother.

It is a terrible grief to me that I could not see him once more — Had we known on Saturday Arthur & I would have been with you ~~o~~yesterday but we feel it would be useless now — perhaps it is best for us to remember his sweet & beautiful face as we always knew it — not worn with sickness. For himself his life had been such a complete sacrifice that I cannot but be sure that he is far happier in the presence of God, that[n] he was or could be here. It is of course for you & ourselves I feel most to have lost such a son & brother. The memory of him, his gifts his goodness & his sacrifice will always live fresh in all our hearts. if only we could have seen more of him in his life. I hope Fr Wheeler will give you his papers — his poems among them — & there was a little rosary we sent him at Christmas — We shall send a cross tomorrow to be laid on his grave. I daresay Fr Wheeler will see to that. Arthur has written to Bridges & Edward Bond — We thought they would wish it.

If it is possible to kiss him for me — do it

With all love my dear parents your loving son
Everard.

10 June 1889 from Amy (Mrs Everard) Hopkins to Mr and Mrs Hopkins

Bodleian, MS Eng. misc. a. 8, fos. 56–8

Addressed to 'Mrs Manley Hopkins | c/o Rev. Fr Wheeler | University College | S. Stephens Green | Dublin. | Ireland'. PM EARLSCOURT S.W. JU 10 89 and H & K PACKET JY 11 89. Mourning paper and envelope.

13, Barkston Mansions, | Barkston Gardens, | South Kensington. [*printed heading*]

My dearest Mr. Mrs. Hopkins

What can I say to you! Only that I wish I could give you a warm kiss of love & sympathy. I know what bitter grief is & so I can sympathise heartily.

He must have been so good! I'm sure he must be happy to be at rest! But for you it is terrible. —

God help you
Your loving
Amy

11 June 1889 from Arthur Hopkins to Manley Hopkins

Bodleian, MS Eng. misc. a. 8, fos. 39–40

Mourning paper

Tre Vean. 80 Finchley Rd | London | N.W.
11th June '89

My dear Father

I have only a few minutes to catch the post, but I write to remind you in case it may ^not^ have occurred to you, that before you leave Dublin it would be worth while to ask Father Wheeler for leave to look into any papers, writings or note books, sketches or what not that Gerard may have left. Probably they would be allowed to pass into your possession.

I believe he kept a Diary. If there are any little Devotional Books, Rebecca would much like to have one.

Of course he had very few personal properties at all, but there must be some few things.

We have sent off this evening a Cross of flowers, to be placed on the Coffin, if in time, or on the grave.

We addressed it however to Father Wheeler, which we thought best.

With our most affectionate loves to Mother & yourself

Your loving Son
Arthur

12 June 1889 from Edward Bond to Mrs Hopkins

Bodleian, MS Eng. misc. a. 8, fos. 41–43^{v}

Addressed to 'Mrs Manley Hopkins | Haslemere | Surrey'. PM RAMSGATE JU12 89 and HASLEMERE JU 13 89.

~~Elm Bar~~
Ramsgate 12 June 89

My dear Mrs Hopkins

Arthur has kindly written to me announcing the sad news of Gerards death. I hardly know how to write to you: but I cannot help sending a line to say how much I feel for you in this affliction which I cannot but fear will touch you very deeply & nearly. I am glad at least that you were able to reach him before his death & I hope that he knew & recognised you. Perhaps some day — if there is anything to tell — you would not mind telling me something of his last hours. I should like to know how my dear old friend died — I cannot help mourning how that for so many years I have seen so little of him but I shall never lose the memory of our early friendship nor my sense of that fine spirituality which distinguished him from his fellows

Words fail me to express the sympathy I w^{d}. fain convey with you & yours. Believe me it is very real & true — & believe me also

Affectionately yours
Edward Bond.

13 June 1889 from Mrs Hopkins to [?A. W. M. Baillie]

Bodleian, MS Eng. misc. a. 8, fos. 44–5

Mourning paper

Court's Hill Lodge | Haslemere
June 13th

My dear Sir,

Before leaving Dublin all the letters Gerard received during his illness — (& which he read & re-read) were brought to me to look over & destroy — I found one from you — & I am not sure whether any intimation was made to you of the course of his illness afterwards — He had seemed to be doing well — but dangerous symptoms set in, which he had no longer strength to resist. His father & I were thankful to be with him for the last few days & to the end, which at the last was peaceful, though he had suffered much for some days. He never lost consciousness, till just the last. — It is a comfort to have seen that all that skill & care could do to save him was done — & to have seen how affectionately he was beloved and respected by every one who knew him there — His funeral was a remarkable one —

For ourselves we are of an age to know that our separation cannot be for very long — & for him he has begun that higher life of which this is but a shadow or a symbol.

— Believe me, dear Sir

Yrs. very truly
Kate Hopkins

14 June 1889 from Frances de Paravicini[1] *to Mrs Hopkins*

Bodleian, MS Eng. misc. a. 8, fos. 46–48v
Addressed to 'Mrs Manley Hopkins | Court's Hill Lodge | Haslemere | Surrey'. PM OXFORD JU 15 89

101, WOODSTOCK ROAD, | OXFORD [*printed heading*]
Friday Evening. June 14.

Dear Mrs Hopkins,

(If you will kindly allow me so to write to you.) I feel that I must send a letter to offer to you our most sincere & deep sympathy in your grief. Father Gerard was, as perhaps you know, our very great & dear friend; & we have felt his death so keenly. It has been a terrible shock. — a sad, sad, loss. And in the midst, my thoughts have been very much with you; for your sorrow must be great indeed.

My Husband was in Dublin for a few days, before Easter, & saw Father Gerard once or twice; & they spent an eEvening together. He thought him looking very ill then, & said that he was much depressed. That day or two seemed to bring back all the old friendship, & give it, as it were, new life. When my Husband came back he spoke of Father Gerard to others; & we had just managed that he should be sent for — back to England — when we heard of his illness. We were hoping to have him in Oxford for some time this summer. Then came the news of his illness; but it was not alarming. I wrote him a long letter, about May 23: but I never knew if he received it or not. Now it is so hard to realize that all is over; & our weak human help & grief so unavailing. I know something of how you must grieve for him. He was so lovable — so singularly gifted — &, in his saintliness, so apart from, & different to, all others. Only that his beautifully gentle & generous nature made him one with his friends; & led us to love & to value him. — feeling that our lives were better, & the world richer, because of him.

I cannot tell you how we sorrow for him, — for losing him; nor how deeply we feel for & with you.

But a time does come, though perhaps not just at first, when we feel so much nearer to those who have gone before. — nearer, because of their more perfect understanding us. All shade of doubting, all faint shadows of indifference — which must come to mar even the nearest relationships here — are cleared away. Only our love & devotion is seen & known. And, living on, day by day, we are apt to forget that "those we love are loved by Another, besides ourselves". When our Lord calls them, & bids them come to Him, there is no less love. — only much, much more. And, very slowly, we begin to understand that "His Mercy is better than life".[2]

One thought has much comfort in it. Although F[r] Gerard's work in the world, so to speak, — his literary work — was always, for him, mixed with a certain sense of failure & incompleteness. Yet he had the life he chose for himself. And, in his religious life, he was very happy. My Husband remembers how he would speak of his enjoyment in the saying his office,[3] & in the quite completeness of his religion.

I hope you will very kindly forgive my writing so much. — I could not help it. And I have had less hesitation, because my letter needs no reply. At such a time I cannot expect you to write.

Again offering you our sincere sympathy, I remain,

Yours very truly
Frances de Paravicini.

[1] Frances de Paravicini, wife of Baron Francis de Paravicini (1843–1920), Roman Catholic convert, daughter of W. W. Williams of Oxford and sister of the Robert Williams for whom GMH wrote essays (see *CW* iv). For the Paravicinis, good friends of GMH in his Oxford years, see the letter of 19 Nov.–2 Dec. 1879 to Baillie and the letter of 15 June 1881. The Paravicinis gave the baptismal font to St Aloysius' in Oxford in honour of GMH.

[2] This last quotation is directly from the Bible, quoting Psalm 63: 3 in the Douay–Reims version. The other comments are steeped in the phrases of the Bible (for example John 13: 34) and hymns, but do not quote directly.

[3] The *Catholic Encyclopedia* entry under 'office' is helpful: 'This expression signifies etymologically a duty accomplished for God; in virtue of a Divine precept it means, in ecclesiastical language, certain prayers to be recited at fixed hours of the day or night by priests, religious, or clerics, and, in general, by all those obliged by their vocation to fulfil this duty. The Divine Office comprises only the recitation of certain prayers in the Breviary, and does not include the Mass and other liturgical ceremonies.'

15 June 1889 from Manley Hopkins to Ernest Hartley Coleridge

Boston College, Hopkins family papers

Mourning paper

Courts' Hill Lodge | Haslemere

Dear Ernest Coleridge,

Your most affectionate letter was welcome & prized. It adds another testimony as to the love Gerard had obtained. In Dublin we found golden opinions on all sides, & devoted friends. All the comfort that such outpourings can give we have, thankfully, received. The funeral services were truly grand. Seventy ecclesiastics &

an immense congregation assisted at them. I know that you will rejoice at hearing that your old friend was honoured as well as loved.

Again thanking you for your letter, accept mine & Gerard's Mother's most kind regards

Manley Hopkins

17 June 1889 from A. W. M. Baillie to Mrs Hopkins

Bodleian, MS Eng. misc. a. 8, fos. 49–51v

Addressed to 'Mrs Hopkins | Court's Hill Lodge | Haslemere'. PM LONDON JU 17 89. Mourning paper and envelope.

22 Sackville Street | London W [*embossed*]
17th June 1889

Dear Mrs Hopkins

I only returned to London this afternoon & having been moving about for the last day or two I could not find time to answer your letter which reached me on Saturday. I cannot express to you how grieved I was to learn from it the death of my dear friend. I had not even heard that he was ill. It is impossible to say how much I owe to him. He is the one figure which fills my whole memory of my Oxford life. There is hardly a reminiscence with which he is not associated. All my intellectual growth, and a very large proportion of the happiness of those Oxford days, I owe to his companionship. It has been a subject of unceasing regret to me that circumstances have made me see so little of him since. His rare visits gave me the keenest pleasure, and were eagerly looked forward to. Apart from my own nearest relations, I never had so strong an affection for any one.

I trust you will not be offended at my intruding my own feelings upon you at this time. I can judge from my own sense of loss, what must be that of those who were nearer to him. If there are any modern photographs of him, and one can be spared, I should esteem it a very great favour if I might have one. I have one which he gave me in the early Oxford days twenty six years ago. He had changed less than most people in the time, but yet a more recent one, if such can be spared, would give me great pleasure.

I hope I am not presumptuous in asking for this, and of course it is conditional on those who have nearer claims being first satisfied.

Believe me

Yours very Truly
A. W. M. Baillie

19 June 1889 from Mrs Hopkins to A. W. M. Baillie

Bodleian, MS Eng. misc. a. 8, fos. 52–3

Mourning paper

June 19th
Court's Hill Lodge

Dear Mr. Baillie

There was a very good photograph done of dear Gerard, ten years ago at Oxford, & I have already written to see if I can obtain some copies. — If, unfortunately it should prove that the negative has been destroyed, I shall have it repeated from our own copy, which is I think the next best thing. — It may involve a little delay, but you shall certainly have one. Thank you for your kind words about him. Your attachment was fully returned, & I remember well the particular look of distress he had when he missed you on his rare visits, & his tone when he said 'Ah, but I havn't seen Baillie'! — It was truly said that friendships are only formed here — but must be enjoyed hereafter.

Believe me,
Yrs very truly
Kate Hopkins

19 June 1889 from Robert Bridges to Mrs Hopkins

Bodleian, MS Eng. misc. a. 8, fos. 59–61v

Addressed to 'Mrs Hopkins | Courts Hill Lodge | Haslemere | Surrey'. PM NEWBURY JU 19 89, CHIEVELEY JU 19 89 and HASLEMERE JU 20 89.

Yattendon Newbury

My dear Mrs Hopkins.

I have not written before because I did not wish to add to your distress by intruding on it, and now that I do write, I hardly know what to say. Since I got the sad news I have thought very much of you and Mr Hopkins, and of the great sorrow which this sad sudden end to Gerard's strange life must be: though you have of course all the spiritual consolation which it is possible to have from the consideration of his simple heart^ed^ ~~and~~ devotion.

To this and your own love for him I know that I can add nothing: but I have thought that I may possess writings of his which you wd like to have copies of: and that it wd particularly interest you to see his last letters to me.

I wrote to Father Wheeler to ask him to return to me any of the letters to Gerard which might still be kept among his papers: and he ~~has~~ in his reply promised to do so, & said that Gerard had [not?] given instructions about his papers etc. From this I think it very likely that whatever there is of ~~inter~~ personal interest will be sent to you, in which case I shd not have much to add. But I shall hear of this perhaps later on from Mr Hopkins, and he will tell me what you wd wish.

I will add nothing now but the expression of my sympathy with you both, and all the family, & I beg that you will not think it necessary to answer this letter before it is quite easy for you to do so.

My mother is away from home or wd join me in my sympathy and good wishes. With my kindest remembrances to Mr & Miss Hopkins believe me your [*?grieved*] Robt Bridges

June 19 89

P.S. I expect my mother will have written to you herself.

19 June 1889 from Adolphus William Ward[1] *to Edward Smith*

Bodleian, MS Eng. misc. a. 8, fos. 64–67^{v}

Enclosed with Edward Bond's letter to Kate of 21 June 1889.

Mayfield | Braemar, | Aberdeenshire. [*last two lines printed*]
June 19th 1889

Dear Ned,

We were rejoiced to see your handwriting again; had you given an inkling of your address you should have heard from me before, but I knew not whether you were at Rome, Capri or elsewhere.

I had seen no notice of poor Gerard Hopkins' death, which truly grieves me. I wish you would at the proper time say to your sister how truly I sympathise with her and hers in this loss. You know how sincere a liking I always had for Gerard, and what a pleasure it gave me to meet him again at Kensington Square some years since. I occasionally heard of him through the Stonyhurst people, and I feel sure that he worked hard and well in the sphere of action which by a kind of destiny, if one may so say, had fallen to him. If so, and if his bent and conscience were in the work, what does it matter now what that sphere was? He did not live for bread alone, but for something better; and respect for his memory mingles with regret for a young life lost.

We are very pleasantly settled here for the summer, though in primitive quarters; and my wife and child are very fairly well. The country is splendid, and if anything should bring you North, a bed will be at your service, if you will give us notice. I am here for health, and cannot yet do much in the way of mountains or indeed hard work of any kind. After Weymouth I tried Manchester, but it would not do, and the College people liberally gave me leave of absence till October. By that time I hope to be all right again; if not, I must seriously think of retirement and a cottage at Hampstead.

Our kindest regards. Where do you live and what have you been doing in the way of pictures? Yours ever

A. W. Ward.

[1] Sir Adolphus William Ward (1837–1924; *ODNB*), professor of history and English literature at Owen's College, Manchester, and principal 1890–7, taking an active part in the founding of the Victoria University, of which he was Vice-Chancellor 1886–90 and 1894–6. Elected Master of Peterhouse in 1900. He wrote on various historical and literary topics, edited (with A. R. Waller) the *Cambridge History of English Literature* (1907, etc.), and was the translator of Curtius, of which GMH said in his letter of 1 Mar. 1889 'I know Curtius's [*history of Greece*] only a little'.

21 June 1889 from Edward Smith to Mrs Hopkins

Bodleian, MS Eng. misc. a. 8, fos. 56–8

Addressed to 'Mrs Manley Hopkins | Courtshill Lodge | Haslemere | Surrey'. PM CHARING CROSS W.C. JU 21 89 and HASLEMERE JU 21 89. Mourning paper and envelope.

U. U. Club
21 June.

Dear Kate

I enclose a note from Mr Ward. You will not be surprised at sympathetic words from him — who has been in former years — as it were one of the family.

Best love. Yr aff. Brother
Edward.

24 June 1889 from Friedrich von Hügel[1] *to Manley Hopkins*

Bodleian, MS Eng. misc. a. 8, fos. 68–70
Addressed to 'Manley Hopkins Esq. | Haslemere | Surrey'. PM LONDON W JU 25 89 and HASLEMERE JU 25 89

My dear Mr Hopkins,

It was quite by chance that my wife heard — in a note from a slight acquaintance, Mrs Felix Moscheles,[2] without any detail of any kind — of your very sad bereavement — a loss which is yours, but indeed also ours. — Even the knowledge of how difficult, indeed impossible it is, to say anything new or that can bring much comfort, must not keep ^me^ from telling you how shocked and grieved my wife and I both are to think that we are never again to have the privilege — for such we always esteemed it — of again looking on the peaceful, spiritual face of your son, and profiting by being for a little in that atmosphere of rare goodness which never left him for a moment. I must look back and look out in my 'Tablet'[3] for a notice, which many a pen, especially among his Co-Religious, would so gladly though mournfully write: but meanwhile I want to write these poor little private lines — as a consolation to myself.

Up here there are many and many that must be feeling for you and yours: Edward Bond especially has, I know, so old and warm a regard for him. And among my own religious people he was, I can assure ^you^, deeply appreciated, his wonderful goodness telling often even quite at first. — I remember my wife once coming back from a Retreat at the Convent at Roehampton, and one of the Nuns telling her that a young Jesuit had recently been saying Mass for them; that he impressed them all so much, they all felt he must be a Saint; this turned out to be your son! —

I know well, my dear Mr Hopkins, how many sacrifices of hopes, all good and some bound up with your deepest convictions, you were called upon to bear in connection with him of whom we all were with you so proud: it is sad indeed that you should be called upon to make the last sacrifice so soon and so completely.

Perhaps you will kindly give our most heartfelt condolences to Mrs Hopkins and your daughters.

I am, my dear Mr Hopkins,
Yours sincerely
Friedrich von Hügel

[1] Friedrich Maria Aloys François Charles von Hügel (1852–1925; *ODNB*), philosopher and theologian. From 1876 to 1903 von Hügel and his wife, Mary Catherine Herbert, made their home in Hampstead.

[2] Margreth Moscheles, wife of the painter and Esperantist Felix Moscheles (1833–1917), who exhibited as Margaret Moscheles at the Royal Academy 1893–1924.
[3] There is no record of an obituary notice in the *Tablet*.

5 July 1889 from Mrs Hopkins to A. W. M. Baillie

Bodleian, MS Eng. misc. a. 8, fo. 71

July 5th
COURT'S HILL LODGE, | HASLEMERE. [*printed heading*]

Dear Mr Baillie

I have just received the photographs from Oxford & I enclose you one at once[1] — They were done in 1879 — & therefore are rather younger looking than he was — but the difference is not much — & the face is just the same in character & expression. Believe me. Yrs very truly

Kate Hopkins.

[1] Not with the letter, but the image was the 'very good photograph done of dear Gerard, ten years ago at Oxford', as GMH's mother describes it in her letter to Baillie of 19 June 1889 (see Pl. V). See also 27 Dec. 1879 to his mother.

6 July 1889 from A. W. M. Baillie to Mrs Hopkins

Bodleian, MS Eng. misc. a. 8, fos. 73–75v
Addressed to 'Mrs Hopkins | Court's Hill Lodge | Haslemere'. PM LONDON W.C. JY 6 89 and HASLEMERE JY 6 89. Mourning paper and envelope

22 Sackville Street| London W [*embossed heading*]
6th July 1889

Dear Mrs Hopkins

I thank you most heartily for the photograph which you have kindly sent to me. It is more like what he was in later years than the old one which I had before, and indeed is a very fair likeness. I shall never forget him, but I am pleased to have something to remind me what he looked like.

With renewed thanks I remain

Yours very Truly

A. W. M. Baillie

6 July 1889 from Frederika A. Reed[1] *to Mrs Hopkins*

Bodleian, MS Eng. misc. a. 8, fos. 76–8

Addressed to 'Mrs Hopkins | Courts Hill Lodge | Haslemere | Surrey'. PM HAMPSTEAD N.W. JY 8 89 and PETERSFIELD 9 JY 89. Mourning paper and envelope

18 Belsize Road.
6.July.1889.

My dear Kate

Thank you so very much for the photograph of dear Gerard — It is a beautiful face — and I value it greatly —

I always have felt the greatest regard for him — and much interested in him — tho' of late years I have been able to see so little of him — but he has always been associated in my mind as one so entirely without guile —

With kindest love I remain
Yours affly
Frederika A. Reed.

[1] Frederika A. Reed (1834–1910) was a daughter of Rear Admiral Frederick William Beechey (1796–1856: *ODNB*) and his wife Charlotte Stapleton (1800–74). She was thus the sister of GMH's aunts Katherine Hannah (Mrs Thomas Marsland Hopkins), Frances Anne (Mrs Edward Martin Hopkins), and Mary Beechey, to whom GMH notes that he should write in his diary of 1864 (*J&P*, 16). Frederika married Frank Reed in 1877.

12 July 1889 from J. W. Watson[1] *to Mrs Hopkins*

Bodleian, MS Eng. misc. a. 8, fos. 79–81^v

Addressed to 'Mrs Hopkins | Haslemere'. PM LONDON W JY 13 89 and HASLEMERE JY 13 89.

3 Palace Gate Mansions
12 July

Dear Mrs Hopkins

Only a few days since did I hear of your son, my dear friend's death. Those who knew him, as I did, in former days, loved him very dearly: & with the affection was also the reverence one feels for the scholar who was certainly the most talented of our time.

I am sure, <u>you know</u>, you have my sincere sympathy & believe me I should have written before only I had not the sad news confirmed until today.

Very truly yrs
J. W. Watson

[1] One of 'the Watsons of Shooter's Hill', Blackheath, whom GMH identifies as the 'kind people of the sonnet' 'In the Valley of the Elwy' in his postcard to RB of 8 Apr. 1879.

20 July 1889 from R. L. Nettleship[1] to Mrs Hopkins

Bodleian, MS Eng. misc. a. 8, fos. 82–84^{v}
Addressed to 'Mrs Manley Hopkins | Court's Hill Lodge | Haslemere'. PM OXFORD JY 20 89 and HASLEMERE JY 21 89.

BALLIOL COLLEGE, | OXFORD [*printed heading*]
July 20 1889

My dear Madam,

Only a short time ago I heard quite unexpectedly of the death of your son Gerard. I do not suppose that you ever heard my name, but he and I were great friends when we were undergraduates at Balliol. Since that time we met but little. This was more my fault than his, and one of the bitterest reproaches that I make to myself is that I did not answer an affectionate letter which he wrote me in 1885.

It is too late now, but you will excuse me for making this poor amends and telling you how much I loved him.

I am yours respectfully
R. L. Nettleship.

[1] (Richard) Lewis Nettleship (1846–92; *ODNB*), philosopher. In turn scholar, Fellow, and tutor at Balliol. See letters of 26 Oct., 1 Nov., and 14 Nov. 1867.

20 July 1889 from Harriett Molesworth[1] *to Mrs Hopkins*

Bodleian, MS Eng. misc. a. 8, fos. 85–87^{v}
Addressed to 'Mrs Manley Hopkins | Courts Hill Lodge | Haslemere | Surrey'. PM NEWBURY JY 20 89 and CHEVELEY JY 20 89.

The Grange Yattendon July 89

My dear Friend

It seems strange that I could have so long abstained from any expressions of sympathy & sorrow on the recent sad occasion but the event was a source of real grief to me. Your, I could almost say our dear Gerards death, tho' I felt his illness was severe (& I always thought him delicate) was unexpected for Robert told me he supposed he was recovering — & the fatal news quite upset me — I looked upon him always as a Holy spiritual, more than an earthly being — & I loved to know & feel he was Roberts real friend. I shall never forget his tenderness during Roberts illness — What I now feel dear fellow is, that it is selfish to repine — for what has he lost? it is more easy to ans^{r} than to calculate his gain. I should so much like to see you all again — especially yourself — for I should love to talk to you about your dear boy — but of course at my advanced age 83, I get more & more indisposed to leave home & I fear I could not tempt you to come & see me — Just now I am expecting my eldest daughter & her husband from India. We shall soon know their movements definitely but often I am alone with my g daughter Mary Plow — & we should be glad to welcome you. I hope your good husband & all your young people are well remember me to especially to your daughters & with love & all best wishes for yourself — believe me to be

My dear friend affecy yours
Harriett Molesworth

[1] RB's mother.

12 August 1889 from Coventry Patmore to Robert Bridges

From Champneys, ii. 248–9.

Hastings, Aug. 12th, 1889.

My dear Bridges,

I can well understand how terrible a loss you have suffered in the death of Gerard Hopkins — you who saw so much more of him than I did. I spent three days with him at Stonyhurst, and he stayed a week with me here; and that, with the exception of a somewhat abundant correspondence by letter, is all the communication I had with him; but this was enough to awaken in me a reverence and affection, the like of which I have never felt for any other man but one, that being Frederick Greenwood,[1] who for more than a quarter of a century has been the sole true and heroic politician and journalist in our degraded land. Gerard Hopkins was the only orthodox, and as far as I could see, saintly man in whom religion had absolutely no narrowing effect upon his general opinions and sympathies. A Catholic of the most scrupulous strictness, he could nevertheless see the Holy Spirit in all goodness, truth and beauty; and there was something in all his words and manners which were at once a rebuke and an attraction to all who could only aspire to be like him. The authority of his goodness was so great with me that I threw the manuscript of a little book — a sort of "Religio Poetae" — into the fire, simply because, when he had read it, he said with a grave look, "That's telling secrets." This little book had been the work of ten years' continual meditations, and could not but have made a greater effect than all the rest I have ever written; but his doubt was final with me.[2]

I am very glad to know that you are to write a memorial of him. It is quite right that it should be privately printed. I, as one of his friends, should protest against any attempt to share him with the public, to whom little of what was most truly characteristic in him could be communicated.

Yours very truly,
Coventry Patmore.

[1] Frederick Greenwood (1830–1909; *ODNB*), author and newspaper editor.

[2] See Introduction, p. lxxii–lxxiii.

16 September 1889 from Robert Bridges to Mrs Hopkins

Bodleian, MS Eng.lett.d.143 [MS Res.d.425], fo. 1

Yattendon Newbury
Sept 16 8

Dear Mrs Hopkins

Thank you for your letter — of course I must see Arthur & Everard. I am very glad that they think that Gerards sketches or studies may be made use of. I can see them* very well when I am in London. [*RB footnote*: * I mean Arthur & Everard] I shall not begin to do anything till I have seen as many of Gerards Roman Catholic friends as I can. Some of them will be in London. & I hope when I have had an interview with one or two of them that they will be more communicative than they are at present.

Arthur need not fear that I shall do anything without his knowledge. I have at present no notion at all as to the sort of thing which the 'memoir' will be.

I am sorry that it is too involved a matter to write on, but I shall be coming to see you as soon as I am in town.

I am with kindest regards yours very truly
Robert Bridges

9 May 1890 from Robert Stewart to Mrs Hopkins

Bodleian, MS Eng. misc. a. 8, fos. 88–90^{v}

Addressed to 'Mrs K. Hopkins | Court's Hill Lodge | Haslemere'. PM DUBLIN MY 9 90 and HASLEMERE MY 10 90.

40 UPPER FITZWILLIAM STREET, | DUBLIN [*embossed heading*]
9 May 1890

^My^ Dear Mrs Hopkins — I do not possess any of your dear Son's handwriting: as you remark, he and I were a good deal together, I found out that he had a great penchant for the art called Counterpoint, so little known & little studied by amateurs, & I offered to look over his exercises without charging him anything — for I thought it a pity that his religious position although an educated & refined man, a position very possibly including something like a vow of obedience & poverty — should interfere with the exercise of a delightful pursuit, like that of Music.

I believe he had some of my books (lent to him) at the time of his lamented death, & I asked one of the priests <whom I knew at the College where he was a professor> to send me any books with my name written within, which might turn up, but I have not heard of any since. I was much attached to your son, & fancy I can now behold his saintly expressive face.

Yours sincerely
Robert Stewart.

14 May 1890 from Robert Stewart to Mrs Hopkins

Bodleian, MS Eng. misc. a. 8, fols. 91–93v
Addressed to 'Mrs K. Hopkins | Court's Hill Lodge | Haslemere'. PM DUBLIN MY 15 90 and PETERSFIELD MY 16 90.

40 UPPER FITZWILLIAM STREET, | DUBLIN [*embossed heading*]
May 14 '90

Dear Mrs Hopkins — I am very much pleased to get your dear, gentle, clever son's photograph: except for a thinness in the lower part of his face, I do not see much alteration in those 11 years — I thought they worked a delicate man like him, far too much: I often heard from him that he was very hard worked, and he did not feed, as a working man ought; my own medical man often urges me to avoid long fasts, and to use small stimulants — Lithea water, flavored with a very little old Irish Whiskey that far famed spirit which Peter the Great of Russia was accustomed to style, "Irish Wine" — of course I am old, & your son was young, but still the truth lies in a moderate use of God's gifts, and I (who teach often 9 hours per diem, and am temperate in the extreme) know that to give lessons all day — alike in Music, as in the Latin tongue ~~of~~ ^in^ which your dear son was so thorough an adept, — "takes (as we say in Ireland) a great deal out of one" — I am sure that you must have seen a good deal of my writing, in the papers of your son.

Once more, thanking you for your thoughtfulness in sending me the picture, which I shall always preserve & value very much,

I remain yours
very sincerely
Robert Stewart

28 May 1890 from Robert Bridges to Mrs Hopkins

MS Eng. lett. d. 143 [MS Res. d. 425], fo. 7
Addressed to 'Mrs Hopkins | ~~E~~ Court's Hill Lodge | Haslemere | Surrey'. PM NEWBURY MY 28 90

Yattendon Newbury.

Dear M^{rs}. Hopkins

I am glad to say that I can at last fulfil my promise and send you the rest of Gerard's letters. I had tried several times to read them: but always had put them down again without much progress: till yesterday, when having returned home after a months visiting among friends, and being unsettled and in the low spirits which I find generally accompanies this change of surroundings, I thought of them: and was surprised to discover that I was in the congenial mood . . in fact they cheered me up altogether.

You will read them with great interest. I have taken out only two or three and those only because they narrated family events etc. and though I might just as well have left them with the rest, I though it better, — in the absence of any reason to the contrary — to respect the understanding on which they were written.

I have erased a name or two — those merely ~~when~~ of persons ^to^ whom I sh^{d} not wish to give any right to have their say.

I hope you are all well at Haslemere. It may interest you to know that my niece Mary Plow is going to be married to R^{ev} H. C. Beeching, the rector of Yattendon. He is a scholar, about 30 years of age. We like him very much.

Keep the letters as long as you wish. I found among them more distinct references of Gerard's state of mind than I remembered. One in particular is very plain. I always consider that he was over nervous about himself, and exaggerated his symptoms — which I think he did. In fact I think that his mental condition was of this ~~nature~~ sort. I may say that I have come round again to more my old state of feeling with regard to his memory. —

It happens that Bell is now publishing my poems. I thought that if I c^{d} make the occasion I w^{d} introduce some of Gerard's verse into the <u>notes</u> of that book and see if the critics noticed it. What w^{d} you think of that?

With kindest regard to M^{r} and Miss Hopkins, yours sincerely R Bridges.
May 25^8^ — 90

P.S.
I have £5 offered to me for a copy of the Growth of Love, by a bookseller. So if you ever want to get rid of your copy send it to me. But I had rather you w^{d} keep it if you wish to.

THE HOPKINS SMITH FAMILIES: AN ABBREVIATED FAMILY TREE

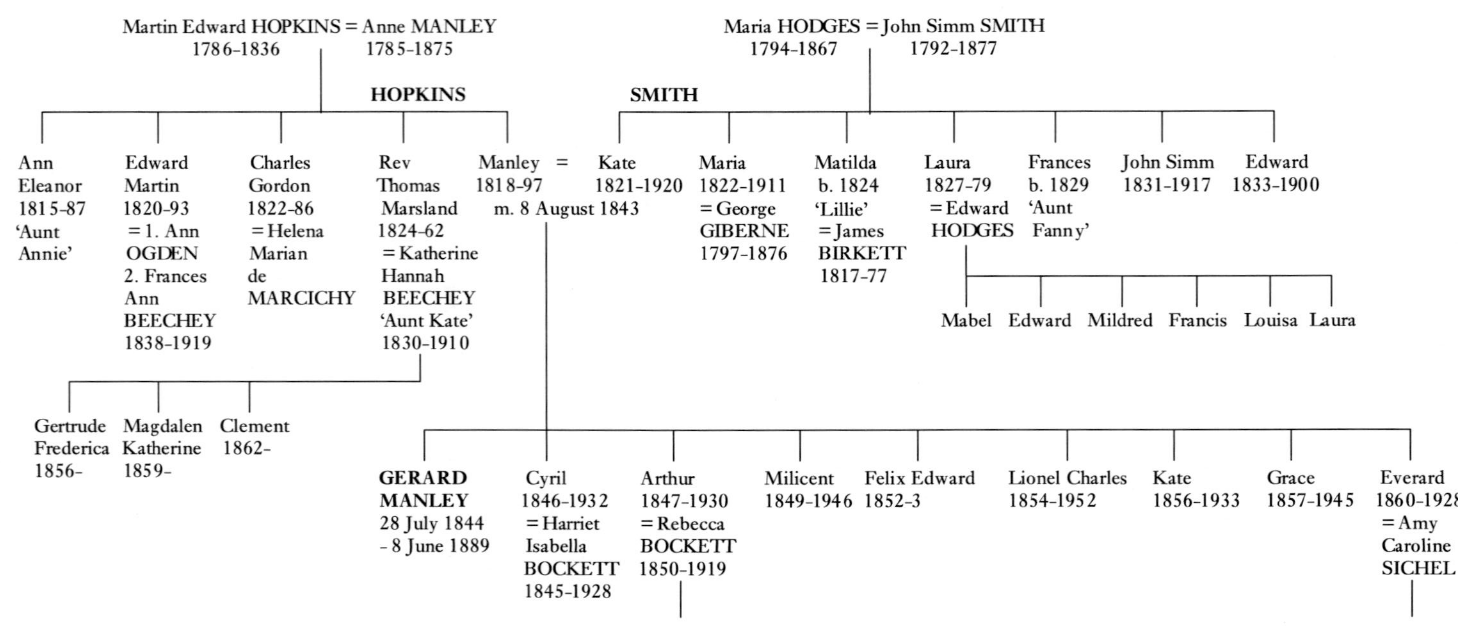

INDEX

Please note that this index does not include items from the List of Letters, nor material from the addresses cited in the headnotes of the letters.